BYZANTINE SAINTS' LIVES IN TRANSLATION

III

THE LIFE OF LAZAROS OF MT. GALESION

Byzantine Saints' Lives in Translation

Series Editor: Alice-Mary Talbot

Previous Titles in the Series

1. Holy Women of Byzantium
2. Byzantine Defenders of Images

THE LIFE OF LAZAROS OF MT. GALESION:

AN ELEVENTH-CENTURY PILLAR SAINT

Introduction, translation, and notes
by Richard P. H. Greenfield

Dumbarton Oaks Research Library and Collection

Washington, D.C.

Manufactured in the United States of America by
Sheridan Books, Inc., 450 Fame Avenue, Hanover, PA 17331 | (717) 632-3535

Library of Congress Cataloging-in-Publication Data

Gregory, the Cellarer.

[Vita S. Lazari auctore Gregorio monacho. English.]

The life of Lazaros of Mt. Galesion : an eleventh-century pillar saint/
introduction, translation, and notes by Richard P. H. Greenfield.

p. cm.—(Byzantine saints' lives in translation ; 3)

Includes bibliographical references and indexes.

ISBN 978-0-88402-272-5 (hardcover: alk. paper)
ISBN 978-0-88402-439-2 (paperback: alk. paper)

1. Lazaros Galesiotes, Saint, d. 1053.
2. Pillar saints—Turkey—Ephesus (Extinct city)—Biography.
3. Monks—Turkey—Ephesus (Extinct city)—Biography.
4. Orthodox Eastern Church—Clergy Biography.
5. Ephesus (Extinct city)—Biography.
I. Greenfield, Richard P. H. II. Title. III. Series.

BX395.L39G7413 1999
270.3'092—dc21
[B] 99-30808
CIP

EU GPSR Authorised Representative
LOGOS EUROPE, 9 rue Nicolas Poussin, 17000, La Rochelle, France
E-mail: Contact@logoseurope.eu

For Anne

CONTENTS

ACKNOWLEDGMENTS

This book is the result of more than fifteen years of intermittent work on Lazaros conducted in London, Oxford, Belfast, Athens, Nauplion, Washington, Montreal, and, for the most part Kingston, Ontario. I would like to thank all the individuals who have given me their assistance and encouragement during the preparation of this translation, as well as the various institutions which have made my work possible. In particular I am grateful to the Advisory Research Committee of Queen's University at Kingston for a grant that paid for some of the travel involved in visiting libraries in 1994 and 1995. Above all, however, I have to thank Dumbarton Oaks for generously commissioning a project which I had long planned but would probably never have realized without their interest. I am indebted to the late Alexander Kazhdan and to Nicolas Oikonomides for their friendly and valuable assistance while I was in Washington in the summer of 1995. I am also deeply indebted to the anonymous readers of the manuscript for their rigorous scrutiny, helpful advice, and generous encouragement; they helped me to avoid many errors and allowed me to make numerous improvements. In addition, I would like to thank the members of the Dumbarton Oaks publications staff and, especially, Robin Surratt and Susan Higman for their care and help in improving this book in many ways. My biggest debt in terms of scholarship, however, is to Alice-Mary Talbot, whose scrupulous editing and vast knowledge, not to mention her great patience, have raised this work to a standard it could not otherwise have achieved. While she, and the others who have helped me, must take much of the credit for things which are right, any errors and misconceptions which remain are, of course, my own. My final thanks are reserved for my wife, Anne Foley, for supporting and putting up with me throughout this seemingly endless project; Lazaros would surely have approved of her patient endurance, and without her, all this, like so much else, would quite literally have been impossible.

LIST OF ABBREVIATIONS

Scriptural Citations

Septuagint (all citations are based on the numbering of L. C. L. Brenton, *The Septuagint Version of the Old Testament according to the Vatican Text,* 2 vols. [London, 1864])

Gen.	Genesis
Ex.	Exodus
Lev.	Leviticus
Num.	Numbers
Deut.	Deuteronomy
Josh.	Joshua
Judg.	Judges
Ruth	
Ki.	Kings
	N.B. 1–2 Sam. in OT = 1–2 Kings in Sept.
	1–2 Kings in OT = 3–4 Kings in Sept.
Chr.	Chronicles (= Paralipomenon of Sept.)
Ezra	
Esth.	Esther
Job	
Ps.	Psalms (first number = Sept. numbering; number in parentheses = OT numbering)
Prov.	Proverbs
Eccl.	Ecclesiastes
Song of Sol.	Song of Solomon
Is.	Isaiah
Jer.	Jeremiah
Ezek.	Ezekiel
Dan.	Daniel
Hos.	Hosea
Joel	
Amos	
Obad.	Obadiah

Jon.	Jonah
Mic.	Micah
Nah.	Nahum
Hab.	Habakkuk
Zeph.	Zephaniah
Hag.	Haggai
Zach.	Zachariah
Mal.	Malachi

Apocrypha

Macc.	Maccabees
Tob.	Tobit
Jdth.	Judith
Sir.	Siracides (Wisdom of Jesus ben Sirach, Ecclesiasticus)
Sap.	Wisdom of Solomon (Sapientia Solomonis)

New Testament

Mt.	Matthew
Mk.	Mark
Lk.	Luke
Jn.	John
Acts	
Rom.	Romans
Cor.	Corinthians
Gal.	Galatians
Eph.	Ephesians
Phil.	Philippians
Col.	Colossians
Th.	Thessalonians
Tim.	Timothy
Tit.	Titus
Philem.	Philemon
Heb.	Hebrews
James	
Pet.	Peter
John	epistles of John
Jude	
Rev.	Revelation

Bibliography

AASS — *Acta Sanctorum,* 71 vols. (Paris, 1863–1940)

AJA — *American Journal of Archaeology*

AnalBoll — *Analecta Bollandiana*

Angold, *Byzantine Empire* — M. Angold, *The Byzantine Empire, 1025–1204: A Political History* (London, 1984)

BHG — *Bibliotheca hagiographica graeca,* ed. F. Halkin, 3d ed. (Brussels, 1957)

Brenton, *LXX* — L. C. L. Brenton, *The Septuagint Version of the Old Testament according to the Vatican Text,* 2 vols. (London, 1864)

Boulhol, *Anagnorismos* — P. Boulhol, ᾽ΑΝΑΓΝΩΡΙΣΜΟΣ: *La scène de reconnaissance dans l'hagiographie antique et médiévale* (Aix-en-Provence, 1996)

BS/EB — *Byzantine Studies/Études byzantines*

Cheynet, *Pouvoir* — J.-C. Cheynet, *Pouvoir et contestations à Byzance (963–1210)* (Paris, 1990)

Delehaye, "Femmes stylites" — H. Delehaye, "Les femmes stylites," *AnalBoll* 27 (1908), 391–92

Delehaye, *Saints militaires* — H. Delehaye, *Les légendes grecques des saints militaires* (Paris, 1909)

Delehaye, *Stylites* — H. Delehaye, *Les saints stylites,* SubsHag 14 (Paris-Brussels, 1923)

Demetrakos — D. Demetrakos, Μέγα λεξικὸν τῆς ῾Ελληνικῆς Γλώσσης, 9 vols. (Athens, 1933–51)

DOP — *Dumbarton Oaks Papers*

᾽Επ.῾Ετ.Βυζ.Σπ. — ᾽Επετηρὶς ῾Εταιρείας Βυζαντινῶν Σπουδῶν

Foss, *Ephesus* — C. Foss, *Ephesus after Antiquity: A Late Antique, Byzantine and Turkish City* (Cambridge, 1979)

Foss, "Twenty Cities" — C. Foss, "Archaeology and the 'Twenty Cities' of Byzantine Asia Minor," *AJA* 81 (1977), 469–86

Gautier, "Évergétis"
P. Gautier, "Le typikon de la Théotokos Évergétis," *REB* 40 (1982), 5–101

Gautier, "Kécharitôménè"
P. Gautier, "Le typikon de la Théotokos Kécharitôménè," *REB* 43 (1985), 5–165

Gedeon, "Γνώσεις" M. I. Gedeon, "Γνώσεις ἐκ τοῦ τυπικοῦ τῶν μονῶν τοῦ Γαλησίου ὄρους," Ἐκκλησιαστικὴ Ἀλήθεια 18 (1898), 27–31, 61–67

GOrThR *Greek Orthodox Theological Review*

Greenfield, *Demonology*
R. P. H. Greenfield, *Traditions of Belief in Late Byzantine Demonology* (Amsterdam, 1988)

Greenfield, "Outer Darkness"
R. P. H. Greenfield, "Fallen into Outer Darkness: Later Byzantine Depictions and Conceptions of the Devil and the Demons," *Etnofoor* 5 (1992), 61–80

Hackel, *Byz. Saint* S. Hackel, ed., *The Byzantine Saint* (London, 1981)

Halkin, "Manuscrits"
F. Halkin, "Manuscrits Galésiotes," *Scriptorium* 15 (1961), 221–27

Harvey, *Expansion* A. Harvey, *Economic Expansion in the Byzantine Empire, 900–1200* (Cambridge, 1989)

Hirschfeld, *Desert Monasteries*
Y. Hirschfeld, *The Judean Desert Monasteries in the Byzantine Period* (New Haven, 1992)

IstMitt *Istanbuler Mitteilungen*

Janin, *Constantinople byz.*
R. Janin, *Constantinople byzantine: Développement urbain et répertoire topographique*[2] (Paris, 1964)

Janin, *Églises CP* R. Janin, *La géographie ecclésiastique de l'Empire byzantin*, I: *Le siège de Constantinople et le patriarcat oecuménique,* 3: *Les églises et les monastères*[2] (Paris, 1969)

Janin, *Églises centres*	R. Janin, *Les églises et les monastères des grands centres byzantins* (Paris, 1975)
JbAC	*Jahrbuch für Antike und Christentum*
Joannou, *Démonologie*	P.-P. Joannou, *Démonologie populaire—démonologie critique au XIe siècle: la vie inédite de S. Auxence par M. Psellus* (Wiesbaden, 1971)
Kaplan, *Les hommes*	M. Kaplan, *Les hommes et la terre à Byzance du VIe au XIe siècle* (Paris, 1992)
Kaplan, "Evergetis"	M. Kaplan, "The Evergetis *Hypotyposis* and the Management of Monastic Estates in the Eleventh Century," in Mullett and Kirby, *Evergetis,* 114–22
Kazhdan, "Ideals"	A. P. Kazhdan, "Hermitic, Cenobitic and Secular Ideals in Byzantine Hagiography of the Ninth to Twelfth Centuries," *GOrThR* 30 (1985), 473–87
Kazhdan, "Ὁ τέλειος μοναχός"	A. P. Kazhdan, "Ὁ τέλειος μοναχὸς ἢ ὁ τέλειος πολεμιστής; ὁ συγκερασμὸς τῶν κοινωνικῶν ἰδανικῶν στὸ Βυζάντιο," *Dodone* 15.1 (1986), 203–16
Kazhdan and Epstein, *Change*	A. P. Kazhdan and A. Wharton Epstein, *Change in Byzantine Culture in the Eleventh and Twelfth Centuries* (Berkeley, 1985)
Kötting, *Peregrinatio*	B. Kötting, *Peregrinatio Religiosa* (Regensberg, 1950)
Laiou, "Sex"	A. Laiou, "Sex, Consent, and Coercion in Byzantium," in *Consent and Coercion to Sex and Marriage in Ancient and Medieval Societies,* ed. A. E. Laiou (Washington, D.C., 1993), 109–221
Lampe, *Lexicon*	G. W. H. Lampe, *A Patristic Greek Lexicon* (Oxford, 1961–68)
Lampsides, "Ἀνέκδοτον κείμενον"	O. Lampsides, "Ἀνέκδοτον κείμενον περὶ τοῦ ἁγίου Λαζάρου Γαλησιώτου," *Theologia* 53.1 (1982), 158–77

Lemerle, "Pauliciens"
P. Lemerle, "L'histoire des Pauliciens d'Asie Mineure d'après les sources grecques," *TM* 5 (1973), 1–144

Leutsch and Schneidewin, *CPG*
Corpus Paroemiographorum Graecorum, ed. E. L. Leutsch and F. G. Schneidewin, 2 vols. (Göttingen, 1839–51; repr. Hildesheim, 1958)

Liddell-Scott-Jones, *Lexicon*
H. G. Liddell, R. Scott, and H. S. Jones, *A Greek-English Lexicon* (Oxford, 1968)

Loparev, *Kratkii otchet*
C. Loparev, *Kratkii otchet o poězdkě na Athon lětom 1896 goda* (St. Petersburg, 1897)

Loparev, "Zhitie" C. Loparev, "Zhitie v. Lazarya Galisieskago," *VizVrem* 4 (1897), 364–78

Malamut, "Bessai" E. Malamut, "A propos de Bessai d'Éphèse," *REB* 43 (1985), 243–51

Malamut, *Route* E. Malamut, *Sur la route des saints byzantins* (Paris, 1993)

MM F. Miklosich and J. Müller, *Acta et diplomata graeca medii aevi sacra et profana,* 6 vols. (Vienna, 1860–90)

Morris, "Political Saint"
R. Morris, "The Political Saint of the Eleventh Century," in Hackel, *Byz. Saint,* 43–50

Morris, *Monks* R. Morris, *Monks and Laymen in Byzantium, 843–1118* (Cambridge, 1995)

Mullett and Kirby, *Evergetis*
M. Mullett and A. Kirby, eds., *The Theotokos Evergetis and Eleventh-Century Monasticism* (Belfast, 1994)

Munitiz, *Partial Account*
J. A. Munitiz, *Nikephoros Blemmydes: A Partial Account* (Leuven, 1988)

Nicol, *"Instabilitas"* D. M. Nicol, *"Instabilitas Loci:* The Wanderlust of Late Byzantine Monks," in *Monks, Hermits and*

	the Ascetic Tradition, Studies in Church History 22, ed. W. J. Sheils (Oxford, 1985)
ODB	*Oxford Dictionary of Byzantium,* ed. A. P. Kazhdan et al., 3 vols. (New York, 1991)
Palladius, *Lausiaca*	Palladius, *Historia Lausiaca,* ed. C. Butler, *The Lausiac History of Palladius* (Cambridge, 1898; repr. Hildesheim, 1967); trans. R. T. Meyer, *Palladius: The Lausiac History* (London, 1965)
Papachryssanthou, "Vie monastique"	D. Papachryssanthou, "La vie monastique dans les campagnes byzantines du VIIIe au XIe siècle," *Byzantion* 43 (1973), 158–80
Patrich, *Sabas*	J. Patrich, *Sabas, Leader of Palestinian Monasticism* (Washington, D.C., 1995)
PG	Patrologiae cursus completus, Series graeca, ed. J.-P. Migne, 161 vols. (Paris, 1857–66)
RE	*Paulys Real-Encyclopädie der classichen Altertumswissenschaft*
REB	*Revue des études byzantines*
RegPatr	*Les regestes des actes du patriarcat de Constantinople,* ed. V. Grumel, V. Laurent, and J. Darrouzès, 2 vols. in 8 pts. (Paris, 1932–79)
REGr	*Revue des études grecques*
ROC	*Revue de l'Orient chrétien*
Schlumberger, *L'épopée*	G. Schlumberger, *L'épopée byzantine à la fin du Xe siècle,* 3 vols. (Paris, 1896–1905)
Seibt, *Skleroi*	W. Seibt, *Die Skleroi: Eine prosopographisch-sigillographische Studie* (Vienna, 1976)
Seibt, *Bleiseigel*	W. Seibt, *Die byzantinischen Bleiseigel in Österreich* (Vienna, 1978)
Ševčenko, "Eastern Provinces"	I. Ševčenko, "Constantinople Viewed from the Eastern Provinces in the Middle Byzantine Period," *Harvard Ukrainian Studies* 3/4.2 (1979–80), 712–47

SM — *Studi Medievali*

Sophocles, *Lexicon* — E. A. Sophocles, *Greek Lexicon of the Roman and Byzantine Periods,* 2 vols. (New York, 1900; repr. New York, 1957)

SubsHag — Subsidia Hagiographica

SynaxCP — *Synaxarium ecclesiae Constantinopolitanae: Propylaeum ad Acta sanctorum Novembris,* ed. H. Delehaye (Brussels, 1902)

Talbot, "Comparison" — A.-M. Talbot, "A Comparison of the Monastic Experience of Byzantine Men and Women," *GOrThR* 30 (1985), 1–20

Talbot, "Family" — A.-M. Talbot, "The Byzantine Family and the Monastery," *DOP* 44 (1990), 119–29

Talbot, *Holy Women* — A.-M. Talbot, ed., *Holy Women of Byzantium: Ten Saints' Lives in English Translation* (Washington, D.C., 1996)

Theodoret, *Hist. Rel.* — Theodoret of Cyrrhus, *Historia religiosa,* ed. P. Canivet and A. Leroy-Molinghen, *Théodoret de Cyr: histoire des moines de Syrie,* 2 vols. (Paris, 1977–79); English trans., R. M. Price, *A History of the Monks of Syria* (Kalamazoo, Mich., 1985)

Thomas, "Evergetine Reform" — J. P. Thomas, "Documentary Evidence from the Byzantine Monastic *Typika* for the History of the Evergetine Reform Movement," in Mullett and Kirby, *Evergetis,* 246–73

Thomas, *Religious Foundations* — J. P. Thomas, *Private Religious Foundations in the Byzantine Empire* (Washington, D.C., 1987)

Thomas and Hero, *Foundation Documents* — J. P. Thomas and A. C. Hero, eds., *Byzantine Monastic Foundation Documents* (Washington, D.C., forthcoming)

TM — *Travaux et mémoires*

Trapp, *Lexikon* — E. Trapp, ed., *Lexikon zur byzantinischen Gräzität* (Vienna, 1994–)

vita Athan. Ath. (A-B) — *Vita Athanasii Athonitae* (A-B), ed. J. Noret, *Vitae duae antiquae sancti Athanasii Athonitae* (Turnhout, 1982)

vita Danielis — *Vita sancti Danielis Stylitae,* ed. Delehaye, *Stylites,* 1–147; English trans. in E. Dawes and N. H. Baynes, *Three Byzantine Saints* (Oxford, 1948; repr. Crestwood, N.Y., 1977)

Viz Vrem — *Vizantijskij vremennik*

Ward, *Sayings* — B. Ward, trans., *The Sayings of the Desert Fathers: The Alphabetical Collection* (London-Kalamazoo, Mich., 1975)

Wilkinson, "Christian Pilgrims" — J. Wilkinson, "Christian Pilgrims in Jerusalem during the Byzantine Period," *Palestine Exploration Quarterly* 108 (1976), 75–101

Wilkinson, *Jerusalem Pilgrims* — J. Wilkinson, *Jerusalem Pilgrims before the Crusades* (Warminster, 1977)

Zacos, *Seals* — G. Zacos and A. Veglery, *Byzantine Lead Seals,* vol. 1 (Basel, 1972)

Zepos, *Jus* — J. and P. Zepos, *Jus graecoromanorum,* 8 vols. (Athens, 1931; repr. Aalen, 1962)

ZslPh — *Zeitschrift für slavische Philologie*

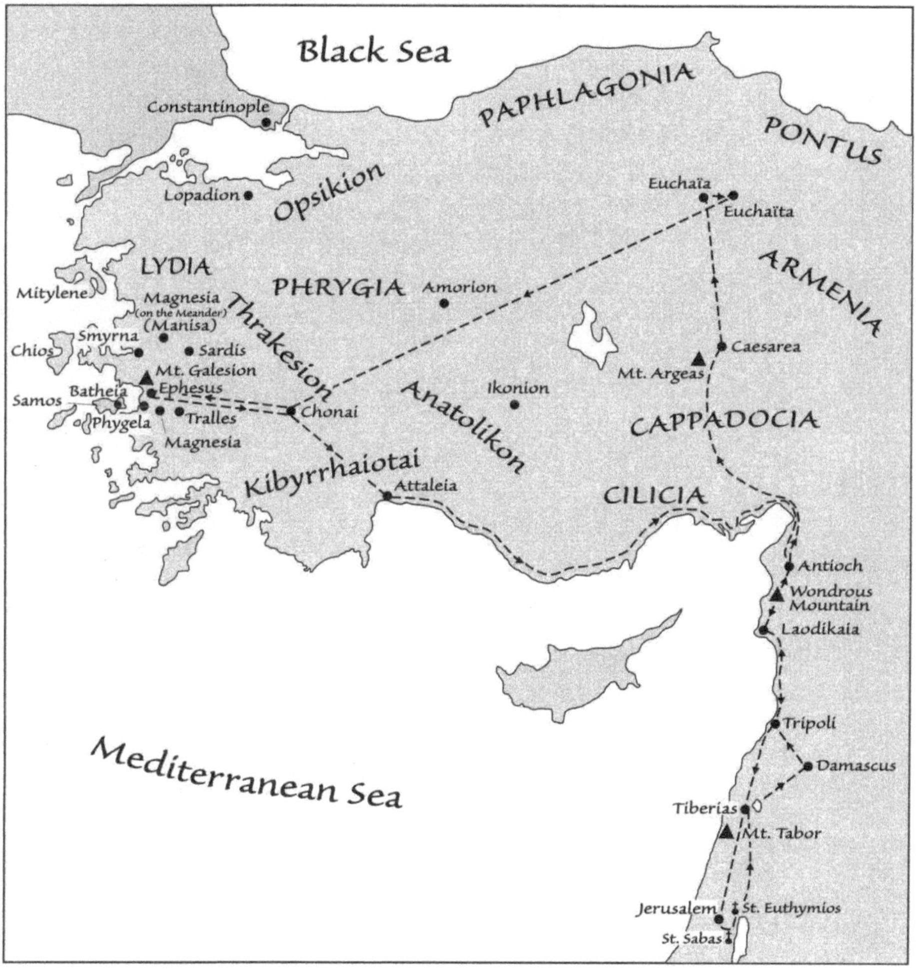

Lazaros' travels and places cited in the *vita*

INTRODUCTION

A. Lazaros' Reputation among His Contemporaries

By the time of his death, in November 1053, Lazaros Galesiotes' reputation for sanctity extended far beyond the region of Ephesus, where he had spent the greater part of his life; he was for many people one of the brightest stars in the Byzantine monastic firmament. This, at any rate, is the impression given by Gregory the Cellarer, a disciple and trusted supporter of Lazaros, who wrote the *vita* that is translated here.

Gregory's account, written shortly after Lazaros' death, is by far the longest, most detailed, and most trustworthy source on the saint; it also forms the basis for most of the other material that has been preserved, and it is thus referred to below as the "primary *vita*." Four other significant sources on Lazaros exist, but these add nothing reliable and, in fact, confuse some issues. The most substantial is a late thirteenth-century reworking of the *vita* by the patriarch of Constantinople, Gregory of Cyprus, who may have possessed an already reworked version of the Life as well as a familiarity with later traditions concerning Lazaros and his foundations. Two other brief sources are apparently related to this version: an epitome drawn from an *akolouthia* of Lazaros, and a slightly fuller *synaxarion* found in a thirteenth- or early fourteenth-century manuscript, now in Moscow. Finally, a section of the Lives of Barnabas and Sophronios (founders of the Soumela monastery near Trebizond), written by Akakios Sabbaites early in the thirteenth century, probably preserves oral traditions concerning Lazaros; it is, perhaps, a slightly earlier, unworked version of the tradition employed by Gregory of Cyprus.[1]

Lazaros' status as a holy man was based chiefly on his extraordinary perseverance as a pillar ascetic or stylite, for he spent the last forty or so years of his life on the barren mountain of Galesion,[2] not far from the city of Ephe-

[1] For a more complete discussion of the primary *vita* and its author, see below section G; on the other source material see below, section H.

[2] The masculine form of this toponym (Galesi*os*) enjoys almost equal support in modern scholarship to the neuter (Galesi*on*), which is used here: Delehaye, Janin, Malamut, Ševčenko, and the *ODB* have preferred the masculine; Halkin, Laurent, Foss, Munitiz, Kaplan, Thomas, and Morris have preferred the neuter. The problem arises because the toponym, both in the *vita* and elsewhere, almost always appears in circum-

sus on the west coast of Asia Minor. An immense and at times emotionally overwhelming impression was made upon visitors by the sight of the gaunt old man standing on the top of his pillar, dressed only in the tattered and ancient leather tunic that was his sole protection from the elements. Unbelievers are said to have converted to Christianity on the spot, while for the pious he provided a living and demonstrable proof that a frail mortal could indeed successfully imitate on earth the life of the angels in heaven. He had in truth become a "living icon" and had shown his contemporaries that there was at least one man alive who was still quite capable of meeting the daunting standards of ascetic practice set by his now legendary predecessors in earlier Christian tradition.[3]

Despite his astonishing feats of ascetic endurance, however, and his symbolic (and at times literal) isolation from his fellow men, Lazaros remained fundamentally committed to the warmer, more human, ideals of Christian

---

stances that do not allow its gender to be determined; it is thus either used with the neuter noun ὄρος (as in the common phrase τὸ Γαλήσιον ὄρος) or else it appears in cases (such as the genitive or dative) that do not allow its gender to be established. I have been able to find only one instance in which it is used unambiguously in the *vita,* Chap. 246, where the phrase εἰς τὸ Γαλήσιον clearly shows that it could be neuter. In several places in the *vita* of Athanasios I by Theoktistos the Stoudite (see A. Papadopoulos-Kerameus, *Zapiski Istoriko-filologičeskogo fakulteta S.-Peterburgskogo Universiteta* 76 [1905], 9–12), and also in the *vita* of Meletios of Mt. Galesion (see Γρηγόριος ὁ Παλαμᾶς, 5 [1921], 613–14), however, it is definitely given as a neuter, and it is on the basis of this evidence that I have favored the neuter form here. My thanks to Alice-Mary Talbot for the references to the *vitae* of Athanasios and Meletios; on them, see below, section I, p. 64.

[3] The Byzantine tradition of stylites or pillar ascetics was a long and distinguished one going back to the 5th century. Begun by Symeon the Stylite the Elder, this striking tradition of extreme asceticism had evidently flourished without interruption down to Lazaros' day, despite opposition during the Iconoclast period. Stylites, who, like Lazaros, also practiced many other forms of asceticism, were venerated at all levels of society for the mastery they showed not only over their own mortal bodies but also over the forces of nature in general. The elevated position afforded by their pillars symbolized the isolation of these remarkable individuals from the concerns and sinfulness of normal material existence and emphasized their status as beings whose way of life was closer to that of the angels than men. Standing midway between heaven and earth, and demonstrably enjoying the supernatural protection and favor of their celestial patrons, they were thus respected and sought out as intermediaries who could effectively present the concerns of ordinary mortals to those who had power at the heavenly court. See especially here, Delehaye, *Stylites,* and, for further references and discussion of their representation in art, *ODB,* s.v. "Stylite."

love, charity, and toleration. His reputation thus also owed a great deal to this softer, caring side of his character that was experienced not only by his close followers, but by the faithful and curious, whether local people or pilgrims and visitors from far away, even overseas, who made the exhausting and sometimes dangerous ascent of the mountain to his pillar. To them, rich and poor, powerful and humble alike, he gave proof of his sanctity by his practical, unquestioning, sometimes extraordinarily generous and often secret acts of charity; he did so, too, by the wisdom and helpfulness of the advice he gave to all who sought his spiritual counsel or who came to him for confession. Visitors went away marveling at his insight and at his ability to relieve the burdens of a guilty conscience.

Furthermore, in spite of Lazaros' great humility and his determined efforts to avoid the praise of men, numerous stories of miraculous acts came to be associated with him during his life: stories of healing, exorcism, protection, provision, insight, and foresight. Before he died, he had thus gained considerable repute as the intermediary, or (for the more simple) actual possessor, of superhuman powers. Not only was he himself demonstrably immune to the wiles and viciousness of the Devil and the demons, whom he could control with a word or a simple gesture, but even his name and the invocation of his prayer became a powerful charm that could produce all manner of effects contrary to nature.

Lazaros' reputation spread rapidly by word of mouth, initially in the immediate vicinity of Ephesus, then throughout western and southern Asia Minor, as well as much farther afield. This process was doubtless assisted by Galesion's proximity to the pilgrimage center of Ephesus and the busy port of Phygela, for those who visited these places on business or in the course of their travels heard of the nearby holy man and were drawn to see him for themselves; they then carried their tales far and wide across the Byzantine Empire and Galesion became a pilgrimage destination in its own right, rivaling its older and more famous neighbor. Casual visitors were not the only ones attracted to this "blazing beacon" of Christian virtue, however. A flourishing community of some three hundred monks sprang up around Lazaros in a number of monasteries on the barren and inhospitable mountain, a phenomenon viewed by the author of the *vita* as the greatest miracle Lazaros performed.[4] Some of these monks carried impressive reports of Lazaros' sanctity on missions to Constantinople and elsewhere, even to some of the further

[4] See Chap. 79; cf. also Chaps. 62 and 85.

reaches of the Byzantine world. Moreover, Lazaros' advice was sought and successfully followed by people seeking to establish communities of their own. The reputation of this particular style of monasticism, as well as of its originator, thus spread beyond the confines of Galesion itself. At the same time this reputation was established by the respect and veneration that Lazaros and his monastery gained among holders of some of the highest political offices in Asia Minor, and this led, in time, to recognition from the imperial court itself. Support, primarily in the form of grants of land and money, from the emperor Constantine IX Monomachos and his mistress Maria Skleraina appears to have assured the survival of the community that Lazaros created on Galesion, and, as this endured and eventually came to be ranked along with the other great holy mountains of the Byzantine world, the memory of its founder's sanctity was upheld.

Lazaros' reputation as a holy man was by no means universally accepted, however, at least during his lifetime and in the period immediately following his death. The *vita* reveals that a distinctly negative attitude existed toward him among members of the ecclesiastical hierarchy of Ephesus, in some neighboring monasteries, and even within his own monastic community. Stories circulated that he was a fraud, or at least that his asceticism was seriously exaggerated for the benefit of visitors. Moreover, instead of the kind, generous, and caring figure so revered by his supporters, these rumors depicted Lazaros either as a tyrannical despot, given to fits of anger and violence toward his monks, or as an incompetent and idle superior who tonsured anyone who came to him and who regularly ignored the needs and the wishes of those in his charge. According to these stories, the monks were beaten, robbed, and starved, while Lazaros himself gobbled up quantities of communion bread when he was supposed to be fasting, guzzled wine, and sat on top of a pillar stuffed full of gold, since he received large and frequent donations from the faithful but never spent a penny on his monks nor gave much away in public to the poor and the hungry. At the same time the life of the community was constantly being disrupted by the antics of frivolous youths and by quarrelsome monks of dubious vocation whom Lazaros was unable to control, as well as by clever and dangerous confidence tricksters by whom he was completely fooled. In settling disputes he would rule in favor of the wrong party, while refusing to listen to genuine and pressing concerns among the brethren, even at times when the well-being of the community was in peril.[5]

[5] See below, section D.

Whatever the impression left by the *vita* and the fact of its ultimate survival, a number of factors suggest that contemporary opinion was divided over Lazaros. The almost total absence of posthumous miracle stories and the paucity of evidence for a major cult or tradition of artistic representation of Lazaros support this view. Indications that disputes over the legal status of his monasteries on Galesion continued for several years after his death, and the evident obscurity into which the mountain fell until the thirteenth century, would imply that there were sufficient doubts in existence, whether or not these were deliberately fueled by those who had their own reasons for opposing Lazaros, to cloud his reputation and prevent him from attaining a permanent place among the greatest figures of Byzantine monasticism.[6]

B. The Principal Events and Chronology of Lazaros' Life

In establishing the course and dating of Lazaros' life there is one seemingly indisputable point of reference: his death on the 7 November 1053.[7] Another relatively certain date is that of the destruction of the church of the Holy Sepulchre at Jerusalem; generally agreed to have taken place on 28 September 1009, this event was witnessed by Lazaros.[8] In addition, the *vita* provides information on Lazaros' age and the length of time he spent in various places. A brief summary of some of the most important points appears in Chapter 254. When pieced together with a number of vaguer hints, this information makes it possible to establish a general, and at times quite detailed, sequence and date for the events mentioned in the *vita.*

Lazaros, whose secular name was Leo, was born in the vicinity of Magnesia on the Meander, the fifth child of parents who appear to have been peasants. The date of birth can easily be determined, although it is not given in the *vita*, since the author states unambiguously that Lazaros was eighty-

[6] See below, section I.

[7] In Chap. 254 Lazaros is said to have died in the year after the creation 6562, Indiction seven. On the exact interpretation of this date, see Malamut, "Bessai," 243–51; cf. Delehaye, *Stylites,* cxv, who construes this as 8 November 1054; Delehaye is also followed by Janin, *Églises centres,* 246 n. 6.

[8] See Chap. 19. The date is that given by the most reliable source for these events, the Christian Arab historian Yaḥyā b. Saʿīd of Antioch, who wrote in the mid-11th century. Some other Arab historians date the destruction to 1007/8, however, and the Greek historian John Skylitzes (writing in the second half of the 11th century) suggests 1010.

six years old when he died on 7 November 1053;[9] straightforward arithmetic thus allows his birth date to be set between 8 November 966 and 7 November 967.[10]

If Lazaros was born in 966/67, it is then quite straightforward to establish the course of his early life from the information provided by the author of the primary *vita*, which is evidently cited by him from reliable sources.[11] At the age of six (thus 972/73) he was sent to a local priest, called Leontios, to begin his education; three years later, aged nine (975/76), he went to study with a notary called George at the nearby monastery of Oroboi; and, after another three years, at the age of twelve (978/79), he went to another neighboring monastery, Kalathai, where his uncle Elias, who had been of considerable influence in his education, was a monk.[12] It was here that the compelling urge to leave the area of his birth for the Holy Land, a goal which was to dominate the early part of his life, first manifested itself in an attempt to run away from the monastery. On this occasion, however, Lazaros was thwarted, and he remained at Kalathai for two years until, at the age of fourteen (thus 980/81), he was sent to another (probably local) monastery, Strobelion, where he stud-

[9] See Chap. 254.

[10] Janin, *Églises centres,* 242, concurs on 967 but then (p. 246 n. 6) argues for 968. Rather similarly Malamut, *Route,* 40, agrees on 967, but (p. 61) also suggests 967–68, a figure again proposed by Thomas (Thomas and Hero, *Foundation Documents,* 148). If, however, Lazaros was born in 968, he would have been at most 85 and possibly only 84 when he died. Delehaye agrees with the basic calculation, although his mistake in dating Lazaros' death to 1054 means he gives the date as 968. For some reason Kazhdan in *ODB,* s.v. "Lazaros of Mount Galesios," suggests that the date is "usually calculated as ca. 972." The only real problem in dating Lazaros' birth to 966/67 is that the tradition preserved in the *vita* written by Gregory of Cyprus, in the epitome, and in the Moscow *synaxarion,* states that Lazaros was only seventy-two when he died (the figure is given in Gregory of Cyprus, chap. 41, *AASS,* Nov. 3:605E; epitome, *AASS,* Nov. 3: 680A; Moscow *synaxarion,* f. 220). If correct, this would mean that Lazaros was born at the very end of 980 or in 981. The reliability of the tradition preserved in these versions as an historical source is dubious, however (see discussion below, section H). Even if it were accepted, the consequent birth date would be very hard to square with the date of Lazaros' departure from Jerusalem (see below). The source of the figure seventy-two, if it is not genuine, is uncertain, but one may note that this number has a certain significance in Greek folklore; see G. K. Spyridake, "Ὁ ἀριθμὸς ἑβδομήκοντα δύο," Ἀφιέρωμα εἰς Κ. Ἄμαντον (Athens, 1940), 409–18.

[11] See below, section G, p. 55.

[12] See Chap. 3.

ied to be a notary under the guidance of a monk called Nicholas.[13] Altogether, Lazaros spent three and a half more years there before he finally succeeded in escaping for the East at the age of eighteen (984/85).[14]

After a visit to the shrine at Chonai and an adventurous journey across Asia Minor, which must have taken several months at least, given the slow and erratic progress of the Paphlagonian monk in whose company he was traveling, Lazaros reached Attaleia on the south coast (presumably sometime between 984 and 986).[15] He spent the next seven years there,[16] associated with a monastery in the vicinity where he was evidently formally tonsured as a monk and took the religious name of Lazaros. There, too, he first demonstrated his ability to pursue the solitary life and formed his own first small community, as well as gaining a considerable local reputation as a holy man. Lazaros stayed at Attaleia until the pressures of his growing popularity became intolerable, and he left to fulfill his life-long dream of visiting the Holy Land. He must have been about twenty-five or twenty-six when he arrived in Jerusalem, sometime between 991 and 993.

Lazaros was to stay in the Holy Land until the church of the Holy Sepulchre was demolished and pressure on the Christian residents from Islamic authorities became too great to bear. For a period of probably six years[17] he

[13] See Chap. 4.

[14] See Chaps. 5–6 (which provide the figure of three and a half years), and 254 (which states that he was around eighteen when he left his homeland).

[15] See Chaps. 8–9. For Lazaros' travels, see the map, p. xx, and also that in Ševčenko, "Eastern Provinces," 745.

[16] See Chap. 14.

[17] The figure of six years given in Chap. 16 seems to refer only to the first period Lazaros spent in the lavra of St. Sabas, not his whole time there. The beginning of Chap. 17 certainly suggests this, and it would appear to agree with my general chronology for Lazaros' life, which places his arrival in Jerusalem somewhere between 990 and 993 and his departure in 1009. If this chronology is accepted, he must have spent much longer than six years at St. Sabas—probably fifteen, at least—the balance therefore having been spent after his return from his temporary stay at St. Euthymios. On this interpretation, Lazaros would have been thirty-one or thirty-two following this six-year initial period at St. Sabas, and the date of his expulsion would be between 996 and 999. It should be noted, however, that the other versions of the *vita* do not agree on the length of time Lazaros spent at St. Sabas, although their accounts are not necessarily incompatible with the outline of events suggested above. Gregory of Cyprus (chaps. 13–14, *AASS*, Nov. 3:592–93) appears to suggest that Lazaros spent six years at the

was a monk at the lavra of St. Sabas, at this time a large monastic community a short distance from Jerusalem; but after disobeying the superior with his determination to pursue a solitary way of life in the desert during Lent, he was expelled. He then moved to the monastery of St. Euthymios, also quite near Jerusalem, and spent an unspecified time in that community before becoming disillusioned with the standards of monastic life there.[18] Helped by his initial sponsor, the archdeacon of the church of the Resurrection in the Holy Sepulchre complex in Jerusalem, he was able to secure readmittance to the lavra of Sabas. His second stay seems to have been most successful: he not only became a fully professed monk, but was ordained priest by the patriarch (prior to 1001)[19] and came to occupy the quite senior position of *kanonarches* in the monastery; at the same time he was developing the rigorous ascetic habits which were to characterize the later part of his life.

Lazaros left St. Sabas and the Holy Land shortly after the destruction of the church of the Holy Sepulchre on the orders of the Fatimid caliph al-Hākim, an event generally dated to September 1009.[20] He would have been forty-two or forty-three when he set out for Asia Minor again, having spent somewhere between sixteen and nineteen years in the Holy Land.[21]

---

lavra before his ordination and then the same number again afterward, apparently giving a total of twelve years for his initial stay, since there Lazaros' ordination precedes his expulsion. The Moscow *synaxarion* (f. 218^v) says that he labored tirelessly in St. Sabas for ten years, a figure which might be taken as referring only to his second stay. Ševčenko, "Eastern Provinces," 723, suggests a period of thirteen years for Lazaros' stay in Palestine but provides no basis for this figure.

[18] See Chap. 17.

[19] The patriarch mentioned in Chap. 17 as having ordained Lazaros must be Orestes Hieremias, who held office from 15 January 986 until 3 February 1006, as the patriarchate of Jerusalem remained vacant following his death until Theophilos took office in 1012. Since this Orestes was apparently also absent from Jerusalem from 1001 onward, having gone to Constantinople as an ambassador from the Caliph al-Hākim to sign a peace treaty with Basil II, and having remained there until his death, Lazaros' ordination must have taken place before his departure; see Schlumberger, *L'épopée* 2:443, drawing on Yaḥyā b. Sa'īd. On the dates of Orestes' patriarchate, see G. Fedalto, "Liste vescovili del patriarcato di Gerusalemme," *Orientalia christiana periodica* 49 (1983), 17.

[20] See above, n. 8, for the date, and the *vita,* Chap. 19, for discussion of this event.

[21] As is argued below, n. 24, Delehaye (*Stylites,* cxv) is surely mistaken in suggesting Lazaros left in 1006, a figure based only on incorrect internal calculations. Malamut

Lazaros traveled slowly northward toward Asia Minor, stopping and making detours to various pilgrimage sites. After crossing into Byzantine territory at Laodikaia, he visited the "Wondrous Mountain" at Antioch where St. Symeon the Younger had lived as a stylite; this visit made a deep impression on him and undoubtedly influenced the subsequent course of his life. From there he traveled up through Cilicia into Cappadocia and then northward again to visit pilgrimage sites in Pontus, before turning west and returning first to Chonai and finally to Ephesus. His long and arduous journey illustrates vividly the problems and dangers of a solitary traveler at the time. If Lazaros fled Jerusalem in the autumn of 1009, he was probably on Mt. Argeas near Caesarea in Cappadocia in the early spring of 1010,[22] and on the way to Euchaïa by early March of that year;[23] as he then had to travel another six hundred miles or more on foot before reaching the Ephesus area, one may conjecture that Lazaros was not back in his home region until late in that year or early in the following one (1010 or 1011).[24]

(*Route,* 119), who gives the date as 992, is evidently confusing this incident with Lazaros' departure from Attaleia. As mentioned above, Ševčenko ("Eastern Provinces," 723) provides no reason for his figure of only thirteen years for Lazaros' stay. Having established the chronology to this point, it now seems clear that the birth date of 980/81, which is required if Lazaros died at the age of seventy-two (as the versions of Gregory of Cyprus, the epitome, and the Moscow *synaxarion* suggest), is untenable. If he had been born at that later date and the chronology of his early life is sound, he could not have reached Jerusalem until 1004 at the earliest, and more probably not before 1005 or 1006; thus there would simply not have been enough time for the minimum ten- or twelve-year residence attested by these sources. On the other versions of Lazaros' Life, see below, section H.

[22] See Chap. 25.

[23] See Chap. 28.

[24] The *vita,* however, states explicitly (Chaps. 30 and 254) that twenty years elapsed between Lazaros' departure from his homeland and the time he returned to it again. Delehaye (*Stylites,* cxv) suggests on this basis that Lazaros must have returned to Asia Minor in 1006 (not 1013 as Thomas [Thomas and Hero, *Foundation Documents,* 148] mistakenly claims), and Janin (*Églises centres,* 242 n. 6) agrees in dating Lazaros' return to Ephesus in 1005; Foss (*Ephesus,* 128) evidently follows Delehaye, while Boulhol (*Anagnorismos,* 124) gives the year as 1004 and Lazaros' age as thirty-seven, although he provides no reason for doing so. These dates are, however, impossible if Lazaros witnessed the destruction of the Holy Sepulchre at Jerusalem in 1009; thus Delehaye's claim that none of the dates he gives "sont contredites par aucun des faits racontés dans la Vie," must be mistaken. If the chronology I have suggested here is correct, then

After a short visit to the general vicinity of his home village and a brief stay at a monastery above the village of Kepion, evidently just outside Ephesus, Lazaros finally settled in the area at a small hermitage dedicated to St. Marina and occupied by two brothers. These men built a pillar for Lazaros, and it was thus here, during his seven years at St. Marina, that he began the career as a stylite which was to bring him such renown. His reputation soon spread and, with the aid of local benefactors, a monastery was constructed to house the disciples who gathered round him. Of particular importance was a wealthy woman called Iouditta, originally from Calabria, who paid for the rebuilding of the church and also adopted Lazaros' young brother Ignatios, who ran away from home to join him during this period.[25] The metropolitan

---

Lazaros had in fact been away from the area for far longer than twenty years: twenty-five at least and perhaps as long as twenty-seven since he ran away from the monastery of Strobelion.

One solution to this difficulty is that the author may be using a very round figure here. Another is that the twenty years he mentions may actually refer to the time Lazaros was away from Asia Minor, that is outside Byzantine territory. This latter suggestion would certainly make some sense since, as was shown above, Lazaros left Attaleia somewhere between 991 and 993. Possibly Gregory the Cellarer heard Lazaros give this figure or found it in the *typikon* (see Chap. 246) and mistakenly took it as referring to the time he was away from his specific homeland in the Ephesus region. Other conceivable solutions raise more problems than they solve: perhaps Lazaros did not really witness the destruction of the Holy Sepulchre (but later claimed this in order to legitimize his departure from St. Sabas) or perhaps his seven-year stay at Attaleia is either a fabrication or a misunderstanding of information contained in the *diatyposis*, given the unlikelihood of an inexperienced young man in his late teens or early twenties having been allowed to do what he is said to have done there.

[25] Chronological problems are posed by the *vita's* statement (Chap. 33) that Ignatios was only about eight when he ran away from home to join his brother. Even if he arrived at St. Marina almost immediately after Lazaros, say in late 1011, then the earliest possible date for his birth would be 1003; Lazaros, however, having been born in 966 or 967, must have been at least thirty-six by then. As Lazaros was the fifth child born to his parents (see Chap. 3), his mother Irene/Eupraxia, even had she started having children at a very early age indeed, would have been at least fifty years old in 1003 and thus past normal childbearing age. Furthermore, since Irene/Eupraxia was still alive long after Lazaros had gone up onto Galesion (Chap. 59), Ignatios cannot have been Lazaros' half-brother by a different mother. There seems to be no simple solution: the easiest way out is to suggest that Gregory the Cellarer must have been mistaken or exaggerating in claiming that Ignatios was only eight when he joined his brother; or possibly Ignatios was indeed born when his mother was very old, either by Lazaros'

of Ephesus also evidently granted some land to the community, an important point when considering later strained relations between Galesion and the ecclesiastical authorities in Ephesus.[26] From the chronology established to this point it would appear that Lazaros began his stay at St. Marina in 1011 or possibly 1012,[27] at about the age of forty-five.[28]

The situation of this monastery beside the main road into Ephesus was not well suited to one who aspired to the ascetic ideals of *hesychia.* After seven years there,[29] Lazaros turned to the neighboring mountain, Galesion, which was quite barren and largely uninhabited; he left his pillar at St. Marina and settled instead in a cave that had been previously occupied by a holy man called Paphnoutios. His first stay lasted for only six months before he was ordered off the mountain by the metropolitan of Ephesus,[30] but he returned shortly thereafter, this time to remain for good. It is important to note, however, in view of the prominence of this problem at the end of Lazaros' life, that the authorities in Ephesus openly opposed his settlement on the mountain from the very start. Lazaros' permanent move to Galesion should be

own father or by a second husband. Other answers are mere speculation and are fraught with difficulties: perhaps Ignatios was an illegitimate child of Lazaros' father (who, although dead by the time Lazaros returned to his home [Chap. 30], could still have been alive seven or eight years before); perhaps Irene was not Lazaros' real mother at all (hence her trouble in recognizing him [Chap. 30]); perhaps Lazaros was *not* eighty-six when he died; perhaps the story of his stay at Attaleia *was* a fabrication or an exaggeration; or perhaps Lazaros *did* later invent the story that he witnessed the destruction of the Holy Sepulchre (on which the dating of his return to Asia Minor and of his establishment at St. Marina depends) and in fact returned much earlier, possibly in 1005 as the *internal* evidence of the *vita* would suggest. The problem is insoluble as it stands but the chronology I have suggested appears otherwise sufficiently sound and coherent for it not to be rejected on this basis alone.

[26] On the possible identification of this metropolitan as Theodore II of Ephesus, see below, Chap. 34; he may also have been the metropolitan who opposed Lazaros' initial move from St. Marina to Galesion, see below.

[27] Depending on when he actually returned to the region and how long he spent at Kepion.

[28] See the *vita,* Chaps. 31–32. Delehaye (*vita,* p. 520 [1]) and Janin (*Églises centres,* 243), who use the date of Lazaros' death and the information given in Chap. 254 but do not take into account the dating of the destruction of the Holy Sepulchre, suggest, respectively, the years 1006–13 and 1005–12 for Lazaros' stay at St. Marina.

[29] See Chaps. 35 and 254.

[30] See Chap. 53.

dated around 1018 or, perhaps more likely (given the six-month trial period) 1019, when he would have been about fifty-two or fifty-three years old.

Lazaros stayed in the cave for a few months at the most before moving onto a pillar which the brethren had built for him nearby.[31] At first he was alone there but, after he nearly died of thirst, a monk went up to live in the cave to look after him.[32] Although the process is not described in any detail in the *vita,* a new community, known as that of the Savior, grew up around Lazaros' pillar and came, in the course of time, to have resident monks and a church.[33] The *diatyposis* (monastic rule) given by Lazaros at the very end of his life limited this community to twelve brothers but, at this earlier time, when it was the only community on the mountain, it may well have been larger.[34] Lazaros spent twelve years at the Savior before moving higher up the mountain to a new pillar, which he had built for him following a disagreement with some of his monks over the constant visits to the community of a nun from Ephesus.[35] This move to his second pillar, that of the Theotokos, must have occurred in 1030 or 1031, when Lazaros was about sixty-four.[36]

The same pattern repeated itself here, with a small community gradually developing around the pillar at this new site,[37] which then became unsuitable

[31] The monastery, and hence, presumably, Lazaros' pillar, was a short distance below the cave of Paphnoutios; see Chap. 52.

[32] See Chaps. 53 and 55.

[33] Chap. 56 shows that people soon started to visit Lazaros there quite regularly. The construction of the church of the Savior is mentioned in passing in Chap. 42 but no details are given. Gregory of Cyprus fills this gap by making Iouditta, to whom the primary *vita* attributes the financing of the new church at St. Marina, responsible for the Savior instead (chap. 25, *AASS,* Nov. 3:598D). My general chronology dates the development of the community of the Savior to the early 1020s.

[34] See Chap. 246. It is not clear if this number includes monks living in the cave of Paphnoutios or in the cell or cells in front of it; certainly there was at least one cell there at a time shortly after Lazaros' death; see Chap. 52.

[35] See Chaps. 57–58.

[36] Janin, *Églises centres,* 243, suggests Lazaros stayed at the Savior from 1012 to 1024.

[37] The *vita* (Chaps. 43, 50, and 64) refers to a number of incidents said to have taken place when Lazaros was living *alone* on the pillar of the Theotokos. This perhaps indicates that a fairly considerable period of time elapsed before the monastery developed there; cf. Chaps. 58 and 61. A tiny chapel appears to be the first development at the site (Chap. 64).

for Lazaros' requirements for some reason. If the tradition preserved by Gregory of Cyprus is to be believed, it became too cramped for his now more ambitious plans, which were to lead to the founding of a third community on the mountain.[38] Certainly the *diatyposis* suggests that the monastery of the Theotokos was only a small establishment at the end of Lazaros' life, of the same size as the Savior.[39] It is unclear exactly how long Lazaros spent at the Theotokos, and it is nowhere stated when precisely he moved up to his last pillar, that of the Resurrection, around which the largest and evidently most enduring community on Galesion was to be founded. The move certainly did not take place before late 1041 (probably not before early 1042) and there are some indications that it may have occurred in mid 1042 or shortly thereafter, when Lazaros was already seventy-five or seventy-six.[40]

[38] Chap. 29, *AASS,* Nov. 3:599E. On this version, see below, section H. Gregory of Cyprus may, however, be confusing or conflating this move with the one from the Savior to the Theotokos, because he describes it as being preceded by the incident in which Lazaros almost died of thirst; according to the primary *vita* (Chap. 55) this happened soon after his move to the mountain and thus when he was still at the Savior. The other incident mentioned, that of the snake sliding inside his tunic (Chap. 67), did indeed take place at the Theotokos.

[39] See Chap. 246.

[40] Chaps. 229–30 provide the crucial evidence establishing the earliest possible date for Lazaros' move to his pillar at the Resurrection. According to the narrative there, the move took place while the anonymous monk, whose escapades form the subject of those chapters, was away from Galesion on the final phase of his adventures. This phase, which involved his absconding from a mission to Constantinople, began at the very earliest in late 1041: he was still in Bulgaria when Peter Deljan was blinded early in that year and evidently "wandered about" for some time after that before making his way back to Galesion, where he remained for another "short" period until he got permission from Lazaros to go on the mission. This must have left before the beginning of June 1042, however, for the monk became involved in the acclamation of Constantine Monomachos as emperor, which occurred early in that month. Chap. 102 also tells the story of a mission that went to Constantinople from Galesion in April 1042 to warn Nikephoros Kampan[ar]es about the insurrection that resulted in the overthrow of Michael V (see Chap. 102). It is unclear how this may relate to the anonymous monk's mission, if at all, but it is conceivable that it was the one from which he absconded; certainly the date accords. Lazaros' move to the site of the Resurrection must thus have taken place between late 1041 (or perhaps April 1042) and the point at which the anonymous monk returned, sometime after June 1042.

Additional, if tenuous, evidence elsewhere in the *vita* corroborates this suggested dating. Chap. 227, which deals with the imposter Dalassenos, may thus refer to a time

Be that as it may, Lazaros, who had evidently been ill for several years,[41] died on his pillar at the monastery of the Resurrection, which by that time had grown into a community of some forty monks,[42] on 7 November 1053, most probably at the age of eighty-six. Gregory the Cellarer says that he had spent forty-one years in all on Galesion,[43] a figure which quite nicely confirms the chronology suggested here if it is taken to include the time he spent at St. Marina, in the foothills, where he established himself in 1011 or 1012.[44]

C. Lazaros as a Person, an Ascetic, and a Teacher

It is often hard to obtain a sense of genuine personality from hagiographical writing, and much of what is said about Lazaros in the *vita* conforms to accepted stereotypes and patterns; nevertheless, there are some fascinating glimpses of Lazaros' character here and the reader is occasionally able to penetrate beneath the simple veneer of pious reputation.

Little is revealed about Lazaros' physical appearance, except that he was evidently a tall man,[45] and, of course, gaunt as a result of his strict asceticism.[46] The harsh regime he followed appears not to have seriously undermined his

when Lazaros was already at the Resurrection, given that the preceding chapter mentions the icons of the archangels that stood at the foot of his pillar there (cf. Chap. 253). As suggested in the footnotes to Chap. 227, a likely date for the incident may be shortly after the accession of Monomachos, that is, in 1042. At the same time, the episode involving Makrembolites (Chap. 101) may have taken place shortly before or at about the time Michael IV died, that is, in December 1041. As Lazaros is stated to be on the pillar of the Theotokos at that time, these two episodes taken in conjunction would also indicate a date for the move sometime in 1042. This would also tie in with the story contained in the other versions of the *vita* suggesting that Monomachos gave Lazaros the money to build the church of the Resurrection, although, as will be seen below (section F.b., p. 41), the question of this funding is very thorny.

[41] See Chaps. 206–7.

[42] See Chap. 246.

[43] See Chap. 254.

[44] It is only a problem if this first period in the area is excluded, for according to my chronology, Lazaros did not actually move up onto the mountain proper, to the cave at what was to become the community of the Savior, until 1018 or 1019: on this reckoning he spent, at the most, about thirty-five years on the mountain itself.

[45] See Chap. 73.

[46] See Chap. 252.

physical constitution until well into his eighties, when he became seriously ill;[47] even to the end, however, his body is said to have remained in remarkably good condition, considering the circumstances in which he had lived.[48]

As regards Lazaros' character, the most obvious aspect is his lifelong devotion to Christian asceticism. His determination to survive on only the barest necessities and to give away to the needy anything he deemed superfluous revealed itself very early in his life,[49] while his first actual experience of solitary asceticism came when he was in his early twenties, at Attaleia.[50] Presumably the patterns of his ascetic life and diet were already being formed at that time, but they became firmly established during his years at the lavra of St. Sabas near Jerusalem, and were applied with increasing strictness after he returned to the Ephesus region.

While in the Holy Land, Lazaros abstained from wine, except at the Eucharist, as well as oil and cheese.[51] These practices continued at St. Marina where, after a period of time, he also excluded bread from his diet (except for communion bread) and lived entirely on raw vegetables and pulses, which were either boiled without oil or merely soaked in water.[52] At the monasteries of the Savior and the Theotokos, he abstained from cooked food on Wednesdays and Fridays, and, during the three forty-day fasts of the Byzantine liturgical year he would eat nothing at all on weekdays. This harsh regime was moderated a little at the monastery of the Resurrection, but he was already in his late seventies then; indeed, these changes may have occurred only when he lost his teeth and became ill during the last three years of his life. At that stage he was eating cooked food, prepared without oil, daily; he also avoided liquids until evening, when he would have drinks that were sometimes hot and sweetened with fruit juice or honey.[53]

Lazaros' devotion to asceticism was not restricted to his diet. He had evidently already taken to wearing the single leather tunic, which was to char-

[47] See Chaps. 206–8, 221, 223; cf. also, Chap. 82 and perhaps Chap. 68.

[48] See Chap. 252.

[49] See Chaps. 3, 4, 8, 23, 24.

[50] See Chaps. 10–14.

[51] See Chap. 17.

[52] See Chaps. 35 and 81.

[53] See especially Chaps. 81–82; but also Chaps. 45, 53, and 55.

acterize his dress sometime before he returned to the Ephesus region.[54] This continued to be the only real clothing he had all the year round while he was on his various pillars, and even this tunic was only changed after years of use, when it was quite literally falling apart.[55] The only other garments he wore were a cowl, scapular, and stole, although, toward the end at least, he also had a woollen cloak.[56] Lazaros had stopped sleeping on a bed while he was at St. Sabas; for the rest of his life, he used a special little chair instead so that he never lay down at full stretch.[57] Even when he was seriously ill he refused any extra comfort in this respect, although his monks tried hard to offer him some relief in the form of a pillow or cushion.[58] He thus strove to attain the ascetic ideal of perpetual watchfulness, keeping vigil all night and, even when overcome by sleep, only dozing lightly while sitting down.[59] At night he would also engage in the spiritual practice of contrition, weeping and wailing while his monks were singing the vigil service in church.[60]

By the time he was on his first pillar at the community of St. Marina, Lazaros had adopted the practice of wearing ascetic "irons" next to his skin. These were a series of heavy pieces of metal, linked together, that tightly enclosed his upper body from shoulders to waist;[61] they were only removed at his death and seem thereafter to have become a relic in the monastery church.[62] He also evidently suffered greatly from lice and other vermin,[63] but it was his endurance of perpetual exposure to the elements that made the greatest impression upon those who saw him.[64]

[54] See Chap. 26.

[55] At least one such leather tunic lasted for twelve years; see Chaps. 35, 82, 112, 208, 235; cf. Chaps. 59 and 252.

[56] See Chap. 35 (for the former) and Chap. 208 (for the latter).

[57] See Chap. 35; cf. Chap. 162.

[58] See Chap. 208.

[59] See Chaps. 53, 59, 225, 248.

[60] See Chap. 185.

[61] See Chap. 35; cf. Chap. 59.

[62] See Chap. 252 for their removal, Chap. 179 for the suggestion of their use as a relic.

[63] See Chaps. 59, 222, 235.

[64] See, e.g., Chaps. 59, 111, 208, 235. Note that in Chaps. 59–60 reference is made to a period during which Lazaros tried hanging his bare feet outside the pillar through a hole in the wall, although he was eventually persuaded to abandon this practice.

The outstanding feature of Lazaros' ascetic practice was thus his confinement on an open pillar for more than forty years, a feat which placed him in a long tradition of Byzantine stylites. He occupied a total of four pillars during this period,[65] spending seven years on the first (at St. Marina) and roughly twelve years each on the last three on Galesion. Each of his pillars was built to order and, from the scant evidence provided by the *vita,* were similar, at least in their basic features. Most notably these pillars were completely open to the elements, lacking a roof to provide shelter from wind, rain, and snow or shade from the sun.[66] However a wall of some sort enclosed the space on top of the pillar, creating the very cramped and confined "cell" in which Lazaros lived. This wall was high enough to obscure him from the view of anyone standing on a platform that had been built adjoining the cell,[67] but when Lazaros stood up, he could be seen by those below and in front of his pillar;[68] he in turn could see a great deal of what was going on within the monastery and in at least some of the surrounding area.[69] The cell had no door[70] but did have a small window giving access to the platform; Lazaros could open it to speak to visitors and receive his food and other needs, but it could also be secured from the inside.[71] It seems to have provided only a limited view of the area immediately outside, as he was unable to see whether more than one person was waiting to talk to him.[72] The window was nevertheless large enough for him to lean out of[73] and, on one occasion at least, for a visitor to thrust his head and part of his body through in order to examine

[65] As did Symeon Stylites the Elder; Theodoret, *Hist. Rel.,* 26.12.

[66] Lazaros' pillar at St. Marina was initially covered but he later had the roof removed: see Chap. 31. For it being open to the elements, see, e.g., Chaps. 111, 235.

[67] See, e.g., Chap. 81.

[68] See, e.g., Chaps. 117, 128, 142. Chap. 225 also suggests that Lazaros could be seen when he was dozing, although it is unclear exactly from what vantage point and whether he was still standing (perhaps propped up in some way) or was actually seated on his special chair; only the latter would imply much greater visibility. Cf. Chap. 59.

[69] See Chaps. 108, 109, and 236.

[70] When Lazaros was dying, entry had to be gained over the wall by means of a ladder; see Chap. 249.

[71] See, e.g., Chap. 219.

[72] See, e.g., Chaps. 88, 103–4.

[73] See, e.g., Chaps. 87 and 120.

the interior.[74] Access to this window was gained by means of a ladder[75] leading to the platform on which visitors could stand or sit;[76] at the monastery of the Resurrection, at least, icons of the archangels stood there.[77]

The cell at the monastery of the Resurrection may also have had a second window that opened toward, and perhaps even into, the church.[78] Such a feature would, as Delehaye argues, explain the puzzling passages in the *vita* that appear to state unequivocally that the pillar was actually inside the monastery church.[79] The obvious solution is that a later church was constructed around the pillar once Lazaros had abandoned it, but Chapter 160 implies to the contrary that the pillar was definitely *in* (ἐν) the church when his successor, Kerykos, moved onto it, even though this man is also said to have always lived without any shelter. Moreover, Chapter 225, at least as Delehaye understands it, implies that Lazaros could be seen, and poked with a stick, from inside the church during a service.[80] If, however, the pillar abutted the side of the church and had an opening through which Lazaros could observe and even participate in the services, this might account for statements suggesting that the pillar was in the church. Moreover, if the opening was simply a small window, rather than a door, it would explain passages clearly indicating that people had to descend the pillar before they could enter the church.[81]

[74] See Chap. 114; Chaps. 75, 107, and 117 also imply that a kiss of greeting could be given through this window.

[75] See, e.g., Chap. 87.

[76] See, e.g., Chaps. 114 (which refers to the "other part of the pillar") and 107 (where a visitor sits while talking to Lazaros).

[77] See Chap. 226.

[78] See Chap. 249. If the brothers were singing in the church when Jonas gave his shout, it is hard to understand how they would have heard him if he was outside and some distance away from the building; on the other hand, if he opened a window directly into the church there would be no problem. Chap. 118 also seems to imply that one of Lazaros' pillars, probably that at the monastery of the Resurrection, stood very close to the wall of the church on one side; cf. also Chaps. 86 and 252.

[79] See Chaps. 157, 159, and 207; for Delehaye's discussion of these passages, see his *Stylites,* cxii–cxiv.

[80] This, however, is certainly not the only possible interpretation: see the text and the notes on the chapter below.

[81] See, e.g., Chaps. 219 and 252.

The height of the pillars is never specified,[82] but they were apparently relatively low. Certainly a normal conversation could be conducted with people on the ground below and Lazaros could easily be heard when preaching or when addressing the monks who would assemble round it.[83] As has just been seen, the pillar at the monastery of the Theotokos, and probably also that at the Resurrection, was certainly short enough to join onto the wall of the choir of the church, even if it was not later completely incorporated into the building. Little is said, either, about the method of construction used in these pillars, although the one at the Theotokos monastery certainly included masonry,[84] and that at the Resurrection apparently incorporated a water cistern.[85] The pillar at the Savior was built in a dry water course,[86] but otherwise it is implied that the pillars stood in the main courtyard of the monastery that grew up around them.

The exact size of the cell is also never stated. The pillar at the Theotokos is said to have been little more than two feet wide;[87] although this measurement may refer only to the pillar itself,[88] there is no reason for supposing that the cell on top of it was very much larger.[89] When Lazaros was dying at the Resurrection, there was room for at least one monk (and possibly more) in the cell at the same time;[90] the evidence implies, however, that there was really no more space than Lazaros required for standing up and for sitting on his special chair, although there was apparently also an area in which he relieved himself[91] and room for putting a pot of food or drink on the floor. Although

[82] Chap. 58 in the *vita* refers to the pillar of the Theotokos as being "elevated" and implies that the one at St. Marina also fit this description.

[83] See, e.g., Chaps. 57, 108, 120, 128, 142; Lazaros could also evidently be reached with a pole (Chap. 225).

[84] See Chap. 58.

[85] See Chap. 222. Delehaye (*Stylites,* clx) interprets this passage to refer not to a water cistern but to a waste pipe.

[86] See Chap. 53.

[87] See Chap. 235; the figure given is "three spans."

[88] See Delehaye, *Stylites,* clv.

[89] Cf. Chap. 114, where the cell is described as "very confined and stifling" by a distinguished visiting ascetic.

[90] See Chap. 249.

[91] See Chap. 81.

Lazaros sometimes wrote in his cell,[92] this was presumably done on his lap and does not necessarily imply the presence of any other furniture. Nor is there mention of any decoration apart from the symbol of the cross that he had himself engraved in one pillar.[93] He did, however, apparently have tokens on hand to give to visitors and probably some coins for the poor from time to time.[94]

Another fundamental aspect of Lazaros' character that emerges from the *vita* is his extraordinary determination. The primary evidence for this is his long and unfailing endurance of the extremely harsh ascetic lifestyle, but his single-mindedness was already apparent in his early life and travels, which are characterized by his refusal to be deflected from his goals by any obstacle, be it relatives,[95] robbers,[96] soldiers,[97] hostile peasants,[98] political rulers,[99] women,[100] demons,[101] animals,[102] lax monks,[103] or intransigent superiors.[104] The same determination is also epitomized by his refusal to consider abandoning his foundation on Galesion despite prolonged and fierce opposition from the highest ecclesiastical and political authorities and from large numbers of his own monks.[105]

Along with this determination, Lazaros also possessed considerable powers of persuasion. He made an excellent impression on those he encountered or who came to see him and this ability certainly assisted him, both in his

[92] See Chap. 67.

[93] See Chap. 59.

[94] See Chaps. 75, 113, 145; cf. Chap. 248, where the rumor that the pillar was full of gold is mentioned.

[95] See Chaps. 3–4, 30.

[96] See Chaps. 9, 23.

[97] See Chap. 15.

[98] See Chaps. 27, 28.

[99] See Chap. 20.

[100] See Chap. 7.

[101] See Chaps. 7, 25, 28.

[102] See Chaps. 22, 25–27.

[103] See Chaps. 4, 8, 17, 24.

[104] See Chaps. 5, 17.

[105] See below, sections D and F.

own career and in furthering the interests of his monasteries. Important and influential people thus became willing helpers and benefactors, among them members of the ecclesiastical hierarchy (like the archdeacon of the church of the Holy Sepulchre in Jerusalem),[106] local lay people (like the Calabrian woman Iouditta at St. Marina),[107] and notable members of the aristocracy and bureaucracy (like Romanos Skleros, or Nikephoros Kampan[ar]es).[108] While the impression Lazaros made late in his life depended to a large extent upon his appearance and reputation, his persuasive abilities predate his celebrity and the establishment of his credentials.[109]

Lazaros' capacity to express himself, in speech and perhaps even in writing, also seem to have been a factor in his influence. Despite his relatively low social background, he had received a good education as a notary in his youth.[110] There are several references in the *vita* to his writing of letters,[111] and these were evidently not only acceptable to people occupying some of the highest positions in the Byzantine world, but also made a considerable impression upon them.[112] Lazaros was clearly not interested in debating theological questions or expounding the finer points of the Scriptures,[113] preferring actions and example to words. The *vita* reveals that he was, nevertheless, a persuasive and memorable teacher, particularly of his monks, who would gather

[106] See Chaps. 16–17; cf. e.g., the metropolitan of Ephesus mentioned in Chap. 34, or the bishop of Philetos, Chaps. 10–11.

[107] See Chap. 34.

[108] See Chaps. 87 and 245 for Romanos; Chap. 102 (cf. Chaps. 105–6) for Nikephoros. For attracting the respect of other important and influential men, see, e.g., Chaps. 101, 103, 105, 107, 118, 119; also, of course, the evident attraction of benefactions from Constantine IX Monomachos and Maria Skleraina, Chap. 245 (cf. 230). Lazaros' contacts with such people are neatly summarized by Morris, *Monks,* 104–5; she also summarizes his benefactors, p. 139; cf. eadem, "Political Saint," 49.

[109] So, e.g., his persuasion of the Armenian soldiers in Chap. 15 or of the emir in Chap. 20, in addition to those mentioned above, like the archdeacon at Jerusalem or the bishop of Philetos.

[110] See Chaps. 3, 4, and 30.

[111] See, e.g., Chaps. 67, 102, 151, 221, 223, 227, and 238.

[112] So his letters to the emperor, which evidently provoked irritation as well as eliciting substantial assistance. Cf. Ševčenko, "Eastern Provinces," 725.

[113] See Chaps. 119–20.

around his pillar to hear him speak or read to them, or who, like some visitors, would receive individual counseling from him.[114] When speaking he liked to make his points briefly but vividly and effectively,[115] and was given to supporting his teaching by reference to patristic examples[116] as well as to the Bible.[117]

Lazaros' great devotion to asceticism does not appear to have completely overwhelmed his sense of humor. The author of the *vita* thus mentions him smiling on a number of occasions and even joking at the folly of his monks or visitors, often as a means of gentle reproach.[118] Similarly appealing to the modern mind is the evidence that Lazaros was a warm, caring person, who was renowned for his benevolence, generosity, and tolerance. He was evidently always concerned with the long-term effect of his actions on the spiritual well-being of those with whom he was dealing, rather than with adherence to strict rules of human conduct and with immediate and superficial appearances of right and wrong. Thieves, for example, were allowed to make off with their ill-gotten gains, were forgiven when apprehended, or were even rewarded with gifts, because Lazaros saw that they were driven to their crimes by the dire economic and social circumstances in which they found themselves; he also believed that generosity would lead more surely to their salvation than would harsh reproaches or punishment.[119] Beggars and other visitors were also treated generously, even when they were suspected of being wrongly motivated or of being outright frauds, and even when this placed serious strains on the resources of the monastery. Indeed, Lazaros went so far as to claim that the real reason God had permitted his foundation to prosper was to look after such people.[120]

The *vita* makes clear, however, that Lazaros' tolerance had its limits and

[114] See, e.g., Chaps. 10, 49, 100, 118, 121, 128, 147, 148, 196, 232.

[115] See Chaps. 101, 105, 119, 122, 184.

[116] See especially Chap. 128; cf. also Chaps. 132–33, 135–37, 144, 148, 157, 162, 163, 186, 210, 216.

[117] See, e.g., Chaps. 181 and 196; but cf. the statement in Chap. 119, which suggests that he tried to avoid too frequent or ostentatious use of such citations.

[118] See, e.g., Chaps. 88, 107, 114, 248.

[119] See, e.g., Chaps. 66, 108, 142, 240, 241.

[120] See, e.g., Chaps. 32, 34, 123, 143, 145, 146, 150, 151, 161, 210, 211, 213, 248. Cf. also Lazaros' devotion to the ideal of Christian charity in his early days in Chaps. 3, 4, 8, 23, 24.

that he was not always amiable and gentle. Thus, when he thought it would be beneficial to an individual or the community at large, he might adopt quite a strict approach to appropriate and proper behavior,[121] and his monks would sometimes be harshly reproved and physically punished for infractions of discipline.[122] Sometimes, too, he would feign great anger for the sake of the effect this might have on the object of his wrath.[123] The *vita* also provides glimpses of genuine and very human irritation and frustration,[124] however, which help to round out his portrait. At one point the author notes that, when roused, Lazaros could be a terrifying man.[125]

Lazaros also gained a reputation for remarkable, indeed sometimes miraculous, insight and foresight, and a number of episodes recorded in the *vita* show that he did possess considerable ability to judge character and to weigh up a particular situation. This allowed him to resolve problems in ways that were not always obvious to those involved; his solutions tended to seek compromise and the best outcome for all concerned (in terms of long-term spiritual benefit), rather than to make definitive judgments in favor of one party or rulings which provided only superficial justice or were based simply on adherence to tradition.[126] This ability also made him very popular as a father confessor; he was able to discern the problems that were troubling people, the sources of the guilt feelings that were making them depressed or miserable, and was thus able to help them unburden themselves of their troubles.[127] He was clearly a very shrewd man, and his biographer is keen to point out that, even though his actions may have appeared at times to be naive or his decisions unwise, he always knew exactly what he was doing.[128]

A final aspect of Lazaros' character to be noted here is his modesty and humility. Possession of such virtues is a standard part of the traditional picture of a Christian holy man, but Lazaros' careful avoidance of praise, his refusal to take credit for his achievements and abilities, and his attempts to practice

[121] See, e.g., Chaps. 91, 95, 118, 119, 147, 148.

[122] See, e.g., Chaps. 11, 49, 57, 77, 182, 183, 188, 194, 195, 203, 204, 224, and 225.

[123] See Chaps. 142, 150, 220.

[124] See Chaps. 202 and 245.

[125] See Chap. 195.

[126] See, e.g., Chaps. 122, 125–26, 127, 129, 131–34, 183, 187, 189, 225.

[127] See, e.g., Chaps. 93, 94, 96, 118, 226.

[128] See, e.g., Chaps. 18, 121, 146, 183, 210.

charity and the like in secret rather than overtly, appear to have been genuine and are borne out by the account of his actions and teaching, at least as recorded in the *vita*.[129]

D. Lazaros as an Eleventh-Century Monastic Leader

Many aspects of Lazaros' character are discernible in the policy and practice he adopted in overseeing the affairs of the monastic communities that formed around him. Here his prime concern was to ensure that the core ideals of cenobitic monasticism were maintained while allowing for the exploration of individual spiritual experience by those who were capable of doing so.[130] His policies and practices thus fit into a pattern detectable in many important monastic foundations of the tenth and eleventh centuries that attempted to blend elements of eremitical and communal life, and which have been characterized as hybrids of cenobitic and lavriote styles of monasticism.[131] Activities

[129] See, e.g., Chaps. 14, 15, 72, 145, 151, 185, 186, 197, 212, 215, 220.

[130] This is perhaps seen most explicitly in Chaps. 180 and 196, but is also implied by many of the passages cited in the following notes. See also the description of Lazaros' style of monasticism in Kazhdan and Epstein, *Change,* 87–88; Kazhdan, "Ideals," 476; and cf. Papachryssanthou, "Vie monastique," 164.

[131] See Morris, *Monks,* 31–63, but esp. 40–42. Morris is, however, perhaps overly determined to place Lazaros in the "lavriote" camp; she thus tends to lay too little stress on his concern to maintain communal aspects of monastic life and to limit the practice of individual asceticism that would take members of his community beyond the normal confines of that lifestyle. For example, Morris states (p. 54) that the monastic habit, with all its symbolism involving tonsure, robes, scapular, and cowl was common in "the great coenobitic houses" but that "this is in marked contrast to Lazaros of Mount Galesion in his hair shirt . . . and vividly marks the difference in <his> monastic approach." Quite apart from the fact the Lazaros is not said to have worn a hair shirt, the *vita* reveals that he actually argued for the preservation of the three levels of monastic habit for his monks (Chap. 130), ensured that a new habit was issued to them each year (Chap. 145; cf. the stipulation in the *diatyposis,* Chap. 246), and wore the cowl, stole, and scapular himself (Chap. 35, although it is to be noted that the passage is taken from the Life of St. Stephen the Younger and applied to Lazaros; cf., however, Chap. 160 where the stylite Kerykos is also said to have worn a scapular and cowl that he made for himself out of wool). In contrast to Morris, see Thomas ("Evergetine Reform," 249–52; Thomas and Hero, *Foundation Documents,* 151–52) who emphasizes Lazaros' struggle to preserve cenobitic forms at a time when these were threatening to break down under the weight of individual interests.

which tended to undermine the communal life of the monastery or attitudes and practices that threatened the equality of its members[132] were frowned upon by Lazaros, who attempted to eradicate them whenever possible. Private acts of worship,[133] refusal to participate in communal meals,[134] the possession of private property or money, and the pursuit of private interests were all condemned.[135] At the same time, the role and responsibility of the superior, in deciding not only matters of communal importance but the minutiae of the lives of each individual in his monastery, was emphasized.[136] For Lazaros, the spiritual well-being of the individual depended upon long experience of, and training in, the communal monastic life, together with the practice of the accompanying virtues, especially obedience.[137] Individual expressions of spirituality were permissible (and perhaps ultimately to be sought), but only when they originated *within* this framework. A number of other stylites are thus

[132] For stress on equality, see, e.g., Chap. 187. This is also implied by Lazaros' condemnation of the possession of personal property; but compare Chap. 227, where a supposed nobleman is said to have been treated with "respect" by the father and the brothers because of his background.

[133] See, explicitly, Chap. 138; cf. also the emphasis placed on the necessity for, and benefits of church attendance by Lazaros (and Gregory the Cellarer), e.g., Chaps. 139, 157, 177, 182, 185, 204.

[134] See, e.g., Chaps. 147; cf. Chaps. 184, 204.

[135] See Chaps. 143, 145, 148, 163, 191–93, 202, 204, 216, 228.

[136] Morris (*Monks,* 42) suggests that Lazaros' "role as *hegoumenos* was, in the lavriote tradition, more advisory than administrative," with the day-to-day running of affairs left to an *oikonomos.* This is certainly the approach envisaged in the *diatyposis,* and may well have become necessary as Lazaros himself became older and the community larger, perhaps after his move up to the monastery of the Resurrection; it is also implied by his evident desire to escape the problems of communal life at the Savior by moving to the (then) remote pillar of the Theotokos. The *vita* clearly shows, however, that, for much of his life at St. Marina and on Galesion he was closely involved in the day-to-day affairs of the monasteries; note, e.g., the apparent requirement that monks coming and going from the monastery should report to him in order to receive his blessing (Chaps. 134, 185, 249); his personal control of monastery business (implied in Chaps. 134, 154, 156, 249); and his involvement in disputes about personal property (Chap. 148) or even the legitimacy of peeling fruit before it was eaten (Chap. 57). My interpretation of Lazaros' role here thus agrees more closely with Kazhdan's view ("Ideals," 476) than with that of Thomas (Thomas and Hero, *Foundation Documents,* 152).

[137] See, e.g., Chaps. 158, 180, 198, 200, 201.

mentioned in the Galesiote community,[138] but permission to adopt such a solitary way of life had to be obtained from Lazaros himself, who would grant it only in exceptional circumstances and with great reluctance, while emphasizing the dangers involved.[139] At the same time he stressed that those who could not aspire to such heights of spiritual achievement were in no sense inferior; their quest for salvation simply followed a different, rather than a lesser, path.[140] Similarly, Lazaros emphasized that those whose backgrounds suited them only to the more menial tasks in the monastery were not inferior to the choir-monks and that each way of life had advantages and disadvantages:[141] all men were equal in the eyes of God and it was merely human vanity and pride to differentiate between them.

Lazaros was concerned with the well-being of his whole flock, not just that of the spiritual stars or those who possessed exceptional abilities. He thus sought to apply and stress in his communities (as in his own life) those elements of the Christian message that emphasized the need to value and care for the weak, the poor, and the less able. There was thus a constant stress on the advantages of perseverance,[142] of determination, and of true asceticism.[143] Moreover, Lazaros' clear devotion to the ideals of toleration meant that he was almost always prepared to give those who failed a second chance, to forgive those who caused trouble for him or the community, and to give the benefit of the doubt in even the most unpromising circumstances.[144]

The *vita* reveals that many monks believed it was perfectly possible to practice their monasticism in ways that ran counter to, and indeed sometimes fell far short of, the ideals espoused by Lazaros; as a result he encountered

[138] So Kerykos (Chap. 159), Nikon, and Merkourios (Chap. 175); Laurentios "the Stylite" (first mentioned in Chap. 71 but also on several other occasions) probably only adopted this way of life after Lazaros' death. Note also the monk who is implied by Chap. 61 to be living as a solitary on the mountain.

[139] See, e.g., Chaps. 175, 189, 196, 197, 204; cf., again, Chap. 81.

[140] See, e.g., Chaps. 181, 187, and 194.

[141] See Chap. 182.

[142] See, e.g., Chaps. 62, 100, 152, 216.

[143] See, e.g., Chaps. 140, 149, 162, 173.

[144] There are numerous examples in the *vita*. See, e.g., Chaps. 66, 99, 100, 108, 129, 142, 143, 152, 188, 201–3, 228, 230, 232, 239, 242. For Lazaros making special allowances for the weak and sick, see, e.g., Chaps. 139, 148, and 149.

strong and determined opposition from within his flock when he attempted to impose those ideals.[145] The *vita* may, then, be seen as providing interesting evidence concerning the state of Byzantine monasticism during the first half of the eleventh century, and in particular may bear witness to a decline at that time in the acceptance of cenobitic forms.[146] Lazaros has thus been hailed as a precursor of reforms that were attempted later in the eleventh century, even though he himself was unsuccessful in some respects in putting his ideals into practice on Galesion.[147]

In this situation Lazaros' policy and practice of monastic management led to his being accused by some of lax discipline, even of sinfulness and corruption,[148] and, by others, of unnecessary rigidity and harshness.[149] Lazaros thus stood between, or perhaps fell between, those who held extreme positions at either end of the Byzantine monastic spectrum. He was opposed, on the one hand, by those who wished to limit monasticism to ardent and completely committed ascetics, and who believed that the pursuit of solitary and individual spiritual goals, independent of control by a superior and free of the constraints of communal existence, was the highest, indeed perhaps the only, true form of Christian life. On the other hand, he ran into trouble with those who saw monasticism as little more than an extension of ordinary life in which the pursuit of personal and individual interests (in terms of the regulation of lifestyle, the conduct of handiwork or trade, and the possession of property and money), and the perpetuation of distinctions of birth, wealth, and education, were to be permitted as a matter of course in a loosely ordered community. Proponents of this view felt that such a community should enjoy the privileges and benefits associated in the Byzantine world with religious establishments, but be unrestricted by many of the more arduous and troublesome controls of traditional cenobitic monasticism.[150]

[145] Chaps. 193 and 202 provide evidence of how extreme this opposition became.

[146] Lazaros himself makes an interesting general comment on this in Chap. 232.

[147] See Thomas, "Evergetine Reform," 249–52; Thomas and Hero, *Foundation Documents,* 151–53.

[148] See, e.g., Chaps. 57, 82–83, 99, 143, 152, 221, 226, 231–32, 240, 248.

[149] See, e.g., Chaps. 138, 143, 148–49, 162, 182, 187, 193.

[150] The difficulties faced by successful monasteries during this period in balancing the practical needs for territorial and economic expansion with the almost inevitable spiritual compromise this required are clearly described and shrewdly analyzed by

Lazaros' relations with his monks were not always easy, and at times became openly hostile, particularly toward the end of his life. While many of these difficulties arose from his views on the fundamental meaning and purpose of monasticism, others appear to have their roots in the particular situation that developed on Galesion. Many monks were pessimistic about the community's survival after Lazaros' death, in view of determined opposition from the ecclesiastical authorities in Ephesus. Moreover, some were unhappy with his desire that his own brother Ignatios take over as superior,[151] and some were disturbed by Lazaros' refusal to understand or act on their concerns.[152] Lazaros was seen as being not only intransigent but also out of touch with the realities of the situation; he thus provoked the opposition of those monks who believed that a simple, legal solution, acceptable to all parties, would be to leave Galesion for the monastery of Bessai, which Lazaros himself had founded nearby. By the end of his life, then, Lazaros' very powerful and determined character and his unwavering conviction of his own divinely inspired correctness had deeply divided his community and nearly destroyed all that he had achieved on Galesion. Yet, history refuted his critics and proved him correct, as the author of the *vita* is pleased to point out, for the monastery, which was the product and epitome of the sterner elements of his character, survived, as did the memory of the saint's warmer, gentler, and more human qualities.

E. Galesion as a Monastic Center

a) Earlier Monastic Settlement on the Mountain

Gregory the Cellarer held that Lazaros' greatest miracle was his establishment of the three monastic communities on Galesion, considering the

Morris (*Monks*, 200–240). Lazaros was evidently caught in this dilemma; his own position was one of refusal to compromise the demands of true *eremia*, while his opponents within his community favored a more practical solution to the problems that arose as Galesion developed into a major and well-endowed monastic institution.

[151] See Chaps. 221 and 202.

[152] On opposition from Ephesus, see below, sections F and G, pp. 36, 38–39, 45–48, 56–57. For expressions of pessimism about the future, see, e.g., in the *vita*, Chaps. 140–41, 245, and 247; cf. also 249. The extent of this pessimism may perhaps be judged by the fact that even such leading figures in the community as Laurentios "the stylite" (Chap. 217) and Gregory the Cellarer himself (Chap. 170) were thinking of leaving Galesion after Lazaros' death.

meager resources with which he began the undertaking.[153] Lazaros was not the first holy man to try to live on the mountain, but he was evidently the first to bring organized monasticism there and to attract considerable numbers of visitors and pilgrims to its hostile and barren environment. Prior to his arrival a number of solitaries are said to have lived on Galesion; indeed Gregory goes so far as to say that there were always monks living on the mountain,[154] although the evidence that he cites apparently relates only to the relatively recent past.

The most notable of these solitaries was Paphnoutios, whose rather lurid story is related at length by Gregory, and who, according to traditions preserved in the monastery, was the first to live in the cave near the monastery of the Savior.[155] It would seem that this was some considerable time before Lazaros arrived, long enough for legendary stories to be associated with him, but not so long that all recollection of him and his successor had faded from local memory.[156] Paphnoutios was followed in the cave, according to this tradition, by the unfortunate shepherd who had accidentally shot him and who afterwards remained there until his own death; this man's skull was still preserved as a relic in the church of the Savior when Gregory composed the *vita,* although Paphnoutios' remains had been translated to Constantinople.[157] Another man is also said to have attempted the solitary life in this cave, and indeed had built a cistern in it for water; he did not remain there, however, but moved to a chapel of the Prodromos, which he also constructed, further down the mountain. Someone else had apparently built a church or chapel, dedicated to the Holy Trinity, somewhere on the mountain.[158]

Apart from these people, who had all gone by the time Lazaros arrived, Gregory was familiar with a tradition that a nun was still living on the mountain when Lazaros took up residence,[159] and a solitary was also living on the pillar of Petra, just above the village of Galesion toward the base of the mountain. Lazaros visited this man on two occasions while moving to Galesion,

[153] See Chap. 79; cf. also Chaps. 62 and 85.

[154] See Chap. 62.

[155] See Chaps. 36–40.

[156] Some major elements of the story are not original. Chap. 45 states that an icon of Paphnoutios still hung in the cave near the end of Lazaros' life.

[157] See Chap. 40.

[158] See Chap. 62.

[159] Ibid.

but the solitary was on the point of leaving to seek a more peaceful spot. The pillar later became incorporated into the general Galesiote monastic community.[160]

b) Lazaros' Primary Foundations on Galesion

The core monasteries of the community on Galesion, those of the Savior, the Theotokos, and the Resurrection, were located quite high up on the mountain, which lay to the north of Ephesus and was notorious for its barrenness and lack of water; it is to be identified with the modern Alamandağ.[161] The *vita* thus reveals that they were well above the village of Galesion and also above the area of Chalkos Halonios, which, in its upper regions in the central part of the mountain, included a difficult pass that had to be negotiated to reach the monastic colony.[162] The *vita* also makes clear that the pillars at the Savior and Theotokos, and the monasteries which came to surround them, were built in a gorge west of the main summit, the Theotokos being somewhat higher up than the Savior;[163] the Resurrection, a larger foundation than the others, was still farther up the mountain, perhaps above the gorge, rather than actually in it.[164] Most travelers to these monastic settlements set out from Ephesus and approached by the main path that ran through the village of Galesion and on up the mountain, but access could also be gained from another direction by a path that came down from near the summit.[165]

Little firm evidence is provided in the *vita* about the plan of any of the monasteries themselves or even about their facilities. They were apparently

[160] See Chaps. 41 and 53. On the location of this pillar and its later inhabitants, see Chaps. 159 and 175.

[161] See Delehaye, *vita*, 502B; idem, *Stylites*, cvi; Janin, *Églises centres*, 241, 248; Malamut, "Bessai," 244; Morris, *Monks*, 40; cf. Foss, *Ephesus*, 120. On the barrenness of the mountain in the *vita*, see, e.g., Chaps. 36, 186, 216, 218, 219, and references to water having to be transported from the river or the cistern at the Savior, Chaps. 45, 91, 174–76.

[162] See Chaps. 77, 154–55; cf. also Chaps. 41 and 56. The journey to these locations was difficult and visitors, at least in the early days, needed a guide; see, e.g., Chap. 46.

[163] See Chaps. 47, 50, 52–54, 58, 169; cf. Chap. 100, which implies that the monastery of the Savior was a very confined and oppressive place to live.

[164] See, e.g., Chap. 174.

[165] See Chap. 64.

unwalled,[166] although there was a definite entrance,[167] and each came to have cells for the brothers; buildings, which included a kitchen[168] and, at least in one or two of the foundations, a guest house where lay visitors were housed separately from visiting monks,[169] probably surrounded a courtyard in which stood Lazaros' pillar and the church.[170] After the monastery of the Resurrection was built toward the end of Lazaros' life, some functions were centralized there: it was thus the location of the pantry from which supplies were distributed to the other two monasteries[171] and probably also of the main guest house, as well as of the *archontarion,* a facility designed to house distinguished visitors and boasting the only real beds on the mountain.[172] Unfortunately, no physical remains have yet been located to allow a better idea of the topography of the monasteries on Galesion to be formed.[173]

c) Other Foundations and Properties Controlled by Lazaros

In addition to the monasteries of the Savior, the Theotokos, and the Resurrection, the *vita* mentions a number of other establishments on the mountain and in its vicinity that were either founded by Lazaros or came to be included within the general compass of the Galesiote community; it also controlled some more distant properties.

During Lazaros' lifetime, Galesion exercised control over, or had very close relations with, three or four monastic communities in the vicinity of the mountain: those of St. Marina,[174] Eupraxia, the Theotokos at Bessai, and the

[166] See Chap. 144.

[167] See Chaps. 207, 243; cf. Chap. 142.

[168] See Chaps. 86 and 236.

[169] See Chaps. 86, 142, 150, 162, and 243.

[170] See Chaps. 49 and 107.

[171] See Chap. 209.

[172] See Chap. 162.

[173] See Foss, *Ephesus,* 130, and cf. W. Müller-Wiener, "Mittelalterliche Befestigungen im südlichen Jonien," *IstMitt* 11 (1961), 112–16.

[174] Chap. 193 shows that St. Marina continued to function in some capacity long after Lazaros established himself on Galesion. Chap. 160, although possibly referring to the early period, may also imply that the community on the mountain continued to enjoy the produce from St. Marina's holdings of arable land on the plain below the foothills. There would seem to be no grounds for claiming, as does Thomas (Thomas

Pausolype.[175] Also mentioned is at least one subsidiary foundation on the mountain itself, the "house of Philippikos,"[176] while another, that of Varva[ni]-tziana, was close by.[177] Other monasteries such as Kampsai,[178] may also have had ties to Lazaros' foundation. More distant properties, such as the *metochion* of Mathaia,[179] the *proasteion* alluded to in Chapter 90 (which was evidently more than a day's journey distant),[180] or the *proasteion* of Pentakrene,[181] are also mentioned.

The convent of Eupraxia must have been close by, probably at or near the foot of the mountain,[182] as was the monastery of St. Marina, which seems to have been across the river (probably the Caystros) from Galesion, on the route to Ephesus.[183] Bessai, too, was evidently quite close, although Chapter

---

and Hero, *Foundation Documents,* 149), that "the metropolitan of Ephesos had evidently reclaimed the administration of St. Marina after Lazarus' departure."

[175] Two of these foundations may, in fact, be the same; see below, section F.a., p. 35.

[176] See Chap. 221. See also Janin, *Églises centres,* 245 and n. 3. Morris (*Monks,* 215) takes *oikos* (house) to refer to a farmstead here.

[177] See Chaps. 91 and 92. A monk, Germanos, who would appear to be from Lazaros' community, was steward when Gregory the Cellarer was writing the *vita.* The monastery may also have possessed an estate at Komothon, which was perhaps not far from this place; see Chap. 91 and also Morris, *Monks,* 215.

[178] See Chap. 221.

[179] See Chap. 144.

[180] The mention in the same chapter of monks going to Lydia to collect grain might conceivably suggest that the monastery owned property there too.

[181] See Chap. 244. Chaps. 90, 246, and 247 confirm that the community possessed a number of *proasteia.* Another named *proasteion,* Epoptine, is said specifically to have belonged to the Pausolype; the importance of this particular property is discussed in section F.a., below, p. 35.

[182] The admission to this convent of a number of female relatives of Galesiote monks would suggest quite close proximity (see Chaps. 74, 164, 201), as would the fact that Eupraxia herself (Lazaros' mother Irene) visits her son on at least one occasion (Chap. 59) and also witnesses the remarkable monk Isaiah "in the middle of the gorge where the cross is set up" (Chap. 199), presumably while on her way up or down the mountain.

[183] The hermitage that was to become the monastery of St. Marina during Lazaros' occupancy lay by a spring in the foothills of the mountain of Koumaron (Chap. 31); this slightly elevated location is confirmed by Chap. 160. Chaps. 34, 36, and 160 also clearly indicate that St. Marina possessed cultivated land on the plain below it and lay quite close to a major road that led directly into Ephesus. This road apparently formed

247 indicates that there was room for several *proasteia* between it and Galesion and that it was separated from the main community on the mountain by a hilly or mountainous ridge.[184] Like St. Marina, it was apparently on the other side of the river at the foot of the mountain in a location both better supplied with water and more suited to agriculture and trade than the main community.[185]

Some of these communities, like the *proasteion* of Pentakrene, were very small indeed,[186] but others, like the convent of Eupraxia or the monastery of the Theotokos at Bessai, were larger. The convent of Eupraxia, which was headed by Lazaros' mother after she had been tonsured by her son, counted among its sisters some female relatives of monks who were members of the community on the mountain.[187] Bessai seems to have been the largest foundation in the area, with more than two hundred monks in comparison to around sixty-four on Galesion.[188]

---

part of the route from Galesion to the city, as Chap. 193 implies, although when Lazaros moved to the mountain from St. Marina (Chap. 53), he had to cross the river before he could begin his ascent of the foothills of the mountain and visit the pillar of Petra that stood just above the village of Galesion. This suggests that Koumaron should not be identified with Galesion. See also here, Janin (*Églises centres,* 242–43), Foss (*Ephesus,* 128), and Malamut ("Bessai," 245–46), who, in light of the above evidence, agree in situating the monastery on the left bank of the Caystros by the main highway north of Ephesus.

[184] See Chap. 247 for further discussion of this information.

[185] See Chap. 218. A certain amount of scholarly discussion has taken place over the question of whether the Bessai (Βέσσαι) of the *vita* should be identified with the Bessai (Βῆσσαι) mentioned by an imperial chrysobull dated to May 1054 (Zepos, *Jus* 1: 637) as being near a place called Ataia and being required to supply one thousand *modia* of wheat a year to the Nea Mone on Chios. Malamut ("Bessai," 248–51) argues convincingly that these two places are distinct, although she does not take into consideration the discussion of the topic in Foss, *Ephesus,* 129 n. 52. Foss suggests that if the Ataia of the chrysobull is emended to Anaia (a port on the Ionian coast just to the south of Phygela; see Chap. 75), then they may in fact be identical; the internal evidence, however, would still appear to place Bessai too close to Galesion for this identification to be convincing.

[186] See Chap. 244.

[187] See Chaps. 164 and 201; cf. Chap. 74. Janin (*Églises centres,* 245) comments briefly on this establishment; see also Talbot, "Family," 129; eadem, "Comparison," 3.

[188] Chap. 246 specifies that there are to be forty monks at the Resurrection and twelve each at the Savior and the Theotokos, for a total of sixty-four. Chap. 79, in

F. Problems Concerning Lazaros' Foundations

a) The Relationship of the Pausolype and Bessai to Galesion

While the *vita* provides evidence for the existence of the monastic communities and properties mentioned in the preceding section, it actually raises more questions than it answers concerning their relationship to Lazaros' principal foundations on Galesion. Many of these problems are probably insoluble, given the present state of the evidence, but they deserve consideration, for they have an important bearing on understanding both the nature of the situation in which Lazaros left the Galesiote community at his death and on some of the motives involved in the writing of the *vita.*

Nothing is said in the *vita* about the formal relationship of either the St. Marina or the Eupraxia communities to Galesion.[189] Some material is, however, provided on the ties of Bessai and the Pausolype to the mountain but it is, unfortunately, problematic. The difficulties are compounded by the fact that most of the evidence is contained in the later stages of the *vita* where the text is sometimes quite badly broken: vital elements have sometimes been lost and accounts break off, tantalizingly, in the middle.

The problem posed by the relationship of the monastery of the Pausolype to both Galesion and Bessai is relatively uncomplicated. According to Chapter 245 of the *vita,* "most of the construction" of the Pausolype was financed by a generous donation of seven hundred and twenty *nomismata* from Maria Skleraina, the mistress of Constantine IX Monomachos. This donation was made "after she had heard about <Lazaros> from her brother," a probable allusion to the visit of Romanos Skleros to Galesion (Chap. 87), a visit which evidently made a considerable impression upon him. In that case, the donation must almost certainly have been made between the accession of Constantine

reference to Lazaros' foundation of the three monasteries on the mountain *and* Bessai, mentions a total figure of three hundred monks. Even if this number also includes totals for some of the other minor foundations, it implies a community of more than two hundred at Bessai, making it a very substantial monastery. Foss (*Ephesus,* 129) agrees with this figure, but Janin (*Églises centres,* 245) seems to be mistaken in suggesting "qu'il ait compté jusqu'à trois cent moines du vivant même de Lazare"; he is followed by Thomas (Thomas and Hero, *Foundation Documents,* 149).

[189] Janin (*Églises centres,* 245) suggests that St. Marina was probably not subordinate to Galesion.

IX and Maria's death, that is between 1042 and early 1046 at the latest,[190] although it is impossible to tell when the project was actually carried out. It is not entirely clear, however, whether this foundation was distinct from the one at Bessai. Janin is noncommittal on the subject,[191] but Malamut has tentatively suggested that the Pausolype should be identified with Bessai;[192] her arguments are certainly cogent, but my own interpretation of the text of Chapters 246 and 247 suggests the opposite.[193] The allusion to the two places in very much the same context in Chapter 245, without any suggestion that they are identical, could be interpreted either way, but, when they are again mentioned together (Chap. 247), it would appear to be precisely for the purpose of contrasting them: Bessai is to depend on Galesion for its support, while the Pausolype is demonstrably self-supporting as it possesses the *proasteion* of Epoptine.[194] One could equally well suggest that the Pausolype be identified with the convent of Eupraxia and speculate that Maria may have intended to fund a female monastic establishment to parallel the male one supported by Constantine Monomachos.

The issues surrounding the foundation at Bessai are far more involved. One of the few definite points which may be established from the *vita* is that the monastery at Bessai was constructed on land granted by the emperor Constantine IX Monomachos for the remembrance of both himself and his mistress Maria Skleraina.[195] The date of this grant, however, is not clear: the text does not establish whether Maria was alive or dead at the time, although the immediate mention in the same passage of her own substantial donation might suggest the former, and thus again give a date somewhere between late 1042 and early 1046.[196]

[190] She died ca. 1045, and certainly before May 1046; see the note in Chap. 245.

[191] Janin, *Églises centres,* 245.

[192] Malamut, "Bessai," 247; she is followed by Thomas (Thomas and Hero, *Foundation Documents,* 149).

[193] See also Seibt, *Skleroi,* 75.

[194] See below, Chaps. 246 and 247 in the *vita* on the considerable problems involved in translation and interpretation of this passage.

[195] See Chap. 245.

[196] A date for the donation prior to the death of Maria Skleraina is also proposed by Malamut, "Bessai," 246, although, as she points out, the actual construction, or at least completion, of the monastery was delayed. Morris (*Monks,* 42) gives a date for the foundation of Bessai between 1046 and 1050 but provides no reason for doing so.

We also know for sure that Bessai was founded by Lazaros himself,[197] while the circumstances that led to the start of the construction of the church of the Theotokos there (and, probably, the monastery as a whole) are also described.[198] Lazaros had had problems with the ecclesiastical authorities in Ephesus from the very start of his career on Galesion when he was ordered off the mountain by the metropolitan very soon after his initial move from the monastery of St. Marina; it was apparently only by taking advantage of this man's absence in Constantinople that he was able to establish himself there permanently.[199] These problems, prompted by Ephesus' legal ownership of the mountain and its insistence that Lazaros and his communities had no rights there,[200] had continued over the years. Indeed, they evidently worsened toward the end of Lazaros' life, possibly following the foundation of his third, much larger (and thus threateningly permanent) monastery of the Resurrection.[201] The worried monks of Lazaros' community, faced by this increasingly determined and unpleasant opposition, first persuaded him to appeal to the emperor to extricate them from their difficulties;[202] then, after this attempt was deliberately thwarted, started nagging Lazaros "rather differently" to found another monastery to which they could retire if they were forced to leave Galesion after his death. The result was the Theotokos at Bessai.

Unfortunately there is no clear indication of the date of these events or the identity of the emperor in question. It is thus impossible to say whether the attempted mission to secure aid from Constantinople on this occasion was related to the interest in Galesion already shown by Monomachos, Maria Skleraina, and Romanos Skleros, or whether it predates this. The phrasing of the brethren's plea to Lazaros in Chapter 239 may suggest that this incident

[197] See Chaps. 216 and 245. Gregory of Cyprus, in his version of the *vita* (*AASS*, Nov. 3:602E–F), suggests that an unnamed monastery, which may plausibly be identified with Bessai (see Janin, *Églises centres*, 244 n. 7), was founded by a disgruntled *oikonomos* as an attractive rival to Galesion, rather than by Lazaros himself. On this version of the *vita*, see below, section H.

[198] See Chap. 239.

[199] See Chap. 53.

[200] See Chap. 245.

[201] In general on such problems of disputed control between lay or monastic founders and local bishops, see especially Morris, *Monks*, 149–54. On Galesion and Ephesus in particular, see also Thomas, *Religious Foundations*, 217; cf. also 157 n. 30.

[202] See Chaps. 238–39.

took place before the specific grant of land for the monastery at Bessai had been made.[203] The monks thus urge Lazaros to "look around somewhere else and find a place <that's> free and found another monastery there," implying that they, at any rate, knew of no specifically designated or even obvious place for such a foundation at this time. In that case one might hypothesize that another mission went to Constantinople, now certainly to Constantine Monomachos, to actively solicit his grant of the land for Bessai.[204]

Whatever the circumstances of its foundation, Bessai had certainly been in operation for at least some time before Lazaros died in late 1053. Quite apart from the imperial instruction (evidently issued shortly before his death) that he himself should move there,[205] there are several accounts of monks already living at Bessai while he was still alive;[206] indeed, Lazaros sent his own brother Ignatios, the future superior of Galesion, there.[207]

One of the biggest problems in the *vita* with regard to the foundation at Bessai is that both Lazaros and Gregory the Cellarer appear keen to cast aspersions on that monastery at every opportunity. By the end of his life, Lazaros was doing his best to ensure its secondary and second-rate status in comparison to his establishments on Galesion; he thus describes Bessai as a place for "tradesmen."[208] He evidently saw it as an appropriate place for monks who could not endure the rigors of life on the mountain and were unable to fulfill his stated ideal of perseverance in the harsh conditions there; it even had diabolical approval, being the place to which the Devil tried to lure a monk who wished to go back up to Galesion.[209] Furthermore, Lazaros' apparent intention in the stipulations concerning Bessai included in his *diatyposis,* even on a charitable interpretation of Chapters 246 and 247, was to

[203] That mentioned in Chap. 245.

[204] This mission could not be one of those mentioned at the end of Lazaros' life, since they obviously postdate the foundation of Bessai; see Chap. 245, e.g., and the discussion below, section F. b., pp. 46–47. Thus the suggestion by Thomas (Thomas and Hero, *Foundation Documents,* 149) that the foundation of Bessai resulted from Lazaros' steward [*sic*] Gabriel's negotiations with Monomachos is to be discounted.

[205] See Chap. 245; cf. Chaps. 217 and 253.

[206] See Chaps. 202, 216–18.

[207] See Chaps. 52 and 221.

[208] See Chap. 216.

[209] See Chap. 218.

ensure that this monastery could not deprive Galesion of its means of support;[210] more plausibly, these stipulations may have been intended to ensure that Bessai stood in a position of complete economic, if not administrative, dependence to Lazaros' own community on the mountain. It was thus specified that Bessai was to receive from the *proasteia* lying between the two foundations only what was surplus to the requirements of the monks on Galesion and, if there were no such surpluses, it was to receive nothing at all.[211] It would appear that Lazaros wished Bessai to be of no concern at all to those who were administering the community on the mountain; even the statement in Chapter 246 that it was to have its own superior may be taken, in this rather negative atmosphere, to be an indication of Lazaros' wish to sever all but the most essential economic ties. Finally, Chapter 217 makes it plain that the church of the Theotokos at Bessai was still unfinished at this time, and it would appear that Lazaros was quite happy for it to remain so.

But why did this hostility arise? How can one explain this negative attitude on Lazaros' part toward an establishment he had himself founded? As his views evidently puzzled even some of his own monks, to judge from the rather angry debate recorded in Chapter 245 of the *vita*,[212] I shall offer only a number of tentative suggestions.

It has already been mentioned that the actual impetus for the foundation of Bessai came not from Lazaros himself and his own vision of the development of his community, but rather from the desire of some (perhaps many) of his monks to find a safe haven from the interference and abuse they were encountering from the ecclesiastical authorities in Ephesus.[213] Lazaros evidently viewed such worries about future security as weakness and interpreted the attitude of these monks as showing both a lack of commitment to the true ascetic ideal and a lack of faith in the divine economy. Thus the imperial grant which provided land and perhaps money for Bessai, instead of furthering La-

[210] On the interpretation of this passage and the crucial question of the translation of the verb διοικεῖν, see below, Chaps. 246–47.

[211] This is also the understanding of Thomas (Thomas and Hero, *Foundation Documents,* 149). For a different interpretation of this passage, see Kaplan, *Les hommes,* 306, and, more fully, idem, "Evergetis," 111; also Morris, *Monks,* 215; for details, see below, Chap. 246 n. 1011.

[212] Cf. also the question posed by the eunuch Stephen in Chap. 216.

[213] See Chap. 239.

zaros' own policies, actually served to undermine them, for it facilitated the establishment of this "lesser" monastery to which disgruntled and "weaker" brethren from the mountain could now go, while still nominally remaining in the Galesiote fold. Furthermore, as the later part of the *vita* shows, it provided Lazaros' opponents, both outside and within his community, with a perfect excuse for putting pressure on him to leave the mountain where his presence was illegal; the situation could be easily resolved were he to take himself and his community down to the establishment at Bessai where he had every right to be.

Lazaros died before the dispute with Ephesus was resolved, and there are a number of interesting hints in the *vita* that this was an ongoing issue at the time of its composition. Problems, which are clearly not unconnected, seem also to have arisen with a now more independent and assertive Bessai. For instance, Gregory the Cellarer's otherwise brief description of the contents of Lazaros' *diatyposis* and his treatment of the discussion that surrounded it is dominated by the topic of relations between Galesion and Bessai. He himself appears to realize that this emphasis is rather strange, and comments somewhat cryptically, after he has finished describing the document, "I have not written <all> this about our holy father's [Lazaros'] rule without good reason, as someone might claim, but so that we may learn the truth from this when we are seeking it."[214] The primary *vita* is also very careful to discount the possibility that Lazaros never signed this document while he was still alive,[215] unlike the later versions of the Life, where this incident has been turned into a posthumous miracle.[216] Gregory the Cellarer takes equal care to establish

[214] See Chap. 246.

[215] See Chaps. 246 and 250.

[216] Gregory of Cyprus' account (chap. 42, *AASS,* Nov. 3:605E–606B) thus tends to the overtly miraculous, for there Lazaros is said to have been found dead (rather than simply unconscious), but then miraculously revived not once but twice—first producing the *diatyposis* that he had himself written, and then signing it. A similar version of this episode is contained in the Moscow *synaxarion* (Moscow, Historical Museum [ГИМ] 369/353, ff. 220–220v; on these versions, see section H, below). It is, however, also possible that instead of being a simple piece of enhancement, what is recorded here might represent a different attempt from that in the primary *vita* to deal with a hostile version of events, presumably supported by Bessai (and perhaps Ephesus), which held that Lazaros had indeed died *without* having signed the vital (and, for Bessai, extremely damaging) *diatyposis,* thus rendering it invalid. To counter this story two different approaches were perhaps taken in the period after Lazaros' death: that of the

both that Lazaros directly approved the finished *diatyposis,* even though he did not write it himself,[217] and that imperial and patriarchal confirmation of it was indeed eventually obtained.[218] Probably stories to the contrary were circulating, along with other malicious gossip about the old man,[219] which aimed to refute Galesion's claim to supremacy over Bessai and the establishment of that foundation as Lazaros' legitimate heir. As things stood at this point, the brethren who remained on the mountain were faced with the unpalatable fact that unless the validity of the *diatyposis* could be established, Bessai could claim both the spiritual and material heritage of Lazaros' work, while they were liable to be left with nothing.[220] Gregory the Cellarer's approach to the subject reflects this need and shows a sharp awareness of the possible implications if the other stories were accepted as reliable. This may lie behind another cryptic comment, in Chapter 223, that the place of the firstborn had been usurped by the second as the result of "some deception." It may also lie behind the author's harping on Lazaros' determination to stay on Galesion at all

primary *vita,* which claimed that Lazaros dictated the document and was still alive when he signed it, although he had to be helped with the signature, and that preserved in Gregory of Cyprus' account, which held that although he had in fact died, he was able to revive miraculously and both produce and make legal the necessary document.

[217] See Chap. 246.

[218] See Chap. 223.

[219] See, e.g., Chaps. 78, 82, 84, 202, 218, 237–38, and 248.

[220] There is good reason for supposing that economic issues were a major factor in the problems between the two foundations. Galesion apparently could not survive without the produce of the *proasteia,* which legally belonged to Bessai, but if Bessai were forced to surrender this produce it would be reduced to economic dependency on Galesion. Failure to secure control of these economic resources could result, in hostile circumstances, in one foundation starving the other out of existence. Lazaros' speech in Chap. 245, in which he refuses to move to Bessai, specifically refers to his unwillingness to take the property of Galesion there. He also argues that since Christ approved the construction of both monasteries, "He can again send whatever is necessary to that monastery [Bessai], just as <He has already done> with this one." Further on, he refers to his conviction that the people of the neighboring villages would always supply the monks of Galesion in dire need. Note, too, the argument of Cyril the *oikonomos* in Chap. 247 and the mention there of a "dearth of necessities" and a situation of "shortage" in the monastery just before Lazaros' death; cf. Chap. 210, which refers to a severe famine in the area at that time. In general on the possibility of monastic establishments dwindling or succumbing entirely as a result of such pressures, whether accidental or deliberately provoked, see Morris, *Monks,* 172–78.

costs, and his refusal either to comply with the imperial order to move down to Bessai or to accept the opinion of brethren who were worried about their future on the mountain once he was gone. Gregory the Cellarer, it would seem, was writing serious polemic, as well as hagiography.[221]

b) The Foundation of the Resurrection Monastery and the Involvement of Constantine IX Monomachos

Lazaros' third and final establishment on Galesion, that of the Resurrection, quickly became the largest and most important monastic community on the mountain, but its foundation involves another set of questions, closely related to those surrounding the monastery at Bessai (and perhaps even more intractable).

The initial difficulty here is that no mention is made of the foundation of the Resurrection monastery in the primary *vita* in its present form. As a result, precise information is lacking, not only about the dating of Lazaros' move from the Theotokos monastery,[222] but also about his motives in establishing that of the Resurrection and the sources of its funding. This crucial gap, however, is filled in all the other versions by various forms of a story linking the foundation of the Resurrection monastery to Constantine IX Monomachos. The outline of this story is that Lazaros predicted to the exiled Monomachos that he would soon become emperor; when this prediction came true, Lazaros, who had received in a vision not only the inspiration for the foundation of the Resurrection monastery but also a clear indication of its site, was rewarded with imperial funding and assistance for its construction.[223]

[221] There is a hint of this same line of approach in Malamut, *Route,* 186: "Sans doute Bessai avait fini par avoir mauvaise réputation, mais l'hagiographe condamne surtout un monastère qui avait échappé à l'emprise de Lazare." To my mind this begs the further question, did it slip or was it pushed?

[222] See above, section B, p. 13.

[223] See the version of Gregory of Cyprus, chaps. 29–31, *AASS,* Nov. 3:599F–600E; for the Epitome see 607E–F; the *synaxarion* version is on f. 219 of Moscow, Historical Museum (ГИМ) 369/353 (τὸν τῆς ἁγίας ἀναστάσεως ναὸν ἐδείματο . . . τῶν ἀναλωμάτων παρὰ τοῦ φιλοχρίστου βασιλέως Κωνσταντίνου τοῦ Μονομάχου ἀφθόνων στελλομένων. ὅς τις δὴ βασιλεὺς πρὸς τὸν πατέρα πλείονα πίστιν ἔσχεν, ὡς προείποντα αὐτῷ ἐν τῇ νήσῳ Λέσβῳ διὰ τοῦ μαθητοῦ τὴν τῆς βασιλείας ἀνάρρησιν). There is also an interesting and possibly earlier variant in the version of Akakios Sabbaites in Lampsides, "Ἀνέκδοτον κείμενον,"167–70. On these versions, see below, section H.

What is perhaps most interesting, and most problematic, here is that a related story appears in Chapter 230 of the primary *vita*. This chapter preserves many details of an episode in which an anonymous monk from Galesion, who is presented by the author as an unscrupulous and highly dubious character, gained the favor of the exiled Constantine Monomachos by predicting his elevation to the imperial throne, using current information (instead of divine inspiration) and a forged letter (which purported to be from Lazaros but which he had actually written himself). The monk went to Constantinople after Monomachos had become emperor, presumably in the second half of 1042, and collected his "reward" consisting of a "quantity" of gold and some spices.[224] Unfortunately, the text breaks off before the end of the story and there is no account of what happened to these riches. The flow of the narrative might suggest that both monk and gold disappeared, at least for a while, but, as the monk himself did eventually return to Galesion, it is conceivable that at least some of the money actually reached Lazaros' community.[225]

Given the parallels between these stories, it may be plausibly suggested that the section missing at this point in the primary *vita* contained some information about the foundation of the Resurrection monastery.[226] But to go further and accept (with the other versions) that Monomachos was knowingly

[224] For further details and discussion, see Chap. 230.

[225] The point of all the stories in the section of the *vita* in which this episode appears (a section which begins after the break at the end of Chap. 223) is to illustrate the wonderful powers of insight and good judgment that Lazaros displayed toward members of his community. For example, Chap. 227 demonstrates Lazaros' good judgment in not tonsuring the imposter Damianos himself (although he does not know he is a fake) and his foresight concerning the man's death. In the case of Chaps. 228–30, which concern the activities of the renegade monk in question here, the climax of the story, from this point of view, may well have been that Lazaros' continued trust in this monk, despite his lengthy and continued record of disobedience and international intrigue, eventually resulted in his return to Galesion together with the crucial and substantial imperial donation to the monastery. A lesser man than Lazaros might well have cut all ties with the monk much earlier, or at least refused him permission to leave the monastery again, and thus have lost out on the eventual rewards he was to bring to the community.

[226] This is certainly the assumption of Lampsides, "'Ανέκδοτον κείμενον," 175. For more on these lacunae, see below, section G, pp. 49–51.

involved in this project or that he gave money to Galesion specifically for this monastery would be highly problematic.[227]

The primary *vita* thus stresses that the unscrupulous monk involved in this episode was working on his own and, far from furthering Lazaros' plans, was actually using Lazaros' name and reputation for his own devious ends; there is thus no reason for supposing that his pitch to the emperor had any connection with Lazaros' ideas for the development of Galesion. Moreover, Chapter 230 states unambiguously that the monk returned to Galesion only *after* Lazaros had "gone up to <the pillar of> the holy Resurrection"; thus Lazaros' plans for that monastery must already have been formulated and the process of establishing this third center already begun prior to the receipt of any imperial grant.[228]

A further difficulty encountered here is that the primary *vita* makes no mention of the Resurrection being an imperial foundation; if this had indeed been the case, it would surely have been of immediate relevance to the ongoing and apparently increasingly unpleasant arguments with Ephesus, as it would have provided Lazaros' community with precisely the legitimacy and support it so patently lacked. If the monastery of the Resurrection had really been founded, or at least constructed, with such obvious favor on the part of the emperor (who was still ruling when Lazaros died), it is hard to see how the difficulties with Ephesus would have continued in the form they obviously

[227] The point then would have been that God, working through Lazaros and both the unwitting monk and emperor, actually arranged the donation for Galesion's benefit and the fulfillment of Lazaros' plans for the monastery of the Resurrection.

[228] Cf. also Chap. 109, which, if it refers to the Resurrection monastery (as it almost certainly does), shows that Lazaros was already on his pillar there before construction of the refectory took place. Gregory of Cyprus' version also indicates that Lazaros had already started or designed the project before he had the money (or sanction) to carry it out; his ability to fund and finish such an ambitious project is worked in as a further miraculous element (chap. 30, *AASS,* Nov. 3:600D). Interestingly too, in the version of Akakios Sabbaites, the visionary experience evidently associated with the foundation of the Resurrection in the tradition preserved in the other versions of the *vita* does not precede the start of the project, as it does in the account of Gregory of Cyprus, but occurs after Lazaros has himself marked out the ground in the presence of the emperor's representative sent to oversee the construction; cf. Lampsides, "'Ανέκδοτον κείμενον," 170. On these versions, see below, section H.

did. Again, if Monomachos really had knowingly approved and financed this project, it would make little sense for him then to have ordered Lazaros to leave Galesion and move to Bessai, especially since the grounds on which he made this decree were that while Galesion "belonged to the metropolitan of Ephesus . . . the site of Bessai had been given to our venerable father by the emperor [Monomachos] himself."[229]

If Gregory of Cyprus' account of this episode (which directly links Monomachos to the Resurrection) is examined more closely, it is perhaps no surprise, in light of the above difficulties, to find that its historicity is immediately cast into doubt by the fact that he apparently makes Monomachos (1042–55) the direct successor of Romanos III Argyros (1028–34). Moreover, his description of Lazaros' vision strikes a false note, for he says that he was "told by an unspoken voice to leave his cell" (ἐξελθεῖν τῆς κέλλης φωνῇ ἀρρήτῳ προστάσσεται) in order to see it, and that he did so "when he was in the open air" (ὡς ἐν ὑπαίθρῳ ἐγένετο); this would be impossible in the version of the primary *vita,* where Lazaros is said to have remained perpetually on his *unroofed* pillar. On the other hand, this detail does tally with both the epitome version and the account by Akakios Sabbaites, which agree that Lazaros lived in a cell on the mountain, rather than on a pillar, prior to the construction of the monastery of the Resurrection. These details lend support to the view that Gregory of Cyprus was here employing a later tradition about the foundation of the monastery of the Resurrection and incorporating it into his reworking of the primary *vita* at a point where crucial information is now missing, rather than reporting anything that had an historical basis. Thus, given the various points outlined here, there would seem to be no reason at all for supposing that Constantine Monomachos was knowingly or directly involved in the foundation of the monastery of the Resurrection.[230]

But what then was the origin of the story of the emperor's involvement in this project? An obvious explanation is that, as has been suggested, the lost section after Chapter 230 in the primary *vita* did indeed include some account

[229] See Chap. 245. Note too that the emphasis on the formal approval given to Lazaros' *diatyposis* by emperor and patriarch would be strange if the monastery of the Resurrection was already an imperial foundation; see Chap. 223.

[230] It is also interesting to note an odd stress in the version by Akakios Sabbaites (Lampsides, "Ἀνέκδοτον κείμενον," 170), which may perhaps be interpreted as an attempt to explain why the monastery of the Resurrection, there depicted as an imperial foundation endowed with great riches, should only have had a mud-brick church.

of how Monomachos' donation to the anonymous monk eventually found its way to Galesion and was used to fund Lazaros' final and most ambitious establishment. In that case the story that the monastery of the Resurrection was built with imperial money was true, but not in the sense that the emperor intended this to happen or even knew what his money had been used for; the Resurrection was thus an imperial foundation in the sense that it had been constructed with imperial money, but it was most certainly not an imperial foundation in any legal sense.

At the same time this speculation does not rule out another possibility, namely that Gregory of Cyprus has here picked up a tradition, also preserved in the other versions of the *vita,* which was deliberately fostered, or even created by Galesion, in an attempt to establish the legitimacy of its position vis-à-vis the foundation at Bessai in its ongoing dispute with Ephesus. As has been made clear already, it would certainly not have hurt Galesion's stance to be able to claim that Lazaros' last and greatest foundation on the mountain was actually built not only with divine sanction (as the result of a vision that specified its precise location), but also with the direct and wholehearted support of the reigning emperor some considerable time before the end of Lazaros' life. In that case the version of the foundation of the Resurrection given by Gregory of Cyprus, and the possibly earlier version in the account by Akakios Sabbaites, may reflect a propaganda campaign waged by the monks of Galesion in their struggle for survival with Ephesus.[231]

Galesion may, however, have been able to employ such propaganda only after Monomachos had died (in 1055), when there was less possibility of its position being openly and damagingly refuted by the emperor himself or of an appeal by Bessai to Constantinople being upheld. Indeed, prior to this, such a refutation would have been a very real danger to Lazaros' followers on the mountain; for if Monomachos was *not* knowingly or deliberately involved in the foundation of the Resurrection monastery, then he may well have believed that the only legitimate imperial monastery under Lazaros' control was

[231] It is perhaps worth noting that Monomachos was also involved at this time in the reconstruction of the church of the Resurrection in Jerusalem (dedicated 1048). The fact that the name of the monastery on Galesion was inspired by Lazaros' own stay in Jerusalem (see Chap. 253) would appear to rule out the suggestion that Monomachos might be associated with it because he had a particular devotion to foundations dedicated to the Resurrection; but this coincidence may perhaps have been useful or even instrumental in fostering the notion of it having imperial patronage.

that at Bessai, since it was for this alone that he had, knowingly and purposely, given a donation of land.

That Monomachos was in fact of this opinion concerning Bessai may also find some support from the admittedly confusing and unclear account in the primary *vita* of the missions that were sent to him from Galesion shortly before Lazaros died. The apparent growth in the opposition to Galesion from the ecclesiastical authorities in Ephesus toward the end of Lazaros' life may perhaps be connected to his foundation of a third community on the mountain and his development of plans for it as a major monastic establishment. While the metropolitan might have been able to ignore two small communities of a dozen monks each and assume that any problems they posed would be easily resolved once their charismatic founder had died, a monastery designed for some forty monks, together with the growing pilgrimage traffic that went with it, was presumably a very different proposition. Faced with this opposition and the resulting fears of his monks, Lazaros, as has been seen, founded the monastery of Bessai as a potential haven for them; this did not, however, alleviate the pressure from Ephesus, which was now perhaps specifically directed at forcing him to leave for his new, legal foundation. Thus, when the worries of the brethren again became unbearable, Lazaros, who was now near death, appealed to Monomachos once more.

Many difficulties of interpretation are posed by the various passages in Chapters 221 through 248 of the *vita* that refer to missions sent from Galesion to Constantinople at the end of Lazaros' life. The most plausible explanation (although not the only one) is that Lazaros' first mission to Monomachos was probably sent in the summer of 1053 and involved the monks Pachomios and Gabriel.[232] The purpose of the mission, from Lazaros' point of view, was to obtain a settlement of the dispute with Ephesus that would favor Galesion and the monastery of the Resurrection and which would carry with it the weight of imperial authority. Monomachos' understanding of the situation, however, was very different from that of Lazaros. The emperor, perhaps encouraged in his opinion regarding the legitimacy of Bessai by the monk Gabriel (who evidently did not share his superior's views on the subject), decided to have Lazaros move to Bessai instead of confirming him in possession of Galesion.[233] Lazaros flatly refused to comply. He sent a letter to this effect to

[232] See Chap. 221.

[233] This is the message conveyed in Gabriel's letter recorded in Chap. 245. It is a course of action that would certainly support the interpretation of Monomachos' posi-

Monomachos by means of the monk Kosmas the Jerusalemite, the condemnatory tone of which merely served to upset the presumably startled emperor, who may not even have been aware of Lazaros' own understanding of the situation.[234] The initial delegation then returned to Galesion, bringing with it a sum of money.[235] Shortly afterward Lazaros died with the situation still unresolved. Another mission must then have gone to Constantinople, taking with it the signed *diatyposis.* This mission, which probably took place quite soon after Lazaros' death and certainly before Monomachos died in 1055, evidently managed to clarify the basis of the earlier misunderstanding and convince the emperor of the legitimacy of Lazaros' position (perhaps because the *diatyposis* now actually existed).[236] The result was imperial and patriarchal approval of the document and thus of Lazaros' own position concerning the foundations on Galesion.[237]

A most interesting point here, given the course of events and interpretation suggested above, concerns the money (*nomismata*) brought back to Galesion by the brethren just before Lazaros' death. If, as seems likely, this was donated by Monomachos, then it must have been given specifically for Bessai, for at the time the emperor had just ordered Lazaros off the mountain and had certainly not yet changed his mind, if he ever did so. In that case this money was presumably given either to ensure the completion of the Theotokos

tion as regards Bessai, outlined above. Thomas (Thomas and Hero, *Foundation Documents,* 149) apparently understands this mission to be related to the foundation and endowment of Bessai; the *vita* (Chaps. 221, 245–46) surely implies, however, that it took place at the very end of Lazaros' life, when Bessai had already been in existence for some time.

[234] See Chap. 223. At this point Lazaros evidently considered sending his brother Ignatios to Constantinople for official recognition as his successor; the plan was abandoned, however, perhaps in frustration; see Chap. 221.

[235] See Chaps. 246 and 248.

[236] See Chap. 223 for these details; the emphasis placed there on the emperor and patriarch actually *seeing* the *diatyposis* may be explained if the lack of such a document was the stumbling block in earlier discussions over the future of Galesion.

[237] Gregory the Cellarer's comment in Chap. 223 about the usurpation of the place of the firstborn by the second suggests, perhaps, that the issue was still not finally resolved, even when he was writing the *vita.* See also here, Janin, *Églises centres,* 246 n. 3; cf. Morris ("Political Saint," 46) who states that "after his [Lazaros'] death letters were speedily despatched to Constantinople," although she cites Chap. 221 (the missions of Pachomios and Gabriel, and Kosmas the Jerusalemite, which clearly occurred *before* Lazaros died).

church at Bessai (and hence to prevent those who wished to stay on Galesion from claiming that they could not move there because it was still unfinished),[238] or else was intended to defray the expenses of the move. Here then may be an explanation of the rather cryptic and confused reference in Chapter 248, which suggests that Lazaros secretly gave the *nomismata* to the *parakellarios* Neophytos before his death (so that he would not die with any money in his possession), with instructions "to give them [the *nomismata*] to the brothers after his death." It is, however, unclear quite what happened, for the money seems to have disappeared for a while, even though Neophytos reportedly fulfilled his instructions. The *vita* may preserve a hint here that the faction within the monastery that remained loyal to Lazaros' views about staying on the mountain at all costs (a faction to which Gregory the Cellarer, and presumably also his *parakellarios* Neophytos, belonged) secreted the money to keep it out of the hands of those who favored the community's move to Bessai. Indeed, by keeping the money from its intended recipients, the Galesiote community may have actually ensured its survival at this crucial point. The possession of a substantial donation might well have allowed Bessai, with imperial backing and cooperation from the authorities in Ephesus, to complete its church and enforce the abandonment of the mountain once Lazaros' charismatic presence was no longer there to protect it. Perhaps too it was this money, when it resurfaced after Monomachos had been won over or had died, which allowed the expansion of the Resurrection monastery sometime after Lazaros' death and helped confirm Monomachos' connection with it.[239]

Although plausible, this interpretation remains hypothetical and it should be quite plain by this point that one cannot hope to resolve in an entirely satisfactory way all the issues concerning Lazaros' various foundations on and around Galesion. The questions surrounding the foundation of the Resurrection monastery and Constantine Monomachos' involvement with Galesion cannot be answered with any more certainty than those concerning the relationship of Bessai or even the Pausolype to the mountain. What is clear, however, is that deep and decidedly murky currents run behind some passages in the *vita*. The reader should be aware of this and of the hagiographer's polemical interests, and thus not take everything at face value.

[238] See Chap. 217.

[239] So, e.g., the construction of additional cells there, which are mentioned in Chap. 110.

G. The Primary Vita *and Its Author*

The present translation of the *vita* of Lazaros by Gregory the Cellarer is based on the edition published by Hippolyte Delehaye in 1910 in the *Acta Sanctorum.*[240] Delehaye's text is edited from a single manuscript from Mount Athos, Lavrioticus I.127 of the fourteenth century, in which the *vita* is found on folios 81 through 293.[241] The manuscript divides the Life into five parts, while Delehaye published it in two hundred fifty-five chapters varying in length from a single paragraph to several pages. A late copy of this version of the *vita* is found in the Athos manuscript s. Annae n. 6, folios 145–307, dating to the eighteenth or nineteenth century.[242]

The scribe of the earlier manuscript has left a note at the end of the *vita* (f. 294) stating that it was copied at the monastery of the Anastasis (Resurrection) in Constantinople for the Great Lavra on Athos. The note also reveals that the text on which the copy was based had come from Galesion, but the manuscript was incomplete, having been seized by the "barbarians" (Turks) when the monastery was overrun; it had then fallen into the hands of a perfumer (μυρεψός) who had torn pages from the book at various places to use as wrapping paper for his wares. How it came to the copyist is not made clear, but, if the perfumer was indeed responsible for all the lacunae in the text, the copyist must have gained possession of the manuscript before too much damage was done, for the gaps, although significant, do not appear to be substantial when compared to the considerable length of the surviving document.[243]

[240] *BHG* 979; *AASS,* Nov. 3:508–88. See also p. 71.

[241] For further information on the contents of this manuscript and its transcription, see Delehaye's introduction (in Latin), *AASS,* Nov. 3:503, 3–4; cf. idem, *Stylites,* cvi–cvii.

[242] Short extracts, primarily of historical interest, were published a few years before Delehaye's edition by Loparev, "Zhitie"; idem, *Kratkii otchet,* 15–21; and by Gedeon, "Γνώσεις." I have been unable to see this last work.

[243] The text of the manuscript note and discussion of it, together with details of the gaps, are published by Delehaye in *AASS,* Nov. 3:503.5; they are also indicated at the appropriate places in the notes to the translation of the text, below. As Delehaye suggests, there must be some question as to whether the copyist, who left blank pages at the appropriate places, received the manuscript in the correct order and thus as to whether everything in the present text occurs in the sequence the author intended. Close examination of the structure of the *vita,* however, does not reveal any serious grounds for thinking that the folios are out of order.

The fact that some of these lacunae occur at points of considerable significance for the history of Lazaros' various foundations, however, when taken in conjunction with the polemical motivation apparent in places in the *vita* and the hostile undercurrents it reveals, raises the possibility that they may be less accidental than the explanation concerning the perfumer would suggest. If the context of the seven major lacunae in the *vita* is examined, it emerges that six of them occur in sections dealing with opposition to Lazaros or problems concerning his foundations,[244] while even a number of the more minor disturbances in the text appear related to the same issues.[245] There may thus

[244] Thus: 1. About two-thirds of f. 207 are missing at the end of Chap. 170, which is concerned with Gregory the Cellarer's plan to leave Galesion and the dangers of the monastery breaking up.

2. Almost all of ff. 236–236v are blank toward the end of Chap. 202, which relates the story of Lazaros' opponents Barnabas and Methodios and the latter's attempt to poison his brother Ignatios.

3. Most of f. 253 and all of f. 253v are blank at the end of Chap. 223, which concerns the missions to Constantinople and elsewhere of Gabriel, Pachomios, and Kosmas the Jerusalemite.

4. Most of f. 262 and all of ff. 262v–263v are blank at the end of Chap. 230, which contains the story of the anonymous monk and the benefactions he secured from Constantine IX Monomachos. This is the section which may have referred to the foundation of the monastery of the Resurrection.

5. Some of f. 270v and all of f. 271 are blank at the start of Chap. 237, which provides details of the suspicions and hostilities shown toward Galesion by the church authorities in Ephesus.

6. Some of f. 279 and all of ff. 279v–281v are blank at the start of Chap. 245, which deals with the mission of Gabriel to Constantinople and the order of Monomachos that Lazaros should leave the mountain for Bessai.

Only the gap between Chaps. 210–11 (a small part of f. 242v and all of ff. 243–243v) cannot be directly related to these issues, because it occurs in the section describing Lazaros' miraculous provision of food. Chap. 210 is, however, explicitly set during the year prior to Lazaros' death and mentions the famine at that time to which reference is also made in the arguments over the future of the community recorded in Chap. 247.

[245] So, e.g., the gap at the beginning of Chap. 90 (the end of f. 149) comes in a story apparently concerning Neophytos the *parakellarios* who was involved in the disappearance at Lazaros' death of the money brought back from Constantinople (Chap. 248). The textual problem in Chap. 141 occurs in a passage discussing the desire of "most" of the brethren to move from Galesion to Bessai after Lazaros' death and their fears about the quality of his successor. The apparent disruption in the text in Chap. 194 could also be linked to the mention of Kosmas Philippikos and his "rebellion," which occurs in the previous chapter. Even the gaps in Chaps. 52 and 53 appear in contexts

be grounds for suggesting that these lacunae are the result not of chance but of deliberate tampering with the text by someone who wished to remove material, which, in the ongoing disputes over Lazaros' foundations, had become sensitive or damaging to their particular position. If this "editing" did indeed take place, one cannot tell when it may have occurred, but it is possible that Gregory of Cyprus, who produced a reworked version of the *vita* in the late thirteenth century, may have been as much in the dark over the content of these missing segments as we are today.[246]

All that is known about the author of the *vita* is what can be gleaned from references to himself in his work.[247] His monastic name was Gregory and, by the end of Lazaros' life, he held the important office of cellarer at the monastery of the Resurrection on Galesion;[248] he had earlier been *trapezopoios,* a position closely linked with the pantry.[249] Clearly, then, Gregory was trusted and respected by Lazaros, and it is also evident that he was especially close to him toward the end of his life; moreover, he firmly supported Lazaros' views concerning the future of the Galesiote community.[250] After Lazaros' death he continued to be a very influential figure in the monastery; his decision to remain on Galesion instead of leaving for Jerusalem, as he at one point contemplated, may have been instrumental in the survival of the community there.[251]

---

that mention Ignatios, Bessai, and the monastery of the Resurrection. However, other problems in Chaps. 25, 34, 63, 64, and 69 appear entirely unrelated.

[246] See below, section H, and also section I, where further doubts about the authenticity of the story of the Turks and the perfumer are raised.

[247] He may also be the anonymous monk of Chaps. 154, 156–58. Material concerning Gregory the Cellarer is discussed by Delehaye in his introduction, *AASS,* Nov. 3: 504A–C.

[248] See Chap. 170; cf. also Chaps. 151, 210, 211 (possibly), 212, and 213. The reference in Chap. 210 may perhaps indicate that Gregory had ceased to be cellarer by the time he was writing the *vita.*

[249] See Chap. 209; on this office in general, see the note to Chap. 82; on the connection with the pantry, see also Chap. 211.

[250] See especially Chaps. 81 and 217; cf. also, e.g., Chaps. 97, 98, 121, 127, 151, 172, 212, 249. In one or two places Gregory does come close to criticism of Lazaros, as in, e.g., Chaps. 191 and 192; and in Chap. 212 he says that he "often" used to argue with him over instructions he received.

[251] See Chap. 170.

The *vita* also reveals that Gregory the Cellarer originated from Constantinople; his mother was still living there and sending letters to him with news from the city after he had entered the Galesiote community, and he had friends there, some of whom visited the monastery.[252] His association with Galesion evidently began while he was still a layman;[253] he did not join the community until Lazaros was on the pillar of the Theotokos (thus after 1030/31), since in Chapter 57 he is unable to draw on his own knowledge to explain why Lazaros left the monastery of the Savior. Gregory's statement in Chapter 224, "this rule [concerning the conduct of the vigil] remained in force down to our own <day>, but I do not know if it is still observed now," poses an interesting question about his situation when writing the *vita,* since his ignorance of this matter implies some separation from the community; unfortunately the start of the chapter is lost, and with it the context, and so it is impossible to suggest a satisfactory explanation. As is clear from the dating of the *vita,* Gregory the Cellarer must have outlived Lazaros by at least five years.

Internal evidence within the *vita* thus establishes that it cannot have been written any earlier than September 1057; in Chapter 98 the author refers to an old friend who was involved in the revolt of Isaac Komnenos against Michael VI Stratiotikos, which formally began with Isaac's proclamation as emperor on 8 June of that year and ended with his coronation on 1 September. Indeed, as Gregory the Cellarer evidently had time to hear of later developments concerning his friend, the earliest possible date for the completion of the *vita* is probably 1058, between four and five years after Lazaros' death.[254] The author himself was a younger contemporary of Lazaros and witnessed many of the episodes he records; moreover, he sometimes cites the eyewitness reports of others who are still alive when he is writing. It is therefore unlikely that the *vita* was written too long after the revolt, making a date after 1057 (but still in the third quarter of the eleventh century) most probable.[255]

[252] See Chap. 97; cf. Chaps. 96, 98, 127. Ševčenko, "Eastern Provinces," 725, points out that, although he came from the capital, Gregory the Cellarer did not trust it as a place for monks.

[253] See Chap. 75.

[254] See further on this the notes to Chap. 98. References to Ignatios as superior (Chaps. 52, 94, and 100), or to brethren who have died since Lazaros' death (Chap. 197), also indicate some considerable time elapsed before it was written.

[255] Gregory the Cellarer apparently joined Lazaros' community while the holy man was on his second pillar at the Theotokos, thus between ca. 1030 and 1042 (see above

The text of the *vita* suggests that Gregory the Cellarer had received a reasonable, though not outstanding education. The style of the work is, for the most part, straightforward and functional, although there are some more sophisticated passages in the introduction, for example, and in some transitional sections; there are no classical allusions, however, or anything to suggest he had more than a good religious education. One or two hints may indicate some medical background,[256] but, if so, this has done nothing to destroy the author's belief in the activity of the Devil and the demons or to suppress his readiness to blame them for all manner of problems, even when these admitted of an ordinary, rather than a supernatural explanation.[257]

The *vita* will undoubtedly seem rather rambling and even disorganized at times to the casual reader, and it is clearly not the work of an author with firmly defined ideas about literary form; Gregory the Cellarer apparently had only a rudimentary idea of the pattern his work was to take before he began to write it. The narrative thus has a general overall structure, which Gregory

section B); even if he arrived toward the end of this period and was a young man in his early twenties when he did so, the *vita* must almost certainly have been completed by the end of the 11th century, by which time he would have been in his eighties. Chap. 75, in which he is referred to as "Father" while still a layman, may indicate that he was, in fact, *not* young when he first came to be associated with the monastery. As A. Cutler ("Under the Sign of the Deēsis: On the Question of Representativeness in Medieval Art and Literature," *DOP* 41 [1987], 147) notes, modern scholars who have worked with the *vita* agree on an 11th-century date. The only exception is H. G. Beck (*Kirche und theologische Literatur im byzantinischen Reich* [Munich, 1959], 701), who dates it to the beginning of the 14th century at the earliest; Cutler suggests that this is either a mistake or unjustified skepticism. In a personal communication to me (of March 1983), Beck stresses that his dating is only hypothetical and admits the strength of internal evidence against it, while still defending it on the basis of the late date of the manuscript of the *vita* and the absence of Lazaros from earlier *menologia.*

256 See, e.g., Chaps. 151, 172, 206; cf. the medical analogies employed in Chaps. 49, 190, 194.

257 For examples of Gregory the Cellarer resorting to a supernatural explanation when this is avoided by Lazaros himself, see Chaps. 28, 52, and 154–55; for general examples of Gregory's belief in the demonic powers, see Chaps. 25, 26, 38–39, 42–52, 55, 56, 63, 67–69, 78–79, 81, 154–56, 166–67, 174, 194, 200, 208, 218–19, 222, 226, 233, 243–44. One particular theme that recurs is that of demons causing people to fall over cliffs; see Chaps. 41, 42, 47, 131, 132, 243, 244, cf. Chaps. 51 and 166. Cf. here Delehaye, *Stylites,* cvii; the demonology of the *vita* was the focus of particular attention in Joannou, *Démonologie.*

outlines, and probably develops, as he proceeds: it is broadly chronological, in the sense that material on Lazaros' early life comes at the beginning and information to do with his later years and the events surrounding his death comes at the end, but, for much of the work, the structure is topical.[258] The impression that the course of the narrative is being decided as it is written would appear to be confirmed by the loose structure within these broader topical segments: there are some substantial digressions and subtopics,[259] and individual episodes follow each other on occasion simply because something that has been mentioned has reminded the author of the next incident he records.[260] Nevertheless, Gregory the Cellarer attempts to give the start and finish of the work some symmetry,[261] to set the characteristic features of Lazaros' life against the traditional patterns of asceticism in the introductory chapter, and to provide a foreshadowing of what is to come in the description of Lazaros' years at Attaleia;[262] there is also some deliberate biblical parallelism, especially toward the end of the *vita,* where Lazaros is equated with Christ in a number of respects.[263] Biblical allusions predominate and there are numerous quotations from both Old and New Testaments, most of which appear to be

[258] See Chaps. 79–80, where Gregory the Cellarer provides an outline of the topics to be discussed in subsequent chapters.

[259] See, e.g., the sections on Paphnoutios, Chaps. 37–40 (described as "seasoning" to the main narrative in Chap. 36); on the "haunted mountain," Chaps. 42–52; or on the anonymous brother, Chaps. 154–58 (which contains its own subsection in Chap. 155).

[260] See, e.g. (among many), Chaps. 84–87, where the story of a monk checking up on malicious rumors about Lazaros' diet leads, by way of the vision this person has at the monastery, to two other narratives concerning incidents in which people see lightning or dazzling light in connection with Lazaros; or Chaps. 91–92, where mention of Varva [ni]tziana triggers recollection of a comparable incident involving another monk from the same monastery.

[261] So perhaps the use of the motif of light in connection with both Lazaros' birth (Chap. 2) and his death (Chap. 252).

[262] See Chaps. 9–14.

[263] This is typical of the *synkrisis* that appears at the end of many *vitae.* See here, e.g., Lazaros' betrayal by Kosmas in Chap. 239, which is compared to Jesus' betrayal by Judas; his food miracles (Chaps. 209, 211–13), which are probably deliberately reminiscent of those performed by Jesus; and especially Chap. 251, which describes the appearance of his corpse when it is lifted down from his pillar in terms that recall the deposition of Christ.

from memory. The abundance of references and allusions to collections of stories concerning the early ascetic fathers presumably reflects Lazaros' own taste for such anecdotes.[264] On at least three occasions elements have been borrowed, without acknowledgment, from other hagiographical sources.[265]

Perhaps because of the hostile context in which the work was composed, Gregory the Cellarer is unusually scrupulous about citing his sources and ensuring that they can be checked by his readers; he outlines his methodology explicitly in Chapters 80 and 205, and throughout the *vita* he habitually identifies his source for a story.[266] For Lazaros' early life Gregory relies on information included in the *diatyposis,*[267] supplemented by his recollections of Lazaros' own (evidently frequent) accounts,[268] as well as by information about his childhood obtained from the monk Leontios who, with his wife, knew Lazaros and his parents at that time.[269] Most of Gregory's sources for the rest of the Life are monks on Galesion, many of whom were still alive at the time of the *vita*'s composition (among them Lazaros' brother, the superior Ignatios);[270] Gregory himself also tells quite a number of stories from his own experience.[271] One or two episodes appear to derive from local lay people.[272]

[264] See above, section C, p. 22. Gregory the Cellarer himself appears to have made particular use of the chapters on Symeon the Stylite the Elder and James of Cyrrhestica from Theodoret of Cyrrhus' *Historia Religiosa,* and of the *vita* of Daniel the Stylite.

[265] Much of Chap. 35, which provides a general description of Lazaros' ascetic lifestyle, is drawn almost word for word from the *vita* of St. Stephen the Younger; some of the "Life" of Paphnoutios (Chaps. 38 and 39) is close to the *vita* of St. Jacob the Monk; and elements in Chap. 243 appear to have been drawn from an episode recorded in the *Apophthegmata* in connection with Makarios the Great (see below Chaps. 35, 38, and 243). As Delehaye (*Stylites,* cviii) points out in relation to Chap. 35, this practice of Gregory the Cellarer "peut inspirer quelque inquiétude" (about the reliability of the text), but, in fact, these appear to be isolated incidents.

[266] For Delehaye's commentary on Gregory's sources, see his introduction, *AASS,* Nov. 3:504C–F; cf. idem, *Stylites,* cvii.

[267] See Chap. 246.

[268] See Chaps. 9, 11, 16, 17, 19, 20, 25, 27, 29, 36.

[269] Chaps. 2–3.

[270] See Chap. 81.

[271] See, e.g., Chaps. 75, 96–98, 205, 212, 214.

[272] Perhaps the Constantine of Chap. 65; cf. Kyriakos in Chap. 243.

On one occasion Gregory says that he is using a written account he has obtained,[273] and Delehaye suggests that he may also have had some sort of written collection of Lazaros' ἀποκρίσεις (responses) before him.[274] This need not necessarily have been the case, however, for Gregory the Cellarer could just as easily have been relying on his own memory, both of specific incidents he had witnessed and of Lazaros' teaching in general, to which he had been exposed on a regular basis over a long period of time. In other places it seems possible that Gregory does rely on information derived from the *diatyposis,* although there seems no reason for supposing that every mention of something which was done habitually or "as a rule" in the monastery, necessarily came from this source.[275] Clearly Lazaros gave oral rulings to his monks in the community on Galesion on particular matters of discipline and administration as these became necessary;[276] over time, such rulings undoubtedly turned into established practice and this may, but equally well may not, have found specific reference in the written *diatyposis* when it was eventually composed at the very end of his life. On some occasions Lazaros also evidently provided more general oral advice concerning such matters,[277] but again there is nothing to suggest that this followed a set pattern and was intended to be comprehensive (a type of "spoken *typikon,*" as it were), or that Gregory the Cellarer's account of such advice need reflect the actual contents of the written *diatyposis.*

There is good evidence that Gregory the Cellarer had clear polemical aims in writing the *vita;* although his main intention was undoubtedly to glorify and confirm Lazaros' reputation as a holy man and miracle worker who lived a life of extraordinary asceticism, he was also concerned to defend his hero from malicious and damaging accusations spread by his opponents and

[273] Chap. 84.

[274] Delehaye, *Stylites,* cvii. The segment most likely to derive from such a source is Chap. 196.

[275] Janin, *Églises centres,* 245, n. 5, suggested that responses to monks found scattered throughout the *vita* represent elements of the "rule"; he cites particularly Chaps. 189–96. The collection of excerpts translated in Thomas and Hero, *Foundation Documents,* 155–65, includes all the possible passages of this type.

[276] See, e.g., Chaps. 135, 138–39, 144, 147, 150, 182, 184–85, 191.

[277] See Chap. 187.

to set the record straight on what he perceived to be the true history and intended status of Lazaros' foundations on and around Galesion.[278]

From Gregory the Cellarer's point of view, and that of the faction he probably represents, it was vital not only to denigrate the position and legitimacy of the community at Bessai as much as possible, but also to downplay any links the emperor Constantine Monomachos may have had to it. Gregory was all too well aware of the dire consequences for the surviving members of the community on the mountain if it were ever established beyond dispute that Monomachos had actually given Lazaros the land for the monastery at Bessai, but had *not* been involved in the foundation of the Resurrection monastery and, moreover, had himself been of the opinion that Bessai was Lazaros' only legal and legitimate foundation. Presumably Gregory the Cellarer could not deny that the emperor had granted land to Lazaros for the construction of Bessai, but in the *vita* he may have attempted to ensure that any other imperial funding which found its way to Galesion could not be claimed by the opposition, and also to imply that any support Monomachos gave to Bessai was in fact due to misunderstanding. Hence then, perhaps, Gregory's treatment of the mission to Constantinople in Chapter 245, in which the monk Gabriel is made implicitly responsible for the emperor's support for Bessai and his order that Lazaros should leave the mountain; hence too the possibly deliberate vagueness in Chapter 248 about the fate of the money that this mission brought back to Galesion and which, if it came from the emperor, must certainly have been intended for Bessai. Finally, Gregory the Cellarer's hostile and derogatory tone concerning the monk who is the subject of Chapters 228 through 230 may also perhaps be explained along these lines. This monk, who perhaps brought to Galesion the money from Monomachos that Lazaros used for the Resurrection monastery, and whom one would expect to be praised by Gregory, is in fact represented as a skilled confidence trickster and charlatan with a dubious record.[279] Gregory's attitude might be explicable, however, if the Bessai faction (possibly even including this monk himself) had subsequently begun to say that this money and everything purchased with it should really belong to Bessai as the only one of Lazaros' foundations the emperor

[278] For examples of Gregory the Cellarer defending Lazaros' reputation, see, e.g., Chaps. 19, 29–30, 56, 64, 78–79, 87, 119, 138, 145, 182, 183, 185, and 231.

[279] So, for example, his involvement in the rebellion of Peter Deljan, Chap. 229.

Monomachos actually considered to be legitimate. By blackening the opposition and by representing both monk and emperor as unwitting tools in the realization of God's deeper plans for the development of Galesion, Gregory the Cellarer is able to deflect this argument.

H. Later Versions of the Vita

Gregory the Cellarer's version of the *vita* is not the only one to survive, although it seems to be the primary source for the others. The most substantial of these other versions is the reworking by Gregory II of Cyprus, patriarch of Constantinople between 1283 and 1289. This version was also published by Delehaye in the same volume of the *Acta Sanctorum,* following the primary *vita;* his edition is based on a fifteenth-century manuscript.[280] One may probably concur with Delehaye in seeing the version of the *vita* by Gregory of Cyprus as an embellished abridgement of the earlier one. The Life has been transformed by the author into little more than an encomium and is thus probably more useful as a witness to the development of the cult of Lazaros than as a true historical source.[281]

It is true, however, that Gregory of Cyprus' version does differ at a number of points from the primary *vita.* While some of the smaller discrepancies are undoubtedly to be explained by the author's carelessness, other more important ones may, as Delehaye suggests, perhaps be due to his possession of a reworked version of the Life (possibly attempting to fill in the lacunae in the manuscript) and/or to his knowledge of later traditions concerning Lazaros and his foundations (possibly developed with specific polemical aims in view). An example is provided by the significant section that describes the role of Emperor Constantine IX Monomachos in financing the construction of the Galesiote monastery of the Resurrection, a foundation said here to have owed its location to a vision seen by Lazaros;[282] another is the overtly miraculous

[280] *BHG* 980; *AASS,* Nov. 3:588–606. The manuscript is the Vatican's Barberiniano VI.22, ff. 283–314. A copy of this text also appears in the same manuscript as the first version, Athos' Lavrioticus I.127, ff. 296–341v, but it is in a later, 18th-century hand.

[281] Delehaye, *AASS,* Nov. 3:508.28; idem, *Stylites,* cviii.

[282] As is discussed above (Section F.b.) the original contents of this lacuna and the origin and motive of traditions that may have arisen to fill it are questions of great importance in considering the relationship between Lazaros' various foundations and their legal and moral claims to represent his tradition after his death. See Chap. 230 of the *vita;* chaps. 29–31 in the version of Gregory of Cyprus, *AASS,* Nov. 3:599F–600E.

account of Lazaros' death at the age of seventy-two (rather than eighty-six).[283] Even where Gregory of Cyprus' version appears to supplement the primary *vita* in important ways, however, there are serious doubts about the historical accuracy of the material it contains.[284] There must, then, be reservations about its ability to add anything of importance to the knowledge of Lazaros' life and foundations already gained from the earlier account.

Other surviving versions of the *vita* are short. A brief epitome drawn from an *akolouthia* of Lazaros, found in the same manuscript as the primary *vita,* was published by Delehaye alongside the two major versions in the *Acta Sanctorum.*[285] The second part of this epitome, at least, appears to be a condensation of the same tradition found in the version by Gregory of Cyprus, since it mentions the vision which led to the foundation of the monastery of the Resurrection and its financing by Constantine IX as well as giving Lazaros' age at death as seventy-two.

An unpublished *synaxarion* found in a thirteenth- or early fourteenth-century manuscript, now in Moscow, also seems very close to the epitome version, although somewhat fuller.[286] It contains a similar account of the foundation of the Resurrection monastery and also includes a version of the events surrounding Lazaros' death, which is close to that in Gregory of Cyprus' *vita.*

A third short, but rather different, source of evidence concerning Lazaros and his foundation on Galesion has been published more recently by O. Lampsides.[287] This text is taken from the lengthy account of the lives of Barnabas and Sophronios, the founders of the Soumela monastery,[288] written by

[283] See Chap. 42, *AASS,* Nov. 3:605E–606B (for Lazaros' death), chap. 41, 605E (for his age). The historical significance of the events surrounding Lazaros' death and the motives of the author of the primary *vita* for stressing that they were *not* miraculous are discussed above, section F.a., pp. 39–40.

[284] So, e.g., the problems cited above, section F.b., p. 44.

[285] *BHG* 980e; *AASS,* Nov. 3:607–608 from Athos' Lavrioticus I.127, ff. 74v–77. Delehaye (*Stylites,* cix) dismisses this work as "absolument dénoué d'importance."

[286] Moscow, Historical Museum (ГИМ) 369/353, ff. 217v-220v. I have been unable to see this manuscript, but am very grateful to Alexander Kazhdan for generously allowing me to use his notes and his partial transcription of this text. See also p. 71.

[287] "'Ανέκδοτον κείμενον περὶ τοῦ ἁγίου Λαζάρου Γαλησιώτου," *Theologia* 53.1 (1982), 158–77.

[288] For more on this monastery, situated some twenty-five miles from Trebizond in northeast Asia Minor, see *ODB,* s.v. "Soumela monastery."

Akakios Sabbaites early in the thirteenth century.[289] Lampsides argues that the account probably preserves oral traditions concerning the life of Lazaros that Akakios himself heard while visiting the monastery of the Resurrection on Galesion. Although the value of this text is probably negligible as a reliable source for the actual details of Lazaros' life, it nevertheless provides some interesting variants and evidence of the development of traditions concerning him in the most successful and enduring of his foundations. Events in the early part of Lazaros' life and career are compressed and somewhat confused in this account and have become more miraculous in the telling; moreover, any mention of Lazaros' travels is omitted. He is thus said to have fled the monastery in which he had been educated and to have moved directly to Galesion at the age of twelve.[290] Interestingly also, no other foundation on Galesion apart from that of the Resurrection is mentioned, nor is Lazaros said to have been a stylite until he took up residence on his pillar there toward the end of his life when he was already over seventy. He and his early disciples are instead said to have lived in crude, dry-stone huts, open at the center and with two roughly apsidal ends, the construction of which is described in some detail.[291] This would suggest that all trace of the other earlier and smaller foundations on the mountain, those of the Savior and the Theotokos, had completely disappeared by the early thirteenth century, while stone huts of the type described were evidently visible, whatever their true origin. Furthermore, if it is accepted that Akakios Sabbaites actually visited the monastery of the Resurrection, it would also appear to suggest that the primary *vita* of Lazaros (and so the biographical details it contained) was not well known at this time, at least to the informant (presumably a member of the community) who lies behind the narrative contained in his account.[292]

[289] For further information, see Lampsides, "'Ανέκδοτον κειμενον," commentary, 158–59, 171–72. The text is edited from the manuscript Dionysiou 268, ff. 483v–491v.

[290] "τὸ ὄρος Κάχλυκον, κατὰ κοινοῦ δὲ Γαλλύσιον" (Mt. Kachlykon, commonly <called> Gallysion), f. 486v, p. 164. The narrative is perhaps influenced by the Life of Daniel the Stylite (see *vita Danielis,* chaps. 2–5).

[291] Cf. the epitome version (*AASS,* Nov. 3:607E), which says that Lazaros "dwelt alone in a stifling and very oppressive cell on the northern part of the mountain" prior to the foundation of the monastery of the Resurrection, and not on a pillar. Cf. also the situation implied for Lazaros by Gregory of Cyprus' account of his vision concerning the Resurrection monastery, above, p. 44.

[292] Lampsides, "'Ανέκδοτον κείμενον," 174, suggests that a possible reason for Akakios' obvious ignorance of Lazaros' travels to the Holy Land was that his visit might

This version includes a fuller and slightly different form of the story concerning Constantine Monomachos' endowment of the monastery of the Resurrection on Galesion.[293] It represents a variant of the tradition found in Gregory of Cyprus' *vita*, although it seems to be more precise in its dating and in its details of the financing and construction of the church; it also appears to tally better with the chronology of the primary *vita,* since Lazaros is said to be in his seventies when this happens. What has survived here is thus perhaps a slightly earlier, unworked version of the tradition which Gregory of Cyprus employs.

I. Galesion after Lazaros' Death and the Development of His Cult

Although the Galesiote community ultimately surmounted its problems and came to flourish and grow in repute in the Byzantine world, not very much is known of its later history. The primary *vita* reveals that a period of extreme uncertainty ensued in the weeks immediately following Lazaros' death. A struggle for control of the monastery, its possessions, and even Lazaros' remains may well have taken place between those who wished to stay on the mountain, those who wished to move to Bessai but still remain independent, and the authorities in Ephesus who wished either to remove an independent community from Galesion altogether or to assert control there themselves.[294] Another point of serious tension that had developed during the last

have been too short to have been told of this. Even if this were the case, it would not explain the omissions and discrepancies in what is recorded; the things that he clearly *was* told show a complete ignorance of events recorded in the primary *vita.* Nevertheless, the *vita* of the founder of the monastery and the *typikon* would be among a monastery's most important possessions, so it would be strange if a copy of the primary *vita* did not remain on Galesion until it was threatened by the Turks and united with the Anastasis monastery in Constantinople (see below, section I, pp. 66–67); certainly the copyist's note (see above, section G, p. 49) would suggest a copy did remain there. It is thus hard to explain the ignorance and confusion of Akakios' informant.

293 Lampsides, "Ἀνέκδοτον κείμενον," 167–70.

294 The immediate response of some of the brethren to the news of Lazaros' death, "Where shall we go? Who can govern us after you as well as you <have done>?" (Chap. 249), clearly illustrates the nature of the uncertainties and doubts troubling them. Evidence of a breakdown in control may be found in Chap. 100, where the eunuch Stephen, who had been ordered to remain at the monastery of the Savior by Lazaros, evidently took the opportunity provided by the latter's death to fulfill his wish to move to the Resurrection monastery; and also in Chap. 204, where an anonymous monk (conceivably the same one who figures in Chaps. 228–30) reportedly set himself up as a "hesy-

phase of Lazaros' life, opposition to the succession of his brother Ignatios as superior of the community, now erupted into actual violence, with an attempt on Ignatios' life.[295] This incident reveals, with striking clarity, the extent to which the situation had deteriorated; even Gregory the Cellarer himself thought of abandoning the struggle and traveling to the Holy Land.[296] But then, somehow (although by what dubious and perhaps desperate means is unclear) the position was significantly altered: Gregory was dissuaded from leaving by one of the elders of the monastery, Ignatios became superior,[297] Lazaros' body remained in a sarcophagus in the narthex of the church of the

---

chast" and refused to participate in the communal life of the monastery after Lazaros' death. Chap. 170, to which reference is made just below, shows that the complete abandonment of the monastery was a real possibility at this time. For uncertainty about the disposition of Lazaros' body, fueled by fears that control of the community would rest with those who possessed it, see Chap. 253.

It is possible that Gregory of Cyprus' story (chap. 35, *AASS,* Nov. 3:602E–F) of the founding of an unnamed, but attractive, rival monastery by a disgruntled *oikonomos* of Galesion may originate in the events of this time. Although the primary *vita* leaves no doubt that Lazaros himself founded Bessai, it probably emerged as a serious rival to Galesion only after his death. To judge from the number of monks who wished to move to Bessai, it seems likely that a considerable exodus from the mountain now took place; this was possibly led by the *oikonomos* to whom the patriarch refers and who thus, in legend, came to be remembered as Bessai's founder. One might note that Cyril, the *oikonomos* in 1053, expresses serious doubts about the viability of Galesion in Chap. 247; he is said to have had no hope of the monastery's survival. Moreover, Chap. 83 shows that by the time the *vita* was being written, Cyril no longer occupied this office, which was instead held by one Bartholomew.

[295] A monk called Methodios, already a proven opponent of Lazaros, reportedly attempted to administer poisoned wine to Ignatios "at the very time of our holy father's death" (Chap. 202). The rebel monk Kosmas Philippikos may possibly have been implicated in this affair, see Chap. 193. Opposition to Ignatios was apparently not something new: the hostility evoked by Lazaros' attempt to make him *oikonomos* of "Philippikos' house" was evidently so severe that Ignatios wished to leave Galesion altogether, but was eventually persuaded by Lazaros to move to the foundation at Bessai (Chap. 221). Cf. also Chap. 141, in which the monks express concerns about finding a suitable successor for Lazaros.

[296] See Chap. 170. Another notable figure in the community, Laurentios (who later became a stylite), also thought of leaving after Lazaros died (Chap. 217); see also Chap. 141, where "most" of the monks are said to have asked for permission to leave at that time.

[297] Several weeks evidently elapsed before Ignatios took over as superior; cf. Chaps. 100, 170. Chap. 52 shows that he remained at Bessai during this interim period.

Resurrection, and the members of the community who were loyal to their dead founder's vision of Galesion stayed on the mountain to continue the fight.

Despite this stabilization of the situation, however, the damage already done to Lazaros' reputation during the disputes that marred the last phase of his life may explain why he did not immediately become accepted as a figure of major importance in the Byzantine cult and why Galesion now entered a phase of relative obscurity. The propagation of damaging rumors about him by the local ecclesiastical authorities in the Ephesus region was undoubtedly harmful in this respect; the alienation of imperial support shortly before his death must also have been detrimental. Almost nothing, then, is known of the history of Galesion or of any cult associated with Lazaros from the middle of the eleventh to the early thirteenth century. No tradition of posthumous miracle-working survives, and only two episodes in the *vita* may be considered in this category.[298] There is no notice for Lazaros in the *Synaxarion of Constantinople,*[299] no record of any contemporary iconographical tradition associated with him,[300] and no evidence that copies of the primary *vita* were made at this time. All that is known is that his body was moved from its temporary resting place to a more permanent tomb on Galesion on 17 July in an unknown year, sometime in the eleventh century.[301]

[298] The first is the granting of an extra day of life to a member of the community as a result of Lazaros' intercession (Chap. 179); the second, the prevention of Ignatios' murder, again by his intercession (Chap. 202). The primary *vita* denies any miraculous element in the production or signing of the *diatyposis* for the monastery, an event treated as a posthumous miracle in other versions (see Chap. 250, and above, section F, pp. 39–40). The production of holy oil on Galesion on "St. Lazaros day" and its employment as a miracle-working substance by the faithful as far afield as Chios (Chap. 76) may refer to an element of the posthumous cult of Lazaros, but this is far from certain.

[299] Lazaros is, however, mentioned there under 7 and 10 November, *SynaxCP,* 204–5.29 and 211–12.43. There is also reference to the translation of his remains under 17 July, cols. 825–26.31 (see immediately below).

[300] There is a 14th-century image of Lazaros as a standing figure in the narthex of the katholikon of Hilandar on Mt. Athos. *The Painter's Manual of Dionysius of Fourna,* ed. P. Hetherington (London, 1974), 60, notes under the appropriate date for Lazaros Galesiotes, 7 November, "Saint Lazarus the confessor, an old man, bald with a long beard." The fact that he is called a confessor and is not depicted as a stylite suggests that only a vague memory of him persisted, unsupported by any firm and original iconographical tradition.

[301] See Janin (*Églises centres,* 246, 247) for references. The transfer must have taken place sometime between 1058 and 1100, since the *vita,* which does not mention it, was

In the thirteenth century, however, perhaps assisted by the emergence of the empire of Nicaea following the loss of Constantinople to the Latins, Galesion entered into a new period of prominence.[302] Akakios Sabbaites visited Galesion and composed his version of Lazaros' Life early in that century, while the Nicene teacher and writer Nikephoros Blemmydes was evidently confined there for a short period of time around 1239.[303] It is, however, to the patriarch of Constantinople, Joseph I (1266–75, 1282–83), who had been superior on the mountain before his elevation, that the community undoubtedly owed much of its enhanced reputation and well-being. Moreover, this patriarchal connection and accompanying influence were continued under Athanasios I (1289–93, 1303–9), who had spent more than eighteen years in the monastery and had been ordained there.[304] Yet another patriarch of Constantinople, Gregory II of Cyprus (1283–89), had been a monk on Galesion; his substantial reworking of the *vita* confirms the distinction enjoyed by this holy mountain during the second half of the thirteenth century.[305] The prominent role played by two other monks from the community, Meletios and Galaktion, in the anti-unionist disputes under Michael VIII Palaiologos, must also have helped to increase the profile of Galesion, which by this time was apparently developing a notable library and was the scene of a productive *scriptorium*.[306] Around 1273, with help from the patriarch Joseph I and the emperor Michael VIII, Galesion acquired as a *metochion* the monastery that

completed at the earliest ca. 1058, while at least one manuscript which does (Coislin. 199) dates from the 11th century.

302 Janin, *Églises centres,* 247.

303 See his *Autographia sive curriculum vitae,* ed. J. A. Munitiz (Turnhout-Leuven, 1984), 1.59 (xxxv); English translation, idem, *Partial Account,* 77–78. See also Janin, *Églises centres,* 247–48.

304 See A.-M. Talbot, *The Correspondence of Athanasios I, Patriarch of Constantinople* (Washington, D.C., 1975), xvii–xviii; cf. eadem, "Comparison," 15; Nicol, *"Instabilitas,"* 197.

305 See here, especially, Janin, *Églises centres,* 247–49; also Foss, *Ephesus,* 129–30. On pride in one's monastery as a reason for hagiographic composition and Gregory of Cyprus' version of the *vita* as an example of this, see A.-M. Talbot, "Old Wine in New Bottles: The Rewriting of Saints' Lives in the Palaeologan Period," in *The Twilight of Byzantium,* ed. S. Ćurčić and D. Mouriki (Princeton, N.J., 1991), 24.

306 See Janin, *Églises centres,* 249; also, Halkin, "Manuscrits," who suggests, however, that Galesion never became a major cultural center. On Meletios see also Nicol, *"Instabilitas,"* 196, and A. Failler, "Mélèce le Confesseur et le monastère Saint-Lazare de Constantinople," *REB* 56 (1998), 231–38.

had been founded in 1241 by Nikephoros Blemmydes at Emathia near Ephesus.[307] The episode further underlines the influence Galesion enjoyed during this period, but a letter of Gregory II of Cyprus reveals that, even then, the monastery continued to have a difficult relationship with the metropolitan of Ephesus.[308]

The resurgence in importance of Galesion in the later thirteenth century was quite remarkable, but it was to be relatively short-lived, for the monastery appears to have been destroyed by the Turks early in the fourteenth century.[309]

[307] See Janin (*Églises centres,* 247–48) and Thomas (Thomas and Hero, *Foundation Documents,* 150). The original source is George Pachymeres, *de Michaele Palaeologo* 5.2 (*Georgii Pachymeris de Michaele et Andronico Palaeologis libri tredecem,* ed. I. Bekker [Bonn, 1835], 1:342.9–13); cf. *RegPatr,* no. 1405. Nothing more is known of Emathia although the site, as described by Blemmydes, sounds as wild and barren as Galesion, which must have been nearby. It was evidently close to Ephesus and also not far from the monastery of Gregory Thaumaturgos, where Blemmydes lived during its construction; see also Munitiz, *Partial Account,* 116–17 n. 73.

[308] See Janin, *Églises centres,* 248; *RegPatr,* no. 1500.

[309] See above, section G, p. 49, on the note in Lavrioticus I.127 to this effect; see also Janin (*Églises centres,* 249–50), who dismisses any suggestion that it may have continued after this date. Foss (*Ephesus,* 130; followed by Nicol, *"Instabilitas,"* 199–200) is probably correct in suggesting that it was plundered and abandoned when Ephesus fell to the Turks in 1304. See also below on possible difficulties raised by this story.

There is a suggestion in John Lazaropoulos' *Miracles* of Eugenios of Trebizond (written in the 14th century) that Galesion had been severely attacked by "barbarians" at a much earlier date, apparently during Lazaros' lifetime (see *The Hagiographic Dossier of St. Eugenios of Trebizond,* ed. and trans. J. O. Rosenqvist [Uppsala, 1996]), chap. 5, ll. 627–28, pp. 238–239); the details provided in this source, however, suggest that some sort of confusion has taken place and little weight is to be placed on the story. Chap. 5 of the *Miracles* claims that the abbot of the monastery of Eugenios, Paul, had been a disciple of Lazaros on Galesion but had "later" fled to Trebizond from the mountain, following the barbarian attack; this part of Paul's career is described in the course of an incident that takes place specifically during the reign of Constantine IX Monomachos (1042–55), and the clear implication is that his flight, and the barbarian attack which provoked it, had taken place quite some time in the past, thus certainly during Lazaros' lifetime. The fact that the *vita* makes no mention at all either of such an important incident or, for that matter, of a Paul among the monks on Galesion, suggests that the story must have become confused. Perhaps the most likely explanation, and one tentatively put forward by Rosenqvist, is that this Paul may be the one mentioned in Chaps. 20–24 of the *vita:* he had probably been a fellow monk with Lazaros in the monastery of St. Sabas and, in company with him, fled the barbarian attacks made on the Christian communities of Palestine around 1009, before going his own way at Laodikaia.

This was, however, not quite the end of Lazaros' foundation, for a chrysobull of Andronikos II provided for the merger of the monastery of the Mother of God on Galesion with that of the Anastasis in Constantinople.[310] Although this document is not dated, Janin suggests the unification may have taken place in the later thirteenth century, since no mention is made of the sack of monastery by the Turks.[311] He also connects it with a further important piece of evidence for the growth in respect for Lazaros and the continuation of his cult in the capital at that time. This is Constantine Akropolites' dedication to Lazaros of a chapel he had purchased (in connection with his restoration of the Anastasis monastery) and his careful prescription for an annual celebration of Lazaros' feast day there, together with a weekly liturgy in his memory to be said by monks from the monastery.[312] Further evidence for the continuation of Lazaros' cult is provided by commemoration of the translation of his head.[313]

As with so much to do with Lazaros and his foundations, however, the evidence outlined here concerning the fate of his community seems to raise more problems than it solves. Was there a single transfer of the Galesiote community to Constantinople? Or was this a long drawn out process? And when did it happen? In the late thirteenth century at the time of Andronikos II's chrysobull? Or only in the early fourteenth when Galesion was sacked by the Turks? If a complete transfer of monks and property from Galesion to the Anastasis in Constantinople took place in the late thirteenth century *prior* to the Turkish sack, it is difficult to explain the story that the sole manuscript of the *vita* of the founder was seized by the Turks when the monastery was de-

[310] MM 5:264–67.

[311] Janin, *Églises centres,* 249. Cf., idem, *Églises CP,* 21, where he suggests that the Anastasis monastery may have been restored as a refuge for the Galesiote monks worried about the Turkish conquest.

[312] The liturgy for Lazaros was to be said every Thursday. See H. Delehaye, "Constantini Acropolitae, hagiographi byzantini, epistularum manipulus," *AnalBoll* 51 (1933), 282–84; Janin, *Églises CP,* 20–22; idem, *Églises centres,* 249; K. A. Manaphes, "Κωνσταντίνου Ἀκροπολίτου, Λόγος εἰς τὴν ἀνακαίνισιν τοῦ ναοῦ τῆς τοῦ Κυρίου ἡμῶν Ἀναστάσεως διαθετικός," Ἐπ.Ἑτ.Βυζ.Σπ. 37 (1969–70), 459–65. See also Thomas and Hero, *Foundation Documents,* no. 46, chap. 8.

[313] Janin, *Églises centres,* 247, 249. The transfer evidently took place on 25 October in an unknown year, perhaps, as Janin suggests, because of the threat posed by the Turks at the beginning of the 14th century, or possibly somewhat earlier in the context of the development of his cult at Constantinople in the later part of the 13th century.

stroyed, for it seems most unlikely that such an important document would simply have been left behind by the monks of the community during a peaceful move to the capital. The authenticity of the story concerning the fate of the manuscript of the *vita,* with its (convenient) explanation for the lacunae in the text, has already been called into doubt,[314] and this might be a further reason for questioning it. On the other hand, if the manuscript *did* remain on Galesion until its sack by the Turks, the simplest explanation would be that there was a two (or more) stage transfer to Constantinople; perhaps one group left Galesion in the late thirteenth century to join the Anastasis monastery but another remained to the bitter end with the monastery's most treasured possessions, including the *vita* and, possibly, Lazaros' head. If that is what happened, then new significance may be found in the otherwise rather awkward fact that Andronikos' chrysobull deals specifically with a monastery dedicated to the Virgin on Galesion rather than that of the Resurrection, as one would expect.[315] A third possibility remains, however, and that is that all these events took place at the same time early in the fourteenth century. In that case the move to Constantinople could not be seen as being simply or largely due to a growth in the prestige of Galesion and its founder in the capital; it would also be a matter of urgent necessity following the sack of the monastery by the Turks.

Whatever is the case, it seems clear that Lazaros' cult, and at least some important elements of his foundation, survived the loss of Ephesus and Galesion to the Turks in the early fourteenth century by being transferred to Constantinople. Indeed veneration for him, or at least some memory of him, survived there until the early fifteenth century, for the Russian traveler Zosima records seeing relics of "Lazarus, bishop of Galesium" in the monastery dedicated to the Lazarus of the Gospels near the Hodegetria. It is, however, far from clear whether these relics actually belonged to Lazaros himself,[316] and, after this, both he and his foundations disappear entirely from the historical record.

[314] See above, section G, p. 50–51.

[315] Cf. Janin, *Églises centres,* 249 n. 3, and note the suggestion in Akakios Sabbaites cited above, p. 60, that no memory or trace of Lazaros' earlier foundations on the mountain remained by the early 13th century.

[316] See G. P. Majeska, *Russian Travelers to Constantinople in the Fourteenth and Fifteenth Centuries* (Washington, D.C., 1989), 379–81, who (p. 381 n. 121) mistakenly associates Lazaros with Syria. Janin (*Églises CP,* 298) suggests that Zosima is referring to a separate monastery dedicated specifically to Lazaros of Galesion, but Majeska

J. Conclusion

Initially, the most striking aspect of the *vita* is undoubtedly its great length, but its importance does not lie simply in its bulk. It is an unusually accessible, instructive, and refreshingly vivid piece of hagiography that not only provides an enormous wealth of material on Lazaros himself, but also much fascinating information concerning Byzantine society in the first half of the eleventh century.[317] The author avoids, for the most part, many of the more stultifying features of the Byzantine genre of hagiography, as well as the embellishments of high-flown rhetorical style that often prove so tedious to the modern reader (and which, for instance, are all too visible in the "improved" version by Gregory of Cyprus). Instead, one finds a clear, comparatively well-rounded picture of Lazaros himself and, in a host of episodes, fascinating glimpses of life in the eleventh century, both inside a monastic community and in the world around it. These glimpses are at times so immediate and so vital that one has the illusion of looking through a window onto that now distant and remote period.

Clearly the *vita* must speak for itself, but one may think here, for example, of Lazaros having his clothes torn off by vicious sheepdogs after he has taken refuge on a rock, wedging shut the door of a lonely chapel to keep

---

proposes that the monastery might have been said to bear this dedication simply due to the confusion arising because relics of Lazaros Galesiotes were housed there alongside those of his biblical namesake. Interestingly, both the earlier Russian Anonymous (early 1390s) and the Armenian Anonymous (late 14th/early 15th century) mention that the relics of a St. Meletios were also preserved in the sanctuary; although the latter describes these relics as belonging to the 4th-century patriarch of Antioch, Majeska suggests that they may have belonged instead to the late 13th-century anti-unionist Meletios (Galesiotes), who was a monk of the monastery. This introduces a further link to Galesion, since Meletios was also a monk on the mountain before going to the capital (Janin, *Églises centres,* 248), and this, surely, is the origin of Meletios' sobriquet "Galesiotes" (rather than a derivation from the unofficial name of his burial place, as Majeska suggests). Was this Meletios venerated at the sanctuary because of some earlier association it had with the founder of Galesion? Or could it be that association of the sobriquet of this Meletios with the name of the biblical Lazaros to whom the church was dedicated, when combined with a memory of Lazaros, led to the false impression received and transmitted by Zosima that relics of Lazaros Galesiotes were displayed there? On this, see Failler, "Mélèce le Confesseur," 231–32.

[317] Kazhdan and Epstein, *Change,* 201, describe the *vita* as "the last great example of eleventh-century hagiography." Cf. here Morris, *Monks,* 70–71.

out the wolves, avoiding seduction by a nun in the narthex of a pilgrimage church, arguing with marauding soldiers or, in his old age, spilling his hot evening drink over his feet and cursing the Devil for having made him scald himself. There is the Lazaros who laughs, who loses his temper, and who bumps heads with a bear in the fog, as well as the Lazaros who meets, and indeed far surpasses, all the standard criteria of Byzantine ascetic virtue.

As well as the shining examples of notable and meritorious monks who grace Lazaros' communities, there are also the lesser brethren with human failings: those who fall asleep in the narthex of the church during morning service, eat to the point of getting sick while celebrating a festival away from the monastery, succumb to the seduction of their host's wife, end up dead drunk beside the path after drinking wine from a broken jar so as not to waste it, sneak around the monastery during church services pilfering possessions from the cells of fellow monks, persuade a flock of goats to follow by using Lazaros' name, or wait with great glee to poke Lazaros with a stick if he should start dozing.

As well as the members of the community who engage in moderate asceticism, there are the madmen and extremists who suffer strange delusions, whip themselves, have their beards pulled out by ice, put rocks in their mouths, stand all night in special harnesses, encourage lice to bite them, and allow maggots to breed in their putrefying sores. There are the loyal, upstanding supporters of Lazaros, and there are the villains: the monks who constantly grumble and argue with Lazaros over his policies; the monks who whisper malicious gossip and spread dreadful rumors about Lazaros; the monk who betrays a desperate mission from the monastery to the opposition in Ephesus; the people sent up the mountain at unexpected moments to check out Lazaros' pillar and to examine him physically for any signs of fraudulence; or the monk who tries to murder Lazaros' brother Ignatios by poisoning his wine.

Finally, while one finds important allusions to historical events and personages in the world outside the monastery, and interesting references to places, practices, and customs, one also catches glimpses of ordinary people, alive and real in that distant world: the priest's wife who is abused by her husband and attempts to get rid of him by using magic to send him mad, only to discover that he has used the potion to celebrate the Eucharist and given it to his whole congregation; the woman who is murdered after the priest to whom she has confessed a love affair reveals her secret to her husband; the man who cannot resist returning to his home after years of exile only to end up accidentally sleeping with his own daughter; the confidence trickster who pretends to be possessed by a demon in order to dupe gullible villagers out of their valuables with the connivance of the local priest; the girl who has been tricked out of her inheritance and then abandoned to her fate on the roads of Asia Minor; the fraudulent nobleman who arranges for his colleagues to act as imperial agents trying to arrest him; the woman who is notorious in her village for her extraordinary meanness; the poor man who is so desperate that he accepts everything he is offered by Lazaros even though he is unable to carry it; the passersby who steal all the beans from the monastery's fields; and the streams of beggars and poverty-stricken peasants who keep coming to the monastery to find something to eat. The characters, to many of whom it is still easy to relate nine hundred years later, continue to step out of the shadows of the eleventh-century *vita* in a colorful, animated procession, and, as they do so, help us to slip back toward the world from which they have come.

NOTE ON THE TRANSLATION

This translation attempts to adhere to the pattern of the original Greek as closely as possible, while at the same time capturing in modern English the atmosphere of vitality and accessibility that pervades most of the text. For the benefit of those unable to compare the translation with the Greek, pointed brackets are used to indicate where words or phrases have been supplied in order to improve the flow or sense of the English. The one notable exception to this practice is in the case of Lazaros' name; Gregory the Cellarer uses it very rarely indeed, but the English requires it to be included so frequently that to bracket it on every occasion where it does not appear in the original would prove an irritation. Figures in square brackets refer to the pages of Delehaye's edition. In general, information concerning textual issues and factual matters is provided in the footnotes; in the interests of clarity and conciseness, however, questions of chronology are dealt with primarily in section B of the introduction, while basic information concerning individuals mentioned in the *vita* is brought together in the Prosopographical Glossary (Appendix B).

The work in progress of Anna Lambropoulou in Athens on a new critical edition of the *vita* of Lazaros, as well as her edition of the Moscow *synaxarion* ("'Ανέκδοτο Κείμενο γιὰ τὸν ὅσιο Λάζαρο Γαλησιώτη," *Theologia* 59 [1988], 588–93), only came to my attention in the final stages of the publication of this translation. It is regrettable that I have been otherwise unable to acknowledge or make use of her work.

BIBLIOGRAPHY

Edition Used for Translation

(BHG 979) *Acta Sanctorum Novembris* 3 (Brussels: Société des Bollandistes, 1910), 508–88.

Related Texts

(BHG 980) *vita* by Gregory of Cyprus, *Acta Sanctorum Novembris* 3 (Brussels: Société des Bollandistes, 1910), 588–606.

O. Lampsides, "Ἀνέκδοτον κείμενον περὶ τοῦ ἁγίου Λαζάρου Γαλησιώτου," *Theologia* 53 (1982), 158–77.

Modern Translations

Partial English translation by P. Karlin-Hayter in *Byzantine Monastic Foundation Documents*, ed. J. P. Thomas and A. C. Hero (Washington, D.C., forthcoming), 148–66.

Secondary Literature

P. Boulhol, ἈΝΑΓΝΩΡΙΣΜΟΣ: *La scène de reconnaissance dans l'hagiographie antique et médiévale* (Aix-en-Provence, 1996), 123–26.

H. Delehaye, *Les saints stylites*, SubsHag 14 (Paris-Brussels, 1923), cvi–cxvi.

C. Foss, *Ephesus after Antiquity: A Late Antique, Byzantine and Turkish City* (Cambridge, 1979), 119–24, 128–30.

M. I. Gedeon, "Γνώσεις ἐκ τοῦ τυπικοῦ τῶν μονῶν τοῦ Γαλησίου ὄρους," Ἐκκλησιαστικὴ Ἀλήθεια 18 (1898), 27–31, 61–67.

F. Halkin, "Manuscrits Galésiotes," *Scriptorium* 15 (1961), 221–27.

R. Janin, *Les églises et les monastères des grands centres byzantins* (Paris, 1975), 241–50.

A. P. Kazhdan, "Lazaros of Mount Galesios," in *ODB* 2:1198.

A. P. Kazhdan and A. Wharton Epstein, *Change in Byzantine Culture in the Eleventh and Twelfth Centuries* (Berkeley, 1985), 87–88, 201, 246–47.

C. Loparev, "Zhitie v. Lazarya Galisieskago," *VizVrem* 4 (1897), 364–78.

E. Malamut, "A propos de Bessai d'Ephèse," *REB* 43 (1985), 243–51.

———, *Sur la route des saints byzantins* (Paris, 1993), 40–43.

R. Morris, "The Political Saint of the Eleventh Century," in *The Byzantine Saint*, ed. S. Hackel (London, 1981), 43–50.

I. Ševčenko, "Constantinople Viewed from the Eastern Provinces in the Middle Byzantine Period," *Harvard Ukrainian Studies* 3/4.2 (1979–80), 723–26, 745.

A.-M. Talbot, "Galesios, Mount," in *ODB* 2:817.

J. P. Thomas, "Documentary Evidence from the Byzantine Monastic *Typika* for the History of the Evergetine Reform Movement," in *The Theotokos Evergetis and Eleventh-Century Monasticism*, ed. M. Mullett and A. Kirby (Belfast, 1994), 249–54.

[508]

The Life, Conduct, and Ascetic Practice of Our Blessed Father Lazaros the Miracle Worker who <Lived> on <Mount> Galesion

1. *He Who fashioned* our *hearts alone, Who understands all* our *works,* as the holy Scripture says,[1] and Who foresees the instability of our minds and how our thoughts tend toward evil things from our youth,[2] has consented in His goodness that contemporary authors should set down in writing the lives, the deeds of contest and asceticism, and the extraordinary and most marvelous achievements of the saints who lived before the law,[3] under the law and in the time of grace,—I mean those of the prophets, apostles, martyrs, and blessed ones. <Such authors have> left <their accounts> like living icons[4] or clean and very clear mirrors for subsequent <generations> in order that when, as the Apostle says, we *consider* their lives and *their behavior* through these <stories>, [509] we may *follow their faith,*[5] and in order that whatever path someone desires to travel he may do this easily and without stumbling, finding his guide therein. For nothing leads so naturally toward the way of virtue or, on the other hand, is so good at making <people> despise all transitory things, whether these bring sorrow or joy, as when <an account of> a life which is virtuous and pleasing to God falls on the ears[6] of those who love Him. For if, as the same blessed Paul says, *bad company ruins good morals,*[7] it is clear that

[1] Cf. Ps. 32 (33):15. This quotation, with the same alterations of αὐτῶν to ἡμῶν, is also used by Theodoret of Cyrrhus as the opening of the introduction to his *commentarius in Amos,* PG 81:1664B.

[2] Cf. Jer. 3:25; 39 (32):30.

[3] That is, the Mosaic law. The meaning is clarified below.

[4] This seems to be a definite allusion to Basil of Caesarea, *epistola* II (PG 32:220); indeed much of the opening segment of this chapter can be read as an expansion of the theme raised by Basil; cf. also Eusebius of Caesarea, *contra Marcellum,* PG 24:764C.

[5] This is a rough quotation from Heb. 13:7. The first section follows the interpretation of the RSV rather than that of the RV, which translates ἀναστροφή (here taken as "behavior") as "conversation."

[6] Cf. Nah. 1:12.

[7] 1 Cor. 15:33, following the RSV translation. The original passage quotes a fragment of Menander's *Thais.* As well as "bad company," the sense of "bad topics of conversation" is also implicit in the Greek; cf. the AV translation, "evil communications."

good <company> tends to lead to good <behavior> and to attune <people's> spiritual condition to what they are hearing.

Who, then, will not think himself miserable when he hears about the lives of the holy men <who lived> before the law and under the law, when he considers, as is likely, what we (who have received the spiritual law, have enjoyed such grace, and have been deemed worthy of the gift of the Holy Spirit) must do if these men (some of whom had only the natural law and the others only the shadowy, written law) exhibited such a scrupulous quality of life? When he has thus reduced his opinion of himself, he will reap much spiritual benefit. Who also would not be warmed when hearing about the deeds and the teachings of the apostles that demonstrate their pure and genuine faith and love? Who again would not have his soul set aflame when hearing of the torments of the martyrs and of the rackings and scourgings and slaughters that they endured for the love of Christ and learn to bear his tribulations nobly for Christ and not to fear the temptations brought against him by his enemies? Who, once again, when hearing about the angelic and superhuman life of the ascetics, and thus receiving the spur of divine zeal in his heart, would not be roused to <follow> the same way of life and would not incite himself to imitate it so as to *leave everything* and eagerly *follow* Christ?[8] For these <ascetics> especially, of all the saints throughout the ages, may perhaps be said to exactly fulfill God's commandments and preserve in themselves unimpaired the images of those who, of old, were illustrious on account of their piety and their other achievements, whether they manifested these by their deeds or their words or their miracles; for we learn from the holy Gospels that to *leave everything* and eagerly *follow* Christ and to be *crucified to the world*[9] is <the way> of those who seek to achieve perfection and those who have fulfilled all the commandments of the law. So this way <of life> reveals their similarity to the prophets and apostles and righteous men, while their struggle against the invisible enemies and the extirpation of their individual will shows their likeness to the martyrs. But what about their guidance of those who are in error and their drawing out of the worthy from the worthless and their display of miracles and the prophetic grace of their predictions?[10] Does not the former

[8] Cf. Lk. 5:28.

[9] Cf. Gal. 6:14.

[10] The general characteristics of the successful ascetic life laid down here are used by Gregory the Cellarer as the pattern for the main areas he considers in his treatment of Lazaros' life.

show their likeness to God and the latter the grace of the Holy Spirit, which has been richly poured out upon them? For the holy hive of ascetics has proved to be a scented meadow, full of flowers, making the souls of all <people> in a variety of ways come to the sweet smell of the good spirit.[11] One <member> of this holy and divinely assembled phalanx is, then, our blessed father Lazaros, whose life and angelic[12] career I have <here> set forth in order to make it known to all, writing in brief because I lack words and knowledge, and simply, in my own amateurish way, but nevertheless truthfully.

2. This man [Lazaros],[13] <who> became a shining, blazing[14] star among those who live as monks, <was> a scion of the Asiatic land, <for he came> from some rural <place> named after the Theotokos, situated somewhere near

[11] This simile would appear to refer to the Λειμωνάριον or Λειμών, the *Pratum spirituale* (Spiritual Meadow) of John Moschos (ca. 550–619), completed by Sophronius of Jerusalem (ca. 560–638). This is a popular collection of stories about monks that enjoyed wide circulation in Byzantine monastic circles; see, especially, the introductory chapter. On this work, see *ODB,* s.v. "Moschos."

The only other known usage of the verb [ἐγ]κατοσφραίνω, in Suidas, has the sense of "scenting out" or "finding" (by scent), but the present translation follows the causal sense of "making one smell at a thing" found in usage of the basic verb in the active voice (see Liddell-Scott-Jones, *Lexicon,* s.v. ὀσφραίνομαι, II). I am grateful to an anonymous reader for suggesting this line of approach. The metaphors of a beehive and a flowery meadow have perhaps become slightly mixed here. Note that "in a variety of ways" renders ποικίλως, which contains a basic sense of "many colored" and thus continues the flower theme in the Greek.

[12] The Greek word ἰσάγγελος actually has the sense of "equal to an angel." It is also used of Lazaros in Chap. 151, below; cf. Chap. 84, where his lifestyle is said to imitate that of the angels (ἀγγελομίμητος), and the conclusion in Chap. 255, where he is described as an earthly angel (ἐπίγειος ἄγγελος).

[13] Lazaros' given name was Leo (see below, Chap. 9), but Gregory the Cellarer, who scarcely ever refers to Lazaros by name in the text, does not use it (apart from the reference in Chap. 9) and clearly thinks of him throughout as "Lazaros" or "the Father," even when describing his early life (see, e.g., Chap. 11). Thus, even before Chap. 9, where clarity and English usage requires a name rather than the pronoun commonly employed in the Greek, I have consistently referred to him by his monastic name to avoid confusion.

[14] The word translated here as "blazing," πυρσοφαής, is not otherwise known although the similar term πυρσολαμπής is used of various holy men; cf. *vita s. Ioannicii (Sabas), AASS,* Nov. 2.1:334A (ἀστὴρ πυρσολαμπής). Lazaros is also described rather similarly as a brilliant beacon in Chaps. 36, 111, and 128.

the borders of Magnesia.[15] His parents were not the sort who care very much about wealth or life's other deceits but <rather> those who live piously, self-sufficiently,[16] and devoutly, and (to put it like the apostle) provide their nourishment by their own hands.[17] Their names were Niketas and Irene, and they had Lazaros, who was truly a son of Victory and Peace,[18] fifth among the children born to them, just like another Job, <who> was *fifth from Abraham;*[19] <like him also> this great man [Lazaros] really was as hard as steel, as his life thereafter showed.[20] When Lazaros emerged from his mother's womb,[21] a light at once shone forth miraculously from heaven and filled the whole interior of the house with an indescribable flash of lightning.[22] Indeed, the people who were there could not stand the brilliance of this light and, leaving the mother with the baby, rushed out of the house and stood somewhere nearby in great fear and trembling. They waited for a little while and then, after that terrible

[15] The context of the whole account indicates that this refers to Magnesia on the Meander; it is thus understood both by Gregory of Cyprus (*AASS,* Nov. 3:589A–B), and by the Moscow *synaxarion,* f. 218. The town was in western Asia Minor a short distance southeast of Ephesus; it is to be distinguished from the other city of Magnesia (now Manisa) further north in Lydia. Foss ("Twenty Cities," 482–83) suggests, on the basis of the *vita,* that the area was "peaceful, prosperous and rustic" at this time. For a fuller account of Ephesus in particular and the area in general during this period see idem, *Ephesus,* 116–37.

[16] The word in Greek is αὐτάρκως. On the connotations of this term here and in the context of middle Byzantine society, see Kaplan, *Les hommes,* 496; cf. 226.

[17] The implication is that they were peasants. The author is apparently referring to 1 Th. 4:11, or perhaps to 1 Cor. 4:12. For a comparison of Lazaros' family background with those of other holy men, see Malamut, *Route,* 68–69.

[18] This is what the parents' names mean. The version of Akakios Sabbaites gives the names of Lazaros' parents as Paul and Eudokia; while Kaplan, *Les hommes,* 496, mistakenly identifies Lazaros' mother as Helen.

[19] Job 42:17. A similar comparison is drawn in the *vita* of Luke the Stylite, who lived in the 10th century: Delehaye, *Stylites,* 198, chap. 3.12–14. Cf. Kazhdan, "Ideals," 478.

[20] Commonly referred to as adamantine in his endurance, Job was used frequently as a model or "type," especially in Byzantine hagiographical and ascetic writings.

[21] Lazaros was evidently born either at the very end of 966 or, more probably, in 967; see the Introduction, section B, pp. 5–6, for detailed discussion of this point.

[22] The language used here may allude to the description of the conversion of St. Paul on the way to Damascus at Acts 9:3; cf. Acts 22:6 and 26:13. Note, too, the rather similar reference to a flash of lightning associated with Lazaros' death, below, Chap. 252.

light had gone away, went back into the house again. When the midwife approached the woman who had just given birth, she found the baby standing upright;[23] he was facing east and had his hands pressed tightly to his chest in the form of the cross. The midwife who delivered him recounted this herself; she was the wife of the great Leontios, the monk who, in turn, told me these things and <all> the rest about Lazaros' childhood and what happened to him up to his departure from his own country for the Holy Land.[24] So, when his parents and those who were there saw these things (as well as what they learned from hearsay), they were filled with wonder and amazement, and from then on began to guess the future well enough and to say that they expected to see something great and auspicious in connection with the child.

3. So the child was raised devoutly and piously by his parents <in a way> not unworthy of their hopes for him. [510] When he became articulate in his speech and had reached the age of six, he was handed over by his parents to the aforesaid priest Leontios at the behest of his uncle Elias, who was a monk in the monastery of Kalathai.[25] Because <this Elias> had also heard by word of mouth about the miraculous character of the child's birth, he said that it had certainly not happened without God's aid, and for this reason he urged the boy's parents to let him receive the proper attention for instruction in the holy letters.[26] After three years had passed,[27] they sent him away for instruction, on the orders of the same uncle, to a notary[28] called George who lived

[23] A similar story is told in the 6th-century *vita* of St. Nicholas of Sion, chap. 2, ed. I. and N. P. Ševčenko, *The Life of St. Nicholas of Sion* (Brookline, Mass., 1984), 22–23.

[24] This does not imply that Leontios was a married monk, merely that he had been married at some time prior to his becoming one; men and women often entered the monastic life after the death of a spouse, or a married couple might choose to be tonsured at the same time.

[25] This monastery must have been in the vicinity of Magnesia and Lazaros' home village; so Janin, *Églises centres,* 242 n. 5; see also Morris, "Political Saint," 45. Delehaye notes some other possibilities that were discussed, and rejected, by Loparev, "Zhitie," 366.

[26] The phrase τὰ ἱερὰ γράμματα refers to elementary education based on religious texts, especially the Psalms; see Talbot, *Holy Women,* 126 n. 47; cf. 167 and 171. On Lazaros' education compared to that of other holy men, see Malamut, *Route,* 70–73.

[27] This makes Lazaros about nine years old at this point; the date is 976 or 975.

[28] The term νοτάριος (notary) can be applied to a range of more or less important officials, both lay and ecclesiastical, who were involved in specialized scribal, secretarial, and legal work. It is evident from Chaps. 4 and 30 that George must have been an ecclesiastical notary. Chap. 4 states that Lazaros received further professional train-

at Oroboi.[29] After he had spent another three years there,[30] his uncle took him to the monastery with him to teach him about church matters and to have him as his attendant.[31] However, when the boy saw that his uncle was well endowed with material necessities but gave away nothing at all from his possessions to the poor, he secretly took whatever he found[32] and gave it to the needy. In the end, because Lazaros continued to do this, there was no way for him to escape detection, for when <Elias> looked for these things and could not find them he began to assail <the boy> with interrogations, blows, and insults; but he bore everything nobly and did not stop his good work. He would also take books from the church and, reading them by himself in solitude, would reap much profit from them.

4. Then divine love entered into Lazaros' soul and he, like the great Abraham, began seeking to become a wanderer from his own homeland and to go to the holy places of Christ's passions.[33] So, one night, he slipped out of the

---

ing as a notary when he was a little older, and in Chap. 30 he is referred to as such. This suggests that he must have been at least relatively well educated in the more secular areas of Greek language and of law. See *ODB*, s.v. "Notary," and in more detail, H. Saradi-Mendelovici, "Byzantine Notaries," *Medieval Prosopography* 9 (1988), 21–49 (41–49 for ecclesiastical notaries in particular). See also here Morris, "Political Saint," 45; eadem, *Monks*, 77.

[29] It is clear from Chap. 30, where Lazaros returns to this place after his wanderings, that Oroboi was also close to his home near Magnesia; see Janin, *Églises centres*, 242, nn. 5 and 7. As Janin and Delehaye note, the Synaxarion for 8 August (*SynaxCP*, 877) refers to the monastery of Oroboi and its saintly abbot Theodosios, although without any indication of place or period.

[30] Lazaros is thus about twelve years old and the date is 979 or 978.

[31] On such practice see Talbot, "Family," 121–22.

[32] A very similar expression is also used of Lazaros' own actions in the following chapter, but also of a thief at his monastery in Chap. 241.

[33] Cf. Gen. 12:1; there may also be some reminiscence of two passages from John Chrysostom in the wording here: *In cap. XII Genes. Hom.* 32.γ´ (PG 53:296), and *In Acta Apostolorum Hom.* 40 (PG 60:282). The theme of Lazaros' thwarted desire to travel to the Holy Land, which runs through this and the following chapters, is reminiscent of a less elaborate incident in the *vita Danielis*, chap. 6.

On the tradition and development of Byzantine pilgrimage to the Holy Land, see especially E. D. Hunt, *Holy Land Pilgrimage in the Later Roman Empire, A.D. 312–460* (Oxford, 1984); Wilkinson, "Christian Pilgrims"; idem, *Jerusalem Pilgrims;* Kötting, *Peregrinatio*, 83–111; *ODB*, s.v. "Pilgrimage." Pilgrimage to the Holy Land from Byzantine territory was certainly encouraged by the victories in the east over the Arabs in the 960s and 970s under Nikephoros II Phokas and John I Tzimiskes, which opened up the

monastery in secret without being observed by anyone and set off on the journey for which he was longing.[34] When his flight became known, however, his uncle sent some people out to search for him without delay. They caught up with him by making inquiries and then returned to the monastery again and took him back to his uncle against his will. When <Elias> had sufficiently chastised him with insults and blows, he ordered those in the monastery to watch him carefully so that he might not leave it at all. After spending two years in the monastery with his uncle,[35] Lazaros was sent by him to the monastery of Strobelion,[36] to a notary called Nicholas, for further education in the professional skill<s> of notaries. This notary was just as heartless as the monk [Elias], for he would give nothing away at all and was <quite> without pity. Therefore, when the pupil saw that his teacher was so untutored in regard to the good, he began without hesitation to teach and admonish him not to be so unsympathetic and miserly toward the poor. However, as Lazaros saw that the man was scarcely swayed at all by his words, he left off speaking and took to action, and whenever he found anything, he did the same with it as he had done with the monk's possessions. When this came to the notary's knowledge, however, he was not angry or annoyed with the boy, as the monk [Elias] <had been>, but instead he was amazed and astonished at the youth's good moral judgment and disposition.[37] Once, in the middle of the night, <Nicholas> woke up and heard the sound of people singing psalms. He got up and went quietly

overland route. The phenomenon of pilgrimage was also developing dramatically in Western Europe precisely at this time. Following the Byzantine successes and the conversion of Géza of Hungary in 985 many more pilgrims could make the journey than before. For pilgrimage from the Western viewpoint, see in particular J. Sumption, *Pilgrimage: An Image of Mediaeval Religion* (London, 1975), esp. chaps. 6–8.

[34] On the motif of flight in Byzantine hagiography, see Malamut, *Route,* 93–95.

[35] This now makes Lazaros about fourteen; the date is 981 or 980.

[36] It is unclear if the nominative should be Strobelion or Strobelios. C. Foss ("Strobilos and Related Sites," *Anatolian Studies* 38 [1988], 168) suggests that this monastery "was probably located in the Maeander valley," because this is where Lazaros was born and spent most of his life. In this assumption he follows Janin (*Églises centres,* 242, n. 5), who also believes that the monastery in question should probably be distinguished from one at Strobilos, a fairly busy port on the Carian coast not far from Halikarnassos (Bodrum). Although neither has any sure evidence for distinguishing the two places, Foss's documentation of other localities with the same or similar names (e.g., on Chios and in Epiros) certainly strengthens the case for the suggestion that the monastery was near Lazaros' home. See also *ODB,* s.v. "Strobilos."

[37] These qualities of Lazaros are praised and illustrated at length below.

to where the boy was, for it seemed to him that the sound was coming from there. As he stood nearby, he heard Lazaros praying and singing psalms by himself, and so he went back and lay down in his bed and fell asleep again praising God. And so, from then on, <Nicholas> no longer treated Lazaros as a pupil but as a teacher. Such a man, then, was Lazaros' teacher.

5. After he had spent three years with <this Nicholas>, however, Lazaros gave him the slip one day and went away.[38] He joined up with some monks and, when he had changed his worldly dress for a monastic habit <that he got> from them, he traveled with them, happy and rejoicing because he had now accomplished his desired goal. But not long afterward his joy was changed to sorrow, for they[39] pursued him again and caught him; they returned, taking him unwillingly <with them>, as on the first occasion.

6. When <another> six months had passed after his return, Lazaros could not bear the burning in his heart and his longing for the holy places of Christ's passions and so, unnoticed, he ran away again.[40] He arrived at a place where there was a monk who had confined himself on a pillar and, when he approached <this man> and told him what he had on his mind, he discovered that he was a good adviser for him.[41] For this <stylite> took off Lazaros' worldly clothes and dressed him in a monastic garment;[42] then, after giving him his blessing, he sent him off to make the journey he desired with many exhortations not to turn back.[43] When evening came, Lazaros did not want to

[38] The verb ἀναχωρέω, here translated as "went away," also has the sense of monastic "withdrawal" in Greek and carries with it here something of that connotation; it is related to the English word "anchorite."

[39] The reference is presumably to a search party from Strobelion but it could perhaps be to the same "people" sent out by Lazaros' uncle Elias on the previous occasion; if so it would confirm the proximity of Strobelion to Kalathai and Lazaros' home village.

[40] Lazaros would appear to have been seventeen or eighteen at this point when he finally managed to leave his home area; the date is thus somewhere between late 983 and 985. On Lazaros' journeys in general, which now begin, see Malamut, *Route,* 40–43.

[41] For parallels in the Lives of other Byzantine saints to this encounter between the future holy man and a wise adviser, see Malamut, *Route,* 97–98; cf. also below, Chap. 9.

[42] This "monastic garment" may refer to the novice's habit, although Delehaye suggests that Lazaros may only have received this when he was in the monastery at Attaleia; see further below on this point, Chap. 9, n. 56.

[43] Compare Lazaros' evident determination not to "turn back" at the end of Chap. 18.

go into a village and so, spotting a small chapel in the middle of the fields, he made his way <there> and went into it; he closed its rickety door and stood, offering up his prayers to the Lord. When he had finished he said a<nother> prayer, sank to the ground and lay down. After he had slept a little, however, he was suddenly awakened by cries of some sort ringing in his ears. Listening carefully he seemed to hear what sounded like wolves standing somewhere nearby outside and howling. [511] He got up, wedged a stone against the door, said a prayer, and then lay down on the ground and slept. In the morning he left there and took the road leading to Chonai.[44]

7. Going on his way, Lazaros found some people originating from Cappadocia who were also heading toward the church of the Archangel. He joined their ranks and went on with them. Now there was a girl with them who was crying and wailing bitterly; when Lazaros saw her, he asked about her and discovered the reason for her sorrowful complaint. According to her she had been tricked by some people and had estranged herself from her family, for, on the advice of these deceitful people, she had taken quite a lot of money from her family home; when they had <thus> led her astray, however, they had taken the money and, abandoning her, had disappeared from sight. Her lament was not, however, so much about these events as because she was terrified and shaking with fear in case she should be disgraced by someone, for she was a virgin. When Lazaros discovered this, he went over and spoke with her; he persuaded her and, through her, those traveling with her to let him take her into his safekeeping until they should reach Chonai. Which indeed he did. Upon their arrival there they found some of her relatives and gave her into their charge so that they might take her back to her homeland and to her parents.

But the wicked Devil, who is indeed the opponent and enemy of the good, saw what happened: that not only was Lazaros himself preserved unharmed from his wicked darts, being protected by the grace of Christ, but also that he had guarded the girl in the same way. Because he was unable to bear his defeat, he hastened to besmirch the purity of Lazaros' chastity by another

[44] Chonai (now Honaz or Khonas) was near the ancient city of Colossae in Phrygia Pacatiana. It was famous for the church of the Archangel Michael, which is mentioned in the following chapter and in Chap. 29 below when Lazaros visited the place again on his return from the Holy Land. The church honored the miraculous diversion of the river, which the archangel was said to have wrought there, and it was an important center for both pilgrimage and trade fairs; see *ODB*, s.v. "Chonai" and "Chonai, miracle at"; Kötting, *Peregrinatio*, 166–71; Malamut, *Route*, 304–5.

such means;[45] but truly he labored in vain. Thus, when night fell, Lazaros stood in one corner of the narthex <of the church of the Archangel> and addressed his prayers to the Lord and then lay down to sleep in the <same> place.[46] But the most Evil One had procured a woman dressed as a nun to approach him and entice him into shameful sexual intercourse; Lazaros, however, got up quickly, as if fleeing from fire, and left the place without saying anything to her. Then he stood in another spot and called on God to deliver him from the many wiles of the Evil One and to contrive to make his journey to the Holy Land an easy one.[47] After Lazaros had thus prayed for many hours, the Lord of all did not disregard his supplication but, in His goodness, delivered him from the war of fornication and enabled him to set out at once in the morning on the journey to Jerusalem.

8. For, while Lazaros was sitting in the narthex after the completion of the early morning service,[48] he saw a monk going into the church to pray. When he came out, Lazaros went up to him and asked him where he was from

[45] Lit. "another such vessel"; cf. 1 Pet. 3:7.

[46] Most Byzantine churches possessed at least one narthex, which was an area, separated from the main nave or ναός, through which one passed from the main entrance. The size of the narthex in relation to the church might vary considerably, but it served a number of liturgical functions including preparation for processional entries, baptism, and the commemoration of the dead. As is clear from the present episode, the narthex might also play an important role in accommodating visitors at pilgrimage sites, as a resting place during the day or overnight, and it could fulfill a similar function at places where "incubation" (the seeking of healing or inspiration during sleep at a sanctuary) was practiced. See further *ODB,* s.v. "Narthex."

[47] The chapter to this point is also translated in Kazhdan and Epstein, *Change,* 246–47, although my translation differs from theirs in certain respects. The episode of the maiden in distress, as is pointed out there, is in some ways parallel to an incident in the epic of Digenis Akritas (J. Mavrogordato, *Digenes Akrites* [Oxford, 1956], 143–59), although there the Devil triumphs over the hero who violates the girl in question. On this parallel see in particular Kazhdan, "Ὁ τέλειος μοναχὸς," 203–5, 216. Laiou ("Sex," 213–15) also mentions the incident during discussion of the Digenis passage; see also Malamut, *Route,* 279–80. Compare, too, the incident recorded in Chap. 15, below.

[48] The word translated by "early morning service" here, κανών, may include a more precise reference to the liturgical "kanon," a set of eight or nine odes or verse paraphrases chanted during the early morning service of "*orthros*" (the Byzantine equivalent of Western matins), but it seems more probable that it is used in this context as a synonym for the service as a whole. See further *ODB,* s.v. "Kanon," "Orthros"; cf. also below, Chaps. 72, 157, 171, 182.

and where he was going. Then, since he heard from the <monk> that he came from Paphlagonia[49] and was traveling to the Holy Land, he fell at his feet and begged him to take him along. The monk encouraged Lazaros to follow him readily, since he had nothing to fear from him, and so he left that place and went on his way with him. But the monk was perverse[50] and did not want to travel straight <there>, or rather he was unable to because of the wicked habit which he had. He would thus turn aside from the direct route and go round on a detour to the villages where he would beg and collect bread and whatever else anyone offered him; he would put these things into a bag and give them to the youth [Lazaros] to carry. Then, wherever they were when evening fell, they would go in, whether it was to a village or a local market,[51] and he would sell these things and pocket the price <he got> for them.

When, however, the youth saw such greed on the part of the monk, he could not keep quiet but began to admonish him, as he had done earlier with the notary, saying to him with humble modesty such words as, "Why do we greedily collect things that we don't need, Father? And, when we collect them, why don't we distribute them among those who are as poor as ourselves instead of wandering around carrying them all day? Isn't the journey hard enough work for us <already>?" Lazaros, however, derived no benefit from addressing such admonitions to the <monk> but instead made him angry <so that> he attacked him with insults and blows; therefore Lazaros stopped speaking and turned to action. When the <monk> went off to beg, Lazaros would give everything away if he happened to meet anyone; <then>, when the <monk> came back and found the bag empty, he would demand furiously and

[49] Paphlagonia ran along the Black Sea coast of northern central Asia Minor.

[50] It is hard to do justice in translation to the Greek word σκολιός, which is rendered by "perverse" here. It could almost be translated into colloquial English by its literal meaning of "crooked" (i.e., "the monk was a crook"), but the Greek also makes a play not only on the man's moral deviousness but also on his tortuous physical progress, which deviates from the "straight" road to the Holy Land; furthermore, it contains a sense of willful and deliberate perversity. In this sort of context, there is also the connotation of diabolical cunning, for the word is often applied to the trickiness of the Devil, especially when conceived as the serpent (on this see Greenfield, *Demonology,* 31, 44–45).

[51] The Greek term translated by "local market" (ἐμπόριον) can indicate quite a wide variety of places. It most likely refers here to a market outside the walls of a rural settlement or to the business district in a town. See *ODB,* s.v. "Emporion."

angrily, "Where are the loaves of bread that I collected by begging all day? Surely you didn't sell them while I was away?" He was thus assuming from his own wicked motivation that Lazaros was the same <as him>; for it is true that we judge others by our own standards. So, when Lazaros heard these things from the monk, he would smile and keep quiet, but the <monk>, seething with anger, would subject him to insults and blows. Lazaros, however, who really was as hard as steel and a skillful boxer,[52] would bear everything nobly, and would not stop virtuously giving <these things> away, just as that other man <would> not <stop> greedily collecting them.

9. Traveling like this they reached Attaleia.[53] There, however, that treacherous man who did not act like a real monk, that imitator of Judas, went to one of the shipowners and, speaking in the language of the Armenians,[54] made an agreement to sell the boy to him. But, by the providence of God, one of the sailors overheard this and, while the monk was still talking to the shipowner, went and informed the youth about these things, for he was not <there> with the monk. As soon as he heard this, Lazaros took off and fled, just as he was. He turned off the main road and quickly started to climb the mountain that lay nearby but, while he was still on the lower slopes, night fell. He began his [512] ascent but, because of the darkness of the night and the great steepness of the mountain, he spent the whole night, as he said, struggling <along> by hand and foot; only when the day had dawned was he able with difficulty to climb up on top. When, however, he did reach the top of the mountain, he found a worn path and went along it. While he was walking along by himself like this, an old monk met him and, when <this monk> had stopped and questioned him and found out all about him, he dissuaded him from <continuing> his journey to Jerusalem because of his youth.[55] Instead he recommended that

[52] Metaphors of the monk as boxer or wrestler are very common in ascetic and hagiographic literature.

[53] Attaleia (Antalya) was a city in southern Pamphylia on the Mediterranean coast of Asia Minor; it was an important naval, military, and trading center at this time with strong links to the Middle East.

[54] There is possibly a hint here (as in Chap. 15) of the general mistrust and suspicion toward Armenians that was common in Byzantine literature, and so perhaps also in real life.

[55] Cf. an incident in the *vita Danielis* (chap. 10), where the young saint is dissuaded from traveling to the Holy Land by an older holy man he meets, although for reasons of political instability, not youth.

he should follow his advice and go with him to his monastery (for the old man was superior of a small flock) and persevere there until such time as there might be no concern over his age. So, persuaded by the old man's words, Lazaros prostrated himself and followed him. After he had spent some time in the monastery he received from that venerable old man the first habit of a monk,[56] and similarly was given the name Lazaros, for previously he was called Leo.[57] And so, as he was well educated in the divinely taught injunctions and precepts by that venerable old man, he became, in a short time, a model and example of every virtue to the brothers there, for he was obedient to all the words of the old man and did nothing whatsoever without his approval.[58]

10. However, when Lazaros learned from the brothers who were there

[56] Lazaros had apparently already been given a "monastic garment" of some sort by the stylite he encountered soon after he ran away from Strobelion (above, Chap. 6), but the precise significance of that habit is not made clear nor is there mention of his taking any vows at that time. If it *was* the novice's habit, then the present, clearly more formal, occasion must refer to his taking the *mikron* or *apostolikon schema,* the habit of the lesser grade of monks that differentiated them from the superior grade, those who wore the *mega* or *angelikon schema.* Lazaros evidently became *megaloschemos* at St. Sabas near Jerusalem, although his rank is there described, rather confusingly, as being *apostolikon* rather than *angelikon* (see below, Chap. 17). Delehaye, however, understands the present passage to refer to the novice's habit rather than to the *mikron schema;* he may be supported by the stress laid on Lazaros' obedience at the end of the chapter, for the novice's habit is described as the "clothing of submission" (ὑποταγῆς ἔνδυμα), and is equated by Lazaros with that of the martyrs rather than that of the apostles or angels in Chap. 130, below. The hierarchical distinction of rank referred to here was apparently quite common, although it was far from being universally recognized or approved in Byzantine monastic circles. See further *ODB,* s.v. "Schema." In Chap. 130, Lazaros himself argues in favor of such a triple categorization of the monastic habit against some of his own monks who are questioning it. In Chaps. 228 and 240 the term *mandyotes* also appears to be used for a novice.

[57] It was normal practice for Byzantine men and women to change their names when they entered the monastic life. Usually, as in this case, the new name began with the same letter as the old.

[58] Despite the fact that he manifestly disobeyed people with authority over him at a number of crucial points in his own life, Lazaros himself demonstrates for the first time here a virtue that he evidently valued very highly in his perception of the monastic life and which he viewed as an essential requirement before a person could advance to higher and more individualistic expressions of that life. Cf. below, Chap. 60 (another example of his own obedience) and Chap. 179 (for an illustration of similarly exemplary obedience by one of his monks).

before him that in the mountain facing the monastery there was a cave suitable for those seeking spiritual peace,[59] he begged the old man <for permission> and went off to take up residence in it. He performed many marvelous labors of asceticism there, but the Enemy of the righteous could not bear these, for every time he attacked Lazaros he was defeated by him; so he crept up on him in another way. The most Evil One thus stirred up some heretics from the village that lay near the mountain (for there were very many of them <living> in it),[60] thinking to drive Lazaros from the mountain by means of them. These <people> would thus come up and attack him with insults and jests, and they even threatened to hit him if he did not quickly leave the mountain; but he bore everything gently and tolerantly, for he was well aware who was inciting them to this action. As a result he did not cease admonishing and encouraging them with kind words until he made them not only stop attacking him but even reject their ancestral heresy, and he thus caused them to join the orthodox church. When he saw them yielding to his words, he wrote to the bishop of Philetos,[61] who received them to communion after they had anathematized their own heresy in church. Some of those who had repudiated <their former beliefs> went to Lazaros and asked to be tonsured by him and to live with him. He was not persuaded to do this <at first>, but they continued begging him more persistently, and so, as he was unable to convince them despite saying a great deal to them, he wrote to the old man and, with his encouragement, received them.[62]

[59] Hesychia (ἡσυχία), the ideal of Byzantine spirituality that underlies all the activities and pursuits of monastic asceticism. See further *ODB,* s.v. "Hesychia."

[60] It is impossible to identify the exact heresy of these people. Lemerle ("Pauliciens," 110), who mentions this episode as occurring in the life of Paul [sic] the Galesiote, is not drawn into suggesting that they may have been Paulicians, although it is quite possible, even likely, that they were dualist heretics of some kind. The Paulicians had lost their political and military standing following their defeat and dispersal by the forces of the central Byzantine administration more than a century before, in the 870s, but there is good evidence for the continued presence of various groups of dualist heretics in different parts of Asia Minor at this time in the late 10th century and, indeed, for long afterward. Cf. below, Chap. 115, where Lazaros converts someone explicitly described as a Paulician.

[61] The bishopric of Philetos came under the metropolitanate of Lycian Myra; see J. Darrouzès, *Notitiae episcopatuum ecclesiae Constantinopolitanae* (Paris, 1981), 7.343, 9.225, 10.274, 13.278.

[62] On this common pattern in Byzantine monasticism by which a *koinobion* grows up around a solitary ascetic, a pattern which is, of course, repeated several times during

11. When the bishop learned what had happened, he went up to Lazaros. He saw him and spoke with him and, since he had profited greatly from the conversation and from the sight of him, decreed that he himself would furnish all Lazaros' needs. Indeed, <the bishop> acquired such faith in him that he bestowed his chasuble[63] on him, although Lazaros gave it back to him for the following reason. Since his fame was spreading to places nearby, a great number of people were going up to him. First of all, as the father himself related,[64] because the mountain was rocky and hard to climb, they constructed a direct path, heating the rocks and then, after drenching them with vinegar, quarrying them out with iron tools.[65] Subsequently, with the cooperation of the bishop, they built a chapel and cells for the brothers close to the cave. Since there were six of them, two of their number were ordained by the bishop. But then, at one of the major feasts, a dispute arose between them as to which one should wear the <bishop's> chasuble, for they also had another. When the father learned about this, he took it and sent it back to the bishop; he then took some hair cloth that he had cut out and sewed with his own hands and gave it to them, saying, "If anyone doesn't agree to celebrate the service with this <on>, he must go away from here." They were unable to argue with him and so, having made obeisance, they accepted this.

12. Once, a man who had the appearance of a demoniac went up to him. Supposedly being aroused by the demon, he said, "I won't go down from the mountain until you've driven me out of <this> creature of God!" and he also spoke much other nonsense. After he stopped yapping and came to himself, the father told the brothers to give him a gift and dismiss him. But the man asked to see the father alone and, when he met with him, said, "If you listen

---

Lazaros' sojourn on Mt. Galesion itself, see Papachryssanthou, "Vie monastique," 164–65.

[63] The *phelonion,* essentially the same garment as the Western chasuble, was worn by priests and bishops over the basic *sticharion* during liturgical celebrations; normally it was made of wool or silk. See *ODB,* s.v. "Phelonion."

[64] The term "the father," used commonly for Lazaros throughout the *vita,* was evidently how his monks referred to him.

[65] The same technique was used to prepare the ground for building a church in chap. 55 of the *vita* of Theodore of Sykeon: see A. J. Festugière, ed., *Vie de Théodore de Sykéon,* SubsHag 48 (Brussels, 1970), 47. It is also described in *The Anonymous Byzantine Treatise on Strategy,* ed. G. T. Dennis, *Three Byzantine Military Treatises* (Washington, D.C., 1985), 60.51–56 (chap. 18). The practice was well known in the ancient world, its most famous employment being by Hannibal in his crossing of the Alps (Livy, 21, 37, etc.); see Dennis for further references.

to me and if you want, I can make you famous and make your monastery rich." When [513] the father said, "How?" he replied, "I'm not possessed by a demon, but I pretend to have this problem.[66] If I find someone established in a church somewhere[67] (whether he's a monk or a layman) who's compliant with my <scheme>, I get him to ask around and find out who has a nice ornament or some other <such> object. After he's found this out and told me the names of these people, I take a cross and go off to some place where it's damp; I then dig <a hole> and hide it there.[68] After several days I make myself appear to be aroused by the demon. I first go into the church and get everyone there to follow me, as though they're under orders from the saint; then I go out with them to the place where I hid the cross by burying it. I dig with my own hands or with a spade, pull out <the cross>, pick it up, and go back to the church. I then begin to call <the people> by name and say, 'Oh, so-and-so, the saint commands you to bring this <particular> object of yours here so that your whole household may not be tormented by demons.' I do this every day and then, when I've gone through them all, I make myself appear to have been cured. Afterwards we split everything that's been brought, I and the person in

[66] This man does not appear to have been alone in using feigned demonic possession as a means of making a living, and the problem evidently remained a persistent one. The canon lawyer Theodore Balsamon, writing in the later part of the 12th century, thus deplores the fact that "many" people who "simulate demonic frenzy for gain" are wandering around the towns of the empire; Commentary on *Canon 60 of the Council in Trullo,* PG 137:716–17; P. Magdalino, "The Byzantine Holy Man in the Twelfth Century," in Hackel, *Byz. Saint,* 59–60; Greenfield, *Demonology,* 93.

[67] The reference is probably to a small private religious foundation of some kind, and the implication is thus not that the person actually lives in the church itself but rather in an associated private dwelling or monastic community to which the church belongs; see below where the charlatan refers to this individual as "the person in charge of the church" (lit. "the master of the church"). The same verb (καθέζομαι) is used in Chap. 28 of a nun similarly associated with a chapel (*eukterion*).

[68] The practice of the burial and rediscovery of the cross described here bears some interesting resemblances to the famous episode of the alleged discovery of the Holy Lance at Antioch by the visionary Peter Bartholomew and the Crusaders (on 15 June 1098), at least as this incident was viewed by detractors (whether Christian or Muslim) who claimed Peter had himself buried it in advance. On the incident, see in general, e.g., J. Riley-Smith, *The First Crusade and the Idea of Crusading* (London-Philadelphia, 1986), 95–96, and in particular, S. Runciman, "The Holy Lance Found at Antioch," *AnalBoll* 68 (1950), 197–205; C. Morris, "Policy and Visions: The Case of the Holy Lance at Antioch," in *War and Government in the Middle Ages: Essays in Honour of J. O. Prestwich,* ed. J. Gillingham and J. C. Holt (Cambridge, 1984), 33–45.

charge of the church, and so I go off again somewhere else." When the father heard all this, he was amazed at the great variety of skills the demons have for doing evil, and at God's forbearance. In reply to the man, he said, "Brother, not only am I myself not going to be misled by you, but I also advise you to stop such wicked behavior; if you can't work, at least support yourself by begging, but just give up this satanic practice!" So Lazaros sent him away, and was not misled into listening to him, or rather to the one who had cunningly contrived by means of that man to involve him in the twin evils of vainglory and avarice,[69] and so to thrust him utterly into the abyss of destruction.

13. On another occasion some people went out to Lazaros from the village that lay near the mountain and asked for his blessing to go to the precipitous part of the mountain to collect honeycombs. The father, however, told the brothers <to bring some> honey and, when they had brought it, said to these people, "If it's honey that you want, look, here's honey! Eat as much as you want and then go back to your homes; but don't go <onto the cliff> there lest you return with a harvest of bitterness instead of the sweetness of the honey." One of them replied brashly to the father, "I've collected many such <honeycombs> and nothing bad has <ever> happened to me, so I'm not worried about going onto the <cliff> now." But the father answered him, "Believe <me>, brother, this time it won't do you any good to go there." However, when Lazaros was unable to dissuade them, despite saying many things, he let them go and do what they wanted. So they went off and, after attaching a rope to the man who had told the father he was expert at this, began lowering him toward the cave. Before he reached it, however, the rope was cut through as if by somebody, <causing> the wretched man <to be> flung down the cliff; he was smashed <on the rocks> and expired at once.[70] So the others went down

[69] The sins that were often seen as being, respectively, the causes of the fall of Satan and Adam and Eve; Gregory the Cellarer, and the original audience, would also probably be inclined to see here a parallel to the temptation of Christ by the Devil.

[70] Although the Byzantines were well versed in techniques of apiculture (see *Geoponica* 15:ii–ix), the method of collecting honey from wild bees alluded to in this chapter is known from antiquity and is still practiced in some parts of the world today. A Byzantine illustration of another of the dangers of the practice, the reaction of the bees themselves, appears in the Venice *Kynegetika* of pseudo-Oppian (Z. Kádár, *Survivals of Greek Zoological Illuminations in Byzantine Manuscripts* [Budapest, 1978], pl. 183, 1), although here the swarm is located in a palm tree, not on a cliff face. Much closer parallels to the practices described here, although from various locations in the Far East, are discussed and illustrated in E. Crane, *The Archaeology of Beekeeping* (London, 1983), 28–31; more details, including accounts of the dangers of falling while collecting

and picked him up, and then, with much weeping and wailing, went off to the village to bury him. But they told everyone about the father's prediction and the words that he had spoken to them <in trying> to prevent them from going there. Those who heard about this were astounded and then were <quite> unable to control themselves; they went up to him, together with their wives and children, singing psalms and holding crosses in their hands. <Indeed>, there was little they did not do, clapping their hands, leaping about, heaping myriad praises on him, and eventually calling him a prophet.

14. These people <started> doing this frequently, however, and so, when the father observed this and that not only would they not leave him alone but were also ascribing to him the reputation of a prophet, he <began to be> afraid lest the praise of men should become an obstacle for him on the way of God.[71] He thus decided to leave that place and travel to the Holy Places, particularly because the old man, who was his guide and teacher, had by this time completed his life; he was, moreover, now of the right age to do this.[72] Lazaros had <by then> spent seven years there engaged in fasting, keeping vigil, and other godly exercises, <practices> that he had not only performed successfully himself and in a manner pleasing to God but had also taught to the brothers who were with him. <Now, however>, he mulled over these points in his mind and then slipped away one night without being observed by anyone, and set out on the <journey> to Jerusalem. He took nothing with him, but left the monastery without bread or any other necessity, with only one tunic, without shoes, and

honey in this way, are provided by S. S. Strickland, "Honey Hunting by the Gurungs of Nepal," *Bee World* 63.4 (1982), 153–61; vivid illustrations of these practices are provided by E. Valli and D. Summers, "Honey Hunters of Nepal," *National Geographic,* November 1988, 660–71; see also, *Archaeology* 48.6 (1995), 39. Kaplan, *Les hommes,* 38, refers to this episode during his discussion of honey in Byzantine agricultural practice, although he does not appear to have fully understood it and mistakenly places it in Chap. 3 of the *vita.* See also *ODB,* s.v. "Apiculture."

[71] Lazaros stresses this danger in his teaching, below, Chaps. 185 and 186, while his own avoidance of praise is described again immediately below in Chap. 15, as well as in Chap. 220.

[72] Lit. "the time of his life now called him to this." Given the figure of seven years for his stay at Attaleia, which is provided in the next sentence, it would appear that Lazaros is at least twenty-four, but probably twenty-five or twenty-six at this point; the date must thus be somewhere between 990 and 993. Malamut (*Route,* 41) agrees, although she suggests more precisely that he was twenty-five and the date 992.

without staff or knapsack,[73] carrying with him only his trust in God. So, he left there and set out.

15. As he neared the great <city> of Antioch, Lazaros saw some people standing in the middle of the road, lamenting over a girl who had just been abducted by the Armenian army as it passed by there. When he found out about this, he immediately started to pursue the<se soldiers>. Reaching the place where they had taken up their quarters, he went up to some of them and asked if they would point out their commander to him. Since they wanted to know why he was looking for him, the father responded, "Some of you have abducted a girl and that's why I'm trying to see him, so that I may take her away, with his backing, after I've looked around and found her, wherever she may be." The words were not even out of his mouth before the men, hearing <the word> "girl," grew angry and began shouting at him roughly, "Abba, an evil demon led you here; be off so that you don't lose your life along with the girl!" The <soldiers> made this angry response in order to frighten him, but the father was not scared at all by their words and instead became even bolder. He replied to them, "I'm telling you straight,[74] that if you don't hand her over to me right now I'm going to go directly to the *katepano,*[75] and then I won't just recover the girl from you on his orders, [514] but I'll also demand your punishment." When they heard these words, the <soldiers> quickly changed their brutality into docility and their brash insolence to humility and started begging him to go away, saying that they would look <for her> after he had gone and would release her when they found her. But as they saw that Lazaros would not be convinced by their words unless he got the girl, they looked around and found her and brought her to him. "Take this girl, Father," they said, "who hasn't been touched by us and hasn't suffered any harm, and go away, <but> give us your blessing yourself in compensation." The father prayed for them and, taking the girl, turned back.

They had not yet reached her village, however, when night overtook them

[73] This alludes to Jesus' instructions to the apostles at Mt. 10:9–10; Mk. 6:8–9; Lk. 9:3, 10:4, and 22:35. There are several other allusions to these prohibitions elsewhere in the *vita,* e.g., Chap. 23, below.

[74] Lit. "in truth."

[75] Although the term *katepano* could, like the parallel term *strategos,* also be used to indicate the governor of a province, it is probably used here simply to indicate a military commander; see further *ODB,* s.v. "Katepano."

in the middle of their journey. Lazaros turned off the road a little way, stopped, and, after he had made a bed in the sand with his own hands, told the girl to lie down there and sleep. When he saw her pleading with him and begging him not to leave her, he said, "Lie down while I go a little way away from you to say my office; after I've finished, I'll come back and lie down near you." So he went away from her and said his office standing up; when he saw that she was asleep, he himself lay down at the spot where he was standing and went to sleep. He woke up in the middle of the night, however, and found her lying behind him, so he got up and stood singing psalms until the morning; and <then> he left there with her and went on his way. When they came near to her village, Lazaros prayed for her and sent her on her way. He continued on his journey, even though she begged him very much to go with her so that she might repay him for the favor that he had done for her; but he, fleeing the praise of men, as has been said, left her and continued on his journey. Thus the incidental task turned out no less <important> to him than the <main> task, and in fact more so, if the word of Christ is true, as indeed it is, that there is no greater love than this, that someone should lay down his life for his neighbor.[76]

16. When Lazaros had reached Jerusalem[77] and had gone round and worshiped at all the holy sites,[78] and indeed all the monasteries <too>,[79] the divine

[76] Cf. Jn. 15:13, which is obviously being quoted from memory since the wording differs from the Gospel text.

[77] It is impossible to tell how long the overland journey of some 750 to 800 miles from Attaleia to Jerusalem may have taken Lazaros; assuming that it was not more than a few months, he would still have been in his mid-twenties when he arrived and the date somewhere between 990 and 993. Malamut (*Route,* 315) suggests a date around 1000.

[78] For details of the itineraries followed by pilgrims in Jerusalem before the Crusades, see Wilkinson, "Christian Pilgrims," 84–97; for the sources in translation, see Wilkinson, *Jerusalem Pilgrims,* and idem, *Egeria's Travels* (Warminster-London, 1981). The *vita* of Lazaros is not referred to in the literature on this subject. Although Wilkinson's itineraries are from a somewhat earlier date (4th–7th centuries) than that of Lazaros' visit, there would seem to have been little change prior to the 11th century. Among surviving accounts of pilgrimage to Jerusalem, the closest to Lazaros' is probably that of Bernard the Monk, who made the journey about A.D. 870, roughly a century earlier (trans., Wilkinson, *Jerusalem Pilgrims,* 142–44). While numerous other accounts and pilgrim guides survive from the early 12th century, these reflect the rather different circumstances that followed the seizure of Jerusalem by the Crusaders in 1099. See also *ODB,* s.v. "Jerusalem"; Malamut, *Route,* 314–16.

[79] The interest shown by Lazaros in the indigenous monasteries of Palestine seems to have been unusual at this time for a foreign pilgrim. See S. H. Griffith, "Anthony

love that had entered his soul made him long to live in the lavra of St. Sabas[80] above all the <other> monasteries there. Then, while he was sitting in <the church> of the Holy Resurrection,[81] the archdeacon[82] of the church approached him and, when he had questioned him and found out about him, he persuaded Lazaros to go home with him. After he had entertained him in a friendly way, <the archdeacon> prevailed upon Lazaros to share his thoughts

David of Baghdad, Scribe and Monk of Mar Sabas: Arabic in the Monasteries of Palestine," *Church History* 58 (1989), 16–19; also Wilkinson, *Jerusalem Pilgrims,* 32.

[80] The Great Lavra of St. Sabas was established in a rocky valley some seven miles southeast of Jerusalem in A.D. 483 by St. Sabas, one of the most notable figures in the early monasticism of Palestine. The lavra expanded over the years to become the most important monastic center in the Holy Land with close links to the patriarchate of Jerusalem. Some five hundred monks apparently lived in the lavra in the mid-9th century and at the end of the 11th century there were still more than three hundred, so it must have been a large establishment when Lazaros spent his years there. The lavra is still in existence. See *ODB,* s.v. "Sabas," "Sabas, Great Lavra of"; Patrich, *Sabas;* also Hirschfeld, *Desert Monasteries,* passim; Wilkinson, *Jerusalem Pilgrims,* 169. On the ancient organization of the Palestinian lavras compared to that of Byzantine monasteries at this time, see also Papachryssanthou, "Vie monastique," 166–73.

[81] This is part of the famous Holy Sepulchre complex that occupied the most important place in the religious life of Christian Jerusalem and was the starting point for pilgrimage itineraries in the city. The Rotunda of the Anastasis (Resurrection), built over the edicule of Christ's tomb, was originally constructed in the 4th century A.D., but the structure Lazaros saw when he arrived in Jerusalem at the very end of the 10th century had undergone several substantial renovations; it must have shown clear evidence of the most recent major repairs, required after it had been seriously damaged during riots in 966, since these took as long as twenty years to complete. Nevertheless, the Anastasis, the final destruction of which Lazaros witnessed (see below, Chap. 19), evidently made a profound impression on him, and he gave the same name to his last and most important establishment on Galesion; see the comment by Gregory the Cellarer in Chap. 253. On the history of the complex and its appearance up to this time, see especially R. Ousterhout, "Rebuilding the Temple: Constantine Monomachus and the Holy Sepulchre," *Journal of the Society of Architectural Historians* 48 (1989), 66–69; V. Corbo, *Il Santo Sepolcro di Gerusalemme* (Jerusalem, 1981), 1:28–139; Wilkinson, "Christian Pilgrims," 88–94; idem, *Jerusalem Pilgrims,* 174–78; also *ODB,* s.v. "Sepulchre, Holy."

[82] The office of archdeacon (ἀρχιδιάκονος) first appeared in the 5th century, and was normally occupied by the bishop's secretary; he could thus be a powerful and influential figure, despite the subordinate position of the diaconate in the ecclesiastical hierarchy. The *Commemoratorium* of ca. A.D. 808 provides a detailed list of the one hundred and fifty staff belonging to the complex of the Holy Sepulchre (a figure which includes some forty resident monks), but there is no mention of an archdeacon as such; fourteen

with him; when he thus learned from him that he had chosen to live in the monastery of St. Sabas, he took him along with him to the lavra. <The archdeacon> gave the superior twelve *nomismata,*[83] according to the rule of the monastery, and thus arranged for him to be received and numbered among the brothers there.[84] Lazaros spent six years in the monastery (as he often told us),[85] holding the office of *kanonarches* together with another brother.[86]

---

deacons are listed, but perhaps the closest official at that time may have been the "secretary who, after the Patriarch, controls everything." Certainly the archdeacon of the *vita* seems to have been influential in assisting Lazaros' career in Jerusalem as we see in this and the following chapter. See further *ODB,* s.v. "Deacon"; Wilkinson, *Jerusalem Pilgrims,* 12, 137.

[83] The *nomisma* was the standard gold coin of the Byzantine world, the equivalent of the earlier *solidus* and later *hyperpyron.* See further *ODB,* s.v. "Nomisma."

[84] There was a long tradition behind the practice of prospective monks donating some or all of their property to the monastery they were about to join. There are records of these *apotagai* (ἀποταγαί) or "entrance gifts" being permitted as early as the time of Justinian, and by the 8th century they seem to have become common and indeed compulsory in many cases, as here. Clearly the practice, which could verge on simony, was open to abuse and various imperial initiatives were taken to prevent or reduce it. This policy was adopted by those concerned with monastic "reform" in the mid-11th century and is thus endorsed by, e.g., the Evergetis *Typikon* (Gautier, "Évergétis," chap. 37, 79–81). In 1096 Alexios Komnenos, in his *De jure patriarchae* (Zepos, *Jus,* 3.409.16–25), was to codify the ban on compulsory *apotagai* or bequests of land in these circumstances while permitting free will gifts (*prosenexeis*); I am indebted to an anonymous reader for these references. Lazaros himself evidently approved of such gifts from those entering the monasteries on Galesion, providing that they were indeed made voluntarily: see below, Chap. 192. On this practice see, in particular, E. Herman, "Die Regelung der Armut in den byzantinischen Klöstern," *Orientalia christiana periodica* 7 (1941), 439–50; Thomas, *Religious Foundations,* 145, 183, 207–8; cf. also Malamut, *Route,* 92.

[85] The figure of six years given here seems to refer only to the first period Lazaros spent in the lavra of St. Sabas, rather than to his whole time there; that is to say, the period prior to his expulsion (see the following chapter). For further discussion, see the Introduction, section B, n. 17. On this interpretation, Lazaros would have been thirty-one or thirty-two when his first stay at St. Sabas came to an end, sometime between 996 and 999.

[86] The *kanonarches* (κανονάρχης) was the precentor of the monastic choir who led the singing and directed choir offices. The position was evidently quite important; see, e.g., Theodore of Stoudios, *poenae monasteriales,* 1.99 (PG 99:1746C); *iambi,* 10 (PG 99:1784B–C). The fact that the monk with whose fate Lazaros is so concerned in Chap. 20 was his fellow *kanonarches* at St. Sabas would appear to indicate either that he must

17. After this, Lazaros <began to be> troubled by the idea that he too should go off with those who used to go out into the desert during the period of the holy forty <days>,[87] but the superior of the monastery would not let him do this. Lazaros was unable to control the burning impulse of this idea,[88] however, so he left without the knowledge of the superior of the lavra and went off into the desert with the others. When he returned, the superior would no longer accept him but expelled him from the lavra and drove him away for being an idiorrhythmic and someone who would rather follow his own wishes than those of his superior.[89] Lazaros therefore left the monastery of St. Sabas and went to that of St. Euthymios,[90] but after spending some time there he withdrew and went back again to St. Sabas for the following reason, which he

have been reappointed to this office after his return from St. Euthymios, or that he held it only during his second stay at the monastery. Gregory of Cyprus (chap. 13, *AASS,* Nov. 3:592F), who gives Lazaros' office as that of *parekklesiarches* or "assistant sacristan" (see below, Chap. 82), places both his appointment to this office and his ordination before his expulsion.

[87] The reference is to Lent. The practice of going out into the desert at this time had a long history dating back to the founders of the monastic tradition in Palestine, such as Euthymios and Sabas. See here Patrich, *Sabas,* 272, cf. 293, and note that this was evidently a privilege reserved for the abbot and those monks he chose to accompany him.

[88] Note the rather similar language used at the beginning of Chap. 6 to describe Lazaros' motivation in leaving Strobelion for the Holy Land.

[89] The term "idiorrhythmic," which is explained exactly in the text here, is found in the context of Byzantine monasticism from the 5th century onward with the same negative connotations. Idiorrhythmics were criticized for going against the tradition of cenobitic monasticism, which was the norm in the Byzantine church. The practice did not find official acceptance until the 14th century when some centers of idiorrhythmic monasticism were established, notably on Mt. Athos. See further *ODB,* s.v. "Idiorrhythmic monasticism." The Byzantine monastic tradition placed considerable stress both on spending a sufficient time under the discipline of the *koinobion* before embarking on a career as a solitary and also on getting "official" permission to do so when the time came; see here Papachryssanthou, "Vie monastique," 161–62. Note that these points have already been made above in the *vita,* Chaps. 4–6, 9–11, 14; they are also reiterated on several occasions below in Lazaros' handling of situations arising in his own monasteries, see, e.g., Chaps. 159 and 175.

[90] The monastery of St. Euthymios was some six miles east of Jerusalem, about halfway to Jericho. It was founded by Euthymios, the father of Palestinian cenobitic monasticism, in the 5th century, the church being dedicated in 428/9. See *ODB,* s.v. "Euthymios the Great"; Patrich, *Sabas;* Hirschfeld, *Desert Monasteries;* Wilkinson, *Jerusalem Pilgrims,* 157.

himself recounted. "I went out," he said, "to a certain place with some other brothers to pick chickpeas, but <some> Arabs with their women and children came along with us.[91] When I saw that they were almost naked and were fooling about in an improper way and saying shameful things to the monks,[92] my mind was quite badly disturbed, so I withdrew from <the monastery of St. Euthymios> and went to the archdeacon and asked him to take me back again to the lavra of St. Sabas."[93] The archdeacon took Lazaros and brought him back to the monastery of St. Sabas <where> he gave the superior a Gospel valued at twelve *nomismata* and arranged for him to be received as on the first occasion.[94] Some time afterward, when the superior saw that Lazaros [515] was making progress in the works of God, he summoned him and persuaded him to accept the dignity of the priesthood, even though he was unwilling; after appointing him to the apostolic and great habit,[95] he sent him with some

[91] Or perhaps, "met us <there>."

[92] The implication that these monks could at least understand Arabic, together with the comment below in Chap. 20 concerning the apparent readiness of Lazaros' fellow *kanonarches* at St. Sabas to associate with "Saracens" and then actually to convert to Islam, provides an interesting witness in a Greek source to the presence of Arabic-speaking monks in the great monasteries of Palestine at this time, despite the typically negative attitude that the account betrays. Such incidents as these may perhaps betray signs of suspicion, if not tension, between Greek and Arabophone monks there; if so this would seem to have been something new (see Wilkinson, *Jerusalem Pilgrims,* 32), but understandable, given the Byzantine successes of the late 10th century and the contemporary situation under the reign of the Caliph al-Hākim bi-Amr Allah. See in particular here, S. H. Griffith, "Anthony David of Baghdad, Scribe and Monk of Mar Sabas: Arabic in the Monasteries of Palestine," *Church History* 58 (1989), 16–19; and, more generally, idem, "The Monks of Palestine and the Growth of Christian Literature in Arabic," *The Muslim World* 78 (1988), 1–28.

[93] The edited text continues the direct speech to the end of the following sentence. It makes more sense, however, to end the direct speech here and to understand the next sentence as a parallel to the similar one that occurs toward the end of Chap. 16, above; in both cases, then, δεχθῆναι is taken as a passive.

[94] It is interesting to note that the archdeacon had to pay a second entrance gift to have Lazaros readmitted.

[95] On the position Lazaros may have occupied in the formal scheme of Byzantine monasticism prior to this, see above, Chap. 9, n. 56, which refers to his tonsuring at Attaleia. The problem here is that the terms *apostolikon* and *megaloschemos* normally refer to two different stages in the monastic progression, the former being applied to

other brothers to the patriarch.[96] With the assistance and testimony of the archdeacon, Lazaros was presented to <the patriarch> who, when he saw that he was arrayed and adorned with the <necessary> virtues, praised him and declared him worthy of the priesthood; he first ordained him deacon, then priest. After he had been made priest by the laying on of the patriarch's hands and had <thus> been greatly enriched in the grace of the spirit, he returned again to the monastery of St. Sabas, and remained there until the uprising of the accursed Agarenes [Arabs] occurred.[97] During all the years he spent in the monastery of St. Sabas, as he himself often said when asked by the brothers, he never drank wine outside the church, nor did he taste oil or cheese or any of the other things which make the flesh fat;[98] nor did he lie on his side but he made a <specially> designed seat and would sit on it when he partook of a moment of sleep.[99]

---

the *mikron schema,* the habit of the lesser grade of monks, the latter to the superior grade, who wore the *mega* or *angelikon schema.* If Delehaye is correct in suggesting that Lazaros was only made a novice at Attaleia, then the present passage is perhaps to be interpreted as meaning that he was elevated through both ranks at once at St. Sabas; certainly Lazaros, and Gregory the Cellarer, were aware of the normal distinctions in this terminology, as Chap. 130 shows, and this might argue against simple confusion here. On the other hand, given the lack of strict formality in Byzantine monastic hierarchy as well as the possibility of local variations, it may well be that the author *is* being imprecise here, or else he is relying on a source that used this particular terminology. In either case he may merely be intending to indicate that Lazaros became a fully fledged monk at this point.

[96] This must refer to the patriarch Orestes Hieremias, who held office from 986 until 1006; see further the Introduction, section B, n. 19, where it is also argued that Lazaros' ordination must have taken place in or before 1001.

[97] See below, Chap. 19.

[98] This passage is probably to be read in conjunction with the attempts made later in the *vita* to absolve Lazaros from allegations that he was less abstemious in his consumption of food and drink than was proper for a prominent ascetic; see below, Chaps. 78, 81–84. Lazaros' diet is also mentioned in Chaps. 35 and 46. Information about the similar diets of other notable ascetics on Galesion is provided in Chaps. 160, 164, 174, 177, and 198.

[99] On this manner of sleeping, see below Chaps. 35 and 165, but especially Chap. 162, where the practice is traced back to an angelic instruction received by the founder of organized Egyptian monasticism, Pachomios. Cf. also the *vita Athan. Ath.* (B), chap. 6.28–30.

18. One day Lazaros, as well as some other <monks> from the lavra, went out into the desert.[100] While he was standing in a <dry> river bed in the middle of the day and offering up his prayers to the Lord, he heard a voice from above, as if from the cliff, saying this to him three times: "Lazaros, you must return to your homeland!"[101] Since he was alone there when he heard this, he recounted it to the fathers after he had gone back to the lavra. He was told by those who knew the place well: "There is a cave above the river bed, and we know that a nun has lived in it for a long time.[102] Maybe she was inspired by God and said this to you." This <was the response of> the elders. Lazaros prostrated himself, said "May the will of God be done,"[103] and went to his cell. But when he went out again from the lavra to the desert of Rouba,[104] according to the custom, and passed the Dead Sea, as he happened to be near the place in which Lot's wife stood frozen into a pillar of salt,[105] he smiled

[100] The version of the *vita* by Gregory of Cyprus (chap. 15, *AASS,* Nov. 3:594A) suggests that Lazaros spent a number of years on a pillar in the Palestinian desert at this point.

[101] The calling of Samuel in the temple would certainly spring to the mind of the Byzantine audience (I Ki. [Sam.] 3:4–8), but the voice from above may also allude to the baptism of Jesus by John in the desert (Mt. 3:17; Mk. 1:11; Lk. 3:22) and perhaps also to the Transfiguration (Mt. 17:5; Mk. 9:7; Lk. 9:35).

[102] Female solitaries were evidently very rare indeed by this time in Byzantine history; see Talbot, "Comparison," 16–17. Two others are, however, mentioned in the *vita,* in addition to the present nun: the extreme ascetic of Chap. 59 (referred to by Talbot), and a nun who was apparently living on Galesion when Lazaros moved there (Chap. 62). Also to be considered here is the woman Irene (of Chaps. 56–57), who was refused permission by Lazaros to live in this way.

[103] Cf. Acts 21:14.

[104] Presumably this was in Lent again; see Patrich, *Sabas,* 126 and 272. The desert area of Rouba (Ruva, Rova, Riva), mentioned in the Lives of various Palestinian saints, was near the Great Lavra of St. Sabas to the east, between it and the Dead Sea; see Patrich, *Sabas,* esp. 51–54. The place is described vividly, a century after Lazaros knew it, in the account of Daniel the Abbot (trans. Wilkinson, *Jerusalem Pilgrims,* 140–41; cf. John Phokas, 329).

[105] For the biblical story see Gen. 19:26. The reputed location of the pillar changed from time to time over the centuries, while the pillar itself was sometimes said to grow and shrink with the waxing and waning of the moon, or as it was licked by animals. According to Epiphanios the Monk, in the late 8th century the pillar was just to the north of the Dead Sea, and this seems to have been the general area in which it was located in the Middle Ages; so, e.g., in the account of Daniel the Abbot at the beginning

when he saw her, and then gave her a slap in the face. "Woe to you, wretched woman!" he said, "What has happened to you?" He did not do this to strike or humiliate the pillar (for how <could he> when it was lifeless and senseless?), but rather he did it to frighten himself, through her example, out of the idea of going back to his own homeland <and so> suffering the same fate, according to the word of the Lord that, "No one who puts his hand to the plow and looks back is fit for the kingdom of heaven." [106]

19. But God, Who loves men, and Who of old ordered Jacob to depart to his homeland[107] and arranged for Moses to return to Egypt again for the salvation of his own people,[108] also (for reasons that He <alone> understands) arranged for this man to go back again to his own country (even though he was unwilling), for the salvation of the many people who have been saved and who are <still> being saved through him until the close of this age.[109] For at that time, with God's permission, the sacrilegious and abominable Agarenes [Arabs] rose up against the Christians and laid waste to almost the whole <civilized> world, together with the monasteries and churches in it.[110] Their leader was a man by the name of Azizes. When this Azizes came into the Holy City [Jerusalem] and saw that the church of the Resurrection of our Christ and

---

of the 12th century (Wilkinson, *Jerusalem Pilgrims,* 148). The pillar that Lazaros saw would thus seem to have been in an area some twelve miles northeast of St. Sabas. See Wilkinson, *Jerusalem Pilgrims,* 164.

[106] The quotation is from Lk. 9:62, although it is not quite exact; it is repeated below, Chap. 63; cf. above, Chap. 6. The same passage is also quoted in the *vita Danielis,* chap. 10 (cf. above Chap. 9, n. 55); and it evidently lent itself to moments of serious decision; cf. Niketas Choniates, *Historia,* ed. I.-A. van Dieten, Corpus fontium historiae byzantinae 11.1 (Berlin, 1975), 427.20.

[107] Gen. 31:3.

[108] Ex. 3–4.

[109] Cf. Mt. 28:20.

[110] This refers to events which took place during the reign of the Fatimid caliph al-Hākim (r. 996–1021). Al-Hākim, who came to the throne as a boy, almost certainly suffered from a severe personality disorder; he is often described as "mad" (or, at best, "eccentric"), although he is believed to have been divine by the Ismā'īlite Druze sect. His instability showed itself particularly in unpredictable and violent political purges and religious persecution of Jews and Christians. These attacks began in 1003 and intensified from 1004/5. Other sources support the suggestion that a large number of monasteries and churches were destroyed or confiscated during this period, at least in Palestine.

God was so beautiful and marvelous, that impious <fellow> ordered one of his dogs (so one might say), who stood out from the others in both physical strength and evil, to climb up (woe is me!) and take down the venerable gold cross that was on the dome, and to throw it to the ground. This servant, who was even more criminal and sacrilegious than his criminal and sacrilegious master, did so. Then that wicked Azizes, after he had reviled our Lord, God, and Savior Jesus Christ a great deal, angrily ordered all <his men> to go up and demolish the church. Almost before all the words were out of his foul mouth, those men, barking like dogs being sent out hunting, rushed up and hurried to carry out their orders. As they began to demolish <the church>, they found some jewelry and gold coins in the cavities[111] in the middle of the wall; these <objects> had been placed there by those people, both men and women, who, moved by their affection for Christ, once came there with the blessed Helen.[112] For this reason those impious men did not stop their demolition until they had completely leveled <the church> to the ground.[113]

[111] Reading ὀπαῖς for ὠπαῖς.

[112] This refers to Helena, the mother of Constantine the Great, who undertook a pilgrimage to the Holy Land in 326–27. This pilgrimage was a very large and public affair, resembling most closely a newly Christianized form of the traditional imperial progress through the provinces. The exact contribution of Helena to the religious development of the Holy Land is difficult to assess, but her pilgrimage probably included the personal foundation and endowment of a number of major churches, or at least the supervision of building works already begun on the orders of Constantine, including the complex of the Holy Sepulchre in Jerusalem. She is also, of course, alleged by tradition to have discovered the True Cross on her visit to Jerusalem. On Helena's journey and her traditional role in the Church, see J. W. Drijvers, *Helena Augusta* (Leiden, 1992), esp. 55–72; also e.g., E. D. Hunt, *Holy Land Pilgrimage in the Later Roman Empire,* A.D. *312–460* (Oxford, 1984), 6–49; *ODB,* s.v. "Helena."

[113] The dating of this event is discussed in the Introduction, section B, n. 8; it is agreed that it occurred within the period 1007–10, probably on 28 September 1009. The most reliable source for these events, the Christian Arab historian Yaḥyā b. Saʿīd of Antioch, reports that the Caliph al-Hākim sent written orders to his lieutenant at Ramleh, Yāroukh, to carry out the demolition of this important Christian monument. Yāroukh's son, Yūsuf, was sent to Jerusalem together with Husayn b. Zāhir al-Wazzān and Abu'l-Fawāris ad-Dayf; after stripping the church, they destroyed as much of it as they could, although some parts proved too difficult to demolish. Other Arab historians generally agree with this account. The Greek historian John Skylitzes, who wrote in the second half of the 11th century, also records the event, but says that the church was destroyed in 1010 by Azizios ὁ τῆς Αἰγύπτου κατάρχων (347.84; the name is later given

When Lazaros and the other fathers saw this (for, as he used to say, he was standing there watching everything with his own eyes), they decided to leave <the Holy Land>. This was not so much because of this incident, but more because of the persecution taking place at that time, for <the Muslims> killed a lot of people, monks and laymen; even worse, many people who were afraid of physical death, alas, died spiritually by denying their faith and calling themselves Saracens instead of Christians.[114] So these men, these lights of the world[115] and imitators of the holy apostles, departed from <the Holy Land> and were scattered here and there throughout the regions of Romania;[116] and <this persecution> was the reason for the dispersal of these men over the whole world, just as long ago the murder of St. Stephen was for the apostles.[117]

20. Since everyone was leaving, the father also decided to depart from

as Azios, 387.12). This name, of course, agrees with that given by Gregory the Cellarer, but its absence in the Arabic sources suggests that both he and Gregory are making a double confusion here: first, mistakenly identifying the leader of the wrecking party with the Fatimid Caliph in Cairo, and second, confusing the Caliph, al-Hākim, with his father, al-'Azīz, who had died on 14 October 996. The church of the Resurrection was eventually rededicated in 1048 after being rebuilt under the patronage of the Byzantine emperor Constantine IX Monomachos (1042–55). See here, M. Canard, "La destruction de l'église de la Résurrection par le Calife Hākim et l'histoire de la descente du feu sacré," *Byzantion* 35 (1965), 16–43 (including a French translation of the relevant Arab sources); H. Kennedy, *The Prophet and the Age of the Caliphates* (London-New York, 1986), 329–37, 379–80; Schlumberger, *L'épopée,* II, 442–44; also R. Ousterhout, "Rebuilding the Temple: Constantine Monomachus and the Holy Sepulchre," *Journal of the Society of Architectural Historians* 48 (1989), 66–78.

[114] See further here, A. S. Tritton, *The Caliphs and Their Muslim Subjects* (London, 1930), 120.

[115] Cf. Phil. 2:15.

[116] Romania here signifies the Byzantine world in general.

[117] See Acts 7:58–8:4, but note that Acts 8:1 specifically excludes the apostles themselves from this diaspora following the death of Stephen. It is interesting that John Skylitzes' brief account of the destruction of the Holy Sepulchre also concludes with the information that the monks from these monasteries were scattered over the whole world (347.88–89). Is it possible that this could indicate a link of some sort between these two works? By referring to the early diaspora here and his stress at the start of the chapter that Lazaros left the Holy Land for God's own purposes, Gregory the Cellarer is perhaps guarding against the charge that Lazaros had run away in the face of persecution and possible martyrdom; further on such defensiveness by Gregory, see the Introduction, section G, pp. 56–57.

<the Holy Land> with another monk called Paul,[118] and go to Rome,[119] so he used to say. While they were still there <at Jerusalem>, however, some bad news reached them, for the monk who used to be Lazaros' [516] fellow *kanonarches* at the lavra of St. Sabas, as the story has already made clear,[120] had denied the Christian faith; the wretched man had abandoned his monastic habit and position and had gone off and become a Muslim. When the father heard this, he was very upset at the perdition of the brother and persuaded Paul to go with him and see this man, wherever he might be. So they went out and found him, and when Lazaros saw him wearing Saracen clothes, he said to him through his tears, "Alas, brother, what do I see? Have you thus scorned your salvation by denying both your faith and your habit? Wasn't it for this very reason that I was always telling you, when you were with me in the lavra, not to make friends with the Saracens? Come, my beloved brother, come and turn back again to our compassionate God, our Lord Jesus Christ, Who does not want the death of a sinner but that he should turn back and live."[121] The father said these words to him and others to lead him to repentance, but the man acted deaf and dumb and could not even look directly at them for shame. When the father saw him in this state, he spoke to him again: "What is it, brother? Won't you answer? Don't you realize that the good Paul <here> has also come for your sake? Give us any answer you want." Scarcely opening his mouth the man replied to the father, "What can I say to you, brother, when I have got myself caught up in such evils? Even if I want to repent and follow you, I cannot, for if it should come to the knowledge of the local emir he would kill me, and you <two> as well. But if you can go and persuade him to

[118] On the dating of Lazaros' departure, see the Introduction, section B, p. 8 n. 21; as is suggested there, Lazaros would have been forty-two or forty-three when he set out again for Asia Minor, probably in late 1009, and would have spent between sixteen and nineteen years in the Holy Land.

[119] On Rome as a site for Byzantine pilgrimage see Malamut, *Route,* 316–17; also, on pilgrimage from the East to the West in the 10th and 11th centuries, see B. Hamilton, "*Orientale lumen et magistra latinitas:* Greek Influence on Western Monasticism (900–1100)," in his *Monastic Reform, Catharism and the Crusades (900–1300)* (Aldershot, 1979), 5:181–216 (repr. from *Le millénaire du Mont Athos, 963–1963).*

[120] See above, Chap. 16.

[121] The last part of this sentence is a loose quotation from Ezek. 33:11, "*I desire not the death of the ungodly, as that the ungodly should turn from his way and live.*" It is also used, in almost exactly the same form, in Chap. 39, below.

let me go, I'll come with you, wherever you want." The father was glad when he heard these words and went off at once to the emir. He saw him and, after much tearful pleading on behalf of the brother, persuaded him with difficulty to give him to them. Then, taking him <with them> at night so that it should not be known to any of the Saracens (for these were the emir's instructions), they started traveling through the desert.

21. After they had got far enough away from the place they had left, they wanted to have a short rest, and lay down on the ground and went to sleep. But that miserable and misguided <former monk> got up <again>, when he saw that they were asleep, and went back, *just like a dog to its own vomit.*[122] When <Lazaros and Paul> woke up and could not find him, they realized what he had done. They understood then that his mind was twisted and that his repentance was not on account of God, just as Judas' was not. Thus, when <Judas> understood what he had done, he returned and cast down the silver pieces, and then, unable to bear his shame, fell into despair and went out and hanged himself;[123] so, in the same way, this man also pretended to repent when he was trapped by force of circumstances, but because he had been blinded by his despair and was unable to perceive the way of repentance and the compassion of Christ, he turned back again to the darkness of perdition. So the fathers got up and continued their journey through the desert, despairing of the salvation of that miserable man.

22. As it was terribly hot in the middle of the day <Lazaros and Paul> grew extremely thirsty, but He, Who long ago made water gush forth from the barren <hill of the> jawbone for Samson when he was fighting and thirsty,[124]

[122] This is a loose quotation from Prov. 26:11; 2 Pet. 2:22. A similar, though not identical version is also given below, Chap. 201.

[123] Mt. 27:3–5.

[124] The reference is to Judg. 15:19. This translation seems to me to be the best way of solving the problems that surround the phrase διὰ τῆς ἀψύχου σιαγόνος. Although it would make sense if διά were taken here in its obvious meaning as "through" or "by means of," it would also imply that Gregory the Cellarer has misunderstood the story in the LXX (and the Hebrew). In the scriptural passage the word for "jawbone" (σιαγών) is used as a proper name for the hill on which the miraculous supply of water occurred, it being the place in which Samson had just slaughtered a thousand Philistines with the jawbone of an ass (Judg. 15:14–16; the etymology is explained in v. 17). The standard text of the LXX thus translates "And God broke open the cistern in the <place of the> jawbone, and water flowed out from it, and he drank" (RSV: "And God split open the hollow place at Lehi [jawbone], and there came water from it; and when

now also miraculously led these men to go to a place where there was water. The water was hidden from the outside by a bramble bush but, when they went inside the bush, they found the water and drank; they then came out <again> and lay down in the shade of the bush.

While they were lying on the ground like this they looked up and saw (just saying and hearing <this> is enough to fill one with horror, let alone seeing it) four lions apparently coming toward them. When they suddenly saw these <lions>, they <stayed> lying <there but> raised the hands and eyes of their souls[125] <in supplication> to God, Who <alone> could save them, and called on Him for help. And, indeed, they did not fail in their request for, just as He miraculously tamed the wild beasts for Daniel,[126] so also did He for them. <The lions> thus came up one by one, smelt them from head to foot, licked them with their tongues and then went by, wagging their tails just like pet dogs do when they see their masters; after <the lions> had drunk and come out of the bush, they did the same thing <again> and then left <the men> and went away. After they had thus been miraculously saved from the beasts, they got up and gave glory to God Who had saved them from the mouths of lions;[127] then they drank some more water and went on their way.

---

he drank . . ."). The translation of διά as "through" at this point would thus perhaps suggest that Gregory has mistakenly understood (or mistakenly remembered) the LXX as referring to God miraculously supplying the water directly out of a jawbone itself, taking the standard text of the LXX as referring literally to an object rather than to a place name; this would have the advantage of making good sense of the qualification "lifeless."

Another possibility is to translate the passage (more literally) as "made water gush forth by means of the lifeless jawbone," in which case it would seem that Gregory must have imagined God using the jawbone to produce the water in some way. Indeed, there is an alternative reading in the LXX at this point which translates as, "And God opened the wound (τραῦμα) of the jawbone." This perhaps suggests that the water was thought to have issued forth from the place where the jawbone had struck the ground when Samson discarded it, in which case the jawbone could be taken as instrumental in the production of the water. Perhaps Gregory knew this alternative reading and took it in this way.

[125] The Greek implies purely mental action here: the men are presumably afraid to move in case they are seen by the lions, but still go through the normal motions of supplicatory prayer in their minds. For such actions performed physically by Lazaros see, e.g., Chap. 28, below. The phrase ὄμματα τῆς ψυχῆς is well attested, see Lampe, *Lexicon,* s.v. ὄμμα, 1.

[126] Dan. 6:16–23.

[127] Cf. Ps. 21 (22):21; 2 Tim. 4:17.

23. For three days <Lazaros and Paul> traveled through the desert, not tasting anything else at all except the water, for they were carrying nothing, no bag, no staff, no bread, nor anything else to eat.[128] <Eventually> they came to Tiberias,[129] <where> they went into the town and received alms from the Christians who lived there. They then left, but three camel drivers, who had seen them as they were about to go into the town, stayed waiting for them to come out and suddenly attacked them and tried to take the bread which the townspeople had given to them. <Lazaros and Paul> took out one loaf and gave it to these men, expecting to get rid of them by giving them this, but they ate it like dogs and started to chase them again. When the father saw that they were chasing them again, he said to Paul, "Let's give them all the bread and be rid of them, because that's why they're following us; <that way> we won't get hurt by them." But <Paul> became very angry with Lazaros and persuaded him to go on without being afraid; then he turned on [517] them, raised his right fist and shouted harshly at them, and thus suddenly made fugitives of the men who had just before been <their> pursuers.[130] So they went on their way without fear.

[128] The absence of equipment and provisions for travel here is again deliberately reminiscent of Jesus' instructions to the disciples in the Gospels; see above, Chap. 14.

[129] Tiberias is on the west bank of the Sea of Galilee (Lake Tiberias) about 70 miles north-northeast of Jerusalem. The main route from Jerusalem to Tiberias ran north to Neapolis (modern Nablus), where it divided, either going to the west via Sebastia (Sabastiya; OT Samaria) or to the east via Scythopolis (Bet She'an; OT Bethshean). If Lazaros and Paul traveled through the desert, however, they probably left Jerusalem to the east, in the direction of Jericho, and then headed up the Jordan valley, rejoining the easterly road at some point. The guide book of Epiphanios the Monk (7th/8th century) apparently refers to a route very much like this and states that it is a four-day journey from the Place of Baptism (just north of the Dead Sea) to Tiberias (see Wilkinson, *Jerusalem Pilgrims,* 121 and map 34, 118). The time given for the journey there would thus tally reasonably well with that indicated by the *vita* of rather more than three days. Tiberias was an important regional center and the *vita* seems to indicate that it still had a thriving Christian community at the beginning of the 11th century; there is evidence that it contained a number of churches (as well as synagogues) in the 8th and 9th centuries as well as a monastery. The town was the pilgrimage center for visiting the sites of a number of New Testament episodes that were located a few miles to the north; most important were those of the feeding of the five and four thousand, and of the Sermon on the Mount, as well as the miracle of Jesus walking on the water. See Wilkinson, *Jerusalem Pilgrims,* 64–66, 174a; cf. Malamut, *Route,* 317–18.

[130] An illustration of the dangers besetting pilgrims and travelers at this time; cf. also in the *vita* the attempt to sell Lazaros into slavery (Chap. 9), or the dangers of pirates

24. After they had gone up and worshiped on Tabor,[131] they went down to Damascus and then traveled through Lebanon <until> they came to Tripoli and so to Laodikaia.[132] Before they left for Laodikaia, however, someone who met them took out a *nomisma* and gave it to them, and someone else <gave them> a bag. Without Paul's knowledge, the father gave this away again to a poor man, thus following properly the word of the Lord, which, besides the other things, forbids carrying a bag.[133] When they got to Laodikaia, they decided to separate. After they had made this decision Paul said to the father, "Come, let's go to a money-changer so that we can split the *nomisma*." But Lazaros replied to him, "If you take my advice, give it to the poor, otherwise do as you think fit; I'm not taking even one obol from it." So, after embracing and praying for each other, they parted. Paul confined himself on a pillar somewhere there, although he did not remain in that place in the end.[134]

(Chap. 228). See further here Malamut, *Route,* 275–77, who comments on this incident among others.

[131] Mt. Tabor was an important pilgrimage site venerated as the location of the Transfiguration, as well as the meeting of Melchizedek and Abraham. Church buildings and a monastery are attested there from at least the 4th or 5th century and accounts speak of three basilicas from the 6th century; by the early 9th century there was a fourth, and Tabor had become the residence of a bishop, even though the monastery apparently had only eighteen monks. The guidebook of Epiphanios the Monk (7th/8th century) speaks of 4,340 steps going up the mountain and notes that it is a single day's journey from Tiberias. Tabor, in fact, is just more than nine miles southwest of Tiberias; it is thus evident that Paul and Lazaros made a deliberate detour from their route to Damascus in order to visit it. See *ODB,* s.v. "Tabor"; Wilkinson, *Jerusalem Pilgrims,* 173.

[132] This route took Lazaros and Paul on a roundabout journey further inland to Damascus (ca. 70 miles northeast of Tiberias) and then back to the coast (at least 90 miles), which they evidently followed between Tripoli and Laodikaia (Lattakia) for a distance of about 110 miles. Following a treaty between al-Hākim and Basil II in 1001 Tripoli remained in Muslim hands, but the frontier with the Byzantine Empire was established just to the north. Laodikaia and its hinterland was thus under Byzantine control. The return of Lazaros and Paul to officially Christian territory may explain both the increase in the charity they received, which is noted here, as well as their decision to separate at this particular point.

[133] See above, Chap. 14.

[134] This raises the question of how Gregory the Cellarer (or Lazaros) knew that Paul did not remain there. It is conceivable that he later visited the monastery on Galesion, but news could have come by way of a visitor from the East (see, e.g., Chaps. 84 and 114), from someone like Kosmas the Jerusalemite who settled in Lazaros' community (see Chaps. 84, 221, 223), or from other monks in the general vicinity who had traveled

25. Upon leaving Laodikaia the father went to Antioch and so to the Wondrous Mountain and the monastery of St. Symeon;[135] then he left there, crossed Cilicia, and came to the region of Cappadocia.[136] When he reached <Mt.> Argeas,[137] he wanted to climb it but he was stopped by those <who lived> there because it was winter.[138] Lazaros, however, put all his hope in our Lord Jesus Christ and His mother and started to climb. When he was halfway up the mountain, <such> a <dense> fog came down around him, as he used

---

to or lived in the Holy Land (e.g., the hostile monk at the Kouzena monastery mentioned in Chap. 84). Cf. below, Chap. 115, where information is evidently obtained about a Paulician, converted in Lazaros' monastery, who subsequently became a monk at St. Sabas at Jerusalem. It is also conceivable that this Paul may have later become superior of the monastery of St. Eugenios at Trebizond in the mid-11th century: see above, Introduction, section I, p. 65, n. 309.

[135] The journey from Laodikaia to Antioch is roughly fifty miles. The Wondrous Mountain (Saman Daği), which is toward the sea to the southwest of Antioch on the river Orontes, was a major pilgrimage site devoted to the veneration of Symeon the Stylite the Younger. The site developed in the second half of the 6th century around the saint's pillar although, by the time of Lazaros' visit, the monastery had evidently been refounded by Greek and Georgian monks in the 10th century. Despite its destruction by the Mamluks in 1260, considerable remains of the complex can still be seen today. See W. Djobadze, *Archaeological Investigations in the Region West of Antioch on-the-Orontes* (Stuttgart, 1986), 57–115; also *ODB,* s.v. "Wondrous Mountain," "Symeon the Stylite the Younger"; P. van den Ven, *La Vie ancienne de S. Syméon Stylite le Jeune* (Brussels, 1962).

[136] The wording of the text here and the fact that Lazaros arrives at Mt. Argeas [Argaios] before going to Caesarea perhaps suggest that he followed the main route westward across Cilicia to Tarsus and then north across the Taurus mountains by means of the Cilician Gates and so to Cappadocia.

[137] This mountain (Erciyas Daği), a snow-capped, extinct volcano, partly responsible for the magnificent scenery in the famous valleys of Cappadocia, is, at 3916 m (ca. 12,000 ft.), the highest peak in Asia Minor. It rises just to the south of Caesarea (Kayseri) and dominates the surrounding landscape. Modern guides describe the climb as tiring, but not particularly difficult apart from the problems normally associated with high altitude; they are, however, presumably referring to an ascent in the summer under good conditions. On Mt. Argaios see *RE* 2:684, s.v. Ἀργαῖον Ὄρος.

[138] As has been seen above, Lazaros probably left Jerusalem sometime shortly after 28 September 1009. The fact that Chap. 28 indicates that he was somewhere beyond Caesarea on his way north to Euchaïta/Euchaneia by 9 March (see below, Chap. 28) suggests that he made his ascent of the mountain early in the spring. It had thus taken him about four or five months, including his stop at the Wondrous Mountain, to cover the approximately 750 miles between Jerusalem and this point on his journey.

to relate, that, even though he strained his eyes, he could not see to the right or left or anywhere else. He did not give up his attempt, however, but bent down and, using his hands to guide him, went on up. While he was climbing like this, he met a bear, as he used to say, and neither he nor it sensed the approach of the other until they came <so close that> they bumped into each other. The only explanation for this was that it was a device of the Evil One intended to frighten him into turning back, or rather of God allowing <this> as a trial of his faith and hope. The <bear> came to a halt at their sudden collision and left the path, while Lazaros went on his way unhindered, heartily singing the Davidic psalms. When he had climbed up <to the top> he found that the door <of the chapel> had been securely barred.[139] He opened it and went inside; when he had prayed, he came out, closed the door securely, and went down the mountain again.

26. After Lazaros had descended <the mountain> and was going on his way, he encountered a flock of sheep. The dogs saw him and began to chase him, so he climbed up on a rock and stood there, thinking that they would be unable to get up. But <these dogs> were raised up by the immaterial dog,[140] so to speak, and sprang from the ground with <great> leaps. They seized one piece each of the leather tunic that he used to wear[141] and tore it apart; then they went running off again, carrying the pieces in their mouths. The father was thus stripped naked by the dogs, but he praised God even for this, before he got down from the rock and went on his way. After he had gone a little

[139] Although it is not stated anywhere in the chapter that there was a chapel or sanctuary at the summit of the mountain that Lazaros intended to visit, this may reasonably be supposed from the mention of something with a barred or closed door there in which he prayed. Gregory the Cellarer has apparently omitted this detail from his narrative or else something has fallen out of the text. The latter seems more likely since the problem occurs close to the end of a folio in the manuscript and because it is unclear why there should be a stress on the door being securely closed. Such sanctuaries on mountain peaks were, as they still are, most often dedicated to Elijah; see *ODB,* s.v. "Elijah."

[140] In other words, the Devil. The Devil and his demons are quite commonly associated with dogs in the Byzantine tradition, although the *vita* seems to stress the link quite heavily, as is apparent from this and the following two chapters (cf. also below, Chaps. 54, 153); it also uses the metaphor of dogs for bad people relatively frequently, see, e.g., above, Chap. 19. See further here Joannou, *Démonologie,* 12; Greenfield, *Demonology,* 101, 122, 133–34, 188; and *ODB,* s.v. "Dogs." In general, see B. Woods, *The Devil in Dog Form: A Partial Type-Index of Devil Legends* (Berkeley, 1959).

[141] Further on this garment, see below, Chaps. 35, 82, and 112.

way from that place, however, he met someone riding a horse; this man felt sorry for Lazaros when he saw him, and took off a patchwork cloak he was wearing over his clothes and gave it to him. The father took this and, after putting it on, blessed the man who had given it to him; he also gave thanks to God for looking after him in this way and continued on his journey.[142]

27. When Lazaros reached Caesarea, he went into the church of St. Basil and prayed;[143] he then left the town and made the journey to the <shrine of> St. Theodore Stratelates.[144] While he was walking along by himself, however, an enormous black dog suddenly jumped out from somewhere and started to follow him; whenever he left the beaten track, the dog would disappear, but whenever he returned to it, he would see it behind him again, barking loudly. As evening was falling, he went into a village, but although he went almost all round it, no one invited him in. Not far from the village he found a cave, and went inside, but the dog came and stood in front of it and barked; as a result, the dogs from the village gathered too and stood there barking with it. The people of the village heard the noise <made by> the dogs and, thinking that a wild animal had gone into the cave, came running up to it carrying swords; then they stood <outside> shouting so that the wild animal (so they thought) would come out. However, when the father let them know with his voice that it was a man inside the cave and not a wild animal, they went away and left him <alone>. In the morning he got up and continued his journey, but the dog could still be seen, barking behind him, until evening came <again>. <Once more Lazaros> went into the village he had reached and went round it, but no one there invited him in, nor did he get even a crumb of bread. He went off to a place where there was a bread oven and, as the ashes were still <hot>

[142] The incident invites a comparison to the famous episode in the *vita* of St. Martin of Tours, where the saint divides his cloak and gives half to a naked beggar; *Vita S. Martini,* 3:1–4, ed. and trans. J. Fontaine, *Sulpice Sévère, Vie de Saint Martin* (Paris, 1967).

[143] Caesarea (Kayseri) was an important military base at this time as well as being a religious center because of its association with the most influential of the Cappadocian Fathers, St. Basil, who was born there ca. 329, became its bishop in 370/71, and died 1 January 379. Nothing now remains of this church. See further *ODB,* s.v. "Caesarea," "Basil the Great."

[144] The shrine was near Euchaïta in Pontus, a journey of some 150 miles almost due north from Caesarea, although it is impossible to tell exactly which route Lazaros followed. On this place and St. Theodore Stratelates himself, see below, Chap. 29.

like coals, he took them out of it and sat down nearby,[145] but the dog again went and stood in front of him and barked [518] so that there too all the village dogs gathered and stood barking with it. Lazaros got up and, picking up <a piece of> the wood which was lying there for use in the oven, <remained> standing there all night, as he used to tell <us>, chasing off the dogs.

28. When daylight came, Lazaros decided not to leave the village that day until the divine liturgy had been celebrated, <partly> because of the solemnity of the day, as it was the feast of the Forty Martyrs of Christ,[146] but at the same time as a test of the uncharitable people <who lived> there. When the time for the liturgy had come, however, and the divine service had been celebrated, <still> no one had given him even a crumb of bread to eat. Then Lazaros realized that they had no concept at all of sharing. He did not get angry or shout insults at them, but raised his hands and his eyes toward heaven and offered up some such words of thanks to God <as these>: "Lord, I give you thanks; and if you should consider me worthy to live in some place where it is clearly your will <for me to do so>, I will not eat by myself the bread that you send me, but I will also serve it as food to all those, rich and poor, who come to me in your name."[147] After he had said this, he left the village.

As he saw a small chapel somewhere nearby,[148] he went to it. He found a

[145] Presumably for warmth since this incident took place in early March, as the following chapter reveals; the glowing coals may also have been intended to help keep the dog away.

[146] The feast day of the Forty Martyrs is celebrated on 9 March, so these events apparently occurred on that date in 1010. It had thus taken Lazaros just over five months to travel from Jerusalem to this point in central Asia Minor, since he set out at the end of September in the previous year. The Forty Martyrs are venerated as soldiers who died when forced to stand naked all night in an icy lake because of their Christian beliefs; the martyrdom was believed to have taken place in the early 4th century during the reign of Licinius, near Sebasteia (Sivas). On the martyrs see *ODB*, s.v. "Forty Martyrs of Sebasteia."

[147] Lazaros fulfills this promise below, Chap. 32. For commentary on this example of the absence of charity in early 11th-century Byzantium, see D. J. Constantelos, *Byzantine Philanthropy and Social Welfare* (New York, 1991), 110, although Lazaros was clearly not, as Constantelos suggests, on his way "to his monastery" at this point.

[148] The word translated as "chapel" here, εὐκτήριον, can be used of any ecclesiastical establishment, ranging in size from a simple chapel to a whole monastery; usually it describes private oratories and chapels as opposed to public buildings that were part of the official church organization. Considerable tensions certainly arose at various times concerning the function and control of such private establishments. It seems clear

nun established in it[149] who, when she saw him, got up and brought him bread and water and made him take some food. After he had partaken of <this> nourishment, he gave thanks to God (for he did everything to the glory of God and, if anything ever happened to him, whether happy or sad, it became an occasion for him to thank God) and then also blessed the nun, before setting off on his way. The dog appeared again, however, following him and barking until it was evening; and then it left him. Thus, even if the father did not say so directly, I conclude that this was not a <real> dog, but an evil demon that had transformed itself into the likeness of a dog, with God's permission, as a trial for the father. For how, if it was truly a dog and not an evil demon, was it able to follow him for those three days and play such tricks?[150]

29. In this way Lazaros reached Euchaïa, <where> he venerated the holy martyr Theodore; then he left and went down to Euchaïta <where> he worshiped and prayed in the church of the holy martyr Theodore Teron.[151] When

---

from the contexts in which the term occurs in the *vita* that the author uses it to indicate a small monastic community of some sort based around an oratory or chapel, but probably without a large, formal complex of buildings. The εὐκτήριον at Oroboi is big enough to have a superior (Chap. 30) and cells, and is also described as a μονή, but that of St. Marina in the foothills of Koumaron (Chap. 31) has only two monks; it is evident from the comment at the end of Chap. 33 concerning this latter place that the author only considers that it has become a full-blown monastery (μοναστήριον) after the construction of cells and a new church. See here *ODB,* s.v. "Eukterion"; and, in general, Thomas, *Religious Foundations.*

149 See above, Chap. 12.

150 The association of the Devil and the demons with dogs was noted above, Chap. 26; they were thought to favor black animals of all kinds, see e.g., Chap. 73, below. See also here *ODB,* s.v. "Dogs," which cites this passage.

151 Theodore Stratelates ("the general" or "commander") is very closely related to the other St. Theodore mentioned here, Theodore Teron ("the recruit"). While Teron was well known in early hagiographical literature, the first references to Stratelates are only found in the 9th century and his biography is clearly modeled on the Life of Teron. By the time of Lazaros' journey in the early 11th century, however, the cult of Stratelates had grown considerably; plausible arguments have been made for linking this development to social factors, particularly the growth in importance of the aristocracy and the military, which had rendered veneration of the humbler Teron less acceptable. Teron was apparently burnt to death under Maximian, whereas Stratelates is alleged to have died under Licinius, but in later hagiography both are said to have killed a dragon, and both are associated with a woman called Eusebia from Euchaïta (Mecitözü or Avkat), which was to the west of Amaseia (Amasya) in Pontus.

While Theodore Teron was firmly linked with Euchaïta, as here in the *vita* (although

he left there Lazaros made his way on foot across the Anatolikon theme,[152] <and so> came to Chonai.[153] He prayed in the church of the Archangel,[154] and then left there with some wandering monks and went down to Ephesus to the church of the Theologian.[155] From there he was on the point of leaving with these men and going to Rome, for the people with whom he was <traveling>

---

there appears to have been no actual tomb in existence), there was evidently disagreement as to the exact name of the resting place of Stratelates' remains. One source thus knows it as Euchaïna (*SynaxCP,* 738), while Skylitzes reports that John I Tzimiskes built a large shrine for Stratelates' relics at Euchaneia in the 970s and changed its name to Theodoroupolis; as we see here, the text of the *vita* gives yet another variant in Euchaïa (Εὐχάϊα), although this is amended by Delehaye (p. 518 [2]; see also N. Oikonomides, "Le dédoublement de Saint Théodore et les villes d'Euchaita et d'Euchaneia," *AnalBoll* 104 [1986], 329) to Euchaïna (Εὐχάϊνα). Later sources appear not to know this place at all and confuse it with Euchaïta. It now seems certain, however, that whatever the exact name by which Stratelates' resting place was known, it was in fact located on the site occupied by modern Çorum, about 20 miles west of Euchaïta, and that it was completely destroyed toward the end of the 11th century. See *ODB,* s.v. "Theodore Stratelates," "Theodore Teron," "Euchaita"; *BHG,* 1750–53m, 1760–73; Delehaye, *Saints militaires,* 11–43; idem, "Euchaïta et la légende de S. Théodore," in *Anatolian Studies Presented to Sir William Mitchell Ramsay,* ed. W. H. Buckler and W. M. Calder (Manchester, 1923), 129–34; Kötting, *Peregrinatio,* 160–66; F. R. Trombley, "The Decline of the Seventh-Century Town: The Exception of Euchaita," in *Byzantine Studies in Honour of Milton V. Anastos,* ed. S. Vryonis (Malibu, Calif., 1985), 65–90; Oikonomides, as above, 327–35; A. Kazhdan, "Hagiographical Notes," *Byzantion* 53 (1983), 544–45; idem, "Hagiographical Notes," *Erytheia* 9.2 (1988), 197–200.

[152] The Anatolikon (Ἀνατολικόν or Eastern) theme was the major administrative province, to the east and southeast of the Thrakesion theme in which Ephesus and Galesion were situated. One of the original and principal themes of Asia Minor in the 7th century, the Anatolikon had lost a great deal of territory by the first half of the 11th century, in particular to Cappadocia and Seleukia in the East.

[153] A journey of some 450 miles. On Chonai, see above, Chap. 6.

[154] On Lazaros' earlier experiences in this famous church, see above, Chaps. 7–8. Chap. 253 reveals that Lazaros was particularly devoted to the cult of the archangels throughout his life.

[155] It was about 135 miles from Chonai to Ephesus. On Ephesus and the surrounding area, see above, Chap. 2. The church of St. John the Theologian, which contained the saint's tomb beneath the high altar, was Ephesus' greatest attraction at this time, although there were other *loca sancta* there such as the cave of the Seven Sleepers, the tomb of Mary Magdalene, and the body of St. Timothy. There was a major procession to the church on 8 May, St. John's feast day, which was also the occasion of an annual miracle of healing dust or "manna," which issued from the tomb. The origins of the

were about to make the journey;[156] however, as he used to say, he was troubled by the idea (<which was> not bad, but indeed very good) of going to the vicinity of his own village and inquiring after his parents, not because he wanted to find out about them, but so that the thought of this would not <continue to> bother him afterward.[157] In fact, however, this action was <due> to the providence of God, in order that the ark (I mean Lazaros' country) might again receive the dove which had earlier flown away from it.[158] So, when he had decided <to do> this, Lazaros said to his companions, "Go on, and I will catch up with you shortly."

30. After they had gone, Lazaros went to Oroboi, to the chapel of George <the notary> who had once been his teacher.[159] He found <George's> son

---

church go back as early as the beginning of the 4th century, but the church of Lazaros' day was basically that built by Justinian and completed in the middle of the 6th century. See *ODB,* s.v. "Ephesus"; Foss, *Ephesus,* 125–28; J. Keil and H. Hörmann, *Die Johanneskirche* [*Forschungen in Ephesos* 4.3] (Vienna, 1951); Kötting, *Peregrinatio,* 171–83.

[156] Lazaros had thus evidently kept to his plan of visiting Rome, which was first suggested in Chap. 20 when he was on the point of leaving Jerusalem.

[157] Gregory the Cellarer's rather awkward explanation here concerning Lazaros' return to his home is presumably intended to avoid the criticism that he had failed to obey the command made in the Gospels, and adhered to by Byzantine monastic tradition (in theory at least), that the true disciple must abandon home and relatives in order to follow the way of Christ; Mt. 19:27–29; Mk. 10:28–30; Lk. 18:28–30. This also offers an explanation for Lazaros' strenuous efforts to deny his identity in the following chapter. Compare, too, the attempts evidently made in Chaps. 18–19 above to counter criticisms of Lazaros' "instability" in leaving the Holy Land. For more on Byzantine tolerance of such "instability" among holy men, particularly in the 13th and 14th centuries, see Nicol, "*Instabilitas*"; and on the question of the monastic ideal of separation from family and its frequent circumvention in practice, see Talbot, "Family."

[158] This somewhat forced allusion is to Gen. 6:8–11, where Noah sends out a dove from the ark in search of dry land after the flood.

[159] For Oroboi, see above, Chap. 3; on the implications of the term "chapel" (*eukterion*) here, see above, Chap. 28. Although it was not specifically stated in Chap. 3 that George was associated with a monastic community during the three years Lazaros spent with him at Oroboi, this is apparently confirmed by the fact that he summons "the superior of the monastery" when he recognizes Lazaros/Leo; cf. the mention of such a monastery in the note there. Boulhol (*Anagnorismos,* 123–26) comments at length on this chapter and provides a French translation of it. On the theme of saints returning to their homes after a long absence ("the sons of Ulysses"), see also Malamut, *Route,* 119–21.

<there> and asked him about his parents and relatives, and also, of course, about his teacher, the boy's father. When the boy heard this from the father [Lazaros], he went to his own father and told him everything, and when he <in turn> heard this from his son, he guessed from his words who it was. He said to the boy, "It's the notary Leo, the son of Niketas and Irene, isn't it? Let's go so that I can see him myself!" <George> came and, when he saw him, recognized Lazaros at once. Lazaros denied it, but <George> put more faith in his own eyes than in the father's words and, without any delay, immediately sent for his relatives and also, of course, the superior of the monastery. They came and also recognized the holy man when they saw him, especially the superior of the monastery, in as much as he was Lazaros' maternal uncle.[160] Lazaros denied it again, but the superior, acting rather sensibly, shut him in a cell and sent for his mother, for she was still alive although his father had died.

When the mother arrived, the superior brought Lazaros out of the cell and stood the son in front of his mother. "Do you know who this is, woman?" he asked. She at first said no, for how could she recognize him [519] when twenty years had already passed since she lost him, especially when he was <so> wasted away by his asceticism and suffering?[161] After she had had a better look at him, however, she began dimly to recognize him[162] and finally realized

[160] Possibly the same uncle Elias who oversaw Lazaros' early education when he was a monk in the monastery of Kalathai, which was also apparently nearby; see above Chaps. 3–4. Even if it is not the same man, the presence of an uncle would nevertheless provide a likely explanation why Oroboi was chosen for Lazaros' first spell of education away from home when he was a boy.

[161] The figure of twenty years given here and also repeated below in Chap. 254 presents some problems for the chronology of Lazaros' life; these are discussed above in the Introduction, section B, n. 24. As is suggested there, Lazaros probably returned to Oroboi in late 1010 or early 1011 when he was about forty-four or forty-five; if my chronology is correct, at least twenty-five years, and possibly as many as twenty-eight, had in fact elapsed since he finally ran away from Strobelion. The fact that Lazaros' own mother found it hard to recognize him, while the others who met him quickly realized who he was, may perhaps be explained by the fact that she had probably seen little of him after he left his home around the age of nine (see above, Chap. 3), whereas they had had much more contact with him during his adolescence. Morris (*Monks,* 81) is mistaken in suggesting that Lazaros was "immediately recognized" by his mother.

[162] Boulhol (*Anagnorismos,* 124 [cf. 126]) sees a probable allusion here to the Pseudo-Clementine *Homilies* 12:23.2 (ed. B. Rehm, *Die Pseudoklementinen* [Berlin, 1992], 1: 185.11–12).

that he was her most beloved <son>; then she ran to him at once and embraced him and kissed him and, with tears of joy welling from her eyes, said what one would expect a mother to say upon finding her dearest son. When Lazaros saw his mother clinging to him like this and was at a loss what to do, he admitted unwillingly that he was <indeed> her son. <News of> this spread rapidly among his relatives and friends and acquaintances, and they all gathered to see him and, at the same time, to share in his mother's joy and happiness over the discovery of her lost son.[163] They spent the whole day like this, and gave glory to God for having deemed them worthy to see a mother thus miraculously made happy by a child; then each of them went back to their homes. The superior invited Lazaros to stay there in the monastery with him because he refused to go home with his mother, even though she implored him a great deal to do so. So he yielded to the superior and remained in the monastery for some days before leaving again and going back to Ephesus.

31. Lazaros entered the town and then left <again> after praying in the church of the Theologian. Led by <God>, who was directing him, he traveled on, and came to a village called Malpadeas.[164] As the day was already <lengthening> into evening, he turned off the road and went into <the village>, where he was taken in by a priest called George.[165] After this man had generously entertained him, he was asked by Lazaros if there was a monastery in the area where he might take up residence.[166] <George> led him to the monastery of the most holy Theotokos, which is above the village of Kepion and is called <the monastery> of Appion.[167] Lazaros went into this <place>, but did not like living there <and so>, directed by the superior of the monastery, he came

[163] There seem to be several allusions here to the parables of the lost sheep, the lost coin, and the prodigal son, both in the final act of recognition by the mother and in the celebrations that follow; see Lk. 15, esp. vv. 6, 9, 20, 23, and 32.

[164] This place is otherwise unknown.

[165] This man evidently remained closely connected with Lazaros' community. He accompanied Lazaros when he first moved permanently onto Galesion from the monastery of St. Marina (Chap. 53).

[166] Lazaros' plan of rejoining his former companions on their journey to Rome has now evidently been forgotten and is not mentioned again.

[167] Or simply "Appionos." Nothing is known of this monastery, but the text would seem to imply that it was still in existence and known to the author of the *vita* later in the 11th century. The village of Kepion was only a short distance from Galesion; see below, Chaps. 55 and 241.

to the foothills of the mountain called Koumaron where there was a spring and also a small chapel <dedicated to> that victorious martyr for Christ, Marina.[168] Here two monks were living, brothers by birth called Hilarios and Leontios. These men took Lazaros in and they both decided that they should live together.[169] After a while, Lazaros persuaded the monks to construct a roofed pillar for him; he moved onto this and spent some time on it, but then decided to take the roof off and live in the open air on this <pillar>, in imitation of the wondrous Symeon.[170] And so he did.

32. Within a short time Lazaros' reputation spread almost everywhere and many people, rich and poor, began coming to him from the villages and towns nearby. He received these people kindly, <thus> fulfilling the vow to God that he had made earlier on;[171] for he would break up and distribute to them the bread that He sent him for his nourishment through the Christian faithful. The monks who were there before <him> saw this <happening> and that the people who lived there were showing more respect for Lazaros, who was a newcomer, a stranger, and unknown, than they were for them, who were locals and well known. So they went to Lazaros and said, "Either stop welcoming everyone and giving away to them in this reckless fashion the things God sends for our use, or else go away from here. If you won't, then we will have to leave ourselves!" The father replied to them, "It's impossible for me not to receive all these people and not to offer them <a share> of what God provides for us; nor am I going to leave here for such a reason. As for you, do

[168] On this sort of "chapel," see above, Chap. 28, n. 148. Marina was a late 3rd-century martyr whose legend describes her victories over Satan and a dragon; these feature prominently in representations of her. See further *ODB*, s.v. "Marina."

[169] The Greek here may allude to Ps. 131 (132):13: ὅτι ἐξελέξατο Κύριος τὴν Σιών, ᾑρετίσατο αὐτὴν εἰς κατοικίαν ἑαυτῷ; "*For the Lord hath chosen Zion; he hath desired it for his habitation.*"

[170] The reference could be to Symeon the Stylite the Elder (ca. 389–459), who established himself on a pillar at Qal'at Sem'ān (see further *ODB*, s.v. "Saint Symeon the Stylite the Elder"), but is more likely to be to Symeon the Stylite the Younger (see above, Chap. 25); the use of the adjective "wondrous" (θαυμαστός) here may suggest that Gregory the Cellarer has him in mind through association with his "wondrous mountain" near Antioch, which, of course, Lazaros had visited on his way back from Jerusalem.

[171] See above, Chap. 28.

whatever seems right to you!" When the monks heard this from the father, they considered <their position> carefully and then, after discussing it thoroughly with each other, left Lazaros there and went away. They went off to the hill called Hypselos,[172] above the village of Legos; they found a place where there was a spring, and there they built a monastery. It is still standing today and bears the name of the monk Hilarion.[173]

33. Not much time had elapsed after the departure of these men before some <others>, who had renounced the world and the things of the world, chose to live together <there> with Lazaros. Indeed, they received the monastic habit from him and were well shepherded by him. When a considerable number were gathered together there, it became necessary to build cells for their repose and <other> needs and also <to build> a house of prayer, for the church that was there before was much too small. As far as the construction of the cells went, some of the Christian faithful became the <monks'> fellow laborers, but the building of the church <was made possible by> a woman called Iouditta, who came from the country of Calabria and lived at "the Beloved" [Ephesus].[174] This woman was brought by her great faith to the father and built the church of St. Marina; she also adopted the father's brother as a son. <This was> Ignatios, who was then a child, but now, through the grace and favor of Christ, is our superior; when he was a boy of about eight, he ran

[172] That is, "High."

[173] Note that the form of the name here is different from that given in the previous chapter (Hilarios); this may be due to a simple error, but perhaps Gregory the Cellarer was mistaken in deriving the name of this monastery from Lazaros' former companion at St. Marina. Morris (*Monks,* 155) is evidently mistaken in suggesting that this Hilarion (Hilarios?) was a spiritual son of Lazaros and one of his successors on Galesion. Kaplan (*Les hommes,* 31) also mistakenly understands this passage to indicate that the monastery of Hilarion was the same place as St. Marina.

[174] It seems reasonable to follow Delehaye's argument here (p. 519 [2]) and take the expression "The Beloved" (ὁ Ἠγαπημένος) as referring to Ephesus. The city had been known as "[the city of] the Theologian" (τοῦ Θεολόγου), after St. John the Theologian, as early as the 9th century, and it would thus be natural for this other epithet of St. John to be applied to it as well (see Jn. 21:7, 20). This is certainly how Gregory of Cyprus understood the term here (chap. 25, *AASS,* Nov. 3:598D). The same expression is used again in Chaps. 56 and 60. See also here Foss, *Ephesus,* 117, 121 n. 21. Note that Gregory of Cyprus attributes to Iouditta the financing of the church of the Savior on Galesion, rather than that at St. Marina.

away from the maternal embrace and came to the father and chose to live together with him.[175] [520] So, by the consideration and favor of God who loves men, the place became a monastery with the building of the church and the cells.

34. <Most of> their food was provided by the faithful Christians who lived nearby, but the metropolitan of Ephesus (<this> was Theodore)[176] also granted them some land to work, because of the faith he had in the father; by working this they also produced quite a lot of food from it. Once, then, they sowed beans in one part, but after these had grown and produced a crop, everyone who passed by there went in and took some because this land was close to the road. When the monks saw how the <beans> were being gobbled up, so to speak, by everyone every day, they went to the father and said that either they should harvest them early, or else that some of the brothers should go and stand there to chase off the people when they were about to go into the <bean field>, "so that we don't lose them altogether," they said.[177] The father did not let them do either of these things, however, but said instead, "Leave them to be eaten by everyone like this, for God is able to make a lot

[175] Chap. 81, below, also reveals that Ignatios was able to report on the details of Lazaros' diet at St. Marina from a time three years prior to his move up onto Galesion; he must thus have been with him in the community there by then, but the implication is that he could not provide any information before that time. Ignatios thus either only ran away to join his brother toward the end of his seven-year period at St. Marina or else (and this seems more likely from what is said in the present chapter) ran away from home earlier, but then spent some time in the care of Iouditta before moving into the monastery. The fact that he accompanied Lazaros when he made his final move up to the cave at the site of the later monastery of the Savior (below, Chap. 53) might also support the idea that he spent some time in this woman's care, for such an undertaking would seem more appropriate to a youth of fourteen or fifteen than to a boy of eleven. Further on the problems of chronology raised by Ignatios' age here, see the Introduction, section B, n. 25.

[176] This Theodore should perhaps be identified with the Theodore II of Ephesus who is listed by M. Le Quien, *Oriens Christianus* (Paris 1740; repr. Graz 1958), 1:686. Delehaye expresses doubts about the trustworthiness of Le Quien's source here, the *vita S. Sisinnii,* but if it correctly suggests that this Theodore was in office when Romanos (III Argyros) was ruling (1028–34), then he would have been the same metropolitan who opposed Lazaros' initial move onto Galesion in 1018 or 1019; see below, Chap. 53. Another, obviously later, metropolitan of Ephesus, Euthymios, is named in Chap. 114.

[177] On the need to protect fields of crops from theft, see also Chap. 243, below.

from a little, just as <He can also do> the opposite." When the time came for harvesting the <beans>, the brothers were urged by the father to go out and cut them, but they did not obey because, as it seemed to them and as it appeared to everyone <else>, there was no hope of getting anything from them. They were persuaded, however, although only with difficulty, and went out; after they had harvested <the beans> and taken them to the threshing floor and broken them up, <they discovered that> they were going to get double <the amount> they had grown.[178] When the brothers saw this miracle, they blamed and criticized themselves, but they extolled Lazaros in their amazement and gave glory to God for the grace[179] of such a marvel. Thus God knows how to glorify and send down His gifts in abundance on those who truly love Him and are eager to fulfill His commandments properly.

35. He persevered there for seven years,[180] standing on his pillar in the open air, burnt by the blazing heat of summer and chilled by the frost of winter.[181] As regards his clothing, he kept his body tightly bound with irons; these stretched from his shoulders to his loins, <which were enclosed> in another circular iron belt fastened to both sides;[182] under his armpits another girdle encircled him, and to this were fastened the middle parts of the irons, which

[178] There is evidently a small lacuna in the text at this point, although the sense is clear. Gregory of Cyprus' version of the *vita* here speaks of the harvested beans, which had previously seemed to be merely husks, overflowing the threshing floor (chap. 23, *AASS*, Nov. 3:597D). For other examples of the miraculous provision or multiplication of food in the *vita*, see below, Chaps. 209–14.

[179] The phrase "the grace" is not in the original manuscript but is supplied by Delehaye.

[180] The same figure is also given for Lazaros' stay at St. Marina in Chap. 254, below.

[181] This element of Lazaros' ascetic endurance is stressed below in Chaps. 111 and 235; cf. Chap. 59. Rather similar descriptions of the conditions in which various ascetics lived are found in Theodoret, *Hist. Rel.*, e.g., 18.1 (Eusebius of Asikha), 21.3 (James of Cyrrhestica), 26.28 (Symeon Stylites the Elder). Most of the present chapter, however, from "burnt by the blazing heat" to "the sacred scapular" is drawn almost word for word from the *vita* of St. Stephen the Younger, Chap. 20, PG 100:1104C; see now M.-F. Auzépy, *La Vie d'Etienne le Jeune par Etienne le Diacre* (Aldershot, 1997), 114.

[182] Perhaps to both of the shoulder "straps"; however the phrase ἐξ ἀμφοῖν τῶν μερῶν might also be taken as "at front and back"; cf. Auzépy's translation of the *vita* of St. Stephen the Younger, chap. 20, p. 207.

came down from his shoulders.[183] He had a single tunic of leather,[184] but he also wore the holy cowl, the stole decorated with crosses, and likewise the sacred scapular.[185] He had a small <specially> constructed seat to rest on, and he would partake of a moment of sleep while sitting on this.[186] His food used to be barley bread and his drink water, but three years before[187] he had even given up eating the bread and <simply> ate pulses and vegetables, some raw and some cooked without oil.[188]

36. Because the father was living in this superior way and thus drew everyone to him like a beacon by the brilliant illumination of his lifestyle,[189] and

[183] Although the general picture is obvious, the precise configuration of the "irons" being described is not entirely clear and the punctuation of Delehaye's text has been emended to allow the present translation; generally such irons seem to have formed a symbolic cross shape, as they are said to have done in the *vita* of St. Stephen the Younger, although the author of the *vita* of Lazaros omits this element here, perhaps suggesting that his irons were slightly different from those described in the hagiographical model. For an illustration of ascetic equipment that would appear to approximate quite closely what is being described here, see Hackel, *Byz. Saint,* 125. For the use of such irons in the patristic tradition, see, e.g., Theodoret, *Hist. Rel.,* 21.8 (James of Cyrrhestica). There may be an indication in Chap. 179, below, that Lazaros' irons were kept as a relic in the monastic church after his death.

[184] Further on Lazaros' leather tunic, see below, Chaps. 82 and 112; he reportedly wore one such garment for twelve years, and he had evidently adopted this style of dress before settling in the region of Galesion; see above, Chap. 26. The *vita Danielis* (chap. 22) makes it clear that St. Symeon the Younger also wore a similar garment, which was allegedly inherited by Daniel. At the same time Gregory the Cellarer is making an allusion, which would also be understood by his audience, to the common use of this phrase to denote the mortal, natural, human body and all that goes with it, thus stressing Lazaros' exposure and "nakedness" on his pillar; see Lampe, *Lexicon,* s.v. χιτών, B.

[185] The word ἐπωμίς in this context indicates the scapular; a normal part of monastic dress, this consisted of a sleeveless outer garment resting on the shoulders and covering front and back. Cf. Talbot, *Holy Women,* 184, 200, 224, 230. See also below, Chaps. 57 and 160.

[186] See above, Chap. 17.

[187] Reading πρὸ for πρὸς. I am grateful to an anonymous reader for this suggestion.

[188] This tallies exactly with what Gregory the Cellarer says below in Chap. 81; he cites Lazaros' brother Ignatios as his source there. Kaplan (*Les hommes,* 31) refers to this description of Lazaros' diet.

[189] Similar images are used of Lazaros in Chaps. 111 and 128, below; cf. Chap. 2, above.

because the monastery was near the road, everyone that passed by there used to go up to him, one for spiritual help, another out of physical need, and another again due to some crisis in his life; but not one of those who went up to him was <ever> seen to return from there without having received the proper medicine for his sickness. For all who went up to him grieving over their particular misfortunes joyfully returned home from him, giving glory to God. When, however, Lazaros saw himself being mobbed in this way by everybody every day, and especially because the monastery, as has been mentioned, lay near the road, and his ears were thus ringing with the voices of travelers and overseers and farm workers in the fields, he began to seek a quiet place that would enable him to get away from the annoyance of this mass of people. Now Mt. Galesion stood right there, and it happened not only to be impassable and craggy and very rugged, but was in addition waterless, and for these reasons was able to offer much tranquility to the person who went there. Lazaros thus decided that it was just the right place for him and he knew that he had to go up onto it and make his home there, especially because he learned from many people that there was a cave on it in which, many years before, a monk called Paphnoutios had ended his days in asceticism. <Now> I have decided that it is appropriate to add the story of this holy man like some seasoning to the present work for the edification of my readers, just as I heard it from our holy father Lazaros himself.

37. This Paphnoutios came from an Athenian family, but left his homeland while he was still young and went off to Rome. He shut himself up somewhere there in a very confined cell and traversed the path of asceticism with success. Adding daily to the wonderful accumulation of his good works, he was raised to the pinnacle of the virtues and thenceforth he became abundantly rich in the grace of the spirit and was proven to be a most holy worker of miracles. Within a short time <Paphnoutios'> reputation spread everywhere and all those who had been stricken with incurable diseases and the attacks of demons started coming to him; through his entreaties to God each person was relieved from the disease afflicting him and returned to his home rejoicing. [521] But because this man was doing so well and his fame was spreading everywhere more <and more> obviously and making him well known to everyone, and because the Lord and God of all was being glorified through him, the situation became intolerable to the Evil One. He was beside himself with rage at <Paphnoutios> and started seeking to contrive some way in which he could trip him up and strike him down. And, as it happened, the Most Evil

One did have the strength, with God's permission, to trip <Paphnoutios> up, even though in the end he was unable to exult in his perdition.

38. For the Evil One took possession of a girl, who was the child of rich parents, and started to disturb her;[190] using her tongue he would shriek and say, "Unless you take me to Paphnoutios the servant of God, I won't come out." When the girl's parents heard this from the demon, they took the child and went to the holy man. As soon as they came near his cell the evil spirit convulsed her and screamed in a loud voice, "I'm coming out of the child, I'm coming out, servant of God," and it came out of her. The girl's parents praised God and thanked the holy man very much and then picked her up and started back toward their own house, rejoicing. But, when they had gone some distance from <Paphnoutios'> cell, the girl suddenly began to be disturbed by the demon again and to call for the holy man by name, just as before. So the parents took her up again and returned to the holy man and, as they were approaching the cell, the demon again let out the same cries as the first time and came out of her. The demon did this a third time and, when the girl's parents saw this, they left her there and went away. But now, when the demon saw that the parents had gone away and had left the girl alone with the holy man, it left off convulsing her and <instead> entered into <Paphnoutios> without being seen. It started to trouble him with illicit thoughts and then it attacked him more <and more> violently until, after it had broken down the strength of his resistance to the idea, it persuaded him to have sexual intercourse with the girl and then actually to murder her. However, when he, like David of old, had already been persuaded by the wicked demon to add murder to lust, God sent his conscience to him, just as <He sent> Nathan the prophet to <David>, and it began to reproach him and to point out more <and more>

[190] As Delehaye points out (n. 1, p. 521), there is a close parallel to this section of the story about Paphnoutios (Chaps. 38 and 39) in the *vita* of St. Jacob the Monk (*BHG* 770); he cites the *AASS*, Ian. 2:869–73 (see esp. 871–73), which gives the Latin text. The Greek text is edited by R. Trautmann and R. Klostermann, "Drei griechische Texte zum Codex Suprasliensis," *ZslPh* 12 (1935), 282–92 (chaps. 8–33); cf. PG 114:1220–30 (where the Greek text breaks off half way through). There is also a summary of it in the *SynaxCP*, 128–30; cf. Laiou, "Sex," 217. In this story the ascetic Jacob, who lives near Samaria, has the possessed daughter of rich and eminent parents brought to him to be cured. As with Paphnoutios, however, he is the ultimate object of the Devil's attack, to which he succumbs by raping and then murdering the girl who has been left in his charge. As an act of atonement he shuts himself up in a tomb, described (significantly, in view of Chap. 39 here) as σπηλιοειδές (Chap. 25, 1.14).

clearly the outrageousness of what he had done.[191] Then <Paphnoutios> began to weep and cry out, "*I have sinned against the Lord,*"[192] and he implored God that his crime might be disregarded and his sin forgiven him.

39. Then the merciful God, Who loves men and does not wish for the death of a sinner but rather that he may turn back and live,[193] saw that <Paphnoutios> was truly repentant, and He did not delay in <bringing about> his salvation. He sent an angel and told <Paphnoutios> to leave Rome and go to Asia, if he wanted to be forgiven his sin, and He gave him instructions concerning the location and the name of the mountain [Galesion]. <Paphnoutios> left Rome at once and came to Asia and, with the guidance of the angel, came up onto this mountain. He entered the cave and spent three years in it, never ever standing upright, never looking up, and never uttering the name of God with his lips, for he was trembling and afraid[194] and, in his extreme humility, thought himself unworthy of the invocation of such a name. <He found> his food from the plants which grew in front of the cave and his drink was the water that trickled down from the rock above it and was caught by that below, lying stagnant where it was hollowed out a little; and to this day the <cave> preserves the name it acquired from the holy man.[195] But when this three-year period came to an end, an angel of the Lord appeared to him and said, "Get up and stand on your feet, and give glory to God because He has forgiven you your sin." After the angel had said these words to him and had left him, the holy man got up, stood upright and offered praise to God according to the angel's instructions. Thereafter he went on living on the mountain, feeding himself on the plants that grew there and begging God that he might either be eaten by a wild animal or else be killed by someone, which <in fact is what> happened.

40. One day, then, <Paphnoutios> climbed up above the cave to a large

[191] See 2 Ki. 11–12. The reference is to the episode in which David makes Bathsheba pregnant and then contrives the death of her husband, Uriah, so that he may marry her. He is reproached for his actions by the prophet Nathan and, although David is forgiven, the child born to Bathsheba is killed by God as punishment.

[192] 2 Ki. 12:13; the statement was originally made by David.

[193] As was noted above, this loose quotation from Ezek. 33:11 appears in almost exactly the same form in Chap. 20.

[194] Cf. Mk. 5:33.

[195] Cf. below, Chap. 41; an icon of the holy man evidently hung inside it once the community of the Savior had developed (Chap. 45).

plant[196] (called the chickpea) in order to gather its fruit to sustain himself. While he was standing <there> collecting this, a shepherd passed opposite the cave with his flock and, seeing him, thought that he was a wild animal; he drew his bow and let fly at him with an arrow, striking him in the ribs. The saint took the blow without a moan and without making any untoward sound; instead he at once set his tongue to giving thanks. Then he twisted his hand round and pulled the arrow out of his ribs while praising God in a loud voice as best he could and climbed down from the plant. The shepherd heard the holy man's voice and went running to the cave; when he saw that he had struck a man, he wanted to kill himself. The holy man, however, restrained him from this impulse by summoning him in a gentle voice and, when he came, made him pick him up and carry him into the cave. After the shepherd had brought him into the cave, the holy man saw him sobbing and weeping bitterly and said to him, "Do not weep, do not grieve over me, brother, for it is not you who have murdered me, but I who have killed myself," and he related everything that had happened to him. <Paphnoutios> then instructed <the shepherd> to bury him, after his departure to God, in the right-hand part of the cave where he used to come in and rest while he was alive; <he also told> him to go away and, [522] when he had settled up his own affairs properly, return to the cave and make his home there. After he had given him these <instructions>, Paphnoutios was silent for a while and then, lifting up his hands, he quoted the <saying>, "Glory be to thee, O Lord my God, Who have thus arranged my affairs so well,"[197] and gave up his holy soul. The shepherd sprinkled <Paphnoutios'> holy corpse with many tears in place of hymns and chants and laid him to rest in the right-hand part of the cave; he went off and settled up his own affairs properly and then returned and entered the cave where he stayed until his death. He too lived a worthy life and received the kingdom of heaven in exchange for the many tears <he shed> over his accidental act of murder. They took the body of the holy Paphnoutios to Constantinople, but some pious people divided up the remains of the shepherd one way and another, and only his holy skull was left behind, which is preserved to this

[196] Lit. "tree" (δένδρον); it would seem, however, that this must be understood here, and shortly below, in the attested sense of a large plant (so the "mustard" [σίναπι] of Mt. 13.32; see Liddell-Scott-Jones, *Lexicon*, s.v. for other examples), since Gregory the Cellarer must have been aware that chickpeas do not grow on trees.

[197] I have been unable to identify the source of this quotation.

day in a vessel, lying in the church of the Savior.[198] God thus knows how to wound the Enemy with his own arrows and, in His love for men, how to heal through repentance those wounded by that <Evil One>; and also how to send that Disgraced One to perdition. Anyway, that is the story of the holy Paphnoutios.

41. Since our father Lazaros, as has already been made clear, was contemplating the ascent of the mountain, he got up in the night without the knowledge of any of his companions and went up toward it. But as he began to climb up he decided that he ought first to go up and see the stylite who was on Petra above the village,[199] for he was ascending from there and had heard that this man wanted to leave his pillar. For this reason Lazaros was going up to him to ask if the place was suitable for his purpose so that, when <the stylite> left, he might move in himself. <Lengths of> wood had been fastened to the rock with other <slats> lying flat on top of them (indeed the peg which is still now to be seen fastened to Petra bears witness to this), and there was a rope tied at both ends on either side, which those going up used as a guide. The father, using the same method, thus started up toward the stylite, stepping on the <slats> of wood; but, when he had already reached the middle of the rock, the rope he was holding with his hand as a guide suddenly broke and he fell on his face onto the <slats> of wood. This was all the work of the Evil One and a contrivance <designed> to kill him by making him fall down from there. But the grace of God, which was always with him and kept him safe everywhere, rendered that <Evil> One's devices useless, for Lazaros stood up and, holding onto the rock with his hands and going little by little, set off <again> toward the stylite. When, <however>, he saw and spoke with the man, he

[198] The name of Lazaros' first community on Galesion, which grew up in the vicinity of the cave where Paphnoutios had lived.

[199] Although the Greek word (πέτρα) could be translated here simply as "the rock," Chaps. 159 and 175 refer to the place as (literally) "the pillar of the rock," in a way which would appear to indicate that the phrase was used as a proper name by the community, presumably to distinguish this natural pillar from Lazaros' constructed pillars elsewhere on the mountain. Delehaye certainly takes it in this way in the text (where the word is capitalized), as does Janin, *Églises centres,* 241. Elsewhere in the present chapter, however, I differ from Delehaye in taking the word as a common noun.

Chap. 159 makes it clear that the village to which reference is made is that of Galesion; mention is made there and in Chap. 175 of at least three other stylites from Lazaros' community who subsequently lived on the pillar. Chap. 175 also appears to indicate that there was a chapel dedicated to the Savior there.

learned from him that the place was unsuitable for spiritual peace, "For I myself," said <the stylite>, "am about to withdraw from this place for this <very> reason."[200] He advised Lazaros to set off for holy Paphnoutios' cave, and so, after he had come down from there, he started up the mountain, singing as he climbed. But when he reached the rock where there is the extremely narrow passage, he finished the office he was singing and, being about to say the prayer, stretched out his right hand and made the sign of the cross on the rock; he kissed it, said his prayer, and <then> passed the place. The cross is still visible now carved <in the rock>, for it was engraved afterward on the father's order as a phylactery for those passing by there.[201] When he reached the cave he went in and looked round and, since it was to his liking, he stayed in it for six months. He used to go out and wander around the mountain, but return to it again and go inside.

42. But who could describe the temptations from the demons which Lazaros experienced while he was living there alone? For, even after the mountain was made into a city and became another heaven, as one might say, with the ceaseless hymn singing and divine liturgies of the monks, some of our brothers experienced these <temptations>, and especially in the cave itself and in the gorge. So I am going to describe a few of the many such <incidents> as evidence for you, so that you may know from these <stories> what sort of temptations the holy Lazaros experienced, when he was alone on this mountain. When the church of the Savior was being built,[202] one of the workmen went out to the lower part of the monastery in order to cut wood for the construction of the church. After he had cut it and picked it up and was about to leave the place, he suddenly saw someone appear before him in the dress of an Ishmaelite [Arab] with wild eyes and <disheveled> hair on his head. This man tried to lure him to the highest point of the gorge by telling him that he would find there whatever wood he wanted, but <the workman> knew from

[200] Although, as Chap. 53 makes clear, he was still there six months later. In Chap. 159 a subsequent stylite is also said to have been bothered by noise from the village, which was evidently just below.

[201] Further on this spot, which is evidently to be identified with the region of Chalkos Halonios, see below, Chaps. 56, 77, 154, and 155; also, perhaps, Chap. 199. It was apparently much feared by the monks in the community.

[202] This is the only mention in the *vita* of the actual development of Lazaros' first community on the mountain, which came to be known as "the Savior" after the dedication of its church. The date is probably thus sometime in the early 1020s.

his dress who he was. When he invoked the father's blessing and made the sign of the cross, the man who was luring him immediately became invisible and he arrived back at the monastery with the wood without having suffered anything bad from the Evil One.[203]

43. A monk called Symeon began begging the father that he might go and live in the cave. The father would not allow him to do this because, as he said to him, he would be incapable of enduring the temptations of the demons. However, when the monk began to pressure the father, arguing forcibly to this end, Lazaros was won over and urged him to go off and live there. So <Symeon> went off and stayed there for some time without being tempted by the demons. But one night, as he stood praying, he saw, so he said, the whole cave filled with sparkling coals.[204] Straightaway then it seemed to him that some <demons> fell on him with a shout and, having laid hold of him, one of his head and the other of his feet, they suddenly hurled him to the ground; and they hit him so <hard> that he became unconscious from such a beating. After they had beaten him a great deal they lifted him up in the air and, taking him to the mouth of the cave, suspended him there until the *semantron* [205] of the church struck; [523] then, when the *semantron* was struck, they threw him to the ground there and went away. The monk came to himself after a little while, got up, and then went running to the <monastery of the> Savior.[206] When he entered the church he did not pray, nor make the sign of the cross on his face, nor prostrate himself to the brothers (as was the rule), but as soon as he entered he fell flat on his back on the floor in front of the icon of the Savior; he lifted up his right hand and <raised> his eyes, which were wild, and began

[203] Other stories of demonic apparitions in the form of ragged men appear in Chaps. 218 and 243; the latter also includes the theme of luring the victim over a cliff, one which appears in several other episodes in the *vita,* e.g., Chap. 47, 131–34. Cf. here also, Chap. 51.

[204] The word translated by "sparkling" here, σπινθηρακοειδής, is not in the standard lexica; it seems to be a mixture of σπινθηρακώδης (Lampe, *Lexicon,* s.v.) and σπινθηροειδής (Liddell-Scott-Jones, *Lexicon;* Lampe, *Lexicon,* s.v.), both meaning "like a spark." Cf. the incident described below in Chap. 49, which refers back to this episode.

[205] The *semantron* was a long piece of metal or wood that was struck or hammered to summon the monks to church and to indicate other important moments in the monastic routine; the device is still in use today. See further *ODB,* s.v. "Semantron."

[206] The monastery of the Savior was evidently a short distance below the cave; see below, Chap. 52.

saying to the Savior things like: "Christ, do You find this good that You let us be tempted like this by the demons?" And, still lying on the ground, he went on saying other <such> things until church finished, as though he were crazy. After the end of the service the brothers stood him up and, after they had made inquiry, found out from him what he had suffered from the demons in the cave. Then they took <Symeon> up and led him off to the father (for the father was then alone on the pillar of the Theotokos),[207] and Symeon recounted to Lazaros everything that had happened to him. The father ordered that the holy Gospel should be read to him and, when one of the brothers had done this in accordance with the father's order, the monk was seen to be sober again and sound in mind as before.[208]

44. Another monk, called John, was praying at night while standing somewhere in the middle of the gorge; he had his eyes and his hands raised to heaven, when he suddenly discovered a sow with her piglets[209] moving about at his feet. This scared him so much and made him <so> afraid, that he gave up his prayer and quickly left the place and never went back there again. Another monk, called Antony, spent some time in the cave, and he too experienced many temptations from the demons there. Once, so he said, they threw stones at him, another time they fell on him and beat him mercilessly, and another time again they called him by name and showed him various illusions.

45. Then <there is> the monk Ignatios (the nephew of the monk Matthew)[210] who, when he was still a boy, went into the cave with another boy to

[207] This would suggest that the incident must have taken place shortly after Lazaros moved up from the monastery of the Savior to his second pillar on the mountain at what was to become the community of the Theotokos; see below, Chaps. 57–58. Chap. 50, which also uses the same phrase, must thus be roughly contemporary.

[208] Reading the Gospels over a victim of possession or demonic assault is a standard exorcistic or apotropaic practice employed by Lazaros on several occasions; see, e.g., Chaps. 47, 70, and 74. On Byzantine exorcism in general and for further references, see *ODB*, s.v. "Exorcism"; in the context of 11th-century hagiography, see Joannou, *Démonologie*, 21–27, 45–46; see also Greenfield, *Demonology*, 135–48, 264–65, 270–71.

[209] The word translated here as "piglets" (χοιρογρύλλιος) is used in the *LXX* for a coney; it seems that elsewhere it was also understood as meaning a hedgehog. It was regarded as unclean.

[210] The term ἀνεψιός is translated as "nephew" here, although the precise relationship it implies is not always easy to define. It may be nephew or cousin; see Laiou, "Sex," 175 n. 2.

draw water. While he was standing over the cistern[211] he saw a man with a terrifying appearance coming down from the part where the conduit is, holding in his hand a stick with an iron tip. <The man> immediately hit him with this. As soon as he had been struck by him, the boy fell to the ground as though dead.[212] When the boy who was with him saw <Ignatios> lying <there> like this, he began to cry and called out to the monk who was there. The <monk> came in and, seeing the boy lying there in this way as though he were dead, prostrated himself in front of the icon of the holy Paphnoutios and said the *trisagion;*[213] afterward he took oil from the lamp and anointed <Ignatios> and made him stand up.[214] <The monk> filled <the boy's> clay pot and led them out of the cave; then, when he had escorted them a little way, he turned back. <Ignatios>, however, was barely able to reach the <monastery of the> Theotokos (for it was from there that he had been sent), and he spent the next eighteen months lying <there> seriously ill. Indeed, his illness was so bad that he was unable to get out of his bed, and had to be lifted by other people and carried in order to relieve himself; this was because his calves were stuck to his thighs. Even worse, however, he was unable to take any food since he would vomit up again whatever he consumed. When the father heard this, he sent some of the brothers and made them carry <the boy> to him, for he was then on the pillar of the holy Resurrection.[215] <Lazaros> gave <Ignatios> some of his own food (it was boiled pulse that he gave him without oil) and persuaded him to eat from it even though he did not want to. Then he gave orders that

[211] The construction and renovation of this cistern is described below in Chap. 53; cf. Chap. 39, above.

[212] There is quite a close parallel to this apparition in the story of Ioannikios, recounted below in Chap. 233.

[213] The *trisagion* refers to the "thrice-holy" hymn, the *sanctus* or "Holy, Holy, Holy" acclamation of Is. 6:3, Rev. 4:8; (ἅγιος ὁ θεός· ἅγιος ἰσχυρός· ἅγιος ἀθάνατος· ἐλέησον ἡμᾶς). It formed part of the eucharistic prayer but could also, as here, be used by itself. See *ODB,* s.v. "Trisagion." Cf. below, Chaps. 107 and 114.

[214] Anointing with various holy oils, often sanctified by proximity to or contact with other holy objects, forms another basic element in exorcistic rituals described in the *vita,* as in standard Byzantine practice; cf. Chaps. 71 and 76, below. Further see, *ODB,* s.v. "Healing," "Oil," "Unction"; also Joannou, *Démonologie,* 24.

[215] This reference to Lazaros' third and final foundation on the mountain dates the story to the last phase of his life, between 1042 and 1053.

<the boy> should be given *paximadia*[216] and wine and, after he had said a prayer for him, dismissed him. So, from then on, <Ignatios> gradually got over his illness and returned again to his former health.

46. The monk Neilos, while still a layman, was told by the cellarer[217] to go out from the <monastery of the> Savior and show the way <down> to some laymen who had come there for a blessing. After he had done this, he left them and started back. But when he was in the middle of the southern stream, suddenly, although it was clear weather and broad daylight, it seemed to get dark around him; indeed <it was> so <dark> that he could not even see himself. He gazed up at the sky and thought that he could see the stars; so, looking carefully at these, he worked out the way to the <monastery of the> Savior from their positions and went on. When he got near the monastery, he turned his eyes to the ground but saw nothing in front of him, for everything was completely dark; the only thing that he <could> see, so he said, was the dome of the church. He knew <then> where he was and began to call out the <usual>, "Bless <me>,[218] Kyris Ioannikios!"[219] (for this was the cellarer's name). When <Ioannikios> replied "Bless <you>!" the darkness left him at once and the stars were no longer shining in the sky, but it was light and day again. So he glorified God Who, through the appearance of the stars, had

[216] *Paximadia* are small pieces of bread baked twice to form hard rusks. See *ODB*, s.v. "Bread."

[217] He is identified below as Ioannikios. The office of cellarer, which was one of the more important in Byzantine monastic organization, primarily involved supervision of the material supplies required by the community and hence required close cooperation not only with the *hegoumenos*, but also with other leading officials such as the *oikonomos*, the sacristan, the guestmaster, etc. The author of the *vita*, Gregory, was himself cellarer at the monastery of the Resurrection (see esp. Chap. 170, below), and he mentions other holders of this office, as well as that of *parakellarios* (apparently the assistant cellarer).

[218] On this common form of greeting between ecclesiastics, see Lampe, *Lexicon*, s.v. εὐλογέω, VI; cf. also below, Chaps. 64, 91, and 208.

[219] The term "Kyris," a form of *kyrios* ("Lord"), is an honorific demonstrating the respect of the layman Neilos for the cellarer of the monastery. It is also used below of the superior, Ignatios (Chaps. 81 and 221); the distinguished lay visitor, Theophylact Sagopoulos (Chap. 107); Pachomios, the *ekklesiarches* of Limnai (Chap. 209); Lazaros himself (Chap. 235); and the visiting dignitary Nicholas (Chap. 238). Another variant, "Kyr," is used for the visiting superior Michael (Chap. 237), and also appears in the nickname "Kyr Eulogesos," used of the monk Nicholas (Chaps. 48 and 178).

miraculously rescued him from the illusion of darkness <caused> by the wicked demons, and went into the monastery.[220] [524]

47. And who can give an appropriate account of what happened to the monk Philippikos?[221] How first the wicked demons made him believe in their illusions and then led him into such conceit that he said, "Angels escort me in procession and bring me into the church."[222] <Later on, however,> when they saw that he had followed the advice of the holy father and had turned away from their deceit, they entrapped him in another way, for they abandoned such illusions and attacked him brazenly, clouding his mind and causing him to lose control of his actions and his speech. For, when he was standing in the church and singing with the other brothers, he suddenly bent his head and his knees and fell onto his face, and he lay there until the brothers made him stand up again. After they had raised him up, however, he stood there, rolling his eyes horribly this way and that. Another time when he was standing singing with the brothers, he was spun round like a bobbin,[223] and he did many other such things that made the brothers who saw them laugh. Once, when <Philippikos> had left the <monastery of the> Savior to go to the father at the <pillar of the> Theotokos and had already reached the middle of the gorge, the demons suddenly grabbed him by the hair and flung him to the ground; they <then> began dragging him toward the eastern part of the mountain. They had already dragged him a considerable distance and were starting to climb up, when the father, who was standing on his pillar, saw him. He sent the monk Meletios (called Mavros [Dark]), who happened to be standing there, to grab hold of him so that the demons would not take him up to the summit and hurl him off; for that was their intention. So the brother ran off very quickly toward him but, when he saw <Philippikos> going up <hill> like that, lying on his back and being dragged by invisible <demons>, he was astounded. He took courage in the holy father's blessing, however, and, invoking this for help, went up to him and stood him up; then, taking him with him, he returned

[220] Compare here stories of demonic blinding related below in Chaps. 52, 174, and 218.

[221] I am grateful to an anonymous reader for suggesting this translation.

[222] Compare the somewhat similar but more elaborate episode described below in Chap. 49 and the parallels cited there.

[223] The rare word ἀνέμη is evidently used of anything that spins round fast, such as a windlass, reel, spool, or bobbin. Cf. Trapp, *Lexikon,* s.v., where the meaning "Winde, Haspel, (Garn)spule" is given.

to the father. Another time again when he had been stupefied by the demons, <Philippikos> left the <monastery of the> Savior and ran to the steep <part> of the gorge, and if the brothers had not run more quickly and grabbed him, he would certainly have flung himself over <the edge>. Often, too, while the <demons> were walking about,[224] they would throw stones at him so that, as a result, he could not go out anywhere by himself. However, the Savior, as He is good, healed this man by the prayers of our blessed father, by the laying on of the holy cross (which had been made by his own hands), and by the reading of the holy Gospel.[225]

48. Another monk, called Sabas, was in his cell when he thought he saw thieves coming into the monastery.[226] He went out<side> and, as he <still> saw them, started summoning the brothers, but the <thieves> immediately became invisible. <Sabas>, realizing they were demons and not men, was terror-stricken and began to tremble. The monk Nicholas, whose other name was Kyr Eulogesos,[227] was also convinced by the illusions of the demons that he was seeing revelations, and, even though he was admonished many times by the father not to believe in them, was not dissuaded. So, since God did not want <Nicholas'> labors to be wasted because he had been led astray by illusions of this kind <caused> by the wicked demons, for he struggled to the best of his ability, He allowed him too to be tested physically by the demons. One night, as he was coming out of his cell, <Nicholas> saw an old man standing in front of him, wearing a tunic made of goat hair (which is usually called a *sthlavinikon*)[228] and carrying a bundle of wood on his shoulders. Just like the monk Sabas, <Nicholas> was also terror-stricken when he saw this man and

[224] An allusion to the activity of Satan as described in Job 1:7.

[225] The imposition of the cross, together with the reading of the Gospel and anointing with holy oil (as noted above, pp. 130, 131), forms the basic element of exorcistic rituals performed by Lazaros; cf. below, Chaps. 70, 74, and 219.

[226] Theft from the monastery was evidently a real threat, either by outsiders (cf. Chaps. 34, 144, and 245), ex-monks (Chaps. 66, 142, 240), or current brothers (Chaps. 108, 241).

[227] The sobriquet "Kyr Eulogesos" would seem to be a pun on the expression Κύριε εὐλόγησον (Lord bless <me>), a request made of the presiding minister by someone who was about to preach or to read from Scripture or the Lives of the saints; it was also written at the start of homilies and saints' Lives, etc. See Lampe, *Lexicon,* s.v. εὐλογέω, VI.

[228] On this word, see N. Oikonomides, "Quelques boutiques de Constantinople au Xe siècle," *DOP* 26 (1972), 347.

started trembling, but the Savior also cured him through the prayers of our blessed father in the same way as Philippikos.

49. Before these three, the monk Gregory (the father of the monk Cyril who became our steward)[229] was also tricked by the illusions of the demons and arrived at the ultimate evil of conceit; indeed, he got so puffed up that he lost his wits. Now, he went into the cave to celebrate holy communion—for he was also priest to those engaged in the <ascetic> struggle,[230] and it was for this reason that the demons cleverly beguiled him—and saw the whole cave glowing like burning coals, just as the monk Symeon <had done>.[231] One time it <happened> like this, but another time, when he was about to elevate the holy <sacrament>, he saw fire descending from above and enveloping the whole cave as well as himself. When he saw these things, he started to be filled with conceit and he went to the father and told him about them with pride and a conceited attitude. The father warned <Gregory> not to believe in such demonic illusions, but his mind had been blinded by them and he began to argue with him. "This is not demonic deceit but an overshadowing of the Holy Spirit," he said. "For look, the Holy Spirit told me that I should go down to the <church of the> Theologian[232] to instruct the metropolitan and all the clergy not to mingle water with the unity of the holy mysteries, but to allow only unadulterated wine <to be used>.[233] And if you don't let me go straightaway, all the Jews are going to come up here. For God also revealed this to me through the Holy Spirit: that water will gush out in this gorge like a river in order to baptize the Jews who are coming to me."[234] After <Gregory> had

[229] The steward (οἰκονόμος) was responsible for managing the properties and estates of a monastery; as such he was a senior monk usually ranked second to the superior in the monastic hierarchy. There is an excellent description of the role of the *oikonomos* in the *typikon* of Kecharitomene (Gautier, "Kécharitôménè," 55–59), and a full discussion of the office in the 11th century, with further references, in Kaplan, "Evergetis," 114–22. See also *ODB*, s.v. "Oikonomos."

[230] A priest from the Savior is said to have ministered to Lazaros when he was alone on his column at the Theotokos (Chap. 64); it seems possible that the reference is to the same man.

[231] See above, Chap. 43.

[232] At Ephesus; see above, Chap. 33.

[233] This refers to the Byzantine practice of adding warm water to the wine during the celebration of the Eucharist; see further *ODB*, s.v. "Zeon."

[234] Quite apart from any other problems in the claims being made here, Galesion was notoriously short of water, as the *vita* makes clear on several occasions.

said these and other such words, the father warned him again and taught him, providing him with references from the holy Scriptures, that monks should not believe such things nor accept them at all.[235] When, however, Lazaros saw that he was not in the least persuaded by his soothing and gentle words, he began to speak more sharply, <using> harsher words like extremely bitter medicine; but <Gregory acted> exactly as those who are deranged by their illnesses often do, for he knocked this <medicine> aside and, getting up in the night without anybody seeing him, went down to the [525] <church of the> Theologian. As soon as the father learned about <Gregory's> escape, he sent some of the brothers to look for him. They went down and, when they found him, took hold of him, tied him up, and returned to the monastery. When he came in sight of the father, however, he started to use his conceited words again and to say to him: "Lazaros, why won't you let me preach the message with which I have been entrusted by God for the salvation of many people?" As the father saw that <Gregory> had been completely enslaved by the illusions of the demons, he gave orders that his feet should be shackled with iron fetters. He also gave him a basket and made him collect the stones from the middle of the courtyard and carry them outside the monastery. When <Gregory> had filled the basket with stones, he took it on his shoulders and went and stood in front of the pillar. Then he called <up> to the father, "Hey, Lazaros, look!" The father put his head out from the pillar and said to him, "What is it?" <Gregory> replied to the father, "Look closely and <you will> understand that it was about me that the prophet David wrote all those years ago under the inspiration of the Holy Spirit; and today indeed his prophecy has reached its fulfillment. For has he not written thus?" <Here> he reached down to his feet with his hand and said, "*They hurt his feet with fetters*";[236] and

[235] Cf. a similar episode in Palladius, *Lausiaca,* chap. 25, where the monk Valens is deceived by demons into thinking he is in league with angels; he then sees a vision in which the Devil appears to him as the Savior in a fiery disk surrounded by a thousand angels carrying lamps. His consequent conceit makes him refuse to receive communion and as punishment he is put into irons for a year. Compare here, too, the somewhat similar episode in the *vita* of St. Martin of Tours concerning the monk Anatolius: *vita S. Martini,* 23, ed. and trans. J. Fontaine, *Sulpice Sévère, Vie de Saint Martin,* (Paris, 1967); this man is also deceived by demons into thinking he has direct contact with heavenly powers, while the story also mentions flashing lights. Given the uneasy relations with the church authorities in Ephesus that are apparent at various points in the *vita,* it is understandable why Lazaros was so keen that this man, with his extreme views, should not be allowed to go and preach there.

[236] Ps. 104 (105):18.

then reaching back with <his hand> to his shoulder, he added, "*his hands slaved in making the baskets.*"[237] The father gave a solemn little smile, however, and said to him, "Very good, and since, as you say, the prophet foretold these things about you long ago, go off eagerly and perform your preordained task with care." So he sent <Gregory> off to work in fetters and gave orders that he should be fed the strictest diet until such time as he forced him to acknowledge <his error> and say with his own mouth, "I was deceived by demons."

50. On one occasion, while the father was still alone on the pillar of the Theotokos,[238] the aforementioned monk Meletios[239] had gone up <to see him>. When he was about to go down from the pillar, and asked permission to descend to the <monastery of the> Savior, he heard the father say this to him: "Aren't you afraid at all when you travel alone at night?" For it was night time then. "No, father," <Meletios> replied, "because of your holy prayers." "<All right>," the father said to him, "but just be careful that you aren't overcome by fear when you reach the point where the two streams join." The brother prostrated himself and said, "Your prayers will help me and I will not be afraid"; and he went down from the pillar. When he reached the spot mentioned by the father, <Meletios> suddenly heard from both parts of the mountain <what sounded> like a lot of horses coming down and the voices of men who were apparently riding the horses. The brother was not frightened at all, for he had been prepared for this by the father's words; so, using the same words, he called back to them, repeating, "I am not scared by your illusory voices because the prayers of my holy <father> are with me." When he said this, they disappeared like smoke. <Meletios> passed the place without being afraid and went <on> down to the <monastery of the> Savior, praising God and being utterly amazed by the father's foresight.[240]

51. <Meletios> was going back to the father on another occasion when he met a man dressed in rags and wearing a sort of little head cloth on his

[237] Ps. 80 (81):6. I follow Brenton, *LXX,* although the Greek could be simply rendered "in the basket," making the quotation more appropriate here.

[238] See above, Chap. 43, where the same statement is made.

[239] If this man is to be identified with the Meletios of Chap. 142, his activities in this and the following chapter may perhaps be explained by the fact that he was in charge of the monastery's horses at some point in his career.

[240] A similar incident is recorded in Chap. 155, below, although that refers to *two* monks traveling at night and no mention is made of Meletios; the passages are so similar, however, that they may be recalling the same episode. Cf. also the story recounted in Chap. 154.

head, which was also ragged and filthy dirty. This person passed him by on the other side <of the path>[241] and then turned off the beaten track, going on foot toward the western part <of the mountain>. The monk assumed that he wanted to go to the father and had lost his way, and called out to him, "Brother, the path that leads to the father is over here." But the man replied, "May God not see him!"[242] When the brother got to the father he told him about the old man. In reply the father said, "In a little while you will learn all about this old man." Toward evening he heard that a shepherd had died after falling from the southern part of the mountain.[243]

52. After the father's death,[244] Cornelius the one-handed was sleeping at noon one day in his cell, which was in front of the cave, when, in a dream, he saw two <demons>[245] come and stand in front of him. One said to the other, "What a young man to be about to lose his eyes." After he had said this, they disappeared from sight, but when <Cornelius> woke up and opened his eyes he found that he could not see anything at all.[246] So he stood in the doorway

[241] The verb in Greek, ἀντιπαρέρχομαι, is used in Lk. 10:31–32 of the actions of the priest and the Levite who ignore the victim in the parable of the Good Samaritan. Some connotations of this story are probably intended here; the man did not simply pass Meletios but actually avoided him. The same allusion is made in Chap. 243, below (see the following note).

[242] The precise point of this negative comment is unclear. Perhaps the hope is that Lazaros will never join the ranks of the blessed in heaven; "May he go to hell!" in other words.

[243] The story, as it stands here, does not make clear the identity of the ragged old man encountered by Meletios. He may simply be the shepherd, whose rather strange actions are to be explained by the fact that he is going to commit suicide. A more likely interpretation, however, is that the author understands him as a demon who is on his way to lure the shepherd to his death; compare especially the demonic apparitions of Chaps. 42, 132, and 243 (cf. Chap. 218) and note that the same allusion found here to the parable of the Good Samaritan is made in the elaborate episode recounted in Chap. 243.

[244] The reference at the end of this chapter to Lazaros' brother Ignatios still being at Bessai when this incident occurred would suggest that it must have taken place not long after Lazaros' death in late 1053; although there were evidently problems concerning his succession to the position of superior, Chap. 100 indicates that only a short space of time elapsed before Ignatios took charge.

[245] Although it is not specified in the text, these are presumably to be understood as demons from the general context of this story.

[246] Compare other stories of blinding by demons in the *vita* in Chaps. 46, 174, and 218.

and called the brothers <out> from the <monastery of the> Savior. When they came up and saw that he was blind, they questioned him and so discovered from him how it was that he had come to suffer this; <then> they took him by the hand and guided him down to the Savior. They led him into a cell and went off and left him. After the brothers had gone, however, the <demons> he had seen before in the cell at the cave came and stood in front of him again and started to tease him, saying, "Is it good sleeping at the cave? Come on then, follow us, and we will lead you back there again and you will get your sight back." They did this for three days and would not let him rest. Then he asked the brothers to take him to the holy Resurrection, but after living on for some days, he died, <still> in this condition. The superior, the brother of our holy father,[247] who was then at Bessai,[248] saw a star burst forth from the mountain and rise up to heaven in a night vision; and he also seemed to hear a voice saying, "Behold, the star of Constantine," for that is what <Cornelius> was called when <he lived> in the outside world. [526]

I have told you these <stories, about> things which happened at various times both in the gorge and in the cave, in a group here so that, as I said before, we may understand the type and number of temptations the father had to endure when he was alone on the mountain, even if he <himself> recounted nothing because of the great humility that he possessed. And indeed, I have told these <stories here>, not all of them <it is true>, but a few among the many . . . in the cave . . . some of them happened in the <monastery of the> holy Resurrection.[249]

[247] This is Ignatios.

[248] On the monastic foundation at this place, mentioned several times in the *vita,* see the Introduction, sections E and F, pp. 31–41. See also Malamut, "Bessai," although the mention of Bessai in this particular chapter of the *vita* apparently escaped her notice (244 n. 8). Chap. 221 explains the circumstances that took Ignatios to Bessai.

[249] This passage is difficult for two reasons: the text is evidently corrupt and, as it stands in Delehaye's edition, there is a problem with the mention of the monastery of the Resurrection. The manuscript contains blank spaces at the end of the first line and the beginning and end of the second line on f. 122v; one must assume that the copyist was either unable to read the original or was perhaps indicating that there was something missing in it. Delehaye mentions the blanks in his apparatus, but does not indicate them in the text. It *is* possible to ignore the gaps and make some sense of the passage as it stands (which is evidently what Delehaye intends), and a possible translation would thus be: "I have recounted these <stories>, although they are not all of them, but <only> a few among the many, <and> some of them occurred in the cave in the <monas-

53. The father spent six months alone on the mountain, as has already been made clear,[250] but, when the metropolitan of Ephesus learned of it,[251] he made him leave the mountain by means of a personal letter and go down again to the <monastery of the> holy Marina, even though Lazaros did not want to <do this>. A little while later, however, when the metropolitan went to Constantinople, the father sent a builder and a monk to renovate the small cistern associated with the cave.[252] The <same> man who <built> the church of the Prodromos, which is called "Marmastos,"[253] constructed this <cistern> long ago. As the story goes, the old man built this <cistern> earlier so that he might live in the cave, and indeed he did live there for some time; <but then>, either because he got discouraged or because God moved him to do this, he left the cave and went down to the aforesaid church of the Prodromos, which, as has been said, he built; and there he died. When this <cistern> had been rebuilt and the winter season began and it was filled by the water that ran down the mountain, the father left the <monastery of the> holy Marina one night; he took with him the priest George (who was mentioned above),[254] his own

tery of the> Holy Resurrection." The problem here is, however, that nowhere in the *vita* is a cave associated with Lazaros' final foundation on Galesion, the Resurrection, whereas the cave of Paphnoutios at the monastery of the Savior is well attested and, indeed, its fearsome reputation is precisely what has set the author off on this particular sequence of stories. It would seem obvious from the context that this is what is being discussed, and Delehaye's reading of the text must thus be dismissed. Instead one may perhaps suggest a reconstruction of the passage along the following lines, taking into account the sections which may have been lost: "And indeed, I have told these stories <here, although they are> not all of the <possible ones, it is true,> but <only> a few among the many; <I have thus only included those that occurred> in the cave <at the monastery of the Savior, together with>, some of the ones <which> happened <in the gorge when Lazaros was living on the pillar of the Theotokos or when he was on his pillar> at the <monastery of the> Holy Resurrection."

[250] See above, Chap. 41.

[251] See above, Chap. 34, on the possible identification of this man as Theodore II of Ephesus.

[252] Chap. 45 makes it clear that this cistern and, apparently, the conduit that fed it, were inside Paphnoutios' cave; presumably it was designed to collect water from the natural source mentioned in Chap. 39. Given the notorious lack of water on the mountain, even this meager supply was important; Chap. 45 reveals that water was carried up from here to the monastery of the Theotokos.

[253] Lit. "marble breast."

[254] See Chap. 31.

brother Ignatios, and three other monks, and went up toward the mountain. Because the river was then in spate,[255] they went down. . . . [256] They crossed <it> by means of the boat. I don't know how he found out <about this>, but he had anticipated it, and was standing on the other side with a <pack> animal as well so that the father might ride it and go up in this fashion as far as the lower slopes of the mountain. He had labored in vain, however, for the father was not persuaded to do this and instead traveled on foot with his companions; he sang the psalms of David <as he went> and <only> reached the place after completing the whole psalter. <On the way> he went up and saw the stylite again,[257] and then, coming down from there, went up onto the mountain. When they got close to the cave they began trying to find it, because it was still dark; but then, while they were searching for it like this, the father <himself> happened to find it. He called out and made them go there too; then he went inside the cave with them and stood there singing psalms until day came. Lazaros blessed his <companions> and then dismissed them, but he asked them <to make sure> that one of the brothers came up once a week to bring him a pot full of water and a few pulses <soaked> in water.[258] So the <others> did obeisance and went down from the cave, but Lazaros stayed on in it until the brothers built him a pillar in the middle of the dry stream bed, open to the air, as he wished.[259] He then went onto this and was *as a sparrow*

[255] This river is probably to be identified with the Caystros; see Malamut, "Bessai," 245.

[256] There is again a problem with the text at this point. As in the previous chapter part of a line has been left blank in the manuscript, presumably indicating a break in the text in the original. Delehaye mentions the break in his apparatus but once again makes no allowance for it in his reading of the text; this causes no difficulties in the present passage, which could be translated "they went down and crossed <it> by means of the boat." It becomes obvious shortly below, however, that some material has fallen out of the text here, for the person who is said to have brought the pack animal to meet Lazaros on the other side of the river appears in the narrative without introduction or identification.

[257] See above, Chap. 41.

[258] This instruction seems to make the renovation of the cistern in the cave, which was described earlier in the chapter, rather pointless, unless it refers to a time, later in the year, when the cistern was already empty. Perhaps Gregory the Cellarer is confusing Lazaros' instructions at this point with those he must have issued when he went up onto his pillar; see below, Chap. 55.

[259] This is the pillar of the Savior.

dwelling alone on a roof,[260] although he kept company with God through his unceasing songs of praise, vigils, and prayers.

54. The Devil, however, who is the enemy of righteous men and the inventor of evil things, could not keep quiet when he saw what <was happening>, and started attacking Lazaros severely with the great variety of his evil contrivances. Once, he gathered his dogs together and attacked Lazaros, with them acting as an armed multitude of soldiers; for the most wicked one thought he would scare him by such an illusion. But his hopes turned out to be futile and in vain, for they discovered that Lazaros was fortified on every side with prayers, armored by his hope in God, carrying the sword of the spirit (which is the word of God) on his tongue, and holding the weapon of the cross in his right hand; so all at once they turned their backs, sought <a way to> escape, and went off howling to report their defeat to the one who had sent them. Another time, they stood on both parts of the mountain at night and threw stones at him, but Lazaros stood <there> again, as though his pillar was an emplacement for a catapult, and hurled prayers at them instead of stones <until> he put them to flight once more.

55. As the most Evil One was unable to trip Lazaros up by using these many various devices, he tried something else. The brother went up as usual and took Lazaros his water with the pulse but, after he had gone, <the Devil> made a scorpion come out and sting the father on the foot. Lazaros jerked his foot at the sudden blow and broke the pot that was standing there, <thus> spilling the water. When the father saw this, he decided not to eat the pulses, preferring not eating at all to eating without drinking. He remained in this state until the Friday without tasting anything at all.[261] But God, Who loves men and does not abandon His own servants in the end, even though He does allow them to be tested for a time, revealed Himself by means of an angel to a layman called Loukianos who lived in the village of Kepion;[262] because of his faith in the father and because he used to entrust his thoughts to him, he was Lazaros' spiritual son. <The angel> said, "You are sleeping without a care, but your father Lazaros is even now on the point of dying from thirst."

[260] Ps. 101 (102):7. The same passage is applied to Lazaros in Chap. 58, below.

[261] Cf. Theodoret, *Hist. Rel.,* 21.24, where a somewhat similar story of the Devil depriving James of Cyrrhestica of water is recounted.

[262] This village has already been mentioned above, Chap. 31, and it is mentioned again in Chap. 241, below.

The brother woke up and knew from the vision in his sleep what had happened to the father; so he got up, took a jar full of water, and went running up to him. When he got <there> he found Lazaros just about to die from thirst, for it was summer time. The father took the water and drank, and when he had recovered [527] he gave glory to God who had thus miraculously sent him the water by means of this brother, just as of old he sent food to Daniel in the <lions'> den by Abbakoum.[263] From that time on God gave Lazaros the grace of controlling and binding scorpions with his own hands[264] and, by stretching out his hand from the pillar to the hands <of others>, of passing it on to those outside. As a result <of this incident> he yielded to the entreaties of the brothers that one of them should go up and live in the cave to assist him because of the obstacles <put in his way> by the Evil One; and so one of them, called Kosmas, went up <there>.

56. After a short time, as Lazaros' fame had again spread among the surrounding places, some people began going up to him. A woman, called Irene, who lived at "the Beloved" [Ephesus] and who had just lost her husband, heard all about Lazaros and went up to him herself. When the woman saw him like that, persevering in that place alone and in the open air on his pillar, she was immediately struck in the heart by the arrow of salvation <and got the idea> that she herself should leave everything,[265] take the holy habit, and, if the father agreed, construct a cell for herself near him and live there with him. However, when the father had heard her <plans>, he would not let her do this right away but <instead> counseled her, gave her a rule for the conduct of her life, and then dismissed her with a blessing.[266] But she really was a disciple of Christ and another Magdalene; she did not want to be separated from the father even for an hour, and kept on going up to him day and night and provided him with anything he might need out of her own resources. But, because the wicked Devil, who does not want to see someone receiving

[263] That is, Habakkuk. For this episode, see Bel and the Dragon, 31–39.

[264] Cf. Lk. 10:19; see below, Chaps. 59 and 67, for examples of Lazaros' use of this power. For another saint who specialized in getting rid of snakes, see the Life of Ioannikios, in *Byzantine Defenders of Images*, ed. A.-M. Talbot (Washington, D.C., 1998), 255–351.

[265] Cf. Lk. 5:28.

[266] Cf. here Talbot, "Comparison," 16–17. The implication is that she now became a nun; see the following chapter.

help from another person, saw this remarkable woman properly organizing her life in accordance with our holy father's honeyed words, he did not want to keep quiet. He therefore beguiled those who lived in the village of Galesion, and especially the one who was their headman in evil rather than in office,[267] and engineered many malicious devices against her and against our holy father in order to prevent her from <following> the way up to Lazaros,[268] and, at the same time if possible, to drive him from the mountain altogether. When he[269] saw her going up to the father every day, he began to slander him to people and say, "She isn't going up to him for spiritual benefit but for sinful and shameful love-making." This is what that unholy and accursed one thought and said about those pure and blameless people. However, when he saw that his words were not achieving the desired effect because of the faith that everyone had in the father,[270] what did he do? He summoned some young men and sent them to sit by the road where the woman of God was going to pass with two other pious women; for she never went up to the father alone. He had instructed them that they should grab the women when they were about to pass by there and do to them that which it is not right to hear. <The men> went off and lay down on the rock where the passage is narrowest,[271] but they fell asleep, and so the women passed by unharmed, while the would-be rapists[272] were seen to be nothing but bad.

[267] The Greek term translated here as "headman" is πρωτεύων. For the significance of this passage in the context of understanding Byzantine village administration, see Kaplan, *Les hommes,* 200; he compares it with the passage in Chap. 63, below, which refers to village *archontes.*

[268] The original audience would undoubtedly detect a word play in the phrase "the way up" (ἄνοδος) here; superficially it indicates the physical path up the mountain, but it also alludes to the woman's spiritual ascent as a result of her visits to Lazaros.

[269] It is not clear whether this refers to the Devil himself or the headman of the village.

[270] Gregory the Cellarer apparently wishes to exonerate the villagers from any hostility toward Lazaros and place as much blame as possible on the headman and his associates; compare also the claim, expressed by Lazaros near the end of his life, that people from the "neighboring villages" would do anything for the monks of his community if they ever needed their help (below, Chap. 245).

[271] Presumably the place referred to in Chap. 41, above; see also Chaps. 77, 154, and 155.

[272] The Greek word used here is φθορεῖς; on the implications of the terms φθορά and φθορεύς, see Laiou, "Sex," 111, 119–20, 127–28, 160, 162, and 169.

57. After the father had spent twelve years at the <monastery of the> Savior, he left there and went up to the higher part of the gorge.[273] I must speak about this matter <now, and explain> the reason why he came to leave the <monastery of the> Savior and go off there, as I have learned it from those who know.[274] The aforementioned blessed woman [Irene] used to go up to Lazaros <even> more frequently after she had been tonsured. One day, when she was there and was standing in the church, the father was standing up on his pillar with the brothers standing round it, and he was rebuking one of them for some fault; this was that, when he was eating a piece of fruit, he had peeled off the skin and thrown it away as no good. But this man, instead of humbling himself as he should have done and prostrating himself so that he might receive forgiveness, dashed off brazenly from the place where he had been standing and went running into the church; there he seized the nun by her scapular[275] and led her out of the church. He brought her before the father and said, "It is this woman who is hurting me and these <others>," indicating to Lazaros the brothers who were standing there, "and not the things for which you are apparently rebuking me." The other brothers backed him up <and confirmed> that this was the case. The father was not upset by that brazen fellow's shameless outspokenness, but grew a little sad, and replied to them calmly and coolly in a sad voice, "It is not this woman who is hurting you, but I, for she only comes up here on my account." After saying this to them, he turned to the nun and said, "Go back to your cell and don't come up here any more." She prostrated herself and then went down the mountain, weeping and wailing at being deprived of the father.[276]

[273] Lazaros now moves to his second pillar, that of the Theotokos. This episode, with its theme of the abandonment by a holy man of one site for another because of pressure from visitors, is mentioned by C. Galatariotou, *The Making of a Saint* (Cambridge, 1991), 79, (although she suggests that Lazaros had spent only eleven years at the Savior and cites Chap. 43 of the *vita*).

[274] The implication is that Gregory the Cellarer did not join the community until after Lazaros had moved to the Theotokos.

[275] On this garment, see above, Chap. 35; cf. below, Chap. 160.

[276] For discussion of the incident described in this chapter, together with other cases of holy men and monks fleeing to the "desert" to escape "the crowd" and scandals, see Malamut, *Route,* 173–80.

58. Several days later the father summoned one of the monks who knew about construction and told him to go up to the higher part of the gorge with two other brothers; he indicated the place to him and <instructed him> to cut down the wild olive tree that stood there and to make a pit near it for burning lime.[277] In the place where the tree stood Lazaros <told him> to build a pillar for him rather like the one on which he was, <that is,> elevated and without a roof. When the brother had finished the pillar just as the father had ordered, <the latter> left his previous pillar one night, without any of the brothers there seeing him, climbed up to the newly built pillar, and got onto it. When the time came for hammering <the *semantron*> for church and the brothers realized what had happened, [528] they all went straight up to him. They saw him there, received a prayer and instructions from him as to how they should live, and then went down again to the <monastery of the> Savior, leaving him there alone. So Lazaros was once more *as a sparrow dwelling alone on a roof* there;[278] he had wandered far off and had lodged in the wilder places, and was awaiting God Who would save him from faintheartedness and from the tempest of the wicked demons and Who would drown the malicious and ill-intentioned designs and contrivances with which they were attacking him every day.[279] For as <soon as> the first night fell, they drew near too, intending to terrify him from the start, and began to throw stones at him; and they continued doing this not only on that night and the following one, but for many <nights> until he put them to flight by hurling prayers at them like rocks.[280]

59. While Lazaros was there, people used to come to him for help, and he heard from some of them that <there was> a woman enclosed on a pillar, who had her feet hanging outside through a hole.[281] When he heard this he

[277] By roasting limestone (calcium carbonate), quicklime (calcium oxide) is produced; when water is applied to this it becomes slaked lime (calcium hydroxide), which forms an important constituent of mortar, plaster, and cement. Lazaros' pillar at the Theotokos was thus evidently a masonry rather than a wooden construction.

[278] Ps. 101 (102):7. Cf. above, Chap. 53.

[279] A considerable part of this sentence is drawn more or less directly from Ps. 54 (55):7–9.

[280] The wording here is very similar to that at the end of Chap. 54, which describes Lazaros' experiences when he first moved onto his pillar at the monastery of the Savior.

[281] Cf. above, Chap. 18, n. 102, on the rarity of female solitaries at this time. This woman is the subject of a note by Delehaye, "Femmes stylites"; cf. also Janin, *Églises*

said to himself, "If a woman, <of> the weak<er> sex has done this for the sake of the kingdom of heaven, then I <too> really ought to do not only this but other, even harder things." So he did this too, and hung his feet out through the wall. The brothers, who were there with his mother, the blessed Eupraxia[282] (for she too was tonsured by him), saw this and went and stood in a circle around the pillar; they tearfully begged him to desist from such an undertaking. "Why are you trying to make us into orphans so quickly?" they said, "Is it not sufficient to stand almost naked on your pillar in the open air as you do, distressed by the cold and the heat, worn out by fasts and vigils, and, in addition, exhausted by the weight of your irons and the biting of your lice, without imposing yet another torment on yourself?" They said these things tearfully in order to persuade him to give up such an undertaking; but instead Lazaros persuaded them by his counter-arguments to stop bothering him about this. For he repeated the <sayings> of the apostle, "*The sufferings of this present time are not worthy to be compared with the glory which shall be revealed in us,*"[283] and, "*In as much as our outer man perishes, so is the inner <man> renewed day by day,*"[284] and, "*Who shall separate us from the love of Christ? <Shall> tribulation, distress, famine, persecution, or nakedness?*"[285] and, "*For thy sake we are killed all the day long*";[286] and as many <texts> again of the same <kind>. When he said all this their grief turned to joy,[287] while their tears, their despair, and their sadness turned to gladness, to delight, and to the praise of God, and from then on they stopped bothering him. The wicked Devil could not bear this, however, and transformed himself into a snake; <then> that most Evil One crawled onto <the father's> feet, thinking to frighten him in this way. But Lazaros was not scared or frightened at all by this; instead he

centres, 242, who assumes that she must have been a contemporary living nearby, and Talbot, "Comparison," 16.

[282] Eupraxia is her monastic name, for she was previously called Irene. As the *vita* later reveals, she had evidently left her home village by this time and had moved to a convent in the close vicinity of Galesion.

[283] Rom. 8:18.

[284] 2 Cor. 4:16. The quotation is not exact, suggesting it is made from memory.

[285] Rom. 8:35. The quotation is again not quite exact.

[286] Rom. 8:36, quoting Ps. 43 (44):22.

[287] There is probably an allusion intended here to Jn. 16:20.

terrified the Evil One by his prayer to God and by the image of the venerable cross, which he had engraved with his own hand on the inside of the pillar, and put him to flight.[288]

60. At that time a monk came to the Beloved [Ephesus] from the West to pray.[289] When he learned this about the father, he went up to him, and when he saw him <doing> this he started to reproach him in quite strong terms. "Isn't the other distress that you suffer from your asceticism enough without adding this exacting and superhuman <endeavor> to it?" he said. "Don't you know that such things often become an occasion for arrogance and pride? Stop doing this sort of thing, then, if you want to be a monk for real!" Since Lazaros really was humble-minded and someone who genuinely strove for obedience, he accepted the rebuke with complete humility; and he obeyed him and drew his feet <back> inside the pillar.

61. Another monk came to the father wearing a hair shirt and told him that he had been on the mountain for many days. "But now," he said, "I feel this compulsion to go into the world outside, not so as to stay there, but just to get a glimpse of the fields and <have> a walk <in them>." "If, as you say, you want to do this because you've become discouraged by being alone on the mountain," said the father to him, "then go to the <monastery of the> Savior and live there with the brothers for as long as you like. But just don't go down from the mountain lest you meet with some unexpected evil." This is what the father <said>, but that <monk> obeyed his own ideas rather than the father's words and did go down from the mountain. After three days he came back and tearfully confessed to the father what had happened to him. For he said, "While I was walking about in the fields, I came across a sheepfold. I went inside and found a bronze pot lying <there>; when I opened it up,[290] I found some cooked meat in it and, since I was hungry, I took it and ate it." The

[288] On Lazaros' power over snakes in general, see Chaps. 55 and 67. The form of a snake is probably that most commonly adopted by the Devil and demons in Byzantine literature, being clearly related to the story of the fall in Genesis. See here Joannou, *Démonologie,* 12; Greenfield, *Demonology,* 37–38, 44–46, 86; Greenfield, "Outer Darkness," 66–67.

[289] Alternatively this could mean "to fulfill a vow."

[290] Trapp, *Lexikon,* s.v. ἀνασκεπάζω, helpfully suggests the emendation of ἀνασκευάσας to ἀνασκεπάσας here.

father forgave him and blessed him, however, and let him go <back> onto the mountain.[291]

62. There was never a time when a monk was not living on the mountain, even before the father came up onto it. The holy Paphnoutios testifies to this and, after him, the shepherd,[292] as indeed also <does> the man who built the church of the Holy Trinity and who constructed, together with it, the church of the Prodromos.[293] There is also said to have been a woman, a nun by her habit, living on the <mountain> at the time [529] when the father came up onto it.[294] All these people, however, saved only themselves by persevering on the mountain; but our blessed father Lazaros, who came up onto this mountain through the providence of God, organized[295] it and caused a previously obscure <place> to become well known and familiar to everybody.[296] He did not only save himself <here>, but others as well, and he continues to save <them> up to the present, <as he will> until the end <of time>.[297] He promised <this to> those who persevered on the mountain, for these are his own words: "He who believes in my Christ (Who has given His blessing to the building of these churches on this mountain) and who perseveres here for His sake, even

[291] The implication of the chapter is that this monk was living as a solitary on the mountain; thus the present sentence may be taken to mean that Lazaros allowed him to return to his former way of life, despite the lapse reported here. It is also implied that at the time of this incident, the monastery of the Savior was still the *only* community on the mountain and thus that the monastery of the Theotokos had yet to develop around Lazaros' pillar.

[292] For the history of Paphnoutios and the shepherd, see above, Chaps. 36–40.

[293] The passage might also be translated: "as indeed also <does> the man who built the church of the Holy Trinity and, again, the one who constructed the church of the Prodromos." The Greek does not make it clear whether the churches of the Prodromos and the Trinity were built by the same man or by different people. The person who built the church of the Prodromos (and a cistern at the cave) was also mentioned above in Chap. 53, but there is no other reference to the church of the Holy Trinity.

[294] On the rarity of female solitaries in Byzantine monasticism, see above, Chap. 18; cf. Chap. 59.

[295] The verb κατακοσμέω may also contain the sense of "adorning."

[296] Cf. here Theodoret, *Hist. Rel.*, 21.4 (James of Cyrrhestica).

[297] Cf. Mt. 28:20. A similar statement was made above in Chap. 19. The basic theme of Lazaros' transformation of Galesion, which is introduced here, is taken up again in Chap. 79, below; cf. also Chap. 85.

if he is careless and lazy but nevertheless perseveres on the mountain because of this hope that he has, will never be deprived of this hope, but will also receive forgiveness for the sins he committed of old in the world."[298] As this narrative proceeds, it will make these things clearer in the proper place; but now, however, let it hold to its present sequence and let it deal with the following matters.[299]

63. Another monk, from the Anatolikon theme,[300] came and said to the father, "I was a prisoner in the land of the barbarians, for I had been captured by them, and I begged God to deliver me from that place.[301] <I swore> that if

[298] A similar statement is attributed to Lazaros below, Chap. 100 (cf. also Chap. 216), and the theme of perseverance on the mountain also appears in several other places during the course of the *vita.* In the following sentence, Gregory the Cellarer apparently acknowledges that he is breaking from his loose chronological sequence here, and thus the use of the plural "churches" in Lazaros' statement could suggest that this particular version of it originates from a rather later period when the monasteries of the Theotokos and the Resurrection had been constructed, perhaps the period referred to in Chaps. 100 and 216. As was noted above, the previous chapter (Chap. 61) would appear to date to a time when the community of the Savior was the only one in existence, while Chap. 64 describes the construction of a small chapel beside Lazaros' pillar at the Theotokos, clearly implying that there was no church there prior to that. It is thus evident that the author has been led into this brief interjectory passage of commentary by reflection upon the story of the solitary monk in the previous chapter, which illustrates the dangers of failing to persevere under the difficult conditions of the mountain.

[299] Gregory the Cellarer now returns to his current theme, which appears to be the illustration of Lazaros' miraculous powers, particularly his control over the forces of evil, his ascetic endurance, and his prescience and good judgment.

[300] See above, Chap. 29.

[301] The story of the miraculous release by Lazaros of the soldier Philippikos from captivity by the "Persians," recounted in Gregory of Cyprus' version of the *vita* (chap. 34, *AASS,* Nov. 3:602A–E), may well represent a reworking of the opening of this episode. It is impossible to tell where this man had been held captive, but the fact that he was heading to the East might suggest it was to the west or the north of Byzantine territory. Since all the stories in this section appear to date to the period when Lazaros was at the Theotokos, the man's release must have occurred in the 1030s or very early 1040s. He might thus have been captured by the Arabs in Sicily and freed during the Byzantine campaigns there between 1038 and 1040, or he could have been captured and later released during the Bulgarian rebellion of Peter Deljan and Alousianos in 1040–41; this would be interesting in the context of the *vita,* as two monks from Galesion were closely involved in those events, thus perhaps explaining how the man had come to hear of Lazaros; see below, Chap. 229.

this happened I would not go back to my home, but would instead put on monastic garb and travel to the Holy Land. And indeed," he said, "as you see, by the grace of God I did escape and I have become a monk. However, now that I am about to set off for the Holy Land, I am being tormented by the idea of going to my homeland on the way, just to have a look at my home." Lazaros replied to him, "Fulfill your vows to the Lord, as you agreed <to do> when you were in trouble, and do not wish any more to go either to your home or your homeland. For it is better not to make a vow than to make one and not fulfill it, especially as you are <now> a monk. Do you not hear the Lord saying in the Gospels that 'no man, having put his hand to the plow, and looking back, is fit for the kingdom of heaven'?"[302] After the father had said this to him, he blessed him and then dismissed him.

The <monk> went down from the mountain but was enticed by the idea <he had had>, or rather by the wicked demon, and he did go off to his homeland. When he got there, he went into a village that lay quite close to his own and a poor woman invited him in to rest. But the author of evil, the enemy who formerly estranged Eve and Adam from paradise by the pleasure of the <forbidden> food, also enticed these <two> with the pleasure of sin and persuaded them to have sex and consummate their sin. After the wretched monk had completed the evil act, he began to ask the woman about his village, about those who were in charge there,[303] and also about those who had gone off to the war with him; as she said she knew all of them, since she herself came from that <village>, he also asked her about himself. But, at the mere sound of his name, she gave a deep groan and her eyes filled with tears. "Oh father!"[304] she sobbed in reply, "Why did you mention that man? You haven't seen him <by any chance, have you>? For the man you just asked about is my father. Not long after he went off to the war (<and I don't know> whether he fell <in battle> or whether he was taken prisoner), my mother also died, leaving me and two other <children who were> boys. As we were small and unable

[302] Lk. 9:62. There are the usual slight variations from the text of the New Testament, suggesting this is quoted from memory. The same quotation, with the same variants, is also used above in Chap. 18.

[303] See Kaplan, *Les hommes,* 200, on the significance of these *archontes;* cf. above, Chap. 56.

[304] In view of the revelation about to be made, this form of address may be understood as being deliberately ironic.

to look after our affairs properly, the people from the village took all our <possessions> and drove us out of our own home. So I left there and came here, and I live, as you see, in this tiny little room, and earn my living by my own hands." When he heard this, the monk looked more carefully at the woman's face, and understood that she truly was his daughter. Then he realized what he had suffered as a result of disobeying the father and obeying the wicked demon, which . . . [305] by not having kept properly to his own rule. He left there without saying anything to the woman about these matters <or telling her> that he was her father, and came <back> to Lazaros to whom he narrated, with a great many tears, all that had happened to him. The father offered him support through his comforting words, gave him instructions <about penance> commensurate with his sin, and let him go off to the Holy Land after he had blessed him; he <also> advised him strongly not to leave there before the end of his life. So the man did obeisance, went down from the mountain, and set out for the Holy Land.[306]

64. As our father was alone in that place,[307] he made arrangements for receiving the blessed sacraments, and they built a little dry-stone apse immediately opposite the pillar;[308] a priest from among the brothers at the <monastery of the> Savior would go and celebrate the holy Eucharist in this <chapel> and so give the blessed sacraments to Lazaros.[309] A <secular> priest called Menas

[305] Something appears to be missing from the manuscript at this point.

[306] See Malamut, *Route,* 293, for comment on this incident.

[307] The reference must be to the pillar of the Theotokos, at a time before a community had developed there.

[308] Or, perhaps, "right against." As Delehaye notes, the same word for "apse," κογχάριον, which literally means a "little sea shell," is also used for an apparently similar chapel in the *Life of St. Stephen the Younger,* PG 100:1101B. As was seen above, Chap. 35, Gregory the Cellarer was obviously familiar with this work.

[309] Cf. Chap. 49, above, which refers to the priest Gregory ministering to the ascetics in the cave at the Savior; perhaps the same man is being thought of here. Although liturgical provisions did exist by this time for the daily celebration of the Eucharist, this never became general Byzantine practice; the traditional days for celebration were Saturdays, Sundays, and feast days. Weekly communion was common for monks, but not for lay people. It is made clear below (Chaps. 83–84) that the sacrament was also reserved for Lazaros during the celebration of the Eucharist in the monastery church; but presumably those chapters refer to a later stage in the development of Galesion. See further *ODB,* s.v. "Eucharist," also "Communion." The mention at this point of

from the village of Samakios[310] also used to go up to the father quite often, as he had great faith in him; on many occasions he too would celebrate the holy Eucharist when so directed by the father, and would give him the undefiled sacraments. One day, however, when <Menas> was going up to the father as usual, he found two bears high up on the mountain, standing in the middle of the path he was about to follow, and fighting with each other. When he saw them, <Menas> stopped still at first, as he was terrified and had no idea what he should do; but then he called the father to mind and, fervently invoking his blessing, [530] began to go confidently on his way. As soon as the <bears> saw him coming toward them, they took off toward the <top of the> mountain at a run, as if they were being chased by him. <So Menas> passed the place without being afraid and went down to the father. When he reached him, he went up and said the <usual> "Bless <me>." Then the father said, "You didn't encounter anything frightening <did you>? . . . [311] <Bears> don't attack someone unless he tries to harm them." <Menas> was amazed when he heard this from the father and told him everything in detail. So he celebrated the holy Eucharist and gave the father the undefiled sacraments; then, after he had received another blessing from him, he went back to his own home, rejoicing and praising God[312] for what he had seen and heard.

65. Another time, <Menas> sent his son, called Constantine (who is still alive and tells the <story>), to the father with honeycombs for him. When the boy was halfway up the mountain he was enticed by the sweetness of the honey and took a small <piece> and ate it. In due course he reached the father and introduced himself to him, <saying> who he was and what he had brought for

---

Lazaros' arrangements for receiving communion should be read in conjunction with Gregory the Cellarer's defense against contemporary critics of his practices, below, Chaps. 78–79, 82–84.

[310] Nothing more is known of this village, although the narrative below would suggest that it was in a different direction from Ephesus; the route from Samakios to the location of the Theotokos thus evidently passed high over the mountain and then approached the pillar from above, whereas the normal route from the city is always referred to as being uphill all the way. Menas, who is not mentioned elsewhere in the *vita*, had a son, named Constantine, who was still alive at the time Gregory the Cellarer was writing and who may well be his source for this incident; see the following chapter.

[311] As Delehaye suggests, something appears to be missing from the text at this point.

[312] Cf. Lk. 5:25.

him. When one of the brothers standing there wanted to take the honey out of the boy's hands, the father called out to him from his pillar, "Don't take it, but let him eat it." When the boy heard these words, he realized that he could not hide from the father what he had done on the way when he was by himself, even though Lazaros said nothing directly to him about this; at the same time he had his own conscience to accuse him (for, even if we are eager to hide our sinful actions from everyone, we are unable to escape the rebuke of <our conscience>), and so he prostrated himself, confessed his fault, and asked for forgiveness. After he had obtained this, he gave the honey to the brother who was standing there, received a blessing from the father, and went back to his own home. <There> he told his father what he (just like his father before <him>) had seen and heard from our holy father.

66. One monk among the brothers, whose surname was Paxamades, was seduced by the demons and left the monastery and went off to the monastery called Avilon.[313] Some time later the Evil One suggested to him that he should go up at night to the <monastery of the> Savior to steal the monks' clothes and anything else he might find in the monastery, for he knew it was the brothers' custom not to have keys to their cells nor for anyone to remain outside the church during the time of the vigil;[314] and a vigil was <taking place> then. So <Paxamades> went up, but when he got near the monastery, he heard the brothers singing, "*By the waters of Babylon, there we sat; and wept when we remembered Sion.*"[315] As soon as he heard this, it was as though he was struck by an arrow. He sat down where he was and wept bitterly, lamenting to himself with words like these: "Oh woe is me, I have been led astray. While these men

[313] The monastery "τῶν Ἀβίλων" is unknown apart from the mention in this chapter; cf. Janin, *Églises centres,* 241 n. 4. In view of the local opposition recorded in the *vita* to the presence of Lazaros and his monasteries on Galesion, it is interesting to note here what sounds like a rival establishment, apparently quite close to the monastery of the Savior and certainly to Galesion. If the goal of the monk's expedition and Lazaros' response can be taken as evidence of economic hardship, Avilon was perhaps faring badly due to competition with the flourishing community founded by Lazaros. Cf. below, Chap. 84.

[314] This vigil (ἀγρυπνία) could refer to the regular nightly service of the monastic hours (*mesonyktikon*), or else to one of the other occasions on which special and more elaborate vigil services were held during the liturgical year, such as on the eve of one of the major feasts. See *ODB,* s.v. "Hours," "Vigil."

[315] Ps. 136 (137):1.

are praising God like angels, how could I come upon them like a robber?"[316] When he had said these <words> and had wept a great deal, he got up and went to the father; and with a great many tears confessed the whole business to him. The father rebuked <Paxamades> as was fitting and then forgave him. He also gave him two *nomismata* and, by means of a personal letter on his behalf to the brothers at the <monastery of the> Savior, he instructed them to provision him from their <supplies>; then he blessed him and dismissed him. So the brother went down from the mountain, rejoicing and weeping at the same time because he had <come to> understand, on the one hand, our holy father's compassionate and sympathetic disposition and, on the other, his own inhumanity and depravity; <and> he went back again to the monastery of Avilon. In the fullness of time, however, he returned to the monastery <of the Savior> where, by the grace of God, he ended his life in a proper <state of> repentance. Thus, in accordance with the holy apostle, our holy father Lazaros also knew how[317] to *overcome evil by good.*[318] And so, indeed, he did.

67. But the wicked Devil started using his evil and malicious contrivances against the holy man again in an attempt to terrify him. He thus changed himself into a snake and, while the father was sitting writing, slithered along his left arm into his leather tunic and crawled into his bosom; when he got there he peeped out, poking out his head in front of him [Lazaros]. The father grabbed this <snake> with his hand, however, and put it to flight by flogging it with the sign of the venerable cross. Then the Evil One changed himself out of the form of the snake and went out of the window like a hurricane.[319] There was also a real snake there which <made> some of the brothers grow sick with

[316] There would seem to be an allusion intended here to the words of Jesus at Jn. 10:1–8: "*He that entereth not by the door into the sheepfold, but climbeth up some other way, the same is a thief and a robber. . . . All that ever came before me are thieves and robbers.*"

[317] Reading ᾔδει for ἔδει.

[318] Rom. 12:21. The same quotation is used below, Chap. 242.

[319] On the common idea of demonic powers appearing in the form of a snake, see the rather similar incident above in Chap. 59 and the note there. The notion of the demon departing in this way is rarer, although related ideas do occasionally occur in exorcisms. On this and comparable departures in contemporary exorcism stories, see Joannou, *Démonologie,* 26–27; cf. Greenfield, *Demonology,* 144; see ibid., 179–80, 226, 230, 232 for less orthodox conceptions linking demons with winds and storms. On Lazaros' power against snakes in general, see above, Chap. 55.

fear when they saw it; but God, through the prayers of the blessed father, made it go away.

68. Once, when Lazaros was sick, the Heir of Darkness[320] changed himself into an angel of light[321] and came and stood above the pillar. "I am an angel of God," he said to the father, "and I have been sent by Him to receive your soul." The father looked up and saw him but, by simply raising his hand to make the sign of the cross, he caused <the apparition> to disperse at once like smoke.[322]

69. The Evil One came in the night to a log, which was lying somewhere near the pillar, and apparently stood <there> chopping at it with an axe. By doing this he did not allow the father to have <any> rest.[323] At the father's order, however, the log was removed from there, and so the <Devil> stopped troubling Lazaros by the noise of his blows. . . . [324]

70. Another man, from Attaleia,[325] whose name was John and whose surname was [531] Kouphalides, also went to the father when he became pos-

[320] The "Heir of Darkness" is the Devil. Gregory of Cyprus also employs this particular description in his version of the *vita* (chap. 18, *AASS,* Nov. 3:595A) and provides some explanation of it there. On the general association of the Devil and the demons with darkness and blackness in the Byzantine tradition see Greenfield, *Demonology,* 24–27; idem, "Outer Darkness," 62–65; Joannou, *Démonologie,* 13.

[321] See 2 Cor. 11:14. Cf. Chaps. 47 and 49, above, and Chap. 208, below. Reference is made to the idea of the Devil or Satan appearing as an angel of light with relative frequency in Byzantine sources; cf. here Joannou, *Démonologie,* 13–14; Greenfield, *Demonology,* 83–84; idem, "Outer Darkness," 67–69. On early non-Christian references to the idea, see, e.g., J. B. Russell, *The Devil, Perceptions of Evil from Antiquity to Primitive Christianity* (Ithaca-London, 1977), 207.

[322] Compare the incident below, Chap. 208, in which the Devil appears in the form of an old woman to Lazaros when he is sick and is similarly dismissed. On demons departing like smoke, a relatively common notion, see Joannou, *Démonologie,* 27; Greenfield, *Demonology,* 15.

[323] The notion of the Devil or the demons making noise, whether vocal or mechanical, to disturb holy men and monks is relatively common in Byzantine sources and has a long tradition going back to the *vita Antonii* of Athanasius. In the present *vita* compare, e.g., Chaps. 50 and 154. Further see Joannou, *Démonologie,* 16–17; Greenfield, *Demonology,* 79–80.

[324] There is a small gap in the manuscript at this point that occupies the last part of f. 133v.

[325] On this place see above, Chap. 9.

sessed by an evil spirit. Within a few days, by the reading of the holy Gospel and the laying on of the venerable cross, he was delivered from the wicked demon that was tormenting him, and returned to his <home> town, rejoicing.

71. Another man from the same town, called Leo, who had a paralyzed right hand, was also miraculously healed by our holy father. But I had better tell his story properly from the beginning, just as I have learned it from the monk Laurentios the Stylite and from others who have heard it directly from the man who was healed. One night, while he was sleeping in bed with his wife, <this Leo> thought he heard some people running about in front of his house and calling, "A thief is taking everything!" As soon as he heard this he got out of bed and went out of the house, but he found no one there; however, he thought he heard the same sort of cries in the distance and so he started off in pursuit toward the source of the cries he was hearing. When he had reached a spot some way from his house, he heard a voice say, "Aren't you going to hit him?" As if someone suddenly struck him, he immediately fell to the ground and lay there like a dead man, but he did just <manage to> call out, "Oh no, I've been murdered!" The people who <lived> in the vicinity came out and brought lights when they heard his cry, and they found him lying <there> as if dead. Since they recognized him, they picked him up and took him home. In the morning his <family> lifted him up and carried him to the church of the Theotokos (which is called the <church> of the Egyptian woman)[326] and laid him there.[327] He spent several days <at the church>, but then <started> speaking <again> and was released from his paralysis as a result of being anointed with holy oil from the lamp of the most pure Theotokos.[328] Only his right hand remained paralyzed; it was so withered and stiff that it appeared to be stuck to his side, while his fingers had dug into the palm with <so> much force <that> they <actually> came out of it <on the other side>. <Leo> went up to the holy man [Lazaros] who sent him back to his

[326] The reference is probably to Mary of Egypt, an early Byzantine holy woman (see Talbot, *Holy Women,* 65–93; also *ODB,* s.v. "Mary of Egypt"). It is not clear, however, why the church should have a double dedication.

[327] Incubation at a church or shrine was regarded, as here, as an appropriate "first aid" treatment by the Byzantines; it could be followed later by other religious or "natural" remedies when the symptoms of an illness or the more enduring effects of injuries became apparent, in this case by anointing with holy oil as a cure for paralysis. See further *ODB,* s.v. "Healing," "Incubation."

[328] On such use of holy oil, see above, Chap. 45; cf. Chap. 76, below.

own home, but several days later Lazaros appeared to him, when he was lying in bed in his house, and said, "In the name of Jesus Christ, *stretch out your hand!*"[329] With these words the father departed, but the patient was immediately rendered healthy. He woke up at once and got out of bed as fast as he could and, when he saw that his hand was healthy and stretched out, he began shouting the "*Kyrie eleeson* [Lord have Mercy]." When the members of his household heard him shouting like this, they got up and lit a lamp; when they saw that his hand was healthy and learned from him the way in which it had been cured, they gave glory to God Who had thus miraculously cured this man through His servant.

72. <Leo> wanted to go into the church after the early morning service[330] to tell everyone about the miracle, but the man who was then *laosynaktes*[331] prevented him from this course of action by saying to him, "If the old man had wanted the miracle to be known, he could have healed you there <on Galesion>, but he did it in this way <instead> because he wanted to avoid the popular acclaim that would result from the miracle. So, if you do this now, everyone who hears <about it> will go up to him because of the extraordinary <nature> of the miracle, and will distress him with their compliments and adulation; for he does not approve of such things." When <Leo> heard the man <say> this, he thought carefully about what had happened to him, <and so> went up to the monastery and kept quiet, letting no one know <about it> except for the metropolitan <of Ephesus>. The latter learned of <the miracle> somehow and summoned <Leo> to him; <there> he told <his story> rather carelessly and not very accurately,[332] so that even the <metropolitan>, upon

[329] The last part of this command is drawn directly from the account of Jesus' healing of the man with the withered arm in Mt. 12:13; compare the very similar wording in Mk. 3:5; Lk. 6:10.

[330] On the early morning service of "*orthros*," the Byzantine equivalent of matins, see above, Chap. 8, and *ODB*, s.v. "Orthros."

[331] The title means literally "assembler of the people" and is presumably used of an official like a verger, beadle, or church warden.

[332] It might appear to make more sense here if the text were emended, under the assumption that the negative has been misplaced; it could thus be translated "<there> he told <his story> with care [not at all carelessly] and very accurately." However one could also explain this rather odd passage, and argue for retaining it, as it stands, by taking into account not only the *laosynaktes'* warning about loose talk, but also the hostility between the ecclesiastical authorities in Ephesus and the foundation on

hearing this, said, "God will have mercy on us through the holy prayers of this saintly old man." Thus <Leo> left the Beloved [Ephesus], along with his fellow citizens, and went back to his own town; but, even though he did not want <to do this>, he <still> proclaimed the miracle to everyone, not by talking <about it> but <simply> by the healing of his hand. The following year he came <back> to the monastery, bringing a letter to the father from the *protospatharios* Leo Basilitzes.[333] The monk Kerykos questioned him and found out his story, and then went up to the father with him. <There> he took hold of <Leo's> healed hand and showed it to Lazaros. "This is your child, father," he said, "whose paralyzed hand here you miraculously healed." The father replied in a brusque voice, "<It was> not I, but God Who healed it." When they came down from the pillar, the brothers questioned the man closely and, indeed, actually touched his hand and saw the scars, which, in particular,

---

Galesion that existed at the time Gregory the Cellarer was writing the *vita.* Thus, if this miracle story had become well known and had later been called into question and used *against* Lazaros in the course of those obviously bitter hostilities, the author may here be defending not only the veracity of the actual miracle, but also Lazaros' deliberately modest and orthodox avoidance of praise for it. So, whatever is being said to the contrary in Ephesus, Gregory is trying to establish the following: a) that the miracle took place; b) that Leo may have been a poor witness, perhaps prone to exaggeration; c) that Lazaros did *not* seek credit and fame for having performed it; and d) that it was in fact the metropolitan himself who was responsible for the story having become known. This general interpretation of the reporting of the episode might also explain the author's obvious concern to establish the reliability of his sources, both at the start of Chap. 71 and at the end of Chap. 72. For the hostility between Ephesus and Galesion and Gregory's polemical motivation in sections of the *vita,* see above, Introduction, sections F and G.

[333] The title *protospatharios* was a high dignity of the imperial hierarchy, which evidently carried with it considerable honor. Until the 10th century it was mainly granted to the commanders of themes, but by the 11th this was no longer the case. This Leo Basilitzes is otherwise unknown, but the fact that Attaleia was probably the capital of the Kibyrrhaiotai theme and was a major military and naval center would perhaps suggest that he held an important imperial office there. Cf. Morris, "Political Saint," 49, although she mistakenly identifies him as the Leo who was the subject of the cure; cf. eadem, "The Byzantine Aristocracy and the Monasteries," in *The Byzantine Aristocracy, IX to XII Centuries,* ed. M. Angold (Oxford, 1984), 115. If the argument in the previous note is accepted, the purpose of mentioning him here may be simply to stress the credibility of the Leo who was the recipient of Lazaros' miracle; if a *protospatharios* entrusts the man with a letter, then the metropolitan cannot claim that he is completely unreliable.

proclaimed the miracle. <Thus> they learned from that <Leo> himself the events which have been written down above, and they passed them on to me in turn, as has already been made clear.

73. Laurentios Halmyrenos, who died not long ago, told me about a rather similar episode. He said that when he was still living in the outside world, his mother told him to go out and fetch their horse, which was in the fields. So he went off and got on the <horse> but, as he was coming <back>, he came to a place where there was a mastic bush;[334] <there>, so he said, he saw a black ox suddenly come charging wildly at him out of the middle of the mastics. The horse shied and bucked when it saw this; it threw him to the ground and then went galloping back again into the fields. <Laurentios> was possessed by a wicked spirit in the fall, and lay there as if he were dead.[335] Some people from the village saw him, for it was not far away, and they went out with his mother and picked him up; they carried him to their church, which was <dedicated> to the holy martyr Prokopios,[336] and laid him <there>, placing [532] the venerable cross on him. He lay like that for two days and nights, unable to regain consciousness at all because of the demon's attack; however, when it was already the third day, he came to in the middle of the night and recovered his senses. He opened his eyes as he lay <there> and looked all around the church, but he was bewildered and quite at a loss for he did not know where he was. While he was lying in this <state>, he saw the doors of the church open suddenly and a tall old monk, wearing a leather

[334] The mastic tree, or lentisc (Pistacia lentiscus), is an evergreen shrub that generally grows as a scrubby bush, although it can become a tree if left undamaged; its resin has medicinal and other uses.

[335] At first it appears as if Laurentios is simply knocked unconscious by his fall and there thus seems no obvious reason for the assertion that he was possessed, since the two conditions are not usually associated in Byzantine thought. It is apparent from the rest of the story in the following chapter, however, that he was both diagnosed as possessed by Lazaros in his miraculous visitation and that he later started to have seizures that were obviously linked to his fall. Although other explanations of mental illness, relying on theories of natural imbalances, were quite widely accepted by Byzantine medical opinion, the most common interpretation of symptoms like those of epileptic seizures was demonic possession; see further *ODB*, s.v. "Insanity"; Joannou, *Démonologie,* 19–20, 44–45; Greenfield, *Demonology,* 89–95, 215–18. In this case, then, it is probably significant that the ox involved is described as being black, the color most favored by demonic powers.

[336] Prokopios was a Palestinian martyr who was believed to have been executed at the start of the 4th century in Caesarea; he eventually became known primarily as a

tunic but bare-headed and without shoes on his feet, came into the church. The <monk> first went and prayed in the sanctuary but then turned and came toward him; standing in front of him, he said to him, "Get up, follow me!"[337] and <Laurentios> got up and followed him. As they left the church the doors closed by themselves. After <the monk> had gone some way from the church with him, he stopped and said to <Laurentios>, "Go home and, in the morning, if you want to be freed from the evil <spirit> that is possessing you, take your mother and go up to Mt. Galesion to the monastery of the monk Lazaros." As soon as the father had said this to him, he vanished from sight.

74. <Laurentios> went home and told his mother everything. In the morning, without any delay, she took him and went up to the father, and recounted the story, just as it had happened. The father told <Laurentios'> mother to go back to her home, but gave orders for the venerable cross to be placed on <the young man> and for the holy Gospel to be read <over him>. Lazaros did this in order to conceal the miracle. Thus after three days during which the cross was placed on him and the brothers read <the Gospel>, the Evil One did not control him <any more>[338] nor did the demon trouble him at all. Indeed, after he had spent some time in the monastery, <Laurentios> asked the father's <permission> and, having been dismissed, went home with

---

military saint and is depicted as such by the 11th century. See *ODB,* s.v. "Prokopios"; Delehaye, *Saints militaires,* 228–33.

[337] This command is reminiscent of the call of Matthew/Levi son of Alphaeus in the Gospels: Mt. 9:9; Mk. 2:14; Lk. 27–28.

[338] Reading πονηρὸς (Evil One) for σταυρὸς (cross). The phrase in the text here, οὔτε ὁ σταυρὸς αὐτοῦ ἐκράτησεν (lit. "the cross did not control him"), is problematical as it stands, for it suggests that Laurentios has not been cured, whereas the following phrase implies the opposite. The word σταυρὸς also occurs in the previous line and an obvious solution is to attribute its repetition to scribal error; it may be that it has been substituted for a different but similar word, e.g., πονηρὸς, thus giving the translation I have adopted. Delehaye indicates in his apparatus that Kurtz suggested an emendation of σταυρὸς (cross) to ταῦρος (bull), presumably to be understood here with reference to the (demonic?) black ox (βοῦς) that initially caused the possession, but this seems unlikely since no further mention has been made of the animal. It is conceivable that the phrase could stand as it is if the verb κρατεῖν ("control," "master," "seize") could have the sense of "give seizures" (i.e., "the cross did not give him seizures <any more>, nor did the demon trouble him at all"), the seizures being caused, of course, not by the cross itself but the demon's reaction to it; one might compare Chap. 219, below, where a possessed man has convulsions and heaves himself off the ground *after* the monks of the monastery have placed a cross upon him. This meaning for the verb is, however, not otherwise attested.

the intention of settling up his affairs and returning to the monastery with his mother's approval and being tonsured. When he had been there for a while, however, upon the advice of his relatives, he abandoned his plan of <receiving> the tonsure, because he was no longer troubled by the evil spirit, and <instead> prepared to take a wife for himself. But, after the <marriage> contract had been drawn up and the matter was already in hand, he was suddenly struck by the demon and thrown to the ground; he frothed at the mouth, rolled his eyes, <twisted> his hair, and did all the things that those possessed by demons usually <do>. <Laurentios'> mother immediately realized the cause of the problem when she saw him, <and so>, after he had recovered, she took her son and went straight to the father with him; she had him tonsured by Lazaros and included in his flock. After this happened, by the grace of Christ and the prayers of our blessed father, the demon left him. <Laurentios'> mother went back to her home, settled up her affairs, and then returned and also received the holy habit from the father. And she is now in the women's convent where she has done well in the course of asceticism and is already nearing the end of her life, due to old age.[339]

75. Once when I was going down from the mountain (for I had been sent by the father to the Kastron [Ephesus][340] on some monastery business),[341] a layman was accompanying me <on the way> down. He struck up a conversation with me and said, "Father, you don't realize what a holy man you have here!" I smiled and said to him, "If we who are close to him, as you say, do not recognize him, how is it that you, who are far removed from him, know him <to be so holy>?" When I said this, he at once put his hand into the opening <of his tunic> and pulled out a lead seal that bore an impression of

[339] On this convent, which was named after Lazaros' mother Eupraxia, see below, Chaps. 164 and 201. Cf. also Janin, *Églises centres,* 245; Talbot, "Family," 129; Talbot, "Comparison," 3.

[340] On the use of "Kastron" (lit. "castle" or "fortress") to refer to Ephesus, see Foss, *Ephesus,* 121–22. The same term is used below, e.g., Chap. 154. As Foss points out, the term indicates the shift of the city during the Byzantine period from the increasingly useless harbor to the fortified hill of Hagios Theologos (Ayasuluk); clearly the use of the term "Theologian" (or its rarer form "Beloved") for the city in the *vita* illustrates the same point. Ševčenko, "Eastern Provinces," 724, is thus probably mistaken in distinguishing this *kastron* from Ephesus.

[341] As the end of the chapter reveals, Gregory the Cellarer was still a layman himself at this time, although it is obvious that he was closely associated with Lazaros' community.

the Theotokos.[342] First of all he kissed it and then made me kiss it too; then he said, "Father, this has preserved me from many perils of the sea through the prayer of holy Lazaros." When I asked about the reason, the man sighed heavily and answered me, his eyes brimming with tears. "I'm a sailor," he said, "and once, when I was with my shipmates[343] somewhere, we were caught in <such> a rough sea that we despaired of our lives. But one of the passengers, when he saw death already at the doors, began to cry out in a loud voice like this, 'Holy Lazaros, make haste[344] and deliver us from our present danger!'

[342] The lead bulla (βούλλα) or seal (σφραγίς), which is mentioned here as being given personally to the man by Lazaros and subsequently worn about his neck as a phylactery, may perhaps represent a Galesiote version of the cast-lead type of pilgrimage medallion known from other pilgrimage centers in this period. The surviving examples of these objects come almost exclusively from the shrine of St. Symeon the Stylite the Younger at the Wondrous Mountain, although some others are associated with St. Mamas. The Symeon medallions are modeled on the earlier clay pilgrimage tokens from the saint's shrine near Antioch, the soil of which was believed to impart a valuable and powerful blessing (εὐλογία). These lead Symeon medallions were produced after the Byzantine reoccupation of the area in the later 10th century and, although the original power of the token, which lay in its fabric, was lost by the transformation into metal, its amuletic properties survived in the iconography that relates them to other Christian artifacts of this type. It is interesting to remember that Lazaros himself visited the Wondrous Mountain during his travels (see above, Chap. 25) and could well have seen such artifacts there. At the same time it should be noted that ordinary lead seals marked with representational stamps were also relatively common by the 11th century, when compared to earlier periods, and the most popular depiction on surviving examples is that of the Virgin. This passage (or the rather similar one below, Chap. 113) may thus simply imply that Lazaros met the man's request by giving him an ordinary seal marked with the image of the Virgin, which he happened to have to hand, just as he gave other visitors coins and the like when occasion merited it (see below, Chap. 145). A seal from Galesion, dated to the 11th or 12th century, has survived; it bears an image of St. Antony and the legend Τῆς μ(ο)νῆς τῶ(ν) Γαλλι[σίου]: see V. Laurent, *Le corpus des sceaux de l'Empire byzantin* (Paris, 1965), 2:151–52, no. 1227. See further here also, *ODB*, s.v. "Pilgrimage medallions," "Pilgrimage tokens," "Seals and sealings"; G. Vikan, "Art, Medicine, and Magic in Early Byzantium," *DOP* 38 (1984), 73–74; idem, *Byzantine Pilgrimage Art* (Washington, D.C., 1982), 39–40; idem, "Byzantine Pilgrims' Art," in *Heaven on Earth: Art and the Church in Byzantium*, ed. L. Safran (University Park, Pa., 1998), 259–60; J.-P. Sodini, "Nouvelles eulogies de Syméon," in *Les saints et leur sanctuaire à Byzance*, ed. C. Jolivet-Lévy et al. (Paris, 1993).

[343] Emending συναντῶν to συνναυτῶν. As Delehaye's apparatus indicates, there are a number of other minor problems with the text in this and the previous chapter.

[344] Taking προφθάνω in the same sense as φθάνω; cf. Jon. 4:2.

Weeping, he cried out again, 'God help us, through the blessing of holy Lazaros who is on Galesion!' And so, against <all> hope, we were saved and were cast ashore, how we did not know. After we had got out of the boat, we asked the man to tell us who this holy Lazaros was, whose name and blessing he had invoked, and through whom God had rescued us from such dire straits. The man told us all about the father and also informed us of the location and the name of the mountain. When we heard, we gave glory to God Who had saved us against <all> hope from such danger through His servant, the blessed Lazaros, and we also thanked the man profusely, since he was the cause of such great good <fortune> for us.

"Some time later we happened to come to Phygela,[345] where I inquired and found out in more detail about the father; I discovered someone from there who knew the monastery and went up with him to the holy man. I saw and talked to Lazaros and confessed my thoughts to him, and <then>, as I was about to go down from him, I asked for something from his own hands so that I might have it as a phylactery and safeguard [533] in every difficulty.[346] He produced the seal which you see and presented it to me. I took it and kissed it and the holy father too, and then went down the mountain. I vowed that, if God should provide me with any <profit> from my voyages, I would take half <of it> back once a year and pay it over into the hands of our blessed father (either myself or by means of someone else if I happened to be somewhere far away and not near the place), so that he might remember me in his holy prayers. From then on, as you see, I've worn the seal around my neck" (for that is how he had it) "and I've been saved from many dangers by it, as I said before.[347] And that's why I said to you, 'Oh, you don't realize what a holy

[345] Phygela (Kuşadasi) is on the coast some fifteen kilometers south of Ephesus. Like the town of Anaea a little farther south, Phygela rose in importance as a port during Byzantine times as the harbor of Ephesus silted up; it was a fortified naval base by 823, and by the early 10th century it had replaced Ephesus as the port and disembarkation point for the city and for Galesion. It is mentioned again below (Chap. 228) as an embarkation point for Crete. On Phygela, see further Foss, *Ephesus*, 123–24; *ODB*, s.v. "Phygela."

[346] Literally "every temptation." A very similar phrase is used in Chap. 113 when an Arab convert asks for the same thing.

[347] There is good evidence for the popular Byzantine belief that the possession of pilgrim souvenirs or "blessings" (*eulogiai*), like the amuletic token referred to here, together with the invocation of particular holy figures, could effect miraculous salvation

man you have here!'" When I heard this story from <the man>, I gave thanks to God for having judged me worthy of seeing such a holy man <as Lazaros> and of coming into his hands, by which, indeed, I was hoping to be tonsured; for I was still counted as a layman <at that time>. But now, by the grace of the merciful God, I have written <down> this <incident> for the benefit of many people.

76. A nun from Chios, who had great faith in the father, used to come to the monastery every year and take a jar of the holy oil produced in the monastery on St. Lazaros' day.[348] When she went back to her own land, she would anoint with this oil everyone who was possessed by any sickness whatsoever, and then would chant the name and the blessing of our holy father; she would banish the sickness at once and the sick person would be seen <to be> well <again>.[349]

77. Indeed, <it was> not only those who invoked our holy father's name and blessing out of faith <who> were themselves saved from dangers and worked salvation for other people; for those also who simply named it as a test found that it achieved their intended purpose. The proof of this claim is close <at hand>. On one occasion Methodios, who is called "the Tall," and

---

from shipwreck and other perils of the sea. Although saints like Phokas, Isidore, and Nicholas were especially associated with protection at sea, it is clear that individuals might invoke a favorite saint in dire straits, and this appears to be what is happening with Lazaros here. As a result of the fortunate outcome of the earlier shipwreck, which was attributed to the invocation of Lazaros, the central character in this episode now carries a medallion of the Virgin which is associated, perhaps only verbally rather than iconographically, with the saint, who has himself supplied it. See particularly here G. Vikan, *Byzantine Pilgrimage Art* (Washington, D.C., 1982), 12–16; and idem, "Guided by Land and Sea: Pilgrim Art and Pilgrim Travel in Early Byzantium," *JbAC* 18 (1991), 77–79, 90–91.

[348] No other passage in this section of the *vita* has referred to a time after Lazaros' death, and so it seems unlikely that this chapter would suddenly do so; the reference thus cannot be to the day on which Lazaros himself was commemorated, even though the power of the oil is obviously associated with *his* name and reputation. Instead the reference is most likely to be to Lazaros Saturday, the Saturday before Palm Sunday, which commemorated the raising of the biblical Lazaros from the dead by Jesus; the festival was evidently one on which baptism and anointment with chrism took place and this latter association may perhaps explain the "production" of holy oil on this day in the monastery. It may be assumed that the festival was celebrated with particular emphasis on Galesion because of Lazaros' name. See *ODB,* s.v. "Lazarus Saturday."

[349] On such use of holy oil, see above, Chap. 45; cf. Chap. 71.

Sabas, who comes from Rizenon, were coming up from the region of Chalkos Halonios.[350] While they were climbing up, they came upon a flock of wild goats grazing. When they saw the monks, the <goats> began to run away from them toward the craggy <part> of the mountain. Sabas said to Methodios, "Let me rebuke[351] them in the father's name and, if they stop running, we'll know <for sure> that our father is a holy man." Although Methodios <tried to> stop him, <Sabas> was not persuaded and cast the binding spell on the <goats>;[352] they stopped still at once and were totally incapable of moving from the spot even though Methodios actually threw stones at them. Then,

[350] The region of Chalkos Halonios is mentioned again by name in Chaps. 154 and 155, and it is evidently also referred to in Chaps. 41 and 56. When taken together, these chapters make it clear that this area lay toward the bottom of the mountain on the route to Ephesus. It was thus above the village of Galesion, through which someone coming up from the city would first have to pass in order to reach it, and evidently included the narrow and much feared pass where the cross was carved in the rock.

[351] The verb in the Greek here, ἐπιτιμάω, is that used by Jesus to command demonic powers in several exorcism stories in the Gospels; e.g., Mt. 17:18; Mk. 1:25; 9:25; Lk. 4:35; 9:42; cf. Jude 9. The word was a technical term in both the Old and New Testaments for the divine threat or rebuke; as such it was regarded as presumptuous by humans to employ it; see G. Kittel, ed., *Theological Dictionary of the New Testament,* trans. and ed. G. W. Bromiley (Ann Arbor, Mich., 1966), s.v. ἐπιτιμάω. By this period the word had clearly taken on magical associations in some circumstances and there is thus a definitely coercive tone to the performance from the start, which is presumably what Methodios objects to (see following note).

[352] The general flavor of the episode seems to warrant the translation here of δεσμός in the particular sense of "binding spell." The concept of "binding" was an important one in Byzantine (and ancient) magic, especially that which was intended to cause harm; it was thus believed that the effects of such magical operations could range from the trivial sort of trick that is witnessed here to much more serious cases involving crippling physical conditions, impotence, lack of success in all manner of situations, or compelling lust. The whole incident recounted here provides interesting evidence of the lack of distinction at the popular level between doctrinally acceptable and unacceptable uses of religious power and of the evident confusion that existed there as to the appropriate attitude to supplicatory, manipulatory, and coercive forms of religious behavior; it also provides evidence (in the reaction of Methodios and his warnings about Lazaros' response if he should find out) of the irritation that was felt toward such attitudes by more "orthodox" representatives of the Byzantine religious spectrum. Cf. the incident recorded below, Chaps. 125–26. In general here, see Ph. Koukoules, "Μεσαιωνικοὶ καὶ Νεοελληνικοὶ καταδεσμοί," Λαογραφία 8 (1921–25), 302–46 and 9 (1926–28), 52–108; also R. P. H. Greenfield, "A Contribution to the Study of Palaeologan Magic," in *Byzantine Magic,* ed. H. Maguire (Washington, D.C., 1995), 138, n. 67.

when <the monks> started to walk on, <Sabas> ordered the <goats> to come after them, and they followed; when they reached the place where the cross is located[353] and stopped, the <goats> stopped too and stared intently at the monks. Methodios told Sabas to release the animals from the binding spell, but he did not want to and said, "They can come into the monastery with us." Methodios answered, "If you do this and the father sees them and finds out the reason why they've come into the monastery with us, he won't just rebuke you[354] but he'll impose a beating on you too, for I know that he's extremely annoyed by such things." Then <Sabas> listened to these words and released the <goats> at once from the binding spell out of fear of the beating; they went running off with leaps and bounds toward the craggy part of the mountain when they were released from the binding spell, while the <monks> reached the monastery astonished by the extraordinary <nature> of the miracle.

78. These, <then>, are the <stories> I have told in abundance about our holy father Lazaros' miracles. There are, however, some people, not only[355] among those outside <Galesion>, but even among those of our own flock, who are sick with disbelief. Some of these do not believe in the miracles because Lazaros did not accomplish them openly but in secret, since he shunned acclaim of men, as I have said many times. Others <do not believe> in the grace (which he received from God on account of his unsullied existence and irreproachable way of life) of foreseeing and foretelling to some people the secret things of their hearts and of speaking about future or anticipated affairs. Others again have acquired such disbelief, or rather wickedness, from <their own> wickedness,[356] that, just as the Jews once <did> to the Lord, they disparage Lazaros as a glutton and a wine drinker.[357] Indeed, what is even worse (I shudder to say it), they also find fault with his partaking of the unde-

[353] The reference to Chalkos Halonios in this passage may suggest that this is the cross at the dangerous pass described in Chap. 41, above, and also mentioned below, Chaps. 154, 155, and, perhaps, 199. On the other hand, the implication would seem to be that it is near the monastery to which they were going; perhaps then it is the cross mentioned in Chaps. 174 and 176, below, which was fixed to an oak tree just above the monastery of the Theotokos on the way to that of the Resurrection.

[354] There may well be a word play intended here, for the same verb, ἐπιτιμάω, is used here as above in Sabas' own binding (or "rebuking") of the goats.

[355] Reading μόνον for μόνων.

[356] Cf. Lk. 6:45; also Mt. 12:35.

[357] Mt. 11:19; Lk. 7:34. A rather similar slander is leveled at Daniel the Stylite, *vita Danielis,* chap. 59.

filed sacraments, stirring a blasphemous tongue against him, and saying that he ordered the priests to put larger portions into the chalice that was being given to him, not in order for him to be blessed, but in order for him to have his fill. But may the Lord God be gracious to them[358] and may the wicked Devil who sows these <ideas> in their <hearts> be set at nought.

79. Therefore, since the Evil One has sown <ideas> of this sort in the hearts of these people and they have caused harm not only to themselves but to others as well by such tales, I am going to bring out into the open the real truth about all these matters as accurately as possible, so that the spread of such evil may not harm many <more> hereafter. I will deal first with Lazaros' food and drink, then with his partaking of the undefiled sacraments, and then again with the grace of prophecy of which he was deemed worthy by God. <As for> the miracles, what needs to be said? For it is <surely enough> by itself for someone to bear in mind how, although he came up alone onto this mountain, without shelter, without shoes, and with only one little leather tunic and the irons which he wore to crush his body, Lazaros was yet able to found the three monasteries <on Galesion> and in addition to construct the monastery at Bessai,[359] to gather some three hundred monks in them,[360] to provide everything they needed, and moreover to maintain so many guests, then as now, in the [534] monastery every day. If someone bears these <facts> in mind, as I have said, I do not think he will find anything superior as far as a miracle is concerned,[361] considering the extent to which Lazaros <lacked> ancestral treasuries or inheritances <when> he founded these <monasteries>, <and that

[358] This evidently reflects a number of Old Testament passages, e.g., Num. 14:19, 20; Deut. 21:8; 2 Macc. 2:7, 22.

[359] For discussion of the foundation at Bessai and its complex relationship to Lazaros' monasteries on Galesion, see the Introduction, sections E and F, pp. 31–41. Note that the construction of this monastery is clearly attributed to Lazaros himself here, while Chaps. 216 and 245 evidently confirm that he was responsible for founding it. This contradicts Gregory of Cyprus' version of the *vita,* which suggests that a disgruntled steward (*oikonomos*) of Lazaros' monastery founded it as an attractive rival to Galesion (chap. 35, *AASS,* Nov. 3:602E–603B).

[360] Chap. 246 indicates that the total number of monks in the three monasteries on the mountain itself was to be limited to sixty-four; the present figure must thus include the residents at Bessai, evidently a large establishment, and probably also those at the other more minor establishments connected with Lazaros' community.

[361] I am grateful to an anonymous reader for suggesting this translation.

he did this> with <only> the help and assistance of some of his relatives and friends.[362] Nevertheless, even if these <facts> are worthy of amazement without any other miracle story, all the same I will have no problem either in establishing the veracity of <those of> his miracles that are unknown to most people or in narrating those which are <already> well known.

80. Therefore, once this narrative has dealt with the <topics> it earlier promised to <discuss>,[363] it will then engage in <consideration> of these <miracles> in sequence. <In this context> I am hesitant to tell the <stories> I have heard from the many brothers who have already died, for I must not call the dead as witnesses (even if the things they told me are true), because of some people's skepticism; instead <I must cite> those who are still living now, so that, if people hear something about the father and do not believe it, they may ask them and so learn the truth from them with their own ears. In this way, then, the<se skeptics> may not disbelieve the other <miracles> I narrate, which those <who are still alive> did not see or hear, and may, as a result, believe the <stories> that those who have already died did indeed pass on to me concerning the father.

81. Our superior, Lazaros' brother Kyris Ignatios, told me the <following> things, when questioned by me, which it would be wrong to pass over in silence. He said that, when the father was still at St. Marina three years before his ascent onto this mountain,[364] he used to abstain completely from eating bread (except for the holy and life-giving <altar bread>) and used to subsist on raw vegetables and soaked pulses; if he ever did have to consume them boiled, he would eat them without oil.[365] From the time he went up onto the mountain, while he was at the Savior and the Theotokos, he used to abstain from any <food> cooked with fire every Wednesday and Friday, and indeed,

[362] In other words Lazaros was not like some other monastic founders who came from rich families and used their own inheritance to endow their foundations; he came to Galesion with next to nothing, but was nevertheless able to attract immense outside support, due to his genuine and obvious holiness, and so create the extensive and flourishing community that evidently existed on the mountain by the time he died.

[363] That is, Lazaros' food and drink, his partaking of the sacraments, and his gift of prophecy, as promised in the previous chapter.

[364] On the implications of this statement for establishing the chronology of Ignatios' early life, see above, Chap. 33. See also the Introduction, section B, n. 25.

[365] Gregory the Cellarer has already made these points about Lazaros' diet in Chap. 35 above.

during the three forty-day fasts, he would take no food at all except on Saturday and Sunday.[366] From the time he went up to the <pillar of the> holy Resurrection he partook of cooked food every day, although without oil, but he did not have anything to drink at all until the evening; for this was always his personal rule.[367] Often, the Evil One, with God's permission, would spill both his food and his drink and would make him spend the whole of that day without food or drink, for he was never persuaded to accept any more. Often too, the Evil One would take the vessels that he used for eating, and would throw them in the place where he relieved himself. His drink was <sweetened with> honey, concentrated must, or grape syrup,[368] if someone brought some to him; but often, as I have said, the Evil One would pour this out and so make him stay <thirsty> until the following evening. Once, when I had taken his drink to him as usual toward evening, and was still standing there after he had taken it and closed his little window, there was a sudden sharp noise like a stone being thrown. I thought the cup that held his drink had been broken, but then I heard the father shaking his tunic with his hand and saying this out loud: "God blast you, Devil, because you've scalded my feet!" I asked him to tell me what the cracking sound had been. The father <replied>, "The most Evil One tipped out the hot drink into my lap and scalded my feet." After he had said this to me, he opened his little window and gave me the vessel he was

[366] Wednesday and Friday were traditional Byzantine fast days, while fasting was not permitted on Saturdays and Sundays. The three major forty-day fasts were Lent (preceding Easter), Advent (or the Fast of St. Philip, preceding Christmas), and the Fast of the Apostles (from the Sunday after Pentecost to 29 June, the Feast of St. Peter and St. Paul). There was also another shorter fast preceding the feast of the Dormition (15 August). On these fasts, see Lampe, *Lexicon*, s.v. τεσσαρακοστή, B.; *ODB*, s.v. "Lent," "Fasting."

[367] The gradual relaxation of the pattern of Lazaros' fasting is presumably related to his increasing age. On his fasting during Lent while he was at the Resurrection, see the following chapter.

[368] The Greek could be simply translated as, "His drink was honey, concentrated must, or grape syrup," but since it seems unlikely that Lazaros is to be imagined *drinking* honey or, indeed, any of these substances in an undiluted form, it may be better understood as referring to various ingredients used to sweeten or flavor his drinking water (ποτός), presumably when it was heated (see immediately below). The Greek word ἕψημα, translated here as "concentrated must" (i.e., new wine or unfermented or partially fermented grape juice reduced by boiling; see Liddell-Scott-Jones, *Lexicon*, s.v., II), could also mean water from boiling vegetables, hence perhaps suggesting some sort of gruel or thin mash, but the parallelism with honey (μέλι) and grape syrup (γλυκύ) in this context surely favors the former meaning.

holding in his hand; it was still whole and not broken at all, which greatly surprised me. I pleaded with the father a great deal, <trying> to make him <let me> bring him another drink, but, as I was unable to persuade him, I made my obeisance, received a blessing, and went down from the pillar. I have written this <down> because it has not come to your knowledge until today, but as for what <comes> next, let the narrative continue <more> directly <without further digression>.

82. After the father went up to the holy Resurrection, he engaged in week-long fasting only during Lent.[369] However, on one occasion, as the monk Ignatios the *trapezopoios*[370] told me, Lazaros decided not to take any food whatsoever for some days, saying to the brothers, "I'm scarcely alive and I can't partake of <any> food <at all>."[371] After he had done this for fifteen

[369] The meaning is not entirely clear. The reference may be to Lazaros' practice, mentioned in the previous chapter, of fasting for the whole week, except on Saturdays and Sundays, during all three forty-day fasts; the implication is, then, that he was too old and frail by the time he was on his pillar at the Resurrection to attempt this except once a year during Lent. Given the following (equally problematic) incident, however, which is obviously intended to illustrate this claim, it is conceivable that this sentence could be taken to mean, "After the father went up to the holy Resurrection, he engaged in fasting for weeks <on end> [or, "for <all> the weeks <prescribed>"] only during Lent"; in other words Lazaros would take no food at all during this period and so was increasing, rather than decreasing, the severity of his fasting when at the Resurrection. See further below in this chapter.

[370] The *trapezopoios* (τραπεζοποιός) basically set the table or acted as a waiter, but other references to the position in the *vita* seem to indicate its holder was a subordinate to the cellarer or to the *trapezarios* (the monk in charge of the refectory), performed some function in the pantry, and was also responsible for taking Lazaros his food. Thus in Chap. 131, the same Ignatios the *trapezopoios* sends a brother out to gather wild leeks on the mountain, while in Chap. 209, Gregory (the Cellarer), who was evidently also *trapezopoios* at the time in question, refuses to give bread to the *parekklesiarches* (assistant sacristan) during a shortage; the holder of the office in Chap. 211 also carries bread from the pantry to the refectory. As the previous chapter makes clear, Gregory also used to take Lazaros his food and drink at one time.

[371] The manuscript reads "Μόλις εἰμὶ καὶ" but a marginal note adds "ἀργὸς ἤγ<ουν> καν<ονισμένος>" and Delehaye incorporates this phrase into the text after Μόλις. It seems clear, however, that the person who wrote the note failed to understand the phrase "μόλις εἶναι," which means "to be scarcely alive"; it is also used in the same way in Chaps. 223 and 233 (cf. Chap. 221). The commentator (and Delehaye) must have taken the passage to mean something like "I am scarcely an idle person, that is <I am> someone who follows the rules, and <so> I cannot partake of <any> food <at all>." This episode should probably be dated toward the end of Lazaros' life when he had

days he was not allowed to go on any longer;[372] for when the monk Kosmas Philippikos realized this <was happening>, he went up to Lazaros and was able to persuade him to take food, although only with much pleading and <many> tears. <This Kosmas> had done the same thing also in connection with the tunic that the blessed man had been wearing for twelve years, because it had become completely ragged, <for he persuaded him> to take it off and put on another, also made of leather.[373] Some people say that they[374] used to give him consecrated bread from the church for food, but they are not telling the truth about this either, and brother Benjamin bears witness <to it>; he was then the *parekklesiarches*[375] and so used to give the sacraments to the father. As has been said, Lazaros never did partake of bread after he forswore eating it. Once a year, however, on account of the prevailing custom at the commemoration of Saint Basil, when the brothers used to make the <flat cakes> which in popular usage are called *lalangia*,[376] they would also make <some> for him

---

evidently become very frail; more specifically it may refer to the time, three years before his death, when almost all his remaining teeth fell out and he nearly died of starvation (Chaps. 206–7).

[372] As was mentioned above, it is not clear whether this implies that Lazaros fasted for fifteen days straight (thus breaking the rule which did not permit fasting on Saturdays and Sundays), or that his fast lasted for three weeks, excluding those days, but that he was now too old and weak to survive sustained fasting even of this kind.

[373] See Chaps. 35 and 112 on Lazaros' leather tunic, a style of dress he had evidently already adopted before he settled on Galesion (see Chap. 26); Chap. 112 also refers to his having worn the same garment for twelve years.

[374] Presumably "the priests" of Chap. 78.

[375] The term *parekklesiarches* (παρεκκλησιάρχης) is not in the standard lexica, but it evidently designates the office of assistant *ekklesiarches* (sacristan); compare the office of *parakellarios* (assistant cellarer) mentioned below, Chap. 248. This interpretation is supported by Chaps. 152 and 209, below, where the same monk, Germanos, is first described as being "entrusted with the job <of looking after> the church" and then as *parekklesiarches* at the monastery of the Resurrection. Gregory of Cyprus states that Lazaros held this office at St. Sabas, rather than that of *kanonarches;* see above, Chap. 16. The sacristan was responsible for the material provisioning of a church but, in monastic organization, was also a senior figure in the administrative hierarchy, with responsibilities for singing and conduct in the church, as well as for more general matters of discipline. See *ODB,* s.v. "Ekklesiarches."

[376] The evidently colloquial term λαλάγγιον is a version of the λάγανον, known from the LXX (Lev. 2:4; 2 Ki.[Sam.] 6:19) and elsewhere, which refers to a thin flat cake usually made of flour and oil; the name, and related forms (like λαλάγγη or λαλάγκιον), presumably arose from the sizzling sound the cakes made when cooking, for the verb

on a griddle;[377] but they would spread the griddle with honey, not with oil. They also used to do this in Cheese-eating Week.[378] These, then, are the <facts> about Lazaros' food and drink.

83. As concerns his partaking of the undefiled sacraments, the elder[379] and priest Neilos said about this, when asked by me, "When I was celebrating and preparing the elements, some of the brothers used to <try> to force <me> to put larger portions into the [535] vessel I was giving to the father with the undefiled sacraments. I myself never did this," said <Neilos>, "because I had no such instruction from the father, but some of the brothers used to do this without being told to by the father. Some of them did it so that they might seize on it as a pretext for criticizing him, but others did it out of pity, imagining, I suppose, that they were really doing something good. For this reason the father often told some of them not to do it, as our steward Bartholomew also attests."[380]

84. A monk called Photios passed on to me in writing (by way of the monk Kosmas who is called the Jerusalemite) the <story> I am about to set down. <This Photios> left Jerusalem and went to Constantinople; he then left there again and came to our monastery as he had heard about the father and

---

λαλαγέω means "to babble or chirp." Such cakes are still made today and are known by such names as λαλαγίτες; they are usually sprinkled with honey or confectioner's sugar. Special bread was traditionally made on St. Basil's day (1 January). The custom continues in contemporary Greece in the form of the "New Year" bread, which is made on this day. On the modern practice, see, e.g., L. K. Hart, *Time, Religion, and Social Experience in Rural Greece* (Lanham, Md., 1992), 204, 221.

[377] Or simply "a <hot> slab."

[378] "Cheese-eating" or "Cheesefare week" (τυροφάγος) was the week preceding Quinquagesima, the seventh Sunday before Easter; it was added to the Lenten fast in the 6th or 7th century to ensure that the period before Easter included a full forty days of fasting. See *ODB,* s.v. "Lent"; and cf. also below, Chap. 213.

[379] Retaining the original γέρων of the manuscript rather than the correction γηραιὸς preferred in the text by Delehaye. In Chap. 217 this Neilos is also described as "our Elder" (ὁ γέρων ἡμῶν), although in Chap. 225, when an incident in his youth is narrated, he is described as being simply "old" (γηραιός) at the time of the composition of the *vita.* He is, obviously, both old and an "Elder" in the monastery. On the role of "elders," cf. Chap. 141, where Lazaros makes provision for the control of spiritual affairs in the monastery by such men after his death and when the superior may be absent. Cf. also Chap. 233 where the monk Isaiah is similarly described.

[380] On the office of *oikonomos* (steward), see above, Chap. 49.

was keen to see him. When he was in the region of Lydia,[381] he went up to the monastery of St. Theophylact, which is called Kouzena,[382] and there found a monk who had also left Jerusalem a long time before. <Photios> asked him about the father as he wished to learn more accurately the <facts> about him. The <monk>, however, opened his mouth and poured forth a great <stream> of abuse and criticism of <the father> into <Photios'> ears; he thus damaged his estimation of the father and upset him badly.[383] But, even though his estimation was shaken in this way by that man's words, <Photios> still did not abandon his desire of going up and seeing the father; for he decided that it was better to trust his own eyes rather than that man's words. So he left there and, when he reached the mountain, went up to the monastery.

When he came in view of the father, he was immediately struck in the heart and was moved to compunction,[384] just by the sight <of him>, and he decided that the things he had heard about him from the monk were false. But, so that he would not have his estimation <of Lazaros> troubled again on account of hearsay, he also decided to learn about the matter for sure by a test. He approached one of the brothers and explained his thoughts <about Lazaros>[385] clearly to him, and asked if he could go into the church alone with him, after the service was over, and look at the elements of which the father would partake. After his request had been met, however, <Photios> found much fault both with himself and with the monk <at Kouzena>; with the latter for having made such innuendoes against the father, and also with himself for

[381] Lydia comprised the general region of western and central Asia Minor that stretched to the northeast of Ephesus and Galesion.

[382] The monastery of Kouzena (τοῦ Κουζηνᾶ), mentioned again below in Chap. 99 (cf. Chap. 105, n. 463), is also referred to by Skylitzes (*Hist.*, 478, 95 [Kedrenos, *Chron.*, 2:610, 22]) as being in the Thrakesion theme, as was Galesion. As Janin (*Églises centres,* 241) points out, this is the only neighboring monastery mentioned in the *vita* which is known from another source.

[383] Note again the evidence of hostility in a neighboring establishment to Lazaros' foundation on Galesion; cf. above, Chap. 66.

[384] Cf. Acts 2:37.

[385] The Greek word, λογισμός, contains a broad range of meaning, including "calculation," "reason(ing)," "mind," and "thought." It has been used a number of times in the chapter to this point and in each case it has been translated as "estimation": Photios' mental perception of Lazaros, in other words, or his thoughts about him; the present translation, with its implication of respect for Lazaros combined with the possibility of doubt attempts to continue that sense into this slightly different context; and at the end of the chapter, where it is translated simply as "thoughts."

having listened to them. When he emerged from the church, he went up to the father. The <latter> saw and spoke with him, and then ordered the monk Elias (for this was the name of the monk who had gone up with him to the father) to take <Photios> to his own cell and to eat with him there, for it was then the middle of the brothers' meal.[386] <Afterward>, when the monk Elias went off to undertake his duties, brother Photios, as he related, was left sitting alone in the cell astonished and quite perplexed. For he was more impressed by our father's angelic way of life and thought it more blessed than all the <others> he had observed, for he was someone who had seen other fathers pursuing virtuous lives in Palestine and Egypt and elsewhere; and he pondered how some people were not afraid to move an abusive tongue against him, considering what sort of man Lazaros was. He was annoyed and perplexed and <his head> was being spun this way and that by his thoughts.

85. While <Photios> was in this <state> he saw an awesome and holy vision, not only in his mind but with his physical eyes as well. He said he saw a building complex[387] between heaven and earth, which boasted wonderful constructions <including> a church and residences, and was extremely beautiful to behold and pleasant as a place to live. Up above this complex, near

[386] *Ariston* (ἄριστον), the meal referred to in this passage, was generally taken early in monasteries, after the morning service of *orthros* (see above, Chap. 8). Although it might be the single meal of the day in some monastic institutions, Chaps. 163 and 239 below make it clear that, on some days at least, the later meal of *deipnon* was also eaten on Galesion. Outside the monastic regime *ariston* was usually eaten at midday. See *ODB,* s.v. "Ariston and Deipnon."

[387] While the basic meaning of the word κτίσις is "something created," and it is thus used primarily in Byzantine Greek to refer either to God's act of creation or to the resulting universe and the creatures inhabiting it, the content of the passage seems to indicate that it is being used here as a synonym for κτίσμα, in the sense of a "building complex" or, perhaps more particularly, a monastic "foundation," due most probably to the extraordinary nature of the complex described. Connotations drawn from the basic use of κτίσις may be intended as well, however, given the context which situates the visionary "foundation" between heaven and earth. Lazaros is, then, being regarded as the κτίστης or κτήτωρ, the founder, a technical term in the monastic and ecclesiastical context (see further *ODB,* s.v. "Ktetor"), but his work is also being set against the background of the original creation of the universe *ex nihilo* by God. The point being made by the vision is thus the same as that made by the author in Chap. 79: that the most visible, the most lasting, and perhaps the most miraculous achievement of Lazaros' saintly life is his foundation and creation *ex nihilo* of the flourishing group of monastic communities that Photios has observed on Galesion. For an overt comparison of Lazaros to God Himself, see below, Chap. 143.

heaven, he seemed to see another complex that was much more glorious and splendid than the former;[388] <indeed> the human tongue is unable to describe its beauty and splendor. Between both complexes there was a ladder set up that flashed more brightly than the sun's rays.[389] The holy father was sometimes to be seen lingering in the lower complex and apparently delivering words of instruction to some people, his lips flowing with honey, at other times ascending the ladder to the habitation near heaven and hastening to enter heaven, his face beaming; then he could be seen descending the ladder <again> and appearing as before; then going back up it again. <The father> astonished the man who was watching by doing this many times. So, when the monk saw a crowd of distinguished people coming along the path, who were astonished at the beauty and the splendor of the residences and were asking each other what these <buildings> might be and whose <they were>, "I was not at a loss," said the monk, "and, as if I had been instructed in <the meaning of> the vision, I answered their questions unerringly. 'What you can see,' I said to them, 'are the constructions of holy Lazaros. His ascension into the height of heaven to the higher construction indicates his progress through spiritual contemplation; while his descent displays his deliberate association and sympathetic interaction with those whom he is leading to God; his reascension <illustrates> his continuous and easy access to God.'[390] But while I was still

[388] Although the vision clearly relates to Lazaros' spiritual achievements, its imagery is undoubtedly based on the successive monastic foundations he had made on the mountain.

[389] The image of the heavenly ladder that appears in this vision has roots that go back to Jacob's dream in Gen. 28:12, but is here most probably to be related to manuscript illustrations of *The Ladder of Paradise* of John Klimax; such depictions enjoyed a vogue in the 11th century, and would thus undoubtedly have been familiar to both the authors here—Photios, who is evidently responsible for the initial written description of his experience (see previous chapter), and Gregory the Cellarer, who has incorporated it in his work. See further *ODB,* s.v. "John Klimax." An allusion may also be intended to the ladder leading up to the top of Lazaros' pillar, which connected the earth below with his "heavenly abode."

[390] The language used of Lazaros here is charged with connotations that relate his activity to the incarnation of Christ. The author (whether Photios himself or Gregory the Cellarer) seems to have Eph. 4:8–10 particularly in mind, but there may well also be a deliberate allusion to Jn. 1:51 in view of the connection mentioned above to Jacob's ladder; cf. also Jn. 3:13. Lazaros' role in the foundation of Galesion and the benefits which this has for the world are again being placed in a much broader context than that of a simple, material human achievement; he is being portrayed, almost like Christ, as an effective mediator of divine grace. For Lazaros compared directly to Christ else-

seeing these things," <Photios> continued, "the owner of the cell [Elias] was suddenly there and tore me away from my vision, for I had been completely entranced and inspired by amazement." This is the account the monk Photios passed on to me by way of another brother, as has already been made clear.

86. Another brother from our monastery, whose name is Nikephoros and who comes from Stratonikia in Lydia,[391] told me something similar. He said that late one evening he was going from the church to his cell and was near the kitchen (for his cell was near the guest house), when there seemed to be a bolt of lightning from heaven. [536] He turned toward the east and saw the dome of the church apparently swathed in fire; the fire then ran down from there like water and went into the father's pillar. When he saw this, the monk was seized by fear and joy at this wonderful sight and went off to his cell glorifying God.[392]

87. Romanos, called Skleros,[393] who was the *strategos* of the region,[394]

---

where in the *vita,* see below, Chap. 251; cf. the comparison to God the creator mentioned above, p. 173 n. 387.

[391] Stratonikia (ancient Stratoniceia-Hadrianopolis, modern Eskihisar), a small inland town of ancient origin, was some sixty-five miles southeast of Galesion. See *RE* 4.1:322–25; suppl. 7:1244–50.

[392] A lay servant of a distinguished visiting monk reportedly had a very similar experience, apparently at the monastery of the Resurrection, the night before Lazaros' death; see below, Chap. 252. Further on the apparent proximity of Lazaros' pillar to the church of the Resurrection, see below, Chap. 118 and the Introduction, section C, p. 18.

[393] This Romanos Skleros was the brother of Maria Skleraina, the mistress of Constantine IX Monomachos (1042–55). He came from an aristocratic family that had significant possessions in the Anatolikon theme and achieved the peak of its eminence at this time. Romanos rose in favor and honor with his sister following the accession of Monomachos to the throne in 1042, and the high office mentioned here evidently formed only one step in the progress of a notable career, which was probably not halted by his sister's death ca. 1045–46 (see below, Chap. 245). There are, however, problems in distinguishing him from other men of the same name in this period. According to Chap. 245, below, he also brought Lazaros' activities on Galesion to his sister's notice, something which resulted in a significant donation from her; however, it is not clear if the visit mentioned here was his only one to Galesion and so that which specifically prompted this development. On Romanos, see Seibt, *Skleroi,* no. 18, 76–85. Cf. *ODB,* s.v. "Skleraina," "Skleros."

[394] The term *strategos* (lit. "general") was used in Byzantine times to indicate the military governor of a theme. By the 11th century the power of the *strategoi* had been considerably curtailed from the peak the office had enjoyed in the 8th century; although still very important men, they had become more numerous and operated under consid-

came up to the monastery to see the father. When he was about to go up to Lazaros, but had only mounted the first rung of the ladder, the father put his head out of his little window. <Skleros> turned back as though he had been pushed by someone and stood holding his head with his hand and bending down toward the ground. Then, after shaking off the faintness that had come over him, he went up to the father. After he had come down from there, he was asked by the brothers what had suddenly made him lurch backward. He replied, "Believe me, brothers and fathers, I'm telling you the truth <when I say> that I saw the father <appear> like fire as soon as he put his head out of the window, and I could not bear the sight; I felt faint, as you saw, and turned back involuntarily. I think," he continued, "that the holy father has as much (and perhaps far more) familiarity with the heavenly emperor, as I myself currently have with the earthly one."[395] But enough of these matters.

88. Since I have said enough in defense of the father's food and drink and, indeed, also of his partaking of the undefiled sacraments, let me now write about the grace of prognostication that was given to him by God.[396] Theodoulos (whom we used to call Raphis [needle], but now call Arrhostos [sick]) told me that toward the beginning of his <monastic> submission he found a *tetarteron nomisma*[397] lying on the ground somewhere outside the

---

erable restrictions, while their role in civil administration was being given over to the thematic judges at about this time (see below, Chap. 102); see also *ODB,* s.v. "Strategos."

The "region" (χώρα) mentioned here probably refers to the Thrakesion theme; see Seibt, *Skleroi,* 79, contra V. Laurent (*Les sceaux byzantins du Médaillier Vatican* [Vatican, 1962], 91), who held that this indicated Romanos was *strategos* of Samos, because the holder of that office had authority over the coasts of the region. The Thrakesion theme stretched inland from the center and south of the west coast of Asia Minor and thus included many rich areas and cities in its territory; the largest of these was Ephesus, although the capital of the theme may have been Chonai. Apart from Lazaros' early journeys, Thrakesion is the setting and focus of interest of most of the *vita.* See *ODB,* s.v. "Thrakesion."

395 The reference must be to Constantine IX Monomachos, who also played an important part in the last phase of the development of Lazaros' community on Galesion; see below, Chaps. 221, 223, 230, and 245, and the Introduction, section F.b. Cf. on this episode, Ševčenko, "Eastern Provinces," 724.

396 See above, Chap. 79, for Gregory the Cellarer's outline of material to be covered in this section of the *vita.*

397 While the *nomisma* was the standard gold coin of the Byzantine world, the equivalent of the earlier *solidus* and later *hyperpyron,* the *tetarteron nomisma* mentioned here

monastery. He picked it up and slipped it into the folds <of his habit>, and then figured out <what he should do>, saying to himself, "If I show this to the father, he'll take it away from me; so I'll buy a psalter with it instead, and then I'll explain it to him and he'll forgive me." After he had thought up this course of action, he then searched around to find a psalter. He found one, but the person who was selling the book wanted a standard *nomisma.* While he was mulling over this problem, a layman whom he knew came to the father for a blessing; <Theodoulos> approached him straightaway, informed him of his problem, and asked him to take the *nomisma* that he had and give him another <in exchange>. The man suggested to him that he should go down to his house, as he did not have a *nomisma* on him then, so that he could change the <*tetarteron*> *nomisma* for him there. So, when the man left the monastery, <Theodoulos> went up to the father and asked untruthfully, as he himself said, if he could go away <to visit> his brother, so that <the latter> might present him with a *nomisma* to buy a psalter. As he was given permission <to do so>, he went down from the mountain, but he did not go to his brother, as he had said, but to the man who had said he would give him the *nomisma.* <Then> he returned to the monastery again, taking this <coin> back with him but still also in possession of the one he had found earlier, for the man did not wish to take it <from him>. He went up to the father and, after he had informed him in the usual way who was standing there, he was asked by Lazaros if his brother had given him a *nomisma.* He replied untruthfully again, "Yes, as a result of your precious blessing." The father asked <Theodoulos> again about this three times,[398] and he replied to each of his questions, "Yes, he has given me <one> as a result of your blessings." The father then opened his little window and asked him if anyone else was standing there. When he learned from <Theodoulos> that no one else was standing there except for him, he

refers to a gold coin issued ca. 965–1092, which was lighter than the standard (*histamenon*) *nomisma,* to which reference is made later in the chapter; at first it was two carats lighter but by the mid-11th century its weight had been reduced by a further carat. It came to be distinguished from the standard *nomisma* by the fact that it was smaller and thicker. The problems of dealing with these different coins are clearly illustrated by the story in this chapter. See especially here M. F. Hendy, "Light Weight Solidi, Tetartera, and the Book of the Prefect," *BZ* 65 (1972), 63–73; the incident in the *vita* is discussed on pp. 65 and 71; see also *ODB,* s.v. "Histamenon," "Nomisma," "Tetarteron."

[398] There is clearly an allusion here to the triple denial of Christ by Peter.

looked at him and smiled, saying, "Go off and thank Christ for sending you both the first and the second <*nomismata*>, since your brother hasn't even given you <the> one you say <he has>." Then the brother saw that it was impossible to escape the father's notice; he prostrated himself in shame, confessed, and begged forgiveness. When he received this he went down from the pillar marveling and, at the same time, giving thanks to God that he had been thought worthy to fall into the hands of such a holy man. This <is the story> brother Theodoulos told.

89. Neophytos, who came from Lydia, also had a *nomisma* no one else knew about, for his brother had given it to him, but he was not able to escape Lazaros' notice either. For the father called him and said, "Lend me the *nomisma* that you have so that I may give it to <this> poor fellow." For a poor man was standing there at that time, begging for alms. At first the brother denied it; "*I* don't have a *nomisma!*" he said. But, as the father pressed his demand and would not relent at all (for he knew exactly what he had), <Neophytos> unwillingly confessed; then he went off and fetched it, and gave it to the father. And Lazaros did the same sort of thing concerning a coin on another occasion <too>.[399]

90. While he was working for the cellarer, the wine happened to run out. Since the servants were away fetching grain in the distant parts of Lydia, and they did not have any <wine> for the next day, as has been said. . . . [400] The monk Bartholomew, who is now our steward, recounted <an episode> which I will now narrate:[401] he was once sent out by the father, along with another

[399] For Lazaros taking money and other things from his monks to give to poor visitors, see below, Chap. 145; cf. Chap. 143, which mentions the opposition this evidently aroused. The right of monks to possess private property was evidently a thorny issue in the community; see also, e.g., Chaps. 148–49, 163, 192–93.

[400] Delehaye, in the published text, evidently understands these sentences to be the introduction to the story of the monk Bartholomew, which begins on f. 149v. The linkage is somewhat awkward as it stands, however, and the fact that there is a gap in the manuscript here at the bottom of f. 149 makes it seem more likely that they are actually the beginning of an episode now lost. Moreover, if the Neophytos of the previous chapter is to be identified with the one in Chap. 248 below, then he also held the office of *parakellarios,* something that increases the likelihood that this passage continues to discuss him. Gregory the Cellarer tells the story of a miracle worked by Lazaros when there was a shortage of wine in the monastery in Chap. 212, below.

[401] The direct speech, which begins here in the published text, is apparently an error.

brother, to one of the monastery's estates.[402] Night fell while they were still in the middle of their journey, so they lodged in a layman's house. After they had eaten and were lying down to [537] sleep, their host's wife, without her husband knowing, climbed into the same <bed> as the brother who was <Bartholomew's> companion and persuaded him to commit sin with her.[403] <Bartholomew> realized what <had happened> and was struck by wicked ideas, for he said to himself, "Oh dear me, what a disaster. If I had a knife I'd get up and murder that woman for the sin into which she's led the brother <who's> with me out of lust; and then I'd leave the house." When he got back to the monastery from there and went up to the father, before he could say anything to him about this <incident, Lazaros> spoke first: "How fortunate for you that you didn't have a knife, since you and your fellow monk, as well as the woman, would have been killed by her husband." After the brother heard this, he told the whole story clearly, <albeit> unwillingly, to the father. Then he prostrated himself and went down from the pillar, <filled> with amazement.

91. The following <incidents> must also be added to those <already mentioned>. Cornelius, who came from Armenia, had the job of <looking after> the <pack> animal that brought the water up from the river to the monastery. On one occasion, however, he went to Komothon with it to fetch wine for the monastery.[404] He picked up the wine and started back but, at some point on the way, he saw the animal turn off the track and so reached out with his hand to strike it with the stick he was carrying;[405] but by chance he hit the jar (what is usually called a flagon)[406] that was hanging from the pack saddle, and broke

[402] That is, a *proasteion* (προάστειον), which in this period and context refers technically to an estate on which the landowner was not resident and which was populated with *paroikoi* or peasant farmers. See *ODB*, s.v. "Proasteion"; Harvey, *Expansion*, xvi.

[403] In discussing the evidently unusual distance at which this *proasteion* lay from Galesion, Kaplan ("Evergetis," 110, n. 38) mistakenly suggests both that the woman was the daughter of the householder and that the monks resisted the temptation.

[404] On the importation of supplies to the monastery from neighboring villages, as evidenced in this and the following chapter, see Foss, *Ephesus*, 120, n. 16; as he indicates, none of the places mentioned has been located. Morris (*Monks*, 215) assumes that the monastery possessed an estate at Komothon (Komothona), but the wording of the *vita* does not necessarily imply this.

[405] A Byzantine would probably recognize an allusion in the wording here to Num. 22:23 and the story of Balaam and his ass.

[406] The word in Greek is φλασκίον.

it. When he saw that the wine was pouring out of the broken <jar>, he ran <up> and grabbed it and began to drink the wine; indeed, he drank so much that he got drunk. With difficulty he continued a short distance[407] but was overcome by the wine; he turned off the path a little way, fell to the ground, and lay there as if dead. Laurentios Halmyrenos and Luke the perfumer[408] passed by there, and one took the monk, the other the beast; they led the <latter> to Varvatziana,[409] the <former> to the village called Voulgarin.[410] When the brother recovered from the wine, he discovered what had happened to him from the people who <lived> there, for he had no idea what had occurred; so he went to Varvatziana, collected the animal, and came <back> to the monastery with the <rest of the> wine. When he went up to the father and called out the <usual> "Bless <me>!" Lazaros said in reply, "Well![411] Should monks lie about dead drunk in the middle of the road?" When he heard this, <Cornelius> unwillingly confessed everything that had happened to him. A layman who was standing there said to the father, apparently by way of apology for the brother, "Father, the brother <only> did this so that the wine would not be wasted." But the father replied, "It would have been better for all the wine to be wasted rather than for him to have got drunk, for drunkards will not inherit the kingdom of God."[412] After the father had said this, the brother made his repentance and sought forgiveness; <this> he received and went down from the pillar straight away.

92. <In> much the same <way>, the monk Germanos (who is now the steward at Varvatziana), <while he> had the job, along with two other broth-

[407] I am grateful to an anonymous reader for suggesting this wording.

[408] Taking this in the sense of "from among <the> perfumers <by trade>," i.e., "a perfumer"; so Foss, *Ephesus,* 120.

[409] This monastery is also mentioned in the following chapter with the same spelling (Βαρβατζιανά), although it is given as Varva*ni*tziana the second time it occurs here. Like so many local places mentioned in the *vita,* nothing further is known about Varvatziana or the nearby Voulgarin. Kaplan (*Les hommes,* 294, n. 105) is surely correct in assuming that Varvatziana was some sort of monastic establishment annexed to Galesion; its steward (*oikonomos*), Germanos, who is evidently a monk of the Galesiote community, is mentioned in the following chapter.

[410] Ševčenko ("Eastern Provinces," 726) and Foss (*Ephesus,* 121) take this name, in the form Boulgarin, to indicate that Bulgarians lived there.

[411] The Greek Καλόν ("well," "good") is clearly ironic here.

[412] Cf. 1 Cor. 6:10.

ers, of <looking after> the horses, went to Targyrou[413] for oil. He took three measures <of the oil> for their own use, and then, after returning to the monastery, asked again for the <oil> they were entitled to by the rule.[414] He too was questioned by the father and confessed all that he had done.[415]

93. Merkourios, who was a skilled plasterer, told me that, while he was still a layman, he had a neighbor who was a painter by trade. This man told him about the father and said, "I went up to Lazaros and, although I did not want to, I confessed to him my past deeds when I was questioned by him. Also," he said, "Lazaros has revealed how long my life <will be>, for he said that it is <to last> for twelve years or more." Indeed, <Merkourios' neighbor> kept track <of the passage of time> and died after living for twelve <more> years. The same Merkourios also told me this: "A monk who had just left the holy mountain,[416] and who was traveling with me when I was leaving the city <of Constantinople>,[417] told me in conversation that a<nother> monk from the area of the holy mountain, who went to Lazaros and confessed what was on his mind, also learned the length of his life from the father. He returned to his own cell and worked out the time; when the day was at hand on which he was actually going to die, he went down to the brothers of the monastery which was there (for he was living alone as a solitary in a cell), and informed <them> of the prediction which the father had made to him and that he was

[413] Τἀργύρου, lit. "the <place> of silver"; or possibly a monastery founded by a member of the prominent Argyros clan.

[414] The implication is that Germanos was trying to obtain a double ration of oil without Lazaros' knowledge.

[415] The Greek verb ἐλέγχω, which is translated by "questioned" here and in the following chapters (93 and 94), also contains the connotations of exposure, accusation, and reproach; Germanos, like Merkourios' neighbor, and the shipowner of the following chapters, is not simply asked about his misdeeds, but it is also implied that these are already known to Lazaros who takes him to task for them, as in the case of Cornelius in the previous chapter (91).

[416] Presumably Mt. Athos, since the *vita* never refers to Galesion in this way; the identification is made more likely by the fact that Merkourios evidently encounters the man a long way away from Galesion at Constantinople.

[417] Although the *vita* sometimes refers to Constantinople by name (e.g., in Chaps. 94 and 95, below) or as "the <city> of Constantine" (e.g., Chap. 84, above), it also follows the common practice of referring to it simply as ἡ πόλις (unquestionably in, e.g., Chaps. 221 and 223). It would thus seem most probable that this is how the phrase is to be understood here.

going to die the next day. He embraced them, addressed his last <words> to them, and then went up to his own cell. On the next day the brothers went <there> and found him dead."

94. Another man, who was a sailor by trade and the owner of a boat, came across the superior[418] and the brothers who were with him in Lopadion,[419] for they had been sent to Constantinople. When he made inquiries and discovered that they were from the monastery of the holy Lazaros, and particularly when he discovered that the superior was Lazaros' brother, he went to the place where they were and, in the presence of some other people and in the hearing of all, he told this <story> about the father. "When I went to him," he said, "I was persuaded to confess to him all the offenses that I committed of old, in the matters about which he questioned me, even though I was unwilling <to do so>. But," <the man> continued, "the holy man also made this prophecy to me, when I was about to depart from there: 'As soon as you return home, you will discover that something sad has happened, but do not despair at this event because it will soon become a source of joy for you.'" And this did indeed happen. For <the man> had a son, about five years old, who died while he was away; [538] but, while he was still alive, the boy had said to his father, showing him the place at the same time, "If I die, bury me here, and build a chapel for me. If you do this you will be able to eat much fruit from the garden that will grow here, and I will be there to give it to you myself."[420]

[418] As is shown just below, this was Ignatios, Lazaros' brother. It is not clear if Ignatios actually held the office of superior at the time the incident occurred, and thus if this episode took place after Lazaros' death, or if Gregory the Cellarer is referring to the position he had come to occupy by the time he was writing the *vita.*

[419] Lopadion (Ulubad) lay some twelve miles south of the Sea of Marmara in northwest Asia Minor at the west end of Lake Apollonia (Ulubad or Apolyont Gölü). It was a relatively important market town and fortress that developed at the site of a strategic bridge on the road to Constantinople from Kyzikos and Abydos, which at this point had also been joined by the highway from the cities and towns of the central and southern West coast, including Ephesus. See *ODB,* s.v. "Lopadion"; J. Lefort, "Les communications entre Constantinople et la Bithynie," in *Constantinople and Its Hinterland,* ed. C. Mango and G. Dagron (Aldershot, 1995), 209–10; also Foss, *Ephesus,* 119.

[420] While the boy's statement refers at one level to the miracles subsequently worked by his coffin (see below), there is also an allusion to the afterlife here, for the Greek word παράδεισος, which literally means a "garden" but is also used for "Paradise," accompanies a reference to the enjoyment of fruit and the suggestion of continued existence after death.

When he got back and found that the boy had died, <the sailor> was not stricken with grief and despondency, but, with thanksgiving to God, constructed a tomb on the spot the child had indicated while he was still alive. He built a chapel on it besides and, after he had moved <the remains> (for the boy had been buried elsewhere), laid him to rest there. Indeed, from that time on until the present day, as the man affirmed to them with oaths, by the grace of Christ, the boy's holy coffin has worked miracles.

95. This <story> must also be told: A woman who came from Constantinople, and was a nun by her habit, cleverly changed her garb into that of a man,[421] and traveled with some of the people who used to go to the Theologian [Ephesus] to pray. As she was near the mountain of our monastery and saw some people going up to the monastery, she inquired and found out about the father, and then went up with the others. When they had seen the father and had heard his homily, they then went off to the guest house to receive a meal,[422] but the father sent one of the brothers and summoned this woman to

[421] As Kazhdan ("Ideals," 474) points out, this is a rare example of the phenomenon of women disguising themselves as men for religious purposes at such a late date in the Byzantine period. On this tradition in general, see particularly E. Patlagean, "L'histoire de la femme déguisée en moine et l'évolution de la sainteté féminine à Byzance," *SM*, ser. 3, 17 (1976), 597–623 (repr. in her *Structure sociale, famille, chrétienté à Byzance* [London, 1981], art. XI). See also, J. Anson, "The Female Transvestite in Early Monasticism: The Origin and Development of a Motif," *Viator* 5 (1974), 1–32; Talbot, "Family," 123; eadem, "Comparison," 10. Deut. 22:5 expressly forbids the practice but, as Anson points out (p. 7), Gal. 3:27–28 might actually be taken as a justification for it. The ideal Byzantine nun was also expected to assume masculine qualities; see Talbot, "Comparison," 9–11.

[422] The Greek word is διάκρισις; for its usage in this sense in the *vita* and elsewhere, see P. Karlin-Hayter, "Lexicographical Notes," *Byzantion* 55 (1985), 589–90; Trapp, *Lexikon,* s.v. διάκρισις, διακρίνομαι. Karlin-Hayter cites most, but not all, of the passages in the *vita* (Chaps. 105, 117, 118 [διακρίνομαι], and 238; cf. Chap. 142) where the word appears in this sense, i.e., a "meal" of some sort customarily offered to visitors to the monastery (hence perhaps something like a "dole" as it existed in Western medieval monastic practice); she also includes without distinction its usage in Chaps. 140 and 246. In these latter passages, however, the word refers to special food allowed the monks as part of the celebration of church festivals, a usage for which Karlin-Hayter cites parallels in the Eleousa *typikon* and the *vita Euthymii* (cf. also the *typikon* of Kecharitomene, ed. Gautier, "Kécharitôménè," e.g., 99.1423; 121.1790, 1798, 1803). As Karlin-Hayter suggests, the use of the word in these latter passages may well imply a "good" or "substantial meal," but there seems no reason for imagining that this sense is also

go <back> up to him alone. When he saw her he said to her, "Why have you done this? Why did you leave your cell with the intention of going to Jerusalem?" (for this was her aim), "Don't you know that you're a woman and shouldn't be going about here and there?"[423] She saw that she could not escape his notice and revealed her whole plan to him. The father said to her, "Go back to where you came from, woman, and don't propose going somewhere <else> from here lest some spiritual or physical harm befall you. For wherever anyone does good, there is the <true> Jerusalem!"[424] <The woman> obeyed the father's words and went back to her own cell again. Some time later she came across the monk Neophytos "the aged"[425] at the Chrysostom[426] and,

implicit in the former passages and that all visitors to the monastery were being treated to "substantial meals." It may thus be helpful to distinguish two slightly different meanings here: a) a "special meal" enjoyed by monks on feast days (and thus probably a "good" or "substantial" one) allowed at the discretion of the superior or founder etc.; b) a more simple "meal" (possibly a "dole") customarily supplied to visitors to the monastery. This latter usage is otherwise unattested; perhaps it was something unique to Galesion, an extension of the former practice resulting from the particularly arduous journey required to visit the monasteries there. Elsewhere in the *vita* the same word is commonly used in its more basic sense to indicate Lazaros' quality of "good judgment" or "discernment."

423 For this particular episode and the evidence it provides of Byzantine disapproval of mobility by nuns at this time, see Talbot, "Comparison," 15; as she points out, Lazaros' final statement is closely paralleled in a speech attributed to abbot Arsenios in the *Apophthegmata,* Chap. 28 (PG 65:97A; Ward, *Sayings,* 12). Cf. here, Malamut, *Route,* 279. On the ideal of monastic stability in Byzantium, see *ODB,* s.v. "Stability, monastic."

424 Lazaros here echoes a common theme of pilgrimage criticism that had been employed from at least the 4th century; this stressed the importance of proper spirituality, which could be practiced anywhere, over the visiting of holy places, which could serve as a means to this end but not as an end in itself. His statement is somewhat reminiscent of a passage in Jerome, *Ep.* 58, "It is praiseworthy not to have been in Jerusalem but to have lived well for Jerusalem"; that passage, along with other parallels, is discussed by G. Constable, "Opposition to Pilgrimage in the Middle Ages," *Studia Gratiana* 19 (1976), 136; cf. also Kötting, *Peregrinatio,* 421–26; J. Sumption, *Pilgrimage, an Image of Mediaeval Religion* (London, 1975), 95f.

425 If this is the same monk Neophytos who figures in Chap. 102, below, he was certainly in Constantinople in April 1042.

426 The narrative implies that this church or monastery was in Constantinople; only one church there is known to have been dedicated to John Chrysostom, on which see Janin, *Églises CP,* 280–81. There was another at Hiereia, to the south of Chalcedon (just across the Bosporos from Constantinople); see idem, *Églises centres,* 36.

when she found out that he was from the monastery of the holy Lazaros, she narrated the whole story which has been told <above> in the hearing of some other people who were also present; and the same brother [Neophytos] has also expounded it to me.

96. A layman called George, who was a friend of mine in the outside world, came to the monastery to be tonsured and asked me to act as an intermediary with the father in this <matter>. After this had happened and he had been tonsured and admitted by the father, he came to me and said tearfully, "This venerable old man really is a great holy man!" When I asked him how he knew this, he replied, "When I went up and was standing in front of the little window of his pillar to make my confession, I couldn't open my mouth and speak because I realized the enormity of my sins, and I went on standing there <like> someone struck dumb and speechless with shame. The father asked me, not just once, but two or three times, <and then>, when he saw that I wasn't answering at all, he opened his holy mouth and uttered first of all that very sin which had tied fast my tongue and my voice, <preventing me> from confessing the rest. He then <named> another <sin> and another again after that, and so, after he had started me off like this, he made me confess all <my sins> to him without being afraid."

97. John, whose surname was Libanos, went up to Lazaros to receive a blessing, for he was about to go off to the Anatolikon theme[427] on the business that had been entrusted to him. He received <this> and went down from the mountain, but I went up to the father to speak with him about this man for I knew him before from the city <of Constantinople>.[428] The father asked me if he had a son in the City and I replied, "<Yes>, he has one about sixteen <years old> whom he has arranged to have educated in letters; but <the boy> is <so> clever that he has surpassed all those ahead of him in his studies." The father asked us to pray for him, "For although," he said, "the boy is <as> clever as you say, he will not last long in this life." Indeed, this happened, for in the following year I received a letter, sent to me by my mother, at the end of which I found the boy's death made known in these words, "And master George, the son of Libanos, died."

Are these sufficient examples to prove sufficiently the grace of prophecy that was given to the father by God, or shall we go on with the account of the rest <of them>? Now, although I am quite clearly guessing at your intention

[427] See above, Chap. 29.

[428] See above, Chap. 93.

in listening <to this>, <I am assuming> that, even if you do not need any more of the many <remaining stories> for certainty and conviction concerning Lazaros' marvelous and abundant grace, nevertheless you will still listen very affectionately and eagerly to a narration of his words and deeds, <simply> because they <are> charming and, indeed, so very pleasant and marvelous; nor would I myself <wish to> appear reluctant <to continue> the narrative. So, then, I must deal with the following <stories>.

98. Kosmas, the son of Konidiares, also went up to the father after being tonsured and received his blessing. When he saw me he recognized me, for he was also an old friend and acquaintance of mine, and he agreed to go off and, after settling his affairs properly, return again to the monastery and live with us. When the father learned this from me, he said, "You won't see him coming back to us as he said <he would>; but after a short time you'll learn that he's rejected the monastic way of life [539] and has once more embraced that of the world, just as his father did." And indeed this did happen, for, during the revolt of Komnenos,[429] he fell in with that man's army (I've no idea where) and, taking off the monastic habit as the father had predicted, he again put on the dress of worldly men and thus went to the city <of Constantinople>. I have learned from some people, however, that <eventually> he became a monk again, but even if this affair did turn out better than Lazaros' reckoning, nevertheless our father's prediction was not wrong.

99. Also a certain Basil, who comes from Smyrna, and is called the son of Blattopolos, was tonsured by Lazaros and spent some time in the monastery.

[429] This passage provides important information for dating the writing of the *vita,* for it shows that Gregory the Cellarer cannot have completed his narrative before late 1057, at least four years after Lazaros' death. The reference is to the revolt of Isaac Komnenos against Michael VI Stratiotikos, which originated in the uncertain political climate following the extinction of the Macedonian line with the death of Theodora in August 1056 and the elevation of the aging civil servant Michael to the throne by surviving members of the ruling faction; it was led by army chiefs, backed by the aristocracy, and it had the support (at least tacitly) of the powerful patriarch of Constantinople, Michael Keroularios. Isaac was proclaimed emperor on 8 June 1057, at Kastamon in Paphlagonia by leading members of the great families of Asia Minor, and the success of the rebels was ensured in a battle near Nicomedia at the end of August of that year. Michael VI abdicated and became a monk, and Isaac I Komnenos was crowned by Keroularios on 1 September 1057. On this episode see Cheynet, *Pouvoir,* no. 80, pp. 68–70; Angold, *Byzantine Empire,* 48–50. On the precise dating of the coronation, see J. Shepard, "Isaac Comnenus' Coronation Day," *BS* 38 (1977), 22–30.

However, since he was not satisfied <here>, he left and went to the Kouzena monastery.[430] Some of the brothers took the father to task because he allowed him to leave the monastery,[431] but he replied to them, "Believe me, he is not going to stay put[432] in the monastery of Kouzena or anywhere else; but, after he has gone round to a great many monasteries, see if he does not come back here again." And to be sure, we <can now> see that he has not stayed either at the Kouzena nor anywhere else for, as the father said <he would>, he just recently returned to the monastery and is living with us.

100. What about the <story> concerning the eunuch Stephen?[433] Does it not match these and similarly show Lazaros' wonderful <gift of> prognostication? For when this man was sent to the <monastery of the> Savior by the father after all the other eunuchs were also collected and sent there because of the problems[434] that arose between them and the rest of the brothers,[435] he

[430] On this monastery, see above, Chap. 84; cf. Chap. 106 n. 463.

[431] There was evidently considerable criticism of Lazaros' policy concerning admission and stability from some of the monks on Galesion who perceived his attitude to be lax and even uncanonical. See, e.g., Chap. 232, where Lazaros also defends his policy, and the Introduction, section D.

[432] The verb προσεπιμένω is not found in the standard lexica.

[433] This monk also figures prominently in Chap. 216, which has a theme similar to the present one. There Stephen wishes to go to Lazaros' other foundation, the monastery of Bessai, but is dissuaded by the father's warnings about that place and his stress, as here, on the spiritual benefits of persevering on the mountain.

[434] It is difficult to do justice to the word σκάνδαλον, translated as "problem" here, for it carries with it the connotation of "occasion for sin" and "(moral) stumbling block," as well as the simpler idea of "an obstacle," "difficulty," or "problem." The latter, however, perhaps captures the idea of "personal problems" in contemporary English, which is certainly appropriate here.

[435] Eunuchs were still important in many areas of the Byzantine administration in the 11th century, although they had begun to lose their control of some of the highest governmental offices by its end. Although they could rise to the top of the ecclesiastical administration (the last eunuch who was patriarch of Constantinople was Eustratios Garidas from 1081–84), it is clear from surviving *typika* that they were excluded from many Byzantine monastic communities at this time. Their needs were met by separate communities specifically for eunuchs. Several such establishments are known: for example, Leo VI, in the 9th century, reserved the monastery of St. Lazaros in Constantinople for them, and a contemporary of Theophylact of Ohrid in the late 11th or early 12th century organized another for them. The reason for such exclusion and segregation seems to have been the fear of sexual, particularly homosexual, temptations, which

was not satisfied with them and begged the father <to let him> go up again to the <monastery of the> holy Resurrection. But the father did not let him. When <Stephen> began to press him, he said to him, "Believe <me>, it is ordained that you will end your life there <at the monastery of the Savior>." And when <Stephen> cited the consequent[436] problems, the confined solitude[437] of the place and the spiritual weariness[438] that afflicted them because of it, the father instructed him: "God is not so unjust," he said, "as to release you from prison only to shut you up in prison again; all we need is patient endurance. For I believe in my Christ, that he who perseveres for God on this mountain, will receive forgiveness from Christ Himself the son of God, for Whose sake he remains persevering in this place, however many sins he has committed in the outside world, and even if he should be negligent.[439] As for the problems, they bring spiritual profit to us if we bear them nobly and with perseverance, because they keep us from imagining we are at all great as a result of our labors for God; and so, if we are annoyed with each other for a bit, but then, after becoming repentant, we severely reproach and criticize

eunuchs could pose for the monastic brethren; being generally beardless (unlike the ordinary monks) they fell into the same category as women and young boys who were similarly prohibited. It is in this context that the removal of the eunuchs from the other communities on Galesion and their segregation by Lazaros at the monastery of the Savior is to be seen. The *diatyposis* limits the number of monks there to twelve (below, Chap. 246). See further *ODB,* s.v. "Eunuchs"; C. Galatariotou, "Byzantine Ktetorika Typika: A Comparative Study," *REB* 45 (1987), 121–22; Kazhdan and Epstein, *Change,* 67, 69–70.

436 Taking μεταξύ in the sense of μετέπειτα (Sophocles, *Lexicon;* cf. Acts 13:42).

437 The word στενομονία is used in the *vita* of St. Stephen the Younger (PG 100:1140A), a work which the author of the present life clearly knew (see above, Chap. 35), to describe the saint's ascetic suffering rather than a place.

438 The term ἀκηδία is notoriously difficult to render in translation except by the rather unhelpful and archaic "accidie," for it has a range of connotations which cannot be included satisfactorily in one or two words; among these are fatigue, inertia, despair, listlessness, and boredom, all of which lead on to other "passions" and mental or spiritual sins. It was always listed among the Seven or Eight Deadly Sins and was regarded as being an affliction to which monks were particularly susceptible. See further, *ODB,* s.v. "Akedia."

439 A rather similar statement is attributed to Lazaros, above, Chap. 62, cf. also Chap. 216. As noted there, the theme of perseverance on the mountain also appears in several other places in the *vita.*

ourselves for not yet having firmly adhered to the path of virtue, that is an indication of humility." Whenever someone who had a problem <of this sort> went up to him, Lazaros taught and counseled him with these <words> and whatever other <statements> usually encourage patient endurance; he <thus> restored and consoled him, and persuaded him to persevere thereafter in this monastery of the Savior. Actually, the aforesaid Stephen did go to the <monastery of the> holy Resurrection after the father's death, but after only a short time had passed he was ordered to go back <to the monastery of the Savior> by the superior,[440] and there he came to the end of his life, just as the father had predicted. Now I could <lengthen this> account by adding to the narrative other <stories> I have learned from some of my brothers; but, to avoid making my narrative overly long, I will omit some of them and turn to the following ones, although these in fact are similar to those just dealt with.

101. Himerios, the relative by marriage of John who is called of Mita,[441] used to recount how the man called Makrembolites[442] went up to the father

[440] Presumably Lazaros' brother Ignatios, see above, Chap. 33. The passage would seem to indicate that a fairly short period elapsed after Lazaros' death before Ignatios took over as superior, although there were clearly difficulties surrounding his succession: cf. Chaps. 52 and 170, and the Introduction, section I, pp. 61–62.

[441] This John also figures in Chap. 103, below. His name is problematical; it could also be "the son of Mita," while Morris, "Political Saint," 49, renders it simply "John Mitas."

[442] The exact identity of this Makrembolites is unknown, although he must be a member of the prominent family of that name which belonged to the civil nobility of Constantinople. The best-known member of the family in this period was John Makrembolites, who was exiled in 1040 for conspiring against the emperor Michael IV (Skylitzes, *Hist.*, 412.79); he was probably married to the sister of Michael Keroularios (later patriarch of Constantinople), who was also involved in the plot, and was thus the father of the Eudokia Makrembolitissa who became the second wife of Constantine X Doukas. It would seem that he was also closely connected to Michael Psellos in some way. See further *ODB*, s.v. "Makrembolites"; Cheynet, *Pouvoir*, no. 50, pp. 51–52 and p. 338; D. I. Polemis, *The Doukai* (London, 1968), 34; Morris, "Political Saint," 48; eadem, *Monks*, 105, n. 46.

Since Lazaros was on his pillar at the Theotokos when he was visited by Makrembolites, the incident must have occurred sometime after 1031, the date he left his pillar at the Savior. As it is unclear when exactly Lazaros moved up the mountain to his final foundation of the Resurrection, it is conceivable that the meeting did not take place until the early 1040s, in which case the Makrembolites who figures in the story may be the well-known John. Certainly the phrase "the man called Makrembolites" might sug-

when he was still on the pillar of the Theotokos. After he had seen and spoken with Lazaros and was about to go down from the pillar, he asked him to pray that he might enter the city <of Constantinople> in good health. The father said to him, "Strive <rather> to enter into the heavenly city in good health, since it is that you must see <instead>." Which indeed is what happened, for he had not yet crossed the borders of the theme[443] when he passed from this life.

102. The father once sent a letter with Isaiah[444] and Neophytos to Nikephoros Kampanes[445] in Constantinople. After he [Nikephoros] had taken it

---

gest that he was a distinguished figure at the time. Further, his eagerness to see Constantinople and his fear that he would not do so because of ill-health could be attributed to the fact that he was in (or was about to return from) exile, possibly following the death of Michael IV in December 1041. Indeed, if that were the case, it might help to establish a date of ca. 1042 for Lazaros' move to the site of the Resurrection (see above, Introduction, section B, p. 13 and n. 40). The contrast between the heavenly and earthly cities here compares quite closely with that which Lazaros draws between heavenly and earthly kingdoms when reproaching another conspirator in exile, Constantine Barys (see below, Chap. 105).

[443] Presumably the Thrakesion theme in which Galesion lay; see above, Chap. 87, n. 394.

[444] Although this Isaiah is probably to be identified with the "elder" Isaiah of Chap. 233, the mission to Constantinople mentioned in that chapter is probably not the same as the present one since another monk (Ioannikios) is said to have accompanied him there.

[445] This Nikephoros Kampanes has long been identified (see, e.g., Loparev, "Zhitie," 376–77; Schlumberger, *L'épopée,* 378–79) with the Kampanares or Kampanarios mentioned by Skylitzes, *Hist.,* 420.87 (Kedrenos, *Hist.,* 2:540.6) as the new *eparchos* or Prefect of the City who was dispatched by Theodora to arrest Michael V in 1042 at Stoudios (see the following note). This clearly puts him at the heart of the action in the events of this chapter and perhaps explains Lazaros' concern for his welfare here. If this identification is correct, then he was also a friend of Michael Psellos, who accompanied him on this mission (Psellos, *Chron.,* 5). As *eparchos,* Nikephoros was a very important person indeed, for the holder of this office ranked second only to the emperor in judicial matters within Constantinople; he was also in charge of police, prisons, commercial and industrial activity, decoration and ceremonial in the capital; see *ODB,* s.v. "Eparch of the City." Lazaros thus clearly had very highly placed connections in Constantinople by this period. For further information on the career of this man, see Seibt, *Bleisiegel,* 175. At the end of this chapter it is stated that he had at one time served as the thematic judge of the Thrakesion theme. He may be the Καμπανάριος ὁ κριτὴς mentioned in the *Peira* 23.6, Zepos, *Jus,* 4; cf. Cheynet, *Pouvoir,* 201 n. 13.

in his hand and gone through it in detail, he turned to the monks, and said, "Fathers, what is this that the holy father has written to me: 'there has been political trouble and uproar in the city but do not be alarmed'? Why did the father write to me when nothing of the sort has taken place in the city?" The brothers said that they knew nothing about it and, after making obeisance, withdrew from his presence. Not long afterward the insurrection of the emperor Michael, who was called Kalaphates, occurred. <This was> when he tonsured the Lady Zoe and banished her on New Sunday; <then> on the Tuesday, when the people rose up against him, there was much [540] bloodshed in the hippodrome at his behest; but on the Wednesday he and his uncle were blinded at the place called Sigma.[446] After he had seen these events <unfold>,

[446] The references here are to the events surrounding the overthrow of the emperor Michael V Kalaphates in April 1042. The information provided by the *vita* accords closely with the fuller accounts of the incident preserved in the historical sources; Psellos, *Chron.*, 5:xvii–li (Renauld 1:96–116); Skylitzes, *Hist.*, 417–21 (Kedrenos, *Hist.*, 2:536–40); Attaleiates, *Hist.*, 1:iv–vi; Zonaras, *Epit.*, 17.19. Only Skylitzes (and Kedrenos) mention Kampanares, however. See further here Cheynet, *Pouvoir*, no. 56, pp. 54–55.

Michael V, whose name Kalaphates (lit. "ship's caulker") came from his father's profession, was a nephew of Michael IV the Paphlagonian and had been adopted by his uncle's widow, the empress Zoe. He came to power with Zoe's support on the death of Michael IV in 1041, but was not content to be a puppet or share his authority with others. Important figures in the previous regime came under attack and were removed from the scene; these included family members, the most powerful of whom, Michael's uncle the eunuch John the Orphanotrophos, was exiled. With the support of another uncle, the *nobelissimos* Constantine, Michael then moved against Zoe and the Patriarch Alexios of Stoudios. On the night of the Sunday after Easter, 18–19 April 1042, Zoe was seized and removed to a nunnery on the island of Prinkipo in the Sea of Marmara, where she was tonsured. Michael had miscalculated his popularity, however, and her treatment led to widespread rioting in Constantinople. Early on Wednesday, 21 April, Michael and Constantine fled from the palace by boat after the mob had broken down the defenses; they took refuge in the monastery of Stoudios in the southwest corner of the city where they were again surrounded by the hostile populace. By this time supporters of Theodora, Zoe's sister, had taken charge of the insurrection, and she dispatched the prefect of the city, Kampanares (see above, note 445), to resolve the situation while her sister (who had been brought back to the city) still hesitated. Michael and Constantine were dragged from the altar and taken a short distance by mule to the area above the Peribleptos monastery, known as the Sigma, where they were publicly blinded before being sent to monasteries. See further *ODB*, s.v. "Michael V Kalaphates," "Zoe"; An-the man who had received the father's letter summoned the brothers and said, "Look, fathers. What the holy father wrote me <about> has clearly happened. For since he did not want to reveal <too> obviously what was going to take place in the city, he disclosed it to me as though it had already happened; but even if he tries to hide himself, I at least, from the day I <first> saw him, <have> regarded and respected him like one of the inspired holy fathers of old." For <this Nikephoros> had seen Lazaros before when he was serving as judge in the theme.[447]

103. When John, who is called of Mita (who was mentioned by me a short time ago),[448] was entrusted with the *episkepsis* of Myrelaion in the Thrakesion theme,[449] he went straight up to the monastery and begged the father to pray for the health of his uncle Eustathios, called of Mita, since he had gout; <he did this> because of the faith he had long had in the father—for he had seen

---

gold, *Byzantine Empire,* 34–35; and on the location of the "Sigma," Janin, *Constantinople byz.*, 424–26. Note that the anonymous monk of Chaps. 228–30 was evidently allowed by Lazaros to go on a mission to Constantinople at about the same time (see below, Chap. 230), although it is not clear how these missions are connected, if at all.

[447] Kampanes thus apparently held the office of judge (κριτής) in the Thrakesion theme sometime before 1042. The thematic judge was at this time entrusted with the administration of the province; it was thus a very senior position (see above, Chap. 87, on its relation to the office of *strategos*). This statement makes it conceivable that he is to be identified with Nikephoros the son of Euthymios who figures in Chap. 106 and who also saw Lazaros while holding this office; see further there.

[448] See above, Chap. 101.

[449] The term *episkepsis* (ἐπίσκεψις), which means literally "care" or "inspection," is a fiscal one. In general it indicates a land lease of some sort involving a group of properties belonging to the state, but it is also capable of more precise definition in some circumstances; this fiscal unit may, for instance, refer to a complex of properties held by the emperor, a member of his family, or another individual, or (and, given the mention of the Thrakesion theme, this is perhaps likely here) it may refer to a fiscal division of a theme. I am grateful to an anonymous reader for suggesting the further possibility that reference is being made here to land held in this theme by the famous Myrelaion monastery at Constantinople, which had estates in Asia Minor (see further, *ODB* s.v. "Myrelaion, Monastery of"; C. L. Striker, *The Myrelaion (Bodrum Camii) in Istanbul* [Princeton, N.J., 1981]). Since this John had also held the office of *dioiketes* (see below, note 450), it is interesting to note that *episkeptetai* (or inspectors) would also supervise the *dioiketai* (or administrators) of *metata.* See here Zacos, *Seals,* 1: no. 3115; cf. also no. 2010, the seal of a *dioiketes* (?) of the *metata.* See also *ODB* s.v. "Episkepsis"; Harvey, *Expansion,* xiv.

Lazaros before when he was *dioiketes*[450] of Ephesus and Artokopeion.[451] After the father had asked John and learned that no one else was standing there,[452] he replied, "We interceded for him again and again,[453] but we learned that he will soon be released from this illness and from the other pains of his body, and will pass over to that <other> painless and untroubled life, receiving the rewards for his righteous labors." For <Eustathios> was a chaste and righteous man who applied himself to almsgiving, and was, besides, a friend to monks if ever anyone was. His faith in our holy father, <which was based> on report alone bears witness to this for, <although> he himself never saw Lazaros, he had a considerable and fervent faith in the father and the brethren because he had heard from his nephew John about his way of life, and he proved <his faith> with actual deeds, for he also furnished the monastery with very many gifts. So much for him; as for his nephew John, whom I have mentioned, after receiving this answer from the father he went down from the mountain. Not long afterward the man about whom the request and the father's prediction was made reached the end of his life.

104. George the flute player, who was also nicknamed Dog, went up to the father together with the aforesaid John and, as that man himself said with wonder after coming back down, heard the father reveal all the wicked things

[450] The office of *dioiketes* (διοικητής) was also a fiscal one, although it seems unclear precisely what functions it involved at this time. In general a *dioiketes* seems to have been responsible for the collection of the land tax. Zacos, *Seals,* 1: no. 2487, p. 1880 publishes the seal of a *dioiketes* from Ephesus of the 9th century. Further on this office see *ODB* s.v. "Dioiketes"; Harvey, *Expansion,* xiii.

[451] The interpretation of the word "artokopeion" in this passage is disputed. Foss (*Ephesus,* 120 n. 17) agrees with H. Ahrweiler ("L'histoire et la géographie de la région de Smyrne entre les deux occupations turques [1081–1317] particulièrement au XIIIe siècle," *TM* 1 [1965], 69 n. 363) in taking Artokopeion as a place name rather than in its literal sense of "a bakery." On the other hand, S. Vryonis (*The Decline of Medieval Hellenism in Asia Minor and the Process of Islamization from the Eleventh through the Fifteenth Century* [Berkeley, Calif., 1971], 10) understands the passage to refer literally to a bakery, in which the case it might be translated "when he was *dioiketes* of Ephesus and was manager of a bakery." Malamut (*Route,* 221) also takes it in this way: John was "préposé aux boulangeries."

[452] But see the following chapter. The point is presumably to stress, once again, Lazaros' modesty concerning his prophetic gifts.

[453] The phrase καὶ ἅπαξ καὶ δίς means literally "once and twice"; cf. 1 Th. 2:17–18, where the expression is also used.

he had done.[454] But when George was also about to go down from the pillar, the father said to him, "Beware, brother, because death is near." <Now>, although George perhaps took the father's words to heart a little at the time, at all events he again persisted in his former <behavior>; he did not refrain from his wickedness nor did he pay attention to his <impending> death as he should have, since the father warned him in this way, for it seems that he still expected to live and was led astray by vague hopes <of doing so>. Therefore the axe of justice caught up with him a short time later[455] and the wretched man really did die.

105. But this <story> must not be omitted either. Constantine, who was called Barys, was sentenced to exile by the emperor Monomachos, for he was suspected of <having designs> concerning the imperial power.[456] When he learned about the father's <reputation>, he wrote a letter and put a considerable amount of gold in a bag with a lead seal, sealing the letter as well;[457] <then, using> a man who was loyal to him, he sent these things to the father, together with one <silk> *skaramangion.*[458] The man who was bringing these

[454] I am grateful to an anonymous reader for suggesting this translation.

[455] A similar expression is also used below, Chap. 201.

[456] Nothing more is known about the Constantine Barys who is the subject of this chapter, although some earlier members of the family are known to have been involved in imperial politics in the early 10th century. There were two serious rebellions during the reign of Constantine IX Monomachos (1042–55), those led by George Maniakes in 1043 and by Leo Tornikes in 1047, as well as a number of others about which little is known; see Cheynet, *Pouvoir,* nos. 61–74, pp. 57–65. It is impossible to determine where exactly Barys fits into this picture, but the wording of the chapter may suggest that he was suspected of plotting a rebellion rather than actually taking part in one; if so his plot would seem to be distinct from the one, mentioned at the end of the chapter, in which Nikephoros the son of Euthymios was implicated; see Cheynet, *Pouvoir,* no. 74, pp. 64–65 and 162. See also Ševčenko, "Eastern Provinces," 725–26; Morris, "Political Saint," 49.

[457] It was a common Byzantine practice to seal both letters and packages for security and privacy; clearly the contents of both letter and bag called for it in this case. A string was tied around the object and its ends were passed through a channel in the lead seal, which was then crushed shut and imprinted by means of the special pliers used for this purpose.

[458] The *skaramangion* was a kind of long undertunic that tied at the waist. It figures in the *Book of the Eparch* and the *de Cerimoniis* of Constantine Porphyrogenitus as a court garment, of costly material and elaborate coloring worn beneath the outer robes; reference is thus made to a σκαραμάγγιον τριβλάττιον or ὀξυπρασινοτριβλάττιον, the

things arrived at the monastery and delivered them into the father's hands; Lazaros <then> ordered the brothers to take the man away to receive a meal, as was the custom. When Lazaros opened the letter, however, he discovered in it that <this Barys> was seeking <some> indication from him as to whether he [Barys] was going to seize the imperial power. <Thus> after the man had been entertained and had gone up to him again, Lazaros took out both the sealed gold and the silk <garment> and gave them back to him together with two *nomismata* for the trouble involved in his journey;[459] and he said to him, "We are not worthy to know such things nor to reveal them to those who ask about them. However, it would have been better if you had not valued these things so highly but rather had put all your trust in God and sought the kingdom of heaven first,[460] according to His word; as for the other things, if it was right for you they would also have been offered by Him when He judged it suitable." Saying this to him, Lazaros dismissed him with a blessing. A short time later that <Barys> who, by himself, was seeking the imperial power, not only failed to gain it, but also lost his own tongue in the attempt. So, see here our holy father's wonderful discernment and his prognostic indication to that man. See how, on the one hand, he was not carried away, ensnared by the gold (for he could have taken it and deceived the man who sent it with false words,

former being a *skaramangion* decorated with three bands of silk, probably purple. The word *blattion* (βλαττίον) is also used in connection with the garment in this chapter when Lazaros hands it back to the messenger; by this time the word had ceased to have any of its original implication of the color purple and had simply come to mean silk. In other words, it was a costly if apparently inappropriate gift. See *ODB*, s.v. "Blattion"; A. Vogt, *Constantin VII Porphyrogénète: Le Livre des Cérémonies* (Paris, 1935), 1:29; and R. Guilland, "Sur quelques termes du livre des cérémonies de Constantin VII Porphyrogénète," *REGr* 62 (1949), 333–48.

459 The dangers involved in his mission are apparent from the comments made by Nikephoros in the following chapter: he had not written Lazaros because he was afraid of being the cause of both his own and his messengers' death should the emperor happen to intercept it.

460 There is a play here on the βασιλεία ("imperial power") for which Constantine is plotting and the βασιλεία τῶν οὐρανῶν ("kingdom of heaven") for which Lazaros believes he should be striving; compare his statement to Makrembolites in Chap. 101, above. One might note that very similar words were used by the emissaries of the patriarch Michael I Keroularios to the emperor Michael VI Stratiotikos on his abdication in August 1057; Michael asks what the patriarch will give him instead of the βασιλεία and they reply, τὴν οὐράνιον βασιλείαν (Skylitzes, *Hist.*, 499.74–75).

as someone else might easily have done), but see rather how he asserted his ignorance (even if he was not [541] <really> ignorant, as the end of the affair shows), and thus avoided the resulting vainglory. On the other hand see how, by saying that it was not good to seek such things, he made clear that <this Barys> had not been deemed worthy of such an honor from above and therefore failed in this <endeavor> and furthermore was subjected to the loss of his own tongue. Such was the story of this man, and so unfortunate its ending,[461] but for the man who will now be spoken of, that is Nikephoros the son of Euthymios,[462] even though he was condemned on the same suspicion by the same emperor to a like exile, things came to a happy conclusion due to his proper and sensible judgment.

106. For, in the place to which he was exiled, <this Nikephoros> found one of the brothers from the monastery. When he had made sure that <the monk> belonged to holy Lazaros' flock, he took him aside and said to him, "Father, I know your holy father very well" (for he had seen him when he [Nikephoros] was judge of the theme),[463] "and I've been wanting to write him

[461] I am grateful to an anonymous reader for suggesting this translation.

[462] Skylitzes (*Hist.*, 471.8–13; Kedrenos, *Hist.*, 602.9–14) supports the present account of the banishment of this Nikephoros son of Euthymios by Constantine IX, and apparently dates it to 1050. He refers to the accusation as a slander (διαβολή), and mentions that although Nikephoros' brother Michael and some other members of his family were also implicated, only he suffered any penalty. This would suggest that the exile of Constantine Barys, whose behavior is here being contrasted with that of Nikephoros, cannot have been imposed on the same occasion. Skylitzes' doubts about the veracity of the charges would seem to be confirmed by Nikephoros' subsequent recall, described in the following chapter. See further Cheynet, *Pouvoir,* no. 66, p. 61.

[463] This information raises the possibility that the present Nikephoros the son of Euthymios is to be identified with either the Nikephoros Kampan[ar]es of Chap. 102, above, or with the Nikephoros the son of Proteuon to whom reference is made below (Chap. 119), since both those men are also said to have visited Lazaros while holding the office of thematic judge. Skylitzes' reference (see previous note) to the present Nikephoros having a brother called Michael might suggest an identification with Kampan[ar]es, since a Michael Kampanarios, evidently a member of the same family, was prominent in the third quarter of the 11th century; see Seibt, *Bleisiegel,* 174–75. On the other hand, there is also reason for identifying the present Nikephoros with Nikephoros the son of Proteuon of Chap. 119: as is mentioned below, note 494, he is probably the Nikephoros Proteuon who was chosen to succeed Constantine IX Monomachos, but was exiled by Theodora and her supporters following the emperor's death in January 1055. The scene of Nikephoros' exile on that occasion was the monastery of Kouzena,

a letter so that he would pray for me to be released from my present plight. But I'm afraid that if this ever came to the knowledge of the emperor then I'd be responsible both for my own death and that of the person bringing the letter. But please, give the holy father this message by word of mouth." This is what <Nikephoros said>, and the brother, when he had returned to the monastery, recounted the whole story to the father. Then Lazaros said to the brother, "In a few days time the emperor will recall the man." And indeed, as had been foretold by him, this happened, for not long afterward an emissary from <Nikephoros> came bringing a letter for the father, which made known his release, and also three pounds of *nomismata.*[464]

107. Once, when Theophylact, called Sagopoulos,[465] was about to go up to see the father, he told one of his young slaves[466] to go and buy fish so that they might have them for dinner when they had gone up to the monastery, "Since," he said, "we shall not find anything like that <up> there." After he said this to <the slave>, <Theophylact> himself set off at once and went up to the monastery. When he had also gone up to the father and, after the *trisagion* and the greeting,[467] was sitting in front of the pillar talking to

---

mentioned twice in the *vita* (Chaps. 84 and 99) and evidently not far from Galesion. While this may make an identification plausible, it necessitates the suggestion of a previous exile, perhaps to the same place, on this, earlier, occasion.

[464] The "pound" (λίτρα) was reckoned to contain 72 *solidi* or *nomismata,* the standard gold coins of the Byzantine monetary system. See further, *ODB,* s.v. "Litra." Nikephoros' gift was clearly a substantial one, being worth over two hundred *nomismata;* by way of comparison, the gift of Maria Skleraina, which evidently enabled Lazaros to build the church of Pausolype, was of seven hundred and twenty *nomismata,* or 10 pounds (see Chap. 245).

[465] For further comment see Cheynet, *Pouvoir,* 225. A Michael Sagopoulos, *protospatharios* and *mystographos,* is known from an 11th-century seal; see V. Laurent, *Le Corpus des sceaux de l'Empire byzantin* (Paris, 1981), 2:68, no. 146. He mentions the Sagopoulos of the *vita.*

[466] Although the word παιδάριον can also mean a young child, the meaning of slave seems more likely here since this individual is referred to as "his man" toward the end of the chapter.

[467] On the form of the *trisagion,* the "thrice-holy" hymn, see above, Chap. 45. Although this hymn was sung at the beginning of the liturgy and the "greeting" (lit. "the kiss," ἀσπασμός) here might refer to the kiss of peace after the Eucharist, the fact that Theophylact is evidently up on Lazaros' pillar at this point (see the following note) makes it unlikely that this passage refers to the celebration of the liturgy in church.

him,[468] the cellarer came to Lazaros and asked him, "What shall I give Kyris Theophylact to eat?" Then the father, joking and smiling, with his eyes on Theophylact, said to the cellarer, "Look, one of his slaves has already arrived at the monastery from the Theologian [Ephesus] and has brought three fish with which he's going to be fed today, since nothing like that is found in the monastery!" These were the father's words; <as for> Theophylact when he came down from the pillar he stood in the middle of the courtyard quite astonished at his statement and at a loss. Only then, while he was in this state, did his man come into the monastery bringing three fish with him just as the father had said. At the sight of them he was completely amazed and said, "Glory be to Thee, oh God, Who has judged me worthy to see and converse with such a holy man."

108. A certain brother went into someone's cell while the other brothers were in the church, took <some> cash <worth> about four *milia,*[469] and went off to his own cell.[470] While he was still on the way, the father called out to him by name from up on his pillar and summoned him. When <the monk> got there, Lazaros said, "Give me the cash which you just took after going into brother Merkourios' cell." As he had no excuse at all, <the brother> im-

---

Instead it would appear that the singing of the *trisagion* and the greeting formed the normal introductory ceremony when visitors came to see Lazaros on his pillar. The same phrase is thus used below, Chap. 114, on the occasion of the visit of Jeremiah, a distinguished Georgian ascetic; cf. also Chaps. 118 and 119 where only the greeting is mentioned. There may also be reference to the ceremony of confession and absolution, which apparently formed the principal part of many interviews given by Lazaros to his visitors, as the *trisagion* was used by the penitent and his confessor before confession (Lampe, *Lexicon,* s.v. τρισάγιος B.4).

[468] That the man was actually up on Lazaros' pillar at this point appears to be confirmed below in this chapter where he is said to have come down from it after his interview. On the structure of the pillar and evidence for the existence of some sort of platform at its top by means of which monks and visitors could approach the access window to Lazaros' "cell," see the Introduction, section C, pp. 17–18. The use of the preposition πρὸ ("before") here thus does not seem to indicate that the man was on the ground in front of (and so below) the pillar, but rather that he was sitting in front of the access window on the platform.

[469] *Milia* here is used as an abbreviation of *miliaresia.* The *miliaresion* (μιλιαρήσιον) was the basic Byzantine silver coin worth one-twelfth of a *solidus* or *nomisma.*

[470] On the danger of theft from the brothers' cells while they were in church, see above, Chap. 66.

mediately took out the cash and gave it to the father; then he prostrated himself and begged for forgiveness, and <asked> that this should not become known to the brothers. The father demanded his word that he would not dare do such a thing again, and when he saw him promise this at once in all sincerity, he gave him forgiveness and dismissed him with a blessing. After the end of church the father summoned brother Merkourios and gave him the cash but, while he told him how the thief had taken it from his cell and how he had recovered it from him, he did not reveal who the thief was, even though <Merkourios> and other brothers pressed him many times to learn who this person might be. I think most of you know this story, but it is more necessary for me to tell the <following one> as further confirmation of what has been written above, since most people do not know it; and so I shall now add it to my account.

109. When the builders were going to construct our refectory, the father, standing on his pillar, sketched out its length and width for <them> by pointing with his right hand.[471] One of the brothers, Matthew by name (and it was he who told me about this), when he saw the plan of the project, apparently found fault with the father in his own mind. Looking up at him, he said, "Why is such effort going to be wasted on this ill-timed work? Where are the <monks> who are going to fill it?" For the brothers were <then> still few and easy to count. "Don't you know," he continued, "that after your death the people who live in the village of Galesion are going to chase us out and make this a barn for their animals?"[472] The father did not show any anger at this speech, nor was he disturbed, but he became thoughtful and as though in-

[471] It is most likely that this and the following chapter refer to the development of the monastery of the Resurrection, the largest establishment on the mountain, housing forty monks at the end of Lazaros' life, according to the *diatyposis* in Chap. 246. It is interesting to note that Lazaros' personal involvement in the detailed planning of the monastery, or at least the church, of the Resurrection also features quite prominently in the version of the *vita* by Akakios Sabbaites (Lampsides, "Ἀνέκδοτον κείμενον," 169, f. 490β). On the other hand, Gregory of Cyprus' version suggests that Lazaros only moved onto his pillar at the Resurrection after the rest of the monastery had been completed (chap. 31, *AASS*, Nov. 3:600E).

[472] The fear that the monastic community on Galesion would not survive the death of Lazaros, particularly because of ecclesiastical pressure from Ephesus, is expressed on a number of occasions in the *vita;* this pessimism evidently grew worse toward the end of Lazaros' life; see the Introduction, section F, pp. 36 and 46, and also below, Chaps. 140–41, 245, and 247; cf. 170, 216–18.

spired, filled, as it seems to me, with the Holy Spirit. He replied to the brother, "You think and speak in this way about this <project>," he said, "but I believe in my Christ that, both while I am still living and after my death, it will be filled with people, not animals." And behold, [542] we all see right up until today, that there are times when the refectory is filled not only once but twice and three times <over> through his holy prayers.

110. The same brother [Matthew] also told me this. After the cells of the monastery were built the father wanted to build others on the western side. When the brothers learned this, they persuaded the aforesaid brother Matthew to go up and persuade Lazaros to abandon the enterprise; for they argued that the monastery was lacking things <it really> needed. The brother discussed this with the father at the wish of the others, and he did at that time persuade him to put the matter aside; but now, after Lazaros' departure to God from this present life, one can see that what the saint planned of old has indeed been fulfilled.

111. Our saintly and holy father was thus like some brilliant and clearly visible beacon, radiating beams of illumination from afar on everyone, whether they lived near or far away from him.[473] He reached[474] those close at hand by words, those at a distance by prayer; or rather, he filled up both with every grace in both ways, while he turned others to thoughts of compunction simply by his holy appearance itself. For in reality that man (to put it more concisely), in his appearance, in his speech, in his action, in the power of his prayer, and generally in every way, was an exhortation to virtue and an example of every good work. For who, when he saw this man on his pillar without shelter in the open air, bravely struggling like some noble competitor with violent winds and rain, with summer's burning heat and winter's chill and actually proving himself a far stronger and more steadfast pillar than that which bore him, who would not at once be amazed and moved to compunction, even if he possessed a heart harder than iron or steel? Indeed, what is far

[473] This is the most developed example of an image that is also used of Lazaros in Chaps. 36 and 128; cf. Chap. 2. On such imagery, see A. Kazhdan and H. Maguire, "Byzantine Hagiographical Texts as Sources on Art," *DOP* 45 (1991), 2.

[474] I am grateful to an anonymous reader for the helpful suggestion that προφθάνων may be taken here in the sense of "reaching." It is also possible, however, that the word be emended to προφαίνων; this would require less extension of meaning and, with its sense of "bringing into the light" or "illuminating," would continue the initial simile of Lazaros as a beacon.

more wonderful, is that Lazaros had such <an effect> not only on people of the faith but even on unbelievers themselves, as my narrative will show.

112. A Jew once came up and saw Lazaros standing like that on his pillar in the open air <dressed> in his leather tunic. <Afterward> he asked about <the tunic> and, when he learned that Lazaros had worn this garment for twelve years without ever having changed it for another,[475] he was astounded at this. "As I see it," he said, "this man really has outdone even the just men of the Old <Testament>; for in the Old <Testament> we discover that Elijah wore only a leather tunic, but he had two and used to change one for the other <so that> he would wear them for no more than six months <each>."[476] Another time, seven other Jews came up to the monastery. As soon as they merely caught sight of Lazaros, they required few words <of explanation> to understand <the quality of> his life, for they too were immediately astounded by the same things as the first man and made the same statement.

113. An Arab,[477] whom the metropolitan[478] of Ephesus had baptized, learned about the father and asked if he might see him; so the metropolitan sent him with an interpreter. When he had come up and had seen the father, his soul was so deeply moved and he acquired such faith, just from the sight of him, that he would not descend from the pillar until he had received something from Lazaros' own hands that he might have as a phylactery and a safeguard against every danger.[479]

114. A monk called Jeremiah, a Georgian by race, who had practiced the eremitic life in Palestine, had just left the desert in accordance with the divine will and had set out for Constantinople. When he arrived in Ephesus on his way <there>, he was kindly received by the metropolitan Euthymios,[480] and

[475] Cf. Chap. 82, above.

[476] The *Septuagint* refers to Elijah's mantle (μηλωτή, a "sheepskin") on a number of occasions: 3 Ki. 19:13, 19; 4 Ki. 2:8, 13–14. His leather belt (ζώνη δερματίνη) is also mentioned at 4 Ki. 1:8.

[477] Lit. "One of the offspring of Agar [Hagar]." The *vita* uses all three terms for Arabs commonly employed by the Byzantines: Agarenes, Ishmaelites, and Saracens.

[478] Lit. "high priest of Ephesus." The following chapter makes it clear that this refers to the metropolitan.

[479] A similar demand, phrased in much the same way, was also made above, Chap. 75.

[480] This Euthymios is clearly a later metropolitan than the Theodore (II ?) who was mentioned above, Chap. 34.

treated with honor on account of the grace of virtue that was clearly manifest in him. Indeed, just to look at, this man was someone who commanded respect, for he seemed, in his dress and his appearance, to be just as they depict the Prodromos [John the Baptist]:[481] he thus had his hair hanging down in twelve braids that reached as far as the small of his back and his abdomen, while his clothing, that is to say his tunic and his scapular with its holy cowl, was made entirely out of hair. <During his visit> he also learned about the father from the metropolitan and the clergy. They persuaded <Jeremiah> to go up to Lazaros so that, when he had carefully observed his <way of life>, he would <be able> to decide if the facts about him tallied with the reports he had heard.[482] So he came up and went to see the father; after the *trisagion* and the greeting,[483] he said to the father, "Please let me touch you at will and examine your circumstances." "Do as you wish," replied the father. Then <Jeremiah> put his head and as much of the rest of his body as he could inside the pillar through the little window and looked carefully at the things that were in it; he did not stop at this, however, but also put his hand inside the father's robe and felt his flesh.[484] When he had withdrawn his <head> along with the rest of his body from the pillar, he stood dumbfounded for quite a long time with his eyes cast down; then he lifted up his head and, looking with astonishment at the brothers (for there were plenty of them there), said, "In truth, brothers, I tell you that it's this man who is a true hermit, and not I, since I haven't yet reached this level of conduct. Indeed, you do wrong, brothers, in allowing the old man to live in such a very confined and stifling cell. Come on then! Let's break down the pillar and get him out!" As he said this he began to push the pillar with his hand, and he turned to the father and said, "Come

[481] John the Baptist was a common figure in Byzantine iconography. For a brief description of his representation in art see *ODB*, s.v. "John the Baptist."

[482] Given the hostility between the ecclesiastical authorities in Ephesus and Lazaros' foundation on Galesion, one may perhaps wonder if the motives of the metropolitan and the clergy in sending Jeremiah up to see, and thoroughly examine, Lazaros are as innocent as they may appear at first glance. This chapter should thus probably be compared with Chaps. 237 and 238, below, which record deliberate attempts made by the authorities in Ephesus to catch Lazaros out and find proof that his asceticism was not all it seemed to be by sending unexpected visitors up to investigate him and his pillar.

[483] See above, Chap. 107.

[484] Cf. an episode reported in Theodoret, *Hist. Rel.*, 26.23, in which a worthy visitor examines Symeon the Stylite the Elder in a rather similar way.

off your pillar and give yourself a little rest. What's the point of such affliction? You've already become dead to the world[485] and no longer have to fear the war of the passions." The father smiled at this but kept silent. In the end, [543] after he had stayed in the monastery for several days and had benefited greatly, this man went back down to Ephesus and told the metropolitan and all the clergy all about the father with complete amazement. "I have never yet seen a man like this one," he said, "either in the desert or anywhere else." These <are> the sort of things <that> this man <said>.

115. Another man, who was a Paulician,[486] came to the father and, when he saw Lazaros, did not need many words <to convince> him to accept the orthodox teaching of the faith into his soul. In fact, he at once completely denied and anathematized the heresy he had loved, and was considered worthy of holy baptism in the monastery at the father's order. Indeed he later became a monk contrary to expectation through the favor of God. For, after he had spent some time in the monastery, he fell into temptation for some reason, or rather he was dragged into error by the shallowness of his will, and, as he was still a layman, left the monastery and went back to his own homeland; however, the benevolent God, by the prayers of our blessed father, <later> caused him to go to Jerusalem and be tonsured in the monastery of St. Sabas.[487]

116. Another layman came to the father for a blessing, along with some

[485] Cf. Gal. 6:14; Col. 2:20.

[486] The Paulician sect, which may well have developed from other early Christian groups in Armenia as early as the 5th century, if not before, was best known to the Byzantines in the strongly Docetic and Dualist form that had become popular and had also developed into a serious political threat to the eastern provinces of the empire by the mid-9th century. Although this immediate threat was crushed in 872, the Paulicians remained numerous in eastern Asia Minor; many were deported ca. 975 and settled in Thrace around Philippopolis, where there was still a very strong and sometimes hostile presence in the early 11th century; it appears that there were also groups of Paulicians and followers of related sects (whether of the original or newer type) still living in the frontier provinces in eastern Asia Minor at this time. It is thus unclear where this particular Paulician may have come from. See further *ODB*, s.v. "Paulicians"; also Lemerle, "Pauliciens" (who mentions this episode p. 110); N. G. Garsoian, *The Paulician Heresy* (The Hague–Paris, 1967), esp. 144, 150; S. Runciman, *The Medieval Manichee* (Cambridge, 1947), esp. 26–62. Cf. above, Chap. 10, where Lazaros in his younger days converts unspecified heretics near Attaleia.

[487] See above, Chap. 16. On the transmission of news about individuals from the East to Galesion see also above, Chap. 24.

others, but, as soon as he simply caught sight of Lazaros, he immediately fell to the ground head first, as though he had been struck in the heart by some missile. He beat his face with his hands and lamented mournfully and bitterly and let loose <such a flood of> scalding tears from his eyes that he even soaked the ground where he had fallen. When he arose from there, he went up to the father, made confession of his sins and received forgiveness; then, justified <in this way>, he too went down from the mountain, as the tax collector <did> from the temple.[488]

117. A woman once came up to the monastery with some other people, and, when she had merely come in view of the father, she too was smitten at heart in the same way. She stood staring fixedly at Lazaros and beat her breast with her hand, while the streams of her tears soaked her dress. So, when those who were with her were called by the brothers of the monastery for a meal according to the custom, she did not go with them. Instead, she replied to those who were summoning her to <eat>, "Leave me to weep for my sins, with the willing athlete <who is> my reproach standing visible before my eyes. For since I have committed <so> many sins, how <could it> not <be> wrong for me to turn to food when I <can> see this holy and pure man standing in the open air on his pillar?" After she had wept copiously, she went up to the father and confessed, with many more tears, the things she had done. <Then> she too received the remission of forgiveness like the prostitute of old;[489] indeed, this woman <now> dared <to do> something almost equal <to her>, for she took the father unawares and, just as that other woman <did with> the feet of Christ, she kissed his holy face, which no other woman had ever dared to do. Thus, after she had washed away the stains of her sins through her confession and her tears, she went on her way in peace.

118. Another man, <who held> the rank of *topoteretes,*[490] also went up to the father. After the greeting he sat down and started to talk about wars

[488] This refers to the parable of the Pharisee and the publican, Lk. 18:10–14; the same parable is also used in Chap. 234.

[489] The reference is to the story of the woman who anointed Jesus' feet in Lk. 7:37–50.

[490] The military office of *topoteretes* was occupied by lieutenants of the most senior commanders in the empire. It is clear from what is said below that the man was acquainted with the steward of the monastery but had not apparently been to see Lazaros before, so he was perhaps a resident of the region of Ephesus and had had official dealings with the steward. See further *ODB,* s.v. "Topoteretes."

and other worldly affairs. The father turned his face toward the wall of the church,[491] however, and let him go on talking while he sat there, but gave him no answer at all. When the man got no response to his words, he took it badly; he got up, made obeisance, and then went <straight> down from the mountain, and did not <even> want to be given a meal[492] according to the prevailing custom in the monastery. Some of the brothers went up to the father after his departure and said, "Why didn't you talk with him, Father? By staying silent you have offended him and he has gone away without receiving any benefit." (For <the man> had said this to the brothers when he was about to leave the monastery.) The father replied, "If he has derived no benefit from our silence, how would he have been edified by a lot of talk?" This is what the father <said>. The man went to the Theologian [Ephesus], however, and came across brother Cyril, who was also our steward;[493] he knew from the past that he was from our father's flock and so approached him. "Because I had heard about your father," he said, "I went to see him and confess my thoughts to him; but quite the opposite happened to me when I went up, for I came down from there hurt rather than helped, <since> he did not exchange a single word with me." The brother questioned <the man> more carefully and, when he learned the subject of his conversation with the father, he understood the matter at once. "That's the reason why the father kept silent and did not exchange a single word with you," he said. "He isn't accustomed to talk to anyone very readily about such things, and especially <not> to those who visit him for spiritual help. But, if you take my advice," he continued, "let's go back together and, when you go up to him, be sure to start off by asking him for spiritual help. Then you'll understand what sort of man our father is!" Convinced by the brother's advice, the man went up with him to the monastery. He went up alone to the father and began to ask him for spiritual help. <Then> the father did open his mouth, and filled the man's ears with salvific and spiritually helpful words that rolled serenely and soothingly from his holy tongue.

[491] The chapter does not make clear when this episode occurred and thus which of the churches on Galesion is meant, but the mention below of Cyril the steward would suggest that this was toward the end of Lazaros' life and thus that the church in question is that of the Resurrection. For Lazaros' pillar being apparently situated very close to the church of the Resurrection, cf. Chaps. 86 and 252 and see the Introduction, section C, p. 18.

[492] On the meaning of the verb διακρίνομαι in this context, see above, Chap. 95, n. 422.

[493] On the office of steward (οἰκονόμος), see Chap. 49, above.

At the same time he filled his heart with as much gladness and joy as was possible, instead of his previous grief. And so that man, <with> his <conscience> sorely pricked, confessed his sins with scalding tears. After he received forgiveness from the father, he came down from the pillar with his eyes still wet with tears. [544] He found brother Cyril standing in front of the church and did obeisance and embraced him. "May <all> go well for you, brother," he said, "because you have been the agent of such good things for me. As a result of your good advice, through confession to our holy father, I have received forgiveness from God for the wrongs I committed in the past." And so, glorifying God, he went on his way.

119. Nikephoros, the son of Proteuon, who had been sent out as judge of the theme,[494] and had long been familiar with the father's reputation, went up to him on foot. After the greeting, as if moved by boldness to jest with the father, he said, "The journey up the mountain is hard, father." He said this because he had come up on foot, as has been mentioned, and was hoping to receive some praise for this from the father. The father replied to him, however, "The way that leads to eternal life is hard and rough and requires much sweat and labor." <Nikephoros reacted> as though he had been struck by this statement, and at once exchanged his lightheartedness for dejection and his inappropriate self-assurance for a <more> modest attitude. He stood there with

[494] As was mentioned above in Chap. 106, n. 463, it is likely that this man is to be identified with the Nikephoros Proteuon, the governor (probably *katepano*) of Bulgaria, who was picked to succeed Constantine IX Monomachos by one faction at the imperial court, but was in fact exiled by the empress Theodora and her supporters following Constantine's death in January 1055. Certainly Cheynet (*Pouvoir,* no. 75, pp. 65 n. 2 and 194) appears to accept this identification, although he mistakenly suggests that this chapter in the *vita* refers to him as "frère de Proteuon." According to Skylitzes, Nikephoros Proteuon's exile in 1055 was to the monastery of Kouzena; this may support the suggestion that the present Nikephoros is to be further identified with the Nikephoros the son of Euthymios whose exile by Monomachos, evidently also in the vicinity of Galesion, is mentioned in Chap. 105 and forms the subject of Chap. 106, above; both held the office of judge of the theme according to the *vita.* Malamut (*Route,* 221) disagrees with this interpretation, and understands the text here to mean that the present Nikephoros was son of the *proteuon* of Ephesus (see above, Chap. 56, n. 267, for an example of this office) who had risen to become judge of the theme. Whatever is the case, it seems unlikely that the present Nikephoros is to be identified with the Nikephoros Kampan[ar]es of Chap. 102. Cf. also here Morris, *Monks,* 105, n. 46. I have been unable to see A. Kazhdan, *Social'nyj sostav gospodstvujuščego klassa Vizantii XI–XII vv.* (Moscow, 1974), 162, which also refers to this man.

his eyes on the ground without daring to look up and gaze directly at the father. Thus a brief spiritual statement may help the person who hears it more than thousands <of words> spouted uselessly, just as this man went away glorifying God after being helped immensely by a single sentence. For our holy man was not talkative or garrulous, nor did he make use of scriptural phrases for the most part or communicate readily with people by <quoting> from Scripture,[495] as <do> some people who love showing off and seeking honor. Instead he would utter his own words simply and plainly and would thus give the greatest assistance to everyone. For his speech was, in the words of the apostle, *seasoned with* divine *salt,*[496] and it used to instill a certain spiritual pleasure and grace in the hearts of those who heard <it>.

120. On one occasion, some men from Attaleia,[497] who had come to Lazaros for a blessing, were proposing some sayings from the Gospels to each other, and each of them was <then> giving his own interpretation of these. But, since they did not agree about the words, they were standing there for a long time, arguing over them. The father, who was leaning out of his little window, kept silent; in the end, however, when they asked him to state which one of them had found the meaning of the saying, he replied, "One <of you> is interpreting this one way, another another way, and another <again> in another way; and that's why I'm not going to say anything to you, except that <while> it would be good to struggle to preserve what we have managed to understand, <with regard to> the things of which we are ignorant, we should either ask God for instruction in the knowledge of them or, if we are not up to this because of the unbelief that is within us, we should seek <the meaning> from a<nother> human being; but <we should> not <do so> contentiously. If we are <still> not able to establish the <meaning> accurately in this way, we should inquire diligently about these things in the holy writings <of the fathers>, for the saints left nothing unexplained, especially the great orator, I

[495] In the *Apophthegmata,* Arsenios 42 (PG 65:105D; Ward, *Sayings,* 16), the abbot Daniel says that Arsenios tried to avoid interpreting the Scriptures although quite capable of doing so. It is possible that the passage may have prompted the train of thought that led Gregory the Cellarer on to the subject of the following chapters. Another parallel between Lazaros and Arsenios is drawn below in Chap. 225.

[496] Col. 4:6.

[497] On the town of Attaleia, in the vicinity of which Lazaros had his first monastic experience, see above, Chap. 9; visitors to Galesion from Attaleia are also mentioned above, Chaps. 70–72.

mean the divine Chrysostom."[498] When the father said this, the men at once stopped their contentious argument with each other and begged his forgiveness, which they received. They <then> acknowledged that they had been greatly assisted by the father's conciseness of speech and went down the mountain, giving thanks to God.

121. Once, too, when I asked the father about such a statement, he answered, "It says this so that the person who is in <monastic> subjection may yield to the will of his superior in everything when he realizes that it is not he himself but the <superior> who will be called to account on his behalf. So, if he had managed <to fulfill> this <subjection> correctly, there would be nothing else <left> for him to strive for or to worry about." With such words the father pricked my stony heart and dismissed me, after he had decided I was worthy of a blessing. Indeed, when I asked a question about some such matter, he would give an answer about something other <than> what I was inquiring about, not out of ignorance, but <because> he was doing this wisely and to good purpose. <He was thus> not <concerned with> how he might explain the matter that had been raised, or how he might demonstrate his own knowledge of scripture, but he was thinking only of this one thing and always looking only to this one <end, namely>, how he might help the person who had asked the question. So, because he judged that it was unsuitable and not the right time for me to be troubling myself with things of this sort, Lazaros brought up the <other topic> instead, about which it was more profitable and essential for me to think.

122. Lazaros was not only accustomed to do this with questions of this sort, but also with those concerning everyday life. A lot of people would <thus> go up to him, especially during the festivals, with disputes among themselves about real estate and various other matters. Often, when he saw them quarreling and exchanging insults, he would keep quiet until he saw them pause in their dispute; then, when he had settled the difference between them

[498] I am grateful to an anonymous reader for a number of suggestions concerning the translation of this passage. The reference is to John Chrysostom (or "Goldenmouth") ca. 340/50–407. Bishop of Constantinople from 398 to 404, he was most famous for his oratorical skills and his copious writings; these were primarily works of biblical exegesis, although he also wrote on many moral topics and other issues important to Christians. As the present passage shows, his reputation continued undiminished in the Byzantine world. See further, *ODB,* s.v. "John Chrysostom."

with a few words, he would send them away, pleased with themselves and thanking God. But these are just a few <stories that> have been recounted from among the many concerning such matters.

123. Who, anyway, would have the strength to tell in detail, case by case, about those who used to go up to Lazaros every day and receive from him appropriate healing and release from the grievous <woes> that were overwhelming them? Or about how many greedy and grasping people who, through his God-given teaching and counseling, not only stopped being greedy and grasping, but rather were even ready to give away their possessions to the poor? Or again, about how many people gave up their sorceries and other wicked practices on his advice and, through repentance, worshiped the God Whom they had previously angered by their wicked deeds?[499] Other people, who were pursuing <evil> arts and satanic practices, were admonished by him to [545] desist from them; when they put forward <the excuse> that they knew no other art by which to make a living, they were designated by him to receive what <they required> for food and their other needs, and <as a result> they were immediately convinced by his words and renounced their most evil practices of this sort. Some, who little by little devoted themselves to the good and developed a desire for virtue, chose to become monks; while for others, their fortunes greatly increased as a result of manual labor and their livelihood became more abundant. A witness from the former <category> is Meliton the flute player,[500] who was tonsured in our monastery after our father's death and ended his life in proper repentance. From the latter <group there is> Constantine, who was called Phlaskas: when he was pursuing <a career> as a flautist he could scarcely get enough to eat, but from the moment he stopped <doing> this on our father's advice and took up manual labor, his fortunes increased so much that he was not only able <to meet> his own and

[499] This sentence appears to allude to Jer. 33 (26):3; cf. Jer. 23:22, 25:5.

[500] As is clearly the case here, instrumental musicians were generally regarded with suspicion and hostility by Byzantine religious sources. This attitude was related to the situations in which such musicians usually performed, for these were generally thought to be lax or immoral, and it was supported both by references in the early fathers and by legal stipulations: Chrysostom thus claimed in his *Homilies on the Epistle to the Colossians* that Christ was necessarily absent from places where flute players were (4.12.6; PG 62:389.52–53), while they, together with players of the *kithara,* were denied baptism unless they abandoned their profession. See further *ODB,* s.v. "Musicians."

his family's expenses adequately and independently, but also to give <alms> to others who were needy.[501] So much for these people.

124. Who <again> would be able to tell in detail, case by case, how those who had fallen into various sins obtained appropriate healing from him in a most discriminating and wise fashion? Some entered the monastic life, while others, who remained in layman's dress and were given a suitable rule of life by him, demonstrated their repentance in compensation for their former sins and received forgiveness from God. But, since those who were guided by him to the way of salvation were numerous and not easily counted, I cannot speak about them, one by one; I have therefore chosen one <example> from among the many, which happened while I was in the monastery, and I have recounted it for the great benefit of those who hear it. I will leave the other <stories> to be told and related by those people who have experienced the actual things that have happened to them; each <may thus> tell his own story and what good he has experienced and make it known to <everyone> else. <As for> the <story> I have promised to tell myself, it will now be set down clearly by me.

125. <There was> a woman from <one> of the villages close to us whose husband was a priest. Because she was beaten and abused by this man every day, whether or not it was appropriate, she came to hate him and, as a result, tried to discover some way to get divorced from him. Indeed, being in this state of mind and completely obsessed by this idea,[502] she confided the matter to another woman. This <woman> proved herself <to be> a wicked counselor to her against her own husband, however, just as the serpent <was> of old to Eve,[503] and the <gist> of her counsel was just as abominable and wicked. "If you want to accomplish your purpose," she said, "you <should> mix polluted blood[504] with wine and give it to your husband to drink, for, when he has

[501] See here the commentary by Kaplan, *Les hommes,* 494. Kaplan evidently takes the adjective αὐλητικὴν here to indicate that Constantine Phlaskas was a courtier; however, the context, immediately following discussion of Meliton the flute player (αὐλητής), and the attested usage of the word, would suggest this interpretation is probably mistaken.

[502] I am grateful to an anonymous reader for suggestions concerning the wording here.

[503] Gen. 3.

[504] Perhaps menstrual blood, although the blood of "unclean" animals was also sometimes employed in Late Antique and Byzantine magic, which was intended, as here, to cause harm.

drunk it, he will at once go mad, and then you will have a legitimate cause for getting divorced from him, because he will be out of his wits."[505] The <priest's wife> was convinced by this wicked counselor (for a woman is easily misled into error), and then became even more aroused by the evil; at the same time, she judged that <her being of> the same gender <rendered this woman> more trustworthy than anyone else whatsoever. That vile woman prepared a potion, just as she had been instructed, and put it in a jar in which her husband used to put the eucharistic wine; this she put in a secret place and <then> looked for an opportunity later on when she might give it to him to drink. But the grace of God, which often makes things turn out for the best in directly opposite ways <from which they were intended>, also arranged the <course> of this affair quite differently. When the <woman's> husband was about to celebrate the holy eucharist, he looked for the jar of eucharistic wine and could not find it, so he popped out of the house, as his wife was somewhere about outside, and asked her if she knew where the jar might have been put. Then, either because she forgot what she had done or else because the words simply slipped out of her mouth accidentally, or, which is nearer the truth, because they were being controlled and managed by God, she said, "Look, and seek, and you shall surely find it!"[506] So the <priest> went back inside and looked more carefully. He found <the jar> and, seeing that it was full of what he took to be unwatered wine (for how could he possibly have conceived of such a wicked business?), he picked it up and went off to create the union of the undefiled and awful eucharistic sacraments with it. But oh, what a miracle! The polluted blood was changed into the holy blood of Christ by the visitation of the sacred and Holy Spirit, and those who partook of it (for the priest and <the> others who also happened to be there received it) not only suffered no <damage> at all to their wits as the woman had thought <they would>, but <actually> enjoyed a <portion of the> salvific sacrament instead. When the woman went

[505] In general marriage was regarded as indissoluble in Byzantine civil and canon law and very few legal grounds for divorce were thus recognized, although practice would appear to have been somewhat more liberal than the letter of the law might imply. The only broadly accepted way of ending a marriage by consent was if both partners agreed to take monastic vows (see the following chapter). Further see *ODB,* s.v. "Divorce." There was a quite widespread belief in the Byzantine world that magic could be employed to provoke insanity.

[506] The Byzantine audience would probably understand an allusion here to Mt. 7:7; Lk. 11:9.

back into the house, she looked for the jar where she had put it away and, since she <could> not find it, realized at once what had happened. Without saying anything to anyone she left the house and went running up to the monastery. <There> she went to the father and revealed the <whole> affair to him with a great many scalding tears because <she was afraid>, according to what she thought and supposed and said, that she had polluted not only her husband and those who had partaken <of the sacrament> with him, but even the holy gifts of Christ as well.

126. The father said to her, however, "Woman, you <may> be quite certain that neither the holy gifts of Christ nor those who have received them have, as you suggest, been polluted, because both have been consecrated by the overshadowing <protection> of the most Holy Spirit. For, although you yourself are not innocent of sin in this <matter>, <still> the <ultimate> aim of everything done by us is <that which is> sought by God." The father said these and other words to the woman and gave her directions <for penance> in proportion to her offense; he <also> ordered her to have nothing further to do with her husband[507] and, if possible, not to return home again but to go <straight> from there to a monastery and be tonsured. Then he dismissed her after he had [546] prayed over her. Her husband, however, went home after celebrating the holy eucharist and, since he could not find his wife, asked <around>. When he learned which way she had gone, he set out after her on the same <route> and came up to the monastery. He found her there, for she had still not yet managed to leave, and began questioning her, because he wanted to know the reason why she had done this. She said nothing to him about the affair, but went up with him to the father and then, turning to <her husband>, said, "Ask the father, and he will tell you why I am here." When the <husband> tried to find out from the father, he replied to him, "It will do me no good to tell <you> why your wife came to me, nor you to hear it. Besides, if you both take my advice, you should renounce everything belonging to your <present> life and take up the monastic life <instead>. For, taking into account what she said to me, I have decided that this would be best for both of you." The <priest> was at once convinced by the father's words without going into <the matter> any further or asking questions. He went off and settled his affairs and then withdrew from the world at the same time as his

[507] Or perhaps more specifically, "ordered her to have no more sexual intercourse with her husband."

wife, both of them entering monasteries. They thus donned the monastic habit and, through repentance, became well pleasing to God. Those <confessors> who are obliged to listen to the <sinful> thoughts of others should be like this, not only <relying> on the stipulations of the canons when they encourage to repentance those who make their confession to them, but <relying> even more on their own good judgment, just as the father did here, and <thus> became the agent of salvation to them both. But <now>, since I have referred to his <good> judgment, I shall recount an affair which I heard from the father himself and which is appropriate here.

127. A layman, who was an old acquaintance of mine from the outside world, encountered me at the Theologian [in Ephesus] and asked me about a similar matter. I inquired if both husband and wife made use of a single spiritual father. He answered, "A <single> one." So I said, "The wife should tell <the spiritual father> about the affair and then he may do as he sees fit about it." When I returned from there, I also let the father know about this. He replied to me, "Oh <dear>! What have you done? Write to the man who spoke with you <and say> that the wife should either confess this to someone else, or should make quite certain that the <spiritual father> will not divulge it to her husband. For something of this sort once happened in the vicinity of Ephesus. <On that occasion> a spiritual father heard the confession of a woman and, because he did not know how to decide[508] the matter from <his own> knowledge, he told the woman's husband. The man <promptly> went off and murdered his wife with a knife. So, do you see what happened then? This is why I told you to write to the man who spoke to you, so that the same thing doesn't happen to this woman." When I heard this from the father, I did his bidding at once, and hastily wrote a letter to the man just mentioned to inform him of the father's advice, as has been said <above>. So matters went as the letter suggested, and nothing untoward occurred in the end, by the grace of Christ. But this <is the sort of> teaching and advice that our holy and inspired father used to give those in the outside world, and he also used to recommend, with the most lofty and spiritual judgment, what each should do.

[508] The verb is διακρίνω. This is related to Lazaros' highly reputed quality of διάκρισις, or "good judgment," the subject of the next section of the *vita* which Gregory the Cellarer is now introducing. The point being made here is that the other spiritual father, like Gregory, lacked this quality that Lazaros evidently possessed so abundantly. On the use of the same word, διάκρισις, for "meal," see above, Chap. 95.

128. Lazaros used to demonstrate his consideration[509] to his own children (I speak, of course, about the monks who surrounded him) <even> more attentively and more frequently, like an affectionate and devoted father. He used to counsel, teach, encourage, reprove, and reproach each one individually and separately, and he would make use of every method and <type of> speech for their correction. He would support the weak <and> raise the fallen; he would encourage <the monks> to run the race vigorously and would further arouse them and make <them do so> even more energetically; at one time he would offer them the <fruits> of his own teaching and would pour forth the streams of his advice from the spring of the gifts of the spirit that welled up inside him; at another time he would introduce supporting texts from the holy Scriptures and would also present <as examples> the marvelous lives and spiritual labors of the fathers who practiced asceticism in earlier <times>, and their great and extraordinary struggles. He would stand up above on his pillar like a brilliant beacon and, holding the book in his hands, would read aloud to everyone the deeds and the teachings of the fathers, which were what he loved to read and to <use for> teaching more than any other text.[510] The brothers often used to pose questions to each other <that arose> either from the holy Scriptures, or from incidents which occurred, such as afflictions, abuses, and other evils of this sort that are usually viewed and named <as such> by most people, or again they would pose questions about the differentiation of sins and sinners; but, when <the brothers> asked the father about these <problems>, they would receive from Lazaros the most marvelous and shrewd decisions[511] <concerning them> and solutions to them. A <case> of this sort is now going to form the subject of my narrative, together with various other ones.

129. One of the brothers asked the father who should be judged superior: those monks who often and continually succumb to the passion of fornication,

[509] The word προμήθεια also contains the sense of "foresight" or "forethought" and thus ties in closely with the subject of Lazaros' good judgment.

[510] The reference here is evidently to a collection of the sayings and deeds of the early fathers, such as the *Gerontikon* or the *Apophthegmata Patrum;* on several occasions in the *vita* Lazaros is shown using illustrations from works of this kind to support his teaching, see the Introduction, section C, p. 22 n. 116. In light of the comment above in Chap. 119 concerning Lazaros' evident dislike and avoidance of ostentatious scriptural citation in discussion and teaching, the passage is unlikely to refer to the Acts of the Apostles.

[511] The word used in the Greek is, once again, διάκρισις.

and attempt to repent, but are entrapped by their <old> habits and fall back into them again; or, on the other hand, those who fall once and for all but who are <then> happy with one object of their passion.[512] The father replied, "None of these people is acting well or irreproachably and, if they were never corrected by repentance, they would certainly be liable to chastisement and punishment; but, I suspect that the frequent sinner would turn more quickly to repentance than the one who has fallen once and for all, and who is happy with just this one object of his passion and is content to stick to this.[513] For the person who has persisted like this with a single [547] object <of passion>, especially if he has already had children as a result, will <only> come to repent with difficulty unless God, Who provides a means even in impossible circumstances, may somehow make things work out as they should, from His deep compassion. On the other hand, the person who keeps on falling and is thus pricked by his own conscience and is also mocked and reproached by <his fellow> men each time, might perhaps change his way of life for the better <more> quickly after he has repented."[514] This <is the> sort of answer the father would give to such a question.

[512] Retaining the original ἐν in place of Delehaye's emendation to ἐνὶ; I am grateful to an anonymous reader for this suggestion. If the emendation is accepted, the passage may be translated "but who are <then> content with just this single manifestation of their passion."

[513] If Delehaye's earlier emendation were accepted, it would seem logical to suggest a similar emendation in the phrase Lazaros here repeats word for word, although Delehaye does not do so.

[514] Thomas, "Evergetine Reform," 251, apparently comments upon this chapter in the *vita* (although he does not cite it specifically by number) and uses it to illustrate his argument that severe disciplinary problems were faced by single-sex communities living under vows of celibacy at this time, problems which were exacerbated by the breakdown of the cenobitic regime. There is, however, no indication at any point in the *vita* of monks cohabiting or engaging in sexual liaisons on the mountain itself; rather the passage should be taken as the response to a hypothetical question perhaps based on actual situations in which monks had broken their vows of celibacy either during a temporary absence from the community for some legitimate reason or after they had left it altogether. The case of Symeon, reported in Chap. 201, thus provides a particularly good illustration of this sort of problem and it is conceivable that the present chapter could be a commentary upon that specific case; cf. also, however, Chaps. 90, 156, 190.

130. Since some of the brothers sometimes used to ask Lazaros about the monastic habit, <as they wanted to know> how the tradition prevailed that it was one thing divided into three,[515] he replied, "The habit is truly a single thing, even if some have distinguished two ranks in it.[516] The division into three ranks that we now <follow> has been prescribed primarily because of the slackness and weakness of this present generation,[517] yet at least <this has> not <been done> entirely at random or illogically, for this can also represent a greater and more lofty model: such a division seems somehow to echo[518] the <heavenly> ranking into these three classes, I mean that of the martyrs, apostles, and angels. So the person who has proved suitable for the rank of the first habit can be reckoned with the choirs of the martyrs, the second with those of the apostles, and the third with those of the angels. Indeed, this is also clear from the everyday names of these, as we usually call them the angelic and apostolic habits and the clothing of submission, which is <another way of saying> martyrdom." This is <what he said> about the habit.[519]

[515] Further on the established gradations of monastic habit in the Byzantine tradition of this period, see above, Chap. 9, n. 56.

[516] This twofold division must refer to the habits or categories of fully professed monks (the *mikron* and *megalon schema*). The dress or rank of the novitiate (referred to below as the "dress of submission" or "obedience") is clearly regarded as somewhat different, although it is still classified under the overall monastic habit when this is used to distinguish people involved in the monastic life, in whatever way, from laymen.

[517] This echoes many disparaging remarks made by Jesus in the Gospels concerning "this generation," e.g., Mt. 12:39, 42, 45; Mk. 8:38; Lk. 7:31. Cf. also the *Apophthegmata* attributed to Antony the Great (23, PG 65:84B; Ward, *Sayings,* 5). Cf. also Chaps. 186 and 232, below.

[518] It is easier to translate this passage if ἐπέχειν is emended to ἐπηχεῖν, an easily explicable scribal error. A translation of ἐπέχειν is possible, along the lines of "aim at," "tend toward," and so "hint at" (see e.g., below, Chap. 138), but this seems rather forced and I am thus adopting the emendation in my translation.

[519] Thomas ("Evergetine Reform," 250–51) comments on this chapter, using it to illustrate his contention that growing awareness of ancient ascetic traditions at this time was causing a questioning of the inequalities and hierarchies that had developed within Byzantine monasticism over the preceding centuries. Lazaros was evidently sympathetic to the call for reform but, says Thomas (p. 252), he felt impotent to institute the desired changes in his own community; here, then, he resorts to a "facile spiritual rationalization" of established practice.

131. A young layman, honored with the rank of *anagnostes*[520] at about the age of eighteen, came to the monastery to become a monk. But, before being tonsured, he was sent by brother Ignatios (who is now our *trapezopoios*)[521] to gather wild leeks and, when he had gone to the area of St. Onouphrios,[522] he fell from the cliff and died. The brothers searched for him and, when they found him, they picked him up and brought him back to the monastery <where> they laid him on the ground in front of the father. So he was laid out <and was the> subject of laments by all the onlookers, not <because> he had died,[523] but rather <because> of the manner of his death and the sorry <way in which his body had been> broken by his fall; for his head and his hands and his feet and every bone in his body had been completely crushed and were covered in blood.[524] While the brothers were thus standing weeping over him, the father saw him laid out like that and said, with a gentle smile, as he looked at the broken body of the brother, "What benefit have you derived from this, <you> wicked Devil? For look, the man you have killed is now numbered among the martyrs, while you have fanned the flames of Geh-

[520] The *anagnostes* or "reader" was a member of the minor clergy who read the texts from the epistles during the liturgy.

[521] See the note in Chap. 82 on this office.

[522] This area of Galesion is also mentioned below in Chaps. 172 and 243 (where another man falls over the cliff at this spot). The place, where there was perhaps a shrine or chapel, most probably derives its name from Onouphrios, an Egyptian hermit who lived ca. 400 A.D. It is possible to deduce from scattered evidence in the *vita* that the cliffs mentioned here stood above farm land near the village of Galesion and thus faced in the general direction of Ephesus.

[523] Excessive expressions of grief over the dead were frowned upon in the Byzantine ecclesiastical tradition as being inappropriate to believers in the Christian teaching of Resurrection. Note Gregory the Cellarer's comment on manifestations of grief over the death of Lazaros in Chap. 249, below. See further *ODB,* s.v. "Death."

[524] The translation here follows the emendation of E. Kurtz, which Delehaye employs in the text, λύθρῳ καθημαγμενα. Good sense could, however, be made of the original Greek of the manuscript (λίθω [*sic*] καθηγμένα) if the second word is taken as a perfect passive participle from κατάγνυμι (properly κατεαγμένα) and the first as a dative of instrument, giving a possible translation "and had been shattered by the stone <of the cliff>"; I am grateful to an anonymous reader for this suggestion. A further possibility is that the participle is from κατάγω (properly κατηγμένα); in that case, the translation would be "and had been reduced <to pulp> by the stone <of the cliff>."

enna for yourself even more!" Some of the brothers who heard this asked him to explain his words more clearly to them. "This man did not go there of his own free will," Lazaros said, "nor did he die because he threw himself <off the cliff>,[525] but <rather> he shed his blood[526] out of obedience, for he was killed by the demons." When he saw that they were still dubious about this, he presented a story that corroborated his words.

132. "There was once a layman who lived <a life filled> with many evils but, toward its end, he eventually brought to mind his death and that terrible and incontrovertible judgment that is coming. So he roused himself and went off to a mountain, on which there was a monastery, to be tonsured as a monk there and to propitiate God by his repentance and tears for the faults he had committed before. However, as he began to climb the path up the mountain, night overtook him <almost> at once and, as he did not know the way, he sank down on the spot where he had been overtaken <by the darkness> and went to sleep. While he was sleeping, someone appeared to him, apparently in the habit of a monk, and woke him up. 'Get up!' <this figure> said, 'Follow me, and I will lead you to the monastery.' The man took him to be one of the brothers from the monastery, and so got up and followed him, without knowing where he was going. But that wicked guide took the man up onto the ridge of the mountain and then pushed him over the cliff and killed him.[527] This much concerning the man was, however, revealed to the superior of the monastery in a dream, for he seemed to see some white-robed <figures> take the soul of the man who had fallen and <start> going up to heaven; but <then> other <figures>, who were dark in appearance, suddenly attacked them and

[525] It is clear from this statement that the brothers' reaction described above was partially due to the suspicion that the young man had committed suicide, something that was forbidden by canon law and regarded as a sin in this period; see further, *ODB*, s.v. "Suicide."

[526] This is perhaps an allusion to the words of Jesus at the Last Supper and thus to the prayer of consecration at the communion; see Mt. 26:28; Mk. 14:24.

[527] The chapter to this point is closely parallel to another, apparently factual, episode recounted in Chap. 243, below. There a layman comes to be tonsured by Lazaros at Galesion but is led over the cliff at St. Onouphrios in rather similar circumstances during the night; in that instance, however, the man evidently escapes unscathed from his fall. It seems quite possible that Lazaros' illustrative story here is based, in its first part, on that incident. For other stories on this theme, see Chaps. 42, 47, 51, and 244.

<tried to> hold back the man they were carrying and to drag him downward. They were arguing and were shouting at the <figures> dressed in the white robes: 'Leave him to us, because he's ours! He's been doing our deeds until now and you've got no reasonable excuse for taking him with you. You've got no <right> to him at all!' At the same time they produced <the lists> of his sins they were carrying in their hands in writing, and <started> enumerating them by type. The radiant <figures> said to the dark ones, 'Yes, it's true; he did do what you say he <did>. But he renounced that <behavior> and came to repent <of it>, and since God seeks the <good> intention of a person, he has accepted his repentance.' However, the dark <figures began> arguing with them again that he had not <yet> managed to make his confession and in fact had not genuinely repented. But, while this was happening, the <superior> heard a voice booming out to them from above and saying this: 'That he had repented and left the <outside> world and forsaken his evil deeds is certainly demonstrated by his action; but that he did not manage to enter the monastery and confess the things he had done and so demonstrate appropriate repentance, <that> is not his [548] fault but yours, who prevented him from <doing> so. But I think that his blood, which has been unjustly shed by you, makes up for <all> the labor and toil that he was going <to do in penance> for his sins.' At this voice, then, those wicked and mean accusers immediately vanished like smoke, while the angels went rejoicing to heaven with the <man's> soul."

133. "The superior of the monastery woke up straightaway, and came to the conclusion that the vision he had seen in his sleep was true and had been shown to him by God. After the dismissal from church, he summoned all the brothers and told them the dream, as it was; since they also agreed that this vision had been revealed by God, <the superior> at once ordered some of them to go out onto the mountain and search for the dead man's body. These <brothers> went out and, when they found his body, brought it into the monastery. They performed the proper <rites> over him according to the rule of the monastery and then buried him in the brothers' cemetery. Now," said Lazaros, "if that man, who was answerable for so many sins, received forgiveness from the God who loves men because he had been killed by the Devil who hates them, how <can it> not <be right> for this <young> man <here>, who did no such thing but died because of his obedience, to be ranked with the martyrs, as I have said <he should be>?" After the father had said this, the brothers were fully satisfied and replied, "<Yes>, it is <right>, father." Then

they carried the brother's corpse out and buried him according to the regulations of the monastery.[528]

134. The brother [Ignatios] who had sent the man out on this errand was, however, very disturbed, as he considered himself to be the cause of his death. "If I hadn't sent him out, he wouldn't have fallen down and died," he said; and, because he could not bear these disquieting thoughts, he went up and confessed to the father. The father said, "This idea is <coming> from the demons; it instills these <thoughts> into your soul in order to make you burden yourself with grief.[529] But you must take no notice of it. Look," he continued, "I'm sending one of you <out> on monastery business right now, but if the person I send should happen to be swept away by the river and drowned, will I be the one who has drowned him? Go along then, and stop worrying about this altogether, because that man has inherited that <eternal> life which is without unhappiness, on account of his unhappy death." The brother had his thoughts set at peace by these words from the father, and went away after making obeisance.

135. This ought not to be overlooked either. The brothers once disagreed during a service, for some of them said they had to sing a *theotokion* during the *troparia* of the feasts,[530] while others did not accept this. So they went to the father and asked for instruction as to what should be done. He <said>, "It is always quite in order to sing the *theotokion;* for, just as the <flavor> of salt is the most useful of all seasonings, so in all Christian hymnody the praise of the Theotokos is the most fitting and necessary <element>. If you like, I'll tell you an appropriate story that corroborates what I'm now saying."

[528] The author perhaps has in mind here a passage from *The Ladder of Paradise* of John Klimax (5:21; PG 88:772c). Although the passage concerns the renunciation of normal burial requested by some extreme ascetics (cf. below, Chap. 246), it speaks of their wish being granted through the light of discernment (διάκρισις), the same quality possessed by Lazaros that is being illustrated in these chapters, and uses the same word as that found here (ἐξοδιάζω) for "carrying out" the body.

[529] I am grateful to an anonymous reader for some suggestions concerning the translation here.

[530] *Theotokia* were hymns directed to the Theotokos; they were sung at some point during many Byzantine services. A *troparion* was the basic form of the Byzantine hymn, or merely a stanza of one. See further, *ODB,* s.v. "Theotokion," "Troparion," also "Kanon."

136. "There was <once> a negligent monk who, for the most part, couldn't have cared less about the spiritual benefits of his actions. However, while he was lazy about these other matters, there was one he didn't neglect and never regarded as trivial: this was that whenever he was singing he would always say a *theotokion* too. For this <reason> alone he was confident that he would be saved. Indeed, he didn't fail in his hope, for at his death God revealed something like this about him to one of the elders. <This man> seemed to see the brother's soul being carried by angels and borne up to heaven, but then some black-colored <figures> suddenly appeared from somewhere and laid hold of it, and <started to> drag it downward. They said to those carrying it, 'Leave this <soul> for us to take, for he always did our wishes!' While this was happening the elder saw a woman dressed in a purple robe suddenly[531] standing there, who said to those who were dragging down the brother's soul, 'It is true, as you say, that he was negligent and used to follow your wishes, but because of his faith and his great love for me, and because he would never sing anything without also saying my *troparion,* I have now stood as a mediator on his behalf before my son and God, and he has granted me this soul. For even I may be worthy to save one soul and snatch it from your grasp.' As soon as she said this the wicked ones let the soul be and fled, and the angels went rejoicing to heaven with it."

137. "There was also another brother in Jerusalem who used to love the Theotokos so much that, wherever he found her holy image depicted, he would bring wax tapers and incense and oil and place them there; thus he would show his devotion <for her> as much as he could. After he had been doing this for a considerable time, he begged the most pure mother of our Lord to let him know in a vision if his practices were acceptable to her. And indeed she did appear to him on one occasion while he was asleep. 'Your practices are good,' she said, 'but they are not acceptable to me because you receive praise from a lot of people <for them>. If you really want to serve me, withdraw and go off into the desert where you won't find either my image or the people who praise you and then I will accept without reservation your faith in me and the disposition of your soul.' After he woke up from his sleep, the brother thought carefully about these things and then, when [549] he had

[531] The Greek word αὐτομάτως also contains the sense of spontaneity, of something happening without any visible cause.

made up his mind,[532] withdrew into the desert at once. While he was there the Theotokos again appeared to him in a vision. 'Now I know that you really do love me,' she said, 'because you didn't disobey me.'"[533] These are the <sort of stories> the father used to tell us, <for> he would always substantiate his decisions[534] concerning the matters we asked him about more definitely with such older examples, and would validate his own words with them.

138. But my account must pass on to the following matters. Laurentios, who is now a stylite, once stood with me in front of the father's pillar and asked him a question about the lamps in the church and those in the cells. The father replied, "The church seems to present an image of heaven <and so> the lights in it <represent> the stars. But as for those in the cells, it seems to me that someone who has acquired intellectual illumination in his heart will have no need of physical <light>. However, if he wants to sing something, and does not know how to say <the words> by heart, or perhaps has some <other> need to read, he should light his lamp until he has finished his office or no longer needs to read, and then he should put it out. For, if a monk goes to sleep with a lighted lamp in his cell, he will be considered a dead man by God.[535] If he has an icon he should take it to the church and should <instead> fix a wooden cross in front of him and say his prayers <before it>;[536] but whenever he enters the church he should kiss the holy icons."[537] The father said this, not to lay

[532] The verb is again διακρίνω, which could perhaps also be translated more literally as "when he had exercised his good judgment" or "his discernment" to bring out its relation to the theme of these chapters.

[533] These stories are clearly related to the type commonly found in the Western collections of *Miracles of the Virgin.* Although these collections began to appear in the West only at the beginning of the 12th century, and continued to flourish throughout that century and the following one, individual stories of this kind seem to have already passed into circulation there in the mid-11th century. It seems certain that their transmission was due to direct contact with Greek traditions of the kind found here.

[534] The word used is again διάκρισις; thus Lazaros' power of good judgment or discernment is once more being illustrated.

[535] The reference is presumably to the custom of leaving a burning lamp or candle in a room with a corpse, but the practical risk of fire was, of course, also considerable.

[536] The implication is clearly that this type of wooden cross should be set up in a monk's cell.

[537] Thomas ("Evergetine Reform," 250; cf. Thomas and Hero, *Foundation Documents,* 152) comments on this passage. His interpretation appears to distort the original emphasis, however, for he suggests that the passage implies that "Lazaros permitted his

down the law, as someone might say <he was doing>, and to ordain <rigidly> that someone should not have an icon in his own cell, but <rather> to promote poverty and thence ensure freedom from distraction for those who obeyed this <advice>.

139. The brothers of the monastery once denounced John, who is called the Smyrnian, to the father for holding a cane while he was standing in church. When the father questioned him, he replied, "As you yourself know, father, I have an infirmity and I can't stand like the rest of the brothers. I have taken to doing this so that I don't leave the church and return to my cell and lie there in sleep and idleness." The father said to him, "Since you are in this <condition>, from now on you may support yourself with two canes if you want, as long as you don't leave the church for this reason."

140. The brothers were once standing in front of the pillar as usual on

---

monks to own their own icons (with votive lamps) for personal veneration in their cells" while urging them "to bring them to the church for worship." It is true that the subsequent sentence states that Lazaros did not rigidly enforce a *ban* on the possession of personal icons and the implication is that monks did in fact continue to own and use such icons. The main point seems to be, however, that he was doing his best to discourage (rather than permit) the possession of private property of any value (such as icons) and the practice of individual forms of worship (such as the personal veneration of icons) which might undermine those conducted communally in the monastery church. By the same token he was apparently attempting to encourage genuine asceticism in his flock and the type of private spirituality which was compatible with true cenobitic monasticism. Such an interpretation of the passage in fact supports, rather than undermines, Thomas' general point, which is to suggest that Lazaros' approach anticipates in some respects the supposed Evergetine reform of Byzantine monasticism later in the 11th century. Cf. here also the similar attitude to lamps and icons in monks' cells revealed in the *vita Athan.Ath.* (B), chap. 44, 179.38–40. The present chapter in the *vita* of Lazaros, like the previous ones and several other passages (see, e.g., the comment in Chap. 96 to the woman who wishes to go on pilgrimage to the Holy Land that the true Jerusalem is simply wherever anyone does good things), demonstrates a stress in Lazaros' teaching on the overriding importance of inner rather than external spirituality, a stress which is, interestingly, also reflected in changes that took place in Western religious attitudes during the same century. As the following chapters make clear, Lazaros' attitudes did not meet with the approval of all his monks; the last instruction in his speech here, when taken in conjunction with the dissension implied in the following sentence, may thus have been intended to counter the dangerous possibility that he could be accused of disliking the use of images in worship in general and hence of being a crypto-iconoclast. Further on Lazaros' style of monasticism, see the Introduction, section D.

the feast day of one of the notable saints. They said to Lazaros, "Father, grant us a special meal[538] for the feast day of the saint we're celebrating now, and send <someone> to buy fish for us." But the father said to them, "This saint did not become a saint through luxury and indulgence, but through fasting and many labors, and so, if we want to observe the feast days of the saints <in a manner> that seems good to God and is pleasing to the saints themselves, we too should imitate their lives to the best of our ability." One of the brothers, called Pachomios, replied to the father, "But as Christ said to the apostles, the wedding guests cannot fast as long as the bridegroom is still with them; but the days will come when the bridegroom is taken from them, and then they will fast."[539] The father realized the brother's intention in saying this; he averted his eyes and his face and, without looking at the brother who had given this quotation, said, "That was <indeed the case> with Christ and his disciples, just as you say; but I believe in Christ my God that after my death you will most certainly lack for nothing."

141. The father said this not only on this occasion but also on many others. The brothers used to receive his words about the <future> somewhat lukewarmly, however, for they did not expect that the monastery that had been established would <continue to> exist after his death, because we would be harassed every day by the people from the metropolis [Ephesus] into moving from the mountain.[540] For this reason most of the brothers, some privately in turn, but others openly in front of everybody, asked for Lazaros' permission to move away from here after his death. He allowed some <to do this>, but on

[538] On the use of the term *diakrisis* in this sense, see above, Chap. 95 n. 422; cf. Chap. 246.

[539] This is a rough quotation; see Mt. 9:15; Mk. 2:19–20; Lk. 5:34–35.

[540] Compare Lazaros' confidence in the face of pessimism by his monks above, Chap. 109; cf. Chap. 110. As is made clear here, this pessimism was a result of the opposition and hostility shown toward the Galesiote community by the ecclesiastical authorities in Ephesus toward the end of Lazaros' life (cf., e.g., Chaps. 237–39). The same feeling of insecurity lay behind the foundation of the monastery at Bessai (see, below, Chap. 239, and above, Introduction, section F.a, p. 36). The desire expressed in the next sentence by "most of the brothers" to move away after Lazaros' death is thus probably to be understood not as a wish to leave the community or the monastic life, but rather to move to Bessai, which, since it enjoyed recognized legal status, might provide them with greater security (cf. Chaps. 216–18, but note Chap. 170, where Gregory the Cellarer himself apparently considers leaving for the Holy Land). On pessimism about the future, see also passages in Chaps. 217, 245, and 247.

others he imposed his death as a bond.[541] Some of them were also saying that his successor as head of the monastery would not be <of> the same <caliber as he was> and would not employ the same spiritual discernment[542] toward those under him; nor would he have sufficient <strength> to support everybody's weaknesses or to guide them as he ought in both spiritual and physical matters. To these the <father> replied, "I know <for sure> that after my death it will <indeed> be possible <for someone> to become the superior in the monastery who, with help from above, will be able to supply you adequately with your physical requirements; you will also be obedient to him in all things, as is proper, and you will have the same trust in him that now you profess to have in me. And for matters of spiritual thought, because the superior will not always be found here, you will have, by the grace of God, elders who know the spiritual way unfailingly from experience and long life; I know that you will not go far astray from the straight <path> if you employ these guides and also communicate your thoughts to them and do everything after asking their advice. And if, as you say, they should banish one of you from the monastery,[543] the one who has been banished should carry on sitting outside the gates for seven days; if, during these seven days, they do not offer this person either food or drink from the monastery, or wish to receive him <back>, he may then leave and go where he wants. For such a man will have been given permission by God and by me <to do so>." With these words, Lazaros restored them and [550] boosted the confidence of those who were doubtful about the future, and he set <their minds> at rest thereafter. But <now> I must relate the following matters.

[541] Lazaros was apparently attempting to ensure that they would remain after his death.

[542] The term is διάκρισις once more.

[543] A slightly different issue from the ones discussed above is introduced rather abruptly at this point, since Lazaros now apparently turns to a question posed by the monks concerning the right of the "elders," after his death, to expel a monk who had perhaps earlier been refused permission to leave in such circumstances by him and who had been required to promise that he would stay on the mountain. The sudden introduction of this issue might possibly indicate that something else is missing from the text here, especially since there are an unusual number of scribal errors in Chaps. 141 and 142. The passage may represent the response to a purely hypothetical question, but it might also refer to an actual incident, familiar to the author, which occurred after Lazaros' death; in that case the allusion above to the occasional absence of the superior from the monastery could also refer to a situation that had arisen at that time.

142. Methodios, who is called "the Tall," once had his cell robbed. He was suspicious of a brother who had left the monastery in the past and had taken up lay life again, and <now> had his home in the village called Kyriou Louka. He suspected that he had been robbed by this man, who had come at night <to do so>. When this became known to the father, he immediately dispatched some of the brothers with orders to seize the man and bring him to him in the monastery. When the brothers had brought him, they stood him in front of the father's pillar and Lazaros, standing up on his pillar, began to castigate him and to accuse him in front of everybody, <saying> that it was indeed he who had stolen the brother's things and no one else. The man stood there shamefaced with his eyes on the ground and defended himself by saying that he had had nothing to do with this at all. Then the father threatened him again, saying that he would cut out his eyes and slash his Achilles tendons and then would throw him into the monastery guest house and keep him <there>, disabled and crippled.[544]

When the man heard such <terrible> threats, he absolutely denied <the crime>, whether truly or falsely, and tearfully offered the defense to the father and the brothers that he was not guilty. While he was standing there weeping, the father told one of the brothers to take him away and lead him to the kitchen and persuade him to have something to eat. He could not be persuaded <to do so>, however, and even refused the food in his great desperation. Then the father, behaving like someone who was very angry, said <even> more sharply to him, "Go! Have some food! I know <exactly> what I'm going to have done to you!" But after he had gone off and been fed, he came up to the father again who admonished him and prayed over him as was his custom, and then dismissed him without doing any harm to him whatsoever.[545] For, <given what> a kind and gentle soul Lazaros really <had>, how <would he have considered actually> making use of retribution, even when <someone> had done something worthy of punishment? Indeed, this man returned to the monastery some time later and put on again the habit he had <previously>

[544] Mutilation formed a normal component of the punishment that might be exacted for theft in Byzantium, although the particular forms of this penalty threatened by Lazaros here seem rather severe. See further, *ODB*, s.v. "Theft," "Penalty," "Mutilation." On the guest house, see below, Chap. 150.

[545] Compare the somewhat similar incident recorded in Chap. 203, below.

discarded; and he died in the monastery of Bessai[546] two years ago now. This was the Meletios whom the superior put in charge of the horses. But these things <happened> later on.

143. At the time, some of the brothers complained when they saw that the father had treated him like this,[547] but others approved. Others said, "<If> he himself gives orders for our cells to be ransacked, why should we blame others <for doing so>?" For the father used to do this to some of the brothers who refused to give up the things they should not have had in their possession.[548] Others again said among themselves, "What's the good of him having gathered together such a crowd <of monks>, when he sits <up> there getting angry with them and being disturbed <by them> every day, and is unable to make them obedient and subservient to his will? And <then>, with these <monks> in this state, he <still> goes on tonsuring others!"[549] As they were saying these things to each other, one of them, John who comes from Smyrna (who was mentioned by me a little <while> ago),[550] replied to the rest. "Why are we talking idly," he said, "standing <around> aimlessly wasting our time with <this> nonsense? Why are we saying these abusive things so thoughtlessly against the father? You don't know anything, but, if you want, I will tell you whom our father follows, and upon whom he tries as hard as he can to model himself, and thus <in what light> his management of our affairs is to be

[546] Malamut, "Bessai," 244, n. 8, does not mention this reference to the monastery.

[547] Compare the reaction of some of the brothers in rather similar circumstances below, Chap. 240; cf. also Lazaros' generous treatment of a thief in Chap. 241.

[548] See below, Chap. 145, for further discussion of Lazaros' habit of doing this. As was noted above, Chap. 138, Lazaros seems to have been engaged in a continual campaign against the possession of private property by monks in his community on the grounds that this ran against true ascetic ideals and therefore those of cenobitic monasticism; at the same time, as is apparent here, he clearly met with determined resistance from some of the monks and even outright hostility; see, e.g., Chaps. 148–49, 180, 191–93, below; and Thomas, "Evergetine Reform," 249–52. The *typikon* of Evergetis, Chap. 27, authorizes the superior to search his monks' cells once a month and to confiscate any possessions he may deem superfluous; they are to be distributed to the needy; Gautier, "Évergétis," 69.

[549] For further criticism of Lazaros' policy of admission to the community and his own defense of his actions, see below, Chaps. 152, 227, 231–32, and 239–40.

[550] Above, Chap. 139. The episode there might perhaps help to explain the apparent change of attitude toward Lazaros' regime he reveals here.

viewed!" When they urged him to speak, he continued, "It's obviously God. It's my considered opinion that our father is an imitator of <God>; <and> I've learned this from his actions.[551] For God, Who formed man and equipped him with much glory and advantage in the beginning, did not put him out of the way when he later proved unappreciative of how rich were His gifts or when he disobeyed His commandment; rather, after He had punished him with the condemnation <following the Fall>, He allowed him to carry on again so that the race of mortals might grow immensely and might fill the ends of the earth, even though He knew full well beforehand that those who would be born of it would commit worse sins than the <first man>. Indeed, from then until the present time He has always been kind and long-suffering toward us, and, even though we disobey His commandments every day, He has not delivered us into eternal perdition, nor has He prevented us from increasing and multiplying immensely. Now, in exactly the same way, our father is disobeyed and <sorely> tried by us every day, but he does not banish us, nor indeed does he refuse to tonsure the people who choose <to become monks>; and, even though he is fully aware of how hard it is to set our minds straight, he is <still> long-suffering, patient, and affectionate, <in the hope> of saving at least some of us." After the brother had said this, everyone immediately agreed with his words. "Yes," they said, "that's absolutely right! You've really hit the mark with your assessment of the father's character and disposition." Those present believed this brother's defense of the father to them to be laudable and intelligently and clearly explained; but they thought that it was especially marvelous[552] and considered it strange that this defense <of Lazaros> should have been made by this <particular> man. For previously he was not readily accustomed to say anything good about the father, but rather, on the contrary, sometimes poured out much abuse against him with his loose mouth and intemperate tongue. But He who of old caused the mouth of Balaam, which that man opened to curse Israel, to bring forth a blessing instead of a curse,[553]

[551] For other comparisons of Lazaros to God and Christ in the *vita,* see above, Chap. 85, and below, Chap. 251.

[552] The use of the Greek word θαῦμα here implies that John's change of attitude may actually be considered miraculous.

[553] Num. 22–24 provides the fullest account of how the king of Moab, Balak, tried to get the seer Balaam to curse the people of Israel before they entered Canaan after the flight from Egypt, only to be thwarted by God Who intervened and made Balaam pronounce a blessing instead; see especially here 23:11. Other references to the incident

now prompted the aforesaid brother [John] to say such things on behalf of the father for the benefit of the other brothers. [551]

144. Someone once came up at night and stole one of the horses <belonging to> the monastery from the stable, together with its saddle; they <then> made off <again>. In the morning, when the father learned about this, he sent some of the brothers out to search for it, but they came back again without finding anything, although they had searched a great deal and made <many> inquiries about it. So, for this reason, they went up together with the other brothers to see the father, and pestered him to allow a wall to be built around the monastery and to have the security of <having> the entrances and exits under <lock and> key. "For we have suffered this <sort of thing> many other times <already>," they said. But the father did not assent <to this>, and said to them, "When saint Sabas attempted to do this in the lavra he founded, he was prevented from <completing> the project at some point in the construction when the Theotokos appeared to him and said to him, 'If you want to have me as a guard for your lavra, let it stay just the same as it was before; but if you <would rather have> the wall, build it as you want!" <Sabas> immediately gave up work on the construction of the wall and left the protection of his lavra to the Theotokos herself. And it's still like that today.[554] So, if we have complete trust and confidence in Jesus Christ and the all pure Theotokos who bore Him, we too have no need of security from walls and enclosures."[555] After Lazaros had said this to the <monks> who were pestering him about the wall, he dismissed them. However, when the feast of St. George[556] arrived and some of the brothers, as was their custom, were about to go off to the *metochion* of the monastery at Mathaia,[557] because there was a church of the aforemen-

(which do not all agree as to the praiseworthiness of Balaam's role) may also be found at Deut. 23:4–5; Josh. 24:9–10; Neh. 13:2; Mic. 6:5.

[554] Patrich (*Sabas,* 192) mentions the fact that the core of the Great Lavra had no walls but makes no reference to this story, which does not appear in Cyril of Skythopolis, *vita Sabae,* ed. E. Schwartz, *Kyrillos von Skythopolis* (Leipzig, 1939). Lazaros had presumably learnt it while he was a monk there.

[555] Note that Chap. 141 refers to monks who have been expelled being required to sit outside the gates of the monastery for seven days. It is, however, possible that Lazaros is quoting there, or speaking figuratively.

[556] This was celebrated on 23 April.

[557] Nothing more is known of this place. A *metochion* was a subsidiary monastery attached to a larger one; it often acted as a base either for supervising distant estates

tioned great martyr there, the father said to them, "Say to St. George, 'Unless the horse is <back> in the monastery tomorrow, I'm not going to celebrate your feast any more after this.'" After he had said this to the brothers, he prayed for them and dismissed them. The next day the horse that had been lost from the monastery was found, with its saddle, grazing on the foothills of the mountain, and making its way up to the monastery. The brother who found it took hold of it and led it up to the monastery; when the father saw it he said, "Look! St. George has given the horse back to us <really> fast!"

145. As I have said many times, when Lazaros did this <sort of> thing, he always used to shun the fame and glory of men. Often, when poor people would come to beg him for alms, they would call him a holy man to this end; Lazaros would, however, reply to the man who had called him this, "I'm no more holy than you are; so struggle, brother, and watch out for yourself so that you don't go to <eternal> punishment along with me!" After he had said this he would not let these people go away empty-handed, but would either <pick out something> from what he himself had to hand, or else would take something from a brother who happened to be there, and would immediately present it to the person who was begging.[558] If he could not find anything to take from someone, he would explain to him, in front of the brothers, that he had nothing, and dismiss him;[559] but privately he would <still> give him something, either <doing so> himself or by means of one of the brothers.[560]

---

or for monks visiting a town. It had its own chapel but, although it might occasionally be a relatively wealthy establishment, it was usually inhabited on a permanent basis by only a small number of monks. See further, *ODB*, s.v. "Metochion."

[558] Cf. Chap. 89, where, in similar circumstances, Lazaros forces a reluctant brother to part with a *nomisma*. Lazaros' great generosity was a recurrent theme in the early part of the *vita* concerning his youth and travels, but examples of the specific practices referred to in this and the following chapter have also been encountered in Chaps. 66, 75, and 113.

[559] I am grateful to an anonymous reader for suggesting the wording of the translation here.

[560] This practice is also mentioned in Chap. 248, below. The context there raises the possibility that, as often seems to be the case, Gregory the Cellarer is actually writing in defense of Lazaros here; hence, perhaps, the stress placed on his refusal of praise, and the concern shown to establish his *secret* generosity. As Chap. 248 makes clear, there were evidently malicious rumors in circulation, even within the monastery, that Lazaros received a great deal of money from benefactors but never spent it or gave it away, so that his pillar was actually stuffed full of gold.

And if none of the brothers there had anything at all to give, he would tell the poor man to go through the brothers' cells and, if he should find a piece of clothing hanging up somewhere there, to take it and leave well satisfied.[561] When he had done this on the father's orders, the poor man would go down from the mountain rejoicing. As for the <monk> who had lost the garment, he might be distressed for the moment, but then, at the time of the <annual> distribution of habits, the father would provide him with a new garment instead of the worn-out one he had lost, if he knew that he needed one.[562]

146. Some of the poor who discovered the father's generous disposition would visit him and ask him to become the sponsor of their children, either <telling him> the truth or else fabricating their story. Lazaros would respond enthusiastically to them, give them what they needed and dismiss them. But he knew the <real> reason why they were doing this. Once, then, someone who seemed to be very hard pressed by poverty came and begged for something from Lazaros, as he said he had no provisions at all. The father took out a *nomisma* and gave it to him and, by means of a personal letter, gave instructions that he should also be given one of the monastery's goats and four measures of wine; he also told the cellarer to give him oil and pulses and cheese, as well as bread and vegetables. In fact, he ordered so many <provisions> to be lavished upon him that the fellow who received them was unable to carry them or wrap them up, and had nowhere to put them at all; and still he said "Yes," when the father asked him if he needed anything else. When the brothers saw the man doing this they criticized him openly for being greedy and insatiable; but the father defended the poor man by saying to them, "Why are we criticizing him? If he wasn't so hard pressed by hunger and poverty he wouldn't do this, especially when being ridiculed by you. You should commiserate with him and have sympathy for him rather than being disapproving and critical." When the father said this, the brothers were put to shame by his words and immediately gave the poor man a hand. So he took everything and went down from the mountain, giving the greatest thanks and glorifying God.[563]

[561] "Well-suited" might be closer to the basic meaning of the Greek word εὐφυῶς here, but it perhaps sounds too much like a pun to appear in the translation.

[562] Reference is apparently made to this practice, which is a regular feature of Byzantine monastic *typika,* in Chap. 171, below, and in the *diatyposis* in Chap. 246.

[563] Morris (*Monks,* 215) comments on this incident.

147. Once, on an important feast day, some of the brothers did not come to the refectory with the rest, as was usual, but took their meal in their own cells.[564] The father learned about this and, after the brothers left the refectory, he called them together <before> him. When he had preached to them from up on his pillar and had gladdened their souls with his sweetest and <most> honeyed words (for the father was accustomed to do this with very few exceptions), in addition to his other preaching and advice, he also issued this statement from above in the hearing of all: "If someone does not come to the refectory with the other brothers on feast days, let him be accursed!"[565]

148. On another occasion some of the brothers denounced the monk Kerykos the [552] shoemaker to the father for having a folding table[566] in his cell. When the father heard <this> he sent one of the brothers who fetched the <table> and set it down in front of the pillar. As plenty of brothers were standing there, including the brother who had the table, the father began to teach, as was his custom, and to say this to the brothers: "The abbot Daniel of Sketis[567] said that many of the monks distributed their property, left their parents, brothers, <and> relatives on account of God and of their sins, and entered into a monastery <where> they did indeed successfully achieve <mastery of> the great virtues. However, they were then conquered by the tiniest <little> things and became objects of evil delight for the demons[568] by acquiring for themselves pouches and chests, in which they kept fruit, sweetmeats, needles, scissors, and belts. These people are condemned as self-indulgent by those who think correctly, and they are accursed according to the scripture. For it

[564] On *ariston,* see above, Chap. 84.

[565] Thomas ("Evergetine Reform," 250) cites this incident as "telling evidence of the breakdown of the cenobitic regime" at this time.

[566] Kazhdan (in *ODB,* s.v. "Tables") plausibly suggests that the doubtful συμβατὴν of the text should be emended to συμβαλτὴν, a term that probably indicates a portable or folding worktable, something entirely appropriate to this context and Kerykos' occupation. Cf. also Lazaros' comment in the following chapter.

[567] Daniel of Sketis was a monk and *hegoumenos* who lived in Egypt during the 7th century. He is known from a collection of moralizing stories, originally written in Greek, which are presented as being told by him or one of his associates. Further see *ODB,* s.v. "Daniel of Sketis." Like Delehaye, I have, however, been unable to identify the source of this particular saying attributed to Daniel.

[568] Or perhaps "they were seized by the least of the demons and became objects of evil delight for them."

says: *cursed is he who removes the landmarks* of the fathers.[569] They will <thus> deserve the fate of Iannes and Iambres and of Ananias and Sapheira, for being their fellow initiates and fellow participants <in the work of Satan>."[570] When the father had said this he added his own decree and issued this statement in front of everyone: "If anyone on this mountain has acquired such a table and keeps it <anywhere> apart from <in> the center <of the monastery>,[571] let him be liable to the same curse!" Then he told the cellarer to pick up this <table>

[569] The reference is to Deut. 27:17; cf. Hos. 5:10. I follow the translation of Brenton, *LXX.* The first part of the quotation from Deut. is exact, but the LXX refers to "his neighbor's landmarks" not those "of the fathers"; the Greek word (ὅρια) translated by Brenton as "landmarks" (Deut.) or "bounds" (Hos.) could also mean "rules," which might be more appropriate in the present context.

[570] Iannes and Iambres are likened at 2 Tim. 3:8 to those who oppose the orthodox faith but will not succeed in perverting it. These men were identified in Jewish and early Christian traditions with the wise men, sorcerers, and magicians of Egypt of Ex. 7:11, 22 who imitated the miracles of Moses before Pharaoh but who, according to a lost tradition, were apparently shown to be charlatans. They are referred to relatively frequently in late antique literature. Ananias and Sapheira, who are the subject of Acts 5:1–11, were a married couple who sold some property to give the money realized to the church; however, they retained some of the proceeds of the sale and, when they failed to tell St. Peter the truth about this, were accused of being caused to lie by Satan. They were miraculously struck dead, one after the other. Cf. also below, Chap. 228.

[571] The interpretation of the Greek phrase "ἐκτὸς τῆς μέσης," translated here as "<anywhere> apart from <in> the center <of the monastery>," is uncertain. Delehaye thought the word μέσης was related to the Latin *mensa* and hence evidently took it here in the sense of a "mess," i.e., the refectory. While possible, this is not the most likely explanation. There are two quite close parallels to the use of μέσης. The first is the common use of the term ἡ Μέση in the *Acts of Athos* to refer to the Protaton in Karyes, the central administration of the Holy Mountain (see, e.g., the *Typikon of Tzimiskes,* in *Actes du Prôtaton,* ed. D. Papachryssanthou (Paris, 1975), 7:125, 126, 129, and p. 206). The second is the use of the same term for the main central thoroughfare in Constantinople (ἡ Μέση λεωφόρος) (see Janin, *Constantinople byz.*, esp. 361–62; cf. also 91 and 97 for evidence of artisans working beside this street). The problem would thus seem to lie in relating these two parallel uses of the term to the situation being described here. The phrase may refer to the central courtyard or "street" of the monastery, and Lazaros is here stipulating that such an object has to be kept (and used) there rather than in the privacy of an individual cell; in other words, the table is to be public rather than private property. The phrase could also be taken as "apart from the common <property of the monastery>" or even "without the consent of the central <administration>" (see Liddell-Scott-Jones, *Lexicon*, s.v. ἐκτός, I.4, for this use of the word).

and take it to the storeroom. But the man who had the table had apparently seen what the father had said and done, and said to him, "Your intention is to set the others straight <by making an example> of me, and that's why you're doing these things to me <so> often." (For Lazaros had shamed him in front of everyone a few days before for possessing a *miliarion*[572] and at another time over a pouch and a cloak.) "Why don't you also do this to the monk Euthymios who has these things <as well>?" The father said, "Don't compare yourself to the monk Euthymios nor to anyone else like him, because he's sick and infirm; that's why I've given him permission to have these things. There's no need to treat those of you who are well in the same way as those who are infirm."

149. Although Lazaros said this, some of the brothers <remained> obdurate and were ill disposed to his words. They retorted by saying to him, "If we're being put under such a curse by you because of these trifling and trivial matters, what's going to happen to the monks of the other monasteries who not only have these things but also have servants and <lots of> money[573] and mules and business dealings and further diversions? Are all of them going to perish?" The father said, "They haven't installed *me* as a judge for the other monasteries. But I do know this <quite> clearly: I didn't come up onto this mountain hoping for that sort of thing, but rather because I'd heard that it was harsh and comfortless and filled with wild animals and snakes and demons, so that I might be tested by these things and so might be able to save my soul. So, if any one of you does not want to persevere here like this and with this aim, but <in the way> that you say, let him go off wherever he wishes. For I've <actually> shown consideration for you, because of your weakness and the

[572] Delehaye believes that the word μιλιαρίου is to be taken as a Hellenized form of the Latin *mil(l)iarium,* and suggests that it refers to a type of bronze pot used for heating water either in baths or in the kitchen. The other items mentioned in this sentence are apparently seen as luxuries or comforts (hence Lazaros' permission for similar things to be used by a sick monk, but not a healthy one), and so this interpretation seems plausible. If, on the other hand, this object falls into the same category as the worktable mentioned above and is hence connected with Kerykos' trade, then the word might be some form of μυλάριον, a small hand mill, perhaps here used for a type of grinder. It is also conceivable that it is a corruption of μιλιαρήσιον or μιλιαρίσιον, a silver coin (on which see above, Chap. 108).

[573] Lit. "*nomismata*" or "gold coins." The implication is that these monks do not simply possess small amounts of loose change, but substantial sums of money.

harshness of this place, and for the most part I've relaxed the strictness of the communal life <here>, in case you should give up because of its great and oppressive intensity and should <thus also> be in danger of falling short of <more> moderate <goals>; for this tends to happen to a lot of people, and especially to those whose spiritual disposition is rather lethargic and irresolute. <For example>, whenever some devout person has brought something to eat, I've let you receive this with my approval as <some> small solace for the body, but not so that you may become completely fixated upon the acquisition of money[574] and tables[575] and other things of that sort, which are <only> appropriate for people who live in the <outside> world and <are affected> by the tumult and cares of everyday life, lest you should be shipwrecked unawares in the harbor while pursuing things far from your calling." Lazaros said these and other words besides in his defense and put forward <these> counterarguments against those who, as I have said, were vexed and displeased by his confiscation <of their possessions>. <By doing so> he not only silenced them, but also made some of them blame and criticize themselves for what they had thought fit to say in direct opposition to him and in disagreement with him. But since my book is focusing now on matters concerning the brothers of the monastery, I must also narrate this <episode>, as it is the right moment for it.

150. Some of the brothers pressed the father to make a rule concerning the visitors who continually arrived at the monastery. <This was> that they should leave after staying for only three days, for Lazaros <usually> allowed someone to stay in the monastery for as long as he wanted to remain there, without being turned away by anybody. Similarly, they also nagged him about the <visiting> monks, and especially the vagrant ones,[576] <and tried to make

[574] See the previous note. Other references in the *vita* make it clear that some brothers did indeed have money of their own from time to time, whether large or small amounts; see above, e.g., Chaps. 88–89, 163, 192, and 193. As these chapters show, Lazaros was evidently opposed to the possession of money by his monks in general and this led at times to considerable friction; in Chap. 108, however, he actually returns money to a brother from whose cell it has been stolen.

[575] Compare the previous chapter; here the normal word "τράπεζα" is used.

[576] These monks were apparently in flagrant breach of the ideal of monastic stability, which, although not rigidly enforced, was still encouraged in Byzantine monasticism. Cf. Lazaros' own early wanderings and Gregory the Cellarer's possible attempts to defend him against such accusations (Chaps. 18–19); cf. also Chaps. 95 and 99. See further, *ODB*, s.v. "Stability, monastic"; Nicol, "*Instabilitas*."

him rule> that they should not be fed in the refectory but in the guest house.[577] As they were unable to convince him, although they had said this forcefully many times over, one day they seized on a reasonable pretext, as it seemed to them, and went to see Lazaros. "As far as the visitors go," they said, "it's not right that the guestmaster does not have <proper> charge of them,[578] either when he serves them or elsewhere. <For example>, he receives the pulses from the cellarer to be cleaned and hands them over to these people but, when they get hold of them, they pick out the good ones and eat them, and leave the bad ones for us. As you don't want to listen to us nor to follow the example of the other monasteries, then at least listen to Christ Himself Who says, '*It is not fair to take the children's bread and to throw it to the dogs.*'[579] [553] Make a rule

[577] The *xenodocheion* or guest house of the monastery was primarily used for lodging visitors but it could also serve as a place for tending the sick; this seems to be confirmed by Lazaros' instruction to Gregory the Cellarer in the following chapter about not expelling sick visitors. Cf. Chap. 142, above, where Lazaros threatens to use it as a prison. Chap. 162 mentions a "monks' guest house" at the monastery of the Resurrection (although apparently a very small one, perhaps no larger than a single monastic cell); it also refers to the later construction of a special facility for distinguished visitors there, an *archontarion,* which evidently contained only two beds; this would appear to indicate, when taken with the present chapter, that visiting monks were housed separately from lay visitors and accorded different treatment, although it is not clear whether distinguished lay visitors were also housed separately from regular ones, who occupied the *xenodocheion,* or whether there was more than one such facility in the three communities on Galesion. The present chapter makes it clear that Lazaros remained firm in his conviction that visiting monks should eat in the refectory with the brothers, although laymen and lay brothers apparently ate in the guest house; cf. the fragmentary episode below in Chap. 211 in which guest monks are apparently being fed in the refectory even at a time of famine (probably at the end of Lazaros' life), and Chap. 213 where lay brothers are fed in the guest house. See further *ODB,* s.v. "Xenodocheion" (which cites this chapter); for other evidence of it also being a facility for the sick at this time, see Gautier, "Évergétis," 81.1166–68. See also here D. J. Constantelos, *Byzantine Philanthropy and Social Welfare* (New York, 1991), 151–52; Kaplan, *Les hommes,* 294 (although note that his footnotes 105 and 106 are inverted there).

[578] The Greek verb used here, ἐπιμελέω, contains both the sense of "looking after" and "being in charge of." The complaint here thus seems to be made on the grounds that the guestmaster is not in control of the visitors (hence my "proper"); however, Lazaros, in his speech to the guestmaster below, deliberately seems to take the word in its other sense of "taking care" in order to reproach those making the complaints.

[579] Mt. 15:26.

that they should spend three days <here> and then leave." After they had said this, the father pretended to be angry with the guestmaster and ordered him to be brought to him. When he had been brought, Lazaros said to him, "Is this how you look after the visiting brothers? Don't you even provide them with water or the proper service you ought to? Don't you know that <news of> the care or the neglect that visitors receive goes directly up to Christ? Believe <me>, if from now on I learn that any visitor has been made miserable by you, you can be certain that you yourself will really be made miserable <as well>! Let the visitors spend three days <here> and then leave, just as my fathers are urging; but, I want the monks <among them> to join them in the refectory, for, even if they are poor and vagrant, they have been made our brothers through their <monastic> habit and they should not eat with the lay people in the guest house." After the father had said this, the guestmaster prostrated himself and asked forgiveness and then, when he had received this, he went off to his work.

151. The <guestmaster's> critics were <thus> put to shame and they too made obeisance and went back to their cells. While they were on their way, they said to each other, "What is it about our holy father that should most amaze us? His angelic lifestyle, the extent of his compassion for the needy and for visitors, or his marvelous understanding and good judgment? He has just made wise and skillful use of this <latter quality> toward us to make us ashamed of ourselves. For could he not have said to us, 'Which of you has contributed anything to the monastery? Doesn't God send everything because of me? Who made you my judges and teachers?' But he didn't say anything like that at all." One of the brothers, called Nicholas Paxamades, said to them in reply, "God certainly knew to whom He was entrusting His people to guide them properly. Don't you see that Lazaros has never ever liked to say 'Someone has come up to the monastery because of me,' or 'Whatever God has sent <has been> through me'? <He doesn't> even <like> to write his name on a letter but instead <simply puts> 'From the humble lavra,'[580] and <says> 'So-

[580] My translation assumes that the phrase ἀλλ' ὅτι ἐκ τῆς εὐτελοῦς λαύρας goes with what precedes it. It might, however, parallel the following statement and mean "<It was> for the sake of th<is> humble lavra," although in that case ἐκ would have to be taken as causal (cf. Liddell-Scott-Jones, *Lexicon,* III.6). The term *lavra* is used elsewhere in the *vita* only of St. Sabas near Jerusalem (Chaps. 16–18, 20, 115, and 144) and never of Galesion; perhaps the implication is that Lazaros signs his letters "<the monk> from the humble *lavra*" with reference to St. Sabas where he spent his formative monastic

and-so came up <here> because of the mountain,' and 'It is on account of the beggars and visitors that God also provides for us.'[581] But woe unto us, for <the father's> life serves as a condemnation of us and on account of him we may justly be condemned before God!" So the brothers went off to their cells while they were discussing these matters with each other. When I went up to the father in the evening, however, he said, "Tell the guestmaster that he should serve the visitors nicely and not force them to go away. And you <too>, if there is a sick visitor, give him generously all he needs from whatever you may have in the cellar;[582] and let him stay as long as he wants. Don't throw him out!"[583] I said, "<But> today you gave orders that <visitors> were to stay for three days and then leave. Are you now saying that they are not to be forced to go away?" "I didn't order this because *I* wanted it to happen or wanted it to be made a hard and fast rule," Lazaros replied, "but <I said it> to calm down the tumult and the clamor of those who are disturbing me with this <business>. Or haven't you noticed how they won't stop bothering me over this every day? Don't they know that it was on account of the visitors and poor people that God allowed this monastery to be <established> in this place and that it's because of them that He also maintains those of us who are persevering here?" When he had said this he deemed me worthy of a blessing and dismissed me.

152. Brother Germanos, who was entrusted with the job <of looking after> the church,[584] once had a disagreement in the church with Isaiah (called

years, but it would make more sense to interpret the disparaging adjective εὐτελής as a modest reference to Galesion, given that the purpose of this passage is to illustrate Lazaros' great humility.

581 This point, repeated at the end of the chapter, is also made by Lazaros in Chaps. 210, 211, and 213 in rather similar contexts concerning doubts about hospitality extended to visitors.

582 This provides the first indication in the *vita* that Gregory, its author, held the office of cellarer in the monastery. His position is confirmed below in Chaps. 170 and 210. On his role in ministering to the sick, see also Chap. 172.

583 The uncertain reading αὐτὸν in the manuscript would seem to make more sense than the αὐτούς of Delehaye's text in this sentence and I am thus following it in my translation. In Gregory the Cellarer's reply the subject does, however, switch to "visitors" in general.

584 In Chap. 209 he is described more formally as being *parekklesiarches* (see above on this office, Chap. 82), evidently in the monastery of the Resurrection. That chapter

"the Short").[585] After the dismissal, he went up to the father and began to abuse him. "It's you who cause these problems," he said angrily, "because you welcome and tonsure the<se> youths and let them stay in the monastery in this disorderly way, causing problems and disturbances, and you don't discipline them or make them learn self-control.[586] Wouldn't it be better if you expelled them, and your flock <thus> lived in peace?" After the brother had angrily said this and other things too, the father gave no response until he knew that his anger had subsided. Then he opened his little window and, looking straight at him, said, "If you were the superior, would you drive them away?" "Yes," said <Germanos>, "because it's better to lose one or two instead of all." The father said to him, "You miserable wretch! You, who consider yourself a spiritual <person> and far more advanced than him, can't patiently endure even one single word. Nor do you humble yourself and prostrate yourself before him so that, by seeing this, he may also benefit from your humility. <Why then> are you seeking these things from him? What if I did force him to leave, as you suggest, and he went off into the world and lost his soul? Tell <me>, who would then have to answer for it? Don't you admire <the fact> that <young men> like this actually persevere and remain on this mountain, and are delivered from the constant problems of the <outside> world? What do you think? If these people were in the <outside> world right now, what would they be doing? God, through His great compassion, is powerful <enough> to make even these <young men> progress little by little in the monastic state. Now then, go and adopt a more humble attitude, and then make repentance to him and ask forgiveness for being the cause of the problem yourself. In that way he too may benefit from your humility." When the brother heard the father <say> this, his <conscience> was pricked and he fell down in front of the pillar and tearfully begged to receive forgiveness. When

---

certainly concurs with the impression given here and in the following chapter that Gregory the Cellarer found Germanos to be a rather difficult man.

[585] Changing the punctuation of the text and taking μετά in the sense of "with" (Liddell-Scott-Jones, *Lexicon,* III.1; it is clearly used in the same way at the start of Chap. 153). As the text stands, the implication is that Germanos went up to the father *along with* Isaiah, which is quite possible but less likely, esp. as Isaiah is not mentioned again as being a witness to the discussion with Lazaros which follows.

[586] Cf. above, Chap. 143, for opposition to Lazaros' admission policy; also below, Chaps. 227, 231–32, and 239–40.

he received this he went down and went straight to the <other> brother to make repentance to him; <thus> he made up with him and they were reconciled with each other.

153. On another occasion again the same brother Germanos had a fight with Ignatios the <nephew> of Matthew. The father sent for him,[587] but, although the brother in question [Ignatios] made repentance to <Germanos>, the latter was not persuaded to forgive him. After he had eaten, and was still being obstinately averse <to doing this>, <Germanos> went off and lay down on his rush mat and fell asleep. In a dream, he saw an Ethiopian come up to him and [554] eagerly embrace him and kiss him like a true friend.[588] When he turned away from the kiss, the <Ethiopian> responded by saying to him, "Why are you turning away from me? Don't you know you're my friend?" As he said this he took hold of him and kissed him. Then he turned round and apparently said to some others, "You come and kiss him too, for starting today he's taken to being a friend of ours and doing our bidding." While the <Ethiopian> was saying this to him, the brother saw black dogs jumping up at his face and licking it with their tongues.[589] He woke up worried and frightened as a result of this, and immediately went running up to the father to tell him his dream. The father replied to him, "Don't you know that people who harbor anger against their brothers and won't forgive them become friends of the demons? So go and make repentance to your brother and be reconciled with him; and stop this demonic habit from now on lest, just as you saw in your dream, you depart with them into the darkness as their friend." <Germanos> prostrated himself, and then went down from the pillar and at once went to the brother and made repentance, and made friends with him.

[587] Or perhaps "appealed to him"; cf. Chap. 203 where the same verb (παρακαλεῖσθαι) is used in this way. I am grateful to an anonymous reader for this suggestion.

[588] The Devil and the demons are frequently associated with black men (or "Ethiopians"), as also below in Chaps. 210 and 233. Further on this association, see *ODB,* s.v. "Ethiopians"; Joannou, *Démonologie,* 13; Greenfield, *Demonology,* 85; idem, "Outer Darkness," 62–65. On Ethiopians in disturbing dreams, see P.-A. Février, "Le maure ambigu ou les pièges du discours," *Bulletin archéologique du comité des travaux historiques et scientifiques,* n.s., 19B (1985), 295 and n. 8.

[589] On demons associated with dogs, especially black ones, see above, Chap. 28. Dogs were generally associated with enemies in Byzantine oneirocritical literature; see S. M. Oberhelman, *The Oneirocriticon of Achmet* (Lubbock, Texas, 1991), 235 and n. 906.

154. Another brother,[590] who used to be sent by the father to the Kastron [Ephesus] on certain business and who used to lodge in someone's house <there> at Lazaros' behest, began to be troubled by an <evil> thought <when he was> there. At first he struggled not to be overcome by such a thought, but when he saw that it was stirring him more strongly, he was frightened that he might be in danger of yielding <to it>, and so he confessed his thoughts to the father. The father said, "If this is what is happening to you, I won't send you there any more." Some days later, <however>, Lazaros called him and sent him there again. The brother said, "Do you <really> want me to go there again? Is this what you arranged with me just a short time ago?" The father replied to him, "Go, and don't be afraid about this, for God will keep you unharmed by such thoughts. Just try hard to complete honestly and trustworthily the tasks I am asking you to do." The brother believed the father's words, and went off after prostrating himself. When he had fulfilled Lazaros' orders, through the grace of God he was no longer troubled by the thoughts that had previously assailed him, and not only then but never again thereafter, even though he was sent there many times by the father. But <once>, while he was returning from there, night fell in the middle of his journey. When he reached the village, Kyriakos[591] saw him and advised him not to go on up <right> then, but to go into his house and stay <there> and go up in the morning. Since he did not usually do this, the brother did not listen to him and instead passed by <the village> and went on his way. When he arrived at the area of Chalkos

[590] This anonymous brother, who is the subject of this chapter and Chaps. 156–58, should perhaps be identified with Gregory himself. As cellarer, Gregory must have been given considerable responsibility and, indeed, he mentions traveling to Ephesus on business, seemingly as a matter of course, in Chap. 75; perhaps significantly, the same expression is used for the city there as in the present chapter. Again, in Chap. 156 he is given the task of organizing food for brothers while away from the monastery on business, something well suited to someone who held the position of cellarer or *trapezopoios.* Moreover, the obvious readiness to seek an explanation for events in terms of demonic activity rather than natural causes, which is apparent here, would fit well with Gregory's own approach elsewhere in the *vita.* If this identification is not made, then it seems strange that Gregory is here so reticent about his source when elsewhere he is generally scrupulous in citing the origin of a story so as not to lay his work open to accusation by doubters (cf. above, Chap. 80).

[591] Presumably the same man mentioned below in Chap. 243. In that case, "the village" mentioned here must be that of Galesion.

Halonios[592] he invoked the father's blessing, made the sign of the cross on his heart and his forehead, and began to climb up the mountain. But when he was halfway up the mountain and had passed the very steep part of the rock where the cross was located,[593] he suddenly heard a noise and a commotion and scurrying footsteps as though something[594] was running away in front of him. The brother was a little bit frightened by this, although he did not completely succumb to fear, and again invoked the father's blessing and crossed himself; then he went confidently on up <the path> with the <words> "God help me through the prayers of my holy father!" ceaselessly on his tongue. When he was near the monastery, however, he was gripped with such cowardice and fear, as he thought he was being pursued by something, that he went running into the monastery gasping for breath. This happened to him because, when he had already reached the proximity of the monastery, he became <over>confident and stopped invoking the father's blessing; for this reason the grace of God withdrew from him for a short while so that he might know who his guardian and his keeper was.

When he reached the father he went up and gave an account of the business on which he had been dispatched; he also told him about this <incident> and asked him at the same time if this was due to demons or to something else, such as wild goats, which normally live on the mountain. The father smiled and said, "Perhaps it really wasn't due to demons but, even if it was, what would that <matter> to you? You didn't go there of your own free will but were sent out by me, and someone who is sent out somewhere by his own father should not fear or worry about physical dangers but should pay attention to <only> one thing, and that is to accomplish honestly and trustworthily what he has been ordered <to do> so that he may not be spiritually rather than physically endangered by straying from his task. And even if he should fall into physical danger, he should not be faint-hearted, but should rather

[592] On this place, see Chaps. 77 and 155.

[593] On the history of this cross, see above, Chap. 41. It is also mentioned as lying on the same route in Chap. 77.

[594] Here and in the second sentence below there is an ambiguity in the Greek plural τινῶν, which cannot be expressed by a plural in English. The monk is unsure exactly what the things are that are running away or pursuing him, and τινῶν can cover the whole range of possibilities, which, it subsequently becomes clear, he was contemplating: people, animals, or demons. The sense of fear is thus perhaps best captured in English by the singular "something."

give thanks to God because the reward stored up for him will be greater." This <was> what the father <said> to the brother, or rather <he did> not just <say this> to him on that occasion, but was always saying this and admonishing and teaching all those who traveled that path and who chose to maintain genuine and true obedience. However, that the rattling noise which was made on the path and which scared the brother was due to no other <cause> but demons, I will try to make clear from another story, which goes like this.

155. <This story concerns> the nephew[595] of the monk John whose surname was Ardagastenos; at the time he was a boy, but he has now reached full manhood and is with us in the monastery; he is also called John, like his uncle. <This John> was <once> coming up to us from there in the middle of the day and, when he came to that same spot, he stopped to venerate and kiss the cross. <While he was doing this>, he heard a sound behind him and, turning round, saw a headless man standing <there>. At this sight the boy was gripped with immense fear and <started> trembling, <but> he called out as clearly as he could in a quavering voice, "God help me through the prayers [555] of my holy father!" The man at once disappeared. Another time, two other brothers were going down there at night and were at the same spot when they suddenly heard the clatter of horses' hooves from the western part <of the mountain> and the shouts of people calling to the horses as it were. However, these men also passed the place unharmed through the invocation of our holy father's blessing.[596] But the death of the monk Daniel at this very spot may perhaps bear witness to what has been said better than anything.[597] And I have actually heard the father himself say that the <monasteries of the> Savior and the Theotokos and the holy Resurrection drove out the demons from the gorge and the <other places up> here, but that some of them <still> liked to lurk in the area of Chalkos Halonios. So much for these things.

156. But the above-mentioned brother, on account of whom we have recalled these present matters,[598] was again sent out somewhere by the father on another occasion, along with <some> other brothers. He reached the place with them and they lodged in a church <there>; a priest was <attached> to

[595] On the term ἀνεψιός, see above, Chap. 45.

[596] Compare the similar episode recounted above, Chap. 50; both passages may perhaps refer to the same incident.

[597] There is no other reference in the *vita* to this person or to this episode.

[598] The anonymous brother (Gregory the Cellarer?) of Chap. 154.

this and he lived quite close to the church. When the brothers were about to go off to carry out the father's bidding, they appointed this brother to make arrangements for their food. He went into the priest's house and started carrying out his job assiduously. But, when the priest's wife saw that no one else was there except for the two of them (for her husband had also gone with the brothers), she came up close to him, and began to talk to him <using> beguiling words, <for> this daughter of the Evil One was trying to entice the <brother> and seduce him into an act of licentiousness.[599] The brother realized her intention from her words, however, and at once took refuge in the father's prayer and invoked this as an aid against her harassment; at the same time he signed himself with the cross and busied himself with the task at hand, while he stayed silent and sang psalms in his head. He met with so much help from our holy father's prayer, and the invocation of this gave him <so much> assistance and kept him <so completely> unharmed from this defilement, that he did not feel that he had experienced <any> passion, not even the notion or the merest thought <of this>. Once or twice he wanted to make a response to shut her up, but he was unable <to do so>, and his tongue and mouth seemed to be held in check as though by a hand. So the brother was protected by the father's prayer in this way and he was able to escape unharmed from the traps of the evil Satan. He returned to the monastery with the brothers without saying anything about this to them, but confessed everything to the father. When Lazaros had heard this <story>, he said to the brother, "If the Devil contrived such things for you, <even though> you did not go there of your own free will but because I sent you, how can those people who leave the monastery of their own free will and confidently venture out unprotected into the world ever escape his grasp?"[600]

157. On another occasion the same brother was standing in the narthex in front of the church door while the early morning service[601] was being sung;

[599] This incident is mentioned by A. Kazhdan, "Byzantine Hagiography and Sex in the Fifth to Twelfth Centuries," *DOP* 44 (1990), 136 n. 65.

[600] It seems impossible to convey in English the full connotations of the Greek word λαβαί (translated as "grasp"), which here has the sense of the "holds" used by wrestlers; the common athletics metaphor for human encounters with the powers of evil is employed once again.

[601] The service of *orthros,* on which see above, Chap. 8; cf. Chap. 72.

as he became drowsy, he dozed off and fell fast asleep while the brothers were reciting the Psalms inside. Then the <brother> seemed to see a man emerge from the sacred sanctuary. The man had flowing hair, and this hair, both in his beard and on his head, was blond <in color>; he was dressed in a purple tunic and was wearing a fillet on his head. Two eunuchs were also to be seen, accompanying him on either side, of whom the one on the right had reddish skin, while the one on the left had rather black hair on his head and a face the color of ripe wheat. The <man> started walking toward the area of the choir, where the father's pillar was,[602] <and then>, on the man's orders, the eunuchs made a distribution of some kind to those who were standing in the choir as they passed by with him. They passed through the two choirs and the central part of the church and so arrived at the door where the brother was standing. <There the man> indicated to the <eunuch> on his right that he should also give the brother something from what he had been giving to those inside. However, when <the eunuch> took out an obol[603] and gave it to him, the other <eunuch> turned to him and said, "Aren't you giving this man a *nomisma* also like you distributed to those inside?" The <eunuch> turned to the <man> who had given the order and looked at him in silence. Then, as though he was addressing both of them, the man replied, "I order gold <coins> to be given to those standing inside the church and singing, but obols to those outside." When he had said this, the three of them suddenly vanished from <the brother's> sight and he at once woke up.[604] Contemplating what he

[602] While this passage, together with those in Chaps. 159 and 207, may imply that the pillar was actually inside the church, and thus that a new building must have been constructed around Lazaros' old pillar at the monastery of the Theotokos after he had moved up to his new one at the foundation of the Resurrection (since his pillar is said always to have been unroofed), it is also possible that the pillar simply adjoined the wall of the church on the outside but had a small window that opened onto the inside. See the Introduction, section C, p. 18.

[603] Another name for the small bronze coin more properly known as a "follis." Its notional value was 1/24th of the silver *miliaresion* and 1/288th of the gold *solidus* or *nomisma*. Clearly a great difference in the value of the largesse is indicated here. See further on this coin, *ODB*, s.v. "Follis."

[604] A similar vision, involving the distribution of various sums of money to monks in the monastery church, appears in the *vita Athan.Ath.* (B), Chap. 28, 156.7–157.39; on that occasion the donor is a woman accompanied by two eunuchs.

had seen, he immediately went up to the father and related his dream to him[605] and at the same time asked him to explain it and tell him whether it had been shown to him by demons or by God. The father replied to him, "Everyone, and especially monks, should distrust dreams.[606] However, what you saw was not <sent> by demons but by God: the person you saw between the two eunuchs was Christ, while they were angels who, on His orders, distribute every day the reward, like gold, to all those who stand and sing inside the church in fear of God and with their minds alert; but they give less, like obols, to those outside as <they are> idlers and sleepyheads. Something similar can be found written down in the *Gerontikon,*[607] <where it says> that God showed this happening every day in the church to one old father, while his eyes were wide open. However, he showed him this so openly because he was a holy man, but he showed it to you in a dream because <you are> an idler and a slacker, to let you know how much punishment you are bringing upon yourself when [556] you leave the church and lie down and go to sleep in the porch. This is why I'm always telling you and the other brothers that you must not miss church." For the father was continually saying, both in private and in public, and especially to the lazier ones, that if someone was unable to say <even> a <single> *trisagion*[608] in his cell over and above <what was strictly required by> the rule he had been given, God would not demand any recompense from him for this, but only so long as he had not been missing church; for someone who had been missing <this> would be considered worthy of blame by God. The father also <said> these things to <the brother> about this.

158. I must also tell this <story>, along with the others about this brother. The feast of a certain holy man was being celebrated somewhere[609] and some

[605] A slight alteration in the punctuation of the text at this point seems to improve the sense of the passage. I am thus reading "καὶ αὐτὸς εὐθὺς διυπνίσθη. Καὶ πρὸς ἑαυτὸν κατανοήσας ὃ εἶδε, πρὸς τὸν πατέρα." I am grateful to an anonymous reader for this suggestion.

[606] Cf. Lazaros' similar comment in Chap. 235, below.

[607] The *Gerontikon* was a collection of stories about the desert fathers. Delehaye here cites the *Pratum spirituale* (see above, Chap. 1), Chap. 105 (PG 87:2009), where two incidents of waking vision are recounted concerning Abba Christopher.

[608] See above, Chap. 45.

[609] Foss (*Ephesus,* 121) assumes that the reference is to Ephesus. If so, it likely refers to the major *panegyris* there, the feast of St. John, celebrated on 8 May (see further, Foss, 126–27). It is doubtful, however, that Gregory the Cellarer would refer either to

brothers were going off there with the father's permission and encouragement. The aforesaid brother asked the father if he too might be given leave to go with the other brothers; the father was unwilling, but nevertheless, as he was pressed very hard by him, reluctantly gave him permission to go. While <this brother> was there, however, his resolve was so badly affected that he came close to consenting to a shameful act. Although he was saved there, for he was protected by the grace of God, he was quite badly hurt somewhere else for, after he had received the undefiled mysteries, he then intemperately ate <so much> food out of gluttony <that> he vomited. When he returned from there to the monastery with the brothers, he confessed to the father everything that had happened. The father said to him, "Didn't I tell you not to go there for this <very> reason?" Then the brother prostrated himself and asked forgiveness for these <offenses> and for Lazaros' blessing to help him in the future. He received what <he asked for> and from then on was well guarded by divine grace; thereafter, as far as he was able, he would do nothing at all without the father's approval. Anyway, these are the <stories> about the aforementioned brother.

159. I must now also speak in some detail in my account about the rest of our fathers and brothers who, at various times in the monastery and on this mountain, have shone brilliantly in the life <devoted> to God, in order that, according to the words of the Savior, the tree may be better known by its fruit, the father from his children, and the teacher from his disciples, as also the branches from the root.[610] I shall focus first upon Kerykos, whom some of you knew. This man, who properly bent his neck to the yoke of Christ and followed the father's wishes most faithfully, proved himself to be a trustworthy and gen-

---

St. John or to Ephesus in the vague way he does here, and so this passage may well refer to some rather less important festival and location, such as the one mentioned in Chap. 144, above: the feast of St. George celebrated at the monastery's *metochion* at Mathaia.

[610] None of these statements is found in exactly the same form in the New Testament. The first reference, to the tree and its fruit, is the closest, being an obvious paraphrase of Mt. 12:33; Lk. 6:44. That to the teacher being known from his disciples is probably to be seen as a reference to Mt. 10:25, "*It is enough for the disciple that he be as his master*"; and that to the branches being known from the root seems likely to recall Rom. 11:16–18. It is less clear what Gregory the Cellarer has in mind as the basis for the father being known from his children, although it may perhaps have something to do with statements in the Gospel of John about the Father being known through the Son, e.g., Jn. 1:18.

uine laborer in obedience. After he had spent time doing various jobs <in the monastery>, he asked the father's <permission> and went off and enclosed himself on the pillar of Petra, which is above the village of Galesion.[611] He lived there for a while, but then realized that it was doing him no good and that he was, on the contrary, being harmed because the place was not suitable for <attaining> spiritual peace.[612] <This was> because, whenever someone says something in the village or elsewhere in the vicinity, it comes <straight> to the ears of the person on the pillar. <Kerykos> made this known to the father and, in accordance with Lazaros' wishes, left that place and went onto the pillar in the church of the Theotokos;[613] for the father was then at the holy Resurrection. Before he <finally> came down from there, however, <Kerykos> had made this <problem> known to the father not just once or twice but over and over again and, as <his request> had <still> not been granted, despite his insistence, what did he do? He was overcome by the idea <of leaving>, or rather he was dragged into this by the wicked demon, and <took> the rope <used for> hauling provisions up to him by means of a winch, tied it around himself under the armpits, and rashly attempted to descend the cliff by himself. But, when he had put his feet out of the window and was on the point of going down, <or> so he thought, he became caught by the hem <of his tunic> on one of the pieces of wood <fixed to> the pillar,[614] and was thus left hanging,

[611] On this place and its use by an earlier stylite, see above, Chap. 41; that occupant of the pillar evidently encountered the same problems as did Kerykos and dissuaded Lazaros himself from attempting to live there when he first thought of moving to Galesion from the community of St. Marina. Chap. 175 reveals that it was also (subsequently?) occupied by at least two other monks from Galesion who had progressed to the stage where they could live as stylites.

[612] Lit. "hesychia."

[613] See above, Chap. 157.

[614] The fact that wooden slats or rungs were attached to the cliff in this location to form some sort of ladder or walkway is mentioned above in Chap. 41. The difficulties Lazaros encountered there show that this construction was already in a dangerous condition at that time, some twenty-five years or more earlier, when he first went to Galesion; this may perhaps explain why Kerykos wanted to go down by rope on this occasion rather than trying to climb. It is not clear, however, whether it is part of this ladder that is described or some other beam or plank used in the construction of the actual pillar itself (whatever form this may have taken) in which Kerykos was living on the cliff. Chap. 207, below, uses the same ambiguous term, ξύλα, apparently in relation to the pillar of the Theotokos, although it perhaps refers there to some element in the

unable either to go up again or to go down, for he was holding the rope with both hands, and was still caught by his tunic on the piece of wood; as a result he was completely helpless and in obvious danger. However, when his hands grew tired and he was about to untie the rope and climb down the crag by himself, <then>, if ever <he was going to>, he invoked the father's prayer with all his heart. At once he felt himself helped, as though by some invisible person, and removed from the danger, for it was as though he had been lifted up a little by someone, <and so>, when he pushed himself <up>, he got back onto his pillar again.

160. From the time this man [Kerykos] left the arena of obedience and turned to the eremitical life he abstained completely from wine[615] and oil, nor did he eat cheese, eggs, or fish. He did not wear two tunics and, moreover, he did not receive one from the monastery as the rest of the brothers normally did, but instead wore a tunic, a scapular,[616] and a holy cowl that he had made with his own hands out of wool. He kept his head uncovered, just as his pillar was, and his feet were bare. The result was that he mortified his body so much with such austerities that he appeared to be nothing but skin and bones to those who saw him, and seemed not to possess any flesh at all. As regards bodily stature, however, he was tall and he surpassed most people in strength so that the <following story> is told about his great physical prowess: He was once bringing back about nine *modioi*[617] of beans by wagon from the threshing floor in the plain to <the monastery of> St. Marina[618] but, when he had al-

---

construction of the church around or beside this. If it is interpreted in this way, then the translation should read "one of the beams of the pillar."

[615] On this abstinence from wine, which was evidently also practiced by Lazaros (see, e.g., Chaps. 17 and 35, above) and other notable ascetics in the community (so Chap. 164; cf. 177, 198), but not by most of the brothers, see Kaplan, *Les hommes,* 33.

[616] On this garment (ἐπωμίς), see above, Chaps. 35 and 57.

[617] The *modios* was a unit of measurement applied not only to quantities of produce but also to the surface area of land; it was also used for indicating the capacity of boats. As the term could indicate quite a range of different quantities whose equivalent weight is the subject of dispute, it is hard to determine the exact weight that Kerykos is said to have carried up to St. Marina. Assuming that the monastic *modios* is being used here, and taking this as equivalent to 10.2 kilos (or 22.4 pounds), the beans would have weighed more than 200 lbs. See further *ODB,* s.v. "Modios," "Litra"; E. Schilbach, *Byzantinische Metrologie* (Munich, 1970), 96–99.

[618] On this place and its development by Lazaros, see above, Chaps. 31–36 and 53; see also the Introduction, sections B, pp. 10–11, and E.c, pp. 31–33. Chap. 34 mentions

ready reached the lower slopes of the mountain <on which> the monastery <stood>, the wagon broke.[619] He himself then put the sack containing the beans on his shoulders, brought it up into the monastery, took it into the barn, and emptied it there. Indeed, many other such tales are told about his feats of immense physical strength. Early on, he was completely illiterate; [557] however, while he was still <practicing> obedience and was pasturing the animals, because of his great love of hard work he learned the basic letters by asking questions, and then, in a short time, he was also taught how to put them together <to form words> and was able to learn the whole orderly pattern of <grammar>.

161. During all the years he spent shepherding the flocks <Kerykos> never ever touched milk unless he happened to be up on <top of> the mountain; however, he gave it generously and without grumbling to all the poor people and beggars who came to him, for he had been instructed to do so by the father. As a result the udders of the animals gave <milk> abundantly like a river in proportion to <the amount> he gave to those who asked for it. This <Kerykos> was <also> once sent by the father to look after a vineyard; he took care of this <task> efficiently and responsibly, but he did not taste even one of the grapes until the vineyard was completely harvested. Then, however, he took one bunch of grapes and went <back> to the monastery, and <there> he ate it after it had been blessed by the father.

162. Another brother called Basil did the same thing with a different fruit, for this was a rule of our monastery that was established from the beginning by the father; <the rule applied> to every kind of fruit, and none of the brothers, either on the mountain or living anywhere down below, was <allowed> to partake of a <particular> kind of fruit until they brought <a

---

that it possessed land used for growing beans. The present chapter evidently refers to an episode that occurred in the past, before Kerykos undermined his physical strength by his asceticism, but it is impossible to tell when this may have happened, for St. Marina evidently continued to function in some capacity long after the development of the monasteries on the mountain; see below, Chap. 193.

[619] The Greek text reads "τοῦ τῆς ἁμάξης ἀρμοῦ κλασθέντος." The word ἀρμοῦ should probably be emended to ἁρμοῦ, which has a range of meanings running through "joint," "bolt," and "peg"; since the text appears to imply there was only one ἁρμός on the wagon it may most likely refer to the joint where the pole was attached to the front axle or the peg holding it in place. It might possibly be a version of the similar Latin term *armus,* which has the basic sense of "shoulder joint" or "side." It is thus unclear exactly what has gone wrong with the wagon, and the translation is deliberately ambiguous, although the text is more specific.

sample> of it into the monastery and it received a blessing in the church. The aforementioned brother [Kerykos][620] (for my narrative must return to him again) thus surpassed most men in his physical strength <at one time>, but he withered his <body> away and substantially reduced[621] it through his ascetic way of life. Indeed, when he was already drawing near to the last days of his life, he too, like the blessed Job, was afflicted with a festering sore;[622] this was so <bad> that the skin and all the flesh of his leg rotted away <leaving> the bone exposed and bare. When the father found out about this, he sent some of the brothers off with orders to bring <Kerykos> down from his pillar. So these men went off, took him down and then, carrying him because he was unable to walk, brought him back to the father at the <monastery of the> holy Resurrection. They laid him down in the cell that is now the monks' guest house,[623] and the father at once made him have some wine, oil, and fish to eat. When the brothers saw him lying there on a bed constructed out of dry stones,[624] with only a rush mat and a ragged haircloth laid underneath him,[625] they felt sorry for him and went to the father. "Father," they said, "order at least one <proper> bed to be brought into the monastery for the comfort of the sick."[626] For not one <proper> bed was to be found in the monastery at all at that time although, after the completion of the *archontarion*,[627] just two were brought up, which were not for the monks but for distinguished laymen who

[620] It seems certain from what is said below that the narrative now returns to Kerykos and that the following account concerns him rather than the Basil mentioned at the start of the chapter, as the marginal commentary in the edited text implies.

[621] The Greek verb ταπεινόω contains not only the sense of physical reduction but also that of humiliation or abasement. Kerykos did not simply allow his body to waste away, but completely controlled and curbed its physical impulses and appetites, which were in opposition to the ascetic lifestyle and ideals.

[622] Job 2:7; cf. also Deut. 28:35.

[623] On this guest house, see above, Chap. 150.

[624] See below, n. 629.

[625] The following chapter reveals that he also had a pillow.

[626] Compare the concern of the brothers for Kerykos here with a similar display of compassion shown to Lazaros himself when he was sick, below, Chap. 208.

[627] Delehaye's suggestion that this *archontarion* was a place in which distinguished visitors to the monastery were lodged is supported by Demetrakos, s.v. ἀρχονταρεῖον, where it is defined as the better furnished rooms for the reception of visitors to a monastery. See also here Malamut, *Route,* 207. The implication is that this *archontarion* was situated at the monastery of the Resurrection.

came up to the monastery; that was why they were put in that building. The father made some such response <as this> to the brothers about the <matter>: "If a monk should die while he is lying on a bed, he should not be thought worthy of burial, because the angel, which long ago spoke to the holy Pachomios, ordered monks not to partake of the sleep they needed while lying on their sides, but while sitting in <specially> constructed seats.[628] It is thus sufficient for us to sleep while lying on a stone couch[629] in this way without worrying about it."

163. The brothers held their peace when the father said this. When the hour of the brother's death had arrived, the father told all the brothers to go to him [Kerykos] so that they might be blessed by him. After they had done so, the brothers embraced him and then stood there singing <the psalm of> "The Undefiled."[630] <Kerykos> lay on his back gazing toward heaven and sang

[628] Pachomios (ca. 290–346) developed the first Christian cenobitic monasteries in Egypt. Palladios (*Lausiakon,* Chap. 32) records how Pachomios was visited by an angel who presented him with a bronze tablet inscribed with the rules to be followed by the monks of his monastery. One of these (32.3) forbade them to lie at full length and ordered them instead to sleep "sitting down on their coverlets thrown over the backs of chairs" (trans. R. T. Meyer, *Palladius: The Lausiac History* [Westminster, Md., 1965], 92). These rules probably belong to a slightly later period than that of Pachomios himself, but Pachomios reportedly slept in a similar fashion and was imitated by others; cf. *vita Pachomii* 14:19–24 (cf. 79.21), trans. A. N. Athanassakis, *The Life of Pachomius* (*Vita Prima Graeca*) (Missoula, Mont., 1975). Lazaros himself evidently always slept on such a chair; see above Chap. 17 (cf. Chaps. 35 and 165). Further on Pachomios, see *ODB,* s.v. "Pachomios," "Pachomian monasteries."

[629] On the word used here (and below, Chap. 168), πεζούλιον, see A. N. Athanassakis and T. Vivian, "Unattested Greek Words in *The Life of Saint George of Choziba* and *The Miracles of the Most Holy Mother of God of Choziba,*" *JThSt* 45.2 (1994), 625; the word appears (in the form πιζόλιον) in the *Life* 19:119, and the authors suggest for the meaning "a terrace wall or bench made of stones." The word is also found in modern Greek in various forms, e.g., πεζούλι, a "low stone wall" or "parapet." Here it clearly refers to the stone "couch" or "bed" on which the brother is lying; this was evidently designed to raise the sleeper above the draughts and damp of the floor but to provide little or no other comfort. Reference is made to stone beds in the *vitae* of a number of Byzantine saints, see, e.g., *vita Athan.Ath.* (A), p. 79, chap. 65.26–28. I am grateful to Alice-Mary Talbot for the references in this note. For a description and illustration of apparently similar stone couches, see Hirschfeld, *Desert Monasteries,* 94–95. Similar structures may still be seen in old Greek houses.

[630] The lengthy Ps. 118 (119), which begins "*Blessed are the undefiled* (ἄμωμοι) *in the way.*"

the response, "*Draw nigh, O God, to my help;*[631] *O Lord, make haste to help me,*"[632] and again, "I have sinned against you, O God; have mercy on me."[633] Philippikos came last of all the brothers; he fell on <Kerykos'> neck and, clinging to him, said tearfully to him, "Please, remember me, the sinner, when you are standing in front of Christ, and make an intercession with Him on my behalf so that He may forgive me my sins. For I know that He will not ignore your request because of the labors you have endured out of love for Him." After he had said this beseechingly three times, <Kerykos> replied to him in a solemn <but> weak voice, "If I do find any liberty of approach there, as you say <I shall>, I will not forget your request." After he had said this, all the brothers bade their last farewell to him and left; they went to the father and made obeisance to him and <then> went to the refectory as it was already time for the second meal <of the day>.[634] After the brothers came out of the refectory, the father ordered one of them to go and see if <Kerykos> was still alive. The brother who had been sent came back and said he still was, so Lazaros sent out another brother again and ordered him to go and put his hand inside <Kerykos'> pillow, take out whatever he found there, and bring it to him. When the brother had done this but was still on his way back from there and had not yet reached the father's pillar, another brother arrived first and announced that <Kerykos> had died. The father took in his hand the things that had been brought to him from <Kerykos> and showed them to the brothers, saying, "These are what were preventing the brother from departing to the Lord, and so, as soon as they were removed, he died at once." They were coins, about sixty *foleis,*[635] a gift which <Kerykos> [558] had received from someone with the approval of the father. The brothers commented that if these <small> coins had prevented <Kerykos> from departing to the Lord, then what <sort of trouble> would those monks be in who had *nomismata* <in

[631] Ps. 69 (70):1.

[632] Ps. 39 (40):13; the word σπεῦσον found here is a variant reading for πρόσχες in the LXX; my translation thus differs slightly from Brenton, *LXX.*

[633] I have been unable to trace the source of this response. It is not a direct biblical quotation although it may be related to Ps. 78 (79):9 and perhaps also to Ex. 10:16–17 and Dan. 9:19.

[634] *Deipnon* was the second meal of the monastic day (when there was one), as opposed to *ariston* which was the first. See further *ODB,* s.v. "Ariston and Deipnon."

[635] On this bronze coin, normally written *follis,* which was also known as the obol, see above, Chap. 157.

their possession> when they departed to <Him>, without having managed to administer them properly?[636] <In response> the father said, "If a *nomisma* is found on a monk who is subject to obedience when he dies, then it is not right for the regular[637] burial rites that are customary for Christians to be celebrated over him." As evidence he cited what happened in the monastery of Gregory the Dialogos.[638] After the father had said this to the brothers, he deemed them worthy of a blessing, and then, since it was evening, he dismissed them to their rest. In the morning, brother <Kerykos> was carried out and buried in accordance with the rule of the monastery. So that was what happened to <Kerykos>.

164. <Then there was> another brother, called John, who came from the Opsikion theme;[639] although <still> a young man, he <held> the rank of priest.[640] He never went down from the mountain after he came up to the monastery, and he abstained completely from wine, oil, cheese, and fish. <Furthermore>, he would not possess <a> gold or silver <coin>, nor even an obol;[641] instead, by making poverty his friend, he sought the inheritance that cannot be lost, <that> of heavenly riches. He was, so I have learned from those who knew him well, the son of poor parents. When his mother received news of him, she too left everything to come to him; and when she saw her son and the place in which he was living, she gave thanks to God. Then she also re-

[636] Compare the rather similar line of argument put forward by the brothers in Chap. 149, above.

[637] There is perhaps a word play here on νόμισμα (gold coin) and νενομισμένος ("proper").

[638] Gregory the Dialogos was the Byzantine name for Pope Gregory I, the Great (ca. 540–604); see H. Delehaye, "S. Grégoire le Grand dans l'hagiographie grecque," *AnalBoll* 23 (1904), 454 n. 2; and *ODB*, s.v. "Gregory I the Great." The *Dialogues,* which he was believed to have written, were translated into Greek, probably by Pope Zachary (741–752), in the 8th century; they were well known in Byzantium. The reference here is to 4:57, the story of the monk Justus who kept three gold pieces; on Gregory's orders he was allowed to die without comfort and was buried in a dung heap because of this breach of monastic rules. Another part of the same story would also seem to lie behind Chap. 200, below.

[639] The Opsikion theme embraced much of the northwest area of Asia Minor, with its capital at Nicaea; it thus lay immediately to the north of the Thrakesion theme in which Ephesus and Galesion were located; see further *ODB,* s.v. "Opsikion."

[640] The minimum age for ordination to the priesthood was thirty.

[641] A small bronze coin; see above, Chap. 157.

ceived the holy habit from the holy father and was sent to the women's convent to the blessed Eupraxia,[642] and there she stayed, traversing the course of asceticism well and in a manner pleasing to God. So much for her. But her son [John], like the above-mentioned blessed Kerykos, also developed festering sores on his foot from <too> much standing, and so he ended his life blessedly and passed over to the <God> Whom he long desired. Not long after this, his mother also followed after her truly marvelous and beloved child, for she also completed the spiritual course in a manner beloved by God. She thus had this <son of hers> as a guide and forerunner in the life <dedicated> to God, and indeed she was even guided by him then, when he preceded <her> on the <final> journey of passing over from this world <to God>. In this way God, in His benevolence, no doubt managed her affairs, so that He might not only show forth *a mother rejoicing over* her child[643] in this present life, in the words of the divine David, but, even better, <one> also <rejoicing> in the future <life>.

165. Another brother, who was also called John, but came from Sardis in Lydia[644] and was advanced in age, shone forth no less than the one just mentioned, and perhaps even more, in his ascetic labors and struggles for God in the monastery of the Theotokos. He pursued <all> the other <goals> and practiced asceticism to the same degree as <the previous John> and exercised the same self-control in everything, but surpassed him as far as standing went and very nearly strove to conquer nature itself. He thus had a rope in his cell with its two ends fastened up <to the ceiling>; he would place this under his armpits and stand up all night, singing psalms and praying to God.[645] Supported by the rope in this way, he would partake of what little sleep he had to have whenever he was forced to do so by nature. When the *semantron*[646] was struck for church, however, he was the first person of all to enter and would

[642] I.e., Lazaros' mother; see above, Chap. 59. On the convent, see also Chaps. 74 (a rather similar episode) and 201.

[643] Ps. 112 (113):9, although that speaks of "children."

[644] Sardis was the major city in the region of Lydia in central western Asia Minor (see also above, Chap. 84), some forty miles northeast of Ephesus and Galesion. See further *ODB,* s.v. "Sardis."

[645] Symeon the Stylite the Elder is said to have tied himself to a beam on his pillar in order to remain standing during the forty days of Lent (Theodoret, *Hist. Rel.*, 26.9). A similar practice is recorded in the *vita Danielis,* chaps. 62–63.

[646] On the *semantron* or sounding board, see above, Chap. 43, n. 205.

never leave until the dismissal, unless nature forced him to do so in some way. After the dismissal from church he would go off singing again to his own cell. <There> he would go inside and complete the office that had been ordained by the father, and he would then give his body a little rest, <although> he never lay down on his side at all, but <sat> in a <specially> constructed seat.[647] When he had had a short rest, he would stand up again and continue singing psalms and praying until the time when the *semantron* sounded the hour. As a result of <too> much standing like this, he hurt his feet, and so he reluctantly gave up his great exertions; he never stopped diligently running the race of asceticism, however, <though> he <now did so> while sitting in his <specially> constructed seat.

166. When the wicked Devil saw himself being heavily defeated by <such> a weak and debilitated body, and his blazing arrows being trampled and crushed beneath <John's> paralyzed feet, and <when he realized> that <John> would not turn his mind away from the remembrance of God, even though he was in such dire straits, he came at him <in a different way> and tried, as he thought, to terrify him. He would lay hold of <John's> feet and pull him out of his seat, and would often seize him and drag him to the door of his cell in order to throw him out. But John would let out a yell and call his servant Gerasimos to <come and> help when he was being hauled around like this by the Evil One. <Gerasimos> would come and see <John's> body moving as though it was being dragged <along> by someone, although he was quite unable to see who was doing the dragging; so he would pick him up, carry him back to his chair again, and put him in it. However, as the Evil One would not allow <John> to get any respite from this kind of trial,[648] he [John] let the father know about it with this brother's help. When Lazaros heard this, he at once summoned some of the brothers and ordered them to go and sing psalms over him and also sing the canon of the Damascene (which people also call the <canon> of the Theotokos).[649] [559] The brothers did this according to the father's orders and <John> received relief from this trial a few days later.

167. A short while after this had stopped <happening>, he who never has

[647] See above, Chaps. 17, 35, and 162.

[648] The Greek word πειρασμός, translated here as "trial," also has the connotation of "temptation" in such circumstances.

[649] John of Damascus was a noted writer of *kanones;* for this particular one, see PG 96:1364–68. See further *ODB,* s.v. "Kanon."

his fill of attacks and machinations against the servants of Christ[650] inflicted another trial on <John>, with God's permission. He made putrid saliva dribble out of his mouth all the time, so much so, in fact, that it soaked the front <of his tunic> and maggots bred in the putrefaction. When the father learned about this from brother Gerasimos, he took a <piece> of woven hair cloth from a<nother> brother and sent it to <John> so that he might wrap it round him to catch the saliva that was running down. That holy old man received the piece of cloth, picked it up in his hand and kissed it, saying tearfully, "Oh holy father, <bless you> for caring about my situation and for considering my <troubles> of importance, <for I'm nothing but> a rotten dog."[651] He put this <cloth> on but, when he realized that it was of no use to him, he took it off and sent it back to the father, indicating that he should send him his prayer instead. The father then sent him some leather from a sack of incense and, when he hung this on his chest from his neck, it caught the saliva that was running down and kept his tunic dry until such time as this trial, too, came to an end.

168. After <John> had spent a whole year sitting <like this>, he was forced to lie down on his side because the whole of his body had by then become as good as dead as a result of his immobility. Of course <he did> not <sleep> on a <proper> bed but on a stone couch, for where could he have found <a real bed> in that place where even now no such thing is to be found?[652] While he was bed-ridden like this, the flesh from his thighs <right down> to the soles of his feet grew cold and became like that of a corpse; at the same time his feet putrefied and became <infested with> maggots, and some <sort of> sore developed on his shoulders that gave off an unbearable stench. Even when that valiant and unyielding man was in this <condition>, however, and was being consumed by such sickness, he did not slacken at all the rule of self-control that he observed, nor did he display any distress, nor did he say anything mean or <betray any> weakness, either great or small. Indeed he also <made a remarkable impression on> those who visited him to

[650] The Devil, that is.

[651] It seems clear from the apparatus that the scribe did not fully understand this statement and there may well be something amiss with it as it stands in the text. The translation, which is necessarily somewhat loose, follows Delehaye's emendations.

[652] For the term πεζούλιον ("stone couch"), see above, Chap. 162; Gregory the Cellarer is presumably referring to the monastery of the Theotokos here, since John is said to have lived there (Chap. 165); he thus excludes the two beds, mentioned in Chap. 162 as having been installed in the *archontarion* at the monastery of the Resurrection.

see and comfort him; for if someone went to the father, whether a layman or a monk, Lazaros would send him to <John> saying, "Go see the new Job." So those who called on him were in fact consoled and encouraged by his words and prepared to bear their <own> trials bravely and gratefully. He would say, "Brothers, if I knew that there were many lords and masters who made this world and ruled over it, and if I were not satisfied with this place, I would perhaps beg one of those <lords> to move me into his area <of control instead>, so that I might find some repose by this move. But, as all earthly and heavenly things, both seen and unseen, are creatures of <but> one God and master, and as all things are ruled and governed by Him, who am I, if it is His will and He wants me to be here for such a long time, to ask Him to take me away from here and move me to another place?" By saying these things (and many similar <words>) to the people who came to him, it was he who encouraged them rather than he who was encouraged by them, and he even persuaded them to bear generously and valiantly the onset of grievous <afflictions>; they would thus be helped by the sight of this man and by his conversation, and they would go off praising God.

169. One day, while <John> was lying there in this way, unable to move, a violent rainstorm burst overhead, and an almost endless flood of water ran down from the summit and the flanks of the mountain toward the monastery, so that it seemed as though everyone would be utterly destroyed by the water.[653] <John> was strongly urged to leave his cell by the <brother> who served him, but he did not listen. "If it's God's will," he said, "and if it's His decision that this should happen, I'll die in this cell." He spent three years in this <state of> sickness and survived our holy father's death by twenty-three days before he, too, passed on to the Lord.[654] Six months before his death, however, he began to experience <periods of> ecstasy in his mind, and often, when brother Gerasimos called him, he was not aware of his voice at all. So, when he came to himself again, <John> said to the brother, "Whenever you see me in that state, sit in my cell if you can, but otherwise leave and go wherever you want. And, even if you see me lying like this for a <whole> week, don't call me at all!" Which is what the brother did.

[653] The monastery of the Theotokos, although above that of the Savior, was evidently still in the gorge (see above, Chap. 58) and so presumably prone to flood damage in such circumstances.

[654] See the note in the following chapter on the dating of John's death.

170. On the very day that <John> was going to die (it was the feast of the holy apostle Andrew),[655] I went down[656] to <see> him, but when the brother went in to let him know that I was there, he found him in ecstasy. The brother called him for a long time, because I made him do so, but he saw that <John> was scarcely aware of him. When he eventually did come to himself, the holy old man said to the brother, "Didn't I tell you that whenever you see me lying like that you should leave me be and not call me at all? So why did you do this now?" The brother replied, "The monk Gregory, the cellarer, has come to <see> you." Then the old man said, "If it's the cellarer, and he wants to see me and talk to me right now, let him come in, because he probably won't be able to see me on another occasion." So I went in and sat down near him and started to talk to him, but after I had finished saying <what I wanted> to say to him, he replied to me, "For the Lord's <sake>, listen to me, <even though I am> a sinner! Don't leave <your position in> the storeroom, and don't withdraw from the monastery for a while on the pretext of [560] going to Jerusalem until <such time as> God may approve the <new> superior of our holy father's flock." (For I had asked him about this.) "For if you leave the monastery, you know, the minds of the other brothers will be badly shaken and, indeed, some will be bound to withdraw too. And because you will have been the reason for their withdrawal, you will have to provide God with an accounting, not only for yourself but also for them, and you will find our holy father opposing you instead of <acting> as your patron, at the terrible <last> tribunal. For you will have been the cause of the brothers' withdrawal and of the subsequent dissolution of Lazaros' monastery, which he has established with <such> great effort."[657]

171. And now let another brother beside these embellish the narrative of

[655] The feast of St. Andrew was celebrated on 30 November. Malamut ("Bessai," 243 n. 5) mistakenly understands this passage to refer to the death of Lazaros himself and discusses the effect this might have on the dating of that event. In fact, when taken in conjunction with the statement in the previous chapter that John outlived Lazaros by twenty-three days, it confirms the date, given in Chap. 254, of 7 November 1053 for Lazaros' death. John of Sardis thus died on 30 November 1053.

[656] This apparently confirms that Gregory the Cellarer was based at the monastery of the Resurrection; he thus had to go *down* to see John at the monastery of the Theotokos.

[657] There is a substantial gap in the manuscript at this point, consisting of two-thirds or more of f. 207.

my account. <This man>, who came from Lydia[658] and was called Nikon, was a <real> peasant[659] <in terms of> his background. Because he was a simple man and was also illiterate, he was set to work in the most menial jobs, but he proved to be as naturally clever and skillful in his inner and more important <behavior>, as he was simple and rather unsophisticated in his outward behavior. <Nikon> thus went to the father on his own <initiative> and asked him to command him to do the <following> as if it was on his [Lazaros'] orders: this was to do obeisance to each person whom he met and to offer his cheek ready to be struck by that person.[660] As the father urged him to do this, he did it for a while but, because some people hit him so violently, he was unable to stand it in the end and gave up the practice; indeed some people struck him so hard that he frequently spat out blood. He would eat what they used to set before the brothers in the refectory,[661] but he never wanted to put on a new robe; <instead> he would take it, just like the other brothers,[662] but would <then> give it away if he happened to meet a beggar somewhere, while he himself would always wear his old ragged <clothes>. When he was questioned about this by the brothers and by the father himself, he would say, "I lost it." His body was so filthy dirty that it seemed to those who saw him <as if> he <must be> always sitting in the furnace of the bathhouse. His flesh was also consumed by a swarm of lice that used to crawl about on the outside of his clothes <as well>; when he picked them off he would not kill them, but would drop them back inside the front <of his tunic> and would say, "Eat from the flesh that God has given you for food." He used to stand in the church like some unwavering pillar and would never sit down at all either in the early morning service[663] or in the vigil,[664] nor would he turn this way and that, but would

[658] See above, Chap. 84; cf. Chap. 165.

[659] In the sense of being completely uneducated and uncultured; a real "hick" in other words.

[660] The New Testament injunction to turn the other cheek uses the same word, σιαγών; cf. Mt. 5:39, Lk. 6:29.

[661] The Greek verb here, παρετίθουν, could be either third person plural (as it is translated) or first person singular. If it is the latter, then the reference is to Gregory, and the implication is that part of his job as cellarer or, perhaps more likely, as *trapezopoios* (a position he evidently held earlier in his career on Galesion [see Chap. 209, below; see above, Chap. 82 on this office]) involved serving at table in the refectory.

[662] On the practice of issuing new clothing to the monks, see Chaps. 145 and 246.

[663] On *orthros,* see above, Chap. 8; cf. Chap. 72.

[664] On the vigil service, see above, Chap. 66.

always face toward the sanctuary with his eyes constantly upraised, standing completely still and motionless. When asked about this sometimes by the brothers, he would say, with his characteristic simplicity and immense spiritual <fervor>, "I'm imagining heaven." Which indeed he was <doing>. Because of this kind of response they used to call him "Ouranios [Heavenly] <Nikon>."

172. <Nikon> developed a sore on the upper part of his foot,[665] but he paid such little attention to it and neglected it <so much> that maggots bred in it; indeed he did not even give up his <habitual> standing and <constant> attendance in church. Even when the father learned about this and ordered me to provide him with treatment, he would not accept it. On one occasion when, on the father's orders, I did <manage to> get hold of him and clean the sore with warm water, he reluctantly allowed the maggots to be removed; but afterward he ran away and <could> not be found to eat his meal at breakfast time.[666] I searched for him and only found him with some difficulty toward evening at the <chapel of> St. Onouphrios.[667] When I asked him to tell me why he had run away, he said, "Unless you stop cleaning the festering ulcer on my foot for me, I'll go away from the monastery and the mountain <altogether>. Anyway, what's <the problem>?" he added, "Aren't we all going to be eaten by worms in the end <anyway>?" When the father learned this from me, he told me not to bother <Nikon> about this any more. So he stayed that way until his death: he did not give his foot any treatment nor, as I have said, did he give up or relax his <habitual> standing and <constant> attendance in church either.

173. In the very hour in which he was going to die, <Nikon> stood with the brothers during compline[668] but, before the dismissal, he prayed and did obeisance to them, and then left and went to the refectory,[669] for he used to sleep on the floor there. He lay down on his mat at the spot where the holy

[665] The precise meaning of the Greek phrase περὶ τὸ σκέλος τοῦ ποδὸς (lit. "upon the leg of his foot") is unclear, but Nikon's comment below implies that the sore was on his foot rather than his leg.

[666] This refers to the earlier meal of *ariston;* on this, see above, Chap. 84.

[667] On this spot, which seems to have been fairly remote and dangerously precipitous, see Chaps. 131 and 243.

[668] This is the service of *apodeipnon,* lit. "the after supper <service>," which ended the monastic day. See further *ODB,* s.v. "Apodeipnon."

[669] The Greek word τραπεζεῖον (lit. "little table") is apparently otherwise unattested in this exact form; it is clearly a diminutive of τράπεζα, and hence may presumably be taken to indicate the refectory.

images of the Theotokos and the archangel Michael extend <their hands> in intercession to the Savior,[670] and peacefully surrendered his soul to God by way of the hands of angels. In the morning, after the brothers had laid him in front of Lazaros' pillar according to the custom, ready to be carried out <for burial>, the father saw him and said, "Behold, a willing martyr! He used to give himself two hundred lashes every day, a hundred in the morning and a hundred in the evening. He did this from the time he gave up being struck by others, but <then>, when he was unable to work because he had developed a sore on his foot, he added to this, for thereafter he used to give his body a<n-other> hundred lashes with a whip throughout the day <as well>. He did this with my approval, for he asked me if God liked someone to beat himself, and when he heard me <say> that He does like it, he took encouragement and continued doing it right up to the present, as though <he was> carrying out an order."[671] <Thus> the holy father testified with these <words> concerning this man who, because of his deeds, was given the most appropriate <nick> name "Ouranios [Heavenly] Nikon."

174. Another brother, who was also called Nikon but came from Phrygia,[672] became well known from his deeds as <being> similar not only in name but also in behavior to the previous one; indeed, one could say <he became> even more <well known>. When this <Nikon> was still a boy and [561] under the authority of his parents, he would secretly leave his home, as I learned from his uncle,[673] and would go off to out of the way places and chapels; there he would stay without taking anything with him to eat until his family went looking for him and he was found. From the time when he came

[670] This passage, from the beginning of the chapter, is translated and discussed in A. Cutler, "Under the Sign of the Deēsis: On the Question of Representativeness in Medieval Art and Literature," *DOP* 41 (1987), 147–48. On Lazaros' special devotion to the cult of the archangels, see below, Chap. 253.

[671] Or perhaps "fulfilling a rule."

[672] Phrygia was the area in southwest Asia Minor between the coastal plains of the Aegean and the central Anatolian plateau. By this period the administration of Phrygia had been divided between the Anatolikon and Thrakesion themes, but it continued to be recognized as a geographical region and was an ecclesiastical province. See further, *ODB,* s.v. "Phrygia."

[673] It is nowhere made clear who this Nikon's uncle was, but Gregory the Cellarer is here following his standard practice of citing sources when his information might be open to doubt; the uncle's identity was presumably known to his audience.

to the monastery and received the monastic habit from the holy father and started upon the way of life <devoted> to God, he never touched wine or oil or anything else fattening;[674] he did not wear two tunics either, or put shoes on his feet. <Nikon> had been sent by the father to the Theotokos to work for the brothers there but, <at that time>, there was a water shortage at the holy Resurrection, although the Theotokos still had some. This <Nikon> would <thus> take water in a pot at night from there, bring it up to the holy Resurrection, and go round the brothers' cells and fill up their pots. He would then go back down again to the Theotokos during the night without any of the others knowing <he was doing this>, except for one brother. Because <Nikon> was doing this, wicked Satan, who is always opposed to good deeds, wanted to blunt his enthusiasm for doing such a good deed and so deprive him of his reward; <at the same time, he wanted> to cause the brothers to lose <even> this small relief <supply> of water. So, when <Nikon> was coming up at night, as I have said, <Satan> sometimes used to throw stones <at him>, sometimes call him by name. <Nikon> was not ignorant of who was doing this, however, and so would make no response to him, but would converse <instead> with God by prayer and by singing psalms, and so would pass by the place without being afraid. On one occasion, when the daylight was <already> fading toward the evening, he was coming up carrying some wine he was bringing to the brothers; but, when he had only just left the monastery <of the Theotokos> and was <still> not far away from it, the Evil One (with God's permission) made him lose <the use of> his eyes <so that> he could see nothing at all.[675] He edged himself forward little by little with groping steps <until> he was just able to find the place where the cross was fixed on the oak tree.[676] There <Ni-

[674] A very similar expression is used of Lazaros' own ascetic practice at St. Sabas, see above, Chap. 17.

[675] Compare other stories of sudden blindness attributed to demonic activity in the *vita*, Chaps. 52 and 218; cf. Chap. 46.

[676] The cross here is certainly to be distinguished from that at the dangerous pass above the region of Chalkos Halonios to which reference is made in Chaps. 41, 154, and 155; that cross was apparently cut into the rock and lay further down the mountain below the monastery of the Savior, while this was evidently situated higher up between the monasteries of the Theotokos and the Resurrection. This is probably the same oak that figures in Chap. 176 and may possibly be identified with the location of the cross mentioned in Chap. 77, but is perhaps not "Philippikos' oak" of Chap. 243, which evidently grew just outside the monastery of the Resurrection to the north.

kon> called out to brother Gerasimos, who was then the cellarer there, and got him to go up with another brother; they lifted him up on their shoulders and took him down to the Theotokos where they led him into his cell and then went off and left him. But while he was lying there on his mat, the demons attacked him in the night and beat him about the head and on the rest of his body so badly that he was unable to hear or speak for a good many days, but lay there, deaf and dumb.

175. At <another> time <Nikon> was troubled by the idea that he should enclose himself on a pillar. He let the father know about this and began pestering him to let him fulfill his personal desire. But the father, who knew that such practices are more dangerous than helpful for the young, decided rather that he should first be made more tractable by <submitting himself to the discipline of> obedience. Lazaros thus ordered him not to speak to anyone at all, except for him, for a period of three years and to climb up to the monastery from the river twice a day, carrying two pots of water; <only> when he had fulfilled these commands properly and in a satisfactory manner could he enclose himself on a pillar. <Nikon> accepted these commands from the father and eagerly set about fulfilling them. He also used to pretend that he was stupid;[677] as a result, both those who met him on the way and the young<er monks> in the monastery used to tease him a great deal and in all sorts of ways when they saw him. He put two stones in his mouth so that he might not speak through force of circumstance or <simply> from forgetfulness, <and thus, even though> he was teased by lots of people in all kinds of ways (as has <already> been mentioned), he never ever said anything.[678] Once, when there was a shortage of wood for the kitchen and everyone, on the father's orders, was going out onto the mountain to bring some back, <Nikon> alone pretended not to want to go. They bullied[679] him badly because of this, dragging

[677] The idea of the holy fool, a saintly person who pretended to be stupid or even mentally ill, formed a distinct element in the Byzantine Christian tradition. Another fool in Lazaros' community, Luke, is mentioned in passing in Chap. 200. See further *ODB,* s.v. "Fools, Holy"; also L. Rydén, "The Holy Fool," in Hackel, *Byz. Saint,* 106–13, esp. 111–12, on such "fools" in the Middle Byzantine period, although he mentions neither one from the *vita;* and Morris, *Monks,* 62, who refers only to Luke.

[678] Abba Agathon is said in the *Apophthegmata* to have kept a stone in his mouth for three years while he learned to keep silence: Agathon, 15 (PG 65:113B; Ward, *Sayings,* 19).

[679] The Greek here uses the same word (πειράζω) that was translated above by "tease." In the Christian context this verb also carried with it inescapable connotations

him about, pushing him and hitting him; in the end, when they saw that he was not willing to go with them, they laid him on his back on the ground and piled rocks on his feet and his chest, and then they left him and went off to <carry out> the work they had been assigned. <Nikon> thus lay there until they returned and allowed him to get up again by taking off the rocks. However, when night fell, he twice went out onto the mountain and brought wood back, <but> without anyone knowing. Indeed, he used to do this often, even <going> to the woods of Levedion,[680] and when his feet split open because of the cold he <could> not be persuaded to wear shoes. Before the three-year period came to an end, however, the monk Merkourios, who was living on the pillar of Petra, departed from this present life; so the father summoned the aforesaid monk [Nikon], released his tongue from its bond <of silence>, and told him to leave and go onto the pillar.[681] <Nikon> did obeisance to all the brothers and received a blessing from them and from the father before he left and went onto the pillar. After he had spent <only> a short time on it, he too ended his life there. They brought him down and buried him in the chapel of the Savior there,[682] for he was deemed a perfect ascetic and *full of* spiritual *days*[683] <despite> still having a youthful body; for he was <only> about twenty years old or just a little more when he died.

---

of temptation and testing. Nikon is thus not only being teased and bullied but is also being tempted and tested, and his refusal to succumb to this demonstrates, even more clearly than his dutiful fulfillment of the father's commands, the exemplary quality of his obedience.

[680] This area is not mentioned elsewhere in the *vita;* it is, presumably, either distant from the monastery or else particularly high on the mountain.

[681] This pillar has already been mentioned several times above. It was evidently occupied by a stylite before Lazaros took up residence on Galesion (see Chaps. 41, 53) and was later used by the monk Kerykos who, like his predecessor, found it too noisy, and left for Lazaros' old pillar in the church of the Theotokos (Chap. 159).

[682] This apparently refers to a chapel dedicated to the Savior, which was at or near this pillar, rather than to the monastery of the Savior. Burial in a chapel or church seems to have been a relatively common way of showing respect for particularly eminent monks, clerics, or lay people, although, as has been seen above, ordinary monks in the community were not buried in such locations. See *ODB,* s.v. "Burial."

[683] That is, "full of spiritual experience." The phrase draws on Old Testament passages that use the expression πλήρης ἡμερῶν ("full of days") when speaking of the death of notable individuals at a great age, so Gen. 25:8 (of Abraham), 35:29 (of Isaac), etc. The *vita* uses the same expression for the death of the venerable Dorotheos in Chap. 177, and of Lazaros himself in Chap. 254.

176. Another brother, who had come to our monastery from another one, was ordered by the father to bring up the water to the monastery from the river by means of a <pack> animal. The <brother> decided to do this with bare feet, even though it was then winter time, for it was the month of December. When the father learned about this, however, he summoned him and ordered shoes to be given to him, which he told him to put on. As the <brother> did not wish to disobey the father, he took the <shoes> and put them on, and wore them until he reached the oak tree,[684] so that his action would not be <too> obvious, [562] but there he took them off and went on down from that point with bare feet; and he did the same thing when he was coming <back> up. He had a long, bushy beard and, as the tip of this got wet from touching the <water> skins and was blown about by the wind, it became frozen; as a result it was pulled off little by little and fell away <until> it had disappeared <altogether>. When this brother had completed with such spiritual zeal the task entrusted to him by the father, he returned rejoicing to his own monastery after he had received the blessing of the father and the brothers.

177. Dorotheos, who <came> from Ikonion[685] and was a priest and <already> advanced in years, was judged worthy of the habit by the father when he came to the monastery. <Despite his age>, he surpassed many of our young men in his eagerness and endurance in performing the tasks entrusted to him, and especially in standing for church <services>. From the time he became a monk he never touched cheese or eggs, and every Wednesday and Friday he kept a complete fast, eating nothing at all; during the three forty-day fasts[686] he would not partake of wine or oil nor anything cooked, except for bread alone. Six years before his death he lost the sight of his physical eyes, but he was enriched <instead> by <the use of> his spiritual eyes, <which were> sharper and brighter. Although he was such an old man that he had become bent with age, he was never absent from a church service; he used to go in first of <all> the other <brothers> and was last out after the dismissal, and he always used to stand and chant enthusiastically, anticipating everyone in the

[684] This is presumably the same tree as that mentioned above in Chap. 174, which evidently stood just above the monastery of the Theotokos on the way to the monastery of the Resurrection.

[685] Ikonion (modern Konya), was situated in south central Anatolia, some 270 miles to the east of Ephesus. It was in the Anatolikon theme.

[686] On these fasts, see above, Chap. 81.

recitation <of the Psalms> and in the *troparia* of the *kanones;*[687] his voice even rose above those of almost all the others. He would go into his cell when he came out of church, close the door straightaway, and stand <there> chanting and praying for a considerable time. He would then sit down for a little and rest, but <afterward> would stand up again and chant until the hammering <of the *semantron*> for church. And so this <Dorotheos>, having lived <in a manner> pleasing to God, departed from this present life *full of* spiritual as well as physical *days.*[688]

178. There are still two of these <notable monks> about whom I <should> speak: I mean Lazaros, who was called "the Short," and Nicholas, whose nickname was Kyr Eulogesos. The <first> of these surpassed almost all those who were striving in the monastery in his attendance at church and in his ceaseless praise of God, both in church and <when he was> alone. He also <excelled> in <the way he would> shed tears and beat his breast, and engage in incessant sighs and mournful lamentations;[689] for he would go out onto the mountain in the evening and stand at a spot well away from the monastery <where> he would spend many hours striking his breast, <performing> genuflections, <shedding> tears, and <uttering> loud lamentations.

179. (Pantoleon, who was very industrious and really did love the poor and love God, also used to do the same thing; indeed, his cell proclaims the harshness and laboriousness of his life.) <Nicholas>,[690] the other one <of these

[687] The liturgical *kanon* was a set of eight or nine odes or verse paraphrases chanted during the early morning service of *orthros.* The odes consisted of an *heirmos* together with additional stanzas, the *troparia* mentioned here, which followed its melody and rhythm. Cf. above Chap. 8, and see further *ODB,* s.v. "Heirmologion," "Kanon," "Troparion."

[688] See above, Chap. 175; cf. below, Chap. 254.

[689] Such open and physical manifestations of grief and contrition played an important part in Byzantine spirituality. The ability to perform them was considered to be a gift from God and the practice thus figures quite commonly in hagiographical literature. It represented the expression of remorse for personal guilt, but it also mourned the sinfulness of humanity in general and the sufferings of Christ. Lazaros' older contemporary Symeon the Theologian ranked this spiritual gift alongside the sacrament of baptism as a requirement for salvation and he encouraged its practice among his monks in Constantinople. See further *ODB,* s.v. "Contrition," and particularly I. Hausherr, *Penthos: La doctrine de la componction dans l'Orient chrétien* (Rome, 1944).

[690] I am taking this to refer back to the Nicholas who was introduced at the start of the previous chapter, against the implication of the marginal comment of the published

two>, was second to none in his obedience, in the integrity of his conduct, in his physical labors, and in <the way he used> to do everything with the father's approval. The result was that, when he was about to die, he asked our holy father to be given one additional day of life (for he was already close to the end), so that he might receive the venerable cross from the consecration, for it was then the Day of Lights.[691] This did indeed happen in accordance with his request. After receiving the venerable cross and partaking of the undefiled sacraments, he raised his hands and said "Glory be to thee, Oh God," and <continued>, "I thank you, holy father, that just as I did my best not to do anything without your advice, so you did not disregard my request." When he had said this and had kissed Lazaros' holy irons,[692] he left the church and went back to his cell, and on the next day he departed to the Lord.

---

text which suggests the whole chapter concerns Pantoleon. It is possible that Delehaye is correct in his interpretation, but it may also be argued that the ὁ δὲ here picks up the ὁ μὲν of Chap. 178 (which is otherwise left dangling), and that it is more reasonable to take the passage in this way than to suggest that Gregory the Cellarer forgot to write about Nicholas altogether, especially since, in the original text, the present chapter division did not exist. In this case the mention of Pantoleon is merely an aside, illustrating the presence at the monastery of another person, besides Lazaros "the Short," who demonstrated the gift of contrition.

[691] That is, the feast of the Epiphany. Celebrated on 6 January, it is one of the most important feasts in the Orthodox calendar and commemorates the baptism of Christ by John the Baptist; its best known ritual involves the blessing or consecration of the waters, which may also involve the throwing in and recovery of a cross, but it is unclear exactly how the standard practices connected with the celebration of the feast may relate to Nicholas' request to receive the cross. See further *ODB*, s.v. "Epiphany."

[692] The passage as a whole is somewhat ambiguous, but it seems quite clear that Nicholas was still in the church when he kissed these irons and thus that Lazaros, who never left his pillar, was not wearing them. (The possibility that Lazaros was still wearing them but could be reached on his pillar through a window looking into the church—see the Introduction, section C, p. 18—seems unlikely: why would Nicholas kiss only the irons if their wearer was also available for his veneration? And would someone so close to death have been physically able to reach Lazaros in this way?) The implication would thus seem to be that the incident took place after Lazaros' death, at a time when his "irons" (described in detail in Chap. 35) were perhaps displayed as relics in the church (cf. Chap. 252, below, which describes their removal from his body after his death but makes no mention of them being replaced before his burial, unlike his leather tunic). For a (critical) example of such a display of "irons" from the 12th century, see John Tzetzes, Letter 104, trans. in P. Magdalino, "The Byzantine Holy Man

180. I have, then, gone through these <accounts> concerning our fathers and brothers here, as I said <I would> at the start of the narrative, so that the <nature of the> tree may be made evident by its fruit and the teacher by his disciples.[693] For <these men> progressed with regard to every virtue as they saw Lazaros' life <set before them> like an original image <for them to imitate>,[694] or rather, as they were most excellently guided and piloted by him. Indeed, one could see a healthy[695] competition among them as, by their ascetic labors, they ran along the *strait and narrow path*[696] with eager feet and hastened in this <way> to reach the wide <spaces> of eternal happiness.[697] For, as has been mentioned, they easily bore the laborious tasks of the ascetic wrestling school by obeying Lazaros' holy precepts and instructions and by following them unswervingly. For, before anything else, this is what he used to teach all those who went to him and chose to live with him, laying down for them, as it were, a fortunate beginning for the progress toward greater things:[698] not to conceal their thoughts from him; not to possess anything, and indeed not to do anything by following their own wishes without his approval; not to do anything in violation of what they were told to do; not to undertake things that exceeded their power, nor to entrap themselves by their own will<fulness> in fasting and keeping vigil or anything else outside the rule of the community.

---

in the Twelfth Century," in Hackel, *Byz. Saint,* 55. In view of Lazaros' great modesty and humility, a characteristic stressed on various occasions in the *vita,* it also seems unlikely that Gregory the Cellarer would depict him as willingly entertaining a request for such miraculous intervention while he was still alive. If this is the case, the passage provides important evidence of a posthumous miracle in the *vita;* cf. also Chap. 202, below, which refers to Lazaros interceding posthumously to save his brother Ignatios' life.

[693] See above, Chap. 159.

[694] The Greek expression ἀρχέτυπον εἰκόνα brings with it many connotations, among the clearest of which is the sense of an original model to be copied by those who seek to emulate it.

[695] The Greek adjective ἀγαθός (lit. "good") also has obvious moral connotations in this sort of context.

[696] Mt. 7:14 (slightly adapted).

[697] The Greek word μακαριότητος contains the sense of "beatitude" or "blessedness," as well as that of simple joy.

[698] I am grateful to an anonymous reader for suggesting this translation.

<Rather>, they were to fulfill the prescribed regulations of the monastery as eagerly as possible in the church, in the refectory, and everywhere else, and were to accept with gratitude what was given <to them>.[699] When they came out of the church or the refectory, they were to keep silence and each go to his own cell while singing to themselves; they were not to gather [563] together and waste time in idle chatter; nor were they to congregate for drinking bouts and feasts; nor were they to leave their own cells out of boredom[700] or for a visit to someone, with each <of them> going off to the cells of the others, unless this was done out of necessity; rather, <each> was to sit patiently in his own cell.[701] Lazaros says <this> so that we may not see or hear or say what we do not want to as a result of leaving our own cells and going into those of others. For it is from this <practice> that slanders, criticisms, and insults <directed> against the brothers naturally tend to develop, <and it is> as a result of these things <that a person's> mind becomes clouded, loses its way, and wanders off from its proper goal. <That> person then neglects to pay attention to himself and <instead> chatters away about the faults of the others, while being <quite> unable to hold himself in check or to recognize his own weakness; he begins to insult the <other> brothers, fight with them, and cause problems every day. These, <then>, along with many others besides, are the things Lazaros used to teach every day, both privately and in public. Finally, <he would> add this <statement> to his words, "If someone keeps to these <guidelines> to the best of his natural ability, and if he gratefully receives whatever the community gives him, both in the refectory and with respect

[699] Here and in Lazaros' speech at the end of the chapter Gregory the Cellarer touches on a theme to which he will return below in Chaps. 191–93: a criticism of the unwillingness of some monks to surrender their personal possessions because they are not content with what they receive from the monastery. Such a refusal is seen as a decline from the standards of true cenobitic monasticism and a primary factor behind problems that the community on Galesion evidently encountered toward the end of Lazaros' life and after his death. Cf. above, Chap. 138, and also the *typikon* of Evergetis, Chaps. 22 and 27, Gautier, "Évergétis," 65–67, 69.

[700] Lit. "akedia" or "accidie"; see above, Chap. 100.

[701] In the preceding passage Gregory the Cellarer has evidently been summarizing stipulations regarding proper behavior in the monastery, which were probably contained in Lazaros' *diatyposis* or *typikon;* see below, Chap. 246. He now clearly switches to a commentary of his own in which he laments and criticizes abuses that he perceives to be the cause of contemporary problems in the monastery.

to his other needs, and is satisfied with them, I believe in my Christ that he will find <a place in heaven> with Antony[702] and the other divinely inspired fathers."

181. Lazaros used to advise those afflicted by physical illness or troubled by some demonic assault not to be faint-hearted nor to fall into despair at such distressful attacks, nor to stir a blasphemous tongue against God. Rather they were to give thanks to Him, bear <their troubles> patiently and bravely while looking forward to their future reward, which would be far more abundant than their present suffering, and repeat to themselves the <words> of the Apostle, *that the sufferings of this present time are not worthy to be compared with the glory which shall be revealed in us,*[703] and that *as much as our outer man perishes so much our inner man is renewed day by day.*[704] He would also recommend <something> like this, "If someone is <forced> by illness to stay in bed, people should not go to see him frequently, but should rather let him be alone in his cell. For while he is alone he may recall his faults and so, when he has wept, may entreat God for forgiveness of them; <but> when he is with many people he may not easily be able to do this." Lazaros would eagerly advise those of the young <monks>, whom he saw to be more eager for asceticism, to mortify their bodies with the harsher and more laborious ascetic practices. On the other hand, he would be accommodating and forgiving toward those <monks> whom he saw to be faint-hearted and less concerned <with this>; he would not overburden them with anything, nor would he be readily moved to criticism of their lack of concern and indifference or of some of their faults (even though he was not ignorant of these), but would himself ridicule and find fault in turn with those who tried to criticize or ridicule this sort of <monk>. For he knew, just as Solomon says, that the criticisms of an ungodly man are <in fact> bruises to him,[705] and that someone may induce this sort of

[702] The reference is to Antony the Great (ca. 251–356), the celebrated pioneer of eremetism in the Egyptian desert and subsequent model for Byzantine ascetic endeavors. He is known primarily from the account of his life attributed to Athanasios of Alexandria. See further *ODB,* s.v. "Antony the Great."

[703] Rom. 8:18. The quotation is exact except for a slight change in word order.

[704] 2 Cor. 4:16. The quotation contains several small variations from the original text.

[705] This is a loose and incomplete quotation from Prov. 9:7: "*He that rebuketh a wicked man getteth himself a blot.*"

man to mend his ways by admonitions and exhortations rather than by severe criticism, especially if the teacher happens to bear out the evidence of his teaching from his lifestyle rather than <just> from his words.

182. To those who asked him about church attendance, Lazaros would make this response: "Those who know the scriptures and stand and sing in the choir are like the reapers in the field, but those who are ignorant and illiterate and don't know how to sing and for this reason stand behind the singers and <merely> listen to the hymn singing <resemble> the <gleaners> who follow behind the reapers and gather up the ears that have fallen down or have been missed. However, while the reapers, <so> it says, often collect tares along with the wheat in their sheaves, the <gleaners> who follow them collect <only> pure wheat. So, even if the daily office of the church is <actually> performed by those who stand and sing in the choir, they certainly don't accomplish this perfectly and without making mistakes, because they sometimes rush through the chants and also sometimes raise their voices at the wrong time and as a result are unable to pay much attention to what they're singing—it's <faults like> these that are to be compared to the tares. However, if those who are illiterate stand <there> soberly and pay attention to what is being sung by the people in the choir, then, even if they don't understand everything, they may still retain securely in their minds what they *have* managed to grasp, for these people aren't troubled by the passions that have been mentioned, except that they may perhaps be weighed down by sleep due to their laziness." By saying <such> things <as> these, Lazaros would humble the arrogance of some, but would strengthen the desire of others to stand resolutely and soberly in church. He would also order the cellarer not to give those who were absent at the start of the early morning service[706] their ration of wine, and sometimes not their food either. He would, moreover, often praise those whom he saw standing resolutely in the church and singing eagerly, and would express his approval <of them> in the presence of the brothers, but he would sometimes do quite the opposite to those who were more negligent and sluggish. He did not do this thoughtlessly, as someone might imagine,[707] but to increase the eagerness of the <former> and stir up the apathy and laziness

[706] On the early morning service of *orthros,* see above, Chap. 8; cf. Chap. 72.

[707] The sentence to this point is contained in a marginal note in the manuscript, but is included in the edited text here by Delehaye.

of the <latter>; for praise is often able to make those who pursue virtue more eager, just as the reverse is also <true>.

183. Moreover, Lazaros would not ignore in an indulgent way those who did unruly things or <committed> acts of youthful folly or were caught in any <sort of> jokes and pranks; instead he would sometimes employ reprimands and [564] threats against them and sometimes even a beating. Those of them, however, whom he saw desisting from their unruliness and turning to reverent and orderly <behavior>, he would encourage still more with admonitions, and he would, in his compassion, deem them worthy of forgiveness for the sins they had previously committed; he would <thus> make them more eager for the good than they formerly were for the bad. On the other hand, he would heal by <quite> opposite <means> those among them who had totally fallen into sin and who argued with him. <Again>, when he saw any of the <brothers> being completely overwhelmed by sorrow, even to the extent that they did not want to take food, *lest such ones,* as the divine Apostle says, *should be swallowed up with overmuch sorrow,*[708] Lazaros used to summon them <to him>. He would first make obeisance to them himself and seek their forgiveness as though he himself had sinned, <then>, when he had cured them in this way, he would dismiss them; for how could someone still be stubborn and obdurate who saw that truly holy head, which was respected by angels, bent before him, unless perhaps he was mad and had lost his wits? <Again>, if one of the <brothers> working on the tasks <in the service of the community> happened to be upset by <another> brother and got into a fight over something and their disagreement was referred to Lazaros, with both men present he would find in favor of the servant who was at fault, or rather would absolve him more than the <other brother>. He used to do this not out of misguided sympathy or from lack of <good> judgment, but to get the <brother who was at fault> to set to work eagerly again because he had stopped being angry and upset, and to actually ennoble the other one, even though he was wronged,[709] in order not to lay the <extra> burden of the trouble together with the job in hand on those who were working at <these> tasks. This is what he used to do

[708] A direct quotation from 2 Cor. 2:7, except that it has been changed from singular to plural to fit the context here.

[709] Presumably by providing him with the opportunity to endure misfortune and injustice patiently and humbly, on the pattern of Job.

publicly, but in private he would do quite the opposite, <for> he would teach and admonish the <servant> to endure his job patiently and not hit his brothers, so that he might not spoil his hard work in this way, whereas he would absolve the other <brother> of blame for the trouble and tell him that God would set aside a reward for him because of this.

184. Lazaros would say to those who asked him about negligence in <observing> the hours,[710] "If a monk partakes of food before he sings his hours, except in great need or some other <extenuating> circumstances, God will consider him <to have done the same> as if someone should strip the hide off seven dead asses and <then> touch food with unclean hands." When they asked if they would also have penalties demanded of them by God for <doing> this, he used to say, "Yes, unless they confess this; for someone may receive forgiveness for whatever <sins> he genuinely confesses from the person who hears his confession, and he should believe that he will also receive this <forgiveness> from God, unless he falls into the same <sins> again." The father would say these things publicly to everyone.

185. Lazaros would, however, give different advice again to those who were taking their turns at the tasks <in the service of the community>. He would admonish and teach them above all else to pursue the task entrusted to them honestly and with great eagerness, and yet not neglect the offices of the hours and the other <church> services. Whenever they were free <to do so> they should go to church and especially to the early morning service and the holy Eucharist, as indeed also the office of vespers;[711] but if they were not free, their mouths and tongues should not be idle and they should sing <something> with their lips, even if it was <only> the *trisagion*[712] or the beginning of whatever psalm should come to mind. If they could not even do this, then they should at least not be at all negligent about <saying> their prayers to themselves. <Furthermore>, if they should find some suitable time during the night, they were immediately to stand up and fulfill the obligation of the

[710] That is, the daily liturgical offices; further on these see *ODB*, s.v. "Hours, liturgical."

[711] More literally, the office of lamp-lighting. Vespers closed the liturgical day, which began with *orthros.* Further on the early morning service of *orthros,* see above, Chap. 8, and cf. Chap. 72; on the Eucharist, see above, Chap. 64; on vespers see *ODB,* s.v. "Vespers" and "Hours, liturgical."

[712] See above, Chap. 45.

day, not only by the recitation[713] of the Psalms, but also by the scalding tears of confession. "For this," he used to say, "tends to help those <who are working on these> tasks more than singing." He would often do this himself for, whenever it happened that he was unable to finish offering up a prescribed office because he had been distracted by many disturbances during the day, the night would <serve as> his <time> for completing the day's work, especially that of the tears. Thus, during vigils, when the brothers used to sing the "Most Merciful,"[714] he himself would spend that time weeping and lamenting. Indeed his lament was so <poignant that it was> like the wailing of a baby or when someone has <the image of> his own corpse before his eyes and recalls it as he weeps and laments. He used to do this so that the sound of his crying would not be heard and would not be known to anyone because all the brothers were gathered in the church at that time and were making a lot of noise, as has been said, as they sang the "Most Merciful"; thus, the raised voices of the brothers used to hide the noise of his weeping and laments. Indeed, Lazaros always used to do everything <he could> to avoid notice and would flee the passion of seeking human esteem in this way, for he knew full well that things that are done <simply for the sake of> showing off and pleasing a person not only fail to provide any benefit for those who do them, but actually <cause> the greatest possible harm; just as furious gusts of wind are in the habit of sweeping away the husks and chaff and winnowing them, so also the praise of men tends to drive away the virtues from <people's> souls. He would thus often ridicule and find fault with some of the brothers, who would make obeisance to him while he was standing up above on his pillar, for being fond of showing off and not acting properly in this because of the <way> they would genuflect to the ground and lie prostrate as they sought to receive his blessing; the same went for those returning from a [565] task or going up for a blessing who made obeisance to him before praying in the church.

186. Other people used to ask Lazaros about the manifestation of overt miracles and say, "How <is it>, when there are some monks still leading ex-

[713] The Greek word used here, μελέτη, contains the sense of a repetitive exercise but also of careful study and meditation.

[714] Delehaye (citing Ducange, *Glossorarium*, s.v. πολυέλεος) notes that this refers to Ps. 134 (135), which bears this name because, when it is sung, it is joined with Ps. 135 (136), which begins, Ἐξομολογεῖσθε τῷ κυρίῳ ὅτι ἀγαθός, ὅτι εἰς τὸν αἰῶνα τὸ ἔλεος αὐτοῦ and continues to praise God's mercy in every one of its twenty-six verses.

alted lives today, that God does not also see fit to work miracles through them as <He used to> with the fathers of old?" The father would reply to them, "God, being just, does all things justly. If He knew that this would not turn out to be harmful but beneficial were it to happen at the present time, He would not refrain from sending down His grace upon us in abundance. But because many people have been destroyed, since they have exalted themselves as a result <of working such miracles> into <a state of> insane conceit,[715] God, for this reason, keeps this grace from us, not because He bears us any ill will, but so that we may not fall into <such> insanity, as has been said, and destroy ourselves; this is especially so with the present generation[716] where there would be scarcely anyone humble <enough> to be saved. For if <God> has given us wings to cross the river, as He revealed to one of the holy men of old,[717] these are <made> of lead and not gold; for we are leaden who have the weight of indolence and vanity lying <heavily> upon us and are melted by the praise of men, just as lead <is melted> by the heat[718] of the fire.[719] Besides," he <would> say, "you should not seek such things from virtuous men; you <should> rather <be looking for> a life that's pleasing to God and pure and irreproachable conduct." This would be his response to those who asked him <about this>, knowing <full well> that, even if <they did> not <do so> openly, they were in fact raising[720] these arguments and putting them forward with reference to him; for they would also say quite openly to him on many occasions, because

[715] The Greek word ἀπόνοια contains not only the sense of madness but also the products of this, particularly in terms of arrogance and presumption; the Byzantine audience would thus definitely see in this warning an allusion to the sin of the Devil, who was believed to have fallen from grace through his irrational and insane pride in seeking to set himself above his creator.

[716] On this expression, see above, Chap. 130.

[717] I have been unable to identify this reference.

[718] Lit. "smell."

[719] A similar statement concerning the effect of praise (although using the image of melting wax instead of lead) is attributed in the *Apophthegmata* to Syncletica, 21; ed. J.-C. Guy, *Recherches sur la Tradition Grecque des Apophthegmata Patrum,* SubsHag 36 (Brussels, 1962), 34; Ward, *Sayings,* 196. Morris, *Monks,* 72, comments on this section of the chapter.

[720] The Greek verb κινέω also contains the sense of "stirring up <trouble>" and "meddling."

of the water shortage on the mountain, that if he would be willing to ask God to produce water he could make it gush forth through his prayer. In order to curb these people's <tongues> he would say, "God knows what's good for us and that it's better for us to be <living> like this than to have running water." He would also offer in his defense the story of the miracle that happened in the monastery of the holy Theodosios, which those who have read his life know.[721] So, this is what <he used to say> to them.

187. People used to come to Lazaros from outside <the monastery> and ask to receive his blessing and rules and regulations from him so that they might found a monastery, gather a community of brothers together, and guide them in a spiritual manner. <To these people Lazaros> would give the following advice: they were to offer themselves as a rule[722] to all those under their pastoral care, and no exceptions at all were to be made concerning food or clothing or any of the other bodily necessities so that they might maintain the law of obedience, firm and unbroken, as a result of their equality in these matters; for, he said, the law of obedience tends to be undermined by inequality.[723] Besides, they were not to give greater honor to those who were stronger because of the vigor <they showed> in their tasks and to despise those who were weaker as though <they were> useless, nor were they to measure the latter against the former; rather they were to do the opposite, and were sometimes to show a little consideration for the weaker brethren and not make demands on them according to the strict <rules> of the community. So he would give this advice and these instructions to them, and a lot more as well, and then would dismiss them with a blessing, as was his custom. Indeed, by

[721] Cf. *Pratum Spirituale,* chap. 80, which tells of a miraculous spring supplying the monastic community on the mountain of Skopelos. Like Galesion, this place had no permanent water supply until Abba Theodosios, the leader of the community, prayed to God with such effect that one was miraculously granted. The story also contains a warning, however, for later on, when a bath house was built, despite Theodosios' misgivings, the spring dried up; it only reappeared when this luxury had been demolished. On this work, see above Chap. 1.

[722] The Greek word used here, τύπος, also carries the sense of "model" or "example."

[723] Cf. also the less detailed description of the treatment of such matters in Lazaros' own *diatyposis,* below, Chap. 246. Thomas, "Evergetine Reform," 251, comments on the present passage, and sees an anticipation of elements of subsequent reform in Lazaros' opposition to obvious inequalities within a monastic community.

acting according to the commandments given to them by our holy father, these people have found benefit in their activities, and are <still> well established and living the monastic life through the grace of God up to the present <day>.

188. The father had already long before put into practice the actions he used to recommend to these people. He was thus always considerate to the weaker <brethren> and sympathetic toward them; or rather, if truth be told, he was similarly disposed to everyone. He would thus never appear to be giving <direct> orders when he was about to send someone out somewhere or entrust any sort of business to them, but <he would act> as if he were giving advice: "You are <quite> capable of going off on this service or of being entrusted with this task," he would say to the brother. If he should see the brother muttering something or being unhappy at what he had been told <to do> because he thought that something bad would happen to him as a result, Lazaros would not force or compel <him to do it>, but would excuse him;[724] for he wanted everyone to do good for their ultimate salvation not by force but persuasion. As a result, he would also often try to correct some of the unruly brothers by teaching and counseling <them; however>, when he saw that such people were not being cured by words <alone>, there were times when he would not hesitate to impose a beating on them, for he was compelled <to do so> both for their own correction and <that> of the others.[725] Afterward, as if he were apologizing to them and to the other brothers, he would say, "Believe me, brothers, I didn't want to discipline you like children and drag you to the good by force; I would prefer you to work for your salvation in obedience to <my> words, but how could I help acting against God's will and my own, when you yourselves forced me to go as far as this, even though, as I have said, I was reluctant <to do so>?"

189. When certain brothers chose to pursue spiritual solitude[726] rather than the <way of> obedience,[727] Lazaros would not allow it, but he would do the opposite with others; for from good judgment and long experience he knew precisely what each person would do well at, or rather (to speak more truly), because he was taught everything by the Holy Spirit. As a result, many

[724] Compare the episode recorded in Chap. 154, above.

[725] Cf. below, Chap. 195.

[726] Lit. "hesychia."

[727] I.e., the cenobitic life.

who were not convinced by his words, but followed their own wishes, realized afterward that the very good at which they were working <so> willfully had <actually> changed into the opposite for them.[728]

190. Again, if one of the brothers assigned to tasks outside <the monastery> happened to fall into some sin and this came to Lazaros' attention, he would not allow the brother to spend any more time there, but would immediately send another <in his place> and bring him back from there. He used to do this so that the brother might not make his wound difficult to heal or even [566] completely incurable by staying <there> any longer, for the continued practice of evil tends to produce this <effect>.

191. Lazaros would advise and urge all the craftsmen to use the profits from their handiwork for the common <good> of the community.[729] However, if one of the <monks> who had ecclesiastical duties[730] wished to spend some of these <profits> on his own wants, whether this was due to weakness or something else, Lazaros would first offer to pay himself for what this person wanted but, if he saw that he was not happy with this <arrangement>, he would allow him to procure what he wanted <with the income> from his own handiwork with his approval; if he realized that the <monk> was <absolutely> set on this, he would let him have his own way, whatever he wanted. On the other hand, if it was an illiterate <monk who wanted to do this, Lazaros> would not allow him <to do so> at all, unless someone who had a <particular> task should do this <extra> work during the time he had off from his <proper job>. For he used to say that he had to make some allowance for those who had the church as their assignment (<in other words, those who performed> the daily church offices), especially because they did not receive anything outside the refectory. "But there's no need to make such an allowance for you, who are illiterate," he would say, "because you don't work in the church and

[728] The same theme is pursued at greater length below in Chaps. 196–204.

[729] Or, less likely, "to contribute their profits to the common fund of the community," so Thomas, "Evergetine Reform," 250, who comments (249–50) on this and the following chapter. Thomas stresses Lazaros' own condemnation of the possession of personal property by his monks, because of the negative consequences he saw this having on communal monastic life, but also his obvious inability to enforce his views over this issue, at least toward the end of his life. Thomas argues that this provides clear evidence for the gradual breakdown of cenobitic monasticism at this time.

[730] I.e., the choir brothers.

actually do get some small <dietary> supplement[731] for the tasks you are entrusted with." For he used to order the cellarer to provide those engaged in these tasks with more food and drink than the others.[732] But our father did <not> do this before he went up to the <monastery of the> holy Resurrection,[733] because, when he was <still> at the <monasteries of the> Savior and the Theotokos, <the monks did> not <do> this sort of thing but held everything in common and no one possessed anything of his own in his cell. Indeed, this rule would have held <good> until now except for the fact that certain of those tonsured in the monastery who <still> had money from the <outside> world were unwilling to give this up completely, because they could not be satisfied with what was provided for them by the monastery.[734]

192. In a similar way, our holy father used to advise and enjoin all those who came to him <to do> this before everything <else>: <namely>, to dispose of everything and give up possession of it and so enter upon the life of <true> self-sacrifice,[735] according to the saying of the Lord.[736] Some were, indeed, obe-

[731] The Greek word here, παράκλησις, has the basic meaning of "consolation," but may also take on the sense of "extra rations" or "dietary supplement." See here Gautier, "Évergétis," 41:469, 475; 43:515; idem, "Kécharitôménè," 93:1328, 1331; 95:1350, 1368, 1373; 99:1427, although in all these instances the word seems to be used of gifts of fish made by the faithful to the monastery. As Gautier points out ("Kécharitôménè," 98 n. 38), this also reflects in some respects the meaning of the term διάκρισις, on which see above, Chap. 95.

[732] Cf. below, Chap. 213, where it is stated that Lazaros ordered that lay people at the monastery should receive the same provisions as the monks, except in the case of wine; of this they were to have only half as much as the brothers.

[733] Gregory the Cellarer is here beginning a lengthy criticism (which continues through the next two chapters) of current practices regarding the possession of personal property in the community. He evidently sees this as being a decline in standards from those which existed during Lazaros' early years on Galesion. In consequence the text, as it stands, does not seem to make sense here, unless a negative is supplied (as I have done in my translation), or perhaps πρὸ is replaced with μετὰ + acc ("the father <only> used to do this after"). This emendation would then establish the necessary contrast between what used to happen at first and what Lazaros allowed to happen in the last period of his life.

[734] Cf. above, Chap. 180.

[735] Lit. "the life of bearing the cross."

[736] This is a loose reference to the saying of Jesus found in Mt. 16:24; Mk. 8:34; Lk. 9:23.

dient to this <advice> and would act in this manner when they entered upon the monastic life; they would distribute some of their <possessions> to the poor and would present the rest to the father and to the monastery. For if one of those who was renouncing <the world> offered him something, Lazaros would accept it, although he did not force anyone to <do> this nor demand that they should give something to the monastery by way of an offering,[737] but he would not turn down what that person was offering of his own accord. Others, however, acting more cleverly, as they thought, decided to retain some of their money for themselves, but eventually their ill-advised possession and use of this <money> caused them to come to an unhappy end. Others again appeared to have renounced all <possessions> but, by forcing the father to rule that they should be given certain necessities by the monastery, they also fell short of the true objective <of the monastic life> without being noticed. For they introduced a great many problems into the monastery as a result and dragged the rest <of the monks> in the same direction; for evil is more desirable than virtue and it is easier for someone to partake of the former than of the latter.

193. An example <of the first kind and of its consequences> is Kosmas, who was also called Polites, while Kosmas Philippikos, is <an example of the second>.[738] <Kosmas Polites> thus kept some of his money with him as he wanted to <continue to> practice almsgiving with it in the future. However, when the father saw him doing this, he would not stop criticizing him and reproaching him for acting badly and improperly; as a result, this <Polites> became vexed by the father's words and began to argue <with him> and express regret concerning the money he had given to the father, <alleging> that he had not administered this <very> well.[739] In the end he fell sick, after he had gone down to the Kastron [Ephesus] to practice his almsgiving there, and was unable to get back up to the monastery; some people brought him up to the <monastery of the> holy Marina, where he died. The father sent out <some

[737] The Greek word is προσένεξις; cf. above, Chap. 16, where the more precise word ἀποταγή is used to refer to this rather doubtful practice.

[738] The identification of the various monks with the name Kosmas and Philippikos who are mentioned in the *vita* is complicated and not always clear; see Appendix B, the Prosopographical Glossary.

[739] Cf. Chap. 248, below, which reveals that Lazaros was maliciously accused by his opponents of being avaricious and that rumors were circulating at the time of his death to the effect that his pillar was stuffed full of gold coins.

of the brothers> and, after they had brought him back from there to the monastery, buried him. <Kosmas> Philippikos, on the other hand, rebelled against the father so much that he withdrew from the monastery not once but twice and waged a war against the brothers. The result was that the father was also forced by this <attack> to act against his own inclination and arouse himself against <this Philippikos>; he <thus> found himself in the same sorry situation[740] as David who of old, so we learn, opposed his own son by force and waged war <against him>.[741] <In fact>, this dreadful <affair> went so far that it came very close to ending in murder.[742] But we all know very well what a difficult and painful life <Philippikos> lived <while> paying the penalty for such shameless actions. And that's the <story> of these <two> men.

194. Since our father knew that certain brothers would not be very simply or easily scared out of their insolent behavior, but would <actually> cling to this <even> more resolutely, he would assail them with harsher rebukes and gibes as punishments for the edification of the others.[743] Lazaros sometimes

[740] Lit. "suffered the same as."

[741] The reference is to the rebellion of Absalom described in 1 Ki. 15–18.

[742] It is unclear whether this refers to an incident mentioned elsewhere in the *vita*. If it does, two possibilities present themselves. If Kosmas Philippikos can be identified with the traitor Kosmas the *taxeotes* of Chap. 239, then it could conceivably refer to the occasion (recorded in that chapter) on which an embassy sent by Lazaros to Constantinople was forcibly stopped and robbed by representatives of the metropolitan of Ephesus and his clergy. On the other hand, the most obvious reference in the *vita* to a murder almost being committed is that in Chap. 202; this concerns an attempt, evidently made at the time of Lazaros' death, to poison his brother (and designated successor as superior) Ignatios. Kosmas Philippikos is not associated with that incident in any way by Gregory the Cellarer (the guilty monk is said to have been one Methodios), but it is perhaps conceivable that he could have been behind the attempt, particularly if he is to be identified with the Philippikos of Chap. 221 who opposed Ignatios' appointment as steward of "his [Philippikos'] house"; moreover, his control of a subsidiary establishment on or near Galesion might also help to explain the circumstances of his serious disagreement with Lazaros.

[743] Although the construction of this whole section of the *vita* is not particularly smooth and is marked by digressions, there seems to be a particularly abrupt transition at this point in the chapter. The opening of the chapter would thus flow reasonably well into the following one, while what now follows seems to have been inserted most awkwardly here unless, perhaps, something has been lost or it has actually been misplaced. Certainly the punctuation in Delehaye's text appears to need some clarification.

observed that people whom he admitted and tonsured who <were already> old when they came to the <monastic> habit from the <outside> world were sad. They would say, "Our lives aren't <long> enough for repentance because we've already wasted all our resources and our physical strength on sins and on the pointless occupations of <everyday> life. What are we going to do from now on <that will be> sufficiently worthwhile? How shall we be able to propitiate God with good deeds of equal value, especially when we've <already> worn out our bodies and are thus unable to endure the exertions <demanded> by ascetic practice?" To rescue them from such unhappiness, or rather from <such> despair (for the Evil One knows that he can bring down the majority <of people> by this means), Lazaros would say comfortingly to them, "God doesn't seek anything else from you except thanks and persistence, and that you don't turn back again to what you've left behind[744] but instead persevere in this place to which He himself has led you, while expecting every day the separation of your soul from your body. Even if [567] death finds you engaged in <such> considerations and meditations, you can be confident that God will not deprive you of the <same> reward <as> those who undertook ascetic exercises and labors <long> before <you did>." He would thus make these people happier and would deliver them from the serious illness of despair, giving them spiritual guidance and calming them with his comforting words as though with soothing medical treatment.[745]

195. As regards those who acted shamelessly and were charged over some transgression in his presence, if this transgression were not well known to the majority, Lazaros would show forbearance and would overlook the occurrence in order not to show the brother up. If, on the other hand, the affair was well known and the harm <done> by this one person was clearly affecting many <others>, he would not be patient but severe, since he judged that this

[744] This warning against turning back to what has been left behind is repeated several times by Lazaros in the *vita,* see e.g., Chaps. 18 and 63. The passage is loosely related to a number of biblical ones, the closest of which are Mt. 24:18; Mk. 13:16; Lk. 17:31, cf. 9:62.

[745] One could give a more modern slant to the translation of this sentence without departing far from the original tone: "He would thus cheer these people up and would <help> them recover from the serious illness of depression, giving them psychological counseling and calming them down by means of his comforting words, as if with therapeutic tranquilizers."

would better suit the needs of the case in question. He would sometimes even order a beating to be inflicted on some of them.[746] For he was <actually> a frightening man, both in speech and in appearance, even if he was known as gentle and mild in his manner as a result of his good character and his <ascetic> struggles.

196. <Sometimes>, as a result of observing Lazaros' way of life, someone was eager to imitate and emulate him as much as possible, or <sometimes> also someone was troubled by the passions of the flesh and wanted to pursue a harsher <regimen> than the cenobitic style of life. If ever <such a person> came to the father and begged him to permit him <to do this>, he would say to him, <as a way of> preparing him in advance, "Be careful, brother, about the course of action you're about to undertake, in case you're unable to follow it through to the end. For many who have begun but have been unable to finish what they started have turned back and have thus manifestly destroyed twice over the things they've done from their own will<fulness> and at the wrong time, not being satisfied with what the *koinobion* has to offer them. But the person who submits to the rule of the *koinobion* and, with unhesitating determination, tirelessly travels the royal road[747] that the fathers have marked out, <that person> doesn't stumble; because he has traveled in a simple <way>, he hasn't stirred up against himself the most crafty and multifarious evil of the demons. A monk," he would say, "has to pay more attention to spiritual simplicity and innocence than to physical asceticism; and he has to avoid the conversation and company of ordinary people, especially of the young, even if he's young himself, because the Enemy has entrapped many <monks> in that way and has then handed them over to destruction.[748] Once he's got them to start out with a supposedly spiritual friendship he's then contrived to ruin them in fleshly corruption, so as to accomplish in them <precisely> what the holy apostle says: *having begun with the spirit you are now ending with the flesh.*[749] For this reason someone should not only not form relationships with

[746] Cf. above, Chap. 188.

[747] This expression is used metaphorically of the *via media* of ethics, which was also applied to the ascetic way of life; see, e.g., Ps. Basil, *Constitutiones monasticae,* PG 31:1349B.

[748] Cf. 1 Cor. 5:5; 1 Tim. 1:20.

[749] Gal. 3:3; the original sentence in Galatians is phrased as a question. Thomas ("Evergetine Reform," 251) interprets this passage as implying that on Galesion, "The

such people[750] but, if possible, he should shut his eyes so as not to gaze openly at their faces lest the Sower of Evil may thus sow some wicked thought[751] in his heart. Rather, he should keep his eyes downcast and pay attention to his own mind, and if ever a <wicked> thought of this kind should develop and then stir in his heart, he should immediately bring his mind back to God, so that by reaching out to Him he may from the start avoid involvement with this <all too> attractive thought; but with his tongue he should chant <these psalms> and make <this> invocation: 'Lord Jesus Christ, son of God, help me. *They have cast me out and compassed me round about;*[752] <*Thou art*> *my joy, deliver me from them that have compassed me.*'[753] And, '*Draw nigh, O God, to my help*[754] and *Judge thou, O Lord, them that injure me.*'[755] If the wicked thought is quelled when he says this prayer he should give thanks to God; but if it should continue to do battle and to press violently, he, in his turn, should contrive as much craft and cunning as the Crafty One himself against this evil so that he may be able to escape the harm <that would come> from giving in to this thought. For since it's better, when comparing two evils, to choose what may be said to be the lesser <of the two>, so one must also change <this particular> thought for another here, such as avarice or vainglory or some other such passion, and, by playing a little trick on the mind through its propensity and desire for this, avoid the violent assault and abusive treatment of

---

practice of forming 'spiritual friendships' with youths flourished, and frequently ended in what Lazaros terms 'fleshly perdition.'" Lazaros is, however, surely talking in general historical terms here, although some particular incident may be in mind; Thomas has rather a slender basis for painting such a black picture of the moral state of Galesion. Cf. also above, Chap. 138 n. 537.

[750] While the basic meaning of the Greek verb προσκολλάω is simply to "stick," "cling," or "be joined to," it is also used in the Bible in a number of contexts that imply marriage or sexual relations: e.g., Gen. 2:24; Eph. 5:31; κολλάω is used in the same context in Mt. 19:5; cf. I Cor. 6:16. The original audience would certainly be aware of this and it certainly seems to be the implication here.

[751] The rest of the passage would suggest that this "wicked thought" is again understood as being sexual in nature. There appears to be an allusion here to the parable of the weeds in the grain field at Mt. 13:24–30 and its explanation at 13:36–43, esp. verses 25 and 38–39.

[752] Ps. 16 (17):11.

[753] Ps. 31:7; the LXX differs here from the English text.

[754] Ps. 69 (70):1.

[755] Ps. 34 (35):1.

the former <wicked thought>. Of course, when he gets up in the morning, <a monk> should strive to offer to God the first fruits of his mind and the first thoughts <that come into his head>. He should <thus> plant his <seed> corn before the enemy can sow his tares, and then toil humbly all day long with his body with all the strength he's got, so that he may also say to God, like the holy David, '*Look upon mine affliction and my trouble; and forgive all my sins.*'[756] In the evening he should make scrupulous confession of the faults that have befallen him throughout the day and, when he lies down on his bed, he should not allow his mind to be subverted by improper thoughts into <considering> any unseemly and unsuitable ideas, but he should compose and focus it through careful study of the holy scriptures,[757] and fix it upon the remembrance of death. Thus, when he's going to sleep he should have a kind of secret agency <at work> as a guard over the wicked thoughts and he should be constantly in communication with this so that his thoughts may not be bewildered by the passions by being unrestrained. He shouldn't take any notice of other people's sins, he shouldn't pass judgments, shouldn't bear ill will, shouldn't <spread> slander nor listen with pleasure to someone else who is spreading it, and shouldn't repay evil with evil if someone has done something bad to him against his will. Rather, he should bear all things patiently, bravely, and without harboring grudges, while accepting also that he should readily forgive those who sin against him and should pardon them, in order that he too may be able to say to God without any inhibition, *Forgive us our trespasses as we forgive those who trespass against us.*[758] One must also take care and watch that one does not shock a brother's conscience by one's appearance, of course, or by one's spiritual practices. <A monk is thus> not to be *deceived by the feeding of the belly,*[759] but he should eat about once a day, keeping to the rule of the monastery; <when he does eat>, he shouldn't gorge himself, but should stop when his stomach still [568] hasn't had enough food. For thus also the fathers decided and ordained that <a monk> should partake of food every day (but <only> a little), rather than fasting for two or three <days> and then stuffing himself with food as a result. As far as clothing goes, he should always make use of more humble <garments>. In short, the person who truly wishes

[756] Ps. 24 (25):18.

[757] Or "recitation <of them>"; see above, Chap. 185.

[758] Mt. 6:12. The Greek word ὀφείλημα literally means a debt.

[759] Prov. 24:15 (LXX only).

to be saved must seek everything that tends toward humility and simplicity and innocence, and avoid things which are grand and have only vain repute. Someone who acts in this way and does <these things>, who places all his hope in God and has confidence in Him as a helper and provider of blessings, instead of in his own zeal and asceticism, prevails over the passions more easily."

197. Some people were persuaded by the father when he said these things and did <indeed> travel the royal road. Others, however, who reckoned that they were being harmed (<at least> as it appeared to them) by <too> much comfort and for this <reason> were longing for greater <challenges>, persuaded *him,* and were allowed to travel the more difficult path. As a result, just as the father said, many <of them> were unable to finish what they had started; they thus turned back and <in doing so> destroyed twice or even three times over what they had previously built up. But all those who were mentally and physically stronger humbly brought their endeavors to a good end. The monk Kosmas, who has just recently died before our eyes at the <monastery of the> Savior, is an example of what I am saying.[760] <I should perhaps note here that>, even if the majority of the brothers who were illustrious in virtue have <already> died, some prior to the death of our holy father and others after his departure to God, there are still some who, through the grace of Christ, are pursuing the virtuous life that is pleasing to God, right up to the present day. I have, however, decided that it would not be a good thing to put either their names or their virtuous deeds individually in writing now, lest, because they are still living and are known to us, I perhaps become both a cause of conceit <for them> or again of jealousy for any of you. Some of the brothers, then, girded themselves with irons, since they wanted to imitate the father even in this, although they were not strong enough to carry on with this practice to the end. Others constricted their waists with rope, as Symeon <did> in the old days,[761] but they too, like the former <brothers>, gave up this sort of undertaking after a short time. In any case, such <practices> do not

[760] It is unclear whether this Kosmas is being cited as an example of willfulness and failure or of humility and success.

[761] The reference is to Symeon the Stylite the Elder who wore a rope made out of rough palm fibers tied round his waist. As this was placed directly against his skin, it cut him quite badly and he was forced to take it off after wearing it for some ten days, although he did not do so of his own accord. See Theodoret, *Hist. Rel.,* 26.5. See further on Symeon, *ODB,* s.v. "Symeon the Stylite the Elder."

normally succeed for the majority in the long run, but <usually> come to a quick end. <This is> either due to physical weakness, since <the body> is unable to meet <the demands of> more severe labors, or else to spiritual weakness, which comes about from a lack of faith and a lack of hope[762] and the man's irresolute purpose; it is also sometimes the result of divine abandonment due to the conceit of the idea, perhaps because the person did not begin these <actions> with humility or is not pursuing them <with it>. Indeed, many people have even caused themselves spiritual damage as a result of being deprived of divine assistance for this sort of reason. As this has unfortunately happened to certain of the brothers in our monastery, I have decided that it is necessary and useful to focus on them and narrate their <stories> for the safety and protection of those who *think that they stand, lest they fall*[763] because of their ignorance. First of all, I will tell you about the monk Isaiah, a story that happens to be full not only of grief but also of joy.

198. From the time he came to stay with the father in the monastery, this <Isaiah> strove, above all else, to keep to the <ideal of> not doing anything without the father's approval. As a result he proved himself to be an *approved workman*[764] in the <path of> obedience, particularly in tasks outside <the monastery>. When he was sent somewhere by the father, he would thus not take bread with him or anything else for his personal requirements apart from the holy father's blessing and his trust in God; and wherever he traveled he would keep impeccably both the rule of the monastery and everything <else> the father had prescribed for him. Every Wednesday and Friday he would keep the vigil and would abstain infallibly from oil, fish, and wine. He never ate cheese or eggs. He used to perform the Sunday vigil in the same way and, because he was illiterate and knew only the fiftieth psalm and the *trisagion,*[765] he would say this psalm a hundred and fifty times all night long,[766] <and>

[762] The Greek word ἀνελπιστία also contains the sense of "despair."

[763] Cf. 1 Cor. 10:12: "Therefore let anyone who thinks that he stands take heed lest he fall." I am grateful to an anonymous reader for pointing out this citation to me.

[764] Cf. 2 Tim. 2:15.

[765] On the *trisagion,* see above, Chap. 45. Ps. 50 (51), which begins "*Have mercy upon me, O God, according to thy loving-kindness*" and is the most important penitential psalm; it is relatively short, containing nineteen verses.

[766] There are one hundred fifty Psalms altogether, so Isaiah apparently repeated the one Psalm he knew until he had completed a recitation equivalent to the whole psalter. I am grateful to an anonymous reader for pointing this out to me.

whenever he had said it three times he would immediately sing a *trisagion*. This was how the monk Isaiah used to live, taking food once a day and drinking three cups of wine (as had been prescribed <for him> by the father if he was invited to a meal by someone out of charity). He <thus> induced many people to <have> faith in him and in the father and, in consequence of this, he also brought back to the monastery many contributions from what had been given to him by the Christian faithful. He thus decorated the three churches on the mountain[767] out of such contributions[768] and he brought many other things into the monastery; and everywhere, both in the town and in many other places, he caused our holy father's name to become better known through his life, which was so pleasing to God.

199. On one occasion when <Isaiah> was going somewhere, he came to a village. Some of his acquaintances there told him about a particular woman who was extremely stingy and hard-hearted, and they said that nobody ever got as much as a single crumb from her house. When <Isaiah> heard them <say> this, however, he invoked the father's blessing and at once went to <see> the woman. Indeed, he approached her so skillfully that he received bread and even an egg from her <own> hands. He then went <back> to the people who had told him about her, holding these items in his hands; he showed <them> and said, "I've got these things from her <very> hands." After <Isaiah> had left the village, [569] these people went to the woman and let her know what exactly had happened and that "the monk didn't do this because he was poor but so that he might lure you into almsgiving." When she heard <this>, she groaned and said, "Oh, woe is me for <being such> a miserable wretch! Other people are worrying about my soul, but I take no thought for myself at all!" After she had said this, she <went> running <off and> caught up with the monk, for he had not yet gone far from the village, and, after pleading with him a great deal, persuaded him to turn back and visit her house. <There> she fell at his feet[769] and begged him to tell her what she had to do to be saved.[770] <Isaiah> taught her many things about almsgiving and then went on

[767] Presumably those of the Savior, the Theotokos, and the Resurrection.

[768] The phrase "out of such contributions" is a marginal note in the manuscript.

[769] Gregory the Cellarer's original audience might find an allusion here to several New Testament incidents, for example the Syrophoenician woman at Mk. 7:24, or Mary, the sister of (the biblical) Lazaros at Jn. 11:32.

[770] Cf. Acts 16:30.

his way, after finally telling her to go to <see> the father. The woman did not delay after his departure, but climbed up and came to <see> the father; indeed, after being taught more fully about these matters by him, she has, ever since then, made her house into another one worthy of Abraham,[771] and has always been very grateful to the monk [Isaiah] for his good guidance. <Anyway>, so that we may not speak at <any> greater length about him, I have learned from some of the brothers, who assured me that they heard this from the blessed Eupraxia herself,[772] that she saw this man with her own eyes, in the middle of the gorge where the cross is set up,[773] carrying burning charcoal <directly> on his bare hands and censing the cross <with it>.

200. But this man, who had so distinguished himself through so many good deeds and had been deemed worthy of such grace, was ensnared and seduced by the bad advice of certain malevolent and wicked men, and <thus> repudiated the commandment of complete obedience and submission and began to embezzle the donations <given> to him for his monastery by the Christian faithful; he also stopped confessing his thoughts to the father <as> meticulously <as he had done before>. Because he was deserted <by God> as a result of these <activities>, he fell into the pit of fornication and, although he confessed his sin (because it became evident to the father) and gave up this <particular> passion, he <still> did not give up misappropriating <donations> and living in the darkness <that results> from not making confession. He lived <on> for five years after this degeneration from his former life, and thus passed away. At his death, with God's permission, he was seized by an evil spirit, and a terrible spectacle was revealed to everyone, for he was convulsed[774] by it and uttered unintelligible cries from his mouth. One day, after he had died and his

[771] This refers to the famous hospitality (*philoxenia*) of Abraham, which stems from the incident recorded in Gen. 18:1–16. There the patriarch offered hospitality to the Lord who appeared to him in the form of three men at the oaks of Mamre. The episode was a popular theme in Byzantine illustration. See further *ODB,* s.v. "Philoxenia of Abraham," "Abraham."

[772] This is Lazaros' mother, who was in charge of the convent near Galesion that bore her monastic name. See above, Chap. 59.

[773] The reference is probably to the cross carved in the rock at the dangerous pass on the way up to the monasteries from Ephesus and Galesion; see above, Chaps. 41, 154, 155, and, perhaps, 77.

[774] The same verb is used in New Testament possession stories; see especially Lk. 9:39; also 9:42 and Mk. 9:20.

forty days <of mourning> had passed, the father summoned the cellarer around dawn and ordered him to make *kollyba* in memory of this monk Isaiah.[775] And on that very night, the monk Luke, who spent his life playing the fool so that he might be found wise in Christ[776] and who was <then> lying in the kitchen, began to say this in a loud voice, "Alas! Poor Isaiah is standing in front of the father's pillar and is calling on the father himself and the brothers to help him." (I <would have> much to say about <this Luke>, if I attempted to write down in detail the <stories> about him.)[777] Then, the following night, the father ordered the brothers to hold a vigil for brother Isaiah. He himself wrote out a pardon for him that evening and gave it to the sacristan,[778] telling him to place it on the holy altar under the altarcloth. The next morning, at the end of the holy eucharist, the father ordered the priest, along with the deacon and all the brothers, to come out of the church and proceed to <Isaiah's> grave. Standing on his pillar, Lazaros gave instructions to the deacon that he should read out his [Lazaros'] pardon of the brother in the hearing of everyone present, and that the brothers should say the *Kyrie eleeson*[779] a hundred times over in a loud voice after <each> reading of this <pardon>. When the deacon had thus read out the pardon five times and the brothers had called out one hundred *Kyrie eleesons* the same number of times, the father ordered him to take one of the stones lying on the grave and place the

[775] The custom of *kollyba,* a practice which derived from ancient pagan funeral meals, was a strong tradition in the Byzantine church. The distribution of these little cakes (which were made primarily of boiled wheat mixed with various nuts, dried fruits, and herbs of symbolic significance), together with the saying of prayers for the deceased, normally took place on three occasions during the forty (or sometimes thirty) days after death, marking stages in the journey of the soul either to God or away from Him. Thereafter the dead were commemorated in this way twice a year, on the anniversary of the death and just before the beginning of the Easter Lent. See further *ODB,* s.v. "Burial," "Death," "Funeral," and "Kollyba." The practice continues in the Orthodox church.

[776] On the tradition of "holy fools," see above, Chap. 175. Perhaps the earliest example of this phenomenon is an anonymous Egyptian nun who is described by Palladius, *Lausiaca,* chap. 34; as was evidently the case with this Luke, she too lived in the kitchen of her convent.

[777] Morris, *Monks,* 62, interprets this sentence as implying that Gregory the Cellarer planned to write about him.

[778] On this office see above, Chap. 82, and note 375.

[779] "Lord have mercy."

pardon under it. After this had been done the brothers came back from there and went into the church, singing the fiftieth <psalm>;[780] <then>, following the blessing, they went to the refectory. But after they had come out of the refectory and the brothers asked the father to tell them about the affair (for no one knew exactly what was going on), the father answered in a rather casual way, "A voice was heard from the grave plaintively saying this: 'Is this <my reward> for all the labor and effort <I> expended for the monastery, that you should now leave me confined <here> in Hades in <these> dark and murky places?'"[781] Although Lazaros was pressed very hard by the brothers to say who it was who had heard this, he would not reveal it. When he was asked by me and by other people if <Isaiah> had received forgiveness, he said, "Yes. I believe in my Christ, that he has attained <it>. For we learn that many things of this sort also took place in the time of the fathers." Anyway, that is the story of the monk Isaiah.[782]

201. Another brother, called Symeon, was watched over by God and remained unharmed by the snares of the Evil One as long as he <followed> the father's advice and was obedient to him, and did everything with his approval. But, from the moment he began to follow his own wishes, or rather the counsels of Satan, he too slid into the abyss of fornication.[783] As a result he left the monastery without letting the father know, and went back to his homeland *like a dog to its vomit.*[784] <Then>, as he himself confessed on his deathbed to the monk Laurentios, who is now on the pillar,[785] [570] <although he did this> reluctantly and <only> after he was compelled <to do so> by <Laurentios>,

[780] See above, Chap. 198.

[781] I am grateful to an anonymous reader for help with the sense of this statement. Cf. Chap. 202, below, where the brothers make a similar point to Lazaros about the monk Barnabas, suggesting that God might forgive him for his sins because of all the labors he had performed in the monastery. On that occasion Lazaros dismisses the suggestion because of Barnabas' lack of repentance.

[782] There is a parallel to the voice from beyond the grave in the episode recounted in the *Dialogues* of Gregory the Great, 4:57. Gregory the Cellarer has already referred directly to this story in Chap. 163, above.

[783] As was suggested above, Chap. 129 may be a commentary by Lazaros on the sort of laxity typified by this individual case.

[784] Cf. Prov. 26:11 and 2 Pet. 2:22; cf. also above, Chap. 21.

[785] On this Laurentios, see above, Chaps. 71 and 138; he is also mentioned again below in Chaps. 217 and 223, and probably in Chap. 253.

he suffered[786] so much <spiritual> harm that he did not pass a single evening free from <some sexual> transgression until he reached his homeland. After some time, however, <Symeon> came back again and returned to the monastery, where he was warmly welcomed by the father; but when he was asked by Lazaros to tell him if he had by any chance suffered any spiritual harm during his absence from the monastery, he concealed <this> and did not confess <it>. <Furthermore>, on the pretext of looking after his daughter (for he had a daughter who is <now> a nun in the convent of Eupraxia of everlasting memory,[787] but he was dead when she took the habit), he used to go down from the mountain and sully <the purity of> his soul, and this, alas, when he was <already> an old man and well advanced in the monastic way of life. Although he was often pressed by the father, he was unwilling to confess his sins in order that he might be corrected, and thus the axe of justice <eventually> caught up with him and cut him down like a tree that does not bear fruit, so that it may not cause the ground <in which it grows> to be idle for <too> long.[788] For death suddenly sprang upon this man like a lion[789] and seized his unrepentant soul that was lying in the black depths of despair. As a result the father sorrowfully made some such statement as this to the brothers after <Symeon's> death: "Believe you me, brothers, the demons have sadly claimed the soul of this old man."

202. <There is> also Barnabas, who was called "the Big" because of his height. He too exhibited considerable enthusiasm at first in carrying out various tasks in a variety of ways, but later, due to the shallowness of his mind, he became swollen-headed and behaved in an arrogant way toward the holy father (or rather, in truth, toward God, if <indeed> insolence against servants may be transferred to their master, just as He said to the prophet of old, "*They have not rejected thee but me*").[790] In fact, <Barnabas> reached such a point

[786] The Greek verb ὑφίστημι also contains a sense of deliberate assent; this spiritual harm did not simply happen to him by accident.

[787] On Eupraxia and her convent, see above, Chaps. 59 and 74.

[788] Cf. Lk. 13:7, and, more distantly, Mt. 3:10; 7:19; Lk. 3:9. Cf. above, Chap. 104, where a similar expression is used.

[789] Cf. 1 Pet. 5:8, "*your adversary the devil, as a roaring lion, walketh about, seeking whom he may devour.*"

[790] 1 Ki. 8:7. The prophet here is Samuel, and the original context of the quotation the rejection of Samuel's corrupt sons by the people of Israel who refuse to accept them as their judges and demand a king instead.

that, after he had also seduced another brother, called Methodios, through his wicked conversations and had made him of the same mind as himself, he left the monastery with him. They went off to Magnesia,[791] to the bishop, and whispered many wicked things in his ear[792] against the holy father and against his brother [Ignatios], who is now our superior.[793] But, even with these men behaving like this, the holy father did not disregard them or stop displaying his <usual attitude>; he thus wrote to them, rebuking them, pleading with them and admonishing them until, with the advice and cooperation of the bishop as well, he had made them return to the monastery. But, as the saying goes, the Ethiopian did not become white, nor was the crab taught to walk straight.[794] They thus caused a lot of trouble for the father and the brothers after returning to the monastery, and in consequence of this each of them at his own particular time received the punishment he deserved. Methodios <received his> because of the wicked business he contrived against the superior [Ignatios]; for, at the very time of our holy father's death, he mixed a poisonous drug with wine and gave it <to Ignatios> to drink in order to kill him, and <would have succeeded> unless God above, Who judges justly, had preserved <Ignatios> from the resulting harm through the intercessions of his brother our blessed father Lazaros; <as it was, Ignatios> did suffer some pain for a while because of this.[795]

Anyway, the man who had dared to do this left the monastery again and returned to Magnesia, <where God> let him be murdered by <some> herdsmen who were pasturing their pigs. <As for> Barnabas, when he had only just arrived <back> and come up to the father from Bessai[796] (for he was <living>

[791] This is presumably Lazaros' home town of Magnesia on the Meander, which was close to Ephesus (see above, Chap. 2), rather than Magnesia in Lydia.

[792] There are strong implications in the Greek of false accusation and malicious insinuation.

[793] For another reference to opposition to Ignatios within the community, see below, Chap. 221. Malamut, *Route,* 134, comments on this episode.

[794] Cf. Apostolius 1:68 and 9:50, ed. Leutsch and Schneidewin, *CPG,* 2:258 (cf. 1:348) and 472.

[795] I am grateful to an anonymous reader for suggesting the sense of this passage. Note the suggestion made in Chap. 193, n. 742 that this attempted murder might possibly be linked to Kosmas Philippikos.

[796] Malamut, "Bessai," 246, discusses the implications this passage may have for the location of Bessai in relation to Galesion, and raises the possibility that this monastery may have perhaps been situated on the boundary between the jurisdictions of Ephesus

there), he asked the father to give him the cell he had previously had on the mountain. The father readily fulfilled his request, but <Barnabas>, instead of going to him, after he had got his cell back, and making confession and asking to receive forgiveness for the sins he had committed against God and against him, went up and <began> putting pressure on him so that he might leave for Bessai again. The purpose <of this visit> was to settle up his affairs there, as he said, not knowing <what was going to happen in> the future; <then>, after he had distributed some <of his possessions> to other people, he would return to the mountain, bringing the rest with him. The father would not allow him to go, however, seeing that he had only just <come back>, or else because he had been instructed by some divine inspiration what the future held for <Barnabas>; instead he advised him to stay quietly in his cell and to send another brother there, whomever he should choose, to do everything that he wanted and then return to him again. But <eventually>, when the father had struggled and fought[797] a great deal and was <still> unable to persuade him or to stop him <doing> what he wanted, he left him to follow his own wishes.

So <Barnabas> went down there and, before he could do even a little of what he wanted, he met his end there without having repented. When our holy father learned of this man's death, he was deeply moved and made some such statement as this about him, at a time when quite a few brothers were standing in front of his pillar: "Oh, wretched Barnabas, you are lost!" Some of the brothers cited in <Barnabas'> defense the labors he had performed in the monastery and expressed the belief that, because of these, God would deem him worthy of forgiveness for the sins he had committed, and they tried to find out what the father thought about this.[798] This <was what> they <suggested>, but the father said to them, "The wretch never ever performed a task honestly, but even so, if he'd <only> managed to confess his sins, God, through His great kindness toward men and His compassion, would have had mercy on him. But since he didn't show any <sign of doing> such a thing and departed bearing <the burden of> his <sins> with him, what real hope has been left to us concerning this man? . . . [799]

and Magnesia, hence the appeal by these men to the bishop of Magnesia rather than to the metropolitan of Ephesus. See also the Introduction, section E, pp. 32–33.

[797] The image in Greek is one of wrestling and boxing.

[798] Cf. above, Chap. 200.

[799] There is a substantial gap in the manuscript at this point. Apart from four words at the top of f. 236, the rest of that folio and all of 236v are blank.

Anyway, I have recounted these stories about the brothers who have already died, [571] for the benefit of my listeners.

203. But what about those who are still alive and have fallen into similar evils? It <would> also <be> good to tell in passing a few <stories> about them for your benefit. But I am really ashamed to relate all the <stories> of these people in detail and, <even> more, I am afraid that by doing so I may become a cause of despair to these men. For many have fallen into despair for this <reason>, and have <either> acquired <an attitude of> shamelessness rather than shame as a result of having their actions exposed, or else they have been consumed by grief. So, in order that these people may not suffer the same <consequences> I will refer to them anonymously as "these people." One <such person>, who fell into some sort of wrongdoing due to his uncontrolled and intemperate attitude, was brought back to the monastery against his will by the father. He was ordered to take off his monastic habit and put on layman's clothes but, as a result of his appeal to the brothers and the father, he was let off such a <severe> sentence. He did not, however, <really> reform himself as our holy father said, for in response to the brothers' pleading on this man's behalf he said, "I don't believe he will reform himself or give up his evil <ways>, even if he now appears to make such promises because of his present difficulties."[800]

204. Another <brother> conducted himself in the same way as Gehazi in <performing> the task entrusted to him,[801] and as a result made himself a recipient of our holy father's curse too;[802] he <now> stands out as an obvious

[800] On Lazaros' power to have a monk accused of wrongdoing brought back to the monastery by force, and on his treatment of the man in question, see the rather similar incident recorded above, Chap. 142.

[801] Gehazi is mentioned in 2 Ki. 4–5 as the servant of the prophet Elisha. The episode in 2 Ki. 5, to which reference is apparently being made here, tells how the Syrian general Naaman was miraculously cured of his leprosy by Elisha. The prophet declined any sort of payment for the cure but Gehazi then deceitfully obtained money and clothing for himself from Naaman. When Gehazi returned from doing this, Elisha asked him where he had been; the unfaithful servant denied going anywhere, but the prophet revealed that he knew exactly what had taken place and so smote him with Naaman's leprosy as a punishment for his actions (2 Ki. 5:19–27). Gehazi is also used as an example in Chaps. 228 and 231 below.

[802] Formal cursing was a normal part of Byzantine life and was employed by ordinary people (particularly for protection of property, contracts, etc.; cf. below, Chap. 246, where such a curse is included in Lazaros' *diatyposis*); it was also employed by

example to everyone <because of> what has happened to him since then. For not only did he fail to derive any enjoyment at all from the gold he thought he would have, but, with the help of this, or rather through it, he actually lost his soul, for alas, he also fell into the mire of fornication.[803] Furthermore, the man who deluded himself after our holy father's death and chose to absent himself from the church and the refectory and the rest of the brothers' meetings and wanted to be called by the vain name of "the hesychast," gradually succumbed to those who were luring him into such things and returned to his homeland. And we all know what happened to him. Moreover, did not the man who lied to the father, heard Lazaros <say to him>, "Don't lie, so that you won't be handed over to the Devil!"[804] and then replied, "Alright! If I *am* lying, so be it!" get what he wanted straightaway? For he was immediately handed over to an evil demon as a lesson to himself and to others. So, brothers, let us avoid lying and following our own wishes, and <instead>, when we have humbled ourselves in the Lord, let us eagerly and faithfully follow in all things those who together with God guide us toward the good, so that we too may not suffer the same fate as the aforementioned individuals. For <the Scriptures> say, "*Ask thy father, and he shall relate to thee thine elders, and they shall tell thee*" <what to do>.[805] But enough of such things.

205. <Now> then, turning my account to our holy father <himself>, I will tell you as much as I can, for it would be impossible for someone to recount in detail everything about that man. How <could they>? For not only are the <stories about him> almost innumerable, but also most of them have not come down to us[806] because those who knew them have died. Furthermore, I cannot even pass on in my narrative all those stories I have been able to learn, partly because their quantity exceeds my capacity to tell them and partly because, in the opinion of some people, what I say myself is not trustworthy without evi-

---

members of the church hierarchy and holy men, who used it to uphold doctrinal and ecclesiastical conformity and moral standards. The practice follows both Old and New Testament tradition, and was thought to invoke the anger of God in consigning the wrongdoer to the powers of evil, as is clearly the case in the episode recorded here. See further *ODB,* s.v. "Cursing."

[803] This may refer to the anonymous brother in Chaps. 228–30; the mention of gold, lying, and the curse of Gehazi may corroborate this suggestion.

[804] Lazaros' words allude to 1 Cor. 5:5 and 1 Tim. 1:20.

[805] Deut. 32:7.

[806] Lit. "come to our hearing."

dence from other <sources>; but <I will tell> those <stories> I have learned from other people who may be trusted, or which I myself have witnessed, or which I have heard from the father himself.

206. The father was once afflicted by a discharge that caused <him> a lot of pain, but when a lancet was applied and an incision made in his neck, pus[807] instead of blood flowed out of the vein, for he had so mortified himself in his body, or rather to the world,[808] that he did not even have a great deal of the <very> blood that sustains life. On another occasion again Lazaros had an extremely painful toothache; he had <already> had seven <teeth> come out at the roots and, while these had fallen out one at a time, almost all <the others> except two <now> came loose and fell out <at once>. Since he was in this condition and was quite unable to partake of any food whatsoever, except for warm water, everyone despaired of <his life>.[809] There was <thus> inconsolable grief and mourning in the community, especially as it had become known to the <brothers> that Lazaros himself had summoned the layman, called Pantoleon, who was in the monastery at that time doing some work, and had ordered him to dig at the back of[810] the apse of the chancel of the church and hastily construct a grave <there>. However, with the brothers in mourning like this and with the father already at death's door, <our> benevolent and merciful God wished to make it clear that although He was going to transport Lazaros in the future to the repose reserved for him in heaven, because he had labored and struggled <in a manner> beyond <ordinary> human nature and strength and had *finished his race* well,[811] He would allow him to go on living this life

[807] Normally the word used here, ἕλκος, refers to a wound or a sore, but it may also imply that this is festering, and the verb ἑλκόω may mean "suppurate"; the extension to this translation thus seems logical, even if it is apparently otherwise unattested. Another possibility, which might make more sense of the passage, would be if ῥεύματος ("discharge") and ἕλκος had become switched; this would make possible a translation as follows: "The father was once afflicted with a festering wound . . . <some sort of> fluid flowed out of the vein instead of blood." Bleeding was a common medical remedy for many afflictions in Byzantine times.

[808] This alludes closely to Col. 2:20; cf. also Gal. 6:14; 2:19; Rom. 6:2.

[809] This may be the same episode referred to in Chap. 82, where Lazaros almost starves himself to death by refusing to eat for fifteen days and is only dissuaded by Kosmas Philippikos.

[810] Or perhaps "behind," i.e., outside the church; the Greek word is ὄπισθεν.

[811] This is a loose quotation of 2 Tim. 4:7; cf. Acts 20:24.

<a while longer> for the salvation of many people. He revealed this as follows in a dream to one of the brothers, called Matthew.

207. For, after the end of the vigil, this brother lay down in his cell for a little rest and fell asleep as a result of his grief over the father and the exertion of the vigil. <While he was sleeping>, he seemed to see himself standing in front of the church observing a eunuch <who approached> the entrance to the monastery on horseback from a northerly direction and came inside. The <eunuch> hurriedly dismounted from his horse and went straight to the church where the monk met him and made obeisance to him, for it seemed that <the eunuch> was <already> known to him. When <Matthew> asked him where he had come from, how he had got there, and why he had come, he replied, "I was with the emperor, and unless I'd hurried and got here first, your holy father would now be dead." He said this to the monk and immediately walked into the church. [572] The monk went inside the church too, and <there> he seemed to see an old man, whom he gathered was a judge, standing in front of the icon of the Savior. Turning his eyes to the right, he saw a woman dressed in black come out of the pillar[812] and, proceeding by way of the three wooden beams that extended upon the bases of the arches,[813] go <over to> the old man. She fell at his feet and made obeisance as if she was thanking him. The monk immediately awoke from his sleep and came to himself; he carefully considered what he had seen, and understood that the father was not going to die from that illness, but <only> after three <more> years had passed, as was

[812] On the possibility that Lazaros' pillar, at least at the monasteries of the Theotokos and the Resurrection, had an opening of some kind directly into the church, or that the pillar of the Theotokos was actually incorporated into the building after he had left it, see Chaps. 157 and 159, and the Introduction, section C, p. 18. In the latter case, this incident must have occurred at the monastery of the Theotokos.

[813] There appear to be two possible alternative meanings for the term ξύλα (lit. "pieces of wood"). One possibility is that these ξύλα are to be envisaged as beams extending from the bases of arches that form part of the construction of the *pillar* and thus perhaps act as rungs of some sort providing access to it; certainly in Chap. 159 when the monk Kerykos jumped off the pillar on Petra he became caught on one of the ξύλα which stuck out from, and evidently formed part of, its construction; perhaps both chapters refer to a similar element in the design of these pillars. Another possibility is that these ξύλα are pieces of wood laid upon the bases of the arches that form part of the construction of the *church;* they may thus be braces of some sort. Whatever they are, the use of ἐπάνω ("upon") at the end of the chapter implies that they are not on the ground.

indicated by <the way> the woman in his vision had walked upon the three beams.[814]

208. Not long afterward Lazaros again fell seriously ill. As he was already getting old then and his body was worn out by his many mortifications, he experienced illnesses more frequently, especially when the seasons changed, for he was constantly being battered by the blasts of the winds and the various fluctuations and alterations in climate.[815] The brothers thus felt sorry for him, and made him a sort of little cushion,[816] which they brought to him. They asked him to take this and place it beneath him, for he had nothing else inside his pillar for bodily comfort except for his leather tunic and his woollen cloak, which served him as a *melote.*[817] After he had come under considerable pressure from the brothers, he opened his little window and saw the cushion, but he immediately closed it again and said, "Get away from me, and leave me to die like this!" Although the brothers pleaded a great deal <with him>, they could not persuade him to take it, and so they went down from the pillar, extremely upset and in tears.[818] Of course, when the wicked Devil saw that Lazaros would not agree to provide his body with the slightest comfort, even when he was so ill, he found himself at a loss and did not know what he should do. So he changed himself into the shape of an old woman and entered the pillar, where he addressed Lazaros, saying, "Bless <me>, father!" The father looked up and, seeing her, said, "Who are you, and who brought you in here?" She <replied>, "I'm someone who has cured emperors and patriarchs and the whole senate.[819] I found out what had happened to you and so I've come to

[814] This would appear to date the illness to ca. 1050.

[815] Cf. below, Chap. 248, where Lazaros' illness, combined with constant exposure to severe winter weather, is given as the immediate cause of his death.

[816] The word in Greek is προσκεφάλαιον, a term that could also indicate "a pillow."

[817] Lit. "a sheepskin" and hence "a rough hairy cloak" worn by ascetic monks: see Lampe, *Lexicon,* s.v. μηλωτή. Gregory the Cellarer is presumably justifying Lazaros' use of this cloak on the basis of earlier ascetic tradition.

[818] Compare the concern shown for the condition of the sick monk Kerykos in Chap. 162, and Lazaros' similarly firm response there.

[819] The senate (σύγκλητος) continued to exist in the 11th century although it had almost entirely lost its governmental powers of Roman republican and, indeed, earlier imperial days; it had also increased considerably in size, perhaps numbering several thousand. The senate's function was now primarily ceremonial and, although it also could advise the emperor, the extent of its real influence depended on the power and

cure you too. Your monks received me, helped me up by way of a ladder, and brought me in <here>, as you see. But <now>," she continued, "let me examine[820] your flesh with my hand if you really want to receive a cure for the illness that afflicts you." But as soon as the father raised his hand to make the sign of the cross (for he was not ignorant of who she was), the old woman immediately vanished like smoke.[821] And when the father had recovered a little from his illness toward evening (for it was midday when the Evil One appeared to him in the guise of the old woman),[822] he told the brothers about this. But <now> let our account pass on to other matters which must be recounted.

209. While I was still in service in the pantry,[823] there was a bread shortage, and there were only five <regular> loaves[824] and four small eucharistic loaves[825] <left> in the pantry. Brother Germanos (who was then *parekklesiarches*)[826] came to fetch his usual two large eucharistic loaves, but when I gave

---

interests of particular rulers. See further *ODB,* s.v. "Senate." The implication is then that this woman is a healer whose ability is sanctioned by influential people; the fact that a woman could be accepted as occupying such a role is interesting.

820 The verb ψηλαφάω can also carry the sense of to "stroke" or "caress," and would thus appear to fit the Devil's plot perfectly here.

821 Cf. Chap. 68, in which the Devil is said to have appeared to Lazaros as an angel of light and was similarly dismissed. Morris, *Monks,* 115, comments on this episode but mistakenly describes Lazaros' assailant as a "beautiful" woman.

822 Midday was a time particularly associated with demonic activity, following Ps. 90(91):6. Interestingly enough, some alternative traditions of demonology also closely linked it with female demons. See further Greenfield, *Demonology,* 20, 104, 189.

823 The Greek word used is ἀρτοθέσιον, lit. the "bread storeroom." The chapter indicates not only that Gregory (the Cellarer) worked in the pantry at one time but that he also held the office of *trapezopoios* (see below). The following sentence implies that this incident took place at the monastery of the Resurrection, where supplies for all three communities on the mountain were evidently centralized.

824 Cf. the version of the miracle of the loaves and fishes in Mt. 14:13–21; Mk. 6:34–44; Lk. 9:12–17; and Jn. 6:1–14. See also below, Chaps. 211 and 213, for further references to this miracle.

825 Lit. "blessed <loaves>." Leavened bread was used by the Byzantines in the Eucharist, as opposed to the unleavened bread or "azymes" of the Western rite. Such loaves could take various forms and were also stamped with a variety of seals; they were often known as *prosphorai.* High-quality bread was usually made from wheat flour, that of lesser quality from barley flour. See further *ODB,* s.v. "Bread," "Prosphora."

826 On this office, evidently that of assistant sacristan, see above, Chap. 82 n. 375.

him the two small ones and kept back the other two, in order to give one to the <monastery of the> Savior and the other to the Theotokos, he did not want to take them unless he could have the other two as well. I refused to do this, and so he left them and went off to the father and said <to him>, "The *trapezopoios*[827] has eucharistic loaves but will not let me have them." The father summoned me by means of a<nother> brother and asked me about this, but when I told him the details of the matter, he ordered the brother [Germanos] to take the two loaves: "So that the other churches may also be ministered to," he said. <Germanos>, however, again refused to take them, as there would not be enough to give to the brothers, so the father said to him once more, "Go on, let the *proskomide*[828] take place with those <two eucharistic loaves you have>; and as for the brothers, *I* will explain the situation to them." When things had reached this point and we were still standing there, as brother <Germanos> was still refusing to come and take the loaves, behold, two monks came into the monastery bringing two mules, one laden with oil and wine, the other with <regular> loaves and eucharistic loaves; they had been sent from Limnai[829] from the *ekklesiarches*[830] (who was then Kyros Pachomios) and his superior.[831] After they had brought these things and put them in front of the pillar before the father, Lazaros called brother Germanos and said to him, "Look what God has sent on account of your lack of faith and contempt! Take as many eucharistic loaves as you want now, and go!" But the brother was unable to look the father <in the face> from shame; he fell to the ground, prostrated himself and sought forgiveness. When he obtained it, he stood up and went off to the church, taking the eucharistic bread <with him>.

210. A year before our holy father's death a severe famine afflicted the region,[832] and one could see a crowd of poor people coming up to the monas-

[827] On the office of *trapezopoios*, see above, Chaps. 82 and 131.

[828] The term "*proskomide*" means the offertory, the preparation of the elements of bread and wine for the Eucharist. See further *ODB*, s.v. "Proskomide," also s.v. "Prothesis," "Anaphora."

[829] This place has not been located. See Foss, *Ephesus*, 120 n. 16.

[830] That is, the "sacristan." On this important monastic office, see above, Chap. 82.

[831] A rather similar incident is recounted in the Life of St. Paul the Younger, chap. 29, ed. H. Delehaye, "Vita S. Pauli Iunioris in Monte Latro cum interpretatione latina Iacobi Sirmondi S.J.," *AnalBoll* 11 (1892), 137.

[832] The famine must thus have occurred in 1052; cf. the reference in Chap. 247 to shortages afflicting the monastery at the time of Lazaros' death.

tery every day. No one who came up left without receiving food, however, and so I said to the father many times (for I was then the cellarer), "<Surely you don't think> all these people are really coming up here to receive a blessing?" The father smiled and said to me, "No, of course <not>! The majority of them <are coming up> to be fed, and for this reason God is [573] sending their food here so that we too may be fed through them."[833] When a shortage of bread occurred in the monastery, I went up to him and said, "What's going to happen <now>? We have no bread for tomorrow." He smiled again and said to me, "Now we've become real monks because we've got no bread for tomorrow, and we should actually give thanks to God for this. For," he continued, "there was once a shortage of bread and the other necessities in a certain *koinobion* <that lasted> for a week.[834] The brothers did not get upset, however, but would go into the refectory when they had sung their office and sit down as usual after saying grace. While they sat there, they would talk about <matters which were> of spiritual benefit and then, when they had said grace again and given glory to God, they would get up <from the table>. They continued doing this every day but, at the end of the week, while they were sitting in the refectory, the Devil appeared to them in visible form as an Ethiopian[835] and said, 'I thought you would have grown angry with God and <turned to> blasphemy because of your lack <of food>, but as I see the opposite is happening, I won't ask leave <from God> to tempt you any more in the future. With these words, he immediately vanished from their sight."[836]

211. . . . When I asked if there were loaves of bread, he replied to me,[837] "Yes there still are." At last he said, "I <can> see something miraculous <happening>, for I'm filling up the basket in which the loaves of bread are usually

[833] Similar statements are attributed to Lazaros in Chaps. 211 and 213, as well as indirectly in Chap. 151.

[834] I have been unable to identify the source of this story.

[835] On the use of this form by the Devil, see Chaps. 153 and 233.

[836] There is a substantial gap at this point in the manuscript, for the small space remaining on this folio (242v) and the whole of the following one (243–243v) are empty; the end of this chapter and the beginning of the next are thus missing. It is unclear if the material in Chap. 211 is to be understood as the conclusion of the present episode or of a different, if parallel, story; Malamut, *Route,* 266, evidently takes the two together.

[837] The person to whom Gregory the Cellarer is talking here would appear to be the *trapezopoios* mentioned below.

put to be carried to the refectory, and I'm taking it and carrying it back to the pantry again from the <refectory>, full of all the leftover fragments.[838] So I assume from what I'm seeing that the loaves are being consumed only by the guest brothers."[839] When the father learned about this miracle from me and from the *trapezopoios,*[840] he again said with his usual beloved humility, "God has arranged <things> for the sake of the poor and the visitors so that we may also eat thanks to them."[841]

212. Another time there was a shortage of wine and there were no more than one and a half *stamnia*[842] in the storage jar[843] in which we usually kept it. I went up to the father and, after informing him of the amount of wine that was <left> in the storage jar, asked him if he would issue orders for me to supply the brothers with eucharistic wine from the church mixed with water; for we usually did this whenever there was a shortage of our normal wine. He would not let me do it, however, but said, "Please go and supply the brothers with the wine that is in the storage jar, mixed with a little water; but if there should <still> not be enough when you have done this, then you can do what *you* are suggesting." So I went down and did as the father said, and then both I myself and the brother who was with me saw a wonderful miracle; for, after I had supplied the brothers in the monastery as well as those in the guest

[838] There is again a clear allusion here to the miracle of the loaves and fishes, which figures in all four Gospels and which, in every version, mentions an abundance of left-over fragments (κλάσματα) being collected: Mt. 14:13–21; 15:32–39; Mk. 6:34–44; 8:1–10; Lk. 9:12–17; Jn. 6:1–14. The previous chapter and the present one to this point may be connected in some way to a section in the *Apophthegmata* (*Anonymous Sayings*), 149, trans. B. Ward, *The Wisdom of the Desert Fathers: The Apophthegmata Patrum* (Oxford, 1975), 42.

[839] See above, Chap. 150, for Lazaros' ruling that visiting monks should be fed in the refectory with the brothers rather than in the guest house.

[840] On the office of *trapezopoios,* see above, Chap. 82. Gregory the Cellarer evidently does not hold this position at the time of this incident, presumably having been promoted to the office of cellarer; it is thus conceivable that the person in question may be the Ignatios who has this title in Chaps. 82, 131, and 134.

[841] See the note in the previous chapter on Lazaros' attitude toward the poor and visitors.

[842] A *stamnion* (σταμνίον) is a small jar or jug used for serving the wine at table.

[843] Lit. "pithos."

house <with it>, the wine in the storage jar was still intact and <exactly> as it was before.[844] When I saw this, I came to myself[845] and realized the <true extent of the> grace which our holy father had received from God on account both of his most pure life which was so pleasing to Him, and of his outstanding endurance and humility. Then my conscience was most sorely pricked, and I condemned myself especially for my deafness and blindness, because I would often argue with him when he gave me orders about such matters. But when I went up to him and told him all about the miracle and sought forgiveness for my disobedience and for arguing <with him>, Lazaros, because he was humble-minded and compassionate and was an imitator of Christ Who was mild and benevolent, kept quiet about the miracle and, after forgiving me and praying over me, dismissed me.

213. <Once>, when there was a shortage of cheese in the monastery on Cheese-eating day,[846] the father sent Nicholas the smith (who has often been mentioned by me)[847] to the village of Galesion.[848] <Nicholas> went but, when he brought <back> to the monastery only one cheese from there, the father summoned me and said, "Please take this cheese and supply the three monasteries with it according to the rule for the day providing the monks with both raw and cooked <cheese>. But <do it> carefully, so that there won't be a short-

[844] There would seem to be another allusion in this episode to Jesus' miracles involving food and drink, this time to the wedding at Cana and the miraculous provision of wine after the original supply had failed; Jn. 2:1–11.

[845] The same expression is used at Lk. 15:17 of the prodigal son when he finally realizes his folly; given the context of famine and shortage here, it seems quite possible that an allusion to that parable is intended and would have been understood by the original audience.

[846] This is apparently a reference to Quinquagesima Sunday, the seventh Sunday before Easter, which was preceded by Cheesefare week (on which see above, Chap. 82); cf. J. van den Gheyn, "Acta Graeca ss. Davidis, Symeonis et Georgii," *AnalBoll* 18 (1899), 250, line 15. Kaplan, *Les hommes,* 42, is surely mistaken in understanding this passage to imply that there was one day a week on which cheese was eaten in the monastery.

[847] It was not uncommon to have a smith working within a monastic community of any size; Chap. 236, below, refers to brothers from the monastery gathering olive roots to make charcoal for use by the smith. See further *ODB,* s.v. "Smith."

[848] On the location of this village, evidently between Ephesus and the foot of the path up the mountain, see above, Chaps. 77 and 154.

age, because the brother who was sent out didn't find another cheese there and didn't bring <another one> back here either." So I picked up the cheese and prostrated myself and was about to go off to the cellar when he called me again and said, "You must distribute it to the lay brothers in the guest house in exactly the same way as you do to the monks." He always used to tell me to do this with all <provisions> that were being given out except for the wine, for whenever the monks received two <measures> he used to order that the lay people should <only> receive about one.[849] So I went off and did as he said and supplied everyone from the one cheese, as with the Lord . . . ,[850] and I collected an abundance of leftover fragments.[851] Once again, when he learned about this from me, he said, "Unless God was <always> multiplying everything <here> for the sake of the beggars and visitors who come up here every day, how could three churches <possibly> have been constructed on this barren mountain, and how could we who are gathered <here> have been able to persevere on it?"

214. Another time there was a dearth of pulses, and as there were none to be found in the cellar except for one plate<full>, the monk Jacob, who was the cook then (as now), went up to the father and told him about this. "Go and take the few vetch-peas[852] which you say are there," said Lazaros, "and cook them, for today they [the monks] will be supplied from those." This did

[849] On Lazaros' stress that visitors should be well treated and on lay visitors being fed in the guest house rather than the refectory, see above, Chap. 150. Cf. also Chap. 191, above, where Gregory the Cellarer mentions that those monks engaged in manual labor received extra rations of food and wine on the father's orders. Some monastic *typika* also lay down that each monk should receive two mugs (*krasobo<u>lia*) of wine; see *ODB,* s.v. "Wine."

[850] There is a small space in the manuscript at this point, apparently leaving room to provide the implied New Testament reference, which is, once more, to the miracle of the loaves and fishes and the baskets of leftover fragments (κλάσματα) collected after all have eaten; see above, Chap. 211.

[851] The Greek is ungrammatical at this point: either κλασμάτων should be read for κλάσματα or περισσεύοντα for περισσεύματα. I am grateful to an anonymous reader for this suggestion.

[852] The Greek term λαθύριον is presumably a form of the ancient λάθυρος, and the modern "λαθούρι." In this case it is a pulse, identified by Liddell-Scott-Jones, *Lexicon,* as *Lathyrus sativa,* the Grass peavine or Vetch-pea. If the precise identification is correct, the plant is actually somewhat toxic, causing back pain and weakness in the legs, and even death in children.

indeed happen. <For> after he had cooked <them>, the monk kept on seeing as many <peas still> in the pot as he emptied out of it, and thus we all ate our fill of them, in accordance with our holy father's statement. And I have truthfully recorded these <stories> about what was miraculously accomplished by the divine power through [574] our holy father, as I was an eyewitness <to them> and <even> an agent in some of them.

215. I must now also tell all the <stories> that have come to my knowledge about the benefit that accrues from the mountain <itself> and, indeed, from this very monastery to you who remain in these <places> steadfastly and in a manner pleasing to God, even if this is obvious to those <of you> who do not have impaired spiritual faculties. <I must>, of course, also <speak> about our holy father's foreknowledge of his death, for this was not hidden from him either (how could it be?), even if he did not openly tell this to anyone but <did so> in a cryptic fashion, out of humility.

216. Stephen the eunuch,[853] who was living at the Savior, went up and pressed the father to <let him> go away to Bessai[854] to live there <instead>. But Lazaros replied to him, "If you want to become a tradesman, then go to Bessai!" The brother replied, "What <do you mean>? Did you found a monastery or a shop?"[855] "I founded a monastery," responded the father, "but I said this to you because <Bessai> is well situated for the provision of material goods, for the give and take <of bartering> and trading, for buying and selling, and <for other> such matters with which true monks should not be involved. But, if you <really> want to be saved, <then> persevere on this barren moun-

[853] Cf. Chap. 100, above, which is similar in theme to the present one. It tells of Stephen's desire to move to the monastery of the Resurrection from that of the Savior and recounts the way in which Lazaros dissuaded him from doing so, partly, as here, by extolling the spiritual benefits to be derived by persevering on the mountain.

[854] On the significance of this chapter in respect to Bessai, see the Introduction, section F, p. 37; cf. Malamut, "Bessai," 246–47.

[855] The Greek word καπηλεῖον conveys the same sense of dubious honesty as κάπηλος, translated as "tradesman" (with a pejorative sense) above. It is the place from or in which such a person operates; cf. here, Malamut, "Bessai," 247. Lazaros also responds to a question about the foundation at Bessai in Chap. 245, below. Note that Gregory of Cyprus, in his version of the *vita* (*AASS*, Nov. 3:602E–F), suggests that a monastery, which may perhaps be identified with Bessai (see Janin, *Églises centres,* 244 n. 7), was founded not by Lazaros but by a disgruntled *oikonomos* as an attractive rival to Galesion.

tain,[856] for a person can't readily find such things here. The fathers <of old> always sought out the deserts and most uncomfortable places, not those which had springs and leafy trees and other physical comforts. For this reason they were well able to subordinate their irrational carnal impulses because they did not easily find the materials that beget the passions. For in the Skete,[857] just as the holy fathers themselves predicted, as long as the place was uncomfortable it abounded in the lodgings and dwellings of the monks but, from <the moment> when, one after another, they began to transport <fertile> soil from elsewhere for growing vegetables and set up trees and cisterns in front of their doors, <the Skete> went into decline and was delivered to destruction."[858] By saying this to the brother, the father immediately made him obedient, so that he no longer wished to leave the mountain but <wanted instead> to persevere on it. Then, after he had prostrated himself and sought and received forgiveness from the father, and indeed a blessing too, <Stephen> withdrew.

217. Our elder, the monk Neilos, brought the same request to the father and pestered him about going off to Bessai,[859] but when he was rebuked by Lazaros he abandoned the idea. Once, too, I learned from one of the brothers that the father wanted to go to Bessai.[860] I was upset over this, because if the father moved to Bessai I would be unwilling to leave the mountain and join

[856] As was noted above, the theme of persevering on the mountain and the spiritual benefits to be derived from doing so appears in the parallel Chap. 100. However it also recurs relatively frequently in the *vita* (see especially Chap. 62, but also Chaps. 149, 151–52, 194), and it seems clear from Chaps. 62, 100, 213, and 217, as well as the present one, that it derives directly from Lazaros himself.

[857] This refers to the original Skete (Sketis), a famous early monastic settlement in Egypt. It was established around A.D. 300 in the Wādī Natrūn to the west of the Nile Delta, probably by Makarios the Great. There are still monasteries there to the present day. See further *ODB,* s.v. "Skete," "Wādī Natrūn," "Makarios the Great."

[858] H. G. Evelyn-White (*The Monasteries of the Wâdi'n Natrûn,* pt. 2 [New York, 1932], 154 n. 3) relates this passage to a remark of Abba Makarios, PG 65:264D. Makarios' remark is not particularly close to what Lazaros says here, however, and it thus remains uncertain if it is what he refers to, although I have been unable to identify any other, more obvious, source.

[859] The phrase "pestered . . . Bessai" is a marginal note in the manuscript.

[860] See further below, Chap. 245. It is revealed there that Lazaros was being instructed to leave Galesion for Bessai by the emperor on legal grounds; he was, however, vehemently opposed to the idea and refused to move. Other reactions to this situation by members of his community are also recorded in that chapter.

him there, but nor could I bear <the idea of> the father being there and my being <thus> deprived of him. When I went up and asked him about this, however, the father replied to me, "God willing, neither you nor I will go there but we will end our lives on this mountain." He was silent for a little while and then said again, rather sadly, "I meant that even if I finished the church there, they <still> wouldn't let us <stay here>."[861] Lazaros also said the same thing about the church and the mountain to the monk Laurentios the Stylite after he was pestered by <Laurentios who wanted> to receive permission to leave the mountain if he became unhappy there after Lazaros' death. The father <also> said to him, "If you want to receive forgiveness from God for your sins, <you must> persevere on this mountain." And not only the holy father used to testify that life on the mountain could lead to the greatest possible spiritual benefit, but indeed even the wicked demons themselves unwillingly used to admit this.

218. For <example>, a monk called Jacob left the monastery but then wanted to return to it some time later; while he was on his way back up to the monastery and had already come close to the river,[862] he encountered an old man dressed in rags. This person questioned the monk and, when he had found out about him, prevented him from <making> the ascent to the mountain and the monastery. Instead he advised him to go to Bessai: "That's the monastery for you," he said, "and <anyway> it's better to go there since you won't be able to stay in this place because they don't have sufficient food or even enough water to drink.[863] Moreover, for some reason the venerable old man [Lazaros] gets angry with the brothers and inflicts intolerable beatings on them every day. And so, because they can't stand this, the brothers are leaving every day." When the brother heard this, he no longer had any desire to go up to the mountain, but decided instead to go off to Bessai, in accordance with

[861] Chap. 239 makes clear that the church of the Theotokos at Bessai was begun in response to harassment from the ecclesiastical authorities in Ephesus and the consequent fears on the part of the brothers that they would have nowhere to go if they were turned off the mountain after Lazaros' death. On this dispute and the relationship between Bessai and Galesion, see the Introduction, section F.a, pp. 34–41.

[862] Malamut, "Bessai," 245, suggests this may be the river Caystros.

[863] If the unnamed rival monastery mentioned in Chap. 35 of Gregory of Cyprus' version of the *vita* (*AASS,* Nov. 3:602E) is to be identified with Bessai, it may be significant that it is described as being in a place which abounded in water, in contrast to the frequently stressed barrenness of Galesion; cf. also Janin, *Églises centres,* 244 n. 7.

the Evil One's advice.[864] As he was going on his way, however, <this> thought occurred to him: "I haven't acted <very> well in coming this far and not going up to the father to receive his forgiveness <before I> go off to Bessai." He turned back when he had this thought, but as <soon as> he came close to the river the Evil One met him again and gave him the same advice as before. After this had happened a third time, however, and the Evil One realized <the strength of> Jacob's desire to go up <the mountain>, he eventually made him lose his eyesight.[865] <After this>, whenever <Jacob> turned round and went toward Bessai he was immediately rid of this disability, but whenever he turned back again and wanted to go up to the mountain he was at once blinded.[866] When the monk saw this <happening>, he realized that it was a contrivance of the Evil One and that the person who was advising him against going up to the monastery was not a man but a wicked demon. He thus sat down on the river bank and remained like that, deprived of his eyesight, until some passersby found him. They questioned him and when they learned what had happened to him, took him by the hand and crossed the river. [575] <Jacob> was released from his disability at once and went up to the monastery rejoicing and glorifying God, <and there> he told the father everything that had happened to him.[867]

219. A youth who had an evil spirit <once> came up with some people who were in the habit of coming to the monastery for a blessing, but as soon as he got close to the monastery he was aroused by the demon and, abandoning his companions, came running inside the monastery. He went up to the father's pillar and began to hammer on his little window with his fists while he shouted, "Open up, <you> louse eater, <you> filthy, naked <man>! Open up! Who are you <anyway>? You're not an apostle of Christ <are you>, because you've brought me here against my will? Aren't I <one of> the <demons> who <come> from the mountain and whom you've whipped and sent away

[864] Gregory the Cellarer lessens the impact of the story somewhat by revealing the true identity of the ragged old man to his audience before Jacob has himself deduced this. For other demonic apparitions associated with ragged dress in the *vita,* see Chaps. 51 and, esp., 243.

[865] Compare other stories of the demons blinding monks in Chaps. 52 and 174, above; cf. also, Chap. 46.

[866] Compare here the demonic darkness that besets Neilos in Chap. 46, above.

[867] For commentary on this episode, see Malamut, *Route,* 185–86.

from here by your entreaties to God?" The Evil One said a lot of things, using the young man's tongue, and he constantly kept on yelling, "Open up!" in a loud voice. <Then>, as the father made no response to him at all, he spat on the window and said, "<You> louse eater, you've made the sign of the cross over me, haven't you?" <After this> he came <flying> down from the pillar like a bird and went into the church where he stood in the narthex, and then, when he had been punished enough, flung the youth to the floor. The brothers brought the venerable cross and placed it on his heart, but he had convulsions and heaved himself up from the floor. "Oh, what have you done, Judas?" he said. "Why have you made the cross of Christ appear, and caused us to be despised and mocked like this by <these> wretched little monks?" When the brothers removed the cross, he immediately leapt up and went inside the nave, where he stood in front of the <icon of Christ> Antiphonetes[868] and began to say in a loud voice to the Savior, "How is it that Lazaros the louse eater, who is naked and has nothing, has been able to build this church of yours on this harsh rock?[869] You promised to leave it untroubled until the end. And <yet now>, because of him, you send angels to it every day as a protection for the monks who surround him." The Evil One said a lot of other things and <then> lifted the young man up off the ground and raised him about two cubits into the air before throwing him <back> down onto the ground from there.[870] And

[868] Lit. "someone who responds" or "the guarantor." A famous miracle-working icon of this type was kept at this time in Constantinople in the church of the Virgin at Chalkoprateia; it was also a type favored by the empress Zoe (1028–50) and evidently enjoyed a vogue under her influence during this period in the mid-11th century. See further *ODB,* s.v. "Christ Antiphonetes"; also A. Kazhdan and H. Maguire, "Byzantine Hagiographical Texts as Sources on Art," *DOP* 45 (1991), 15–16; B. Hill, L. James, and D. Smythe, "Zoe: The Rhythm Method of Imperial Renewal," in *New Constantines,* ed. P. Magdalino (Aldershot, 1994), 225.

[869] The use of the phrase "build this church of yours on this harsh rock" (σου τὸν ναὸν τοῦτον ἐν τῇ στερεᾷ ταύτῃ πέτρᾳ οἰκοδομῆσαι) would appear to be deliberately ironic. The adjective στερεός has the basic meaning of "solid" or "firm" and thus, while the demon complains of the monastery being built in such a barren and harsh place, it nevertheless testifies unwittingly to the fact that Lazaros' church is, like the entire church of Christ, founded on a solid rock. The Byzantine audience would hence see here an obvious allusion to the famous passage in Mt. 16:18, "*You are Peter* (πέτρος) *and on this rock* (πέτρα) *I will found* (οἰκοδομήσω) *my church.*"

[870] The cubit (*pechys*) was a unit of linear measurement which ranged between 46.8 cm and 68.5 cm, depending on the circumstances in which it was being used. See *ODB,*

so he stopped yapping. Thus the Evil One, against his will and plainly for all to see, proclaimed the truth for the benefit of those who were listening, even though this was not his intention. For that most Evil One thought that with such words he might deceive the father into saying or doing something that would lead to pride; but he engineered <all> this in vain.

220. Once too, on another occasion, when someone of this sort was standing in front of the pillar and saying such things, one of the people standing there asked the father about what <this person> was saying. He replied to his questioner, "It's a demon who's talking nonsense, so one shouldn't pay attention to it." Lazaros was thus always covered all over with the armor of humility, so that he hated and avoided praise and eulogies in the same way that another person might turn away from recriminations and insults.[871] One of the monks thus once wrote a hymn on him, but when the father learned about this, he immediately summoned the brother and asked him for the hymn. When the <monk> denied <having> it, because he was frightened, Lazaros threatened him, saying that if he found it anywhere he would order it to be burned on his head, <but> he then released him from further interrogation.

221. But I do not want to say any more about these matters <now>, seeing that my work is becoming rather long. Instead I will change the <subject> of my narrative to <stories> concerning our holy father's foreknowledge of his death. Our holy father's brother, Kyris Ignatios, who is now our superior, was appointed steward[872] at the house of Philippikos[873] by the father; but then, because Philippikos and some other brothers took offense at him and the holy

s.v. "Pechys." The youth is thus flung to the ground from a height of some three or four feet.

[871] Cf. above, Chap. 14.

[872] On this office, see above, Chap. 49.

[873] The implication is that this Philippikos was in charge of some sort of subsidiary monastery on the mountain, a fact which may explain the circumstances of his serious disagreement with Lazaros; Janin (*Églises centres,* 245 and n. 3) points out that this establishment must have been reasonably important if it had its own steward. In contrast, Morris (*Monks,* 215) takes *oikos* ("house") to refer to a farmstead here; it is unlikely, however, that Lazaros' brother Ignatios, whom he was clearly grooming as his successor on Galesion, would have been appointed *oikonomos* of such a place or, if it was merely a farm, that his appointment would have provoked the serious dispute it evidently did.

father because they suspected that the father was doing this from nepotism, <Ignatios> resigned from this position and also wanted to withdraw from the monastery and go to Kampsai[874] because of these problems.[875] However, the father would not allow him either to leave the monastery or go to Kampsai, but instead he urged him to stay at Bessai and make that his resting place,[876] so that he might live there as he wanted to. <Ignatios> was not convinced <to do this, so> the father said to him again, "Go and do as I tell you, because you're going to be in charge of this monastery before very long." Which did indeed happen. When he heard the father <say> this, <Ignatios> obeyed and immediately went where Lazaros ordered him.[877] Again, when the father sent Pachomios and Gabriel and <some> other brothers to the city [Constantinople] and elsewhere in connection with certain affairs of the monastery,[878] they were afraid that he might die during their absence, since he was scarcely <still> alive then, so they went up to him and let him know this. Lazaros, however, told them to go and not worry about this at all. "That certainly won't happen until you've all returned," he said to them. Which is what did happen.[879] When he had said this and had <thus> persuaded them <to go>, he said a prayer as usual and dismissed them. And <then>, after the departure of these brothers, when Lazaros was sending the monk Kosmas, called the Jerusalemite, to the

[874] A monastery of Kampsai is otherwise unknown but it was presumably not on the mountain; cf. Janin, *Églises centres,* 245 n. 4. The name, which means "baskets," might indicate the means of access to a particularly inaccessible foundation. A place called Kampsa is recorded on the western side of the Kassandra peninsula in the Chalkidike (*RE* 10:1842), but it is unlikely that it is referred to here.

[875] Ignatios' wish to leave the monastery altogether is presumably prompted by the seriousness of the hostility toward him, as can be seen from the attempt made on his life at the time of his brother's death; see above, Chap. 202; cf. 193.

[876] The word ἀνάπαυσις also contains the sense of a place where one may find tranquillity and respite from trouble.

[877] Ignatios is mentioned in Chap. 52, above, as still being at Bessai sometime after Lazaros' death.

[878] On the missions to Constantinople mentioned in this chapter, as well as others at or after the end of Lazaros' life (cf. below, Chaps. 223, 245, 246, and 248), see the Introduction, section F.b, pp. 46–47. There is no evidence for suggesting as Thomas (Thomas and Hero, *Foundation Documents,* 149) does that this Gabriel was Lazaros' steward.

[879] Chap. 246 reveals that Lazaros fell into his final illness as soon as they returned.

city [Constantinople] with a letter for the emperor,[880] he said to him, "Take the monk Ignatios with you too, and tell the emperor to make him <the next> superior." When the brother heard these words, he was terrified and said to Lazaros, "What <do you mean> by saying this? You're not going to die, <are you>? For if that's the case, I won't [576] leave the monastery at all." "Go," said the father to him, "for that certainly won't happen until you've all returned." <Then>, when <Kosmas> was about to go and went up to receive a blessing from Lazaros, he also asked him whether Kyris Ignatios was going to accompany him, as he had told him previously. The father replied to him, "You go, and leave him; for if God wants him to be the superior, He'll certainly make him <it>."[881] After he had said this to <Kosmas>, he at once prayed over him and <then> dismissed him.

222. In addition to his illness at this time, another trial was inflicted upon Lazaros by his tempter, and this was a triple one, that is to say, by lice, bugs, and ants. For the former proliferated into such a multitude that they were scurrying about on the outside of the pillar; while the ants in turn came out of the oak tree, which stood some way away from the pillar, and got inside the pillar by running up through the water cistern,[882] as if they were being sent to it and guided <there> by someone. The brothers tried very hard to keep them out and devised <all sorts of things>, but <in the end>, as they were unable <to do so>, they cut the tree down, even though the father did not give them permission to do this. The brothers cut it down, against the father's wishes, because they saw how much he was suffering from <the insects>.

223. When the father was still just barely alive, I went up to <see> him. "Oh!" he said to me, "If only you could stop the brothers from coming up to <see> me instead of letting them <do so>, for I can't give each one of them an answer <any more> because of my illness." I said to him, "But, father, the brothers are afraid of you suddenly dying and thus leaving the monastery

[880] Since these events take place at the very end of Lazaros' life, this must be Constantine IX Monomachos (1042–55).

[881] Malamut (*Route,* 160) mistakenly suggests that Ignatios actually went to Constantinople to be confirmed in the position of superior.

[882] This is the obvious meaning of the phrase λάκκος τοῦ ὕδατος, although Delehaye (*Stylites,* clx) suggests that it may perhaps refer to a waste pipe ("tuyau de dégagement"); cf. also Chap. 81, which mentions an area in the pillar in which he used to relieve himself.

without having issued a rule[883] nor having made any arrangements for the <other> two monasteries." "They mustn't be afraid of anything of the sort," the father said, "for there'll be a rule and the emperor and the patriarch will see it."[884] He also made the same declaration to Laurentios the Stylite: "You'll see the rule with an imperial seal <on it> after my death." And behold, just as the holy father foretold it, both to me and to the monk Laurentios, we do now possess this, sealed with an imperial seal, and the emperor and the patriarch did see it and did take <the matter> in hand.[885] And even though some kind of deception has <now> taken place and the second<born son> has received the blessing instead of the firstborn,[886] nevertheless for a time the one who was blessed as the firstborn was really blessed and our holy father's statement about this was not mistaken. The brothers <thus> went to the city [Constantinople], saw the emperor, and settled everything satisfactorily, for they found that the emperor was agreeable to their <requests> in every way, even though he had been irritated with them a little while before on account of the letter that the father had sent to him with the monk Kosmas, which had reproved his wicked and unreasonable deeds. . . . [887]

[883] The Greek word used here is διατύπωσις (*diatyposis*); the same term is used throughout this chapter and also below, Chap. 246, for the rule Lazaros actually dictates.

[884] Or perhaps, "are going to provide this"; for the verb ὁράω used in such a way, see Liddell-Scott-Jones, *Lexicon,* s.v., II.2; they cite Gen. 22:8 as an example. The verb θεάομαι, which appears just below in the present chapter, would then presumably be used in the same sense of "provide" or "see to." Janin (*Églises centres,* 246) understands the present passage to indicate a visa.

[885] Or, more literally, "the emperor and the patriarch saw it and held it in their hands."

[886] Cf. Gen. 27, which recounts how the aged Isaac was tricked into blessing his younger son Jacob instead of his firstborn son Esau. It is unclear to what exactly Gregory the Cellarer is referring here, although it is probably the dispute between Galesion and Bessai over the legitimate succession to Lazaros' tradition, a dispute which must still have been ongoing at the time the *vita* was composed; see the Introduction, section F.a, p. 40.

[887] For discussion of this passage in relation to the various missions to Constantinople at or after the end of Lazaros' life, see the Introduction, section F.b, pp. 46–47.

Infuriatingly, there is a substantial break in the manuscript at this point. Most of f. 253 and the whole of f. 253v are blank. The end of Chap. 223 is thus lost and other material is evidently missing too, for Chap. 224 begins in the middle of a description of

224. < . . . > When he had done these things he would stand for a short time, while he sang and prayed, until the *semantron* sounded for church; and so the vigil was completed as if in sequence, as <I have> said. This rule remained in force down to our own <day>, but I do not know if it is still observed now.[888] These <then are the details> concerning the regular vigil <as it was kept> by the brothers who lived alone. As for <the vigil> in church, if anyone happened to fall asleep while they were standing up and singing, and so stood <there> without singing, the father used to order another brother to give him a slap; when he had been woken up in this way, he would go on singing.

225. This being the case, a monk called Neilos, who was a young man then but who has now grown old, tells the <story of how> he, more than anyone, used to be overwhelmed by sleep. As a result he also used to be slapped more than the others, and so began to be roused <to anger> against the father. But the father summoned him (whether he was inspired by God in this <matter>, or realized what <was happening> from certain signs or <simply> did so through his own good judgment) and said, "Whenever you see me dozing, wake me up by striking me with the reed pole." For there was a reed pole standing there for use with the candles.[889] When <Neilos> heard

---

vigil practices. Gregory the Cellarer has evidently completed his section on Lazaros' foreknowledge of his death (see above, Chap. 221) and passed on to consideration of other matters to do with Lazaros' gift of insight and good judgment as this was applied to members of his community; although not apparent in Chap. 224, this theme emerges in the following chapter, which runs on from it, and continues in one form or another to Chap. 232.

[888] The lack of knowledge admitted here by Gregory the Cellarer is interesting since it would appear to have important implications for his situation at the time the *vita* is being written; unfortunately, the fact that the context of this chapter has been lost makes it impossible to evaluate satisfactorily.

[889] This is the way Delehaye (*Stylites,* cxii) understands this rather awkward passage; he thus takes the reed pole (κάλαμος) as a sort of long taper or spill, presumably used for lighting candles high up in the church. He further infers from this that the incident must have taken place inside the church and thus that Lazaros could observe, and be observed by, those taking part in the services by means of a second little window in his pillar opening into the building; see further, Introduction, section C, p. 18. The fact that Lazaros *summons* Neilos to him here, however, may suggest to the contrary that neither the interview nor the setting of the incident was in the church. In that case the reed pole in question could perhaps have been used for lighting candles in front of the icons of the archangels that stood before his pillar (Chap. 226). Or perhaps it has no liturgical connotation at all, for the word κηρίον can also signify a honeycomb as well

this, he received Lazaros' instruction with joy, and said to himself, "The time has come when I can pay him back for the slaps I've received on his orders." And indeed, when the vigil was performed as usual, this man, who previously had been sleepy, was <now> alert and wide awake.[890] And so, as soon as he saw the father dozing—for one could never see him sleeping on purpose because in the daytime Lazaros was being bothered by many lay people and monks, and at night he was keeping vigil, either alone or with the brothers, and, just as it has been written that the holy Arsenios would put the sun behind him, whenever he was going to stand for a vigil, and would stand <there> singing until he saw it in front of him again,[891] so the father would conduct the vigils with the brothers in the same way. For this reason, Lazaros, who exercised so much power himself over nature, would be overpowered by nature and would fall into a doze for a short time. So (as has been <already> said), when the aforesaid young man saw Lazaros dozing, he immediately ran and grabbed the reed pole and went off <as> fast <as he could> to strike him. But one of the brothers, who was <also> named Lazaros, saw him rushing to strike the father in this bold and shameless way; he reached out his hand and stopped <Neilos'> assault by holding onto the reed pole, and he berated him severely for his insolence. <Neilos>, however, having failed in his objective, turned his anger <instead> on the man who had stopped him, because he had prevented him from doing what he so badly wanted <to do> to the father. But he did these things because he was young then and more rash in his impulses, and was <thus> driven by foolishness. Now that he has grown old, however, he has realized the wickedness[892] of his action [577] to such an extent that he <now> blesses the man who prevented him and, because he blames himself, confesses his irrational irritation against the father to everyone, and seeks to receive <their> forgiveness.

226. The monk Meletios, whom I have mentioned many times, was sent

as a wax candle; the sentence could thus be translated "For there was a reed pole standing there which was used for <getting> honeycombs." In that case the κάλαμος would not be a flimsy reed but a long and reasonably sturdy pole, perhaps a bamboo cane. On methods of collecting wild honey at this time, cf. Chap. 13.

890 Cf. 1 Pet. 5:8.

891 Arsenios the Great (354–445) was a scholar and tutor to the sons of Theodosios I who eventually retired to Egypt to become a notable hermit. The passage in question may be found in the *Apophthegmata,* Arsenius, 30 (PG 65:97C; Ward, *Sayings,* 12); a similar practice is ascribed to Symeon the Stylite the Elder in Theodoret, *Hist Rel.*, 26.24.

892 The word ἀτοπία in Greek also carries the sense of absurdity and impropriety.

down below by the father on some tasks. He returned from there in the evening and went up to <see> the father; but while he was standing in front of the pillar at the little window and making his report to the father <about the errand> on which he had been sent out, Lazaros pressed him to confess in detail everything which had happened. <Meletios>, however, did not want to tell the father one of the things that had happened to him, hiding it like a snake in its lair. "I'll make my confession about this tomorrow," he said. But as the father would not dismiss him until he actually did confess this one <bad> thought, <Meletios> was trapped and, as there was nothing else he could do, he divulged this too. As soon as his confession of the <bad> thought had come to an end, there was a sudden crash, so that the brother thought the icons that stood there had fallen to the ground,[893] and he thus called to the monk Cyril to bring a lamp. But at the moment the noise occurred, the father let out a shout, "Begone to the darkness, Devil!" When the brother brought a lamp, they saw that the icons were standing in their proper place and nothing was lying below. The father was asked by the brother what had made the noise. "It was the demon," he said, "which had been preventing your confession of the <bad> thought." After the monk Meletios had gone down, the monk Cyril came up, and he too asked the father about this. The father replied to him, "It was the demon which had been preventing him from confessing his <bad> thoughts. When it saw that I'd forced him to confess everything, it changed itself into the shape of a weasel[894] and started to come inside my pillar through the little window. But when I made the sign of the cross over it, it immediately fell out of the pillar onto the ground like lightning[895] and made that noise."

227. A layman, who was distinguished from most people by his handsome <appearance> and physical strength, <once> came up to <see> the father. His name was Damianos, <or> so he falsely said, and he further claimed to be the nephew of Thalassenos.[896] This man begged the father profusely to

[893] For a further reference to these icons that stood before Lazaros' pillar and which were evidently of the archangels, see below, Chap. 253.

[894] Following Delehaye's emendation of μυγάλης, "shrew," which appears in the manuscript, to γαλῆς "weasel" or "pole cat" (or, perhaps, as in modern Greek, simply "cat"). This certainly makes more sense of the following sentence, for it is hard to imagine a shrew making the sort of noise which was heard by Meletios and Cyril.

[895] Cf. Lk. 10:18.

[896] Thalassenos is almost certainly a form of the name Dalassenos, which belonged to a powerful family of this period. The family first came to prominence in the later part of the 10th century and occupied important positions, especially in the East, where

tonsure him at once, but he <soon> realized that the father would not agree to this, although it was clear that Lazaros had never refused to perform this rite on anyone else.[897] So, what did he do? He went down to the Theologian [Ephesus] and found some men of the same type as himself. He <then> got them to go up to the father and look for him, allegedly because they had been sent by the emperor to do so. Thus, a few days after he had come <back> up, these men came up looking for him, just as <Damianos> had instructed them. When he saw them descending[898] on <the monastery, Damianos> went up to

---

several members, including the originator of the clan, Damianos, held the post of governor of Antioch. In the earlier 11th century the most notable of the Dalassenoi was Constantine who, despite losing favor at court and being arrested and imprisoned under Michael IV (1034–41), was nevertheless evidently almost chosen as the new husband of the empress Zoe in 1042 in place of Constantine IX Monomachos (see also below, Chap. 230). The family continued to hold prominent offices throughout the century; one of its best-known members is Anna Dalassene, who married John, the brother of Isaac I Komnenos, and was the mother of Alexios I. The present man—who was an imposter, as the text makes quite clear (although it nowhere suggests why, in that case, he should have wished so desperately to be tonsured as a monk)—was likely impersonating a real member of the family, probably the eldest son of either Theophylact or Romanos, brothers of the above-mentioned Constantine and sons of the original Damianos. See especially here J.-C. Cheynet and J.-F. Vannier, *Études prosopographiques* (Paris, 1986), 75–115, although Cheynet mistakenly assumes that the Damianos of the *vita* is the genuine article (his no. 9, pp. 88–89); cf. idem, *Pouvoir,* 226 n. 151, 295 n. 66. See also *ODB,* s.v. "Dalassenos" and "Dalassene, Anna." Psellos (*Chron.,* 6:12) also comments upon the handsomeness of Constantine Dalassenos. Malamut (*Route,* 202–3) also discusses this episode.

The date of the incident is unclear, although its position here, toward the end of the *vita* and alongside other events which happened near the end of Lazaros' life, may suggest that it is contemporary with them. Since the man's story was evidently found to be credible, it must relate to a period when the Dalassenos family was out of favor. The most obvious period for this, following the arrest and exile of Constantine Dalassenos in August 1034, may be too early. Another likely occasion would perhaps be that of the plot by Constantine's brothers and another of his nephews, Adrian, against Michael IV in 1038–39, following which the conspirators were exiled (see Cheynet, *Pouvoir,* no. 41, p. 47), but if the incident is contemporary with those around it in the *vita* then it may refer to general suspicion of the family following Constantine's unsuccessful bid to marry Zoe and the rise to the imperial office of his rival Constantine IX Monomachos in 1042.

[897] I am grateful to an anonymous reader for suggesting this translation.

[898] The implication would seem to be that these men are approaching the monastery from above, rather than by the normal route from Ephesus below, presumably to make their activity look like a real attempt to take Damianos by surprise and arrest him.

the father as if he was terrified and, trembling, said to him, "Look, father, those people coming here are coming for me; they want to arrest me and take me back to the emperor." And he pleaded with Lazaros to tonsure him that very minute, before the men should descend on <the monastery>. The father was scarcely convinced <to do so>, but he nevertheless summoned some people and told them to take the man away to a secret place and then tonsure him and put the <monastic> habit on him. For, as his life later showed, the man was not worthy to be invested <with the habit> by the father or <to have this done> inside the church. The men supposedly dispatched by the emperor to search for <the fellow> arrived after the brothers had done this according to the father's orders; but, when they saw him wearing the monastic <habit>, they let him be and went away <again>. <Damianos> spent some time in the monastery, and was treated with respect by all the brothers and by the holy father himself since he was believed to be the nobleman he said he was. But although he was being <treated> with respect, <the fellow> took no notice of this; <instead> he devised a wicked plan by which he persuaded the father to send some of the brothers with him so that, as he falsely suggested, they might accompany him to his home, sell off all his possessions,[899] receive their <monetary> value, and then return to the monastery again with him. When they reached the vicinity of Amorion,[900] however, this <Damianos> gave them the slip. The brothers looked hard for him but, when they were unable to find him, they left there and came <back> to the monastery, loudly criticizing the father. Philippikos did so especially, for he was there too. Some time later the father learned that this <Damianos> had changed back again into secular garb and was in Chonai.[901] By means of a personal letter <that he sent> with Barnabas and Nicholas Paxamades, he made <this> clear to him: "You should know, brother, that you will soon come to a bad end unless you return to the monas-

Chaps. 64 and 207 show that it was possible to get to the monastery from above and from the north.

[899] Cf. Mk. 10:21; Lk. 12:33, 18:22; Acts 2:45, 4:34–35.

[900] Amorion is the modern Hisar, near the town of Emirdağ in central Asia Minor, some 225 miles east of Galesion. It became important as a military center in the 7th century and gained in repute under the "Amorian" dynasty, founded in 820 by Michael II, who came from the place. It was destroyed by the Arabs in 838 although, as a result, it also became famous for its Forty-Two Martyrs who refused to convert to Islam. At this time it was a bishopric but otherwise unimportant. See further *ODB*, s.v. "Amorion."

[901] On this place, see above, Chap. 6.

tery again and propitiate God, Whom you have angered by your rejection of the angelic habit,[902] through genuine repentance and by donning once more the same holy habit." When the man received the holy father's letter, he read it and <then> replied to him through the brothers, "If it is God's will, I will come to you after Easter. And whatever you want <me to do>, I shall do it." So the brothers returned and reported this to the father, but he replied to them, "Woe is he! What has become of him? Because he didn't come with you right away he won't last as long as Easter, nor <will he> ever come here again." The father said this about him because he was inspired by God, and, not long after, his words were fulfilled. [578] For the wretched man was murdered with a knife by his own manservant in the second week of Lent, and thus met a wretched end in accordance with our holy father's prophecy.

228. Another man was also tonsured by the father with the same <sort of> intention as the previous fellow, or even worse.[903] He too deceived the father and, taking one of the brothers with him, went off as far as Phygela[904] to find a ship and cross over to Crete; for he falsely claimed to come from there although, in fact, as it subsequently emerged, he was from the Phialitai.[905] Anyway, after he reached <Phygela>, as I have said, he also gave the brother the slip.[906] The brother looked hard for him but, as he was unable to find him, he too returned to the father. Some time later the man himself returned <from there> and came back to the monastery and the father; <now, however>, he was decked out in the apostolic habit <even though> he had only been tonsured by the father as a *mandyotes.*[907] He was asked by the father,

[902] Although his expression may be used as a technical term for the habit reserved for the higher grade of monk (see above, Chaps. 9 and 130), it probably refers to the "monastic habit" in general here.

[903] See above, Chap. 204, for the suggestion that the first monk of that chapter is to be identified with the central figure of this section of the *vita* (Chaps. 228–30).

[904] On the port of Phygel(l)a, see Chap. 75 n. 345.

[905] It is not certain what place of origin this indicates, although it could conceivably mean that the man actually came from Phygela itself. It less likely refers to Phialia (modern Phigaleia) in the west central Peloponnese.

[906] Malamut (*Route,* 278) understands this to mean that this man gave his companion the slip after they had gone to Crete.

[907] The *mandyas,* from which this term derives, was a cloak worn over the basic monastic tunic. It would seem from the passage here and from the distinction made elsewhere in the *vita* between different types of monks and their habits (Chaps. 9 and 130)

"Where have you been?" but instead of telling the truth and asking forgiveness for having lied before when he deceived the father, he now piled wickedness upon wickedness[908] and added a lie to a lie. "I went and took all my <possessions>," he said, "and put them in a boat; but, as I was making the voyage over here, <we> encountered pirates about halfway through it and I lost everything. However, through your holy prayer, I was able to escape their clutches and, as you see, I've returned unhurt to the monastery." The father, who knew that the <fellow's> excuse was a fabrication, smiled and said to him, "Glory be to the holy God Who has saved you from such trouble and has caused you to be delivered safely to the monastery again." Some time later he went to the father and asked to be given another brother so that they might go to the Western regions on a mission.[909] At first the father would not agree, but said to him, "Sit in your cell, brother. For this won't do you any good." But then, after he had been pressured and pestered a great deal by this man, Lazaros gave him the monk Meletios[910] and let him travel where he wanted. He strictly ordered him not to embezzle any <funds> at all from this mission, however, and said, "If people who are sent out on a mission follow the orders of the person who sends them out and do not embezzle <funds> from it, God will rank them with the apostles. But if they disregard the orders of the person who has sent them and then, when they have embezzled <funds>, lie <about it>, they will

---

that the term *mandyotes* in this context must indicate a novice, since the "apostolic" habit in which this man reappears is evidently proper to the lower rank of professed monks, rather than to the superior one whose members wore the "angelic" habit. It would thus be equivalent to the "clothing of submission" mentioned in Chap. 130, and it may perhaps be surmised that people of this rank wore the *mandyas* over ordinary lay clothing. Delehaye points out that Ducange knows the term and defines it, s.v. Μανδύας, as *monachus parvi habitus;* at least this does not contradict the implication of the present passage, even if it does not give the same depth of meaning. Compare the similar passage in Chap. 240 (cf. also Chap. 242), and see further *ODB,* s.v. "Mandyas," "Novice." Malamut (*Route,* 278) understands the first part of this passage as indicating that the man returned "richly dressed."

[908] This is an adaptation of Ps. 68 (69):27.

[909] The Greek word διακονία has generally been translated in this work as "task," but in the context of this chapter as a whole it would also seem to hold the additional connotations contained in the English word "mission." The following narrative certainly makes it clear that the brother did plenty of preaching, although not quite on the lines Lazaros intended.

[910] His return from this mission seems to be discussed in Chap. 230, below.

be condemned along with Ananias and Sapheira,[911] with Gehazi, [912] and with Judas."[913] After the father had said this, he gave the man his blessing and let him go on his way with the brother. The <fellow> obeyed these orders and warnings until he had gone down the mountain but, after that, who could recount everything that wretched man did <which led> to the destruction of his own soul? For he used to say, "The father who has sent me out on this mission is a prophet and, because he has the gift of prognosis and precognition, he predicts to all the people who come to him what will befall each <of them> in the future. And so, because he has also given me this gift[914] through prayer, he has sent me out to teach and to prophesy to everyone about everything."[915] By saying this <sort of> thing he persuaded almost everyone that this was <indeed> the case, especially when they heard the father's name <mentioned>. And <in fact>, when he was questioned by them, either about past or future matters, he often spoke the truth in what he said, whether the demons were arranging this, so that he might believe them once and for all, or whether this happened <purely> by chance. So, because he had been deceived by the wicked demons with such lying statements, he simply became another false prophet.

229. Traveling in this way, <the fellow> reached the region of Bulgaria, where the rebellion of Dolianos was then under way.[916] So, when he had

[911] Acts 5:1–11. Cf. also above, Chap. 148. The same verb translated as "embezzle" in this chapter (νοσφίζω) is also used of their actions in "keeping back" some of the proceeds from the sale of their property.

[912] Gehazi figures in 2 Ki. 4–5. See Chap. 204; cf. also Chap. 231.

[913] Mt. 27:3–5; Acts 1:16–20.

[914] Lit. "grace."

[915] There seems to be deliberate alliteration in this speech in the Greek on the sounds "pr" and "p." I have attempted to preserve this as far as possible.

[916] The reference is to the rebellion of Peter Deljan (rendered in Greek as Deleanos or Dolianos). This man, claiming to be a grandson of the tsar Samuel, led a major revolt against Byzantine control in Bulgaria in 1040–41. The revolt also spread to much of northern and central Greece and seems to have spawned widespread political unrest, both against the ailing emperor Michael IV and his powerful brother, John the Orphanotrophos, who had introduced unpopular tax reforms. It is unclear exactly where the monk was when the episode recorded in this chapter took place; although he could have been in one of the towns in central Greece seized by Deljan, the fact that it is said to have been in "the region of Bulgaria" makes it unlikely. On the other hand, the place could be Dyrrachium, which was taken by one of Deljan's generals, Kaukanos

reached this <area> and had gone into a town <there>, the *strategos*[917] of the place, who had heard about him, sent <someone> out and summoned the monk to him. When <the monk> came, <the *strategos*>, who was about to go to war with the Bulgarians, asked him when it would be good to undertake this affair. He replied, "Let me <have> tonight, and I'll tell you about it tomorrow." In the morning he went to the *strategos* and said, "If you want to achieve victory, you should engage them on Sunday." For it was then Wednesday. The <*strategos*> believed the false prophet's words and proclaimed this to the whole town too; and <then> everyone could be seen flocking to the imposter and treating him with great respect and reverence, as though he <really> were a holy man and a prophet. When Sunday arrived, the *strategos* took his whole army and went to the monk; then, after they had shown <due> reverence to him and had received his blessing, they went out of the city with the *strategos* at their head. When the engagement took place, however, the <*strategos*> was the first to fall and, at this sight, the others immediately turned and fled; the Bulgarians pursued them and killed almost all of them. The survivors and the remaining townspeople searched for the monk so that they could lynch him, but he found this out from someone, gave everyone the slip, and left the town. He <then> went off to the Bulgarians, and there was somehow introduced to Dolianos; [579] he stayed with him, encouraging him with his deceitful words, until he [Dolianos] had been blinded by Alousianos.[918] <The fellow> thus fled again from there and continued to go from place to place, leading <people> astray and going astray <himself>.[919]

(Skylitzes, *Hist.*, 411), following the elimination of Deljan's fellow rebel and rival Tichomir, who had been based there. On the religious atmosphere surrounding events in this rebellion, see, e.g., Skylitzes, 413–14 on the siege of Thessalonike; cf. also A. Miltenova and M. Kajmakamova, "The Uprising of Petar Deljan (1040–1041) in a New Old Bulgarian Source," *BS* 8 (1986), 227–40. Further on the rebellion in general, see Cheynet, *Pouvoir,* no. 45, p. 49 (cf. nos. 46–48, pp. 50–51), and pp. 388–89; also *ODB,* s.v. "Deljan, Peter." Cf. on this episode in the *vita,* Ševčenko, "Eastern Provinces," 726.

917 That is, the military governor. On this office, see above, Chap. 87.

918 Son of the Bulgarian tsar John Vladislav, this Alousianos joined Deljan's rebellion in 1040 and became co-ruler of the rebel forces. He quarreled with his partner during the siege of Thessalonike, however, and took the opportunity provided by the expedition of the Byzantine emperor Michael IV in 1041 to blind Deljan and change sides. See further, Cheynet, *Pouvoir,* no. 51, p. 52, and p. 388; *ODB,* s.v. "Alousianos."

919 There is a play on words here in the Greek between πλανῶν ("leading astray") and πλανώμενος ("going" or "being led astray").

230. When the people <started> searching for <this fellow> in order to lynch him, the monk who was with him[920] left the city and returned to the monastery where he reported everything to the father. Some time later the man himself came to the monastery and was generously admitted by the father. He stayed in the monastery for a short time, but <then> again persuaded the father, by assertions and dreadful oaths, to send him to the city [Constantinople] on a mission for the monastery, along with another brother. <The fellow> also slipped away from this <brother>, however, and went on alone; he deceived a lot of people with his false words, and did not return to the monastery again until the father had gone up to the <pillar of the> holy Resurrection,[921] and then <only> reluctantly and unwillingly. While he was traveling around like this and was in the vicinity of Smyrna,[922] he learned that they were <in the process of> declaring Monomachos emperor, so he embarked on a ship and went to Mitylene, for <Monomachos> had been banished there.[923] He forged

[920] This is presumably still Meletios; see above, Chap. 228.

[921] This statement is important in providing a rough indication of the date of Lazaros' move to the monastery of the Resurrection, something which is not otherwise discussed in the *vita* as it now stands. See further the Introduction, section B, p. 13, where it is suggested that it may have taken place in late 1041 or, more probably, sometime in 1042. As is noted there, it is unclear how this monk's mission may relate, if at all, to that of Isaiah and Neophytos (above, Chap. 102), who were sent to Constantinople by Lazaros in April 1042. It may appear tempting to suggest an identification of the present monk with the Isaiah of Chaps. 198–200 (and perhaps that of Chap. 102), given that there are some quite striking similarities in the dubious conduct of their role as emissary from Galesion (especially if the present monk is indeed the man referred to at the start of Chap. 204 and thus, like Isaiah, fell into fornication after embezzlement); there is, moreover, the coincidence of timing here. The information provided on the background of each man differs, however, and this, together with the fact that Gregory the Cellarer does *not* name the present monk or the one of Chap. 204, would seem to rule out this possibility, intriguing as it might be.

[922] Smyrna, modern Izmir, was some 40 miles to the north of Galesion on the west coast of Asia Minor. It was a major naval base which, like Phygela, grew in importance as Ephesus declined. See further, *ODB*, s.v. "Smyrna."

[923] The future Constantine IX Monomachos had been exiled to Mytilene (modern Lesbos) by Michael IV (see Cheynet, *Pouvoir*, no. 39, p. 46), but the latter died in December 1041, shortly after he had returned in triumph from his victory over Peter Deljan's rebels. He was succeeded by his nephew Michael V Kalaphates, who was himself overthrown in the troubles of April 1042 (on which see above, Chap. 102). Constantine was called back to the capital in early June 1042 and was crowned emperor on the

a letter, as though it was from the father, and gave this to him. The gist of the letter was as <follows>: "God has revealed to me that you will be ruling as emperor in a few days time; and behold, what God has disclosed to me, I have <now> made known to you. But you must <be sure to> remember us when you are in power." Monomachos received the letter and read it; he <then> took the monk aside and said to him, "Father, do *you* know what the holy father wrote to me?" "Yes," he replied, "I know <what he said>, for he also told me to tell you this by word of mouth." Then <Monomachos> said to him, "Go and say to the holy father, 'If it's God's will, and what you have written does <indeed> happen to me, <then> write to me when you learn this and whatever you want I shall do it for your monastery.'" The monk, who was a <real> rogue, said to him, "I know the father will send me to you again, but how will I be able to see your imperial majesty?" Then <Monomachos> summoned his manservant and said to him, "If God wills it, and what the holy father has written to me does take place, and I am <indeed> ruling as emperor, you must <be sure> to recognize this monk, so that if he ever comes and you see him, you are to bring him in to me." After he had said this, <Monomachos> dismissed <the fellow>, who embarked on a boat and returned to Smyrna again. Some days later, when he learned that they had made Monomachos emperor, <this monk> left Smyrna by boat and arrived at the city [Constantinople] where, with the assistance of the emperor's manservant, he was granted an audience with him. When <Monomachos> saw <the monk>, he received him with great joy; he gave him a great quantity of gold and some spices,[924] and sent him back rejoicing to the father with a letter. So <the monk> left the emperor's presence and, after he had embarked on a ship, went to Smyrna again. . . . [925]

---

twelfth of that month after he had married the empress Zoe (see Cheynet, *Pouvoir,* no. 60, pp. 56–57).

[924] The Greek word ἄρωμα ("spices") may also mean "incense" or "perfumes." It probably does not refer to "arable land" here (cf. Liddell-Scott-Jones, *Lexicon*, s.v. [B]), a usage attested only in ancient Greek, although this certainly would have interesting implications for the details and timing of Monomachos' support for Galesion and/or Bessai. Gregory of Cyprus (chap. 30, *AASS,* Nov. 3:600D) understands it in the former sense and so does Malamut (*Route,* 279), although earlier (p. 154) she takes it as "land."

[925] Infuriatingly again, there is a considerable gap here at this crucial juncture in the manuscript; some two-thirds of f. 262 together with all of ff. 263–263v are blank. For

231. Now, if some busybody should comment on the fact that the father, despite being holy, used to admit such men <to the monastery>, <or> again on the fact that he did not know he was being duped by them, I do not think that person has any real reason to be puzzled <by this>.[926] Thus Gehazi, who was with the prophet Elisha, was an avaricious and perverse man,[927] while Judas, who was with Christ, was also <such> an avaricious man and a crook that, for this <very> reason, he became a traitor to his own teacher and ultimately even resorted to committing suicide by hanging himself. Again, we hear of many such people at the time of the apostles, but no one who has any sense will find fault because of this with the holy men with whom those evil ones were associating, nor will he hold them partly to blame for the wickedness of those <bad> men. On the contrary, he will rather praise and marvel at the holy men, but will deem the wicked ones <truly> wretched, because they were not willing to change their evil disposition despite <living> alongside such <good> men. Anyway, the father's <powers> of prophesying and foreseeing or of searching the hearts of those who came to him were not absolute; for that is a property that belongs by nature to God alone, and to those to whom He reveals <these things> when He wishes. As for the father, it was <enough for him> to keep, as far as he could, the commandment of Christ which says, "*Him who comes to me I will not cast out,*"[928] and to be kind and long suffering and patient with those who do <us> injuries.[929]

232. The monk Kosmas Philippikos, however, whom I have often mentioned, was assailed by many evil thoughts against the father when he saw such things <taking place>. And so, because he could not bear being disturbed like this by these thoughts, he went up and said to Lazaros, "Have the fathers really ordained, as <is now the case here>, that if someone comes <to you>, you should admit <him to the monastery> and tonsure him right away without <further> investigation, especially young boys and country bumpkins who

detailed discussion of possible interpretations of this chapter and how it may relate to the history of Lazaros' foundations, see the Introduction, section F.b, pp. 42–45.

[926] Cf. the reference to Philippikos' criticism of Lazaros in this context in Chaps. 227 and 232; cf. also the criticisms voiced in Chaps. 143, 152, 239, and 240.

[927] Gehazi is mentioned in 2 Ki. 4–5. See Chaps. 204 and 228.

[928] Jn. 6:37.

[929] The author alludes here, in both idea and vocabulary, to the advice contained in such New Testament passages as 1 Cor. 13:4; Eph. 4:2, 32; Col. 3:13.

don't <even> know their right hand from their left?[930] Or <should this happen only> after <someone> has spent three years <in the monastery> when, on the one hand, the superior will have <gained> sufficient experience of the resolution and determination of the postulant, and, on the other, the postulant <will have gained sufficient experience> in turn of monastic conduct and <this> way of life?" The father gently replied to him and said without <any> anger, "I know myself that these accusations you make against me have a basis in fact. But you don't realize how idle our generation has become and how unenthusiastic and obstinate <it is> about turning toward the good.[931] A person doesn't deliberately choose to enter monastic life of his own accord <nowadays> unless God, in His great goodness, permits him to fall into a crisis of some sort; <only> when he has come to reflect on what will happen in the future as a result of this <situation> will he despise the worthlessness of the present <life>, and decide to come to the life <which is led> for God. But supposing someone who *has* been able to flee from the world like this comes to me and seeks to become a monk, and I, as you suggest, do not tonsure him but make him wait like that for a <period of> time; and <suppose> that tiny spark, which God in His benevolence has in some way kindled in his heart, as I have said, should <then> be snuffed out, won't <that person> return to the world and be keen to take up his former lifestyle again [580] (or <perhaps> a worse one)? And how can I not tonsure <these> youths and country people[932] when I admit them? I think of myself as being a gardener who plants different plants; I water them and provide the other care <they need> to the best of my ability. And insofar as they flourish and come to bear fruit, glory be to the holy God Who has made them grow and brought them to maturity. However, insofar as they become sickly and fruitless or wither away completely due to their own negligence, I don't think *I* will be held responsible or condemned by God for this." Philippikos had nothing to say in reply when he heard these <words>, and so he prostrated himself and sought forgiveness. After receiving this <forgiveness>, he went down from the pillar, weeping and sorely pricked <at heart> as well as amazed and astounded at the father's good judgment.[933] Now, the

[930] Cf. Jon. 4:11.

[931] Cf. above, Chap. 130; also Chap. 186.

[932] The same word that was translated above as "country bumpkin," ἄγροικος, is used here, but the context is obviously less pejorative.

[933] The quality of διάκρισις again.

things I have recorded <here> about our holy father's most sublime and spiritual good judgment <are> just as I heard them with my own ears from Philippikos himself.

233. This might be a good time to reveal <something> as well about the care and zeal which Lazaros demonstrated for saving souls, and especially for those <of the monks> who were serving in obedience to him. The monk Isaiah was once sent out to the city [Constantinople] together with Ioannikios (who was mentioned by me much earlier <in the narrative>).[934] When they arrived in <the city>, they took lodgings in the house of a widow who had great faith in the father from what she had heard <about him> and who lived in what is called Maurianos' portico.[935] One day, the horse-racing was being held, and brother Ioannikios went there without <getting> the approval of the elder [Isaiah]. On his return he was asked by the elder where he had been without his approval (for he had been assigned by the father into service and obedience to <Isaiah>), and he immediately confessed where he had been. The elder was annoyed with him and said, "You've behaved badly by going to such a satanic spectacle." But <Ioannikios>, instead of prostrating himself and begging forgiveness, <began to> argue, in his ignorance, and said, "What's satanic about seeing men and horses running <around>?" When he said this, the monk Isaiah became still more angry and threatened to tell the father everything upon their return <to the monastery>.[936] After they had eaten, brother Ioannikios, who was still being recalcitrant, got up and began to climb up to the upper part of the house[937] to sleep, but when he had reached the top of the ladder he suddenly fell to the ground and began screaming, "Oh, <no>!" As soon as the monk and the <other people> in the house heard this, they rushed to him as quickly as they could. They found him lying on the ground like that, continually shouting "Oh, <no>!" so they picked him up and laid him on the

[934] Presumably the Ioannikios of Chap. 46. The events of this episode are discussed by Ševčenko, "Eastern Provinces," 725 and 726.

[935] The μακρὸς ἔμβολος τοῦ Μαυριανοῦ was a major thoroughfare that ran north from the Bakers' Quarter, just to the west of the Forum of Constantine, downhill toward the Golden Horn (Janin, *Constantinople byz.*, 43, 93). It was thus within easy walking distance of the Hippodrome, lying perhaps half a mile or so northwest of it.

[936] This might also be translated "If they should ever get back <to the monastery>"; Gregory the Cellarer perhaps has the end of the story in mind.

[937] The word ὑπερῷον may signify an "attic," "loft," or simply "spare room" at the top of a house; it was normally, as here, reached by means of a ladder.

bed. They asked him to tell <them> what had happened to him, but he was unable to reply because of the pain he was in, so they left him alone; a little <later>, after he had stopped screaming "Oh <no>!" they asked him again. He answered <now>, and tearfully said to the elder, "Forgive me, father, for having sinned against you and against God and for having gone off to the satanic spectacle of the horse-racing without <seeking> your approval." The elder forgave him and <then> asked him again what had caused this to happen to him. <Ioannikios> replied, "I was going up the ladder and had reached the last rung when I saw an Ethiopian standing in front of me with a stick in his right hand.[938] The man didn't say anything to me but instead struck me with the stick he was holding and then vanished. I fell to the ground and started screaming 'Oh, <no>!' because of the pain and distress <I was in>. But please, pray to God on my behalf, to forgive me this sin!" This is what the brother tearfully said to the monk Isaiah. <Isaiah> prayed for him and gave him support and encouragement with comforting words, and he stayed there with him until he had concluded all the business on which he had been sent. <Then>, when he was about to return to the monastery, he told the woman to take care of <Ioannikios>, who was unable to go with him since he was barely alive <by that time>. <Isaiah> embraced and bade farewell to <Ioannikios who> tearfully pleaded with him to ask the holy father to pray to God for him so that the sin he had committed without his approval might be forgiven. <Isaiah> then parted from him, left the city right away, and took the road for the monastery. <Ioannikios> lived for six days after <Isaiah> left, but <then> died.

234. The monk Isaiah found out about this while he was on his way, and so, on his arrival at the monastery, he told the father all that had happened to the brother and also, of course, about his death. When the father heard this, he ordered the priests to say a liturgy every day for forty days on behalf of the brother.[939] For <Ioannikios> was one of the <true spiritual> contestants and never ever disobeyed a command from the father. He was a heathen[940] and had not been baptized when he <first> came to the father at the monastery,

[938] Compare the incident recorded in Chap. 45, above.

[939] On this period of mourning, see above, Chap. 200.

[940] Lit. an ἐθνικός. Compare episodes in which other non-Christians come to visit Lazaros, above, Chaps. 112 (Jews), 113 (an Arab), and 115 (a Paulician). It is unclear what Ioannikios may have been before his conversion.

but, after he had been baptized at the holy father's behest at the <monastery of the> holy Marina[941] and then had been tonsured by him, he demonstrated such faith and obedience toward the father that he single-handedly worked on *all* <the different> duties <required> of the brothers.[942] <Ioannikios> would thus get up along with everyone <else> and would stand for the office in church until the canon was completed. But, as soon as he left the church, he would go and fetch wood and water, mix up the flour <into dough>, and then, if it was the right time for this, would light the oven and bake the bread; he would then come into the kitchen and perform the task of cooking for the brothers. After he had done <all> this <just> to start with,[943] he would go into church and would celebrate the holy eucharist; for, with a great deal of effort on his part, he had also learned his letters, and so had been judged worthy of the rank of the priesthood. [581] Because of these superior qualities he possessed in comparison to the other brothers, <and inasmuch> as even he <was> human, <Ioannikios'> mind became filled with pride and he did not heed the elder [Isaiah]. He was thus handed over to be tested by the Enemy, so that he might realize what he had done, and not go away empty-handed, like the Pharisee, as a result of <over>confidence about his way of life, but might rather go away justified to God, like the tax collector, after he had humbled himself with much weeping, as a result of being humiliated by this small offense.[944] At the same time this also happened for the benefit of the other <brethren>, so as <to demonstrate> that if someone should be handed over by the father or another superior to someone <else>, then he should not despise that man, but should manifest the same faith in him that he would <normally> observe toward his <own> superior. And that's how it is, as the fate of the brother shows. But I am <now> going back to the father and matters concerning him.

235. One winter there was a torrential rain storm and then a north wind

[941] On the origin and development of this monastery by Lazaros, his first in the area, see above, Chaps. 31–36.

[942] As is made clear below, the point appears to be that Ioannikios worked with equal diligence at both manual and ecclesiastical duties, something which was apparently unusual; cf. above, e.g., Chaps. 182, 183, and 191.

[943] Lit. "received this first fruit."

[944] This passage refers to the parable of the Pharisee and the tax collector, Lk. 18:10–14. The same parable is also cited above, Chap. 116.

started blowing so that the puddles of water in the hollows of the rocks and the ground froze solid because the wind was so bitterly cold.[945] A shepherd, who was looking after the sheepfolds <in which he had> his animals on the mountain at that time, saw what had happened and thought of the father. "How can Kyris Lazaros stand the brutal force of this bitter winter storm[946] when his pillar has no roof?" he said to himself. But while he was thinking about this, another thought came to him, <namely>, "The pillar is not uncovered just now, for when the monks see such distress, they spread something over it to protect Lazaros from the force of the winter storm and remove it again after the storm has passed. The <shepherd> fell asleep while he was thinking these <thoughts> about the father, for it was evening, and, in his sleep, he saw himself standing in front of the pillar. He seemed to see the whole gorge burning with fire. Looking up toward the pillar, he saw two eunuchs, wearing shining robes and with swords in their hands, walking along above the church, and between them he seemed to see a woman dressed in purple.[947] They came walking toward the pillar and then, while the <eunuchs> stood there respectfully and reverently on either side, the <woman> came round onto the pillar. While the <shepherd> was <standing there>, amazed and puzzled at the sight of the woman, he heard a voice from an invisible source saying, "Why are you standing <there> amazed and puzzled at the sight of <this> woman? She's the one who is sheltering him and keeping him warm and safe from the force of the winter storm." At the same time as this voice came to him, the <shepherd> saw the woman take the mantle from her shoulders and cover the pillar <with it>. When he woke up, he was amazed at the sight <he had seen> in his dream and, as soon as it was daylight, he left the spot where he was staying and went down to the Theotokos. He went to the father and recounted the dream in a crude and unpolished way, just as he had had <it>. But the father replied to him, "You shouldn't put any faith at all in dreams,

[945] Although this chapter evidently refers to a time when Lazaros was still at the monastery of the Theotokos (see below), it should be compared to the description of the circumstances of his final illness in Chap. 248, below.

[946] The Greek word χειμών has the sense of both "storm" and "winter," although the two may be combined, as is apparently the case here.

[947] The vision is of the Theotokos (the patron of the monastery), accompanied by two archangels. On Lazaros' devotion to the cult of the archangels, see below, Chap. 243.

because they <come> from demons."[948] He said this by way of humility, since, unless he was <protected> in the manner the man had seen in his vision, how could he have persevered on that pillar, <which was only> three spans wide,[949] standing in the open air in a single small leather tunic, with his head uncovered and his feet bare, exhausting his body in addition by fasting and vigils and with the weight of his irons, and afflicted by both heat and cold as well, of course, as by the swarm of lice <that covered him>?[950] Surely, even if he had been <made of> stone or iron, he would have been worn away by <the passage of> time; but this <mere mortal>, through his hope and faith in our Lord Jesus Christ and in His mother who is the unwavering hope of the faithful, was supplied with strength and was watched over and protected by them, and thus nobly bore all these things, just as if <he really was> as hard as steel.[951]

236. Some of the brothers went up onto the mountain to the north of the monastery to pull up wild olive roots to make charcoal for use by the smith.[952] While they were standing there uprooting these, an enormous boulder suddenly started rolling down toward the monastery with a great rumbling <noise> as though it was being pushed by someone, <although I don't know> whether it had <in fact> been shaken loose by the <brothers> or whether <this had happened all> by itself, or rather whether it had been dislodged by the wicked demons with God's permission. The father, who was standing up on his pillar, shouted loudly at the brothers who were digging out the wood, and the boulder, which was coming down <the mountain> and was already poised over the cells, went past sideways behind them (oh, what a miracle), as if <it had been> controlled by a hand. When it came to the south <of the monastery> it went back up <the slope> a little and then, rolling down from there,

[948] Cf. Lazaros' similar comment in Chap. 157, above.

[949] The span or *spithame* was a Byzantine measure of length, which could vary between 20.8 and 23.4 cms. Three spans would thus give a width for the pillar of somewhere between 25 and 28 inches. See further *ODB*, s.v. "Spithame"; cf. also Delehaye, *Stylites*, clv.

[950] Compare the similar descriptions of Lazaros' extraordinary way of life found in Chaps. 35, 59, and 111.

[951] Cf. Chap. 2.

[952] A smith called Nicholas was mentioned in Chap. 213. On the use of charcoal in Byzantine times, see *ODB*, s.v. "Metallurgy," "Smith." Large monasteries commonly had their own artisans of this type.

came to a halt in front of the kitchen where it barely struck the door with its edge and knocked it down. One can infer from this alone what it would have done to the cells and the brothers in them if it had fallen directly onto them, for some of the brothers were inside at the time. But that rock, like a living and rational being, <acted> as if it respected and revered the father's shout to the brothers that it had prompted; <thus> after being checked[953] in its <headlong> charge, it soared <into the air>[954] and, in the end, changed direction. . . . [955]

237. . . . The father climbed right up on to the top[956] of the pillar and called to the superior by name, "Bless <me>, Kyr Michael!" At the sight of him, these people immediately dismounted from their horses and went up to him. The father asked them the reason they had come up to <see> him and why <they had done so> at such a time, and they replied, "We came up to <see> you as we happened to be passing by here." <Then>, while they were

[953] The verb ἀναχαιτίζω has the literal sense of being yanked back by the hair and may also be used to describe a horse suddenly rearing up. The image here is perhaps that of a runaway horse being brought under control by Lazaros.

[954] The verb κουφίζω has the sense of "being" or "making light"; the boulder literally "made itself light."

[955] There is a break in the manuscript at this point; a small part of f. 270v and the whole of 271 are blank. It is hard to tell how much material is missing here, but clearly the beginning of Chap. 237 has been lost and evidently with it the introduction to a new subsection of the *vita,* for Gregory the Cellarer here turns to events connected with the open hostility of the ecclesiastical authorities in Ephesus to the presence of Lazaros' communities on Galesion toward the end of his life (Chaps. 237–39). The general context of these episodes would appear, however, still to be that of Lazaros' care and concern for the monks in his charge, for this theme obviously recurs in Chap. 240 and thereafter.

[956] The verb ἀνέρχομαι is used throughout the *vita* (as indeed it is in the following sentence) to mean "go up" or "ascend," and it almost always describes people either climbing up the mountain or going up (by ladder) to the top of the father's pillar to see him. The implication of its use here might thus seem to be that Lazaros had left the pillar for some reason and was now *returning* to it. This is, however, most unlikely, given the explicit claims that he never left any of his pillars once he was on them and the atmosphere of suspicion concerning his asceticism in the present chapter. The translation here thus follows the assumption that the verb is used here, together with the adverb ἐπάνω, to indicate that he climbed up higher than usual on the pillar, perhaps onto the parapet around it. This was presumably done so that he could see his suspicious visitors and be seen by them more clearly than usual.

standing there, they began examining the pillar <to see> if they could see anything for which they had been sent <to look>.[957] But although they investigated[958] very thoroughly, they saw nothing of what they expected; and so they prostrated themselves and, after requesting and receiving a blessing, they went down the mountain. When they arrived at the Theologian [Ephesus], they reported [582] what they had seen and heard to the metropolitan and everyone <else>. But even then the treacherous servants of the Evil One were not convinced and <refused> to keep quiet, for they <started> saying that the superior had lied about these things because he was thinking of himself and wished to glorify Lazaros.

238. Again another man was sent out by the metropolitan; this man, who was called Nicholas and later became the steward to the bishop of Batheia,[959] is still alive and tells the story of this affair. So, after <Nicholas> had reached the mountain he made the ascent with difficulty as the path was completely concealed by snow, for it was then winter time. When he was already close to the monastery, he got off the animal he was riding and was tying it to one of the trees that stood there, when one of the brothers, who had been sent to him by the father, came and said to him, "Kyris Nicholas, the father bids you tie up your animal and come here." When <Nicholas> had come in sight of the father, Lazaros said to him,[960] "Go to the kitchen so that you can get warm and receive a meal." For this was always the father's custom, and whatever

[957] As was noted above, the context of this episode is lost, but what is left makes it clear that the narrative concerns a hostile visit (like the one described in the following chapter) apparently designed to prove that Lazaros' famed asceticism and life on the pillar were actually fraudulent, or at least less rigorous than they appeared to be. Lazaros' question above about why these men had come to see him at "such a time" (whatever this may have been) presumably indicates that the visit was deliberately timed so that it would be unexpected, thus ensuring that no "cover up" could be carried out. Cf. also above, Chap. 114, for another examination carried out by a distinguished visitor at the instigation of the metropolitan.

[958] The Greek verb περιεργάζομαι also has the implication of both meddling and time-wasting.

[959] As Delehaye notes, this is probably modern Vathy, the main town on the Greek island of Samos. The island is separated from the coast of Asia Minor by a narrow strait and lies just to the south of Ephesus. The office of steward or *oikonomos* in this context refers to the important clerical official in charge of administering the financial affairs and property of the bishopric. See further *ODB*, s.v. "Oikonomos."

[960] The sentence to this point appears in the margin in the manuscript.

time anyone came up to the monastery he would tell them to receive a meal. The man refused to do this, but <instead>, just as he had been instructed, went straight up and stood there examining <everything> carefully <to see> if he too could see anything he had been sent <to find>.[961] After he had examined <everything> thoroughly enough, however, and was going to descend from the pillar, the father made him go and receive a meal. <Nicholas> did this and <then>, after he had eaten, went <back> up and told Lazaros <all> about the affair. After he had thus received a blessing, he went down the mountain, and he too went and reported what he had seen and heard to the metropolitan and the others. But since those wicked and spiteful men[962] would not stop inciting the metropolitan and his entourage every day to expel the father from the mountain, the brothers realized that these people would not let them live in peace, for they used to mistreat them in various ways and would make fun of them and hurl abuse when they met them. They thus went and nagged the father to write to the emperor so that he might extricate them from this difficult <situation>. And indeed, the father was persuaded <to do so>; he thus wrote and, after he had given the letter to some of the brothers, sent them off to the emperor.[963]

239. But one of the brothers of the monastery, called Kosmas, <now> acted exactly like Judas, for when the <aforesaid> brothers had already left the monastery, he also left the company of the <remaining> brothers after supper,[964] descended the mountain, and went off to the Theologian [Ephesus].

[961] Nicholas' urgency is presumably again to ensure that no "cover up" takes place while he is in the kitchen, and Gregory the Cellarer is keen to stress this fact to prevent critics from voicing the same suspicion. This also probably explains Gregory's emphasis that sending people to the kitchen for a meal was normal practice and not a means to get this particular man out of the way.

[962] Some information on the identity of these men, who are presumably the same "treacherous servants of the Evil One" mentioned in the previous chapter, must have been contained in the lost section preceding Chap. 237.

[963] While it is clear that this mission and the events of this and the following chapter are associated with the later stages of Lazaros' career on Galesion, although probably not with the very end of his life, it is impossible to fit them more exactly into the chronology of the *vita.* For an exploration of some of the possibilities, see the Introduction, section F.b, pp. 36–37.

[964] On *deipnon,* see Chap. 163, n. 634. There is, of course, a direct allusion made here to Judas' departure after the Last Supper in order to betray Jesus.

And, after he had gone into the city, he informed the metropolitan and his clergy about everything. <Then> those men seized upon this good excuse and persuaded the metropolitan to send <people> in pursuit of the brothers. When <these men> had caught up with the <brothers> and grabbed hold of them,[965] they manhandled them with a lot of jeers and insults, and, taking <from them> all they were carrying,[966] returned <to Ephesus>. The brothers returned unhappily to the monastery and complained bitterly against the father for having admitted and tonsured such a man <as this Kosmas>, for he used to be a *taxeotes.*[967] But the father defended himself by saying to them, "You mustn't be unhappy and upset because of this, either with me or with the brother <himself>. For unless it was God's will we wouldn't have been prevented <from doing this>." With these words he soothed their great agitation and calmed down the situation. But <the brothers soon began to> nag him again, <although> in a different way, saying, "The metropolitan's people will never let us stay here in peace, especially after your death. So, while you're still alive, you have to look around somewhere else and find a place that's free and found another monastery there, so that if the metropolitan's people *don't* let us stay here after your death, as <we> say, <then at least> we can go there." <The brothers> persuaded Lazaros to act in this way, by saying this, and out of this came the initiative for building the church of the all holy Theotokos at Bessai.[968] But <more> on that later.

Now, since the monk Kosmas (who became a traitor, as the story has already made clear) knew our holy father's benevolent and sympathetic disposition, he returned <from Ephesus> after a time and came back to the monastery. When the brothers saw him they were extremely upset, so they went to the father and said that he should not admit him <to the monastery> as he

[965] Again, the language is reminiscent of the arrest of Jesus in the garden of Gethsemane, following his betrayal by Judas; cf. Mt. 26:50.

[966] I.e., the letter to the emperor.

[967] A *taxeotes* was an official who generally functioned as a police officer or bailiff acting for a magistrate, although the position could also have a more obviously military character. The precise significance of the term, which in this particular context seems to be somewhat derogatory, is unclear.

[968] Chap. 217, above, which also apparently refers to this church, reveals that it had not been completed at a time just prior to Lazaros' death. It is unclear whether reference is being made here simply to the church of the Theotokos itself or to the whole monastery at Bessai.

was a second Judas and a traitor who had betrayed his own teacher. But the father said to them, "If we don't readmit a man like ourselves who has fallen and repented, how will God admit us, who fall incessantly every day, when we repent?" After the father said this and since the brothers had nothing to say in response to it, they unwillingly agreed to admit the traitor into the monastery again. Our holy father had the same attachment to this <Kosmas> as someone might have toward a dear and true friend, but that man, even though he used to speak <words of> peace in the open (to put it like the divine David), never stopped whispering slanders against the father when he went outside <the monastery>.[969] As a result he met an end appropriate to such a character and disposition, for he was not deemed worthy to die in the monastery but <rather> in the <outside> world, without telling[970] anything to any one at all or having sought or received forgiveness from anyone. Anyway, that's <all> about him.

240. Another monk stole from the monastery due to his wicked habit, or rather disposition, and then went away. Some time later he returned again and the father generously admitted him. As he did this on many occasions, the brothers finally rose up against the father and said, "If you admit this man, we're leaving!"[971] The father replied to the brothers, "Let's admit him one more time, but if he doesn't stay,[972] and leaves the monastery, then, just as you wish, <if> he should come back again, I won't admit him any more." As the brothers were persuaded <by this compromise>, they allowed the man to live with them in the monastery when he had been received <into the community> again. [583] Not long afterward the brother fell sick and this <illness actually> became a basis for <the restoration of> his spiritual health, for, weeping profusely, he made confession to the father and all the brothers of his past evil deeds, and fervently begged to receive forgiveness. When he received this, he became an "apostolic" <monk> on the father's orders, for he was <previously

[969] The allusion would appear to be to Ps. 27 (28):3: "*Draw not away my soul with sinners, and destroy me not with the workers of iniquity, who speak peace with their neighbors, but evils are in their hearts.*"

[970] Presumably the implication is that he died without "confessing."

[971] Compare the criticism of Lazaros voiced by the brothers in rather similar circumstances in Chaps. 142–43, above.

[972] The verb φυλάσσω could also mean "take care" or "watch out" here.

only> a *mandyotes,*[973] and so he departed to the Lord, weeping and rendering great thanks to God. After his death the father said to the brothers, "Look, brothers, what a penalty we came close to incurring for destroying the brother's soul. For if we had not admitted him just now, he would have gone off into the world and would have died there, completely unrepentant."

241. A layman from the village of Kepion[974] came up to the father and asked to be admitted to the monastery so that he might live with the brothers and work alongside them for his food and the other necessities of life, for he was stricken with terrible poverty, <or> so he said. After the father had admitted him, he handed him over to the cellarer so that he could work with him in the bakery and on other jobs in the monastery. But this <fellow>, who was well practiced in a habit he had apparently acquired earlier, stole whatever he could find without the cellarer noticing and sent this to his mother by way of a lay acquaintance of his. When the cellarer looked for the things this man had stolen and could not find them, he questioned him <about this>. The man immediately denied <everything>, but as he went on doing this on many occasions, the cellarer <began to> press him and said, "Nobody else is doing this except you!" The man was afraid that he might be exposed and <thus> might suffer some ill treatment from the cellarer and the other brothers, so he went up and asked the father to release him so that he might go home again. The father blessed him and did release him but, in the night <before> he was going to leave, the <fellow> took a sack full of flour and two pairs of hides[975] and went out of the monastery and hid them. In the morning, when he was about to leave, the cellarer, who was suspicious of him, went out and stood <there> somewhere, watching him carefully. Then, when he saw him leave and take the sack and the hides, he went running up to the father and told him all about the affair. But the father replied to him, "Let him go, and don't chase after him <and try> to catch him. For he's <just> a poor man." He thus

[973] Compare the similar passage in Chap. 228, above, and the comment there.

[974] This village is presumably to be identified with the Κηπίον mentioned above in Chaps. 31 and 55, although here it appears to have a plural form (Κηπίων).

[975] Delehaye, following Ducange, suggests the meaning of "hide" for the word πετζία. A similar form, πετζίν, is indeed attested with this meaning, but since these πετζία are described as being in pairs, it seems conceivable that shoes of some sort may be intended here, perhaps something like πέδιλα ("sandals" or "shoes").

stopped <the cellarer> from making any trouble for the thief at all, and by his action fulfilled the saying that the Lord spoke to the disciples, "*of him who takes away your goods do not ask them again.*"[976]

242. The monk Nicholas, the brother of the monk Lazaros who was nicknamed "the Short," left the monastery not <just> once but twice, and then returned again and was generously admitted by the father. When he was about to do this a third time, however (as if he was being pushed <into this> by the Evil Instigator), and had got his outer garment ready in the evening for his departure, he was stricken with a very severe pain in his heart in the middle of the night. At dawn, then, <Nicholas> too confessed his sins through a brother <monk>, and, after becoming a *megaloschemos,*[977] he departed to the Lord in a properly repentant state within seven days. Thus <true> holy men know how to *overcome evil by good*[978] and to redeem those who are in the depths of sin through their forbearance and merciful consideration <for others>. So, those <are> the <stories> about the father's compassionate disposition and the forbearance he used to show to sinners, which I have also described elsewhere to a certain extent. But I must now speak in detail about the miracles he worked on many after he went up to the holy Resurrection.

243. A layman <once> came to the monastery to become a monk. But one night, before he had been tonsured, he was lying asleep outside the monastery, to the north under the oak tree (which is still standing there now and is called Philippikos' <oak>),[979] when someone suddenly appeared and <started> calling him. He woke up and, peering <around>, saw a short[980] person dressed

[976] Lk. 6:30.

[977] That is, a fully professed monk of the superior grade; see Chaps. 9 and 130. Cf. also Chap. 228.

[978] Rom. 12:21. Cf. above, Chap. 66; the use of the same quotation here as well as mention of the Devil may suggest this Nicholas should be identified with Nicholas Paxamades.

[979] Note that here, as in Chap. 244, the victim sleeps under a tree, something that is sometimes associated in modern Greek folklore with supernatural danger; see, e.g., R. and E. Blum, *The Dangerous Hour: The Lore of Crisis and Mystery in Rural Greece* (New York, 1970); esp. 132–33 (nos. 33–35); cf. 104 (no. 38) and 112 (no. 66); cf. also J. C. Lawson, *Modern Greek Folklore and Ancient Greek Religion* (Cambridge, 1910; repr. New York, 1964), 154–56.

[980] Cf. Lk. 19:3 where the Greek phrase τῇ ἡλικίᾳ μικρὸν is used of the tax collector Zacchaeus.

in old, ragged <clothes> standing in front of him.[981] <This figure> said to him, "Come <with me>, the cellarer's calling for you!" The man got up straightaway and followed him but, when they reached the monastery entrance, his wicked guide *passed by on the other side.*[982] The man said to him, "Let's go in here to see the father." But the Evil One replied, "I can't go in there, because of the man you mentioned. But come <with me>, I'll take you to where the cellarer is." As they were going along the man saw innumerable little oil bottles[983] hanging round the belt of the <person he was following> and, in the middle of them all, one which was bigger than the rest. Also, although it was night time, there seemed to be a light around them. The man said to the Evil One, "What are those?" "I bring oil in them for the brothers," he replied, "and season their pots."[984] When the man asked about the big one, the Evil One

[981] Although demonic apparitions are associated with ragged dress on other occasions in the *vita* (see Chaps. 51 and 218), this element, like several features of the story that follows here, is apparently drawn from a rather similar episode recorded in the *Apophthegmata* in connection with Makarios the Great (Makarios 3, PG 65:261–63; Ward, *Sayings,* 106–8). There Makarios sees Satan appear in the form of a man, dressed in a cotton garment; it is full of holes, and from each hole a small flask is hanging. When questioned by Makarios, Satan says he is going to visit the brothers who live nearby in order to arouse their memories, and that he is taking food in the jars for them to try. On his way back he is again stopped by Makarios and reports that he has been turned away by all except one, Theopemptos, who is his friend. Makarios then goes and gives Theopemptos some good advice about countering these attacks by Satan, and learns, when he meets the Devil again, that this has worked, much to the latter's chagrin. The episode, and Lazaros' commentary upon it, recorded in Chaps. 131–33, above, should also be compared here.

[982] The use of the verb ἀντιπαρέρχομαι here is an allusion (absent in the *Apophthegmata* version) to the parable of the Good Samaritan in which the priest and the Levite do the same thing to the man who has been robbed: Lk. 10:31–32. The same expression is also used in Chap. 51, above, another apparently similar episode.

[983] The Greek word, λικύνθια, is clearly a rendering of that which appears in the same context in the *Apophthegmata,* ληκύνθια. As Delehaye suggests, it would seem to be a variation of the plural of ληκύθιον, a diminutive of λήκυθος, and must hence indicate a small oil flask (so Liddell-Scott-Jones, *Lexicon*). While these flasks are said to contain food in the story in the *Apophthegmata,* here they are specifically described as being used for transporting oil.

[984] The Greek word χύτρα ("pot") generally refers specifically to a cooking pot of some sort (cf. above, Chap. 61), but since it seems certain that the monks on Galesion did not possess their own cooking utensils, the phrase "season their pots" is probably not to be taken literally here; it is perhaps most likely to be connected to the role of the

said again, "That's Philippikos' <bottle>."[985] While he was talking like this, <the man> was following the Evil One, imagining that they were going to the guest house, for the Evil One had told him that was where the cellarer was, but <instead> they went past <it> and into the precipitous area of St. Onouphrios.[986] When they had reached the ridge and <the man> had already put his foot out <over the edge> so that he would fall head first down the cliff, that evil guide, along with his false light, immediately vanished from sight. When the man saw this <happen>, he cried out as loudly as he could, "Theotokos, help me, through the prayers of [584] holy Lazaros!" As he said this, he found himself standing on the ground at the bottom <of the cliff>. Although he had no idea what had happened to him, he was happy to be where he was, and remained standing there; and because he thought he was standing somewhere near the monastery he began to call out for the monks. Now Kyriakos Galesiotes[987] and another man happened to be nearby as they were keeping watch over the cultivated fields;[988] when they heard the man shouting like this, they first thought that it was a demon imitating a human voice in order to deceive them. But when they heard him shouting some more, Kyriakos' companion said to him, "I'm going to see what it is." <Kyriakos tried to> stop him, however; "Don't go there," he said, "in case it's a phantom and makes a mockery of you." But <his companion> did not listen to him and took his

Devil in the *Apophthegmata* version in rousing suppressed memories. The apparition is perhaps given plausibility in the context of the *vita* if one remembers the monk Nikon's nocturnal transportation of water from the Theotokos to the Resurrection mentioned above in Chap. 174.

[985] A person who heard this story and was aware of the version in the *Apophthegmata* would understand that this implied that Philippikos, like Theopemptos there, was a particular friend to the Devil.

[986] On this place see above, Chaps. 131 and 172. The former chapter records the story of another man who fell over the cliff at this spot with less happy consequences.

[987] This is probably the same man who was mentioned above (Chap. 154) as offering hospitality to a monk in "the village" on the way up to the monastery from Ephesus. In that case the fields mentioned here must lie at the foot of the mountain in the general direction of the city.

[988] On the need to protect fields of crops from theft, compare the episode of the bean field recorded in Chap. 34. Morris (*Monks,* 215 n. 32) apparently understands this passage to refer to "two monks supervising the plowman," although there would seem to be no grounds in the text for this interpretation.

stick and went off toward the voice. When he drew near he called out to the man, "Who are you?" In reply the man began to say, "Is such <behavior> good, fathers? Does the holy father teach you to play tricks in this way on people who have just arrived at the monastery?" As he was saying this, <Kyriakos' companion> suddenly reached out with his hand and grabbed him and so dragged him back to their tent. The <two men> questioned him and <thus> found out from him all that had happened. And in the morning Kyriakos took him along with him and went up to the monastery, and he told the father and the brothers what had happened to him.

244. The monk Cyril the shoemaker[989] and the monk Theodoulos the stonemason <both> experienced something <rather> similar. For <Cyril> was sent out on some business by the father to the *proasteion*[990] of the monastery called Pentakrene, along with the monk Cyril who <later> became our steward.[991] It was already evening when he arrived, and he went to sleep under a tree outside the house, <although> his companion went to lie down inside. <While he was asleep> his fellow monk appeared to him, or so he thought, calling to him to get up. "Come on," he said, "let's go into the church and celebrate the holy Eucharist, for so-and-so's asked us to do so." He woke up and, not even putting shoes on his feet because he was being hurried by the <other monk>, got up immediately and followed him. The <demon>, which had appeared in the guise of his fellow monk, seemed to him to be wearing priestly robes and to be holding a censer and a pan of coals in his hands; swinging the censer as he walked along, he urged him to follow him quickly. But when <the monk> reached a precipitous place, God, Who wished to save

[989] Another shoemaker, Kerykos, was mentioned above, Chap. 148.

[990] On this term, see Chap. 90.

[991] Although the second monk, Theodoulos, may be the central character of this story and be accompanied on his mission by Cyril "the shoemaker," who must thus be identified with Cyril "who became our steward," this is perhaps unlikely. The translation thus assumes that the μὲν at the beginning of this sentence indicates that Gregory the Cellarer intends to tell two stories here: one about Cyril the shoemaker and one about Theodoulos the stonemason, although the latter has now been lost in the substantial gap in the manuscript at the end of the chapter. The central figure of the present story is thus Cyril the shoemaker, who is deliberately distinguished by this epithet from the other Cyril who accompanies him on his mission, the senior monk Cyril "who became our steward."

the brother from meeting a violent death by being pushed over the cliff by the Evil One, made a woman from the village cry out, for her son had died that night; and as soon as the cry occurred, the Evil One, with his fantastic shape and false light, disappeared. When the brother saw this, he realized what had happened. He first invoked our holy father's prayer for help and then called out for his fellow monk and the vinedresser who was also there. Although they barely heard him, they went out and found him turning around this way and that in the middle of the scrub[992] without knowing where he was or where he was going. For, although it was night time when he went off with the Evil One, it had appeared to be day<light> to him and he had thought he was walking along a beaten track. So, following the voices of the monk and the vinedresser with difficulty, as <I> have said, he was able to go to them, and told them about the affair.[993]

245. . . . The monk Gabriel persuaded the emperor to issue a *prostagma*[994] to the father,[995] formally instructing him to move from the mountain to Bessai, because the mountain belonged to the metropolitan of Ephesus whereas the site of Bessai had been given to our venerable father by the emperor him-

[992] The word φρύγανον can also mean firewood, and the monk could perhaps be thought of as wandering about among piles of this outside the house, but the context of the story, in which the demon has led him away to a precipitous place, would suggest uncut "scrub" or "brush."

[993] There is a substantial gap in the manuscript at this point consisting of a small part of f. 279 and the whole of ff. 279v–281v; that is the equivalent of almost a whole page of the edited Greek text. At least some material on Lazaros' later miracles seems to be missing: if my interpretation of the first part of this chapter is correct, then a similar story about Theodoulos the stonemason has been lost; at the same time, Gregory the Cellarer referred to "the miracles he worked on many" at the end of Chap. 242, but only two are now described. It is also clear that the context has changed in Chap. 245 and thus that Gregory's introduction to the last section of the *vita,* which covers the end of Lazaros' life and the events surrounding this, has disappeared.

[994] Reading προστακτικῶς for προστατικῶς (I am grateful to an anonymous reader for this suggestion) and understanding the phrase γράψαι πρὸς τὸν πατέρα προστατικῶς as implying this. The emperor is persuaded to issue an official administrative order (*prostagma*) recognizing the legal rights of the metropolitan of Ephesus over Galesion and forcing Lazaros to move from the mountain. See further *ODB,* s.v. "Prostagma."

[995] Reference is evidently being made here to the mission of Gabriel and Pachomios mentioned in Chap. 221. On its relationship to the other missions sent to Constantinople from Galesion around this time (Chaps. 221, 223, 246, 248), see the Introduction, section F.b, pp. 46–47.

self for the remembrance both of himself and of Maria, who was called Skleraina.[996] Indeed, this woman also sent seven hundred and twenty *nomismata* and one of the imperial <sacred> furnishings[997] to the father after she had heard about <him> from her brother; in fact, most of the construction of the Pausolype[998] was <carried out> with this money.[999] Brother Gabriel also sent the father a letter that pointed out the benefactions made by the emperor to the monastery and how God had assisted him in everything through his [Lazaros'] prayers. <This letter> also <added>, "Since the emperor has written <instructing> you to go to Bessai and leave the mountain of Galesion because

[996] This refers to Constantine IX Monomachos' mistress, Maria Skleraina, who was provided with the official title of *sebaste,* and lived in the palace alongside the empress Zoe. The visit to Lazaros of her brother, Romanos Skleros, is described above, Chap. 87 (see the note there for further information on the family), and it is stated just below here that it was he who told her about Lazaros. As the present chapter clearly states that the foundation was established for the remembrance of *both* Constantine and Maria (not simply in memory of the latter as Janin evidently understands it, *Églises centres,* 244), the donation of the land on which Bessai was constructed could have originated before Maria's death, thus sometime between June 1042 (the date of Constantine's succession) and early 1046 (by which time she was dead). On the dating of Maria's death, see N. Oikonomides, "St. George of Mangana, Maria Skleraina, and the 'Malyj sion' of Novgorod," *DOP* 34–35 (1980–81), 243. Further on her in general, see Seibt, *Skleroi,* 71–76 (no. 16); *ODB,* s.v. "Skleraina." There is no ground for supposing, as Morris ("Political Saint," 48) does, that she ever consulted Lazaros personally.

[997] The term ἔπιπλα is evidently used here with the same sense it possesses in monastic *typika* (see, e.g., the Evergetis *typikon:* Gautier, "Évergétis," 17.56, 63.842, 71.984). Cf. also the 9th century *vita* of St. Euthymios the Younger: L. Petit, "Vie et office de saint Euthyme le Jeune," *ROC* 8 (1903), 197.17, where mention is made of gifts of ἔπιπλα σηρικὰ καὶ σκεύη ἱερὰ ("silk furnishings and holy vessels"). Seven hundred and twenty *nomismata* are ten pounds of gold; cf. above, Chap. 106. The passage is mentioned by A. Harvey, "The Theotokos Evergetis and Eleventh-Century Monasticism," in Mullett and Kirby, *Evergetis,* 133.

[998] That is "<Our Lady> the ender of sorrows" or "the Consoler"; it is presumably an epithet of the Virgin (so Janin, *Églises centres,* 245). The Pausolype is mentioned again in Chap. 247, where it is made clear that it was not just a church but a monastic foundation; it is not revealed, however, whether it was for men or women. For discussion of the possibility that it is to be identified with Bessai or perhaps the convent of Eupraxia, see the Introduction, section F.a, p. 35.

[999] Although the grant of the land on which Bessai was built was not *necessarily* made before Maria Skleraina's death, the gift which enabled the Pausolype to be constructed evidently was.

the place belongs to the metropolitan, you must take all the monastery's possessions and all the brothers and go there <instead>." But when the father heard this, he said, as though he was talking to the man who had written to him, "I'm not going to go to Bessai because of what you say or because of the emperor's letter, nor <will I take all> the monastery's property <there>. <It is> Christ Who has approved the construction of both this <monastery> and that one, and He can again send whatever is necessary to that monastery [Bessai], just as <He has already done> with this one." When the brothers heard this statement, however, some <of them> were very upset, for quite a lot of them had the intention of going off to Bessai. One of the brothers, Isaiah who was called "the Tall," replied to the father and said, "The name of Galesion will last until your death, but after you've died it will disappear." But when the father heard this he lost his patience, even though he could tolerate a great deal, and retorted reprovingly to <Isaiah>, "God will obliterate your name from this monastery after my death," he said, "but not that of Galesion." And this did indeed [585] happen. For, after our holy father's death, <Isaiah> withdrew from the monastery and went off to <that of> St. Gregory, while the name of Galesion is <still> on everyone's tongue and is more widely celebrated <than ever>. After the father had said this to brother Isaiah, brother Cyril again replied, "Don't be angry with the brother, father, for the bishop of Tralles,[1000] the steward of Ephesus,[1001] said the same thing to me too, only a few days ago."[1002] Then the father said to the brother, "Neither the bishop of Tral-

[1000] Tralles (just over a mile north of the modern Aydin) lay some 28 miles inland from Ephesus on the north bank of the Meander. It was a bishopric throughout the Byzantine period. See further *ODB,* s.v. "Tralles."

[1001] On the office of *oikonomos* in this context, see above, Chap. 238. The grammar implies that the bishop of Tralles and the steward of Ephesus are one and the same person, and this seems to be a historical possibility. Thus, for an example of one member of the church hierarchy acting in this capacity for a higher one, see N. Oikonomides, *A Collection of Dated Byzantine Lead Seals* (Washington, D.C., 1986), 80–81, no. 79: a seal of Demetrios, metropolitan of Cyzicus, grand *oikonomos* (of the patriarchate) and *synkellos.* The seal dates to this period (ca. 1029–before 1039).

[1002] It would seem clear from the text that the bishop of Tralles had said the same thing as Isaiah, namely, that Galesion would only survive until Lazaros' death and would then disappear; in other words, it was a threat made in the context of the dispute between the authorities and the community on the mountain. Kaplan ("Evergetis," 111) is thus presumably mistaken in suggesting that the bishop of Tralles and the *oikonomos* of Ephesus (whom he takes as two distinct people) were here urging Lazaros to have

les nor his metropolitan <can do this>. And even if <all> the metropolitans and emperors in the world get together, they won't have the strength to obliterate the name of Galesion, because God founded it, and thus no <mere> man can obliterate it! I tell you, even if people come into it and steal everything the monastery has, they still won't be able to destroy it. But if just one of the brothers living here goes down into the neighboring villages and says that the <monks> who are persevering on Galesion lack the necessities <of life>, the people <from those villages> will bring to the brothers who have stayed put here whatever food they require." When the father said this, the monk Nicholas the scribe[1003] responded, "If that's the case, <then> what need was there to found Bessai?" "What do you think?" the father said to him, "Is it <really> sinful to praise God there as well as here?" [1004]As no one had anything to say in reply to Lazaros, they prostrated themselves one by one to him and went back to their cells.

246. But, when the brothers whom the father had sent out to the city [Constantinople] and elsewhere returned to the monastery, Lazaros immediately fell into the sickness that <finally> released him from the present life, just as he had told them <would be the case>, as was mentioned above.[1005] Eight days before his death he summoned the aforesaid Nicholas the scribe and instructed him to write a rule.[1006] So after this brother had asked about

all his monasteries accorded the same *autodespotos* legal status that Bessai, with its imperial backing, enjoyed; he recognizes the problems inherent in his interpretation, however, by saying that they did so even though they "had most to lose" were such recognition to be granted. In the context of the dispute it seems to make no sense at all for representatives of Ephesus to suggest that Lazaros should gain imperial protection for the very monastery they were seeking to control or destroy, since this would have put it out of their grasp.

[1003] Lit., "*grammatikos*." Technically this word meant a scholar but it came to indicate a scribe and to be an alternative term for a notary (see above, Chap. 3). Later, and possibly even by this time, it could refer to the secretary of a monastery. See further *ODB*, s.v. "Grammatikos."

[1004] Cf. Lazaros' response to a rather similar question posed by the eunuch Stephen in Chap. 216, above.

[1005] This probably refers to the mission of Gabriel and Pachomios, mentioned in Chap. 221 (cf. Chap. 245), since similar wording is used there to describe it.

[1006] The term used throughout this chapter is *diatyposis.* On important evidence to be gleaned from this chapter on the method of composition of monastic *typika,* see Thomas, "Evergetine Reform," 252–54; Thomas and Hero, *Foundation Documents,* 151.

each <item> that he had to write in the rule and had ascertained this from him, he went off and wrote it out, and then brought it <back>. When he read it through to him, the father was pleased with it and said that it was fine. But <now> I must indicate here the principal <elements> of this <document> that the father commanded the brother to write. It thus contained an account of how the father left his own homeland and reached the Holy Land; it then described how he arrived at this mountain, by the providence of God, after his return from <the Holy Land>, and how he went up and constructed the three monasteries on it and <subsequently> gathered the monks in them and governed them, as best he could, up to the present time. Then it also <spoke> about the *proasteia,*[1007] which God sent from the Christian faithful, <and stated> that these should <nominally> belong to Bessai (for it was prescribed that it should have a superior too),[1008] but that they should <first and foremost> provide support for Galesion.[1009] There were to be forty brothers at the

[1007] On this term, see above, Chap. 90.

[1008] The implication is probably that, although there was no superior at Bessai during Lazaros' lifetime, there was to be one after his death. Certainly there is no mention of anyone holding such an office in the *vita* as it now stands; when reference is made to the community at Bessai, it seems to be regarded in this respect in much the same way as Lazaros' other foundations on Galesion (see, e.g., Chaps. 79, 142, 202, 216, 221). The instruction that Bessai is now to have its own superior is thus perhaps best understood in the context of the rivalry between the two establishments that had developed out of the disputes over the legality of Lazaros' settlement on Galesion and which was evidently ongoing at the time Gregory the Cellarer was writing the *vita.* As was suggested in the Introduction, section F.a, pp. 39–40, Gregory's handling of the *diatyposis* in this chapter is apparently governed by such considerations. This stipulation may thus perhaps be seen as part of an attempt on Lazaros' part to ensure the separation of Bessai from Galesion as far as possible (see also below in this chapter), and thus to prevent it claiming to be the legitimate heir of his foundation and tradition, to the detriment (and even possible destruction) of Galesion itself.

[1009] The translation of this passage, and a number of related ones below, is crucial for understanding the relationship between Galesion and Bessai in particular, but also that with the foundation of the Pausolype. It is unfortunate that it is not entirely straightforward. Commentators, such as Janin (*Églises centres,* 246), Malamut ("Bessai," 247), and Kaplan (*Les hommes,* 339, cf. 306), as well as Karlin-Hayter in her translation of this passage (Thomas and Hero, *Foundation Documents,* 164), evidently take the verb used here, διοικεῖν, in its most obvious sense in such a context, that is, "to administer." The problem is that the verb appears here in the active voice (διοικῶσι), while their interpretation requires it to be taken as a passive, thus: "the *proasteia* . . .

<monastery of the> Holy Resurrection, twelve at the Savior, and twelve at the Theotokos. The superior, with the <due> consideration and approval of the brothers, was to choose one of them, who was capable of properly administering the <affairs> of the monastery, and he was to make him steward and entrust him with full responsibility for the monks on the mountain, <but> he was not to be troubled by those at Bessai or be hindered in anything. Once a year, however, at the end of the month of August, the superior was to make inquiries of the <steward> and, if he should discover any surplus from the income of the *proasteia,* he was to take this and return it to Bessai; but if he should find no surplus, he was to leave the <steward> alone and was not to trouble <him or> demand to have anything back from him, so that he might not put any constraints on the <monks> living here <at Galesion>,[1010] <at least> on this account.[1011] <The document> also contained <regulations>

should belong to Bessai, . . . but . . . should *be administered* at Galesion." There is no obvious parallel for διοικεῖν being used in this way in the active voice; it should probably be taken instead in another attested sense: "to support" or "to provide for" (Liddell-Scott-Jones, *Lexicon,* s.v., I.2; cf. also Gautier, "Kécharitôménè," 39.322, 349, of servants being supported by the monastery). Not only does this make grammatical sense here, but it also accords well with the context, which has to do with the income derived from *proasteia* (evidently in kind rather than money) and the use of this income to ensure that "no constraints" were placed on the Galesiote monks; the following chapter clearly shows that the constraints Lazaros has in mind are to do with provisioning. The translation of this passage also affects the interpretation of the parallel passage in Chap. 247, where the brothers raise doubts about the issue and Lazaros responds to them; see further there.

[1010] Thomas ("Evergetine Reform," 253) is surely mistaken in understanding this passage to refer to the peasants living in the area; as he says, such a concern would be "unusual." Cf. Thomas and Hero, *Foundation Documents,* 151, where Thomas speaks of the "monastery's dependents," but note that Karlin-Hayter (p. 164 there) translates this passage more ambiguously as "reducing those settled here to hardship." The wider context would appear to indicate that it refers instead to the well-being of the monks of Galesion, who are not to be starved out by being deprived of the vital produce originating from these *proasteia.*

[1011] For a different interpretation of this passage from that provided in the Introduction, section F.a. p. 38 (which sees it in the context of rivalry between Galesion and Bessai), see Kaplan, *Les hommes,* 306, and, somewhat more fully, idem, "Evergetis," 111. Kaplan (who sees the passage in terms of hostility between Galesion and Ephesus) suggests that the transfer of surplus produce from Galesion to Bessai was designed to keep it out of the hands of the metropolitan of Ephesus, since Bessai was an imperial foundation which thus "enjoyed sovereign (*autodespotos*) status"; Kaplan's position is

about the daily regimen of the brothers, as well as about the special meals[1012] on feast days. Again, concerning their clothing and footwear and their other requirements, <it> similarly <prescribed that> the steward at the time was to supply these things to the brothers without fail, "Just as I myself have done hitherto," he said. When the brothers asked him about this later, he said, "Yes, let the church office remain unchanged, just as it is <now>. But after you have dragged my wretched body <out> by the feet, throw it into the gorge as food for the beasts of the earth and the birds of the air."[1013] And at the end, as is customary in <monastic> rules, the man who wrote this put a curse by the three hundred and eighteen divinely inspired fathers[1014] and <warned> that whoever should dare to alter or transgress even one single syllable of this will[1015]

---

also followed by Morris (*Monks,* 215). For a discussion of an apparently similar relationship and "division of labor" to that envisaged here between *hegoumenos* and *oikonomos* in some other monasteries of this period and slightly later, see Kaplan, "Evergetis," 114–16.

[1012] On this use of the Greek word διάκρισις in this sense, see above, Chap. 95; cf. in this context, Chap. 140.

[1013] The last part of this sentence draws on a number of Old Testament passages: Deut. 28:26; 1 Ki. 17:46; Ps. 78 (79):2; Jer. 7:33, 19:7, 41 (34):20; Ez. 29:5; 39:4. Only Ez. 29:5 has the beasts and birds in the same order, however. Lazaros (or Gregory the Cellarer) almost certainly also has in mind here a passage from the *Ladder of Paradise* of John Klimax (5:21; PG 88:772c), which refers to some ascetics begging to be treated like animals instead of humans when they died and thus to have their bodies flung into a river bed or left to be eaten by wild beasts. There seems to be another allusion to the same passage in Chap. 133, while Lazaros' request is mentioned again in Chap. 253. The inclusion of this whole statement here by Gregory perhaps implies that some omissions in the original document were later clarified orally by Lazaros. If so, it would appear that these included general arrangements for the daily offices and specific arrangements for the disposal of Lazaros' body. The first part of the statement may, however, refer only to special arrangements for church services following Lazaros' death, in which case its purpose is simply to request that there be no alteration to the daily pattern of worship then just as there is to be no elaborate funeral: Lazaros' humility and avoidance of human glory continues even in death.

[1014] This is the traditional (though probably not actual) number of the fathers who attended the 1st Council of Nicaea in A.D. 325. The same curse is included in several surviving *typika:* see, e.g., the final words of the *typika* of Evergetis (Gautier, "Évergétis," 95:1382–83) and of Pakourianos (idem, "Le typikon du Sébaste Grégoire Pakourianos," *REB* 42 [1984], 91:1199–1200), both of the 11th century.

[1015] The Greek word here is διαθήκη.

would have our holy and divinely inspired father Lazaros as his accuser on the terrible day of judgment before the tribunal of Christ. <Now> I have not written <all> this about our holy father's rule without good reason, as someone might claim, but so that we may learn the truth from this when we are seeking it.[1016] As a result of his illness, however, Lazaros was unable to lean out of his little window or take <this document> in his hand in any other way and sign it, and it thus remained unsigned until the day on which he was going to die. For neither the <monk> who had written this and was keeping it nor any other brother could make him sign it, nor did they dare <do so>, because they were all still hoping he would live.[1017] For who of us expected to see his death? And indeed, even after he had died, many <ordinary> people found this impossible to believe, even when he was lying <there right> before their eyes.

247. When some of the brothers also <started> saying that the [586] monastery's *proasteia* should provide support[1018] for Bessai <and not for Galesion>,

[1016] This rather cryptic comment may perhaps again be interpreted as referring to the dispute with Bessai (cf. Chap. 223, above); see the Introduction, section F.a, p. 39.

[1017] On the importance of this, see below, Chap. 250.

[1018] The same verb, διοικεῖν, which was discussed at some length in the previous chapter, is again used in the active voice here and in Lazaros' speech which follows; in both cases a similar translation to that above is proposed. A further complication now arises, however, for Lazaros makes the point in his argument that the monastery of the Pausolype is αὐτοδιοίκητος. Trapp, *Lexikon,* s.v., gives the most obvious meaning for this word (which is absent from the other lexica) of "sich selbst verwaltend, unabhängig" ("self-administering" or "independent") and Demetrakos, s.v., understands it in precisely the same way. Karlin-Hayter (Thomas and Hero, *Foundation Documents,* 164) also takes it this way, "As for the Pausolype monastery, it is self-governing," as does Kaplan (*Les hommes,* 306), "le monastère de Pansolype [*sic*] . . . est, en fait, complètement indépendent, au moins pour la gestion (αὐτοδιοίκητος)," and Thomas ("Evergetine Reform," 250; cf. Thomas and Hero, *Foundation Documents,* 149, where he applies this word to Bessai). Malamut ("Bessai," 247) simply leaves it untranslated, and Janin makes no comment. If, however, the cognate word διοικεῖν is used here in the sense of "supporting," then it would seem reasonable to suppose that αὐτοδιοίκητος could also be taken as "self-supporting" or "self-sufficient." Indeed, in the context, this makes perfect sense. What appears to be the subject of discussion here is the provisioning and supply of the monastery, and thus brother Cyril (significantly the current *oikonomos* or steward of Galesion) responds to Lazaros' argument by saying that the problem is that he [Lazaros] is assuming there will be a plentiful supply of provisions for the foundation when all the evidence at the time points to the fact that it is desperately short of both food and water (themes which recur several times in the *vita:* cf.,

the father replied, "No. All the <*proasteia*> on this side of the ridge[1019] that separates this monastery from that one [Bessai] are to provide support for <the monastery> here. And, as I've said, the superior will have the authority to take from the <monks who are> here <on Galesion> and return <to those who are> there <at Bessai> only those <agricultural products> that he finds are in surplus after making inquiries of the steward once a year, and nothing more. But the monastery of the Pausolype[1020] is self-supporting, as you all know full well, since it possesses the *proasteion* of Epoptine. For since God has approved the foundation of that monastery, because He is good, He has also taken care to arrange things so that it can support itself." Brother Cyril <then>

---

e.g., Chap. 218, where Bessai is contrasted very favorably with the situation on Galesion; note also chap. 35 in Gregory of Cyprus' version, *AASS,* Nov. 3:602E–F). Moreover, the word αὐτοδιοίκητος is paralleled in the following sentence by the phrase τὰ πρὸς αὐτάρκη διοίκησιν, something which clearly suggests "self-sufficiency" rather than "self-government." The concept of αὐτάρκεια was a key one in Byzantine society for both peasant and aristocrat and, at heart, it contains precisely the ideal of "self-sufficiency" (see especially, and at length, here Kaplan, *Les hommes,* 493–522). If Bessai and the foundation of the Pausolype are not identical (see Introduction, section F.a, p. 35), then Lazaros is here contrasting the self-sufficient position of the latter with that of the former, Bessai, which must depend on the charity of the superior of Galesion for at least some, if not most, of its support. This would certainly fit in with Lazaros' apparent intention (and Gregory the Cellarer's evident determination) to do all he could to ensure the survival of Galesion and prevent Bessai from becoming a serious rival or alternative to it by rendering the latter a completely subsidiary (and indeed, second-rate) establishment. On the other hand, even if the Pausolype *is* to be identified with Bessai, the point here is presumably that it does not need the support provided by these *proasteia* (since it is "self-sufficient" in that it possesses Epoptine), whereas Galesion most definitely does.

[1019] For discussion of the meaning of the Greek word used here, ζυγός (or, ζυγόν), which basically means anyone and then anything which lies across or athwart something else, see Malamut, "Bessai," 245. She is surely correct in interpreting it as a line of mountains or hills, rather than the "pass" envisaged by Janin (*Églises centres,* 246), although the two are, presumably, not incompatible. One might conceivably translate it as "<natural> barrier," thus including both hills and, apparently, the river (Caystros?) that separated the two establishments. Malamut discusses the location more widely ("Bessai," 244–46).

[1020] The Pausolype was mentioned in Chap. 245 as having been mostly constructed with funds donated by Maria Skleraina. On its possible relationship to Bessai, see the Introduction, Section F.a, p. 35.

said,[1021] "You<'ve assumed> a great abundance <of material supplies> when writing in the rule about our needs and our regimen, but I don't know, or rather I'm at a loss <to know>, where or how we'll be able to find these things as easily as that." The brother said this because of the dearth of necessities and the shortage in the monastery at that time[1022] and because he had no hope that the monastery itself was going to continue to exist after Lazaros' death. When <Cyril> said this, the father replied to him, "I believe in my Christ, that if you do exactly what I've laid down <in this document>[1023] then you'll have an abundance of everything." He was also asked about a superior and said, "You'll make <superior> whomsoever God wants." So much for this.

248. And so Lazaros was finally[1024] mortified in his body, so to speak, not only by his illness, but also by his abstinence from food and his vigils and the harshness of the winter. For, from the time that he was afflicted by his illness, in addition to the lack of food and the vigils with which he was contending while in distress from his illness, he also had to deal with the rigors of a winter storm. For it was then the month of November. For, as Lazaros had been soaked by the rain that fell then in torrents, when a north wind blew after the storm had passed,[1025] this caused him a great deal of additional distress, as <I> have said. Three[1026] days before his death, Lazaros summoned the monk Neophytos, who was then the assistant cellarer,[1027] and, taking out the *nomis-*

[1021] If this is Cyril the steward, then some indication is given of the high level within the community at which concern was being felt over Lazaros' determination to keep the monastery on Galesion at all costs. Compare the desire of Laurentios (later the Stylite) to depart if he should survive Lazaros (Chap. 217) and, e.g., the doubts expressed by the monk Matthew and other brothers in Chaps. 109–10.

[1022] Cf. Chap. 210, which refers to a severe famine in the area at this time.

[1023] The Greek verb διατάσσω has the sense of making a bequest or a testamentary disposition when used in the middle voice, as here, and it thus refers explicitly to the rule Lazaros has had written.

[1024] The Greek adverb τελείως also has the sense of "completely" or "absolutely"; both meanings are implicit here.

[1025] Reading παρέλευσιν for παρέλευσεν.

[1026] Reading γ′ οὖν with Delehaye. The manuscript simply has ἡμερῶν γοῦν, which could be translated as "<some> days before his death."

[1027] The term *parakellarios* is not found in the standard lexica but this meaning seems reasonably certain; on the apparently analogous office of *parekklesiarches* (assistant sacristan), see above, Chap. 82.

mata that the brothers had recently brought back from their mission,[1028] he gave them to him with instructions to give them to the brothers after his death.[1029] Which the brother did indeed do. <Now> no other *nomisma* was found in his <possession> except for these which, as has just been mentioned, the brothers had recently brought back from their mission. <He did this> so that the people who had wickedly gossiped about him and had actually not been ashamed to label him as avaricious might <themselves> be put to shame in this <way>. They used to say this because, while they saw what was given to him by the faithful Christians, yet they never saw what <he spent> for the support of both the monastery and the monks, as well, of course, as what he used to give away secretly to the poor. As a result, even some of the brothers of the monastery used to say that his pillar was stuffed full of *nomismata.*[1030] The father often heard this and would say jokingly and smiling at them, "Anything *I* have is yours. And no doubt after my death you'll find it inside my pillar as you say!" After he had died, however, they not only failed to find a store of *nomismata,* as they had expected,[1031] but even discovered that those <*nomismata*> that the brothers had recently brought were missing <too>, because for fifteen days he had given all this <money> to the poor without anyone knowing.[1032] For poor people were often standing in front of his pillar

[1028] This apparently refers to the mission to Constantinople of Gabriel and Pachomios mentioned in Chaps. 221, 245, and 246, since the latter chapter seems to indicate that Lazaros fell into his last illness immediately after they returned.

[1029] Lazaros' determination not to die while in the possession of money should be related to his stern words on the subject in Chap. 163, above.

[1030] Cf. here the criticism of Lazaros' financial administration by the monk Kosmas Polites in Chap. 193.

[1031] Delehaye includes in the text here a phrase found in the margin of the manuscript (μόνον <οὐχ> ὡς αὐτοῖς ἐδόκει προαποκείμενα) and I have duly translated this; its insertion at this point does nothing to simplify interpretation of this difficult passage, however, especially as it has had to be emended by Delehaye to make good sense, and it may thus be better to omit it. Without it the text might be rendered: "they did not find any *nomismata,* but even discovered. . . ." Further on this marginal phrase and the difficulties of the passage as a whole, see the following note.

[1032] While this sentence does make sense as it stands, the last statement is problematic. The apparent implication of the present text is that during the fifteen days before he died, Lazaros gave away to the poor all the money in his possession, *including* that brought back on the mission and given to Neophytos. In that case, however, it directly contradicts the statement, made a little above, that Lazaros told Neophytos to give this

begging to receive something from him and, although he used to appear to send them away <empty-handed>, he secretly used to give them[1033] whatever his resources permitted,[1034] either himself or by way of a brother.[1035]

249. The moment for Lazaros' departure had now come. Some of the brothers, whom he was sending out to the Kastron [Ephesus] for some things the monastery needed, thus went to him to receive his blessing so that they might leave, but he said to them, "Don't go down this evening because of the vigil." For it was Sunday <the next day>.[1036] And when one of them went up toward dawn to ask Lazaros if he would give them the order to go—this was

particular sum of money to the brothers after his death, "which the brother did indeed do," and that "no other *nomisma* was found in his possession *except* that brought back by the brothers." There are a number of mistakes, alterations, and additions in the manuscript at this point and it seems quite possible that something may have dropped out of the sentence or been switched around, producing this apparent inconsistency. Furthermore, as was argued in the Introduction, section F.b, pp. 47–48, the rather uncertain history of this perhaps important donation and the vagueness of Gregory the Cellarer's narrative concerning it may be related to the rivalry between Galesion and Bessai, to factional disputes within Lazaros' community, and to the related question of the original purpose for which it was intended, making this passage particularly prone to tampering. The most likely solution is that the last part of the sentence was not originally intended to refer to the money brought back by the brothers, but only to that already in Lazaros' possession. Indeed, the marginal note mentioned above, which shows that its author was also having problems with the text at this point, may well have been intended to suggest precisely this solution. Delehaye has had to emend the note in order to make sense of it in the text, but in its unemended form it may be translated "only the <money> they thought had been stored up beforehand." It thus seems likely that the author of the note was referring to the last part of the sentence and that Delehaye was mistaken in inserting it where he did. In sum, it seems clear from the chapter as a whole that Lazaros himself deliberately created the impression that the money brought back by the brothers had been given away, along with the rest, but that it in fact resurfaced sometime later in the possession of those whom he wanted to control it and not in the hands of his opponents.

[1033] The phrase παρεῖχε τούτοις is found in the margin in the manuscript.

[1034] There would seem to be an allusion here to Acts 11:29 in the wording of the Greek.

[1035] See above, Chap. 145, where reference is also made to this practice by Lazaros.

[1036] The text here appears to disagree with the clear statement below, Chap. 253, that Lazaros died on a Sunday. The difficulty may be resolved, however, by taking the present reference as an explanation of the vigil, which took place on the Saturday evening in preparation for the Sunday, hence my translation.

Jonas who used to be troubled by an evil demon but who, they say, was immediately set free from the scourge of the Evil One by entering the pillar and touching the holy body of our blessed father[1037]—when, <then, this man> went up and asked him <about this>, the father ordered him to bring a ladder and enter the pillar. The brother did so and, upon entering the pillar, found Lazaros sitting on his little seat, as though he were asleep. Thinking that he had <already> died, because he did not answer when called, <Jonas> opened the little window in the pillar that looked toward[1038] the church and called out through his tears, "Brothers, the father's died!" The brothers were just beginning to sing the ninth ode then,[1039] but when they heard this cry[1040] they all immediately stopped singing and, instead of the melody of the ode they had been singing, they raised a doleful tune; <then>, weeping and striking themselves as they beat their breasts, they went running out of the church and up to the pillar. Other brothers, who had brought lights (for it was still dark),[1041] entered the pillar by the ladder, and they too found Lazaros sitting like that, with his hand on his right cheek and looking as though he was asleep. When the brothers saw him sitting <there> like that they began to call him and say with tears, "Bless us father, open your eyes and look at your children,[1042] open

[1037] Cf. the *vita Danielis,* chap. 97, where Daniel also cures a demoniac at the time of his death.

[1038] Or perhaps "into" the church. On this point, see the Introduction, section C, p. 18.

[1039] The text has "the ninth hour (ὥραν)" here, but this would appear to be problematic since Jonas' discovery of Lazaros' critical condition occurred just before or perhaps during the early morning office of *orthros* (lit. "dawn") while it was still dark: it would thus be impossible for the brothers to be singing the office of the ninth hour (nones), which fell in mid-afternoon. Furthermore, it is stated below that Lazaros actually died after receiving communion around the second hour, quite early in the morning. There is a plausible suggestion by a later hand in the margin of the manuscript that the text should perhaps be emended here to "the ninth ode" (ᾠδὴν) and the translation follows this emendation; cf. also the use of ᾠδῆς in the following sentence. On the Byzantine hours of the day, see *ODB,* s.v. "Hour."

[1040] Lit. "statement."

[1041] Cf. Mary Magdalene's visit to Jesus' tomb on the first day of the week while it was still dark; Jn. 20:1.

[1042] Part of this sentence is supplied by Delehaye from an abbreviated marginal note in the manuscript; the author probably has Is. 60:4 in mind here ("*Lift up thine eyes round about, and behold the children gathered*"), although the wording appears to

your lips and grant us forgiveness for the sins we have committed against God and against you." When the brothers who were standing in front of the pillar heard these doleful words [587], they too began to say tearfully to the father, "Give us an answer, father, and grant forgiveness to <us> wretches. Alas, what is this dreadful thing that has happened to us? Where shall we go? Who can govern us after you as well as you <have done>?" But this is what those who were childish and faint at heart like me said, while those who were more advanced in asceticism encouraged themselves and the others by saying, "Glory to the Holy God, Who makes everything <happen> to our advantage, as He <alone> knows <how to do>."

250. While the brothers were engaged in <doing> this, the father quietly opened his eyes and looked at them, and when they saw this they began, one after the other, to call out in a loud voice, "Forgive us, father!" When this cry arose from them, the father raised his right hand a little and, moving his lips in a similar way, granted each of them forgiveness. They also brought the rule for him to sign, but since he did not have the strength to take it in his hands and sign it, the monk Cyril, who was also inside the pillar, put the pen in the father's hand and then, guiding it while the father moved it a little, signed this <document>.[1043] Lazaros remained like this, as if he were asleep, until the sec-

draw also on 4 Ki. 19:16; Bar. 2:17; Dan. 9:18 in the first part; cf., in the second, Bar. 5:5.

[1043] The text of the *vita* thus quite clearly indicates that Lazaros is still alive at this point, albeit extremely weak. The tradition found in the version by Gregory of Cyprus and in the Moscow *synaxarion*, however, contains an evidently enhanced and miraculous account of these events. There Lazaros is already dead, and the distraught monks believe that he has left them no *typikon*. In response to their pleas, however, the corpse is reanimated; it first produces the document from inside its clothes and then, when they discover that it is still unsigned, proceeds to sign it for them (Gregory of Cyprus, chap. 42, *AASS*, Nov. 3:606A–B; Moscow, Historical Museum [ГИМ] 369/353, ff. 220–220v). Cf. here Kazhdan, "Ideals," 476; his article in the *ODB*, s.v. "Lazaros of Mount Galesios"; and Kazhdan and Epstein, *Change*, 88. One may perhaps see in this different tradition a simple hagiographic enhancement, presumably designed to assist with the slightly awkward fact that there are no obvious posthumous miracles recorded in the primary *vita* (see above, Introduction, section I, p. 63), but it is also conceivable that an older tradition could lie behind Gregory of Cyprus' account, one which took a slightly different line from the primary *vita* in dealing with a hostile version of events which held that Lazaros had indeed died *without* having signed the vital *diatyposis*, thus rendering it invalid. Further on this possibility, see the Introduction, section F.a, pp. 39–40.

ond hour,[1044] when he received the undefiled sacraments, for one of the priests among the brothers of the monastery had celebrated the holy Eucharist in the righthand part of the narthex. <Then>, as in an untroubled and gentle sleep, he surrendered his holy soul to the Lord through the hands of holy angels, and both lay down and slept[1045] the sleep of eternal repose which all the saints in Christ sleep <so> well.

251. But when they had lifted up Lazaros' body on the pillar and let it hang suspended <there> in order to bring it down, oh, what a truly dreadful[1046] mist and gloom dimmed both the spiritual and corporeal eyes of the brothers, oh what a cloud of despair, oh what a fount of tears, and nothing else could be seen among them all at that time except for woe and lamentation and inconsolable weeping. Moreover, <the image of> my Jesus was reproduced again in the sight of that sacred body, and it really seemed as if He could be seen being taken down from the cross once more.[1047] Of course this greatly increased the <brothers'> lamentation and their wailing mounted even more intensely. For who could have passed by that sight without <shedding> tears? Who would not have been bitterly pricked at heart and let fall scalding tears when he saw that dead body hanging down from the pillar, that body which even before his [Lazaros'] death had been mortified through his asceticism and had wrestled down the bodiless enemy? <Who would not have wept> when he saw those eyes <now> closed which had opened the eyes of <so> many people to consideration of their future blessings and which by pouring out perpetually flowing tears had dried up the dark sea of the passions? <Who would not have wept to see now> shut up and silenced that mouth, those lips, and that tongue which had opened the mouths of <so> many and had moved their tongues to the praise of God? <Who would not have wept to see now> hanging down toward the <ground> those hands which <so> blessedly were always raised up to God and had set <so> many people free from the hands of

[1044] The second hour is still quite early in the morning.

[1045] Cf. Ps. 4 (5):8: "*I will both lie down in peace and sleep.*"

[1046] Lit. "great" (πολλῆς).

[1047] This marks the culmination of the parallels Gregory the Cellarer has been drawing for some time in the *vita* between the end of Lazaros' life and that of Jesus. There may also be some reminiscence of the *vita Danielis,* chap. 99, for Daniel's body was affixed to a plank and displayed vertically to the onlookers "like an icon"; and of Theodoret, *Hist. Rel.*, 26.28, where Symeon the Stylite the Elder's body is said to have remained upright even in death.

demons and of wicked men; and those feet <now> become motionless that had run along *the strait and narrow path,* as the Gospel has it,[1048] and which had caused the feet of <so> many, who had <previously> been tottering about in sin and sliding rapidly toward the pit of destruction[1049] due to their despair, to be set most securely on the firm rock of hope and faith? <And who would not have wept when he gazed> upon all the other parts of his body, with which, to speak like the apostle, *he had glorified God,*[1050] and upon his venerable head, <now> hanging down just like that of the One Who formerly was hung upon the cross for our sake? Thus numerous causes of lamentation arose <then> for the brothers in every way.

252. But when they had brought him down in this way from the pillar by way of the ladder, they took Lazaros into the church, and placed him on his back on the floor. They then took off the leather tunic he was wearing and one could see a strange and extraordinary sight <if one looked> at him; for his body, which had been wasted away by the great austerities and hardships of his asceticism, was cleaner and in better condition than the bodies of people who pamper themselves every day with baths and luxurious living and other self-indulgence. While they were unfastening the irons which he wore,[1051] a distinguished monk, who had just then come to the monastery from Constantinople to see Lazaros, was standing there. When he saw the father's body and his irons and his leather tunic, he turned to those standing near him and said, "This monk is truly great. I don't think <another> such man could be found on earth today." This monk had a layman with him to serve <him>, and this man went out on the night <before>[1052] Lazaros was to die and, as he himself told us in the morning, saw fire come down from heaven like lightning and surround the church and the pillar; the flame then gathered together into a single <ball> and, running along like water, went inside the pillar.[1053] As <I>

[1048] Cf. Mt. 7:14.

[1049] Cf. Is. 14:23: "*a pit . . . for destruction.*"

[1050] The allusion would appear to be to a combination of 1 Cor. 6:20 and, perhaps, Rom. 6:13, 19.

[1051] See above, Chap. 35, for a detailed description of these; cf. also Chap. 179.

[1052] Lit. "in which." The translation accords with the fact that although he clearly collapsed during the night, Lazaros did not actually die until later the next day.

[1053] The monk Nikephoros is reported to have seen a very similar sight in Chap. 86, above. Cf. also the blinding flash of light which fills the house at the moment of Lazaros'

have said, this man, told us what, by God's grace,[1054] he had seen. <Then>, after they had unfastened Lazaros' irons and removed them from his <body>, they sponged off our holy father, according to the rule of the monastery, and dressed him in his leather tunic again. They then lifted him onto a bier and carried him into the narthex, where they set him down; and, after they had celebrated the usual <rites> over him, he remained there unburied until the following day.[1055]

253. The brothers then <started> discussing and trying to decide where they should bury him, because when they had asked him about this he had told them to throw his body into the gorge [588] as food for the birds and the beasts.[1056] The monk Laurentios said,[1057] "When I went up to <see> him just a few days ago, Lazaros asked me if the place near my cell where the rosemary bush stands would be suitable for making his grave, so that we shouldn't suddenly <have to> start <doing this>, he [Lazaros] added, and <thus> not be able to prepare it as we <would> wish." But some of the brothers said, "We must take him to Bessai, because, if he's buried here, the metropolitan might <claim to> have control over us for that reason." After the brothers had discussed this matter a great deal among themselves, they decided to bury him in a sarcophagus[1058] and to put this in the narthex on the righthand side of the

birth, above, Chap. 3; the author may well be emphasizing a symmetry he sees in the events accompanying both the birth and death of the saint.

[1054] Lit. "as seemed good to God."

[1055] The preparation of Lazaros' body, as described here, is discussed in the *ODB*, s.v. "Funeral." The *vita* appears somewhat unusual in its concentration on the ritual preparation of the body, as in the absence here of memorable last words or a vision. Further on the accounts of the deaths of holy men and women, see D. Abrahamse, "Rituals of Death in the Middle Byzantine Period," *GOrThR* 29 (1984), 125–34; see also G. K. Spyridakes, "Τὰ κατὰ τὴν τελευτὴν ἔθιμα τῶν Βυζαντινῶν ἐκ τῶν ἁγιολογικῶν πηγῶν," Ἐπ.Ἑτ.Βυζ.Σπ. 20 (1950), 72–171; and Ph. Koukoules, "Βυζαντινῶν νεκρικὰ ἔθιμα," Ἐπ.Ἑτ.Βυζ.Σπ. 16 (1940), 3–80, although none of these make use of the present *vita*.

[1056] See above, Chap. 246.

[1057] This is presumably Laurentios the Stylite, although this chapter evidently shows that he did not move onto a pillar until after Lazaros died (cf. above, Chap. 138).

[1058] Although burial in true sarcophagi was relatively common in Late Antiquity, it had become rare by this time and was generally reserved for the rich and famous. In the 11th century, however, simpler and less costly sarcophagi were used of the type

church until such time as there should be a superior; then, in accordance with his decision, they would do whatever he decided was best. They <thus> made a sarcophagus from *incorruptible wood,* or cypress <in other words>,[1059] and laid his sacred body in it on the aforesaid righthand side of the narthex; afterward they enclosed it with slabs of marble. This was on the eighth of November, <the day> on which the feast of the great Archangels is celebrated.[1060] For Lazaros died on the seventh of that month, <which was> a Sunday, and I do not think his demise and burial occurred merely by chance on those days. <Thus this in fact happened> so as to make it perfectly clear that, just as he left his own homeland because he was moved by zeal for Christ and arrived at that place where there was, and still is, the house of His resurrection,[1061] and <then>, after he had returned again from there according to the divine will, constructed on this mountain this very church <that bears> the name of the holy Resurrection, so Christ also translated him from earth to heaven on this holy day which commemorates the resurrection.[1062] Furthermore, the festival of the holy <and> incorporeal <angels> followed immediately after Lazaros' burial <rites> because his holy and revered soul, <now> released from the bonds of the flesh, is celebrating the everlasting and blessed feast and festi-

---

apparently described here, made of wood enclosed with stone slabs. Burial in the narthex of the church (as elsewhere in the building) was also not uncommon, especially for more notable people. See further, *ODB,* s.v. "Sarcophagus," "Burial." No indication is given as to what *did* eventually happen to Lazaros' remains.

1059 The Greek phrase rendered here as "incorruptible wood" (ξύλα ἄσηπτα) also appears in Ex. 25:5. It is variously translated into English there as "shittim wood" (AV) or "acacia wood" (RSV), and the tree to which it refers is generally taken to be the *Acacia tortilis,* rather than the *Cupressus sempervirens* indicated here.

1060 Strictly not just of the archangels but the *Synaxis ton Asomaton,* or all heavenly incorporeal beings. The archangels recognized by the Christian church were Michael, Gabriel, and Raphael. See further, *ODB,* s.v. "Archangel," "Asomatos."

1061 The reference is to the church of the Holy Sepulchre in Jerusalem, further on which see above, Chap. 16. The apparently strange wording of the reference here may perhaps be explained by the fact that the church, the destruction of which Lazaros had himself witnessed (Chap. 19), had recently (1042–48) been reconstructed by Constantine IX Monomachos; see R. Ousterhout, "Rebuilding the Temple: Constantine Monomachus and the Holy Sepulchre," *Journal of the Society of Architectural Historians* 48 (1989), 66–78.

1062 Sunday was held to commemorate the Resurrection.

val in heaven along with those <angels> and it stands there with them and offers up the thrice-holy hymn[1063] to the God of all. For, even while he was still alive, the blessed <father> used to honor the holy festivals celebrated for the incorporeal <angels> in a special and different <way> from those of the other saints, and he held them in great reverence; he had also made a rule that the brothers should hold vigils for them. "These <archangels>," he would say, "are God's servants and our unsleeping guards and we must revere and honor them to <the best of> our ability." And the icons of the holy archangels that were painted in front of his pillar are also a sure proof of his love for the incorporeal <angels>.[1064]

254. Thus our blessed and divinely inspired father Lazaros, *full of* human and spiritual *days,*[1065] ended his life excellently and in a manner most dear to God after he had lived for eighty-six years altogether.[1066] He was <thus> about eighteen years old when he left his homeland, and twenty years went by before he returned to it again by the divine will; he <then> spent seven years at the <monastery of> St. Marina[1067] and forty-one years on Mt. Galesion.[1068] He

[1063] Lit. the "*trisagion* hymn." The allusion here is to the "Holy, Holy, Holy" acclamation of God by the seraphim at Is. 6:3, and by the "four living creatures" at Rev. 4:8. On the liturgical trisagion, see above, Chap. 45. When he describes Lazaros' soul standing and singing to God with the other heavenly beings, Gregory the Cellarer probably has Rev. 14:3–5 in mind; cf. also Rev. 5:9; 15:3.

[1064] On the location of these icons, cf. above, Chap. 226. In connection with Lazaros' devotion to the cult of the archangels, it is perhaps worth noting that he evidently underwent a formative experience as a young man in the narthex of the church of the Archangel Michael at Chonai (above, Chap. 7). On his return to Asia Minor from the Holy Land he revisited Chonai and prayed in the church there again (Chap. 29). Chap. 173 also records an image of Michael in the refectory.

[1065] On this expression and its origin, see above, Chap. 175; cf. also Chap. 177.

[1066] This does not tally with the age of seventy-two given in the version of the *vita* by Gregory of Cyprus (chap. 41, *AASS,* Nov. 3:606E), in the epitome published by Delehaye (*AASS,* Nov. 3:608A), or in the Moscow *synaxarion* (Moscow, Historical Museum [ГИМ] 369/353, f. 220). There are, however, serious problems with the chronology if the age provided by the primary *vita* is rejected, quite apart from questions about the reliability of these other sources; see further the Introduction, section B, p. 6 n. 10. Ševčenko, "Eastern Provinces," 723, mistakenly states that Lazaros died at the age of eighty-one.

[1067] The same figure is given above in Chap. 35.

[1068] See the Introduction, section B, p. 14.

died, as I have said, on the aforesaid seventh <day> of the month of November in the six-thousand five-hundred and sixty-second year after the creation of the world, indiction seven.[1069]

255. This <then> was the career, this the life of that *earthly angel and heavenly man,*[1070] our blessed father Lazaros. He kept on earth to the *strait and narrow path,* as the Gospel <has it>,[1071] and has <thus now> passed on to the open spaces and ever-enduring life in heaven,[1072] <where> he stands with the angels in the presence of the holy and life-giving Trinity, receiving abundant rewards for his many labors. <There> he constantly and eagerly intercedes on behalf of us who speak his praises on earth, so that we may receive from God release from the grievous <ills> that oppress us and <forgiveness> for the sins we have committed, and in order that we too, after we have made holy remembrance of him with spiritual joy and have eagerly striven to emulate his life as far as we can, may offer up praise to the Son and the Father and the Holy Spirit, now and always, for ever and ever. Amen.

Thanks <be> to God who accomplishes <all> good things.

Lord Jesus Christ, Son of God, have mercy on me.

[1069] That is, 7 November 1053. See further on this date Malamut, "Bessai," 243–44, and the Introduction, section B, p. 5.

[1070] Cf. John Chrysostom, *De poenitentia,* PG 49:291.2.

[1071] See Mt. 7:14. Delehaye indicates that there is a small lacuna in the manuscript at this point.

[1072] Cf. the rather similar passage above, Chap. 180.

APPENDIX A

Chronological Outline: Lazaros' Life and Related Events

Date	*Events*	*Byzantine rulers*
		963–69 Nikephoros II Phokas
966/67	Lazaros is born near Magnesia on the Meander.	
		969–76 John I Tzimiskes
972/73	Lazaros begins his education with the local priest Leontios (age 6).	
975/76	Lazaros begins studies with the notary George at Oroboi (age 9).	
		976–1025 Basil II
978/79	Lazaros joins his uncle Elias in the Kalathai monastery (age 12); he makes his first attempt to run away.	
980/81	Lazaros moves to the Strobelion monastery and studies to be a notary with the monk Nicholas (age 14).	
984/85	Lazaros runs away to the East (age 18); he visits Chonai and travels across Asia Minor.	
ca. 984–86	Lazaros reaches Attaleia and avoids enslavement; he enters a monastery near Attaleia, where he remains as a monk and then a solitary for seven years.	
ca. 991–93	Lazaros arrives in Jerusalem (age 25/26); he enters the monastery of St. Sabas.	
ca. 996–99 [?]	Lazaros is expelled from St. Sabas after which he enters the monastery of St. Euthymios; he later returns to St. Sabas, where he is made *kanonarches.*	

1001 or before	Lazaros is ordained deacon and priest by the patriarch of Jerusalem, Orestes Hieremias.
ca. 1003 [?]	Lazaros' brother Ignatios is born.
1009 (Sept.)	Lazaros witnesses the destruction of the Holy Sepulchre in Jerusalem; he leaves the Holy Land shortly thereafter (age 42/43).
late 1009/ early 1010	Lazaros visits the "Wondrous Mountain" at Antioch; he then travels through Cilicia to Cappadocia.
1010 (spring)	Lazaros travels to pilgrimage sites in Pontus.
late 1010/ early 1011	Lazaros returns to the Ephesus region; he visits Oroboi and stays briefly at the monastery of Kepion.
1011/12	Lazaros begins his seven-year stay at St. Marina (age 45); he moves onto a pillar and is joined by his young brother Ignatios.
1018/19	Lazaros has a six-month trial stay in the cave of Paphnoutios on Galesion; he is ordered off Galesion by the metropolitan of Ephesus, but later returns to remain there permanently (age 52/53).
1019 [?]	Lazaros moves to the pillar of the Savior; he nearly dies of thirst, but is saved by the layman Loukianos of Kepion. The monk Kosmas moves from St. Marina to the cave of Paphnoutios.
1020s	The community at the Savior gradually develops.
	1025–28 Constantine VIII
	1028–34 Romanos III Argyros
	Lazaros is visited frequently by the nun Irene from Ephesus, causing local ill-feeling and opposition within the community.
1030/31	Lazaros moves to the pillar of the Theotokos (age 64). The incidents in which the monk Symeon is assaulted by demons in the cave of Paphnoutios, the monk Meletios hears demonic horsemen, and an anonymous solitary leaves the mountain and eats meat occur shortly thereafter.

1030s	The community at the Theotokos gradually develops; a dry-stone apsidal chapel is built near Lazaros' pillar; his mother (tonsured as Eupraxia) is now living in the region of Galesion.
	1034–41 Michael IV
	Lazaros attempts to live with his feet exposed until visited by a Western monk who dissuades him from doing so. Also during this period, the snake crawls onto Lazaros' feet, the ex-prisoner accidentally sleeps with his daughter, Menas encounters the bears, Constantine brings the honeycombs, and Himerios witnesses the visit of Makrembolites.
1040	The anonymous monk and the monk Meletios travel to Bulgaria and become involved with the rebellion of Peter Deljan (Dolianos). They return separately to Galesion in late 1041 or early 1042.
late 1041/42 [?]	Lazaros moves to the pillar of the Resurrection (age 75/76).
	1041–42 Michael V
1042 (April)	The mission of Isaiah and Neophytos with a letter from Lazaros to Nikephoros Kampanes arrives in Constantinople at the time of the overthrow of Michael V Kalaphates.
	1042 Zoe and Theodora
1042	The anonymous monk visits Constantine Monomachos in exile on Mitylene, and he "predicts" that Constantine will become emperor; after this has happened (June 1042), the monk claims a reward of gold and spices in Constantinople.
	1042–55 Constantine IX Monomachos
1042–46	Romanos Skleros visits Galesion [?]; Maria Skleraina makes a donation for the foundation of the monastery of the Pausolype; the Theotokos at Bessai is founded [?]. The young monk Ignatios suffers a crippling illness and then is cured by Lazaros. The monk Kerykos moves from the pillar of Petra to Lazaros' old pillar of the Theotokos.

1050	Lazaros suffers a serious illness and loses his teeth; he orders the layman Pantaleon to dig a grave for him in or behind the apse of the church at the Resurrection.
1053 (summer?)	Lazaros sends the monks Pachomios and Gabriel to Constantine IX Monomachos; Lazaros sends a letter to Monomachos by Kosmas the Jerusalemite.
1053 (7 Nov.)	Lazaros dies (age 86); his body is placed in a sarcophagus in the narthex of the church of the Resurrection.
1053 (30 Nov.)	The outstanding ascetic John of Sardis dies; on his death bed he persuades Gregory the Cellarer to stay on Galesion.
late 1053/ early 1054	Lazaros' monasteries undergo a period of confusion; Ignatios remains at Bessai for a time and then becomes superior. Cornelius the one-handed becomes blind at the Savior and dies at the Resurrection; Stephen the eunuch moves to the Resurrection but is then ordered back to the Savior, where he dies.
1053–55	A mission from Galesion to Constantinople with the signed *diatyposis* gains imperial and patriarchal recognition.
1054	The schism between the Eastern and Western churches begins.
	1055–56 Theodora
	1056–57 Michael VI
	Laurentios Halmyrenos dies; the monk Basil, son of Blattopolos, returns to Galesion.
1057	Kosmas, son of Konidiares, becomes involved in the revolt of Isaac Komnenos.
	1057–59 Isaac I Komnenos
	The monk Meletios dies two years before the composition of Lazaros' *vita.*
1058–75 [?]	Gregory the Cellarer composes Lazaros' *vita.*
before 1100 (17 July)	Lazaros' remains are transferred to a permanent location on Galesion.
early 13th c.	Akakios Sabbaites visits Galesion; the *vita* of Barnabas and Sophronios is written.

ca. 1239	Nikephoros Blemmydes is confined on Galesion.
mid-13th c.	Joseph I, future patriarch of Constantinople, is superior of Galesion.
ca. 1273	Galesion acquires the monastery of Nikephoros Blemmydes at Emathia as a *metochion.*
mid to late 13th c.	Athanasios I and Gregory II of Cyprus, future patriarchs of Constantinople, and prominent anti-unionists Meletios and Galaktion are monks on Galesion.
late 13th c.	Gregory II of Cyprus reworks Lazaros' *vita.*
late 13th/ early 14th c.	The epitome and Moscow *synaxarion* versions of Lazaros' *vita* are produced; the chrysobull of Andronikos II provides for the merger of the monastery of the Theotokos on Galesion with that of the Anastasis (Resurrection) in Constantinople; Constantine Akropolites dedicates a chapel to Lazaros in Constantinople and issues regulations for the celebration of his cult; Lazaros' head is translated to Constantinople.
ca. 1304	Galesion is sacked by the Turks.
14th c.	The earliest surviving manuscript of Lazaros' primary *vita,* Athos, Lavrioticus I.127, is copied.
early 15th c.	The Russian traveler Zosima records seeing relics of Lazaros in Constantinople.

APPENDIX B

Prosopographical Glossary

The list includes persons named in the *vita* who were directly involved with Lazaros and Galesion. Numbers in parentheses indicate the chapter in which the person under discussion appears; those in italics indicate that the reference is in a note in that chapter.

Antony

A monk on Galesion, who spent some time in the cave of Paphnoutios, where he was subject to demonic temptation (44).

Barnabas [1]

"The Big"; a monk on Galesion who became arrogant and fell out with Lazaros. He left Galesion (with Methodios [2]) for Magnesia, where he spread malicious rumors about Lazaros and Ignatios [1]; eventually persuaded to come back by Lazaros, he lived first at Bessai and then on the mountain. Still unhappy, he persuaded Lazaros to allow him to return to Bessai, where he died unrepentant. Despite appeals by some fellow monks after his death, Lazaros refused to exonerate him. He is probably to be identified with Barnabas [2] (202).

Barnabas [2]

A monk on Galesion who was sent by Lazaros (along with Nicholas [3]) to Chonai with a letter to "Damianos." He is probably to be identified with Barnabas [1] (227).

Bartholomew

A monk on Galesion, he was steward at the time Lazaros' *vita* was composed. He is cited as a witness to Lazaros' eucharistic practice. He also observed a woman seduce a companion monk while lodging on his way to an estate of Galesion and subsequently experienced Lazaros' gift of insight (83, 90).

Basil [1]

The son of Blattopolos and a monk on Galesion. He was tonsured by Lazaros but left for the Kouzena monastery and then various other places. He returned shortly before Lazaros' *vita* was written. He is possibly to be identified with Basil [2] (99).

Basil [2]

A monk on Galesion who tended fruit for the monastery. He is possibly to be identified with Basil [1] (162).

Benjamin

A monk on Galesion who was *parekklesiarches* at the end of Lazaros' life. He was still alive when Lazaros' *vita* was written, but he apparently no longer held that office (82).

Constantine [1]

The son of the priest Menas at the village of Samakios near Galesion. He was still alive when Lazaros' *vita* was written. As a boy, he ate honey that he was taking to Lazaros (65).

Constantine [2] IX Monomachos

Byzantine emperor from 1042 to 1055. He had as his mistress Maria Skleraina, sister of the Romanos Skleros who visited Lazaros at Galesion. He supposedly had his elevation to imperial power foretold to him by an anonymous monk (Chaps. 228–30) while still in exile on Mitylene in 1042. He later (after June 1042) rewarded this monk in Constantinople with gold and spices. Constantine also granted Lazaros the site of Bessai for remembrance of himself and Maria. He exiled Constantine [3] Barys and had his tongue cut out for treason. He received a delegation from Galesion, headed by Gabriel and Pachomios [3], in [?] the summer of 1053, on which occasion he was persuaded by Gabriel to issue a *prostagma* instructing Lazaros to move from the mountain to Bessai. Lazaros sent him a letter [?] of refusal via Kosmas [3], which annoyed him by its critical tone. He later saw the *diatyposis* and settled the affairs of the monastery satisfactorily (*87,* 105, *221, 223,* 230, *245*).

Constantine [3] Barys

After being exiled by Constantine [2] IX Monomachos, he wrote to Lazaros concerning his political schemes and sent him substantial gifts, which were rejected (105).

Constantine [4] Phlaskas

A flautist who gave up his profession on Lazaros' advice and prospered as a result (123).

Cornelius [1]

"The one-handed"; a monk at the Savior whose secular name was Constantine. He was apparently a young man at the time of Lazaros' death, and soon thereafter was blinded by demons and died at the Resurrection (52).

Cornelius [2]

A monk on Galesion from Armenia. He was in charge of the pack animal used to carry water and other things. He drank too much wine after he broke a flagon he was transporting (91).

Cyril [1]

The son of Gregory [1] and a monk on Galesion at [?] the Resurrection. He was steward at the end of Lazaros' life. He convinced a disgruntled *topoteretes* to return to Lazaros for spiritual advice, and he heard the sound of the demonic manifestation following the confession of Meletios [3]. Before he became steward he was sent on business to the *proasteion* of Pentakrene with Cyril "the shoemaker" [2], whom he rescued from demonic peril with the aid of a local vinedresser. He supported the position of Isaiah [5] and repeated the doubts expressed by the bishop of Tralles, steward of Ephesus, that Galesion would not survive after Lazaros' death. Cyril criticized Lazaros' assumption of the abundance of material supplies when composing the *diatyposis,* and he helped the dying Lazaros to sign the *diatyposis* (49, 118, 226, 244, 245, 247, 250).

Cyril [2]

"The shoemaker"; a monk on Galesion who was sent on business with Cyril [1] to the *proasteion* of Pentakrene. He experienced a demonic dream, as a result of which he nearly fell off a cliff (244).

Damianos Thalassenos [Dalassenos]

Using this name and claiming to be a member of the distinguished Dalassenoi clan, this imposter sought refuge on Galesion and was reluctantly ordered to be tonsured by Lazaros. He later absconded from a group of monks near Amorion, provoking criticism of Lazaros' admission policy from Philippikos [4]. He reverted to lay life at Chonai, where he received letters from Lazaros (carried by Barnabas [2] and Nicholas [3]) and promised to return to the monastery on Galesion. His early death was predicted by Lazaros. He was murdered by his man-servant (227).

Daniel

A monk on Galesion who died in the Chalkos Halonios area (155).

Dorotheos

A monk on Galesion who came from Ikonion. A priest and already old when he entered the monastery, he became an exemplar of monastic virtue despite being blind for the last six years of his life (177).

Elias [1]

Lazaros' uncle and a monk in the monastery of Kalathai. He directed the course of Lazaros' early education and was his third teacher (when Lazaros was ages 12 to 14). He is probably to be identified with Lazaros' anonymous maternal uncle who was the superior of a monastery at or near Oroboi at the time of Lazaros' return from the Holy Land (3–4, 30[?]).

Elias [2]

A monk on Galesion who conducted the visiting monk Photios to Lazaros and entertained him in his cell (84).

Eupraxia

See Irene [1].

Eustathios

"Of Mita"; The uncle of John [4] and a benefactor of Galesion. He suffered from gout, and his death was predicted by Lazaros (103).

Euthymios [1]

A metropolitan of Ephesus (114).

Euthymios [2]

A monk on Galesion who was, due to his poor health, allowed some personal possessions by Lazaros (148).

Gabriel

A monk on Galesion who took a letter from Lazaros to Constantine [2] IX Monomachos in Constantinople (along with Pachomios [3] and other monks) in [?] the summer of 1053. He persuaded the emperor to issue a *prostagma* to force Lazaros to move from Galesion to Bessai, and he also wrote to Lazaros himself urging his compliance (221, 245).

George [1]

An ecclesiastical notary. He was resident at Oroboi, where he was associated with a chapel. He was also Lazaros' second teacher (ages 9 to 12). He had a son (3, 30).

George [2]

A priest in the village of Malpadeas, near Ephesus and the village of Kepion. He accompanied Lazaros on his final move from St. Marina to Galesion in 1018/19 (31, 53).

George [3]

A lay friend of Gregory the Cellarer. He became a monk on Galesion (monastic name unknown) and was [?] alive when Lazaros' *vita* was written (96).

George [4]

A flute player, nicknamed "Dog." He visited Lazaros in the company of John [4]; Lazaros revealed his evil deeds and foretold his death (104).

Gerasimos [1]

A monk on Galesion at the Theotokos who was a servant of the old ascetic John [9] during Lazaros' last years. He was still alive after Lazaros had died. He is probably to be identified with Gerasimos [2] (166–67, 169–70).

Gerasimos [2]

A monk on Galesion and a cellarer at the Theotokos. He helped Nikon [2] after he had been blinded near the monastery. He is probably to be identified with Gerasimos [1] (174).

Germanos [1]

A monk on Galesion. He was a steward at Varvatziana when Lazaros' *vita* was written, and earlier had been in charge of the horses. He attempted to cheat on his oil ration. He is possibly to be identified with Germanos [2] (92).

Germanos [2]

A monk on Galesion and *parekklesiarches* at the Resurrection. He had a disagreement in the church with Isaiah [2] and then complained to Lazaros about his toleration of lax behavior. He had a fight with Ignatios [2] and then experienced a demonic vision when he refused to forgive him. He also had a dispute with Gregory the Cellarer (when he was *trapezopoios* at the Resurrection) over the distribution of communion bread and then complained to Lazaros and refused to listen to him until miraculously shown the error of his ways. He is possibly to be identified with Germanos [1] (152–53, 209).

Gregory [1]

A monk and priest on Galesion, probably at the Savior. He was the father of Cyril [1] the steward. In the cave of Paphnoutios, he was deluded by demons into believing he had a divinely inspired mission to preach a change in eucharistic practice at Ephesus and to convert the Jews. He was imprisoned and punished by Lazaros after disobeying his orders. He is possibly to be identified with the anonymous priest from the Savior who ministered to Lazaros when he was first on the pillar at the Theotokos (49, 64[?]).

Gregory [2]

The Cellarer. He is author of Lazaros' *vita* (see the Introduction, section G).

Hilarios

A monk and the brother of Leontios [2]. He was resident with Leontios at the chapel of St. Marina, where they were joined by Lazaros and built his first column. They later left and founded a monastery on a hill called Hypselos, above the village of Legos (31–32).

Himerios

A monk on Galesion [?]. He was a relative by marriage of John [4] and a witness of the visit of Makrembolites to Lazaros at the Theotokos (101).

Ignatios [1]

Lazaros' younger brother, who, after Lazaros' death, became superior of Galesion, a position he still occupied when Lazaros' *vita* was written. He left home to join Lazaros at St. Marina (age 8), where he was initially adopted by Iouditta. Ignatios is cited as the source for information on Lazaros' diet at St. Marina. He accompanied Lazaros on his final move from St. Marina to Galesion in 1018/19. He was sent, at some point, on a mission to Constantinople with other brothers and was appointed steward at the "house of Philippikos" by Lazaros, but resigned after opposition from Philippikos [3] and others on the ground of nepotism. Ignatios sought to leave Galesion for Kampsai but was persuaded to go to Bessai instead because Lazaros predicted that he would soon become superior of Galesion. Lazaros apparently thought of sending him to Constantinople in the [?] summer of 1053 to obtain imperial confirmation for his succession, but he never actually did so. Ignatios survived a poisoning attempt by Methodios [2] at the time of Lazaros' death, and he remained at Bessai for a short time afterward, before returning to the mountain as superior. He saw a vision concerning the monk Cornelius [1] (33, 52, 53, 81, 94, 202, 221; cf. the Introduction, section B, n. 25).

Ignatios [2]

A monk on Galesion at the Theotokos and the nephew or cousin of the monk Matthew [1]. He was a boy at the time Lazaros was at the Resurrection, between [?] 1042 and 1053. He was struck down by a crippling demonic illness while collecting water in the cave of Paphnoutios. He fought with Germanos [2]. He is possibly to be identified with Ignatios [3] (45, 153).

Ignatios [3]

A monk on Galesion. He was *trapezopoios* during Lazaros' later life and [?] when his *vita* was written; he is cited as a witness to Lazaros' fasting. Ignatios felt responsible for the death of a young layman whom he had sent out to gather wild leeks on the mountain, but he was comforted by Lazaros. He is possibly to be identified with Ignatios [2] (82, 131, 134).

Ioannikios

A monk and priest on Galesion and cellarer at [?] the Savior. He was a heathen when he first came to Lazaros at St. Marina, but was then baptized and tonsured by Lazaros. He eventually became a priest. A model of all types of monastic practice and virtue, he worked primarily in the kitchen. Lazaros sent him to Constantinople in the company of Isaiah [4]. He went to the horse races without Isaiah's approval and, having refused to admit his fault, suffered a (demon-assisted) fall, from which he died some days later (46, 233–34).

Iouditta

A native of Calabria and resident at Ephesus. She built a new church at St. Marina for Lazaros' community there and adopted Lazaros' younger brother Ignatios (33).

Irene [1]

Lazaros' mother. She gave birth to Lazaros, her fifth child, in 966/67 and to Ignatios (at an advanced age) in or after 1003 [?]; she was widowed prior to 1010/11. Irene initially failed to recognize Lazaros on his return to Oroboi. She was tonsured by Lazaros and took the name Eupraxia during or before his time at the Theotokos (probably in the 1020s or early 1030s). She attempted to dissuade Lazaros from extreme asceticism, and witnessed Isaiah [3] cense a cross with burning charcoal that he held in his bare hands (2, 30, 59, *74*, 164, 199, 201; cf. Introduction, section B, n. 25).

Irene [2]

A woman of Ephesus widowed in [?] the early 1020s. She became a nun and visited Lazaros frequently at the Savior, arousing local hostility and opposition in the community. This caused Lazaros' move to the Theotokos, and she was banned from Galesion by Lazaros ca. 1030 (56–57).

Isaiah [1]

A monk on Galesion who, along with Neophytos [3], in April 1042 took a letter from Lazaros to Nikephoros [2] Kampanes in Constantinople. He is probably to be identified with Isaiah [3] and [4] (102).

Isaiah [2]

"The Short"; a monk on Galesion and a rather unruly youth who had a disagreement with Germanos [2] (152).

Isaiah [3]

A monk on Galesion who was an exemplar of obedience and other monastic virtues although illiterate. He was a reliable emissary to the outside world from Galesion and was renowned as a solicitor of donations, which, among other things, paid for the decoration of the three churches on the mountain. Isaiah was responsible for spreading Lazaros' reputation. He later embezzled donations and fell into fornication. He died in agony and apparently haunted the monastery until he was formally provided with posthumous forgiveness by Lazaros. He is probably to be identified with Isaiah [1] and [4] (197–200).

Isaiah [4]

An "elder" on Galesion who was sent by Lazaros to Constantinople with Ioannikios. He reprimanded Ioannikios for visiting the horse races while there, but then forgave him and comforted him after he suffered what was ultimately a fatal fall. He is probably to be identified with Isaiah [1] and [3] (233–234).

Isaiah [5]

"The Tall"; a monk on Galesion at [?] the Resurrection who expressed doubts about the survival of Galesion following Lazaros' death because of his refusal to move to Bessai. Lazaros predicted he would leave Galesion; he withdrew to the monastery of St. Gregory after Lazaros' death (245).

Jacob [1]

A monk on Galesion who cooked at [?] the Resurrection. He still held this position when Lazaros' *vita* was written. He participated in the miraculous multiplication of peas. He is possibly to be identified with Jacob [2] (214).

Jacob [2]

A monk on Galesion who attempted to return to the mountain after leaving but was temporarily blinded by the Devil in the guise of a ragged old man when he refused to go to Bessai instead. He is possibly to be identified with Jacob [1] (218).

Jeremiah

A Georgian ascetic from Palestine who visited Ephesus on his way to Constantinople. He was deeply impressed by Lazaros' great virtue after having visited him and examining him physically; he later reported his findings to the metropolitan of Ephesus, Euthymios (114).

John [1]

A monk on Galesion who had a demonic experience in the gorge (44).

John [2] Kouphalides

A layman from Attaleia who was cured of possession by Lazaros (70).

John [3] Libanos

A friend of Gregory the Cellarer from Constantinople who received a blessing from Lazaros before going to the Anatolikon theme on business. The death of his son George was predicted by Lazaros (97).

John [4]

"Of Mita"; he was a relative by marriage of Himerios, nephew of Eustathios. He saw Lazaros when *dioiketes* of Ephesus and Artokopeion. He visited him again in the company of George [4] after being entrusted with the *episkepsis* of Myrelaion in the Thrakesion theme (101, 103, 104).

John [5]

The "Smyrnian"; a monk on Galesion who was allowed by Lazaros to use a cane to support himself in church after criticism from his fellow monks. Despite his reputation for hostility to Lazaros, he stoutly defended him against critics on one occasion (139, 143).

John [6] Ardagastenos

A monk on Galesion who was the uncle or cousin of John [7] (155).

John [7]

A monk on Galesion who was the nephew or cousin of John [6]. He entered the monastery on Galesion as a boy but was an adult when Lazaros' *vita* was written. He had a demonic experience on his way up the mountain (155).

John [8]

From the Opsikion theme, he was the son of poor parents. He became a monk, priest, and outstanding ascetic on Galesion at an early age. His mother entered the convent of Eupraxia after he was tonsured. He died of complications arising from sores on his foot caused by his asceticism; his mother died shortly after he did (164).

John [9]

From Sardis in Lydia, he was a monk and an outstanding ascetic at the Theotokos on Galesion. He entered the monastery at an advanced age. After injuring his feet through his asceticism, he became progressively incapacitated and suffered various (demonic) afflictions that he bore in exemplary fashion, being exhibited by Lazaros to visitors as a second Job. He persuaded Gregory the Cellarer not to leave Galesion after Lazaros' death. He died on 30 November 1053 (165–70).

Jonas

A monk on Galesion at [?] the Resurrection. He was going on business to Ephesus with other brothers when he discovered that Lazaros was dying (7 November 1053) and announced this to the community. He was cured of demonic illness by entering Lazaros' column (249).

Kerykos [1]

A monk on Galesion who took Leo [1] to Lazaros to show him the effects of his miraculous healing. He is probably to be identified with either Kerykos [2] or [3] (72).

Kerykos [2]

The shoemaker. A monk on Galesion who criticized Lazaros after he had been publicly shamed and had had various personal possessions confiscated. He is possibly to be identified with Kerykos [1] but not Kerykos [3] (148).

Kerykos [3]

A monk on Galesion who was a distinguished ascetic of great physical strength. He was a stylite on the Petra pillar, and then at the church of the Theotokos. He died at the Resurrection of complications from a severe sore on his leg. His death was held by Lazaros to have been delayed by his possession of some small coins. He is possibly to be identified with Kerykos [1] but not Kerykos [2] (159–63).

Kosmas [1]

A monk at St. Marina who moved to the cave of Paphnoutios on Galesion to look after Lazaros when he was first on the column at the Savior in [?] 1019. He is possibly to be identified with Kosmas [2] (55).

Kosmas [2] Philippikos

A monk on Galesion who persuaded Lazaros to eat when he was unable to sustain a fast at the end of his life and to wear a new leather tunic. He twice withdrew from the monastery. He "waged war" on the brothers, causing Lazaros to have to defend himself by force; the affair nearly ended in murder (perhaps a reference either to the intercepted mission of Chap. 239 or the attempt to murder Ignatios [1] in Chap. 202, if to an episode mentioned in the *vita*); he lived a difficult and painful life as a result. He was upset by Lazaros' admission policy, which he considered lax and uncanonical, but was convinced by Lazaros' defense of it. Kosmas [2] is said to have been mentioned often in Lazaros' *vita,* but certain identification with others called Kosmas or Philippikos is hard. He is possibly to be identified with Kosmas [1] (given his later influence over Lazaros); with Kosmas [6] (if cited as a bad example); with Kosmas [7] (given reference to his hostility); with Philippikos [3] (given his opposition to Ignatios' appointment as steward of his "house"); with Philippikos [4] (given his criticism of Lazaros for admission of the charlatan "Damianos"); and with Philippikos [5] (given that he was the supposed recipient of the Devil's largest bottle of oil) (82, 193, 232).

Kosmas [3]

"The Jerusalemite"; a monk on Galesion, he passed a letter from the monk Photios to Gregory the Cellarer and carried a condemnatory letter from Lazaros to the emperor Constantine [2] IX Monomachos as a follow-up to that taken by Gabriel and Pachomios [3] in the [?] summer of 1053. He is possibly to be identified with Kosmas [6] (84, 221, 223).

Kosmas [4]

The son of Konidiares and an old acquaintance of Gregory the Cellarer. He was tonsured as a monk and considered joining the community on Galesion, but subsequently reverted to lay status and took part in the revolt of Isaac Komnenos in 1057 (98).

Kosmas [5] Polites

A monk on Galesion who argued with Lazaros about his continued possession of money and criticized Lazaros' financial administration. He fell sick at Ephesus and died at St. Marina; he was buried at [?] the Resurrection (193).

Kosmas [6]

A monk on Galesion who died at the Savior shortly before the composition of Lazaros' *vita* (197). He is cited as an example, but it is unclear whether of good or bad attitude and practice. He is possibly to be identified with Kosmas [3] (if a good example) or with Kosmas [2] (if a bad example) (197).

Kosmas [7]

The *taxeotes;* a monk on Galesion, he betrayed to the metropolitan of Ephesus a mission sent by Lazaros to the emperor. He later returned to the mountain and was readmitted by Lazaros despite opposition from other monks. He continued to slander Lazaros and died away from the monastery without making a last confession. He is possibly to be identified with Kosmas [2] (in view of his opposition to Lazaros) (239).

Kyriakos Galesiotes

An inhabitant of the village of Galesion, he offered hospitality to a monk returning to the mountain at night. He was keeping watch with a companion over fields at night when he heard and then rescued a layman who had been led by the Devil over the cliffs at St. Onouphrios (154, 243).

Laurentios [1]

A monk on Galesion, he became a stylite, but evidently only after Lazaros' death. He was alive when Lazaros' *vita* was written and is the source for the story of Leo [1]. He questioned Lazaros about lamps in the church and cells, and heard the confession of Symeon [2]. He sought permission from Lazaros to leave the mountain for [?] Bessai if he was unhappy after his death, but was dissuaded. He heard Lazaros' promise that a signed and sealed *diatyposis* would exist when he died. He reported Lazaros' wish to be buried at a spot near his [Laurentios'] cell (71, 138, 201, 217, 223, 253).

Laurentios [2] Halmyrenos

A monk on Galesion who, as a layman, was possessed by a demon after a fall from a horse and cured at the monastery after seeing a vision of Lazaros. He became repossessed after planning to marry instead of entering the monastery, but was cured again when tonsured by Lazaros. With Luke [1], he assisted the drunken monk Cornelius [2]. He died shortly before Lazaros' *vita* was written. His mother became a nun in the convent of Eupraxia after he was tonsured and was still alive, though old, when Gregory the Cellarer was writing (73–74, 91).

Lazaros [1]

"The Short"; a monk on Galesion who was an exemplar of church attendance and contrition. He was the brother of Nicholas [6] and is probably to be identified with Lazaros [2] (178, 242).

Lazaros [2]

A monk on Galesion who once prevented Neilos [2] from striking Lazaros when he caught him dozing. He is probably to be identified with Lazaros [1] (225).

Leo [1]

A layman from Attaleia who was cured of paralysis by a vision of Lazaros following a visit to Galesion. He told his story to the metropolitan of Ephesus and a year later brought a letter to Lazaros from the *protospatharios* Leo [2] Basilitzes (71–72).

Leo [2] Basilitzes

Protospatharios at [?] Attaleia who entrusted Leo [1] with a letter for Lazaros (72).

Leontios [1]

"The great"; a monk and priest who is cited as Gregory the Cellarer's source for Lazaros' early life. He was Lazaros' first teacher (ages 6 to 9 in 972/73–975/76). His wife acted as midwife at Lazaros' birth (2–3).

Leontios [2]

A monk and the brother of Hilarios. He was resident with Hilarios at the chapel of St. Marina, where they were joined by Lazaros and built his first column. They later left and founded a monastery on the hill called Hypselos above the village of Legos (31–32).

Loukianos

A layman who lived in the village of Kepion near Galesion. He was a "spiritual son" of Lazaros, and saved him from dying of thirst when he was first on his column at the Savior in [?] 1019 (55).

Luke [1]

The perfumer. A [?] monk on Galesion who assisted Laurentios [2] with the drunken monk Cornelius [2] (91).

Luke [2]

A monk on Galesion considered a holy fool. He reported that he had heard the complaining spirit of Isaiah [3] (200).

Makrembolites

Unidentified, but evidently an important member of this prominent family. He visited Lazaros at the Theotokos (101).

Matthew [1]

A monk on Galesion who was the uncle or cousin of Ignatios [2]. He is possibly to be identified with Matthew [2] and [3] (45, 153).

Matthew [2]

A monk on Galesion and a critic of Lazaros who expressed skepticism about survival of the community and hence plans to build a large refectory and additional cells at [?] the Resurrection. He is probably to be identified with Matthew [3], possibly with Matthew [1] (109–10).

Matthew [3]

A monk on Galesion who had a vision, when Lazaros was sick ca. 1050, predicting that he would live for three more years. He is probably to be identified with Matthew [2], possibly with Matthew [1] (206–7).

Meletios [1]

"Mavros" (Dark); a monk on Galesion at [?] the Theotokos who saved Philippikos [1] from demonic assault. He heard demonic sounds in the gorge between the Theotokos and the Savior. He met a demonic [?], ragged man on the mountain. He is probably to be identified with Meletios [2], [3], and [4] (47, 50–51).

Meletios [2]

A monk on Galesion who returned to lay life for a time in the village of Kyriou Louka. After being accused by Methodios [1] of robbing his cell, he was arrested and threatened by Lazaros but then released; he subsequently returned to the monastery and was later given charge of the horses. He died at Bessai two years before Lazaros' *vita* was written. He is probably to be identified with Meletios [1], [3], and [4] (142).

Meletios [3]

A monk on Galesion, probably at the Resurrection. He was sent out from the mountain on an errand by Lazaros. He witnessed a demonic manifestation when compelled by Lazaros to confess something he wished to hide. Gregory the Cellarer says this Meletios has been mentioned many times in Lazaros' *vita*, so he must be identified with some, or perhaps all, the others of this name (226).

Meletios [4]

A monk on Galesion who was sent by Lazaros to accompany the unscrupulous monk in Chap. 228–30 on a mission to Bulgaria. He became involved in events connected with the rebellion of Peter Deljan (Dolianos) there in 1040, before leaving the other monk and returning to Galesion. He is probably to be identified with Meletios [1], [2], and [3] (228, *230*).

Meliton

"The flute player"; a monk on Galesion tonsured after Lazaros' death. He had died by the time Lazaros' *vita* was written (123).

Menas

A priest at the village of Samakios near Galesion. The father of Constantine [1], he visited and ministered to Lazaros when he was first on the pillar of the Theotokos. He met bears on the mountain (64–65).

Merkourios [1]

A plasterer and monk on Galesion and a source of stories about Lazaros' foresight. He was [?] still alive when Lazaros' *vita* was written. He is conceivably to be identified with the unnamed monk of Chap. 58 who knew about construction (93).

Merkourios [2]

A monk on Galesion who had money that was taken from his cell by a fellow monk returned by Lazaros (108).

Merkourios [3]

A monk on Galesion who later was a stylite on the Petra pillar until his death, when he was succeeded by Nikon [2]. He is not to be identified with Merkourios [1], if the latter was still alive when Lazaros' *vita* was written, for Nikon predeceased Lazaros (175).

Methodios [1]

"The Tall"; a monk on Galesion who remonstrated with the monk Sabas [2] when he used Lazaros' name to place a binding spell on some goats. He accused the former monk Meletios [2] of robbing his cell (77, 142).

Methodios [2]

A monk on Galesion who was persuaded by Barnabas [1] to leave Galesion for Magnesia, where they spread malicious rumors about Lazaros and Ignatios [1]. He was persuaded to come back by Lazaros, and he tried to poison Ignatios at the time of Lazaros' death. He again left for Magnesia, where he was murdered by swineherds (202).

Michael

The superior of an unnamed monastery. At the behest of the metropolitan of Ephesus he unexpectedly visited Lazaros (in the company of others) and examined his column for evidence of fraud (237).

Neilos [1]

A monk on Galesion. When still a layman he was employed by the cellarer Ioannikios at the Savior as a guide for visitors to the mountain. He is possibly to be identified with Neilos [2] (46).

Neilos [2]

A monk, priest, and elder on Galesion, where he had lived since his youth; he was still alive, though old, when Lazaros' *vita* was composed. He is cited as a witness to Lazaros' eucharistic practice. He sought to leave the mountain for Bessai but was dissuaded by Lazaros. As a young man he had problems staying awake in vigil and once attempted to strike Lazaros after being told by him that he could do so if he caught him asleep during the vigil. He is possibly to be identified with Neilos [1] (83, 217, 225).

Neophytos [1]

A monk on Galesion from Lydia. He had a brother and was forced to give a *nomisma* to the poor by Lazaros. He [?] worked for the cellarer. He was still alive when Lazaros' *vita* was composed. He is probably to be identified with Neophytos [2], [3], and [4] (89, 90[?]).

Neophytos [2]

"The Aged"; a monk on Galesion who at the church of Chrysostom in Constantinople met a nun who had visited Galesion. He was still alive when Lazaros' *vita* was written. He is probably to be identified with Neophytos [1], [3], and [4] (95).

Neophytos [3]

A monk on Galesion who accompanied Isaiah [1] on the mission to Nikephoros [2] Kampanes in Constantinople in April 1042. He is probably to be identified with Neophytos [1], [2], and [4] (102, 248).

Neophytos [4]

A monk on Galesion and *parakellarios.* Three days before Lazaros' death he was secretly entrusted by him with the money brought by monks returning from a mission to Constantinople in summer/fall [?] 1053. He later gave it to the brothers, as instructed. He is probably to be identified with the Neophytos [1], [2], and [3] (248).

Nicholas [1]

A notary at the monastery of Strobelion. He was Lazaros' fourth teacher (in notarial skills) (ages 14 to 17 or 18) (4–5).

Nicholas [2]

"Kyr Eulogesos"; a monk on Galesion who was an exemplar of monastic virtues. He suffered demonic delusions before being cured by Lazaros and was the subject of a (probably posthumous) miracle performed by Lazaros that allowed him an extra day of life, in which case he must have outlived Lazaros. He is possibly to be identified with Nicholas [4] or [7] (47, 178–79).

Nicholas [3]

"Paxamades"; a monk on Galesion before leaving for the (nearby?) monastery of Avilon. He planned to rob the monastery of the Savior but confessed to Lazaros instead and eventually returned to the Savior, where he died. He praised Lazaros' humility and management of the monastery. Lazaros sent him (along with Barnabas [2]) to deliver a letter to "Damianos" at Chonai. He is probably to be identified with Nicholas [6], possibly with Nicholas [4] (66, 151, 227).

Nicholas [4]

"The smith"; a monk on Galesion sent by Lazaros to the village of Galesion for cheese. He is said to have been mentioned often in Lazaros' *vita,* so he is probably to be identified with either Nicholas [2] or [3], possibly with Nicholas [6] (213).

Nicholas [5]

A steward to the bishop of Batheia. He was still alive when Lazaros' *vita* was written. He visited Lazaros in the snow, at the behest of the metropolitan of Ephesus, to look for evidence of fraud (238).

Nicholas [6]

A monk on Galesion and a brother of Lazaros [1]. He twice left the monastery but returned each time and was readmitted by Lazaros. He fell ill while preparing to leave a third time and subsequently died. He is probably to be identified with Nicholas [3] (since there is a parallel mention of the Devil, and the same quotation from Romans is used in both Chaps. 66 and 242); also possibly to be identified with Nicholas [4] (242).

Nicholas [7]

"The scribe"; a monk on Galesion at the [?] Resurrection. He was involved in a discussion with Lazaros over his refusal to move to Bessai from Galesion. He composed the *diatyposis* following Lazaros' instructions (245–46).

Nikephoros [1]

A monk on Galesion who hailed from Stratonikia in Lydia. He saw lightning run from the dome of the church into Lazaros' pillar [?] at the Resurrection. He was alive when Lazaros' *vita* was written (86).

Nikephoros [2] Kampanes

He is to be identified with the Kampanares or Kampanarios who was *eparchos* or city prefect of Constantinople in 1042. He had seen Lazaros when serving as thematic judge of Thrakesion. He received a letter from Lazaros in April 1042, carried by Isaiah [1] and Neophytos [3], predicting the political upheavals in which he [Kampanares] was involved at that time. He is possibly to be identified with Nikephoros [3], the son of Euthymios, but probably not with Nikephoros [4], the son of Proteuon (102).

Nikephoros [3]

The son of Euthymios, he had seen Lazaros when serving as thematic judge. While banished by Constantine [2] IX Monomachos, he communicated with Lazaros, who predicted his recall. He subsequently donated 216 *nomismata* to Galesion. He is possibly to be identified either with Nikephoros [2] or [4] (105–6).

Nikephoros [4]

The son of Proteuon, he visited Lazaros when he was thematic judge. He was probably the governor of Bulgaria who nearly succeeded Constantine [2] IX Monomachos in 1055 but was exiled to the monastery of Kouzena in the vicinity of Galesion. He is possibly to be identified with Nikephoros [3] (119).

Niketas

Lazaros' father. He died prior to Lazaros' return from the Holy Land in 1010/11 (2, 30).

Nikon [1]

A monk on Galesion who was a peasant from Lydia. He was an exemplar of monastic virtue and various forms of asceticism, including self-flagellation. He died before Lazaros (171–73).

Nikon [2]

A monk on Galesion from Phrygia who was an exemplar of monastic virtue and ascetic practice, including acting the holy fool. He carried water to the monasteries, and was temporarily blinded by a demonic assault. Bullied by other monks, he became a stylite on a pillar of Petra following the death of Merkourios [3]; he died a short time later, aged only ca. 20, and was buried in the chapel of the Savior near [?] Petra. Gregory the Cellarer knew his uncle (174–75).

Pachomios [1]

A monk on Galesion who questioned Lazaros' refusal to allow a special meal on a feast day and apparently did not think the monastery would survive Lazaros' death. He is possibly to be identified with Pachomios [3] (140).

Pachomios [2]

An *ekklesiarches* of Limnai, an unknown place evidently near Galesion. With his superior, he sent bread, oil, and wine to the Resurrection during a shortage (209).

Pachomios [3]

A monk on Galesion who took a letter from Lazaros to Constantine [2] IX Monomachos in Constantinople (along with Gabriel and other monks) in the [?] summer of 1053. He is possibly to be identified with Pachomios [1] (221).

Pantoleon [1]

A monk on Galesion who was an exemplar of contrition, industriousness, and other monastic virtues. His cell, which in some way demonstrated the harshness of his life, still existed at the time Lazaros' *vita* was written (179).

Pantoleon [2]

A layman who was doing some work at the monastery of the Resurrection in 1050 when Lazaros became seriously ill. He was ordered by Lazaros to dig a hasty grave for him in or behind the apse of the church (206).

Paphnoutios

An ascetic and predecessor of Lazaros on Galesion. A native of Athens, he lived as a solitary at Rome. He raped and murdered a girl in his care and atoned in the cave at the site of the Savior on Galesion until his untimely death. He gave his name to the cave or the spring there. His relics were translated to Constantinople (36–40, 41, 62).

Paul

A monk who was Lazaros' companion during his journey from Jerusalem to Laodikaia in late 1009. He subsequently became a stylite near Laodikaia for a time and [?] later became superior of the monastery of St. Eugenios at Trebizond (20–24).

Paxamades

See under Nicholas [3].

Philippikos [1]

A monk on Galesion at the Savior who was deluded and assaulted by demons and was apparently tempted to suicide by them. He was cured by Lazaros (47, 48).

Philippikos [2]

A monk on Galesion at [?] the Resurrection. He was the last of all the brothers to embrace the dying Kerykos [3] and requested his intercession in heaven (163).

Philippikos [3]

A monk on Galesion who took exception, along with others, to what he saw as nepotism in the appointment of Lazaros' brother Ignatios as steward of his [Philippikos'] "house." He thus appears to have been in control of some sort of subsidiary establishment on Galesion. He is probably to be identified with Philippikos [5], possibly with Philippikos [4] and Kosmas [2] (in view of his serious rebellion, which may have involved violent opposition to Ignatios) (221).

Philippikos [4]

A monk on Galesion who criticized Lazaros for admitting the charlatan "Damianos" to the monastery after the latter had absconded. He is possibly to be identified with Philippikos [3] and Philippikos [5], and Kosmas [2] (in view of his opposition to Lazaros) (227).

Philippikos [5]

A monk on Galesion who had an oak named after him. He was the supposed recipient of the Devil's largest bottle of oil. He is probably to be identified with Philippikos [3] and possibly with Philippikos [4] and Kosmas [2] (in view of his opposition to Lazaros) (243).

Philippikos [6]

A soldier miraculously released by Lazaros from captivity by the "Persians" before becoming a monk on Galesion (Gregory of Cyprus, chap. 34, *AASS*, Nov. 3:602A–E, perhaps reworking part of the story contained in Chap. 63 of the *vita*).

Photios

A monk from Jerusalem who visited Constantinople and then the Kouzena monastery, where he heard damaging rumors about Lazaros. At Galesion he checked Lazaros' eucharistic practice and had a vision of him in the cell of the monk Elias [2]. He left a written account with Kosmas [3] (84–85).

Sabas [1]

A monk on Galesion who saw demonic thieves entering the monastery. He is possibly to be identified with Sabas [2] (48).

Sabas [2]

A monk on Galesion who hailed from Rizenon. He put a binding spell on goats by using Lazaros' name. He is possibly to be identified with Sabas [1] (77).

Skleraina, Maria

The mistress of Constantine [2] IX Monomachos and sister of Romanos Skleros; Monomachos granted land for Bessai to Lazaros for remembrance of both himself and her. Following Romanos' visit to Lazaros, she donated 720 *nomismata* (and an imperial sacred furnishing), which were used for construction of the Pausolype (245).

Skleros, Romanos

Brother of Constantine [2] IX Monomachos' mistress, Maria Skleraina. He was prominent in the 1040s and, as *strategos* of the [?] Thrakesion theme, he visited Lazaros at the Resurrection and had a visionary experience of him (87).

Stephen

A eunuch and monk on Galesion at the Savior and the Resurrection. He was sent along with other eunuchs to the Savior by Lazaros. He was talked out of leaving the Savior for Bessai by Lazaros. He moved to the Resurrection after Lazaros' death, but was swiftly ordered back to the Savior by Ignatios [1]. He died shortly after Lazaros (100, 216).

Symeon [1]

A monk on Galesion who lived in the cave of Paphnoutios at the Savior, where he was assaulted by demons. He is possibly to be identified with Symeon [2] (43, 49).

Symeon [2]

A monk on Galesion who fell into the sin of fornication and went home for a time, though he later returned to the monastery. He died suddenly in an unrepentant state. He had a daughter who became a nun at the convent of Eupraxia after his death. He is possibly to be identified with Symeon [1] (201).

Theodore

A metropolitan of Ephesus (probably to be identified as Theodore II). He granted land to Lazaros at St. Marina but was probably the man who opposed Lazaros' move to Galesion in 1018/19 (34; cf. 53).

Theodoulos [1] Raphis/Arrhostos

A monk on Galesion who found money and experienced Lazaros' gift of insight. He was alive when Lazaros' *vita* was written (88).

Theodoulos [2]

"The stonemason"; a monk on Galesion who experienced a demonic attempt to lure him into falling over a cliff [?]; the account of the episode is now lost (244).

Theophylact Sagopoulos

He visited Lazaros and witnessed his power of discernment concerning the fish he had told his slave to bring to the monastery (107).

INDEX OF PEOPLE AND PLACES

For specific monasteries and churches, see the cities or places in which they are located in the Index of People and Places. For monasteries and churches in general, see the General Index. Numbers in square brackets refer to identifiers used in Appendix B.

GENERAL INDEX

INDEX OF NOTABLE GREEK WORDS